THE SELECTED LETTERS OF
TENNESSEE WILLIAMS

VOLUME I • 1920–1945

BY TENNESSEE WILLIAMS

PLAYS

Baby Doll & Tiger Tail
Camino Real
Cat on a Hot Tin Roof
Clothes for a Summer Hotel
Dragon Country
The Glass Menagerie
A Lovely Sunday for Creve Coeur
Not About Nightingales
The Notebook of Trigorin
The Red Devil Battery Sign
Small Craft Warnings
Something Cloudy, Something Clear
Spring Storm
Stairs to the Roof
Stopped Rocking and Other Screenplays
A Streetcar Named Desire
Sweet Bird of Youth

THE THEATRE OF TENNESSEE WILLIAMS, VOLUME I
Battle of Angels, A Streetcar Named Desire, The Glass Menagerie
THE THEATRE OF TENNESSEE WILLIAMS, VOLUME II
The Eccentricities of a Nightingale, Summer and Smoke, The Rose Tattoo, Camino Real
THE THEATRE OF TENNESSEE WILLIAMS, VOLUME III
Cat on a Hot Tin Roof, Orpheus Descending, Suddenly Last Summer
THE THEATRE OF TENNESSEE WILLIAMS, VOLUME IV
Sweet Bird of Youth, Period of Adjustment, The Night of the Iguana
THE THEATRE OF TENNESSEE WILLIAMS, VOLUME V
*The Milk Train Doesn't Stop Here Anymore, Kingdom of Earth (The Seven Descents
of Myrtle), Small Craft Warnings, The Two-Character Play*
THE THEATRE OF TENNESSEE WILLIAMS, VOLUME VI
27 Wagons Full of Cotton and Other Short Plays
THE THEATRE OF TENNESSEE WILLIAMS, VOLUME VII
In the Bar of a Tokyo Hotel and Other Plays
THE THEATRE OF TENNESSEE WILLIAMS, VOLUME VIII
*Vieux Carré, A Lovely Sunday for Creve Coeur, Clothes for a Summer Hotel,
The Red Devil Battery Sign*

27 Wagons Full of Cotton and Other Plays
The Two-Character Play
Vieux Carré

POETRY

Androgyne, Mon Amour
In the Winter of Cities

PROSE

Collected Stories
Hard Candy and Other Stories
One Arm and Other Stories
The Roman Spring of Mrs. Stone
Where I Live: Selected Essays

Tennessee at Acapulco, summer 1940.

"Somehow I feel very sure of a great power in me these last few days and I know it is only waiting - waiting a little while - to emerge in something constructive. A great dammed up emotional energy which cannot be entirely dissipated by little things."

—*Tennessee Williams, letter to Joseph Hazan, August 23, 1940*

THE SELECTED LETTERS OF

TENNESSEE WILLIAMS

VOLUME I • 1920–1945

EDITED BY

ALBERT J. DEVLIN AND NANCY M. TISCHLER

A NEW DIRECTIONS BOOK

For our spouses, Molly and Merle,
with love and thanks.
—the Editors

The Selected Letters of Tennessee Williams, Volume I, is published by arrangement
with The University of the South, Sewanee, Tennessee.

Book design by Sylvia Frezzolini Severance
Manufactured in the United States of America
New Directions Books are printed on acid-free paper.
First published clothbound by New Directions in 2000
Published simultaneously in Canada by Penguin Books Canada Limited

Library of Congress Cataloging-in-Publication Data

Williams, Tennessee, 1911-1983.
    [Correspondence. Selections]
    The selected letters of Tennessee Williams / edited by Albert J. Devlin
and Nancy M. Tischler.
        p. cm.
    Includes index.
    Contents: v. 1. 1920-1945
    ISBN 0-8112-1445-1 (alk. paper)
    1. Williams, Tennessee, 1911-1983—Correspondence. 2. Dramatists,
American—20th century—Correspondence. I. Devlin, Albert J.
II. Tischler, Nancy Marie Patterson. III. Title.
    PS3545.I5365 Z48 2000
    812'.54—dc21
    [B]   99-087398

New Directions books are published for James Laughlin
by New Directions Publishing Corporation,
80 Eighth Avenue, New York 10011

CONTENTS

LIST OF ILLUSTRATIONS

Frontispiece, page iv: Sombrero photograph, Acapulco, 1940. By permission of the Harry Ransom Humanities Research Center, University of Texas at Austin (hereafter HRC).

Page 1: "Dady" holding "king dakin," with Tom Williams, ca. 1921. By permission of the Harvard Theatre Collection, Houghton Library, Harvard University. Fredric Woodbridge Wilson, Curator.

Page 6: Tennessee Williams drawing, caricature of Rose Williams as a "Wido." By permission of the Rare Book and Manuscript Library, Columbia University (hereafter Columbia University).

Page 13, top: Tom on board the *Homeric*, New York, 1928. By permission of the HRC.

Page 13, bottom: Tom on a hayride at the University of Missouri. *Savitar*, 1931. Courtesy of Allean Hale.

Page 48, left: Grand, Rosina Otte Dakin. By permission of the HRC.

Page 48, right: Grandfather, The Reverend Walter Edwin Dakin. By permission of the HRC.

Page 67: Rose with Tom and an unidentified friend, early 1930s. By permission of the HRC.

Page 89: Tom and Jiggs. By permission of the HRC.

Page 129: Edwina Dakin Williams. By permission of the HRC.

Page 137: 722 Toulouse Street, New Orleans. Courtesy of the Williams Research Center, Historic New Orleans Collection.

Page 167: Tennessee and Jim Parrott, 1939. By permission of the HRC.

Page 198, top: "Spud" Johnson at Taos. By permission of the HRC.

Page 198, bottom: Mabel Dodge Luhan, Frieda Lawrence, and Dorothy Brett at Taos. Courtesy of Henriette Harris.

Page 203: Tennessee, Anne Bretzfelder, Fred Melton, and Donald Windham, New York, 1940. By permission of the HRC.

Page 243: Meeting of the Playwrights' Seminar at the New School, New York, 1940 (Piscator Papers). By permission of Morris Library, Southern Illinois University, Carbondale.

Page 249: Tennessee Williams drawing, "<u>Then</u> c/o Wells-Fargo." By permission of the HRC.

Page 291: Publicity portrait of Tennessee for *Battle of Angels*. Photograph by Vandamm Studios. By permission of the Billy Rose Theatre Collection, New York Public Library for the Performing Arts.

Page 325: Cogan House, Provincetown, 1941. Courtesy of the Lyle Leverich Collection.

Page 349: Tennessee Williams drawing, caricature of G.B. Shaw. By permission of Columbia University.

Page 365: "Gag" photograph celebrating Tennessee Williams's award from the American Academy of Arts and Letters, New York, 1944. Photograph by George Platt Lynes. Courtesy of the American Academy of Arts and Letters, New York.

Page 409: Howard Baer cartoon, "I really came here to write a play." Courtesy of *Esquire*.

Page 423: Dakin Williams. By permission of the HRC.

Page 445: Tennessee at Santa Monica, 1943. By permission of the HRC.

Page 515: Tennessee Williams's illustrated cover sheet for "A Balcony in Ferrara." By permission of Columbia University.

Page 563: Howard Barnes presenting the New York Drama Critics' Circle Award to Tennessee Williams, New York, 1945. Courtesy of the Richard Freeman Leavitt Collection, University of Tennessee.

INTRODUCTION

To date the editors have collected 2,800 letters, notes, telegrams, and other pertinent documents written by Thomas Lanier (Tennessee) Williams from 1920 until his death in 1983. Of these, approximately half fall into the years treated by Volume I, 1920 to 1945, which culminates with the "smash success" of *The Glass Menagerie*. From available letters, notes, and telegrams written during these years, some 900 in all, the editors have selected and annotated 330 for publication.

The selected correspondence traces Williams's youthful visit to Clarksdale, Mississippi, his continuing life in St. Louis, and residence at three midwestern universities with as little repetition as possible and with as many hints of an artist's life in the making as the early letters permit. Tom's wandering began in earnest in 1939 and necessarily complicated the process of selection by virtue of a larger cast of correspondents and intensified artistic endeavor. The letters of the later period are intended to catch the alternating rhythms of life on the road, at the Williams's unhappy home in St. Louis, and upon the Broadway stage. With such tieless young casuals as Jim Parrott, Joe Hazan, and Paul Bigelow, Williams dropped his stiff domestic style and wrote a more colloquial and sexually vivid line. To such Broadway figures as Lawrence Langner and Theresa Helburn, directors of the Theatre Guild, he often wrote with an undertone of restlessness and dread—work of the "blue devils" that periodically assailed him.

The editors have taken care to document both the literary foreground and the early production history of the two major plays of the period: *Battle of Angels*, which closed ingloriously in Boston in 1941, and *The Glass Menagerie*, whose long and uncertain gestation came to brilliant issue in Chicago and New York. Successive drafts of the plays can be followed in the correspondence, as can Williams's slowly advancing knowledge of his craft. Illustrating the life and the works, then, with coverage and nuance, and with as little editorial intrusion as possible, has guided the editors in selecting Tennessee Williams's correspondence—a record of "that fatal, inevitable forward motion in life" (ca. August 18, 1940) to which the subject committed himself again and again.

◆

Williams's first known letter would establish patterns for the next two decades of correspondence. Written in 1920 from the rectory of St. George's Episcopal Church in Clarksdale, the letter is addressed to Edwina, Tom's mother, by an eight-year-old traveler who has already felt the rigors of the road: "I was awfully tird when I got on the train." Edwina had wisely arranged the first of her son's many escapes from the dreaded "City of St. Pollution" to which the family moved in 1918. Tom's brief return to Clarksdale set the pattern for later travel to the bohemia of New Orleans and to a succession of seaside havens, where he seemed to answer a question that he would pose rhetorically in *The Glass Menagerie*. "You know," Tom Wingfield says of Malvolio the Magician, "it don't take much intelligence to get yourself into a nailed up coffin. But who in hell ever got himself out of one without removing one nail?" Volume I of *The Selected Letters* is a manual of survival, of deft and repeated escape from "two-by-four situations." None was more complicated than Tom's "Life with Mother and Father, with Rose and Dakin," a long-running domestic tragedy that supplied the playwright with the essentials of speech, gesture, and a pervasive undertone of apprehension and defeat.

Of the letters collected in Volume I, more than a third were written by Williams to members of his immediate and extended family. His maternal grandparents received a weary visitor in 1920 and then again in 1935 in Memphis, when clerical work at the Continental Shoe Company led to physical and nervous collapse. Williams's correspondence with the Dakins is tonally distinctive and bespeaks the aura of calmness and reserve within which they apparently lived. To "Grand," Rosina Otte Dakin, he wrote on Mother's Day in 1936 with a tenderness that is rarely found in the fifty-odd letters written to Edwina. To "Grandfody," the Reverend Walter E. Dakin, Tom wrote as a schoolboy so anxious to please his scholarly grandfather that he obscured his academic failures, beginning with his delayed graduation from high school in 1929. If there is tension to be found in the Dakin household, it can be read in references to the economic sacrifice and self-denial of Grand, mute testimony to her parched and burdensome role as the wife of an Episcopal priest in the South.

Conflict in the Williams household in St. Louis was closer to the surface and far less dignified. Edwina's fine profile was marred in a door-slamming episode with Cornelius, who also enraged (Rose) and terrified (Tom) his two older children, while lavishing favor upon the third (Dakin). Cornelius elicits from Tom carefully phrased accounts of money spent and money required, of grades hopefully foreseen, with only traces of humor. Cast as the ogre of the household, Cornelius is often evoked in correspondence by coded references to his health and periodic hospitalization, a chronic drinker's signature, and to his periodic absence on business travel, a respite for the weary family.

For the prude and the social climber in Edwina, Tom crafted letters that bespoke a choir boy's innocence and that claimed acceptance by leading families and literary figures encountered on his travels. The many letters written to Edwina, the second largest group in Volume I, are complicated rhetorically by her unfailing support of her son's literary adventure and by the mixture of ignorance and intolerance with which she apprehended his goals. Neither Edwina nor Rose, Tom complained to the Dakins in 1936, could appreciate the "modern" humor of "Twenty-Seven Wagons Full of Cotton," a story of seduction that Edwina forbade her son to send "to anybody." Several years later, Tom assured his agent, Audrey Wood, that "I have always gotten along rather well with female ogres" (July 30, 1939). The ogre in question was Frieda Lawrence, but Edwina had surely been good preparation for Williams's handling of D.H. Lawrence's formidable widow, as well as of such volatile actresses as Miriam Hopkins and Laurette Taylor. The result in correspondence with Edwina are filial letters curiously flat and devoid of emotion but informed by a deep regard for the binding effect of family relations.

It was with Rose Williams that the family chronicle gave the most profound evidence of its literary potential. Hints of Rose's instability abound in letters written in 1926 from All Saints' College in Vicksburg, Mississippi, where she felt "nervous as a cat" and banished from family and friends. During the next decade her condition worsened, until she was institutionalized in 1937 and diagnosed as schizophrenic. Superbly revealing is a letter that Tom wrote to his sister in 1927 at the time of her informal, and unproductive, debut in Knoxville. "We miss greatly the clatter of kettles, hissing of steam, and splash of water which signify your presence in the house. Except when Dakin is hammering or my type-writer clicking, everything is deathly still. We are all very sensible to your absence." Rose

Williams's abortive courting in a southern city and the "frivolities" (November 19, 1927) of her bath and boudoir anticipate with uncanny precision both the argument and the intimate feminine imagery of *A Streetcar Named Desire*—which is underway as Volume I of *The Selected Letters* concludes. Her "absence," made final at the time of her lobotomy in 1943, is not close to the surface of the letters, nor does her presence at Farmington State Hospital draw Tom frequently upon his visits to the so-called "parental roof" in St. Louis. And yet the typewriter never stopped "clicking." "Homage to Ophelia," written in 1944 as a foreword to the play *You Touched Me!*, is a moving apostrophe to Rose, "luminous and delicate," as was her legendary antecedent in verse. The family letters, while giving evidence of a sad, unvarying domestic history, preserve a lyrical core of memory that sustained Williams during his prolonged apprenticeship and maturity as a writer.

◆

Acquiring Audrey Wood as agent was the decisive event in Tennessee Williams's early career. Their first meeting in New York in 1939 remains legendary, as does her reputation for candor: "One of my virtues, unfortunately, is extreme honesty and I cannot at this point promise you any kind of a quick sale on anything . . . although I do say I think you are highly promising." Within several months she sold a piece to Whit Burnett's prestigious *STORY* magazine, a "fortress" that Williams had failed to breach since his first submission in the early 1930s. Thereafter Audrey Wood became Williams's most trusted reader and his most persistent correspondent in Volume I. Her honesty led her to predict that a long, rambling scenario "would emerge much more an emotional monologue than a full-bodied play." The more "exciting" synopsis of *Battle of Angels* brought a promise to "go screaming down the street like a mad woman and deliver you a sale" if you can make "this play come alive." Both judgments were rendered in the first year of her agency, and they must have convinced Williams that the diminutive "Miss Wood" was a unique blend of commerce and good artistic taste. She was also an excellent listener, as can be inferred from the tone of their ensuing correspondence.

In late 1941, in the aftermath of *Battle of Angels*, Williams described his thin skin to Audrey Wood while thanking her for a testimonial (from John Tebbel, managing editor of the *American Mercury*) that she had tipped into a recent letter of hers. "I don't believe anyone ever suspects how completely unsure I am of my work and myself and what tortures of self-doubting the doubt of others has always given me" (ca. September 24, 1941). In a following letter, Williams tilted his sensitivity toward stoicism, telling Wood that "I have lived behind the mobile fortress of a deep and tranquil pessimism for so long that I feel <u>almost</u> impregnable" (ca. October 7, 1941). Torture and tranquility, exposure and protection, publicity and reserve—the regularity of this "see-saw" motion, as Williams would later describe it to Wood, was already familiar to the agent by 1941. But these and other such letters addressed to Wood were also an occasion for Williams to objectify and adjust his own "precarious balance of nerves" (ca. September 1, 1942) as no other correspondent would allow him to do. She might not be an infallible "Court of Human Relations," as Williams wrote in 1946, but Wood's personal and professional stability and her reserved friendship were crucial elements in Williams's maturing as a writer.

♦

Volume I of *The Selected Letters* ends with the validation of a literary life that nearly failed to beat the heavy odds arrayed against it. Thomas Lanier Williams entered the University of Missouri in 1929 as the Great Depression began. Three universities and nine years later he graduated as war in Europe gave every indication of engulfing the world. In 1939 he reached New York in time to observe the demise of the Group Theatre, whose playreader, Molly Day Thacher, admired his work, and of the Federal Theatre Project, which might have produced his early topical plays had its funding not been cut by a partisan congress. "I got the stuff to go ahead," a young Odets character says, ruing the fate of his and Tom Williams's generation in being set aside as it were and reduced to political abstractions. It was within this context of apparently bad generational luck that "Tennessee" Williams used letters to equip his new identity with a countervailing ethic of honesty, beauty, and endurance.

Honesty was a means of defending the "dreamer" that Amanda Wingfield would brand "selfish" in *The Glass Menagerie*. The alternatives were mulled by Williams in letters and journal entries and found insupport-able: a dreary commercial life in St. Louis, a repetition of his sister's illness and institutionalization. "Aloneness," not self-sacrifice or family regard, he observed to his friend Joe Hazan, would allow the artist to realize his "one ineluctable gift, to project himself beyond time and space through grasp and communion with eternal values." But the approach to beauty would require "infinite patience, endurance. We must make a religion of that last thing - endurance" (September 3, 1940). Williams seldom if ever spoke to his hard-boiled agent about Beauty unvarnished, but Audrey Wood herself had overcome significant odds to establish a thriving agency, and she could easily identify with the religious value that her strange young client had placed upon "endurance." His aesthetic language—quaint by today's academic standards—may have come from abroad, from D.H. Lawrence primarily, but it was the "wreckage" of American family and civic life that supplied the tenacity that Audrey Wood and all of his correspondents admired. "We are always looking down on the bourgeois," he wrote to an impressionable Joe Hazan in 1940, without fully realizing that his own virtuous identity as a writer had been formed in their midst, among his "own kind of vague, indefinite folks" (October 21, 1939).

AJD
June, 2000

EDITORIAL NOTE

Volume I of *The Selected Letters of Tennessee Williams* is intended to provide complete, authoritative texts and to preserve as much of the form of the original correspondence as is compatible with publication. The heading for each letter begins with a reference number followed by the correspondent's name, the letter's place of origin and date, and a bibliographical description of the original manuscript, including its present location.

The editors have preserved, and marked SH (Stationery Headed), the names of hotels, boats, railways, and family and friends with which many of Williams's letters are imprinted. His own notations of address and date have also been preserved, but the editors have often intervened to provide more accurate or complete information. When only an approximate date could be established, the editors have used the abbreviation ca. and placed it within square brackets to signify an insertion. When we could amend an incomplete date or supply a missing one, we dispensed with the marker ca. but retained the bracket. When a postmarked envelope has been preserved and could help to date an otherwise undated letter, we have given this information in the heading and identified it with the abbreviation PM (Postmarked). To solve the many problems of dating in Volume I, the editors first considered the internal evidence of the letter itself and then such other aids as Williams's concurrent correspondence, his recipient letters, letters written among members of his immediate and extended family, and especially his journal, which begins in March 1936 and continues with only a few significant lapses for the remaining years of Volume I.

In the vast majority of cases, the published letter texts are based upon original manuscripts that have been examined by at least one of the editors. The few exceptions to this rule are noted in the bibliographical description which follows the date line in each heading. The vast majority of letters are also published here for the first time. Those printed in *Remember Me to Tom* (1963), Edwina Dakin Williams's memoir, have been reprinted with the original manuscripts serving as copy texts and in several cases with the full letter text restored. Only in one instance (letter #195) has a letter been censored to guard the privacy of a living person. The use of ellipsis is Williams's own practice and functions as an alternate system of punctuation rather than as a sign of omission. Several editorial changes in lineation reflect a sharply competing principle of economy in preparing Volume I. In his typed correspondence, Williams used a block form with double spacing to indicate paragraph breaks. The editors have followed the design of his autograph letters in which paragraph breaks are marked by indentation. We have also printed closings and signatures on the same line and in some cases regularized their punctuation. The salutations are unedited.

Williams's erratic spelling—more than 100 errors of his can be found in Volume I, the majority in violation of the most basic rules of orthography—has not been corrected, save in the case of mechanical or inadvertent error, nor has his capitalization or punctuation been standardized. The intrusive convention [*sic*] is not used in editing the letter texts. Rough syntax has been smoothed occasionally by the insertion, in square brackets, of omitted function words or other elements needed to create a readable text. In no case, however, has an insertion been made where the author's intention is not entirely clear. Square brackets have also been used to convey information, in italics, about the condition of the manuscript: [*end of letter missing*]. Strikeovers and cancellations have been retained when they are decipherable and revealing.

Bracketed annotations follow nearly every letter and are not keyed to a footnote or other visual system of identification. This decision was made to discourage the usual discontinuous practice of letter reading—one that occasions undue intrusion into the letter itself and requires that the reader constantly break its pace and mood to consult an editorial language of explication. The annotations are not, however, without design. Some few, especially those that inaugurate a unit of letters, begin with a statement of orientation before taking up specific items in the letter. Each annotation is paragraphed to reflect the letter's internal order of elements that have been selected for treatment, and these frequently are identified by strategic quotations from the letter itself.

In writing the annotations, the editors have used a wide variety of sources, including quotations from letters of Williams not selected for inclusion (usually because of their repetitive or perfunctory nature), from his unpublished journal, and from correspondence among members of his immediate and extended family. Each of these sources is identified and may be consulted by readers who wish to supplement the annotations. Dates for Williams's extensive works are given parenthetically in the annotations, according to the following practice: Non-dramatic texts are dated by their first appearance in print or, if unpublished, by their manuscript date and provenance. Dramatic texts are dated by their first major performance unless otherwise noted. To keep the reader apprized of Williams's complex body of work, we have repeated the dating of texts with the first mention of each in the seven parts of Volume I.

The great majority of persons, events, and texts mentioned in the letters have been identified to the extent that their importance seemed to warrant. The few persons whom we have failed to identify no doubt deserved a better fate. More extensive biographical treatment has been given to each of Williams's correspondents upon the occasion of the first letter addressed to each. Thereafter briefer identification has sufficed.

ACKNOWLEDGMENTS

The editors are indebted to the following scholar-critics who have made basic contributions to the study of Tennessee Williams. First, of course, is Lyle Leverich, Williams's authorized biographer, whose singular perseverance led to the publication of *Tom: The Unknown Tennessee Williams*, in 1995, the award-winning first volume of a distinguished biography. Lyle Leverich's death in 1999 has deprived the editors of a source of friendship and guidance. Lyle, we are sure, would have it remembered that his young friend Paul Jordan gave unusual aid and support in the years following the appearance of *Tom* and thus made a unique contribution to his continuing research.

To Tennessee Williams's primary bibliographers the editors also owe a large debt of gratitude. In the 1960s Andreas Brown laid the foundation for the massive Williams collection at the Harry Ransom Humanities Research Center, Austin, Texas. No serious Williams scholar can proceed very far without acknowledging the forethought of "Andy" Brown and his logistical marvel. Drewey Wayne Gunn continued the work of description with the first significant listing (1980, revised edition, 1991) of Williams's vast corpus, and George Crandell gave it definitive form in his 1995 bibliography—in its own right a marvel of accurate and efficient description.

The editors found valuable biographical and bibliographical material in *Tennessee Williams' Letters to Donald Windham, 1940–1965*. Published in 1977 and ably edited by Donald Windham, the collection is often a revealing counterpoint to letters appearing in the present edition. The journal of Tennessee Williams, forthcoming from Yale University Press under the editorship of Margaret Thornton, provided a similar function and is quoted by special arrangement with Yale University Press.

The preponderance of letters printed in Volume I are drawn from three institutional sources: Harry Ransom Humanities Research Center, University of Texas at Austin; Harvard Theatre Collection, Pusey Library; and Butler Library, Columbia University. At the Humanities Research Center, special thanks are due Linda Briscoe, Bill Fagelson, Pat Fox, Cathy Henderson, Peter Mears, Barbara Smith-La-Borde, and Tara Wenger; at the

Harvard Theatre Collection, Michael Dumas, Annette Fern, and Frederic Woodbridge; at the Butler Library, Jean Ashton, Gwynedd Cannan, and Bernard R. Crystal.

Other collectors, institutional and private, who kindly supplied letters or research material include the Alderman Library, University of Virginia (Gregory Johnson); American Academy of Arts and Letters (Kathryn Talalay); Beinecke Library, Yale University (Patricia C. Willis); Cleveland Play House (Scott Kanoff); DeGolyer Library, Southern Methodist University (David Farmer); Houghton Library, Harvard University (Leslie Morris); Huntington Library (Cathy Cherbosque); Kent State University Library (Jeanne Somers); Lilly Library, Indiana University (Heather R. Munro); McKeldin Library, University of Maryland; Morris Library, Southern Illinois University (Karen D. Drickamer); Olin Library, Washington University (Kevin Ray); Princeton University Library (Margaret Sherry); Southern Historical Collection, University of North Carolina at Chapel Hill; Harriet Holland Brandt, Burbank, California; Dan Isaac, New York; the late James Laughlin, Norfolk, Connecticut; Jordan Massee, Macon, Georgia; Fred Todd, San Antonio, Texas; Charles S. Watson, University of Alabama; Dakin Williams, Collinsville, Illinois.

The editors are also indebted to a hardy band of survivors who knew Williams during the years treated in Volume I and have shared valuable information and memories: Horton Foote, Wharton, Texas; Joe Hazan, New York; Mary Lois Filsinger Kessler, Landrum, South Carolina; Jordan Massee, Macon, Georgia; Jim Parrott, Miami, Florida; Anne Bretzfelder Post, New York; Mary Helen Gilliam Raspberry, Helena, Arkansas; William Jay Smith, Cummington, Massachusetts; Esmeralda Mayes Treen, Henderson, Nevada; Mary Hunter Wolf, Hamden, Connecticut.

Five years of preparation have revealed special friends of *The Selected Letters* whom we wish to acknowledge. Matthew J. Alofs began work on the project in 1998, first as a member of the University of Missouri Undergraduate Mentorship Program, later as research assistant, proofreader, and indexer. His formidable knowledge of Williams often led him to infuse seemingly mundane tasks with discovery and innovation. George Crandell, Peggy Fox, Allean Hale, and Don Lamm read parts of the work in progress and provided astute criticism, often saving the editors from errors both of omission and commission. Allean Hale, in particular, interrupted her own valuable research to answer editorial questions and to give friendship and support during the preparation of Volume I. The late James Laughlin was still actively the president and publisher of New Directions when *The Selected Letters* was undertaken. For his support the editors are particularly thankful. Richard F. Leavitt, compiler of *The World of Tennessee Williams* (1978), advised the editors on the selection of photographs and supplied several from his own extensive collection. Jordan Massee gave valuable papers to the editors and patiently answered questions about his friendship with Tennessee Williams in the early 1940s. Esmeralda ("Ezzie") Mayes Treen shared memories of growing up in St. Louis and of her friendship with Rose Williams. To the University of the South, copyright holder of the works of Tennessee Williams, the editors are grateful for permission to edit and publish a two-volume selection of his correspondence. The playwright's brother, Dakin, was a generous friend to the editors, giving access to important family papers and answering questions that no one else could presume to address.

Professor Devlin's work as co-editor was supported by an NEH senior fellowship, a Rose Cowles Research Fellowship, Humanities Research Center, University of Texas at Austin, and grants from the University of Missouri Research Board and Research Council. Professor Tischler received a Cline Fellowship from the HRC and a grant from the Institute for the Arts and Humanistic Studies, Pennsylvania State University. Generous assistance was supplied by reference and special collections librarians at the University of Missouri: Anne Barker, Anne Edwards, Margaret Howell, Hunter Kevil, and Michael Muchow, as well as by an efficient Interlibrary Loan staff headed by Marilyn Voegele. Research assistance at the University of Missouri was given by Hilary Aid, Penny Couillard, Jennifer Goodon, Cliff Manlove, Kimberly McCaffrey, Julianne Ramsey, Elizabeth Thomas, Sarah Trippensee, and Peter Van Leunen. The editors value especially their collegial interest in the "Letters" project. To the late Charles Mann, Chief Librarian of Rare Books and Manuscripts at Pennsylvania State University, Professor Tischler offers thanks for his assistance. To Peggy Fox, vice president of New Directions, and to Sylvia Frezzolini Severance, book designer, the editors are indebted for their care and perseverance. Finally, Jennifer Zarrelli transcribed the letters with her typical competence and good cheer.

The following archivists, librarians, research assistants, and other distinguished informants have provided much valuable assistance, for which the editors are thankful: Anne Armour, University of the South; Laurence G. Avery, University of North Carolina at Chapel Hill; Bridget Aschenberg, International Creative Management, New York; Alma Bennett, Clemson University; Sheppard Black, Ohio University; Robert Brady, Hickman High School, Columbia, Missouri; Mary Ellen Brooks, University of Georgia; Jackson Bryer, University of Maryland; Lauren Bufferd, Chicago Public Library; Garrett Carter, Lake Forest, Illinois; Kay Cattarulla, Dallas Museum of Art; Eva de Chazal, Columbia, Missouri; Nena Couch, Ohio State University; Rosemary L. Cullen, Brown University; Edwina Dodson, Clarksdale, Mississippi; Weldon Durham, University of Missouri; Peter Dzwonkoski, University of Rochester; Elaine Engst, Cornell University; John Fick, Quincy, Illinois; John T. Fisher, MD., State College, Pennsylvania; Jack Frick, New Orleans; Danielle Gierer, Church of St. Michael and St. George, St. Louis, Missouri; Diana C. Haskell, Newberry Library; Bill Heaton, Lyon, Mississippi; Robert Hines, New Orleans; Kenneth Holditch, New Orleans; Mary Huth, University of Rochester; James H. Hutson, Library of Congress; Jill Alene Jiminez, Cleveland Museum of Art; Linda Keown, Hickman High School, Columbia, Missouri; Philip C. Kolin, University of Southern Mississippi; Jackie Kopatz, School District of Clayton, Missouri; Richard E. Kramer, New York; James B. Lloyd, University of Tennessee; Colleen R. Mallet, Vassar College; Dennis C. Martin, Hawthorne (California) Public Library; Sharon Perry Martin, Dallas Public Library; Panny Mayfield, *Clarksdale Press Register*; Remy McBurney, New York; Robert McCown, University of Iowa; Robert W. Melton, University of Kansas; L. Rebecca Johnson Melvin, University of Delaware; Wilbur E. Meneray, Tulane University; Janie C. Morris, Duke University; Fran Murphy, University of Iowa; James E. Murray, School District of University City, Missouri; Brian Parker, University of Toronto; Rev. Gene Phillips, S.J., Loyola University (Chicago); Rebecca Roberts, University of Alabama; David Savran, Brown University; Helen Sheehy; Bill Short, Rhodes College; Jeff Sirkin, Harvard Law School Alumni Center; Gary Lee Smith, University of Missouri; Tonya Stitt, University of Missouri Alumni Association; Kathi A. Strickland, Texas Department of Health; Dan Sullivan, Minneapolis; Suzy Taraba,

University of Chicago; Andrea Telli, Chicago Public Library; Neda Thompson, University Park, Pennsylvania; Ralph Voss, University of Alabama; Raymond Wemmlinger, Hampden-Booth Theatre Library; James L. West, Pennsylvania State University; Linda White, Clarksdale (Mississippi) Public Library; David Witt, Harwood Museum, Taos, New Mexico.

ABBREVIATIONS

AL	Autograph letter unsigned
ALS	Autograph letter signed
APCS	Autograph postcard signed
ca.	about
Conversations	*Conversations with Tennessee Williams.* Ed. Albert J. Devlin. UP of Mississippi, 1986.
Houghton	Houghton Library, Harvard University
HRC	Harry Ransom Humanities Research Center, University of Texas at Austin
HTC	Harvard Theatre Collection (Pusey Library), Houghton Library, Harvard University
Leverich	Lyle Leverich, *Tom: The Unknown Tennessee Williams*. Crown Publishers, 1995.
n.d.	no date of publication
PM	Postmarked
qtd.	quoted
SH	Stationery headed
TL	Typewritten letter unsigned
TLS	Typewritten letter signed
TLSx	Typewritten letter signed copy
TTr	Typewritten transcript
TW	Tennessee Williams
Windham	*Tennessee Williams' Letters to Donald Windham, 1940-1965*. Ed. Donald Windham. Holt, Rinehart and Winston, 1977.

PART I
1920-1932
CLARKSDALE · ST. LOUIS · COLUMBIA

Overleaf: "Dady" holding "king dakin," with Tom, ca. 1921.

1. To Edwina Dakin Williams

[106 Sharkey Avenue]
Clarksdale, Miss.
Feb. 28, 1920
[ALS, 3 pp. Columbia]

Dear mother

I met Grandfody right at the train. soon as the chicken gets of her nest I am going out to get the eggs. I liked Mr. moss awfully much. but I was awfully tird when I got on the train. And he wanted me to go in the chair car with him and read the paper. I could have stayed in my berth just as well but he insisted on me going in the chair car. I was about hafe past nine when I got in bed. tell Rose fussy the big old Plymouth Rock turned out to be a Roster so Grand killed him and ate him. Grandfody said he made fine chicken saled and dumplins Laura Grands cook came running in asking Grand for protecion. Because her husband had beat her. they began to fuss so much that both of them moved out of The servants house. All the chickens are going in danger of lossing there heads if they dont lay any eggs. send my love to Dady and Rose And kiss Sonnie for me.

Love from Tom

[TW wrote as an eight year old from the rectory of St. George's Episcopal Church in Clarksdale, Mississippi, where his family had lived for several years before moving to St. Louis in 1918. "Grandfody" and "Grand" are the Reverend Walter Edwin (1857-1954) and Rosina Otte Dakin (1863-1944), his beloved maternal grandparents.

TW returned to the small Delta town of Clarksdale because of Edwina's uncertain health and his own poor adjustment to "the City of St. Pollution" (*Conversations*, p. 180), as he later described his home in the North. In September he entered the fourth grade at Oakhurst Elementary School and in the spring was promoted to the fifth, which he would resume at the intimidating Field School in St. Louis.

"Dady" is Cornelius Coffin Williams (1879-1957), who married Edwina Estelle Dakin (1884-1980) in Columbus, Mississippi, in 1907. He joined the International Shoe Company in 1914 as a traveling salesman and became an assistant sales manager for the Friedman-Shelby Branch in St. Louis in 1918. Rose is TW's older sister and "Sonnie" his infant brother, Walter Dakin Williams, born in St. Louis on February 21, 1919. Mr. Moss was a family friend who reportedly accompanied TW to Clarksdale.]

2. To Rose Isabel Williams

[106 Sharkey Avenue]
Clarksdale, Miss.
March 15, 1920
[ALS, 2 pp. Columbia]

Dear Rose

I am glad Mother got a girl. tell Mother that the church is thinking about having a vested choir. tell dady Grandfody said not to send my bicycle. I found a nice soft ball up in the attic for sonnie. tell mother Grand got the money for My stockings I found fussys head in the back yard and gave it a nice burial I hope king dakin Isent so cross as he used to be. tell him I am coming to take his throne away from him in to months. Our peach trees are blomming. And the flowers are up in the yard I tried to make a garden in the back yard but the chickens ate all the seeds up excuse my writting but because I am writting fast Grandfody chopped up a barrol an to rats ran out.

love from Tom

[TW's older sister Rose was born in Columbus, Mississippi, on November 19, 1909, and died in Tarrytown, New York, on September 4, 1996. She also revisited Clarksdale and spent at least a part of the 1921-1922 school year with her grandparents. On February 24, 1922, she casually wrote to Edwina that "Mrs. Wingfield stocked our store room" (HRC). It was a name that TW had also heard in Clarksdale and would later use in *The Glass Menagerie* (1945) to evoke his own domestic history.

The "girl" was a servant and "king dakin" TW's usurping infant brother. "Fussy," now defunct, was the Plymouth Rock that turned out to be a rooster. She reappeared as a proper old hen in TW's screenplay for *Baby Doll* (1956).]

3. To Edwina Dakin Williams

[106 Sharkey Avenue]
Clarksdale, Miss.
May 27, 1920
[ALS w/ illustrations, 2 pp. Columbia]

Dear Mother.

Please urge Grand to come on The 15th of June. If you don't she will wait till Autumn. Grandfody wants her too and I do too. Tell Rose. I think she will do it for her because Rose has intire power over Grand.

I had Just saved up nine hole dollars. When Grandfody made me put five in The bank. We are invited out to the country.

Grand Might go to memphis on The train and leave memphis on a boat I hope she will. With love

Tom

[Trips to Edwina's household in times of illness or other adversity were a familiar pattern for Grand. TW later described her as casting a "spell of peace" over "the furiously close little city apartment" where his family lived an embattled existence. "'Grand' was all that we knew of God in our lives!" ("Grand," 1964).]

4. To Rose Isabel Williams

[106 Sharkey Avenue
Clarksdale, Mississippi]
[ca. May-June 1920]
[ALS w/ illustrations, 6 pp. Columbia]

Dear Rose

I am incloseing my Ranbow paper I will send you something more interesting next time because this is Just an advetising paper. next time I will write you about Janes wedding. and of how poor Jane was fooled. tell dady That one of his friends Mr friedman now works at a wholesale store named friedman and Schultz here. he says he used to know dady. please remember. Please tell Mother That I am in The sixth table in division and multiplying. And am having Geography. smalbox is terrerbele in Clarks dale. our neighbors have it who are The neils. and Grandfody and I got vaccinated and it dident hurt a bit its like pulling out a tooth. you get awful scard and when it over you find out it don't hurt a bit. Grand is awful scard because she thinks That shes going to take it but if she uses a little Christen sience I don' think she will tak it love

from Tom

[Signed by "Thomas Lanier Williams," the "more interesting" number of the "Ranbow" comic paper consists of two ruled pages with a leading caption on page 1, "Drive out sufregets who are women voters because they don't no even who they

are voting for." "Poor Jane" is identified in the cartoon narrative on page 2 as "Mrs Jane h. Rothschild," a "sufreget," who "is afraid Miss Rose Williams will paint up so much That she will get all The million men." The story ends with Rose, pictured as a "WIDO," having "her tenth husband. all the Rest commided suicide because she was so strict."

In March B.W. Friedman was elected president of Friedman-Schultz, a newly incorporated wholesale shoe company in Clarksdale.

Shortly before TW's arrival in Clarksdale, the *Daily Register* reprinted a lengthy article (February 13, 1920) on the healing power of Christian Science. On June 1 Dr. L.D. Harrison, the city health officer, reported seventy-five cases of "smalbox" and urgently recommended vaccination. TW oddly, if precociously, connected these events, prompted perhaps by discussion of "Christen sience" overheard in the rectory or on pastoral visits. His formal schooling began in September, suggesting that earlier study had been centered in the rectory.]

5. To Edwina Dakin Williams

[106 Sharkey Avenue]
Clarksdale, Miss.
Oct. 17, 1920
[ALS, 2 pp. Columbia]

Dear Mother.

I am getting along fine in school. My report was all ones and twos which means good and perfec. A few days ago I went out to Lyon and spent the day with a little boy named David Bobo. I got my bycicle about three day ago. and Mary helen Gilliam has one to. and we ride every day together and have lots of fun Miss Ruby neill iss my teacher she has red hair and is awfully strict but not counting that shes awfully nice. tell Rose her bride dolls head was saved we will send it. With much love

Tom

[TW's fourth grade report card shows that he excelled in reading, spelling, and geography, was fair to good in composition and arithmetic, and was promoted to the fifth with an overall rating of "good."

TW's playmate in the nearby hamlet of Lyon was David Ivey, the informally adopted son of Mr. and Mrs. Charles Bobo. TW used "the odd name" (originally Beaubeau) of this prominent Clarksdale family in his story "The Yellow Bird" (1947) to signify an irrepressible pagan beauty and freedom.

Mary Helen Gilliam Rasberry has recalled riding her bicycle with TW, but she had few memories of the visiting boy himself to share with the editors.]

6. To Rose Isabel Williams

[106 Sharkey Avenue]
Clarksdale, Miss.
Oct. 30, 1920
[ALS, 4 pp. Columbia]

Dear Rose.

I am doing fine at school. My report was all ones and twos.

I don't like Miss Neill any more because she calls Me preacher. We had a spelling Match with the other forth Grade and the ones that missed had to sit down and I was among the few that were left standing. A minstral came to town to-day and passed the school house and the boys threw rocks at it and hit a old colerd woman with her bow. Edward Peacock invited me to his birthday party. There is a little boy named Paul that lives down the street from us who is very nice.

Mary Helen Gilliam has a bicycle and I ride with her every day.

Grandfody and I go to the movies on Friday and Saturdays. The rectory has been paperd and painted. With much

love Tom

[Such teasing as Miss Neill's gave title to TW's story "De Preachuh's Boy," in which a "delicate" nine year old is mocked as "'Sis-sy, Sis-sy'" (n.d., HRC). In 1996 a local resident who knew TW as a child stated that he was "mercilessly" taunted by classmates and suggested that his "strain of melancholy" may have been "gained right here in Clarksdale."

Edward P. Peacock, Jr., lived in a large Victorian house near the Episcopal rectory. The "pet name" of his younger sister, Mary Edmunds, was "Baby Doll," later to be overlaid with suggestiveness and controversy occasioned by the film. The "nice" little boy was Paul Strode.

The stage and film stars at the Marion Theatre gave Walter Dakin and his grandson a periodic escape from the rectory, an outlet that TW would later describe in his journal as "the usual anaesthesia" (August 8, 1937).]

7. To Walter E. Dakin

[6254 Enright Avenue
University City, Missouri]
[ca. 1927]
[ALS, 2 pp. HTC]

Dear Grandfather,

Being of thrifty Quaker lineage, it is opposed to my nature to throw away this good piece of paper simply because it has the remnant of a french lesson on its back - and so I'm utilizing it for this letter, with apologys.

As Grand has informed you, Mother got through her very serious operation quite well according to the reports we have received. We haven't seen her yet. The doctor said that it would be dangerous for us to visit her as she had to be kept absolutely quiet. We feel now that she has survived the operation and these first two days, she will surely get through allright.

The morning of the operation was certainly an anxious one for us. We waited two hours while she was on the operating table. Grand had intended to bring a prayer-book for us to read out of but in her habitual flurry, she got the hymnal instead. However we read appropriate hyms and the good Lord seemed to receive them just as well.

The nurse reports on Mother's condition night and morning. The reports today were that she was comfortable and was kept asleep most of the time.

Dakin is behaving himself as well as he is constitutionally able. Rose and I are co-operating in house-work for Grand and the maid continues to come and so everything here is well-ordered. Hoping that you are getting along alright,

Lovingly, Tom.

[The intervening years saw the Williams family move several times before settling, in June 1926, on Enright Avenue in University City, the so-called "tenement" setting of *Glass Menagerie* fame. TW had graduated from Ben Blewett Junior High and was probably a junior at University City High School when this letter was written. "U. City" was a middle-class western suburb of St. Louis that modestly advanced Edwina's social design and gave her sons access to a superior education. In *Memoirs* (1975) TW recalled only the dreariness of the cramped, unhappy quarters that his family would occupy for nearly a decade: "An ugly region of hive-like apartment buildings . . . and fire escapes and pathetic little patches of green among concrete driveways" (p. 16).

Edwina printed page 1 of this letter in her memoir, *Remember Me to Tom* (1963), and without dating it precisely or identifying her operation (probably a hysterectomy), said that "the rest of the letter has been lost." Page 2 (beginning with the third sentence in the third paragraph and showing a canceled French lesson at the top) was found by the editors at the Harvard Theatre Collection in 1995. Contrary to reports, the full letter text shows that Rose was not shielded from news of Edwina's "serious operation" while away at school in Mississippi. The letter may date from 1927 after she completed the spring term (her last) at All Saints' in Vicksburg.]

8. To Rose Isabel Williams

SH: Thomas Lanier Williams
6254 Enright Avenue
St. Louis, Mo.
[November 19, 1927]
[TLS, 4 pp. Columbia]

Dear Rose,

Aunt Belle sent us a letter giving a list of your engagements and, believe me, you are certainly going to be busy! You are probably right this minute at that tea which Aunty is giving for you. If you're not too tired when you get this, write us a letter and tell us how it went off. We are intensely interested, of course.

Your new evening dress came out this morning. I don't greatly admire the color of it - a strange green - but perhaps it matches your eyes. Mother says she thought it was blue when she saw it in the store. But I don't see how. It's just as green as cats' eyes.

To-day is Saturday and I have been busy all morning finding a family "who would appreciate a Thanksgiving dinner" from St Andrew's society. I have finally found one who lives down by Tenth St. - scene of the Italian gang-fights - and I think I shall ask for an armored car to deliver it with.

Miss Florence made out a menu for me to use and, believe me, she was economical about it. One stalk celery, 5 potatoes, 3 apples!

Mother and Dad were out last night and are going out again to-night. Imposing on me, making me stay in with Dakin two nights in succession on the week end! I think I shall choke Dakin to-night and go out anyway.

Mother and I admonish you not to eat all the cake and Ice cream set before you because if you do you won't last a week!

Dad tried your bed night before last, but he didn't sleep well on it so last night he went back to his own, saying that yours brought him bad luck. While he was in your room he demanded an explanation of all your cosmetics which were left in the closet. He was shocked at the number. Also he wanted to know what you did with that doll which was sitting on your bed. He seems to have no understanding of feminine frivolities.

You will be glad to know that I am sticking to my own neat little hole-in-the-wall and am not desecrating your sanctified boudoir.

We miss greatly the clatter of kettles, hissing of steam, and splash of water which signify your presence in the house. Except when Dakin is hammering or my type-writer clicking, everything is deathly still. We are all very sensible to your absence. It has gotten much warmer outside since you left. I certainly hope it has gotten warm for you in Knoxville. You don't want to go to partys with a red-nose, I'm sure.

The most momentous happening since your departure was Dakin's breaking of a window in a near-by apartment. Dakin doesn't seem at all depressed over it. Although the owner was very angry. It happens to be the house of one of Dakin's enemys - the breaking was done by accident, though. I guess it will have to be paid for.

With love to Aunt Belle and Ella, and wishing you the happiest time of your life,

yours lovingly, Tom.

[Rose Williams made her informal debut in Knoxville to take advantage of the social prominence of her aunt, Isabel ("Belle") Williams Brownlow (1883-1938), the younger sister of Cornelius. She recorded a month-long gala of parties, luncheons, and debutante balls in her diary (November 18-December 20, 1927, HRC), but the visit failed to produce a suitor for the hopeful eighteen year old. She "was never quite the same," TW stated in *Memoirs*: "A shadow had fallen over her that was to deepen steadily through the next four or five years" (p. 117). His warning about diet alludes to her chronic indigestion.

At least twice TW linked Rose and Blanche DuBois in describing the origin of *A Streetcar Named Desire* (1947). Rose's abortive courting in a southern city and the "frivolities" of her bath and boudoir anticipate with uncanny precision both the argument and the intimate feminine imagery of *Streetcar*.

Miss Florence, the divorced mother of TW's close friend Hazel Kramer, was a boisterous, unconventional woman whose company and support TW often sought, to Edwina's dismay.]

9. To Edwina Dakin Williams

SH: The Biltmore
Madison and Vanderbilt Avenues, New York
PM: Grand Central Station, New York,
July 2, 1928
[ALS, 6 pp. HRC]

Dear Mother,

I am dead tired! It is after eleven o'clock and this Biltmore bed looks as seductive as Paradise to the damned. Even so, I am going to write you this short letter to tell you the marvelous time that I'm having and the perfectly dazzling prospects for our four-day stay in N.Y. We have just concluded dinner with a multi-millionaire, one of Mrs. Watson's partners, in his seven room suite at the end of the hall. Dinner served in princely style by the foreign waiter!

Grandfather is perfectly thrilled. And of course I am! This man is a partner of <u>Wrigley's</u>! The first thing he did was to offer us some chewing gum. Tomorrow morning Grandfather and I are to have our breakfasts served in our room. At noon we meet Mrs. Watson and motor out to her magnificent Country Estate. In the evening we attend a performance of The Show Boat.

The rest of our program is not made out. Except that we are to attend The Three Musketeers Grand Opera Tuesday night.

<u>Also</u> Mrs. Watson has assured Grandfather that if Gov. Al Smith, who

rooms at the Biltmore at present, comes here, she will give Grandfather an introduction to him.

Really, I wouldn't be a bit surprised if Mrs. W.K. Vanderbilt didn't call at the door this next instant!!

What almost knocked me over during the dinner was when Mr. Cummings told me that I was sitting at the same table, in his private suite, where the Prince of Wales had sat during his stay at the Biltmore in 1921!

Did that kill me!!

Mrs. Watson is a lovely woman but I've never known anyone to talk with the rapidity that she does. She can't seem to get the words out of her mouth fast enough to suit her.

Well, we had a perfectly splendid trip up here on the train. I wish I could tell you all the things we're going to do here, but I don't know myself yet.

Tomorrow morning Grandfather & I are going to do a little excursioning on our own - around the main Blvds, on the buses etc.

In the meantime, the strongest smelling salts couldn't keep me awake.

Love to All, Tom.

[Before sailing for Europe, TW and his grandfather were entertained in New York by Jessie Watson, a partner in the Biltmore chain and a Dakin family friend. Their "excursioning" led them to Wall Street and the Battery and in the evening to the Ziegfeld Theatre for the original version of *Show Boat* (1927). The tour was one of many that Walter Dakin conducted for friends and parishoners, and it was also the first trip abroad for his seventeen-year-old grandson. Dressed in knickers, TW looked very much the waif of the party in a photograph taken on the deck of the *Homeric* and reprinted in *Memoirs*. The party sailed on July 6 and reached Paris in time to celebrate Bastille Day. On July 20 the tour continued to the south of France, then to the principal Italian cities, including Rome, Venice, and Milan, followed by Montreux, Cologne, Amsterdam, and London. By early-September TW was back in University City preparing for his final regular semester of high school.]

Smartly dressed in knickers, Tom on board the "Homeric" with Grandfather's touring party, 1928.

Tom on a hayride with "Ezzie" Mayes at the University of Missouri, ca. 1931.

10. *To the Williams Family*

SH: White Star Line
On board S.S. "Homeric."
PM: Southampton Paquebot,
July 13, 1928
[ALS, 8 pp. HRC]

Dear Family,

We are now approaching the British coast and of course we are antic-ipating that first glimpse of Europe with a great deal of pleasure. I begin to understand how Columbus felt when he came into sight of the West Indies.

An immense flock of gulls - very picturesque birds which have the remarkable faculty of standing perfectly still in the air - have been follow-ing the ship all day. Also we have passed several other boats - which gave us quite a thrill, since for 6 days we had seen nothing but the desolate vast-ness of the sea. Last night was the first unclouded sunset and it was glori-ously beautiful. The whole western sky and sea looked as though it were streaked with flame. Afterwards the clouds, which always come up in great numbers from the water where the sun sinks, assumed gorgeous coloring.

A few nights ago we saw northern lights which looked like enormous search lights across the sky.

The voyage has been extremely pleasant but you can imagine that we will all be very glad to set foot on our natural element once more.

The first day out I was just desperately sea-sick but have become fully adjusted to the ship's motion since then and am now quite well and ready to enjoy the delights of Gay Paree.

For the past three evenings there has been dancing aboard the ship. In our party there is a young widow who is studying theatrical dancing under the great Ned Wayburn in N.Y. I have had her for a partner and we have got along splendidly. We have really become quite celebrated aboard the ship. She has taught me the finale hop - one of those stamping dances - and since I have quite a penchant for stamping anyway, as Rose knows, we do it very well.

There is a saloon aboard the ship which offers all kinds of alcoholic drinks. And believe me, there is never a lack of customers. Everynight there's at least half a dozen choruses of Sweet Adeline sung from the bar-rail trou-badours. Grandfather, himself, keeps his tongue pretty slick with

Manhattin Coctails and Rye-Ginger Ales. I have tried them all but prefer none to plain ginger-ale and Coca Cola. So I'm afraid I'm not getting all the kick out of this boat that the others are getting.

I do not want to miss the first sight of land and so I will end up this letter and go out on the deck.

Hoping that you are all enjoying a pleasant summer and wishing that I could enclose some of the pleasures that I am having,

Yours lovingly, Tom.

[In *Memoirs* TW described the "widow" as a dancing teacher who "was enjoying a conspicuous flirtation" with a member of the party who resented his presence. "'You know his future, don't you?'" he reportedly said to the woman, within TW's hearing. "Mystified" at the time, he nonetheless remembered the prediction of homosexuality with "singular clarity" (p. 20).

The "great Ned Wayburn" was a Broadway director-choreographer whom Audrey Wood, TW's future agent, recalled in her memoir, *Represented by Audrey Wood* (1981): "In my mind I can still see this corpulent man, perched on his chair, eating a large piece of roast beef with his fingers as he watched his tired chorus girls dance on and on below, with no break for their food."]

11. *To Hazel Kramer*

SH: Hotel Rochambeau
4 Rue La Boëtie, Paris 8e
[July 15, 1928]
[ALS, 2 pp. HTC]

Dear Hazel,

We are just preparing to leave on a sightseeing excursion around the town. I just feel compelled to avail myself of this splendid stationary.

Paris is simply sublime, Hazel. Absolutely nothing like it. I'm enjoying it like everything.

Saw the most charmingly wicked show last night - Les Folies Bergéres. I will tell you all about it when I get home.

We are doing more delightful things! Dining at the Ritz! Going to the Grand Opera!

Last night was the festival celebrating the fall of the Bastille. The streets were gorgeous with Chinese lanterns flags and all sorts of decorations. Bands and dancing in the streets. Paris is certainly the gay city.

We start this morning with a long sight-seeing trip.

So I must now terminate this letter.

Je suis le votre,

Avec une couer plein d'amour, Tom.

[TW met Hazel Kramer in St. Louis when he was eleven and she nine: "Some young hoods were . . . throwing rocks at a plump little girl. I went to her defense . . . {and} thus began my closest childhood friendship which ripened into a romantic attachment" (*Memoirs*, pp. 14-15). Neither family encouraged the relationship, although it remains unclear whether TW's father, Cornelius, or Hazel's grandfather, Emil Kramer, or both, took steps to end it when the friends reached college age. Hazel never fully shared TW's "attachment," "un coeur plein d'amour," and in 1935 he sadly learned of her engagement to Terrence McCabe, whom she met while attending the University of Wisconsin and later married.]

12. *To Edwina Dakin Williams*

SH: Hotel Rochambeau
4 Rue La Boëtie, Paris 8e
19 Juillet [1928]
[ALS, 6 pp. HRC]

Dear Mother,

I have just imbibed a whole glass of french champagne and am feeling consequently very elated. It is our last evening in Paris which excuses the unusual indulgence.

French champagne is the only drink that I like here. But it is really delicious.

We have certainly had an exciting time in Paris. We've done practically everything there is to do. It takes me about fifteen minutes every evening to write up all our daily activitys.

Today we went to the Louvre and out to Versailles. Our morning at the Louvre permitted only the most limited [*omission*]

Versailles is a perfect wonder-land. It was thrilling to see and walk among those places with such romantic historical connection. We stood upon the balcony upon which Marie Antoinette boldly faced the mob which came to threaten her life. We looked into the secret passageway through which she fled when the crowd of enraged citizens broke into her boudoir. The palace is exquisite throughout. All the ceilings are covered with rich paintings - the walls inlaid with gold. We walked down the long hall of mirrors, with its resplendent chandeliers and windows opening out upon the beautifully landscaped garden. It is the room in which the peace treaty of the Great War was signed. We saw the very table that it was signed upon.

What appealed to me the most was the park in which Marie Antoinette found retreat from the court life which she detested. It was in this park that she played milk-maid. We saw all the rustic little buildings in which she amused herself. Also, the huge, gold carriages in which she rode on fête days.

The most beautiful part about it, though, is the surrounding woodlands. They surpass for natural beauty any woods I have ever seen. They are filled with little streams and waterfalls and down the steep banks which are on either side of the road, there are thick, beautiful vines.

We have seen the two notorious Parisian shows - The Folies Bergére and the Moulin Rouge. The both completely live up to their reputation. No American show would dare to put over the things that they did. It was, however, more artistic than it was immodest. Anyway, when you're in Paris, you might as well leave all dispensable conventions behind.

I can easily see why some people look upon Paris as the whole world. It really is marvelous. We went to the famous Grand Opera a few nights ago and saw the opera of Romeo and Juliet. The music was very beautiful.

We proceed tomorrow morning to Marseilles - Thence to Nice, where we will probably get to do some salt water swimming.

Do you know I have'nt had a real bath since arriving in France? I feel disgraced. Baths are considered rather a vanity here, I believe as no hotel rooms, except those of exclusively American patronage, are equiped with bathtubs. I keep fairly clean only by use of the sponge and little foot-tub.

Grandfather insists that I retire early this evening but I don't know how I can manage it on top of all the champagne and my late hours of the past week.

We take the train tomorrow at seven, though, so I suppose I had better submit.

Yours - with love to all - Tom.

[TW's summary of "daily activitys" was an early instance of his penchant for journal writing. The notes were probably the basis for a series of ten travel sketches
(October 30, 1928-April 16, 1929) that he wrote for his high school paper, the *U.
City Pep*. The second, "The Tomb of the Capuchins," leads earnestly with the statement that "these monks were all at one time very decently interred" (November 12,
1928).

TW gave no hint in letters or published sketches of the crisis that he later
described in *Memoirs*: "It began when I was walking alone down a boulevard in
Paris. . . . Abruptly, it occurred to me that the process of thought was a terrifying-
ly complex mystery of human life. I felt myself walking faster and faster as if trying to outpace this idea. . . . At least a month of the tour was enveloped for me by
this phobia about the processes of thought, and the phobia grew and grew till I
think I was within a hairsbreadth of going quite mad from it" (p. 20).]

13. To Edwina Dakin Williams

SH: Hotel Terminus
Montreux (Suisse)
5 August 1928
[ALS, 4 pp. HRC]

Dear Mother,

Montreux is the most delightful place that we have yet visited. It even
surpasses Nice and Sorrento, each of which we had thought perfection. It is
situated right on the shores of beautiful lake Geneva and is surrounded by
the gigantic, snow-capped Alpine mountains. I do wish that our visit could
be prolonged at least a week. But our schedule is relentless - we have to leave
at six o'clock tomorrow morning. The change of weather from hot Italy to
chilly Switzerland was of course very decided - but also very welcome.

Today we went by motor boat up the lake shore to the romantic old
Castle of Chillon. The trip was one of the most pleasant we've taken. The
castle was not at all dismal as we had expected but really quite attractive
with its court-yard filled with flowers and its large bushes. If captivity for
life were imposed upon me, I should prefer the Castle of Chillon to any
other prison. It is preserved very nearly as it was originally, several centu-
rys before. We were shown the places where Byron, Shelley, Dickens and
H. Beecher Stowe had scratched their names on the walls; the stone pillars
and iron rings to which the famous prisoner of Chillon and his six com-

rades were strapped; also the deep pit into which the condemned were tossed, to suffer slow death by starvation. I volunteered to go down in the hole to see what it looked like - but when informed that there would be no way out, I withdrew the offer quite hastily!

This afternoon Benton A. and myself went up to the Montreux-Plâge, a splendid bathing-beach, much nicer than either Nice or the Lido at Venice, in which I also swam. The clear, fresh water was agreeable to taste - unlike the salt. It was also much more invigoratingly cool. Afterwards we wrapped up in huge Turkish towels and smoked cigarettes on the smooth terrace. Had a wonderful time. I do wish that Rose could have been along to enjoy this lake with us.

You do not need to feel the least bit concerned over my safety as long as I am with Grandfather. He is the most apprehensive person imaginable. He is perfectly terrified if I step off the train for a second during a thirty minute stop and at the dinner-table, whenever fish is served, he hollers down the table, as if he had discovered dynamite, that there are bones in the fish. I am given detailed instruction as to how the fish should be dissected and the bones taken out.

He is almost as bad about me as another lady in the party is about her luggage. She gets hysterical whenever her bag is taken out of her sight and lately has almost insisted upon carrying her own trunk.

Venice and Milan were both exquisite. We visited the great cathedral at Milan three times in our one day there - it was so beautiful. Decidedly the finest piece of architecture we've seen anywhere. We are still shopping - we will soon be as laden down as Marley's ghost! In a short time now we will be starting home.

Love to All, Tom.

[TW echoes the title of Byron's poem "The Prisoner of Chillon" (1816) in describing the dungeon where François Bonivard was imprisoned in 1530 for defending Swiss liberties against the Duke of Savoy.

Thomas Benton Abbey, Jr., of Webb, Mississippi, and his mother were members of the touring party.]

14. *To the Williams Family*

SH: Hotel Schweizerhof / Christl. Hospiz
Koln A. Rhein / Viktoriastrasse 11
[ca. August 10, 1928]
[ALS, 7 pp. HRC]

Dear Mother, Dad Etc.,

We have just arrived in Cologne after our delightful all-day trip on the Rhine. The scenery was beautiful - rolling hills, surmounted by the ivy-grown ruins of castles. There were many points of legendary & historical interest all along the way such as the Mouse tower of Bingen where the old Bishop of Bingen was supposed to have been devoured by the rats and the Lorelei rocks where according to the old German myths the beauteous mermaid Loreleis bathed in the sun, singing their siren songs to the incautious sailors who ventured near. Grandfather said he dared them to show themselves but his boastful valour went untested. The Loreleis were either busy house-keeping or else did not consider us worthy prey, for we were allowed to pass unmolested. Many picturesque little German towns were stretched along the banks, all with cobbled streets, turreted churches[,] high, gabled roofs and chimney pots and bright flowers. It certainly looks like the land of the fairy-tales. The Germans impress me as being much more good-natured and kindly than the people of the other countrys we have passed through. The Swiss are much like them. We enjoyed our visit in Switzerland immensely. I have written you a letter from Montreux. Interlaken was also extremely attractive. The tremendous Swiss Alps were of course magnificent. We took two splendid trips - one out to a glacier and the other through beautiful Lauterbrunnen Valley to some marvelous water-falls. There was a cave in the glacier, carved right through the solid ice. It was most interesting, although rather chilling and dampening, to walk through the ice-walled tunnel. It was dazzling bright from the intense reflections of the sun and a clear, beautiful blue in color. In our eagerness to get some good camera pictures, Benton and I clambered consider[ably] beyond the danger line on the top of the glacier and the Swiss guide became almost frantic, since the day was unusually warm and the ice slippery. Fortunately Grandfather was not present. If he were, he would surely have collapsed.

We got down quickly enough as soon as we realized that we were the cause of all the wild excitement below. I imagine that Grandfather & I will arrive back in St. Louis on about September 1 or 2.

Your letter telling about the astonishing installment of frigidaires just arrived after having gone through almost as many places as we have. Your other letters arrived somewhat more promptly but not all in their chronological order.

We are just about dead from our long trip. I can hardly keep my eyes open. Since we have a lot of sightseeing on for tomorrow morning, I imagine I had better get into that nice bed upstairs with the thick feather quilt!

Love to All, Tom.

[The Mouse Tower and the Lorelei were familiar tourist sights on the Rhine, but their legendary associations with death may have reminded TW of his own morbid fears: "My phobia about thought processes had reached its climax" in the cathedral in Cologne, he recalled in *Memoirs*: "Then a truly phenomenal thing happened. . . . It was as if an impalpable hand were placed upon my head, and at the instant of that touch, the phobia was lifted away as lightly as a snowflake though it had weighed on my head like a skull-breaking block of iron" (p. 21).]

15. *To Walter E. Dakin*

[6254 Enright Avenue
University City, Missouri]
[September 1928]
[TLS, 1 p. Columbia]

Dear Grandfather,

I feel deeply penitent for having been so slow in writing you. However you know that during the first quarter of one's senior year, he is exceptionally busy. I expect to get off a letter to Mrs. Watson directly after finishing this one - which I know you are pleased to hear.

A very thrilling event is now impending in the house-hold. For the first time in our dramatic social history one of us is going to attend the V.P. Ball - in the dress circle! It's Rose, of course. She has been invited to go by a Mr. Mathewson who works down at Dad's office and with whom Rose has had several dates of late. He is a very nice, attractive fellow and Rose is as excited over going with him as the ball itself. She received the invitation this morning along with the accompanying V.P. favor which this time was a very handsome set of bridge playing-cards.

Rose is going to wear her orange evening dress with all the Tulle drapery. I suppose Grand will recognize the description. Also, she has had her evening cloak cleaned and expects to wear that. It came out surprisingly well and Mother and I were gratified to see some in the windows down town which were the exact style, length and brocaded silk material and with the same kind of white fox collar and cuffs. She's going to look the berrys.

Mother and I have been given seats, too, but as usual they are way up in the peanut gallery. I suppose we shall be able to see Rose dance, however at the conclusion of the ceremonies. It is going to be a particularly elaborate ball this season, since it is the golden anniversary. The decorations will be beautiful.

I was awfully glad to get the exquisite little picture of the Lady of Shallot. I hope that you will make the scrap-book and that you will let me see it when it is finished. I found the little diarys I had written. At first I thought that they had been lost. I am going to re-write them on the typewriter sometime soon.

Write soon, as we are anxious for news,

Much love, Tom.

[The Veiled Prophet was a pageant of romance and chivalry created by the business leaders of St. Louis. Based upon the New Orleans Mardi Gras, the annual festivities included a parade and fairs and ended with a formal ball that was the preëminent event of the fall season. Rose Williams held a coveted ticket of admission to the "dress circle," or main floor, but she was not a debutante maid of honor and would be seen only "at the conclusion of the ceremonies."

In 1878 the first visual representation of the Veiled Prophet (a leading citizen chosen each year to preside over the carnival) showed a heavily armed figure, masked and robed in white and wearing a pointed hat, who closely resembled a klansman. In the 1960s the Veiled Prophet was attacked for racism and exclusiveness and lost much of its membership.

The "little diarys" are probably the same summary of "activitys" that TW made during his trip to Europe (see letter #12).]

16. To Walter E. Dakin

[6254 Enright Avenue
University City, Missouri]
[November 22, 1928]
[TLS, 2 pp. Columbia]

Dear Grandfather,

Dakin and I are having our Thanksgiving holidays from school now and enjoying them very much. We all had our Turkey Dinner out at the club. It was a huge dinner, perfectly delicious, and we ate enormously. There was only one other party out there besides ourselves so we practically had the club to ourselves. Rose and I had a nice time dancing after the dinner to the victrola. Afterwards Dakin and I went to see a real good picture-show. So the holiday was very adequately celebrated.

Graduation is getting very close, of course. I received my class ring last week. For an inexpensive ring, only five dollars, it seems quite handsome. It is dull gold, silver and black with the school emblem engraved on it. Mother and I have decided that I should wait until the beginning of the school year, in September, to enter the University. It is much simpler and easier than entering in January. Besides, to jump directly from high-school into college would be rather breath-taking. There is such a big difference, of course.

Aunt Belle has sent Rose and I both a very warm invitation to visit her in Knoxville some time this Spring. She has written us two letters and she promises us a marvelous time. Of course Rose is simply wild to go. I would like it myself. However I have been thinking about taking a short business course after graduation; also of doing some post grad. work in my Latin so that I will go over to Washington with a full four-year course of it to my credit. I shall only have completed three years and a half at the time of my graduation. If I went in May and didn't stay long, I suppose the visit wouldn't interfere.

Have any of your investments been affected by these fluctuations on the stock market? My economics teacher was saying yesterday that periods of great "inflation" were often followed by panics and that people should invest very cautiously. I suppose, however, that you have got your fortune invested just as securely as possible. It's generally wise, though, to investigate now and then.

Economics is a subject I just started this term and it interests me a great deal.

I have always before been so ignorant about business, finance etc. It is considered a very difficult subject but so far I have done well in it.

I have been reading a good number of biographies this year, which I am sure you will commend. Probably you remember how I picked up that volume of Ludwig's Napoleon on the boat and liked it so well that the owner had to ask me for it. I tried to get it at the library but it was out. Instead, I got a life of the Kaiser Wilhelm by the same author. Since then I have read several others of celebrated literary personages. I have one at home now about Shelly, whose poetry I am studying at school. His life is very interesting. He seems to have been the wild, passionate and dissolute type of genius: which makes him very entertaining to read about.

Rose and Mr. Matthewson just returned from the picture show and all the family has retired to the back of the house, to give them undisputed sway. Last Saturday they went out to the Country Club's Thanksgiving dance. Rose wore her green evening dress and Mother's red shawl which we brought her from Europe. They looked awfully well together.

Rose is hoping to receive a fur-coat this Xmas but so far there have been no indications that she will. Mother has promised to exert her influence. I do hope that she can get one. They give so much eclat to a girl's appearance.

If you give me a Xmas present this year, I would like something to wear. Something bright and snappy in the way of a scarf, socks, or ties. Mother and Dad are planning to go to see Mary Roger's friend. They live right in the neighborhood. Rose thinks that she would enjoy meeting them. They are really more nearly Rose's contemporaries than Mother's.

Write us real soon.

Yours very lovingly, Tom.

[At first TW planned to attend Washington University in St. Louis. His enrollment at the State University of Missouri in Columbia was due in part to its well-known School of Journalism.

Emil Ludwig wrote both *Napoleon* (1926) and *Wilhelm Hohenzollern: The Last of the Kaisers* (1926). *Shelley: His Life and Work* (1927), by Walter Edwin Peck, may have been TW's source for the "dissolute" genius.

It was at the Woodlawn Country Club, where the family celebrated

Thanksgiving, that Rose had danced with "Mr. Matthewson," probably Colin W. Mathieson, an employee of the Friedman-Shelby Branch. In 1981 TW recalled his sister's "love" for an "ambitious" young man who worked at the International Shoe Company, who "paid her court," and then "just didn't call anymore." That, he concluded, "was when Rose first began to go into a mental decline" (*Conversations*, pp. 330-331).

In the same interview, TW attributed the young man's retreat to a scandal that had damaged Cornelius's position with the company in December 1936 (see letter #62), an unlikely concurrence in view of the advanced state of Rose's illness at this time. Whether attempting to improve the dramatic effect of his sister's desertion or merely confusing chronology, TW had long ago derived the powerful and recurring figure of the disconsolate lady-in-waiting from Rose's failure in love.]

17. *To Walter E. Dakin*

[6254 Enright Avenue
University City, Missouri]
[January 31, 1929]
[ALS, 2 pp. HTC]

Dear Grandfather,

I suppose you have already received news of that momentous event in my career - my graduation from high-School! I received my report cards this Monday. I had passed all my exams, very creditably. In a few days I am going to register in one of the two fine business schools here. I think I will take a course in short hand and type-writing. I am also going to continue my course in Latin at the High-School so that when I enter the University in Sept. I will have had a complete 4 years of Latin and also an extra cred-it to my account.

I have bought the Tuxedo which you gave me money for. It is very handsome, satin lapels and trouser stripes and a silk, brocaded vest. It fits very nicely. The Prom will take place in just a week now.

Last night Rose went out with her friend Mr. Mathewson, to the musi-cal comedy, My Maryland, at the Shubert Theater. She said it was an awful-ly cute show. Both she and mother are going to see the Strange Interlude which comes next week. It is the play written by Eugene O'Neill - you probably remember that it was in New York while we were there. Its unusual feature is that all the actors speak their thoughts, showing the decided difference between what people <u>say</u> to others and what they <u>think</u> in reality. It is tremendously long - begins at 5:00 o'clock and lasts till 11:00, with only a short intermission for dinner.

The editor of the school-paper, who is in my Latin class, wants me to continue my writing for the paper. I have just concluded an article on Pompeii this evening which I will send to you as soon as it is published.

With much love to you and Grand,

Tom.

[TW did not graduate from University City High School on January 24, as planned, but on June 13, 1929 (as reported by Leverich). He removed two incomplete grades in the spring term and graduated fifty-third in a class of eighty-three. Internal evidence suggests that TW wrote this letter after January 24 and therefore misled his grandfather about the "momentous event." The apparent deception was continued in an April letter to Walter Dakin that alludes to TW's being "out of High-school" (see letter #18).

While *My Maryland* (1927), an operetta with a Civil War background, played at the Shubert Theater, attendance records were set at the American for the Theatre Guild production (February 4-16) of *Strange Interlude* (1928). TW echoed popular reports of the extravaganza, but when he later wrote about the play in a college paper, he described Eugene O'Neill's use of asides as "obvious" ("Some Representative Plays of O'Neill," n.d., HRC).

"The Ruins of Pompeii" was published in the *U. City Pep* on February 5, 1929.

This letter is dated January 31, 1929, in a hand that does not appear to be TW's.]

18. To Walter E. Dakin

[6254 Enright Avenue
University City, Missouri]
April, 1929
[ALS, 6 pp. HTC]

Dear Grandfather,

I suppose that this is a birth-day letter your birth-day being so imminent. Mother and I were wishing we were with you so that we might all celebrate it together. Do birthdays impress you as much as they do me? I suppose you've had enough to make them seem very common-place. My eighteenth birth-day, just passed, certainly seemed very impressive to me. Being eighteen and out of High-school makes you feel very mature.

Dad has been traveling a good deal lately and with both him and Rose absent, this seems a most quiet and reposeful house-hold.

I suppose you have already received letters from Rose, describing her marvelous times in Knoxville. We received one containing her picture, published on the society page of a Knoxville paper. We thought it was remarkably good for a picture taken by a news-paper photographer. It was a profile picture - and Rose has a very handsome profile which even a news-paper camera could not fail to reveal.

She seems to be going just as much as when she visited there in the winter. Mother feels anxious, somewhat, about her having enough endurance for such an active life as she is leading there. However, as long as she's having a good time I don't see how it can hurt her.

She wrote about having been out with Rose Comfort. She said she was "perfectly adorable" and that Aunt Belle and Ella were charmed with her. She belongs to one of the best sororities and drives a cute sport roadster. Of course Grand will be pleased to hear how well she's getting on. I think it's nice that she and Rose should meet again. Perhaps John T. will invite Rose to visit her sometime.

Our Spring weather here is unusually pleasant. I have heard that the rivers are pretty high. But I don't suppose there is much danger of another flood like the one a year ago.

I hope you and Grand are both well,

Yours very lovingly, Tom.

[Rose described her present visit to Knoxville as "perfectly marvelous," but her indigestion led her to say that she would "never be entirely well" until she stopped "eating lobster croquetts and rich deserts" (letter to Edwina, April 31, 1929, HRC). A later examination at Barnes Hospital in St. Louis would reveal that her indigestion was "solely nervous" and that she had "no serious organic trouble" (see letter #35).

The "adorable" Rose Comfort (first step-cousin once removed of Rose Williams) was the daughter of John Tate Raulston and his first wife, Comfort Tate, both of Winchester, Tennessee. His second wife was Grand's sister, Estelle. "John T." had "the dubious distinction," as TW put it, of presiding over the famous "'Monkey trial'" ("Grand") in Dayton, Tennessee, in 1925. A lay preacher in the Methodist Episcopal Church, he was a fierce critic of Clarence Darrow, who defended John T.

Scopes against the charge of teaching evolution in his high school biology class. TW would later dedicate the play *Not About Nightingales* (written in 1938) to Darrow. He also used the Comfort family name in *Baby Doll*.]

19. To Walter E. Dakin

[6254 Enright Avenue
University City, Missouri]
[ca. September 1, 1929]
[TLS, 1 p. HRC]

Dear Grandfather:

I am leaving for school exactly one week from today and I am awfully busy making the final preparations; going to the dentist's, getting clothes and all other necessary equipment. Mother is going up with me to spend one day to see that I am properly settled. She acts as though I were leaving for war instead of for college.

We are having fearfully hot weather here - we have all been wondering how you were standing it down in Mississippi. But I suppose you are willing to suffer any degree of temperature as long as it is for the good of the cotton. I am trying to get a lot of exercise before I go off to college so that I will have more weight and be in better condition - this last week I am going to play lots of golf and go swimming as frequently as I can.

I think Grand plans to leave in about a week, too, so your summer-bachelorhood is about over. There isn't the slightest news now, Grandfather, but there'll be plenty next week, after I am settled at Columbia and I will find time to write you a letter then. If you happen to have any particularly kind thoughts of me this winter, say it with a shirt or a neck-tie. You know college boys are generally pretty clothes-conscious and I haven't any too many to be conscious of.

Rose still thinks of motoring down with Virginia in October - provided her stomach trouble is sufficiently improved.

Lovingly, Tom

[The University of Missouri is located 125 miles west of St. Louis in "the charming town of Columbia" (*Memoirs*, p. 24). Known locally as "Little Dixie," the area had a southern way of life that resembled the small-town setting of TW's Mississippi childhood. In his first semester he lived at Effie Graham's boarding house and studied French, Geology, Composition, Citizenship, and the mandatory R.O.T.C. His academic work was uninspired, but he absorbed the college scene, storing material that would later be used in stories and plays. It was at MU that his eccentricity also took root, particularly his dependence upon others for the necessities of life and his resistance to such cumpulsory duty as R.O.T.C. Although TW made no lasting personal or professional friendships at Columbia, he found there a timely refuge from the parental storms in St. Louis.]

20. To Rose Isabel Williams

[1004 University Avenue
Columbia, Missouri]
[ca. September 14, 1929]
[ALS, 2 pp. HTC]

Dear Rose,

I have just returned from the College Chorus try-outs. I went just as a spectator, along with some girls next door and Harold, my roommate. But after hearing the pitiful efforts some of the boys made to sing, I had courage to make a try myself and to my surprise, the voice teacher accepted me as a first bass - after a great deal of deliberation. Of course I'm awfully pleased to get in, since the members of the chorus have lots of fun from what I hear. We give concerts in the churches and on school fête days. I will have some use, now, for my tux.

The instructor said my greatest difficulty was in reading notes. He played the bass and the soprano notes together and my voice often made leaps into the soprano.

All day I have been trying to get my military uniform - they are now being issued - but haven't yet succeded. We have to wear them 3 mornings a week when we drill. I will get a lot of kick out of being dressed up like a soldier. I will have my picture taken in it with my little camera and send you one.

Friday Miss Graham is taking all of us on a picnic to Rollins Springs near here, in her car.

That's all the news at present. Write me what you are doing.

Love, Tom

P.S. Tell Mother that the chorus fee is $3.00 for music, etc. It would be more than I have on hand, at present.

[TW had two roommates at MU named Harold. The first, Harold Edmund Carroll, lived at Graham's boarding house in the fall of 1929, while the second and more important, Harold Arthur Mitchell, lived at the Alpha Tau Omega house in 1930 and was memorialized as Mitch in *A Streetcar Named Desire*. He became TW's best friend at MU, although he left after the winter semester of 1931.

TW did not take well to military dress. William S. Bell wrote to him on December 28, 1958, and asked if he were the same "T.L.W." with whom he had roomed at MU and who "made me very mad by calling my Chi Omega Sweetheart 'Bouncing Bubbies?'" He added in friendly reminiscence, "Are you the TLW that looked so lousy in your R.O.T.C. uniform?" (HRC). Bell pledged Alpha Tau Omega in 1931 and was also a member of the Pershing Rifles, a drill company selected from men "outstanding in their military work" (*Savitar*, 1932).]

21. To Cornelius Coffin Williams

[1004 University Avenue
Columbia, Missouri]
Monday, Sept. 23, 1929
[ALS, 4 pp. HTC]

Dear Dad,

I was certainly pleased to get your letter and the check. I spoke to Miss Graham about the arrangements for paying her and she said that she had just written you about it.

I think if you will add about $1.50 to your monthly check to Miss Graham, that will cover the laundry expense. Of course there will be some variation in the amount sent to the laundry. If it costs any more than that, I can pay the difference from my allowance. I am pretty economical with my laundry. I had only 3 shirts in the laundry last week and 2 pairs of socks, besides my pajamas etc. So far I haven't had any clothes pressed. And they are still in pretty good shape.

Yesterday I attended a dinner at the A.T.O. house. I liked some of the men there a great deal. They are building a large new chapter house now which will be completed in a couple of months.

I wouldn't be at all sorry to get a bid - although I'm just as comfortable here as I could be anywhere, I suppose. Miss Graham's meals are really delicious and the crowd in the boarding-house are very friendly. I could not have hoped for a nicer rooming place.

Saturday night Miss Graham, a Math. teacher and some of my fellow-roomers drove over to Jefferson City - 30 miles - in Miss Grahams new Buick roadster. I was the only one besides Miss Graham who could drive so she appointed me chauffeur. And we made a great night of it. Miss Graham isn't at all the typical old maid. She has as much life as any co-ed in Columbia.

I enjoyed seeing the beautiful State Capitol in Jefferson City, situated on a high bluff over the Missouri river. Sunday morning, before leaving for the frat. dinner, I drove over to the Columbia air-port where we saw some planes, participating in an air derby from Kansas City to some place in the East.

So far I have had no difficulty with my school work. I like my French particularly. The course is in translation of modern French short-stories.

I hope things are going well at the house - and at home.

Affectionately yours, Tom.

[Pleas for money were a staple item in TW's letters to Cornelius, a well-compensated employee of the International Shoe Company but a reluctant supporter of his son's education: "When I was about to set off for college in the early fall of 1929 suddenly there wasn't any money for the tuition; if it hadn't been for Grand coming through with a thousand dollars right in the nick of time, I couldn't have gone" (*Memoirs*, p. 24).

TW did not attend rush week when the Greek houses made bids to prospective pledges. It was through his father's "intervention" that Alpha Tau Omega contacted TW and invited him to pledge.]

22. To Edwina Dakin and Cornelius Coffin Williams

[1004 University Avenue
Columbia, Missouri]
Thursday, Oct. [3] 1929
[ALS, 4 pp. HTC]

Dear Mother and Dad,

I have some very big news for you in this letter. I have just pledged the Alpha Tau Omega. They invited me to supper last night and afterwards took me up to the council chamber where I was asked to join the frat, and offered a pledge pin. I have never accepted anything with more alacrity. I have been over to the A.T.O. house several times and I liked the fellows there a great deal. They are just completing a new chapter house - one of the finest on the campus. I don't think I could have made a better frat. They are very cordial and congenial. And they are not stereotyped, like the members of some frats. They don't limit their membership to a single type of fellow. It is one of the oldest and largest national fraternities - was started in 1865, right after the Civil War, in Richmond, Va. Its purpose was to help cement the friendship of the North and South.

They recited the whole history to me last night.

As soon as I re-entered the parlor, wearing the pledge-pin, the whole chapter swarmed around me with congratulations. I had never felt so important.

I think they will want me to move in as soon as the new house is opened. That will be near the end of next month. I have not broached the subject of moving out to Effie. Perhaps you could come up and negotiate with her, when the time comes.

From what I hear, living in a Frat is more expensive than boarding out. However, the social advantages of being a fraternity man are certainly great enough to warrant the extra expense. A non-frat man is practically "out of it" in Columbia, as I have found in the past month.

In business and social life after you are out of the University, belonging to a fraternity is still a very big asset.

A young man whom Mr. Morris, son of the shoe salesman, brought around to see me, is also being rushed by the A.T.O.

I expect I will have to go to parties and dances every week, as the pledges are always given lots of entertainment.

I am awfully sorry that Rose has had to go back to the hospital. I surely hope they finally succeed in curing her of her long trouble. Tell her that I want to have her up here as soon as she is able. Attractive sisters add much to one's prestige in a fraternity.

There are quite a number [of] older men - including some faculty members - in the Frat. The Dean of men, Mr. Heckel, who teaches my Citizenship, is a member. There is no further news.

Lovingly, Tom.

["Surely," TW noted in *Memoirs*, the brothers "had never encountered such an eccentric young man, let alone pledged him" (p. 26). The names of three fellow pledges, James Connor, James Dobyne, and John Venable, would reappear, respectively, in *The Glass Menagerie*, a story entitled "The Resemblance Between a Violin Case and a Coffin" (1950), and *Suddenly Last Summer* (1958).

Rose's "long trouble" may have been exacerbated by her last visit to Knoxville. Typically her "marvelous" times with her aunts led to self-doubt and depression when she returned to University City.]

23. To Cornelius Coffin Williams

[1004 University Avenue
Columbia, Missouri]
Monday, Oct. 14, 1929
[TLS w/ autograph postscript, 2 pp. HRC]

Dear Dad,

I haven't yet heard from Mother or Rose whether you have returned from Knoxville - nor how Aunt Ella is. I hope that the lack of further news about her indicates that she is improving. I was awfully sorry to learn how seriously ill she was and I am anxious to hear how she is now.

Not knowing how long you would be in Knoxville, I have delayed thanking you for the golf-sticks. I surely was glad to get them: and I have been using them pretty often. Harold, my room-mate, played in the finals of the University golf tournament. He is teaching me a lot about the game.

Friday afternoon my Geology class went on an expedition trip to a marble quarry near here, to make a study of the rock. In my scientific zeal, I climbed up the side of the quarry. After I had gotten some distance up, a piece of rock to which I was holding started to crumble and I slid to the ground, about twelve feet. I wasn't hurt a bit, except for some scratches, but the leg of my pants was ripped over half the way up. I think I suffered nearly as much from embarassment as I would have from a sprained ankle or wrist. Fortuneately the pants were just a pair of khaki ones that I had borrowed for the trip from Harold. He enjoyed the joke so much that he didn't mind the loss of the pants.

I found a couple of very good fossils on the trip. They were of little sea animals that had been imbedded in the rock thousands of years ago, when the rock was on the bottom of the ocean.

Geology is a hard subject - but very interesting.

I am surely glad that Rose is coming up. Please remind her that if she wishes to see the game she had better send me the money for her ticket immediately. It is $2.50. If she sends the money now I can reserve the seats and, therefore, probably get better ones.

Miss Graham said that you had sent her the check for my board but that you hadn't included anything for the laundry. If you wish, I will have her send you the bill and you can enclose the amount with my allowance. Miss Graham says she doesn't care when I pay it. She is keeping the charges listed.

I was sorry to have been out when Mother called last week. I had been to the library, doing some reference work in Geology. Tell Rose they have no fiction in the library, so she need not be afraid that I was reading novels there.

Hoping you and the rest of the family are well,

Lovingly, Tom.

PS Give my thanks to Mother and Dakin for the fudge. It was so good that it only lasted 15 minutes.

[Cornelius's older sister, Ella Williams (1875-1958), was operated on for appendicitis and recovered from a grave condition.

Neither the lesson in geology nor the adventure at the stone quarry was lost upon TW's later characters. In *Battle of Angels* (1940) Myra Torrance remarks that "ten thousand years from today we'll just be little telltale marks on the side of rocks which people refer to as fossils." And in *A Streetcar Named Desire* Blanche DuBois proposes "a moonlight swim at the old rock-quarry," a rendezvous adjoining the campus that was reserved for "Night Classes" (*Savitar*, 1930).

Recurring symptoms and hospitalization frustrated Rose's plan to visit Columbia on October 19 for the football game with Drake.]

24. *To Rose Isabel Williams*

[1004 University Avenue
Columbia, Missouri]
Nov. 3, 1929
[ALS, 4 pp. HTC]

Dear Rose,

I hope that you are not reading this letter in a hospital bed! You surely ought to be out of it by now.

Your picture was delivered to me yesterday and I haven't anything of which I am prouder. It is certainly a beautiful picture. One of the fellows in the house said you were too good-looking to be anything but a movie-actress.

I am surely delighted that you are thinking of coming up to visit me. Why not make it the week before Thanksgiving? We could ride home together for the Thanksgiving holidays.

I think that would be just grand!

I've been obeying strictly your injunctions to "study hard and keep awake". I haven't missed a single 8:00 class. I have to study hard this term, since one of the conditions of my A.T.O. initiation is to make an average of M. A large number of my fraternity brothers have been pledges for 2 or 3 years because of their inability to meet that requirement. Of course I don't wish to share their fate.

I know that my frat. initiation won't be as bad as some of [the] jokes played on me in this house. Yesterday morning some of the boys burst in the room while I was dressing and shoved me down the stairs, out the front-door and into the yard with nothing on but my shirt, socks and a pair of track pants. Can you conceive of anything like that, outside of slap-stick comedy?

To one of my natural modesty and bow-leggedness it was terribly embarassing - especially as there was quite a crowd of co-eds passing along the walk at the time.

The track pants were the stunning blue-and-white striped ones.

My muscles are rather sore this evening from horse-backing. I rode for two-hours, circling around the pole at every pace from a walk to a gallop. I should be a master equestrian before long -

I have been quite well - haven't had a single cold since coming here. That is doing awfully well, for me.

Now, please don't disappoint me again about coming up for a visit. Write me soon the date of your coming -

Very lovingly, Tom

[Predictably the grade "M" meant that "the student ranks among the medium students." TW may not have missed "a single 8:00 class," but his transcript shows that he was assessed one negative credit hour for eighteen other absences in the fall.]

25. To Rose Isabel Williams

[1004 University Avenue
Columbia, Missouri]
[ca. November 17, 1929]
[ALS, 4 pp. HTC]

Dear Rose,

I am surely ashamed of not having written until now. I have had less time than usual, though, as the frat. has established a new ruling for pledges of studying 3 hours every evening in the frat study-hall. It just came into affect this week. I think this regulation will help my grades a lot. One of the fellows in the house is an expert in geology, my most difficult subject, and he is giving me some free tutoring.

One thing I can say for the A.T.O. house is that they don't encourage laziness in their pledges. They have a supervisor stationed at each end of the study-hall and they don't allow us to lift our noses from our books for a minute. They are making practically all of the pledges sign up for some form of competitive sports. The last time I was there one of them asked me if I could run two miles. Not knowing what was up, I answered that I supposed I could. He said "alright, you are signed up for cross-country racing."

I don't believe training for it will start for a couple of months, though.

I am surely in an embarassing dilemma with both your and Hazel's birthday coming this week and I without sufficient funds to buy either of you a birthday present. I suppose I can count on your forgiveness. But I don't know about Hazel's.

Ask Mother if she could buy me a book - send it to Columbia, so I could send it to Hazel from here. I will repay her out of my next months allowance.

I am particularly poor at present, due to someone's having taken $3.00 from my trunk one night while I was at pledge meeting. I am really having quite a time keeping possession of some of my things here.

I am delighted that you will be here the end of this week. Will you arrive Friday - or Saturday. Make it one or the other, please.

Bill Kiefaber has offered to take me home in his ford for about ½ train fare. Would you like to go with him? It has been washed, polished, repaired and looks 100% better.

With love to all, Tom.

If Mother will get that book for me, I would like either The Methodist Faun by Anne Parrish or A Farewell to Arms by Ernest Hemingway.

[William Otto Kiefaber, of St. Louis, graduated from MU in 1931 with a degree in Business. Recast as "the merchant Kiefaber of Laurel," he testifies against Blanche DuBois in *A Streetcar Named Desire*.

The protagonist in Anne Parrish's novel *The Methodist Faun* (1929) is a sickly, insecure artist who is beset by an over-protective mother, lives in a stagnant, intolerant town, and has a divided sexual nature. The novel's message to Hazel Kramer, to whom TW had reportedly written a letter proposing marriage on his first night in Columbia, is stated in chapter 1: "I'm sensitive, and that means suffering. I'm different, and that means loneliness."]

26. To Rosina Otte and Walter E. Dakin

SH: Mrs. Cornelius C. Williams
6254 Enright Avenue
Saint Louis, Missouri
Nov. 1929
[ALS, 6 pp. HTC]

Dear Grand and Grandfather,

Everybody here at home is complaining about my laziness at writing. Mother tells me that I have written her only one letter since the time I was here last - almost 3 weeks ago. I had no idea it had been so long since I had written. I am even worse about writing you, I believe. Now that I am at home, with no class bells to listen for and no homework to do, I will write you what I have been doing with myself these last weeks.

I have been studying 3 hours each week-day night at the frat house. Compulsory study is a new pledge regulation. Although 3 hours of uninterrupted studying everynight is rather irksome to me, I feel its a good thing as it surely ensures thoroughly prepared lessons. Some of the older frat brothers are quite helpful to me in subjects which I find difficult. It is a matter of great concern to the actives what grades the pledges make, since it reflects upon the frat. Therefore, they make every effort to spur us on.

Last Friday I took part for the first time in competitive athletics. I was one of the five ATO fellows representing the frat in the cross-country races. We had to run 2½ miles, in competition with five men from each fraternity. I was quite dubious of my ability to stick it out, as I had never done any racing in High-school. But to my surprise, I was right there at the finish although not conspicuously near the front of the field.

Military drill has been discontinued for the winter months. In the meantime everyone has to sign up for some form of physical exercise - I selected "equitation", as I had already done some riding with my artillery class and had enjoyed it. While I am here, in Saint Louis I think I will get some riding boots. I already have the pants.

Rose is still suffering from her indigestion but is much better than she was before going to the hospital. I have made her promise to visit me in Columbia early in December. I want her to be there for the two ATO dances, celebrating the opening of the beautiful new house. They are to be on two consecutive nights - the 13th and 14th - both of them are formals, so you see that my tux which you gave me last winter will be serving me well. I am also going to wear it on the 12th at the chorus recital at the Methodist church, at the ceremony celebrating the formal installation of the Church's big new organ. The program is going to be all Christmas songs, most of them being of the early Christian era. Many of them are quite attractive.

I think I will move in the new frat house right after Xmas. I may start taking my meals there now. It is a 4 story building of mansion-like size built in the English style. It is going to be exquisitely furnished. It will only cost about $10.00 more to live there than it does in my present boarding-place.

My room-mate - an artillery student-officer - and I want to make our room as attractive as possible. I wonder if you have any framed prints which might be suitable - just one or two - if so, I would surely be pleased to get them.

Wishing you a joyful Xmas season -

Very lovingly, Tom.

[TW wrote to the Dakins while on Thanksgiving recess. He later confirmed Rose's (apparently successful) plan to visit MU in December in a letter to Cornelius (December 11, 1929, HTC), and in the following January he moved into the new A.T.O. chapter house on Richmond Avenue.

The Christmas "recital" at the Missouri Methodist Church was delayed until January 7, 1930, when the "new organ" was ready for use. The University Chorus, with "Thomas L. Williams" in the bass section, was accompanied by the University Orchestra under the direction of Professor George Venable.]

27. To Rose Isabel Williams

[1004 University Avenue
Columbia, Missouri]
[January 12, 1930]
[ALS, 2 pp. HTC]

Dear Rose,

My stationary is again exhausted, which is not surprising as it always serves the whole house. Until Mother sends me a new supply, I will have to write my letters on this typewriter paper.

This is the last week before the term finals so it will be a very busy one for me. I am almost sorry that I was excused from study-hall as I find study comes harder when one knows he can do other things. However, I will use all my force of will and make myself study 3 hours every night, as I really need them.

I was greatly amused by your letter describing Hazel's party. After such a wild revel, I wonder that you are even in a condition to write letters. I received letters from Hazel and Ezzie. Both of them pronounced the party a "howling" success. They said that you looked "darling".

I spent all yesterday - from 9:00 in the morning 'til 4:00 in the afternoon - working at the frat house. I had to polish the floors in Mrs. Eckert's, the chaperon's apartment, and the parlor, and the stairs from second floor to basement. It is the most tedious work imaginable. I had to get down on my knees and apply wax with a cloth over the whole surface of the floor; then get a polishing-brush to rub over it until it glistens. I think in a month or two I will qualify as a male house-servant.

I was so tired this morning - Sunday - that I could not get up in time for Church.

Tell Mother to please send me some more stationary soon as I still have a few Xmas letters to write. I am hoping to see her soon in Columbia. I can move the 25th.

With love, Tom.

[Hazel Kramer and Esmeralda (Ezzie) Mayes were St. Louis friends of TW and Rose. Ezzie, the daughter of a physician, graduated from prestigious Mary Institute, enrolled at MU in the fall of 1930, and continued to share friendship and literary interests with TW. He used her given name in the plays *Spring Storm* (n.d., HRC) and *Camino Real* (1953).

Esmeralda Mayes Treen has described the "revel" as a formal dance that she, Hazel Kramer, and Maureen and Ivy Jennings, high school students all, hosted at the Forest Park Hotel on January 4, 1930. "I would say the dance was a great success," she told the editors: "We let it be known at Washington U. that no one would be barred. We all knew students there and we wanted a crowd of 'stags.'" She added that "Rose was a very pretty girl and was always dressed well. It is probable that she looked 'marvelous.'"

Mrs. Blanche Eckard was the A.T.O. chaperon.]

28. To Rosina Otte and Walter E. Dakin

[1004 University Avenue
Columbia, Missouri]
January 21, 1930
[ALS, 7 pp. HTC]

Dear Grand & Grandfather,

My latest supply of stationary has been exhausted and I am forced to write on this type-writer paper until Mother sends me a new box.

We are having the term finals this week. I am devoting myself almost entirely to study. So far I have had my French and English exams. I had no difficulty with either of them. The only subject over which I feel any anxiety is my Geology exam which, however, doesn't come until the end of the week and I have plenty of time in which to arm myself against it.

This is my last week in the boarding-house. This Saturday morning I'm planning to move into the frat. house. Miss Graham's has been pleasant, but I'm sure I'll enjoy living in the frat house better as there will be a much nicer crowd of boys to live with.

Mother in her last letter said that she was expecting to come up to see me the end of the week. She wants to supervise my moving and to get acquainted with my fraternity brothers and the chaperon.

We have had a temperature as low as 16 below zero here this week. It has been snowing at frequent intervals the last 4 days and the streets and sidewalks are almost impassable. It looks quite beautiful, though, as there is not enough smoke in Columbia to make it dirty.

I received a box of home made candy from Rose yesterday and a cute little black marble ash-tray with a tiny red hippopotamus on it. In the same mail I received a beautiful picture of Esmeralda Mayes, taken by Ashen-Brenner, about the best photographer in St. Louis. It did much to lighten the gloom of exam week.

I do not expect to make more than one change in my course for the next term, which starts Monday. I am going to take Zoology or Botany, having finished my Geology. I am going to continue my French. Next term I will be in the Advanced department. I think I will make it my minor.

This afternoon I am going to the organ concert in the Methodist Cathedral being given to soothe the nerves of the students during this anxious week. The organist is Mr. Jolliff a piano instructor in the School of

Fine Arts and the Worthy Master of my fraternity. He is a splendid musician. He will occupy the room right across from mine in the frat house.

I have written as much as I have time to for the present.

Please let me hear from you soon. You needn't worry about my exams as I am determined to pass them and have done pretty well (knock wood) so far.

With lots of love, Tom.

P.S. I don't believe I have thanked you, Grandfather, for the Xmas money. It was awfully kind in you and it did a great deal to make my holidays pleasant.

[TW's first-semester grades, his best at MU, were "Superior" in Composition, Citizenship, and French, "Medium" in Geology, and "Inferior" in R.O.T.C.

In 1940 TW recalled a scatological use of Ezzie Mayes's "beautiful picture": "My room-mate {at MU} seemed to find it disconcerting, because one evening when I came home he had changed its position to one directly above the toilet, and underneath it had printed this unkind caption - 'If Nature's Remedy don't work, take a look at this!'" (letter from TW to Lawrence Langner, n.d., Yale).]

29. To Edwina Dakin Williams

[Alpha Tau Omega House
Columbia, Missouri]
Feb. 5, 1930
[ALS, 2 pp. HTC]

Dear Mother,

The week is almost over again without my having written you. The only thing that flies faster than the days here is my allowance.

There are only a few minutes before the dinner bell is due to ring so I must limit this letter to a page. This evening I have a date with a Phi Mu girl. I suppose we will go to the dance at Harris's cafe or the picture show. Fortuneately the Phi Mus have moved into their new house just around the corner so I am spared some of the expense of taxi fares.

Yesterday evening I attended a meeting of the Columns editorial board, which publishes the school literary magazine. There was a very attractive crowd there. We read and voted upon stories submitted to the magazine and afterwards talked and played the piano.

For tomorrow evening I have a dinner engagement at the Columbia Country Club with Mr. Jolliff and Mr. Austen, my french teacher. I was amazed when Mr. Jolliff told me of the invitation as I had never imagined Mr. Austen had any amicable feelings toward me. I'm still quite mystified. Write soon and have Rose send the candy she promised.

Love, Tom.

[Advising the board of *The Columns*, joining the Missouri Chapter of the College Poetry Society, and entering writing contests was apparently the extent of TW's literary involvement at MU. There is no sign that he was active in the Missouri Workshop, which produced student and professional plays and depended upon a large volunteer staff. He audited a course in modern drama taught by Robert Lee Ramsay, perhaps the only professor at MU who recognized his talent, but did no formal course work in theatre. Admission to the School of Journalism in the fall of 1931 brought heavy course loads that may have curtailed further campus literary activity.]

30. To Edwina Dakin Williams

[Alpha Tau Omega House
Columbia, Missouri]
Feb. 16, 1930
[ALS, 5 pp. HTC]

Dear Mother,

I was sorry to learn from your letter that you were without a servant. I am hoping that by this time you have found someone to replace Mattie. I suppose in a way it's a relief to have her off your hands as she always had such an uncertain temperament.

I am in a dilemma about my laundry. I have to pay for it by the lot, sending it to the laundry, as they refuse to give charge accounts to the students. Dad suggested in his letter that some boys in the house might know of a laundress. However, all of those who do not have their laundry done at Dorn-Cloney's, the town laundry, send it to their home's, to be done there. They say that it is cheaper for them to send it home. I was wondering if you would like me to do that. I can get a special laundry box of brown canvas and mail it home every week or 10 days at a cost of about .15¢ for postage. Quite a number of boys are doing this and find it quite satisfactory. Dorn-Cloney's charges are somewhat higher than those in Saint Louis, I believe, so it would save money.

I am forced to use more clothes here than at the boarding house. It is a house regulation that we should come to dinner every evening in a fresh shirt, preferably white. I have a large pile of laundry now and don't know what on earth to do with it. So please write me soon whether I should send it home - or what!

I am sorry to use so much space in my letter upon the prosaic subject of laundry. But you can see that it is a real problem to me.

I am taking Mrs. Eckard to Church this morning so must hurry and get dressed.

Rose and Dad upbraided me in their letters for using up all my month's allowance so soon. However, the $2.00 which Dad sent me was really a part of my allowance as I had paid that out for my laundry. I think I will not be entirely broke for some time, as I am being strictly economical - no dates!

Until it snowed two days ago, I had been playing golf in the afternoons again. The snow seems, fortunately, to be disappearing pretty rapidly. A couple of buttons have come off of my winter coat and it is beginning to show need of a cleaning, so I will be glad to get my light coat, when you send it.

I discovered the coat to my blue summer suit - which I had thought to be lost. I now have that suit intact and will have it cleaned as soon as I am able and will wear it this Spring.

While passing the bulletin board yesterday evening I noticed a sign posted by a girl stating that she had found a pair of horn-rimed glasses and would hold them for the owner. I think quite possibly they are mine and I will call for them. I only wish that she had posted the sign in time to save me from getting a new pair.

One of the boys in the house told me the other evening that he had met a boy from Clarksdale who spoke of having known Grandfather and said that he would like to see me. His last name, I believe, is Goin. Another boy here is in the same law frat as Don Cramer who lived next to us on Cates ave.

I enjoyed the magazines and music sent by Rose and will write to her real soon. I was surely distressed to learn that she had been ill again.

With lots of love, Tom.

[TW did not tell Edwina how he solved his laundry "dilemma" and met the A.T.O. "house regulation" for dining attire: "I would wait until the other boys on the floor had descended to the great dining hall in the basement. Then I would scurry into somebody's room and snatch one of his white shirts and wear it down to dinner and return it, surreptitiously, when the meal was over. I was not very clever at this and was soon found out" (*Memoirs*, pp. 26-27).]

31. To Rose Isabel Williams

[Alpha Tau Omega House
Columbia, Missouri]
March 8, 1930
[ALS, 3 pp. HTC]

Dear Rose,

We are having a conclave at the house this week-end - delegates are visiting here from all the chapters in the province, and so the house is terribly crowded. We had a formal dance last night. There were no stags invited, so it was rather a heavy affair. I had to dance with my date most of the evening. After the dance was over I had to spend almost the remainder of the night searching for a place to sleep - so this morning I am too tired to move, almost.

It is surely sweet in you to write me so faithfully and to send such delicious candy. Both boxes were enjoyed hugely. I congratulate you on your cleverness in thinking of the "Glass" placard.

I think it is wise in you to have a vaccination before coming here. The epidemic seems to be gotten under control; however there is still danger for a person who is susceptible to the disease. My vaccination did not take. At least I don't suppose it did, for the only reaction was a little inflammation and itching. If yours does take you needn't feel embarassed about it. At the dance last night there were some girls present with swellings nearly the size of eggs upon their arms. Practically all of them wore vaccination bandages.

It surely makes me happy to think that I will see you and Hazel next week-end. If only I could get you a date for the dance! But it simply can't be done, as all the dates were in before you mentioned coming up. I hope, however, that you will find something just as nice to do Saturday evening. We will see what we can do about it.

I think it would be nice if Hazel and I and you and Bill could have a double date Friday evening and go out to the Coronado or some other dancing place. I wish that you could stay a few days longer but I suppose Hazel will have to have you go home with her.

I'm sorry to hear that Dakin is so ill - hope it isn't serious. I will enclose a little note to him in this letter.

With love to all - and much to you, Tom.

[Esmeralda Mayes Treen has recalled that her circle of friends, including Rose, often gathered at private homes to socialize and play bridge. Rose's clever "'Glass' placard" may have been a place card designed for such an occasion. Treen also noted that it was common for her friends to collect and exchange glass figurines such as those that eventually found their way into *The Glass Menagerie*.

An outbreak of smallpox in February led the *Columbia Missourian* to run a front page story entitled "Girls Rush to Clinic After Seeing Picture of Smallpox Ravages" (February 18, 1930).

Hazel Kramer was TW's date and Bill Kiefaber may have been Rose's.]

32. *To Walter Dakin Williams*

[Alpha Tau Omega House
Columbia, Missouri]
March 8, 1930
[ALS, 4 pp. HTC]

Dear Dakin,

I guess you think I'm an H— of a brother, letting your 11th birthday go by without any sign of being aware of it. However, circumstances were such that I was totally unable to send you a decent gift. As soon as I get back to Saint Louis - sometime this Spring - I promise to take you to any show you want to go to and buy you an ice-cream soda. Lock this letter in your trunk as a written statement of the debt so that I won't be able to laugh it off when the time comes.

I hear from Mother & Rose that you have been ill recently - first reports were that you had measles - later a "severe infection of nose, throat, and eyes". Rose says you were very greatly alarmed one evening for fear that the bumps on your face would be a permanent mar to your beauty. When one's face is his fortune - as in your case - you cannot blame him for being very concerned over it.

I hope you are well now and able to get back to school.

Yesterday afternoon I made an attempt at golf. And was I rotten! My tee-offs were just about as long as the average croquet shot. To save my self respect, I'm blaming it on the fact that the grounds were rather wet and my one golf ball was cracked. However - if you get a little practice - I'm afraid you'll find me an easy opponent the next time we play each other.

Yesterday was certainly my busy day! I know you would have enjoyed seeing how hard they worked me yesterday morning getting the house ready for the big conclave. I had to wax and polish floors in my own room and a room across the hall - wash my windows, move furniture downstairs to get the floor ready for dancing that night, and run about a thousand errands. I am surely learning the penalty of good nature around here.

This evening I am going to the Big Six track meet. It will decide the championship in track sports - such as high-jumping, running, pole-vaulting, etc - of the six universities in the Big 6 conference. It will be a very thrilling event. Probably you have already heard that Mizzou won the basket-ball championship this year. I saw every game that was played in the home field-house.

To assure myself that you will answer this letter, I'm warning you that if I don't get a letter from you within a week my promise about the picture-show and the soda will be automatically cancelled!!

Well - don't get into any trouble,

Lovingly, Tom.

[The schools of the "Big 6 conference" were Missouri, Iowa State, Kansas, the Kansas Aggies, Oklahoma, and Nebraska, winner of the indoor track meet that TW planned to attend.]

Grand, Rosina Otte Dakin,
and Grandfather, The Reverend
Walter Edwin Dakin

"My first eight years of childhood
    in Mississippi were the most
    joyously innocent of my life,
    due to the beneficent homelife
    provided by my beloved Dakin
    grandparents, with whom we
    lived."
        —Tennessee Williams, *Memoirs*

33. To Cornelius Coffin Williams

SH: Thomas Lanier Williams
Alpha Tau Omega House
Columbia, Missouri
March 15, 1930
[ALS, 6 pp. HTC]

Dear Dad,

As usual, I must begin this letter with apologies for not having written it sooner. I know that you and Mother have just cause for complaint about my negligence in writing. It is quite a common failing among college students. One boy moved out of the house 2 weeks ago. He is still receiving letters from his parents at this address so apparently has not yet notified them of his moving.

We are almost as crowded this week-end as last, when the conclave met here. There is a basket ball tournament among High school teams from all over the state in Columbia - and each fraternity house is having to provide food and shelter for one of these teams. We have one from the Ozarks region to our extreme chagrin. They eat just like cattle, spilling things all over the table. They celebrated their victory last night by getting drunk on the corn whisky they brought up with them. Their subsequent good-humor kept the whole house awake.

I believe in your letter you asked about a check which you gave Mother to pay to the house at the time when I moved in. That covered my monthly dues - for November, December, January, plus some extra assessments for dances and a Christmas gift to the house from the freshmen. In that letter I got your check for the monthly house-bill which I gave to Mr. Eirman, the commissary. Also, received the check for $15. to cover my allowance and laundry - for which I thank you.

Could you send me a pair of black low shoes, Dad? The brown ones I got during the Xmas holidays are still holding out, but in military drill we are given demerits if we don't wear black shoes.

I am going to the bus station in about half an hour to meet Rose and Hazel who are coming up for the week-end. I am afraid Rose will not get very much fun out of the visit, as her friends John and Martha Berkeholder are going home for a visit over the week-end. I will surely enjoy seeing her, though.

I am writing on the stationary which Mother sent me this week.

Having one's name on his stationary is a real economy as it makes it last about twice as long.

Hoping you are all well,

Lovingly, Tom.

34. *To Edwina Dakin Williams*

SH: Thomas Lanier Williams
Alpha Tau Omega House
Columbia, Missouri
May 1930
[ALS, 6 pp. HRC]

Dear Mother,

I suppose you were justly wrathful when you arrived in Saint Louis and found that I had forgotten to phone Dad to meet you. I was quite ashamed of myself when I remembered the next morning. There are some mitigating circumstances, however. My roommate and several others in the house started drinking beer as soon as all the Mothers got out of the house Sunday afternoon. They went to a restaurant and got so hilariously drunk that the proprietor had to call out the police. Warned that the police were coming, they went to another restaurant to continue the carousel. The police finally overtook them in the Davis tea-room. There was quite a brawl in which Anderson one of the men in the house was hit over the head with a police club. Of course the whole house was in a furore over it; we had to stay up all night cajoling the drunkards. The Dean of Men, Mr. Heckel, found out about it and I'm afraid some of them will be kicked out of school.

Yesterday afternoon I drove to Kansas City with Herby Fick, the band leader, & Joe Warren. We got there about 5:00; went to a show, had dinner and afterwards to a dance-hall at which Herby was trying to secure an engagement. Joe and I were given complimentary tickets to the dance. We stayed there until 1:00; Got back in Columbia at 4:00 in the morning.

We didn't get to see much of the city but it seemed awfully attractive.

I have a story in the May issue of the Columns. I will send you a couple of copies of it.

In this letter I'm enclosing the pictures we took. On the whole, they are pretty good - particularly the ones of you.

By the way - I have a T.L. for you. Bill Reese, a boy from Saint Louis, said you must have had a "very carefree life" to be looking so "young and pretty".

Very lovingly, Tom.

[A senior from Quincy, Illinois, Herbert Fick was an A.T.O. brother active in campus politics and musical productions. He later reportedly formed a band in Quincy called "The Redhots." Joe Warren, of Wichita Falls, Texas, was a member of TW's pledge class.

"A Lady's Beaded Bag," a sketch about a "trash-picker" who finds treasure in an "ash-pit," appeared in *The Columns* in May. Earlier in the spring TW's first-known play, "Beauty Is the Word," won a sixth-place honorable mention in the annual Dramatic Arts Club contest sponsored by Professor Ramsay. Set in the South Pacific, the one-act features a beautiful young woman named Esther, whose hypnotizing dance averts a native uprising and reproaches the bleak theology of her missionary aunt and uncle. Perhaps anticipating the dangers of playwriting, TW concluded that Esther "was safer" with the natives "than she would be with an audience in a New York theater." A report of the play's being performed at the time is unfounded. It was first published in 1984 in *The Missouri Review*.

Edwina had received a "T.L.," "Trade Last," from Bill Reese and now owed him a compliment in return.]

35. To Walter E. Dakin

SH: Melbourne Hotel
Grand Avenue and Lindell Boulevard
Saint Louis
June 16, 1930
[ALS, 6 pp. HRC]

Dear Grandfather,

I reported to work here at the Melbourne - our business headquarters - a little early this morning and I'm using the extra time to get off my long-due letter to you.

This job of selling Pictorial Review subscriptions is extremely strenuous and not at all suited to my personality, as you can easily imagine. It is a good experience, however, and the salary of $21.00 a week comes in handy. It is house to house canvassing from 9:00 in the morning till 8:30 at night. It is quite exhausting. At the end of each day I wonder if I will be able to endure another day of it. There is so much unemployment and poverty that selling magazine subscriptions is difficult even for an experienced salesman. Some of the people I encounter are terribly disagreeable - we have been canvassing in the worst districts of the city. I don't imagine that I will remain at this work very much longer. I wish that I could find some work of a more congenial sort. It's very hard, though, to get jobs this summer.

Rose's clinical examination at Barnes' proved that her trouble was solely nervous. She is now under the care of a nerve specialist. It is a relief to know that she has no serious organic trouble. However, her condition is pretty bad - virtually a nervous breakdown. Of course she is very nervous and unreasonable. She had a quarrel with Dad last night and became so furious that she left the house and spent the night with Miss Florence who happened to be visiting us. She declares that she will not come back. However, I think she will change her mind. Her trouble is certainly a great worry to Mother and Grand and myself but I think the doctor will be able to get her out of it. He has given her a schedule to live by which should be effective in relieving her nerves. I suppose Grand will [omission] you the details of it.

I surely appreciated your gift of shirt and pyjamas. I was greatly pleased with them both.

Dakin has been planning [to] go to the Y.M.C.A. camp for children - at which Karl Harford is working this summer. It opens in two weeks.

What are you planning to do this summer? Going to Florida? I hope you will have a pleasant vacation.

Yours very lovingly, Tom.

[The June 1930 number of *Pictorial Review* (1899–1939) carried the usual mix of women's fashion, advice, and recipes, as well as the first installment of *The Silver Swan*, a "brilliant novel dealing quite frankly with international marriage." In *The Glass Menagerie* just such an "exciting" new serial is announced by Amanda Wingfield, a far more lively solicitor of magazine subscriptions than her real life son. Within two weeks TW was "summarily dismissed" (*Memoirs*, p. 28) from his summer job.

Rose's "quarrel" with Cornelius was the subject of a pacifying letter from Edwina to her father: "Cornelius wasn't himself when he ran Rose out of this house last Sunday night and was very sorry afterward" (June 23, 1930; qtd. in Leverich). Long estranged from her husband by this time, Edwina wrote to calm and reassure her parents rather than defend Cornelius.

The Harfords of nearby Webster Groves, Missouri, were related to the Williams family on the Dakin side. Carl G. Harford, TW's second cousin, graduated from Washington University Medical School in 1933 and later served on the faculty. In 1969 Dakin Williams reportedly sought Harford's advice on committing TW for psychiatric care at Barnes Hospital.]

36. To Walter E. Dakin

[6254 Enright Avenue
University City, Missouri]
PM: St. Louis, July 24, 1930
[TLS, 3 pp. HRC]

Dear Grandfather,

The heat wave has returned here with all of its original vigor. For several days we have been having temperature several degrees over a hundred. More people have died of heat prostration here than during the flu epidemic.

The short pyjamas you sent me have been a great comfort these hot nights. I am so pleased with them that I'm going to get some more of them if they are obtainable in the Saint Louis stores.

Rose and I - as you have probably heard - are taking a business course together at Rubicam's business school. Rose finds the work very difficult, which is only natural, as it has been so long since she has been in school and had any mental discipline. I think she will eventually "get" it, however, although it may take her longer than the regular 6 months. It seems to be of some effect in taking her mind off of her stomach - which was the doctor's principal idea in recommending the course.

I hope that you are not suffering too much from the heat. I would certainly like an opportunity to see you again this summer but I suppose you are planning to spend your vacation some place where it is cool.

Dakin has started a miniature golf course in our side yard. It seems to be prospering; he charges 2 cents a round, and he has already made nearly a dollar off of it. The only disadvantage is that it attracts quite a large crowd of noisy kids right beneath our windows.

Yesterday afternoon Esmeralda Mayes invited me to her country club where we spent the afternoon sun bathing and swimming. It was certainly pleasant relief from the heat.

I haven't yet fully planned the course I am going to take at school next term but I will tell you about it as soon as I have.

Grand and Mother are both sustaining the weather pretty well.

With much love, Tom.

[Rose's formal education ended in 1927, apparently without graduation, after brief stints at Soldan High School and Hosmer Hall in St. Louis (1925) and four terms at All Saints' College in Vicksburg, Mississippi (1925-1927).

Rose's therapeutic course at Rubicam Business School was recast in a well-known episode in *The Glass Menagerie*. Ezzie Mayes, who joined TW and Rose for summer classes, has recalled the intimidating experience: "For typing we sat in a pool and practiced phrases such as 'All good men come to the aid of their country.' If there was one mistake the OGRE who ran the class humiliated you in front of the entire class. It almost killed Rose." In the following January Rose was reportedly a student at Hadley-Crow Vocational School, which may also have contributed (as Allean Hale speculates in unpublished research) to TW's treatment of his sister's abortive business career. Examples of Rose's typing exercises have been preserved at the Humanities Research Center.

This letter was written on stationery imprinted with the name Thomas Lanier Williams and the address Alpha Tau Omega House, Columbia, Missouri.]

37. *To Rose Isabel Williams*

SH: Thomas Lanier Williams
A.T.O. House
Columbia, Mo.
Jan. 22, 1931
[TLS, 1 p. HRC]

Dear Rose,

Here is another note, to accompany my laundry box, even briefer than the first, due to the fact that this is the eve of Exams. Prayers Requested!

I am glad to hear that you have decided upon our dance for the occasion of the "crusade"; if the three gentlemen are not too particular about sleeping conditions, which may or may not be good, they can be easily accomodated at the house.

I have been living a life of virtual retirement, in order to get my numerous papers done. I wrote about 6000 words last night.

I have really gotten my fill of over-stuffed courses and am going to act with much more caution in my next semestre's enrollment.

I appreciated the oranges and the tie enclosed in my last laundry. The oranges were quite juicy and the tie in excedingly good taste. The house has stopped furnishing soap so I would like to receive a bar, preferably Woodbury's, in my next.

Scott Ware, the English Proff., mentioned having received a letter from Carter stating that he was coming here with you. Carter's Dad was Scott's god-father and cousin.

Much love to All, Tom

[Carter Johnson was one of the "gentlemen" visitors to MU and probably the object of Rose's "'crusade.'" In 1932 she archly described herself and Johnson as "Smoking, Dancing, Card playing Sunday School teachers," but their dating was underscored by Rose's complaint that "he seems so afraid that I won't make a favorable imprint on the family" (letter to TW, April 2, 1932, HTC).

TW's grades were uniformly "Medium" in fall 1930, save for the familiar "F" in R.O.T.C. One of "over-stuffed courses" was probably General Zoology.]

38. *To Walter E. Dakin*

SH: Thomas Lanier Williams
A.T.O. House
Columbia, Mo.
Monday, September 14, 1931
[TLS, 2 pp. Columbia]

Dear Grandfather,

I am sure you must have come to regard me as a very prodigal grand-son, for my having failed to write you in such a length of time. I excused myself from all letter-writing this summer on the grounds that I was too busy. And then when my vacation-time came, August 15, and I left for a couple of weeks of recreation at the Y.M.C.A. camp in the Ozarks, I played just as hard as I had been working, and consequently all my letters were still further deferred. I am back at school now, and Rush-week, the most exciting period of the whole year, is concluded - there are still several days before classes begin and in that interim I shall be able to discharge myself of all letter-writing obligations.

Considering the fact that I had never done any office-work before, I believe I acquitted myself pretty well at the shoe company. I did order-listing and typing - the experience was very valuable, and I hope I may be able to get the job again next summer, if nothing better presents itself. I feel that I was excedingly lucky in getting the job, since I was practically the only fellow in the house who did work this summer. A good number have not been able to return to the University this Fall because they were not able to earn any money - it will be difficult, I am afraid, to keep the house open, with ten less men than last year. We have pledged a considerably smaller number this year than previously, since so many cannot afford fraternities.

I am entering the School of Journalism this Fall and so I am anticipating this school term much more than those past. I know that I will take a great deal more interest in the work and I am certainly going to put more effort into it.

I think your plan of going to Florida this winter is splendid. I hope that Rose can manage to go with you as it would do her a great deal of good. She appeared this summer to be [in] a good deal better condition than the summer before and I think a few months in Florida would complete her recovery and make her strong enough to get into some kind of work, which she needs more than anything.

I suppose the cotton situation in Mississippi is very depressing right now. I hope that your income isn't suffering much from it.

I am too tired out from this gruelling Rush-week to write a longer letter, but I am going to be less remiss, hereafter, in my letter-writing, so you may expect to hear from me again before very long.

With love to you and to Grand, Tom.

[Clerical work at Continental Shoemakers, a branch of the International Shoe Company, gave TW a foretaste of life "at the bottom of our social architecture" ("Random Observations," December 1941, HRC), as he would later describe it. The summer job was arranged by Cornelius, who was becoming more insistent that TW and Rose undertake their own support.

Walter Dakin's travel plans reflect his earlier retirement in 1931 as the rector of St. George's Episcopal Church after nearly fifteen years of ministry. So beloved were the Dakins for their "cultural influences and loyalty to friends" (*Clarksdale Daily Register*, April 8, 1931) that wealthy parishoners offered them an apartment to prevent their leaving Clarksdale after retirement.]

39. To Rose Isabel Williams

SH: Thomas Lanier Williams
A.T.O. House
Columbia, Mo.
Saturday A.M. [December 5, 1931]
[TLS, 2 pp. HRC]

Dear Rose,

It seems, despite all my most solemn resolutions, I can't cure myself of my negligence in writing. You have not written, either, this week. Is Culbertson's method consuming all of your time these days?

I have had to write a series of papers in journalism this week, all several thousand words in length, and my fingers dont feel natural off of the typewriter keys. I am trying my best to maintain an S standing in my journalism courses. I have been able to do that, so far, except in my advertising course. I hit a quizz pretty well in that a few days ago, which may help me considerably.

I attended the Arts and Sciences banquet last night where Ursula Genung was announced as the winner of the Mahan poetry contest. She had written a perfectly exquisite group of sonnets and she read them before the banquet guests composed of distinguished professors and educators [from] all over the country. She looked lovely - and is certainly a brilliant girl.

Are you still intending to visit me the week-end before the holidays? If you are, I will see about getting you a room in Ursula's rooming-place.

I finally bought Hazel a birth-day gift - an inexpensive gold chain. I must write her a letter to accompany it and explain the delay.

As you can readily understand, I am very anxious to hear from you concerning the situation on the home front. Has the spirit of Quiet Night now descended?

Tell Mother I received my laundry and wish to extend my compliments to the laundress for the excellent way in which she did my shirts. They were very nicely starched, for the first time. I will send home some laundry this afternoon.

Very lovingly, Tom.

P.S. I just called up Ursula to congratulate her and she said she would like to have you occupy her room if you came up. So you would probably not have to pay any room rent.

I got your copy of the Ballyhoo. It is really a riot. Everybody in the house is reading it.

[By citing "Culbertson's method," TW chided Rose for preferring bridge to letter writing.

Ursula Genung, a sophomore from Kansas City, won second place in the poetry contest and read a single sonnet at the College of Arts & Science banquet on December 4. She reportedly dated TW and may have contributed to the figure of Myra in "The Field of Blue Children" (1939), a story with a Columbia setting.

"The spirit of Quiet Night" had not descended upon Edwina and Cornelius, who were openly and bitterly divided at this time. TW dramatized such marital discord in the one-act play "Hot Milk at Three in the Morning," in preparation for the 1932 Dramatic Arts Club contest. A revised version entitled "Moony's Kid Don't Cry" appeared in *The Best One-Act Plays of 1940* (1941) and was TW's first published drama. The original play appeared in 1984 in *The Missouri Review*.

The racy cartoons and parodies of advertisements printed in *Ballyhoo* magazine (1931–1939) appealed to an audience of nearly 2 million readers after its founding in 1931. The December number satirized sensational reportage with the headline, "211 Slain by Shovel Fiend in Penthouse Orgy."]

40. *To Cornelius Coffin Williams*

SH: Thomas Lanier Williams
A.T.O. House
Columbia, Mo.
Jan. 29, 1932
[TLS, 1 p. HRC]

Dear Dad,

Registration for the second term commences Monday; I still have another examination to take and have been so absorbed in studying for it that I delayed until now writing you concerning the fees for the coming registration. There is the usual fee of thirty dollars for hospital, library and Incidentals, five dollars for enrollment in Journalism school, and ten dollars to cover the expenses of books, which is less than formerly, as I will not need so many. This makes a total of $45. Will you please send the check special delivery so that I shall be able to register Monday, in time to get into the preferred classes, and get everything straightened out before the next term begins?

I suppose there have been complaints at home about the infrequency of my letters since Christmas. I have been having to prepare term papers several thousand words in length, and naturally haven't felt like doing any writing outside of that.

I hope that the Red Goose is now flying out of the black clouds of depression.

With love to all,

Lovingly, Tom

[The "Red Goose," a rare levity in TW's correspondence with his father, refers to a line of shoes sold by Cornelius. They "are half the fun of having feet," or so the advertising copy claimed.]

41. To Edwina Dakin Williams

SH: Thomas Lanier Williams
A.T.O. House
Columbia, Mo.
March 5, 1932
[TLS, 3 pp. HRC]

Dear Mother,

I enjoyed a great deal getting your letter and the enclosed clippings. Although a full-fledged member of the College Poets of America society, the writing of poetry has never been one of my most glittering talents. If I find among my various Mss. anything of a suitable nature, I shall send it, however, and trust to a sense of fraternal obligation upon the part of Scot Ware to award it the prize.

I thought Grandfather's prayer very impressive and well-composed and am glad that his fine qualities are so well appreciated in Clarksdale. I don't see why they should consider moving to Memphis, just because their house is temporarily vacant. With the present signs of a possible return to prosperity, they should wait upon the chance of getting it rented again to a more satisfactory tenant.

How the devil did Grand scrape together $250. in these times of famine? For ways that are dark and tricks that are vain....I almost suspect her of embezzling church funds!

I was given recently a highly unsatisfactory regular "beat" in my reporting class - the daily reporting of prices in local produce. It is considered an honor to be given a regular beat by the editor, as it is supposed to indicate that he holds you to be reliable, but I should, in this instance, preferred to have remained unhonored, rather than have the burden of listing every day the prices of light and heavy hens, sour cream, eggs, and geese - which of course offers no chance for creative writing. I am hoping, though, that he will elevate me to a better "beat" after a while.

Mrs. Eckard and I have been attending the Christian Church together the last three Sundays. I go there because there is a choir composed of sixty Christian college glee-club members, which makes the music delightful, and the preacher is the most intelligent in town. The service differs very little from the Episcopalian.

It is not unusual for the delivery of grades to be so long delayed. You remember, they were not sent last year till near the end of the summer - or rather about the middle. They will probably be sent out in a few days, however. Although I did not make any poor grades, the fact that I was taking such a large course, 22 hours, which is 5 in excess of the number that can be taken with credit, I could not put very much time in upon the individual courses, and suffered accordingly, in the grades that I received.

During examination week I had a series of stys on one of my eyes and going to the school oculist, was informed that one of my glasses was no longer correct, and I would have to get it changed. He gave me the new prescription, which I have had filled by an optician here in town, whose bill I am enclosing, in the hope that you can help me with it. Since I had the examination made by the university oculist, the charge is only $2.50 for the single lens.

The two ties which you sent me recently were extremely good-looking.

I have been writing all afternoon and consequently failed to get my laundry off again. I will send it Monday.

With much love - and with birthday greeting - delayed but none the less cordial - to Dakin,

Tom.

[Edwina had apparently urged TW to enter a writing contest judged by Coleman Scott Ware, an English instructor who lived at the A.T.O. house, hence the "fraternal obligation."

Walter Dakin's "prayer" marked the bicentennial of George Washington's birth and was published in the *Daily Register* for "the spiritual benefit" (February 23, 1932) of Clarksdale.

The celebrated local "preacher" was the Reverend C.E. Lemmon, father of the Williams scholar Allean Hale.

The money scraped together by Grand approximated the fees and expenses for one semester at MU. There was no formal charge for tuition. TW's fall 1931 transcript shows 16.5 hours, not 22, and a grade point average that fell slightly below "Medium."]

42. To Edwina Dakin Williams

SH: Missouri State
Sunday, May 15th [1932]
[TLS, 2 pp. Columbia]

Dear Mother,

I have taken your reproof about letter-writing very earnestly and am trying my best to reform.

I have written three letters this Sunday afternoon, in spite of the fact that the place is swarming with chattering parents who are down for our family get-together, which, by the way, you were most remiss in not attending. You have no idea all of the charming and elegant society which you might be mingling amongst here. There was a particularly large group this year, due, no doubt, to the urgent need of distraction from business and domestic worries engendered by the great business elevation and the unusually inviting aspect of some good meals for nothing.

We had a real banquet this noon, caviar in anchovy paste, spring chicken, and strawberry short cake.

I think this may have relieved somewhat the shadow of the famous "Federal Raid Upon A.T.O. house" which lurked upon most of the parental brows.

This being the time of year when a young man's fancy fondly turns to thoughts of getting a job, I have written to Mr. Fletcher, and am hoping he will find some form of occupation for me. I leave school the fourth of June, a few days later than before.

Not having visited my native Southland in quite some time, Grand and Grandfather's generous invitation was strongly appealing, and I should like to go if circumstances, meaning the expense and the if and when of a job, permit my going.

I am enclosing the program of the One-Act play contest. I did not have time to finish the play that I was working on during the holidays, which I think might have won in the contest, but I turned in a considerably shorter and lighter manuscript, a domestic satire, titled, "HOT MILK AT THREE IN THE MORNING" which was given honorable mention, with the criticism that it contained no stage diagram and that the speeches were too long.

Indiscourageable, I have turned in a short story in that contest, which is also for a $100. prize. It is called "BIG BLACK: A MISSISSIPPI IDYLL" - you see, I am returning to reminiscenses of my native locale for inspiration, which is another reason why I should like to visit there for a short time.

I hope that all of the family are well. My laundry will probably be late again, as having been routed from my room by the visiting mothers, I could not gather it Sat.

With much love, Tom.

[In April federal prohibition agents raided illegal stills and speakeasies in Columbia and visited Greektown as well, according to reports in the 1932 *Savitar*: "The ATO's tell us that the recent revenue officers' raid happened somewhere between the Tri-Delt and DU houses."

Mr. Fletcher was a friend of Cornelius and a manager at Continental Shoemakers, where TW had worked the preceding summer.

TW's final semester at MU ended on a dismal note. "Hot Milk at Three in the Morning" and "Big Black: A Mississippi Idyll," won only a distant honorable mention (#13 and #5, respectively) in campus writing contests. His grades in the School of Journalism also fell sharply: two "Mediums," three "Inferiors," and a "Failure" in R.O.T.C. Presumably it was the last grade that enraged Cornelius and led him to withdraw his son from school after the grade report arrived in June.

The "native" locale in "Big Black" (1985) was a generalized one of "blistering" southern heat, "level cotton fields," and "a gang of Negroes" breaking rocks for a new road "south of Jackson." More incisive was TW's portrait of Big Black, a charismatic laborer who was treated with sympathy and understanding, and familiar racial bias.]

43. To Editor "Oscar" Zilch

[6254 Enright Avenue
University City, Missouri]
August 19, 1932
[TLS, 1 p. HRC]

DICTATOR OF FASHION COMMENTS ON STYLE

Thinking that a few hints on sartorial effects would not hurt any of the brothers, the editor of the LINK delegated the job of fashion tips to the one and only T.L. "Red Goose" Williams.

Brother Williams sets down his fashion hints in the following letter to the LINK:

August 19, 1932.

Dear Editor Zilch:

Having been laid up the past few weeks with a crack[ed] upper jaw and a number of semi-detached molars, I was truly grateful for the heartening tribute of a letter from my journalistic colleague. Also, for the overwhelming compliment of being asked to contribute an article to the LINK. But, why, my dear Oscar, of all subjects from the mating instincts of the walrus to the latest inside dope on the Alpha Chi's and why Ezzie can't go swimming did you select me to write on sartorial hints. Is it possible that the honorable editor, whose memory has always equalled that of the proverbial elephant, has forgotten those occasions during the past year when, within that sacred temple of friendship, before the bros. assembled, I was reprimanded by ye worthy master with all the severity at his command, for having entered the dining salon of an evening in such a state of disarray - sans socks and with vest unbuttoned - that I seemed to be giving an impression or impersonation of the mad genius.

I think that it would have been far more suitable if I had been asked to expound in Jules Laverne style, FROM SHOWER TO DINNER TABLE IN THREE SECONDS, and the question of proper dress delivered into the more competent hands of our esthetic pedagogue, Pottsy Batchelder, now sojourning in the cultural center of Boston, who could design as a rush week uniform, I presume, some very charming ballet costumes of black silk sprinkled with pink and blue and yellow dots, in which we might embrace

our prospective - shall I say victims? - to the airily symphonic strains of
Narcissus.

But, since you have in your superior wisdom seen fit to impose this
office upon me of Worthy Arbiter of Fashion, I have done my best in the
following.

No seersuckers (oh those nasty, vile things) and leave the flannels with
the loud stripes at home . . . and emerald studded belts are not in this year
. . . but tab shirts are . . . and look nice, too . . . and don't forget your white
flannels . . . but no diamond rings . . . nor any trick a la Bell hats . . . nor
any Tahitian sunrise motiffs in the neckwear . . . and Holmburg hats will
be good this fall . . . and bring along your white shoes . . . and summer
ties . . . and linen suits if you can afford to have Bill Ridgeway charge them
for a year or more, Predock . . . and I don't have to chew beer . . . I can just
smell it and pass out together with R.S.C.(?).

> Yours fraternally,
> The Red Goose,
> Worthy Arbiter of Fashion.

["Editor Oscar Zilch" was TW's contribution to a running gag well known to readers of *Ballyhoo* magazine, including the A.T.O. brotherhood (see letter #39). Elmer
Zilch, head of an advertising company, and his protean family (Rufus, Norman,
Otto, et. al.) of vice presidents appeared regularly in *Ballyhoo* to give zany advice
and contribute to the slapstick humor.

TW's "semi-detached molars" were the result of a diving accident at the
Westborough Country Club.

It was Jules Verne who wrote *Around the World in Eighty Days* (1873).

TW alludes to his friend Ezzie Mayes and to A.T.O. brothers Lowell
Batchelder, William S. Bell, William O. Predock, and Ramon S. Carrington
("R.S.C."). William H. Ridgeway was the proprietor of the St. Louis French Dry
Cleaning Co. in Columbia.

In effect this was a letter of farewell probably written after TW learned that he
would not return to MU for his senior year. The text printed above follows the version published in *The Link* (SUMMER SAUSAGE) *Official Organ of Gamma Rho
Chapter of Alpha Tau Omega* (Columbia, Mo.), p. 4.]

44. To Walter E. Dakin

[6254 Enright Avenue
University City, Missouri]
[Summer 1932]
[TLS, 1 p. HTC]

Dear Grandfather

I am surely grateful to you for your kindness and trouble in writing down that very interesting string of coincidences in your letter, just received. I agree with you that they form a very good nucleus for a mystery story, and as soon as I have an available time, I shall try to fashion them into one. I want to commend you for your vivid and interesting account of it. Submitted just as you wrote it, it would make a very acceptable manuscript, I think.

My great handicap at present is lack of time. I have, of course, no opportunity for personal writing during the day, and in the evenings my tired nerves make it necessary to give my time chiefly to rest and recreation, and the little writing I manage to squeeze in is mostly of the poetic genre. Some week-end, however, I am planning to type off a few short stories, and shall very probably include this one. I am, of course, very much disappointed that I cannot return to the University this Fall, but have hope of going back next year - I would love to be able to get my degree at Columbia University in New York, but that may be hitching my wagon to too high a star. I was somewhat disappointed in the Missouri School of Journalism. They do not give the student a chance to do the type of writing he is best fitted for, but stick him into whatever job suits them. I was compelled to report quotations on the poultry market and undertakers notices most of the time my last term, which was not very edifying work. I am trying to save some money toward going to Columbia - which is the country's very best school of journalism.

Before leaving for Florida, or whatever winter resort you are considering, do try to visit St. Louis for a while, as we are all very anxious to see you again. I shall try to write a longer letter some evening when I am less tired.

Very lovingly, Tom.

[Determined that his "fantastic older son" (as TW saw himself in the paternal eye) become self-sufficient, Cornelius had arranged for TW's job as a clerk-typist at

Continental Shoemakers. The menial job, priceless in Depression-era St. Louis, paid $65 a month and lasted for nearly three years, a period that TW viewed both as a "season in hell" ("Random Observations") and as a valuable exposure to working class life. The experience was later recast in his "serious comedy" *Stairs to the Roof* (1945).]

PART II
1933 - 1938
ST. LOUIS • MEMPHIS
IOWA CITY • CHICAGO

45. To Harriet Monroe

SH: 6254 Enright Avenue
Saint Louis, Missouri
March 11, 1933
[TLS, 1 p. HRC]

Miss Harriet Monroe

Will you do a total stranger the kindness of reading his verse?

Thank you! Thomas Lanier Williams

[At Continental Shoemakers, or so legend has it, TW wrote poems on shoe boxes, met a fellow worker named Stanley Kowalski, and discovered a flight of "stairs to the roof" where he could dream of escape from "the City of St. Pollution." He began to meet the young and often radical literary society of St. Louis and formed an important relationship with Clark Mills, a promising poet who attended Washington University.

TW's plea to Harriet Monroe (1860-1936), editor of *Poetry* (1912-present), would evolve into a famous curtain line, but at the time it may have recalled her intention in founding the distinguished magazine of verse: to unearth "smothered geniuses, who might be waiting for a hearing." TW published forty-odd lyrics from 1933 to 1938, nearly all in collegiate and little magazines, but he did not appear in *Poetry* until 1937. It was, he knew, "as hard to get rich on poetry as fat on vinegar" (letter to the Dakins, October 28, 1933, HRC).]

46. To William A. Martin

SH: Continental Shoemakers
1509 Washington Ave.
St. Louis, Mo.
Oct. 18, 1933
[TLS, 1 p. HRC]

Dear Mr. Martin:

I suppose the Fall number of your magazine is now in preparation, and I hope that the enclosed Mss. are not too late for consideration.

I should like to give you the names of two young poets whom I knew at the University of Missouri, and whose work would surely be creditable to your journal; Roberta Mansberger, who won the Mahan Poetry Contest at the University in 1931, and James Freedman, who won it in both 1932 and 1933. Miss Mansberger lives in Colorado, Freedman in Kansas City. Both are graduates, and their exact address could be secured, if you are interested, by writing either to the English Department or the Registrar's office of the University. Both of these appeared several times in the publication of the College Poetry Society of America. Both of these young people had an originality and a technical finish which I think would rank them high among experienced professional poets . . . especially Miss Mansberger, whom I thought a real genius. If you can get in touch with them, I think it would be fortunate both for you and for them.

Very Sincerely, Thomas L. Williams

[William Martin (1902–1974) was a local merchant who published *Inspiration: A Journal for Aspiring Poets and Poetry Lovers* (1931-1933). He informed TW in July that "Under the April Rain," his elegy for the St. Louis-born poet Sara Teasdale, had won first place in the "'Spring Number'" (July 20, 1933, HRC) contest. Her recent suicide had shocked St. Louisans and led TW to strain for a commemorative rime: "Her ashes we scattered upon the sea, / As song is spilt on air; / But under the April rain she is free, / She is silent, and does not care!"]

47. To the Editors of STORY

SH: Thomas L. Williams
6254 Enright Avenue
Saint Louis, Missouri
Jan. 7, 1934
[TLS, 2 pp. HRC]

Editors of STORY

This being my second offering to STORY ("a tale of two writers" was the first), the time may be ripe to introduce myself. My real name is Thomas Lanier Williams, under which I have contributed verse to a number of small journals, without doing the name or the journals a great deal of good. I am now twenty-two, and have not had a story published since I was seventeen, when I sold a story about an Egyptian queen to WEIRD TALES magazine, an achievement which I never tried to repeat. Lately I have been trying The Little Magazines and have received a number of very polite letters and warned against the influence of Erskine Caldwell. STORY magazine is my particular star, of course.

I have studied journalism at the University of Missouri and am now working for the International Shoe Company, till the newspapers discover my talent.

STELLA FOR STAR is an effort to cast a highly fanciful light upon what an old English professor of mine once described as "one of the greatest enigmas in the biography of English literature".

If a rather sentimental treatment can still be tolerated at times, as Emmet Gowan's excellent story in the present issue seemed to indicate, I have some hope that you may like this story.

Very sincerely yours, T.L. Williams

[Whit Burnett (1899–1973) and his wife Martha Foley (1897–1977) founded *STORY* magazine in Vienna in 1931 and published the first American number in April 1933. To date they had rejected "A Tale of Two Writers," whose title page identified "T.L. Williams" as "Undiscovered" (n.d., HRC), and would soon return "Stella for Star" (n.d., HRC).

Published in *Weird Tales* in 1928, "The Vengeance of Nitocris" is TW's first known story to appear in a commercial magazine. Nitocris, the "Egyptian queen," avenged the death of her brother Pharaoh by arranging a mass execution of the nobles and priests of Thebes who had killed him.

"Stella for Star" was based upon Jonathan Swift's unconsummated love for Esther Johnson and her frustration and languishing death. Blanche DuBois alludes to this strange impasse in *A Streetcar Named Desire* (1947) when she cites the story's title in reference to her sister Stella. The story remains unpublished, but in January 1935 it won first place and a ten dollar prize in a St. Louis Writers Guild contest (see letter #49).]

48. To Walter E. Dakin

SH: Thomas L. Williams
6254 Enright Avenue
Saint Louis, Missouri
June 19, 1934
[TLS, 2 pp. HRC]

Dear Grandfather:

It is too bad I have to wait till vacation time to write letters, but that is just the way it is. This is the first week of my vacation and I am spending it quietly and economically at home. The second week I am taking in August and hope then to go up to Chicago or the Ozarks. Since the club has been opened to us without charge for swimming, tennis, and golfing, we have all the pleasure of a summer camp right within a few minutes drive of home.

As you know, I have gotten a little roadster to drive around in. I know a second-hand car is supposed to be an awful expense. But I had this one examined thoroughly before I bought it and it proves to be a real economy. It runs twenty miles on a gallon of gas and all the parts are in good condition and will not require any replacements or repair for some while at least. It gives Rose, and Dakin, and I a chance to get out to the club every evening. Formerly we had to go everywhere on the street-car except when Dad happened to leave his car at home.

I am spending my mornings writing, now that I am on my vacation. I am sending a good many stories out, and hope to have some acceptances before long. I have some poetry coming out in the July-August issue of VOICES, the big New York poetry magazine, which I will send to you when it is issued.

This coming Sunday we are driving Rose up to the Sunday-school convention at Columbia. Mother and I are driving back that evening but Rose will stay a week. She always has a good time up there.

I hope you and Grand can get away from that hot city some time this summer. You would find it at least a little cooler here in Saint Louis. We would love to have you spend some time here, or in Chicago where we could visit you. I am glad that you are thinking of renting your house and going to Florida. It would be great for you. And if I become a successful writer one of these days, I will take the first air-plane down there myself and we'll have a cottage on the beach.

With much love to you and Grand, Tom

[Scatterbolt was the "roadster" used for trips to the Westborough Country Club, and with TW at the wheel it frequently ran out of gas and needed rescue.

Of the two-dozen or so stories that TW wrote and/or submitted for publication from 1933 to 1938, only one, "Twenty-Seven Wagons Full of Cotton" (1936), was accepted and saw publication during this time. A story accepted in 1934 by Jack Conroy, editor of *The Anvil* (1933-1935), an important radical magazine published in Moberly, Missouri, was apparently rejected by his successor. The poems "After a Visit" and "Cacti" appeared in the August-September 1934 number of *Voices* (1921-1965). Harold Vinal, the editor, shared Harriet Monroe's belief in giving voice to the new poets, but he deplored the harsh diction of modern poetry and was mocked by E.E. Cummings for his dullness. TW met Vinal in New York in 1940.

The "Smoking, Dancing, Card playing" (letter from Rose to TW, April 2, 1932, HTC) Sunday school teacher Rose Williams attended the Episcopal Summer Conference of Church Workers at Stephens College in Columbia, June 24-29. One topic of discussion was "Family Relations."]

49. To Josephine Winslow Johnson

[6254 Enright Avenue
University City, Missouri]
Feb. 2nd [1935]
[TLS, 2 pp. Washington U.]

Dear Miss Johnson:

As you are the only member of the Writers' Guild with whom I have any personal acquaintance, I am addressing this note of thanks to you and hope you will extend it verbally to the rest of the Guild and the contest judges. Receiving first prize came to me as a complete surprise. In the telephone message the night before there was nothing to indicate I had gotten more than honorable mention and I certainly expected no more. In fact, when the speaker preceding you gave a list of the better stories and mine was not among them, I thought I must have come out very badly indeed. Even when you made your criticism of the prize-winning stories I had no inkling of my good fortune until you made some reference to a book on Swift. Consequently, when the prize was actually awarded I think I was too dazed to show the proper amount of gratitude.... While this success doesn't necessarily mean I'm a good writer, since Guild members were excluded from the contest, it certainly gives me more encouragement than anything else I've achieved in writing thus far!

This story about Jonathan and Stella is a good cross-section of my writing, as it shows my best and worst characteristics. It is full of bombastic irrelevancies, the characters aren't logically developed, and the romantic spirit, like Stella's garden, is almost unbearably sweet. But I was only trying to create a single, poetic effect and think I may have succeded a little in doing that.

By the way, how do you manage to cross your ankles and fold your hands so reposefully while sitting on a stage? There is something beautifully mysterious about that!

Very sincerely, Tom Williams

P.S. I am going to copy below a few lines of poetry by LI PO, 14th century Chinese poet whom I've just discovered. I thought they were so fine I wanted to share them with someone who especially likes poetry. I tried reading them to my sister last week, she was knitting a sweater, and listened to them without missing a stitch, so I feel that was wasted effort.

The Rabbit in the Moon pounds the medicine in vain,
Fu-Sang, the tree of immortality, has crumbled to kindling wood,
Man dies, his white bones are dumb without a word
When the green pines feel the coming of the spring. . . .

    *   *   *   *

Little I prize gongs and drums and sweet meats,
I desire only the long ecstasy of wine, and desire not to awaken. . . .

    *   *   *   *

Tonight I stay at the Summit Temple,
Here I could pluck the stars with my hand,
I dare not speak aloud in the silence,
For fear of disturbing the dwellers of Heaven!

    *   *   *   *

Why do I live among the green mountains?
I laugh and answer not, my soul is serene:
It dwells in another heaven and earth belonging to no man.
The peach trees are in flower, the water flows on. . . .

[Josephine Johnson (1910-1990) was born in Kirkwood, Missouri, a suburb of St. Louis, and attended Washington University. She painted, wrote verse and fiction, supported leftist causes in the 1930s, and later taught at the University of Iowa (1942-1945). She made the Guild's award to TW shortly before learning that her first novel, *Now in November* (1934), had won the Pulitzer Prize.

Translations by Ezra Pound (1915) and Arthur Waley (1919) had stimulated interest in Li Po, an eighth-century Chinese poet of the High T'ang period, and led to the appearance of his poetry in later anthologies and collections. TW's quotations (see letter #50) appear to follow Shigeyoshi Obata's rendering in *The Works of Li Po* (Dutton, 1922).]

50. To John Rood

[6254 Enright Avenue
University City, Missouri]
[ca. March-April 1935]
[TL draft w/ autograph addition, 1 p. HRC]

Dear Mr. Rood:

Thanks for your sympathetic letter and helpful criticism. Like most young writers, I lack the ability to criticize my own work and even my best friends can't tell me. Sympathetically critical letters are a courtesy I have received only from Martha Foley and the Little Magazine editors. Yours was particularly helpful. I am glad you rejected the stories, as I certainly don't want to publish inferior stuff.

Tonight I stay at the Summit Temple.
Here I could pluck the stars with my hand,
I dare not speak aloud in the silence,
For fear of disturbing the dwellers of heaven.

Chang Chow in dream became a butterfly,
And the butterfly became Chang Chow at waking.
Which was the real—the butterfly or the man?

[John Rood (1902-1974) edited *Manuscript* (1934-1936), a respected little magazine based in Athens, Ohio. In late-March he returned the stories "Blue Roses" (March 1935, HRC) and "His Father's House" (n.d., HRC), along with an unidentified play, but he advised TW to "just keep on writing. It is remarkable how one begins to <u>know</u> what is right" (March 22, 1935, HRC). In September he accepted "Twenty-Seven Wagons Full of Cotton," forerunner of the one-act play (first published in 1945) and of the film *Baby Doll* (1956). Rood became a distinguished sculptor and taught for many years at the University of Minnesota.]

51. To Josephine Winslow Johnson

[1917 Snowden Avenue
Memphis, Tennessee]
May 17, 1935
[TLS, 1 p. Washington U.]

Dear Miss Johnson:

Some clippings from St. Louis newspapers recently arrived, telling about your having received the Pulitzer Prize. I was certainly delighted to read about it and want to offer you my congratulations. I've been out of touch with things down here in Memphis, recuperating from an illness which forced me to quit the shoe business. I hadn't read an account of the Pulitzer prizes in the newspapers (haven't been reading newspapers or anything till just lately) but now I've collected all the available St. Louis clippings and am pasting them in my literary scrap-book.

I guess you're very happy and you certainly should be very proud. But I suspect you received the honor with more composure than I received mine from the Writers' Guild.

I've hardly touched my typewriter in the past two months, since my heart and nerves have been playing these disturbing tricks on each other, but now that I'm feeling more settled inside, I'll probably start writing my head off again. There're so many fascinating things to write about down here. You should visit these southern plantations! Every one down here seems to have a history that you could write volumes about. Recently visited William Faulkner's home. In his home-town they call him "The Count" because he's so stuck-up. Seldom recognizes anyone on the street. But I think he's just absent-minded, like me and most other great writers. He's now conducting an air-circus. Does stunts in his airplane with a negro parachute-jumper every Sunday afternoon. So everyone in Mississippi thinks he's crazy. . . .

Hope I may see you some time, when and if I get back to St. Louis.

With all best wishes, Tom Williams

[TW wrote from the Dakins' retirement home in Memphis where he spent the summer recovering from nervous and physical exhaustion. In *Memoirs* (1975) he recounted several bouts of hypertension that culminated in late-March with an admission to St. Luke's Hospital while on a birthday outing with Rose. He resigned from Continental Shoemakers and received a priceless "twenty-fourth birthday gift": a "permanent release from the wholesale shoe business in St. Louis" (p. 39).

TW seems not to have read *Now in November*, Josephine Johnson's novel of Depression-era life on a small Missouri farm.

At the time of TW's visit to Oxford, Mississippi, "The Count" William Faulkner was less an "absent-minded" genius than a beleaguered husband saddled with debt and writing his own "head off" to pay the bills.]

52. *To Walter Dakin Williams*

[1917 Snowden Avenue
Memphis, Tennessee]
June 25, 1935
[TLS, 1 p. HTC]

Dear Dakin:

Your letter arrived just this morning and was quite a sensation. Everything about it was exceedingly admired, penmanship, literary style, and most of all the news about your grades. Grand and grandfather were beaming with pride. I don't know how I looked, but my complexion must have turned rather green, especially when you mentioned the honorary pin. What kind of pin was it, by the way?

You seem to have a very bad case of Urch-itis, even reading books for him during the summer. I should think you would find old Victoria pretty dull after Queen Bess and her various "thieves".

Summer is arriving at Memphis. It is just beginning to get comfortably warm. Miss Shapiro and I have fitted out a studio-solarium in our back-yards and yesterday had lunch under the peach trees with a few other guests. As you know, we collaborated on a play that is going to be presented. I wrote the play and Miss Shapiro wrote the prologue and epilogue which were almost bad enough to spoil the whole business. It has been accepted by the Garden players, however, and is now being rehearsed almost every night at the Shapiros. The leading lady bawls her lines so loudly that she sounds like she is selling fish. I am intending to take a part in the first act, a street scene, in which all kinds of pedestrians cross the stage. I will probably be the blind-man with the tin cup and dog. Not a very difficult part but quite sufficient for my dramatic capacities.

I am getting along quite well down here. I still have to rest a good deal but am feeling stronger. I'm sorry to hear Dad has been sick and hope he's now well. When you go to camp let us know what you're doing up there.

Grand and grandfather send their love to you and the rest of the family,

Lovingly, Tom

[Erwin J. Urch ("Urch-itis"), a history teacher at University City High School, held advanced degrees from the University of Chicago and Chicago Theological Seminary. He reportedly taught both TW and Dakin, the latter a diligent student at sixteen.

TW's first staged play, "Cairo, Shanghai, Bombay!" (n.d., HRC), was written in collaboration with Dorothy Shapiro, a young neighbor of the Dakins, and produced by The Garden Players, on July 12, "on the great sloping back lawn of a lady named Mrs. Rosebrough" (*Memoirs*, p. 41). Set in an unnamed seaport town, the one-act concerns a young sailor and a pick-up named Aileen whose dreary lives lend romance to the faraway lands of the title. Cairo they pronounce "Kayro" after the Illinois river town, in a refrain of humorous naivety and pathos. Their plan to elope is blocked by the sailor's friends and the woman left alone on the stage with her grip as the lights go out.

The director, Arthur B. Scharff, has recalled that TW "didn't talk much" at rehearsals, nor did he object to the cutting of "verbose" lines. The script, from which Shapiro's "moralistic" prologue was also cut in rehearsal, did not lead Scharff to attribute "any great talent" (interview, n.d., Virginia) to the collaborating authors.

This letter was first published in Edwina Dakin Williams's memoir, *Remember Me to Tom* (1963), p. 71.]

53. To Edwina Dakin Williams

[1917 Snowden Avenue
Memphis, Tennessee]
Aug. 17, 1935
[TLS, 1 p. Columbia]

Dear Mother:

We were all pleased to hear you're planning to come down, but I wish you would postpone the visit till the last week-end in August or the first in September. The Perrys have promised to take me down to their 10,000 acre plantation. I was hoping to go next week-end and would be very reluctant to miss it as that is my only opportunity to study the life on a Mississippi plantation. Also there are a number of other things I wish to do before returning to St. Louis. I've been intending to interview the local editors about newspaper work, but have had to put it off on account of the heat which has been simply exhausting and I am just beginning to feel human again after this long period of nervous prostration. The last few week-ends I have spent out in the country. I have made some awfully nice friends here who have been splendid about taking me places. Last two week-ends Mr. Hollifield has taken grandfather and I down to Maywood Mississippi where there is a fine artesian swimming pool. The sun and fresh air have helped me tremendously. Today (Saturday) I spent at Mrs. Rosebrough's where we are producing another play. She has a huge garden and private swimming-pool. I think it would be much better if you waited another week - or two, when it will be considerably cooler and Grand and I both could drive back with you. You see, I'm anxious to enjoy this southern atmosphere as long as possible.

Grand and grandfather are both well. Grand went down town yesterday and bought two coats and three dresses. Today we got a big crate of peaches sent by the Rhodes from Virginia. They are certainly lovely friends. They have written us several letters. Thursday evening Grandfather had a bridge party. He invited over two tables, to Grand's and my consternation: neither of us felt like entertaining that evening.

We are quite interested in the new house and dog. I hope the pup has a tractable nature.

With love to all, Tom

[The Perry plantation in Tunica County, Mississippi, may have provided important background for *Cat on a Hot Tin Roof* (1955). Tipped into an early draft of *Cat* (as Brenda Murphy has noted) is a newspaper clipping (n.d., HRC) that reports G.D. Perry's rise from manager to wealthy landowner in the Delta. His wife and nine children (the five boys short-necked) are pictured with Perry who had just purchased thousands of additional acres north of Clarksdale.

Joseph Phelan Hollifield wrote the one act from which TW's first full-length play, *Candles to the Sun*, evolved in 1937. They also collaborated on an intermediate draft entitled "The Lamp, A Drama of the Southern Coal Fields" (n.d., HRC), perhaps in the summer of 1935, with TW doing most of the writing and Hollifield supplying locale. The play was set in the Red Hills area of Alabama and treated a family of oppressed miners facing the rigors of a strike.

Peyton Rhodes was a professor of Physics at Southwestern in Memphis, later its president, who helped TW gain access to the college library.

In the autobiographical story "Grand" (1964), TW described a summer incident not mentioned in his letters. Fearing dependence, Grand had saved $7,500 in bonds by dint of self-depriving economies. Her naive husband was bilked (perhaps blackmailed) of the nest egg by "nameless con men" and in a backyard ritual of expiation burned "all his old sermons." Curiously 150 are nonetheless preserved at The University of the South.]

54. To Rosina Otte and Walter E. Dakin

[6634 Pershing Avenue
University City, Missouri]
Sept. 1, 1935
[TLS, 3 pp. HRC]

Dear Grand and Grandfather:

I know you will be interested in hearing about our trip and arrival so I am writing you at once, even though I have to borrow some of Rose's fancy stationary. We had a very pleasant, uneventful trip. The weather was ideal for driving. We stopped at Cape Girardeau and had lunch at the beautiful Marquette Hotel there while Dad was visiting one of his salesmen. After lunch Rose and I took a walk around the business section and down by the water-front which was very old and quaint. We got in St. Louis about 4:30 and went immediately to the Dog Hospital to get Gypsy who nearly went wild with excitement when he saw the folks. I have never seen any people so Dog-crazy as they are. They all talk baby-talk to him, even Mother, and during dinner when he was locked up on the back porch none of them could eat comfortably because he was crying. He really is a beautiful dog, black and white and shiney as silk.

The house is perfectly lovely, even prettier than I expected. It is Colonial style throughout. The living-room is gorgeous. It has a big crystal chandelier and crystal candelabrums on the long white mantal, built-in book-cases on either side of the fire-place. It is one of the most charming small homes I've ever seen. We found everything in perfect order, the grape arbor loaded with ripe grapes and the rose garden in full bloom. The place seems so quiet and spacious and dignified after our sordid apartment-dwelling that it doesn't seem like we're the same people. I'm sure you'd be just crazy about it if you were here. The street is quiet as the country. But only a half block from the campus and city car-lines.

In spite of everything being so nice I surely miss Memphis. I felt like I was saying goodbye to an old friend when we crossed the river and I saw the Memphis skyline disappearing in the river mist. I don't think I will ever become so attached to any other city. But I guess that was just because I had such a pleasant, restful time down there.

Grandfather, Dakin says to tell you he hid your candy in the top-drawer of the front room book-case. He was afraid that Rose would get into it, you know. Hope you've found it before now.

The whole family enjoyed their visit with you so much, especially Dad. We can hardly wait for you all to come up the 1st of October, so please don't disappoint us about that.

I think the trip home, with all the fresh-air, did me good, as I'm feeling much better this evening than I did during the week-end. I'm going to take a hot-shower now and go to bed early.

Please remember me to all my friends and acquaintances in Memphis, especially those whom I was unable to tell goodbye.

With much love from, Tom

[Rose's "fancy stationary" is headed by a silver horizontal bar with a dark blue centered device bearing her initials.

The new rental house was still in the unfashionable suburb of "U. City," but it was near Forest Park and Washington University and had a spacious residential air. With an end to "sordid apartment-dwelling," Edwina's goal of respectability was signally advanced.

TW did not return to Continental Shoemakers in the fall. In *Remember Me to Tom*, Edwina described his thirty-odd months in the warehouse as "absolutely useless work" required by a bullying father. He continued to read and write (primarily stories and verse), meet literary friends, and audit evening courses at Washington University in preparation for his senior year.]

55. *To Rosina Otte and Walter E. Dakin*

[6634 Pershing Avenue
University City, Missouri]
March 12, 1936
[TLS, 1 p. HTC]

Dear Grand and Grandfather:

We are in the throes of spring house-cleaning here. Both Susie and Edward are busy. All the floors are being waxed, windows clean[ed], stairs carpeted, Etc. As you may have heard, Mother is having all the daughters over this Monday for an afternoon tea. It is going to be a big affair. We are having a caterer prepare the food - Dorr & Zeller. They will make the coffee and take care of everything. We are having cakes and ices and candies and over a hundred open face sandwiches. If there is enough left over Rose is going to entertain a few friends after the party.

It is quite spring-like here. Our elm trees are budding. We also discovered yesterday that we have a pussy-willow. It is blooming in the backyard. A pleasant surprise. I bet Memphis is beautiful, too, this time of year. It is such a relief to be through with that terrible winter. We had to get another supply of coke, though. Just a few days ago.

I'm getting along fine with my university subjects. Lately I've been thinking of getting my degree, if possible, and then applying for a teaching job in some small town high-school. I believe a B.A. degree would be sufficient for that. And I know I could teach high-school English. I don't believe I would have to acquire many more credits. In my short-story class there are two real writers. One writes for STORY and the other for MANUSCRIPT. They have both been offered contracts by book publishers and are working on novels.

Everybody is well except Gypsy who has insomnia and woke Rose up twice last night. I'm going to take him out for a walk this evening when I mail this letter. Perhaps that will make him sleep better.

                    With much love from us all, Tom

[Edwina was active in the Daughters of the American Revolution and later in the spring became regent of the Jefferson chapter. Asked to join at this time, Rose said that she preferred "to come in on the Williams side of the family" where there were "so many interesting ancestors" (letter to Ella Williams, n.d., HRC).

This letter coincides with the beginning of TW's journal on March 6, 1936. Several days later, in contradiction of his rosy report to the Dakins, he described a case of "nervous heart" in Professor Webster's short story class that had left him feeling depressed and isolated. With typical aplomb he "took a pill" and resolved "to control" (*Journal*, March 10, 1936) his nerves. The unpublished journals were continued with only a few significant lapses for the remaining years of this collection. They are held primarily by the Humanities Research Center and are forthcoming from Yale University Press.

This letter was first published in *Remember Me to Tom*, pp. 79-80.]

56. To Harriet Monroe

6634 Pershing Ave.
University City, Mo.
March 27, 1936
[TLS, 1 p. HRC]

Dear Miss Monroe:

I was surprised and delighted by your selection of "My Love Was Light". It is the kind of poem which I write most naturally but am always afraid editors will find too much in the traditional style. Nearly a year? A breath-taking expanse of time! But I will try to be patient - - and time punctuated by the monthly arrival of POETRY is bound to pass more quickly. The Wednesday Club's twenty-five dollar poetry prize, which I won this week with a sonnet sequence, affords me the luxury of a subscription.

Thanking you again many times,

Very truly yours, Thomas L. Williams

P.S. In your current issue (March) the poems about the "tragedian" rooster and the "Locusts" struck me as being especially fine.

[TW's first acceptance by a major literary magazine was noted quietly in the journal. Following Harriet Monroe's death in September 1936, *Poetry* continued to publish a weighty list of contributors, including Allen Tate, Wallace Stevens, Elizabeth Bishop, and Edmund Wilson, and in June 1937 two rather conventional lyrics by Thomas Lanier Williams: "My Love Was Light" and "This Hour."

On March 25 the "tired, elegant old ladies" (*Journal*, March 29, 1936) of the Wednesday Club awarded TW the first prize of twenty-five dollars for his sequence entitled "Sonnets for the Spring."]

57. *To STORY Publishers*

[6634 Pershing Avenue
University City, Missouri]
April, 1936
[TL draft, 2 pp. HRC]

Dear STORY Publishers:

As I am obviously not one of your favorite contributors (the score so far is twenty-two to nothing in your favor) I have no reason to suppose that you might be interested in my comments on the short story situation, but am going to make some just the same.

I have been a contributor and subscriber for the past two years and my many personal rebuffs (all of which were more or less deserved) have neither discouraged nor soured my spirit - I still think STORY is unsurpassed in its field. There is just one thing that troubles me: what has become of your once-vaunted interest in the experimental short story? If I were not terribly fond of STORY and devoted to what I think (perhaps mistakenly) are STORY'S best interests I would not risk your displeasure by bringing up such a question.

I know the position that you are in. The magazine BUYING public is not - alas - interested in experimentation! Of course there's still another angle to the situation. Successful writers (with the brilliant exception of Saroyan and one or two others) are AFRAID of writing experimental stories. They have too much to lose. For the most part they've quit hoboing, dish-washing, Etc. They've developed a high standard of living - comparatively speaking - they've gotten married and developed soft, luxurious tastes along with several new mouths to feed! They depend on their writing for their living. So they don't dare write anything but what they're pretty sure the public wants. The result is that most of the literary experimentation is now being done by incompetent young nobodies like myself who have absolutely nothing to lose, no money, no reputation, no public or editorial favor by writing any way they damned please! Of course our experimental stories don't get into print - I've even given up submitting mine to editors - and I don't contend that American letters are suffering great injury on that account. Nevertheless the situation seems painful - short fiction is falling into a rather tedious, colorless rut of episodic naturalism. There's nothing wrong with episodic naturalism. It is, in fact, excellent, marvelous!

But it must not become a mere formula, practiced in an imitative, slavish fashion by writers who don't even understand its meaning. The door ought to be kept open - no matter what comes in! Stories like "The Night Reveals" (which is not episodic naturalism) are very good, entertaining stories - but do they belong in an ADVANCED magazine? I would rather see them in the "Saturday Evening Post"! That is where they would earn the most money and gain the most general attention. . . . [end of letter missing]

[TW wrote to "the invincible fortress of Foley and Burnett," who, he thought, were becoming "regular Babbitts" (*Journal*, March 31, 1936). His criticism was a reply to Whit Burnett's self-congratulatory note in the April 1936 number that claimed a history of publishing "serious" writers "without regard for commercial standards." By citing William Saroyan, TW made invidious contrast between such a bold experimental story as "The Daring Young Man on the Flying Trapeze," which Burnett published in 1934, and the present lead ("The Night Reveals" by Cornell Woolrich), which he thought little more than pulp fiction. TW first appeared in the highly regarded *STORY* magazine in 1939.]

58. To Rosina Otte Dakin

> [6634 Pershing Avenue
> University City, Missouri]
> May 10, 1936
> [TLS w/ autograph postscript, 2 pp. HRC]

Dear Grand:

This letter is addressed exclusively to you, since it is Mother's day. I hope you didn't think we had failed to remember you on this occasion. As a matter of fact, nobody realized it was Mother's Day until Rose came home from Church and mentioned that it was. Then I wondered if anybody had written to you and nobody had so I am now trying to make amends for this inexcusable lapse on our part. Dad is out of town now on a three weeks' trip to the West coast and Susie is taking a week's vacation so mother and Rose are kept pretty busy with the cooking and housework. Today we took our Sunday dinner out. We went to the Dean Sisters and had hamburgers and cold drinks which were delicious - but made us appreciate the dinners Susie usually cooks for us on Sunday! Gyp didn't have anything to eat, though he was in the car with us. He begged so pitifully that the waiter finally brought him out some scraps of ham and a lump of sugar - which seemed to satisfy him.

Yesterday Dakin and I took a trip to the country. A young girl whom I met at the Wednesday club - she writes poetry - had invited me out for the afternoon. We had lunch and Dakin went horseback riding. It is a lovely country home on the Missouri River and they have invited me to come out whenever I wish. They're awfully nice, cultured people.

It is beautiful around our place now. The ivy is out, covering the house, the grape arbor blooming, and the roses right on the verge. The grass keeps me busy. I have to mow the front and back yard several times a week. I didn't know a yard could be so much trouble. However it is worth it. We are going to put up our croquet set in a few more days.

This next week-end Mrs. Ver Steeg is driving Rose, Dakin and I out to her country place on the Mississippi. We're taking a picnic lunch and will spend the day out there. Dakin thinks the little girl, Patsy, is crazy about him - he gets more conceited every day! He has been given a part in a play at school. An English part so he is cultivating the English accent and Piccadilly air which is an awful trial on the rest of us.

We are looking forward to seeing you some time this summer.

With much love from us all, Tom

Best wishes for the holidays to Grandfather, Tom.

[In *Tennessee Williams: An Intimate Biography* (1983), Dakin Williams recalled that the St. Louis artist Florence Ver Steeg had once repeated a remark of Rose's, ca. 1935, about the rumored Jewish blood of the rector of St. Michael and St. George's Episcopal Church. Confronted by Dr. Karl Morgan Block for spreading false rumor, Rose was deemed unfit to teach in the Sunday school and relieved of her duties. Upset and humiliated, she required hospitalization once again. When Block later accepted the post of Bishop Coadjutor in California, Edwina commented to the Dakins that "he'll make better bishop than pastor" (April 29 {1938} HRC).

This letter was first published in *Remember Me to Tom*, pp. 81-82.]

59. To Wilbur L. Schramm

[6634 Pershing Avenue
University City, Missouri]
[ca. June 16, 1936]
[TLS, 1 p. HRC]

Dear Mr. Schramm:

I've just returned from the Mid-West Writers' Conference in Chicago where I rather hoped I might find some representatives of American Prefaces. But Mr. and Mrs. Rood were about the only editors present. You were wise in staying away. As might be expected, the conference seemed more concerned with politics than literature and was so exhaustingly dull that I left immediately after the morning session and did not return. I found the Chicago lake front much more edifying. All this hullabaloo about Fascist repression seems like so much shadow-boxing to me at the present time. The fiercest of our revolutionary writers are now receiving monthly checks of well over a hundred dollars from the Government for activities which they themselves describe as mainly "boondoggling" - so I cannot feel that the Fascist peril is very imminent at this moment!

With me at the "conference" was Clark Mills (McBurney) who I think is probably the most distinguished of the very young American poets. He says you have some poetry of his and I'm anxiously waiting to see it.

Here's a very innocent sort of love story with a sunny atmosphere which you may find appealing in contrast to the pervasive gloom of my other contributions. It comes a little out of season but I personally have always enjoyed spring stories best in the dead of winter.

Sincerely, Tom Williams

[Wilbur Schramm (1907–1987) was an English professor and the founding editor of American Prefaces (1935–1943) at the University of Iowa. He had written encouraging letters of rejection to TW, predicting that he would soon "burst out and write some fine stuff" (May 6, 1936, HRC). The "innocent" love story submitted with this letter was apparently rejected and remains unidentified.

The Chicago Writers' Group had called for meetings on June 13–14 to discuss the threat of fascism and to protest the midwestern writer's indentured relation to the East. Richard Wright, Nelson Algren, and Jack Conroy, the radical novelist-editor well known to TW in St. Louis, also attended the "exhaustingly dull" conference. "'Boondoggling'" refers to artists receiving aid from Federal Arts programs being implemented by the Roosevelt administration.

The Chicago trip was "a ghastly fiasco" that led TW to record a divided "impression" of Clark Mills (McBurney). As a poet he was "brilliant," as a person "conceited, spoiled, bigoted, childish and painfully lacking in a sense of humor" (*Journal*, June 16, 1936), or so TW thought. Mills did not use McBurney, his surname, professionally.]

60. To Rosina Otte and Walter E. Dakin

[6634 Pershing Avenue
University City, Missouri]
August 30, 1936
[TLS, 1 p. HTC]

Dear Grand and Grandfather:

Dakin and I have just returned from a delightful two weeks at camp in the Ozarks. It was nicer this year than I have ever known it. We had everything, even a mild tornado, by way of diversion and escaped some of the worst heat, according to reports at home. Dakin gained some weight and we are both feeling fine. We produced three plays which I wrote and Dakin acted in. The last one was an old-fashioned melodrama and for the heroine we had a little Ozark girl that waited on the tables whose accent and manners were just perfect for the part. She pronounced villain as "vill-yun" and was so dumb she didn't realize the play was supposed to be funny, which made it all the funnier.

It rained just the day before we returned and has been pretty cool here since then. I hope the heat has broken in Memphis also. It must have been awful to have to conduct services in such weather.

While I was away I got a letter from Simon & Schuster publishing company that published Josephine Johnson's "Now In November". They said my short story in "Manuscript" was excellent and wanted to know if I were working on a novel and said if so they would like to see it. So I think that I will try to write one during my spare time - just a short one. It is easier to sell a good novel than a good short story. I've also had a story tentatively accepted by "American Prefaces" which O'Brien the short-story critic considers the most promising new literary magazine.

It is certainly lovely of you to offer to send me to Washington. But I don't want you to do it if it would mean sacrificing things that you need. I think I could complete my work in another year and of course I could get out of the physical education on account of my irritable heart. At camp I met a Washington U. Junior who said he wanted me to write for the school literary magazine and join the Poetry Club. He's an editor of the magazine. I think my contacts at the University would be extremely helpful. I'm going to get in touch with some newspaper editors pretty soon and perhaps in another year they will have a place for me or something else will open up.

Jiggs and the others are all quite well.

With much love, Tom

Tom with Jiggs, one of many family pets.

[TW's return to "the awful screech of trolley wheels and polite, constrained city voices" could only improve his memory of the Ozarks. Homelife remained tense and he was often possessed by "a little crazy blue devil" (*Journal*, August 30, 31, 1936) of fear and depression.

One of the camp "plays" is a burlesque of the balcony scene in *Romeo and Juliet*. To Romeo's punning gallantry, "What fragrance floats upon the air! / Is it the rose—or Juliet's hair?" a shopworn Juliet replies, "I got six ounces for a dime / at Woolworth's. Don't it smell sublime?" (n.d., Dakin Williams Collection).

The *Manuscript* story was "Twenty-Seven Wagons Full of Cotton," but Edwina and Rose did not think it "excellent," as TW complained to the Dakins: "Mother and Rose are not used to modern writing and were very displeased with the subject, which is an affair between a crude Arkansas couple, and so Mother forbids me to send the magazine to anybody. . . . It is supposed to be humorous but she and Rose don't take it that way" (August 6, 1936; qtd. in *Remember Me to Tom*, pp. 82-83).

TW considered writing a short novel for a contest sponsored by the publisher Little, Brown. *The Apocalypse* would treat college students faced by the revelation of spring, but he could not expand his "ideas" (*Journal*, August 7, 13, 1936) to novelistic length and soon dropped the project.

"Ten Minute Stop" (1985), the story "tentatively accepted" by *American Prefaces*, was returned in early-October with "some preposterous suggestions" (*Journal*, October 7, 1936) for revision. Edward J. O'Brien, editor of the annual series *The Best Short Stories*, had described *American Prefaces* as "the most promising new magazine" of 1935.

On June 22 the Washington University registrar advised TW that he would be admitted as a "Student Not Candidate For a Degree." This report differed considerably from the optimistic prospect for graduation that he described to his grandfather in an earlier letter (n.d., HTC) and repeated in the present one. On September 15 he received a tuition check of $125.00 from the Dakins that allowed him to enroll in sixteen hours distributed over English, Greek, French, Political Science, and Physical Education.

Jiggs, successor to Gypsy, was the latest and most petted of the Williams family dogs.]

61. To Rosina Otte and Walter E. Dakin

[6634 Pershing Avenue
University City, Missouri]
[ca. November 15, 1936]
[TLS, 2 pp. HTC]

Dear Grand and Grandfather:

I hope you excuse the infrequency of my letters. I know infrequency is a mild term - but I just don't seem to have a spare moment. All my mornings, including Saturday are taken up at the University and I have three courses which require a tremendous amount of outside reading. For one course I am having to read all of O'Neill's plays to make a term paper on his work. In another I am having to read all of Sophocles' tragedies and in my French course I am kept busy reading Voltaire, Etc. Then I have a lot of outside activities. I am working in the "Thyrsus" dramatic organization as a play "prompter". I have to attend all the rehearsals for the plays they are putting on as well as rehearsals for my own play at the Mummers'. That is now over, thank Heavens. Then I am on the swimming team and have to swim every afternoon from four to five-thirty. I think it is good for me to be kept so busy. Sometimes I get terribly tired and have to spend an afternoon in bed but on the whole I am feeling much better.

I know you will be glad to hear that Rose seems much better. Her mind seems to be functioning much more clearly. She is working around the house and going out a little. She went to Church Sunday and to a D.A.R. meeting. She is taking more interest in things. But is terribly ill tempered. She and mother are constantly squabbling over things. I think it would be good for her to go away for awhile since she and Mother are so incompatible. It would be nice if she could visit "Clare" in Florida.

I hope you will change your minds about coming up here. I still think you could find a reasonable place or else stay with us. I think that would also help Rose.

We are still having a delightful Fall. The chrsanthemums are now blooming. I hope Grand has not sold her farm. I think that sly John T. is trying to put something over on her. There will probably be a big inflation period if the present trends continue and the land may increase in value a great deal. Otherwise why are they so anxious to make a deal? Of course that is something that you would have to investigate for yourselves. I wouldn't do anything without first visiting the farm and getting first hand information about it.

With much love from us all, Tom

[TW considered the present fall his "happiest season" (*Journal*, November 15, 1936) since the spring of 1931 at MU. His one-act play "The Magic Tower" (HRC) had won a contest sponsored by the Webster Groves Theatre Guild and was performed successfully on October 13. His "play at the Mummers," a local theatre group directed by Willard Holland, was a curtain-raiser ("Headlines") written for Irwin Shaw's anti-war tract *Bury the Dead* (1936), which opened in St. Louis on November 11.

Rose's improvement followed "neurotic sprees" in which she fancied herself "an invalid," talked "in a silly dying-off way," and trailed "around the house in negligees." It was a "disgusting" (October 7, 1936) performance, TW wrote in the journal, for which he later asked God's forgiveness. His criticism of Rose grew out of a literary party that he gave in late-September in the absence of their parents. William Jay Smith, then a student at Washington University, has recalled the scene: "Pale and trembling, in a fluffy dress, Rose drifted down the stairs, apparently knocked off kilter by some of the rough language she had overheard" (*The New Criterion*, March 1996). She later complained to Edwina and was rebuked by TW for betraying him. A coolness ensued.

TW felt that the "sly John T." Raulston, Grand's brother-in-law, might cheat her of inherited farm property in East Tennessee that he managed for the estate.]

62. To Walter E. Dakin

[6634 Pershing Avenue
University City, Missouri]
[ca. December 8/19, 1936]
[TLS, 2 pp. HRC]

Dear Grandfather:

Just received your letter and glad to know you may pay us a visit. Rose is home from Barnes and in a distinctly better frame of mind. Of course she is not normal and probably has not been for a long time but is not ranting around like she was before. She types, practices piano and does housework but still has odd delusions such as thinking Mrs. Wright next door is her half sister and that the family is responsible for her ill health but does not talk about it except occasionally. Her doctor seems to do wonders with her. She is crazy about him. It is very trying for all of us, especially mother, but is just one of those things which have to be taken. We hope she will gradually return to normal.

Dad is just about on the point of buying that house in Davis place. It is a swell place, not nearly so isolated as it sounds. The street car into the city and the bus are both just a block from the house, the car goes right by the University and connects with downtown lines. It has an upstairs and downstairs (basement) sitting rooms and also a sun parlor. Three baths with showers. Very ritzy neighbors but none of them <u>close</u> which would be an advantage, perhaps, with Rose in her present condition.

The "Mummers" are planning to produce my long play soon as I finish rewriting it, sometime this winter. I hope you will get to see it.

Dad is going down to Knoxville next week and will try to talk Ella into taking Rose in her shop if Rose gets well enough to. The Doctor thinks it would be good for her and she doesn't want to stay home.

With much love to you both, Tom

P.S. I've had this letter in my desk about a week. Most of the information is no longer valid. Dad was laid up in the hospital for a week with an injured ear as Mother has no doubt informed you. He is now out. It doesn't look like we will get the new house. And his trip to Knoxville has also fallen through or will be postponed till later.

The salesmen sent an enormous bunch of flowers to the house. Roses, chrysanthemums, and gladiolas sufficient to decorate several rooms.

Rose seems a lot brighter and better. A couple of days ago she applied for a job as dress <u>model</u> at Scruggs but they told her she was too short. I am glad to see she felt like applying, though. She and mother went to Mrs. Ver Steeg's bridge party at the Woman's Club a few days ago.

Au Revoir -- no more paper!

[Of Rose's hospitalization Edwina wrote to the Dakins: "The only thing I can see that the doctor has done for her is to start her to smoking" (December 6, 1936, HRC). She added in a following letter that Dr. Alexander had told Rose "'she needed to get married,'" and that "she has been raving on the subject of 'sex' ever since" (Monday {January 25, 1937} HRC). TW wrote at the time: "Tragedy. I write that word knowing the full meaning of it. We have had no deaths in our family but slowly by degrees something was happening much uglier and more terrible than death. Now we are forced to see it, know it. The thought is an aching numbness - a horror! I am having final exams but can't study. Her presence in the house is a——" (*Journal*, January 25, 1937).

The "long play" is *Candles to the Sun*. Shortly after the new year, TW noted that it was "practically done" and that he and the director, Willard Holland, had agreed that the ending should be one of "mingled sadness and exaltation" (*Journal*, January 3, 1937).

Edwina was awakened on the morning of December 10 by a call that Cornelius had suffered a "'head injury'" and was being treated at Barnes Hospital. A fellow salesman, she incredulously wrote to her mother, "<u>bit</u> a piece of Cornelius' ear off" (December 12, 1936, HRC) in a drunken card game. Although hushed up, the episode weakened his position at the shoe company and delayed the family's attempt to find a job for Rose in Knoxville.]

63. To Willard H. Holland

SH: ~~Rose Isabel~~ Williams
6634 Pershing Avenue
Saint Louis, Missouri
[ca. mid-April 1937]
[TLS, 2 pp. HRC]

Dear Willard:

I have just read Hynds review of the new period play - and I think it rather nasty and completely unjust. The play - while not hilarious - was an artistic triumph. It was distinctly the most even, well-knit play you've put on. Everything was in perfect keeping and consistency, there was not a single thing that struck off-key. The reason the audience was so unresponsive during the first act Thursday night was the novelty of the thing: though announced as a period piece, few of them had wits enough to realize they were seeing an exact reproduction of the play as it was played and not a cheap burlesque. That was the artistic thing about the show and unfortunately neither of the reviewers quite realized it - though McPherson gave a pretty decent review comparatively. Frankly none of the male actors turned in a very striking job but then nothing was bungled and the total effect was very pleasing from start to finish.

APRIL, ETC. is progressing nicely. I think it is potentially better than "Candles" as the subject is one which I can handle better - it is purely characterization. I have written 84 pages so far and there is still one whole scene not written so it will probably run about the same length as the Candles. Of course the dialogue is pretty crude at this stage - the first draft - but I may bring it over early next week to let you have a look at it. I will call you.

I also have written some new one-acts under the compound title of "American Blues" which you might be interested in.

I made my stage debut last week in the Moliere. I was not at all nervous - actually enjoyed myself on the stage - which surprised me tremendously as I had always fancied myself a hopeless victim of stage-fright. Instead of being frightened by the full-house I was stimulated and found myself ad-libbing both lines and action - so now I am a full-fledged Thespian!

I saw McPherson at intermission Thursday night. Introduced him to Jane Garrett whom he had admired extravagantly in Candles - he told me she was an actress of professional calibre. Last night he was urging her to try Broadway. Well - I think she is good myself.

Don Ellinger has spoken to me twice about getting you to give a performance of "Candles" on campus under auspices of A.S.U. - procede at your own discretion - I am not much interested in that bunch and I am rather tired of "Candles". I have not even felt like re-typing the Ms. yet.

Will see you soon, Tom

[Willard Holland (1908-1963) was a native St. Louisan who directed the Mummers (founded ca. 1928), a semi-professional group that staged TW's first two full-length plays. An aspiring actor, Holland later moved to Hollywood where he held a variety of jobs, including dialogue director for Universal Studios. TW remembered him as a socially-conscious director whose work was always "charged with electricity." The Mummers he also admired for a youthful "romanticism" that epitomized the "benevolent anarchy" ("Something Wild," 1949) of art. The "period play" directed by Holland was Clothilde Graves's late nineteenth-century comedy *Three in a Row*, and the "nasty" reviewer Reed Hynds of the *St. Louis Star-Times*.

Candles to the Sun opened in St. Louis on March 18 and was a hit with audience and reviewers alike. Jane Garrett played the role of Star, the daughter of an exploited mining family in Alabama, who falls in love with Birmingham Red, the strike leader. The play dealt "with group welfare as opposed to individual welfare," TW said in a contemporary interview, but he had no direct knowledge of miners or their plight and had not followed through on an earlier plan "to visit some real coal-mines in Illinois" (letter to Walter Dakin, September 15, 1936, HRC). The critic Colvin McPherson was impressed nonetheless by TW's "sound knowledge of locale" (*St. Louis Post-Dispatch*, March 19, 1937). A first edition of *Candles* is planned by New Directions.

The new play, *April Is the Cruellest Month*, drew its provisional title from *The Waste Land* (1922) by T.S. Eliot and appropriately enough concerned the dawning and frustration of love. On April 25 TW planned to give Holland a draft of the new play about which he felt "very uncertain" (*Journal*, April 25, 1937).

American Blues was a "compound title" for various one-act plays collected in 1939 and 1948. Those submitted to the Group Theatre in 1939 were not in each case the same ones published in 1948 (see letter #101).

"Competent" was the reviewer's judgment of TW's role in Molière's *Les Fourberies de Scapin* (1671), which opened at Washington University on April 7. His academic record was deficient, however, and he was placed on probation on April 20.

Don Ellinger was an organizer of the American Student Union (A.S.U.) at Washington University. In the preceding September the pacifist group had mailed a letter to incoming freshmen that was harshly critical of the R.O.T.C., for which Ellinger's scholarship was revoked. TW alluded to the well-publicized incident in "Headlines," his curtain-raiser for *Bury the Dead*. *Candles to the Sun* was an attractive vehicle to Ellinger's "bunch," but TW felt "a natural uncongeniality" for such "professional 'againsters'" (*Journal*, November 11, 1936) and resisted political commitment. *Candles* was not produced at Washington University.]

64. To Willard H. Holland

[6634 Pershing Avenue
University City, Missouri]
[ca. May 1937]
[TL draft, 2 pp. HRC]

Dear Willard:

I've just been reading over the new drama. It really is a mess. I hadn't realized it was so bad or I wouldn't have let you see it. I'll have to work on it at least two months before I let you see it again, it is in such a thoroughly chaotic state. None of the characters seem to speak quite naturally, the atmosphere is either hysterical or dull. I guess it needs a great deal more mental incubation than I've had time to give it so far - I've just been working on it the past six weeks and that sporadically. However I think it contains the germ of something really good: if I work on it all summer it may turn out surprisingly well: on the other hand, I may have to discard it altogether. I think your idea of the contrasting outdoor scene between Helen and Dick a good one and will use it to open the play. The second outdoor scene could come at the beginning of the second part - after intermission - to give an effective contrast. The idea of the play as I see it now is simply a study of Sex - a blind animal urge or force (like the regenerative force of April) gripping four lives and leading them into a tangle of cruel and ugly relations.

Hertha is destroyed by it. Helen loses her lover and makes a marriage of convenience. Arthur's passion for Helen makes him ruin a fine relationship and go into one which has a purely physical basis. Dick is the only one that gets out of the muddle, and he only at the sacrifice of his love for Helen. It is a tragedy of sex relations, but the final effect should not be completely grim, for while Helen and Arthur are not an ideal match, they will probably manage to make a reasonable adjustment. Hertha is the martyred one.

It is going to be a terribly hard thing to handle but if it works out right will be worth the effort.

[TW blended Columbia and Clarksdale locations to form a Mississippi Delta setting for *April Is the Cruellest Month*. The "outdoor scene" recommended by Willard Holland was probably based upon a lovers' leap near the MU campus that is still frequented by students. In a later version (ca. April 1938) entitled *Spring Storm*, Helen Critchfield became Heavenly and lost even a "marriage of convenience." The "martyred" Hertha, named for a Missouri co-ed, formed the sensitive, introspective contrast to Helen's more conventional role. Hertha's suicide in "the freight-yards," an undisguised allusion to *Anna Karenina* (1875–1877), would reappear as an alternate ending for *A Streetcar Named Desire* (see letter #327).

The echo of Eugene O'Neill, especially of *Strange Interlude* (1928), in TW's naturalistic language and "tangle" of sex relations may reflect the prestige of O'Neill's recent Nobel Prize, as well as TW's reading of his plays at Washington University in 1936. The roving life that led O'Neill to Buenos Aires as a young man may also be echoed in Act One, when Dick tells Helen that he would "rather take a cattle-boat to South America" than conform to her routine expectations of marriage.]

65. *To Rosina Otte and Walter E. Dakin*

SH: Rose Isabel Williams
6634 Pershing Avenue
Saint Louis, Missouri
PM: St. Louis, July 13, 1937
[TLS, 3 pp. HRC]

Dear Grand and Grandfather:

It is almost too hot to breathe on this second floor so you will excuse for writing a very brief letter. This is the first really bad weather we've had. I hope it doesn't extend to Memphis.

At last we've just about selected a house. The lease is not signed yet but the agent assured us it would be. It is on 42 Aberdeen Place, one block west of Skinker and about two blocks South of the Washington University Campus. It is a fine location. It is just one block from Forest Park and right on the City Limits carline. I have not been inside the house yet so cannot describe the interior. It is somewhat larger than this house, as it has a third story.

I am delighted that you will get this vacation at Monteagle. It is lovely of Mrs. Saunders to take you. I hope you'll stay the whole summer. I think Grand ought to have a change.

I have had a terrible affliction all last week, poison ivy. My face has been like raw beef. It kept me from sleeping several nights but now is beginning to disappear.

I suppose mother has written you about my Greek course being cancelled. I was the only student who enrolled for that course so of course they could not afford to give it. They returned the tuition. I can take it next Fall if I go back to school then. Perhaps it would be more sensible to take it then, anyway, as it would save money.

I sure hope you can rent your house this Fall and come up here. Why don't you make up your minds to do that? Grandfather, you would enjoy living in this location. It is within walking distance of the art-museum and the zoo - just one block from the park and the street car makes it convenient for going downtown. It is also a short walk from the University. It has the same number of bedrooms as the present house plus a servant's room on the third floor. The owner is in Miami Florida and we won't know definitely for a couple of days if he has accepted the terms.

Tonight Dakin and I listened to a radio broadcast of Hamlet. Did you know they are giving a series of Shakespearean plays over the radio? The next one will be "Much Ado About Nothing" with Leslie Howard in the leading role. You should find out if it will be heard in Memphis and listen in. It is a national hook-up so I feel sure you can get them.

Grand, I hope you will not over-do yourself in this hot weather and that you will have a good rest at Miss Janie's cottage. We visited Rose this week. She looked well and seemed in pretty good spirits but would not stay outside long on account of her "relatives" who she thinks are on the grounds.

Dad is planning to drive up to Knoxville after we move. He will take Dakin with him. Then Dakin is going to the Y.M.C.A. camp in the Ozarks to rest up before school commences. He seems to be getting along very well with his typing.

I have been working on my new long play which Mr. Holland says he will produce next Fall. That is about all I've done this week besides applying lotions on my poison ivy. I never dreamed that a skin eruption could be such agony. Thank heavens it is beginning to heal!

We got a letter from Isabel saying that Aunt Ella had gotten a job at the Y.W.C.A. in Knoxville.

I hope you are going to have a pleasant time at Monteagle.

With much love from us all, Tom

[The new rental house in the wealthy suburb of Clayton was a sharp rise above University City where the family had lived since 1926.

TW failed Greek in the winter semester and earned D's in three other subjects. More "ignominious" was the failure of his one-act play "Me, Vashya!" to be chosen for presentation in William Carson's English 16. In a note appended to the script, and presumably written by the instructor, Carson attributed the rejection to the vagaries of judging and to the difficulty of casting Lady Vashya, "perhaps the first of {TW's} slightly deranged heroines" (n.d., Washington U.). TW blamed Carson for the fiasco and described him as a typical Washington University professor, "the stronghold of the Reactionaries!" (*Journal*, June 4, 1937).

In March Rose's condition worsened, and in April the family attempted to place her in Highland Hospital in Asheville, North Carolina, the state, TW noted, where his family had "originated" and would make a "triumphal return!" (*Journal*, April 7, 1937). She went instead to St. Vincent's Sanitarium in St. Louis County, where she began an institutional life of nearly sixty years duration. Her present "good spirits" had been absent in May, however, as Edwina informed the Dakins: "Her face looked so yellow and bloated and she was so full of delusions . . . that I see she has not improved. . . . The visit made Tom ill so I can't take him to see her again. I can't have two of them there!" (May 11, 1937, HRC).

In June, Rose was diagnosed as schizophrenic, and in late-July she became "violently insane" (letter from Edwina to the Dakins, Monday {August 2, 1937} HRC) and was placed in isolation. For medical and financial reasons, she was transferred on July 31 to Farmington State Hospital, seventy-five miles south of St. Louis, to begin insulin shock treatment. "Why must a child of God have dementia praecox?" (*Journal*, June 24, 1937), TW asked at the time of her diagnosis.

The new play, *Fugitive Kind*, was "laid in a flophouse" (*Journal*, June 5, 1937) in a large midwestern city modeled upon St. Louis. A return to the documentary realism of *Candles,* it projects youthful idealism and love against a familiar 1930s backdrop of economic depression and social injustice. With a hint of later critical notices, TW described the play as one that "smooths out but does not develop" (*Journal,* July 6, 1937).

Monteagle, in the mountains of southeastern Tennessee, is near the University of the South where Walter Dakin studied theology as a young man.]

66. To Wilbur L. Schramm

SH: Thomas Lanier Williams
42 Aberdeen Place
Clayton, Missouri
August 22, 1937
[TL draft, 1 p. Virginia]

Dear Mr. Schramm:

I know it will surprise you to learn that I am intending, if possible, to enter the University of Iowa this Fall. I first conceived that notion while talking to Mr. Blandford Jennings, English and Dramatics teacher at a local highschool, who told me he thought I would be greatly benefited by study in Prof. Mabie's department at your University. As you will see from the enclosed clippings, I have been pretty much absorbed in writing plays for the past two years. I had a long regional drama presented here last spring - the one reviewed - which is now in the hands of a New York agent. I have completed two more long plays since then, one of which will be produced by the same group about Christmas. I feel, like Mr. Jennings, that I need some laboratory work in a good dramatics department and have been told that yours is unexcelled.

My problem is the usual one of insufficient funds. I have enough to manage the tuition and part of the living expenses but will need to secure some part-time employment to provide the rest. Twenty or thirty dollars a month would be enough. I am writing this letter to enquire if you know of any work I could do in Iowa City. I have had three years office experience, type proficiently, and will undertake any kind of work. Perhaps you could mention my case to Prof. Mabie or others in the department.

I know that this request is presumptious, but you have been so good about reading and criticizing my short-stories that I have formed a deep confidence in your good nature. I will be tremendously grateful for any help that you may be able to give me.

Sincerely,

[TW may have been encouraged to attend the University of Iowa after his sonnet, "The New Poet," appeared in *American Prefaces* in April 1937. Later in the summer he drafted a letter to the registrar, stating a wish to finish his degree at Iowa "because of its dramatic and other literary advantages" (n.d., Virginia). Edward C. Mabie was the formidable head of Speech and Dramatic Arts.

The plays completed since the March production of *Candles to the Sun* were early drafts of *April Is the Cruellest Month* and *Fugitive Kind*. The "New York agent" who held *Candles* was Olga Becker, a former board member and actor for the Mummers.

This letter survives in multiple drafts at the University of Virginia, suggesting its importance to TW.]

67. To Clark Mills

[St. Louis, Missouri]
[September 22, 1937]
[ALS, 2 pp. *Journal*]

Dear Clark:

I am seated in a coach bound for Iowa City - it is 11:45 P.M. - and I feel such a prodigious excitement - in spite of a double sedative - that I must communicate my feelings to someone or else <u>blow up</u>. I know you will be disappointed not to hear from me after I get to Iowa City where I will really have something to write about - perhaps I can continue the letter from there or else write a new one. But of course the <u>important</u> thing is that I am actually going - I never really believed in its possibility until I got on the train!

I spent this evening with Bill Smith and the Filsingers. We drank great quantities of beer, criticized Bill's new verse - which is rather good, shows progress - and laughed almost continuously. I felt quite hysterical with joy over my imminent departure. I want you to know that I have already purchased a pint of good whiskey to fortify myself against the rigors of a northern winter! I have a feeling that I am not going to be at all precise this winter, despite B.J.'s warnings. I will probably call up Schramm and Mabie soon as I get in town and invite them both out on "a colossal binge".

Bill and I called up your mother tonight and she said she had recovered from her illness which I'm sure you are glad to know. I will at least add my address to this letter when I get to I.C. so you can drop me a line before sailing - I'm anxious to know how you come out with Bishop. My regards to Salvan.

Sincerely your friend, Tom.

[Clark Mills (1913-1986) earned undergraduate and graduate degrees in French at Washington University in 1935 and 1937, respectively. An early friend and mentor of TW, he was a promising poet whose work began appearing in national magazines in the mid 1930s. He campaigned for modernism and undoubtedly helped to wean TW from such latter-day Romantics as Sara Teasdale and Edna St. Vincent Millay. TW wrote to Mills shortly before his friend sailed for France to study at the Sorbonne.

Before leaving for Iowa, TW visited Rose on September 12 and found her "in remarkably good spirits," although she was "swollen and exhausted" from the insulin treatment. "I beg whatever power there is to save her and spare her from suffering" (*Journal*, September 15, 16, 1937).

Insulin Shock Treatment (IST) was introduced in 1933 and all but abandoned by the mid 1950s as a dangerous and ineffective procedure. As administered in Missouri state hospitals, the treatment consisted of daily sessions, lasting for eight weeks, in which insulin was injected to produce a hypoglycemic state of coma. IST was thought to moderate or cure symptoms in fairly recent cases of depression and schizophrenia.

William Jay Smith earned degrees at Washington University in 1939 and 1941 and became a highly respected poet, translator, and teacher of creative writing, as well as a lifelong friend of TW. The sisters Catherine and Mary Lois Filsinger were students, past and present, at Washington University and nieces of Ernst Filsinger, who married Sara Teasdale in 1914. Mary Lois Filsinger Kessler has recalled for the editors TW's buoyant good spirits that summer and likened his distinctive laughter to a "little wild goat's." The "warnings" were those of Blandford Jennings, an English teacher at Clayton High School.

Albert J. Salvan and Morris G. Bishop were professors of French, respectively, at Washington University and Cornell, where Bishop later served as the chairman of Mills's Ph.D. committee.

This letter was written in TW's journal and apparently never mailed to Mills.]

68. *To Edwina Dakin Williams*

[225 North Linn Street
Iowa City, Iowa]
[September 23, 1937]
[TLS w/ autograph postscript, 1 p. HRC]

Dear Mother:

All I have done so far is to find a rooming and boarding place. This is my first evening here. The Quadrangle was completely filled up with a long waiting list so I had to walk all over town to locate a suitable place. However I am very well-satisfied with this place. I get both board and room here. I will enclose the contracts for you to examine. They appear rather complicated. The board is $21. a month, in advance. The room is ten, making a total of $31. for room and board. The meals are excellent. So far my room is the only one taken so I have plenty of privacy. It is convenient to the campus and to the downtown section. I can pay my board till the end of this month and you can send me the money for next month on the 1st - $21. The room rent I have paid up for a month in advance - ten dollars - so you needn't send a check for that till the end of Oct.

I am delighted with the town. It is very much like Columbia, small and friendly, but the campus is much larger and handsomer. It is on both sides of the river which is about the size of the Meramec. Registration is tomorrow and Saturday. After that I'll have more to tell you of course.

I find on unpacking that I have left only two articles at home, my shaving brush and tooth brush. I'll buy a new tooth-brush but wish you would send me the shaving brush with my new suit when it arrives. In meantime I can use some brushless shaving cream.

It is already raining here! It seems to be intermittent, however, so I may be able to make the mail-box this evening.

I hope Dakin is getting along all right at Washington. I'm sure he would like this University much better. It is by far the nicest campus I've seen.

Will write again early next week.

Lovingly, Tom

P.S. You had better keep the "contracts" -

[With a student body of 8,000, Iowa was a larger and more vibrant campus than Missouri or Washington University. Norman Foerster directed the School of Letters, and Paul Engle, a young poet on the faculty, would soon lead the Writers' Workshop to national renown. Under Edward C. Mabie, the University Theater had gained a strong reputation and moved into superb new quarters in 1936. Paintings by Grant Wood, a member of the Graphic and Plastic Arts department, supplied the titles for several of TW's one-act plays: "American Gothic" (Summer 1937, HRC) and "Daughter of Revolution" (n.d., HRC).

Dakin Williams had an unhappy start at Washington University when he was not rushed by a fraternity and considered withdrawing. He later pledged Tau Kappa Epsilon.]

69. *To Edwina Dakin Williams*

225 N. Linn
Iowa City [Iowa]
Sunday Evening [October 3, 1937]
[TLS, 2 pp. HRC]

Dear Mother:

Apparently people in the Dramatics Dpt. are not supposed to be Godly as they even have us working on Sunday morning. I am taking part in a "living newspaper", a series of skits dramatizing current events. I play a negro chairman of a church convention condemning Hugo Black and the Ku Klux Klan. First rehearsal this morning.

My registration was held up five days because my credits had not come from the University of Missouri, only from Washington. I had to wire Columbia to have the credits forwarded. I wrote Holland about this delay and he apparently became very alarmed because he sent Prof. Mabie, head of Dramatics Dept., a long telegram urging him to admit me and also got Colvin McPherson, dramatic crit of the Post-Dispatch, to send a Special Delivery letter. All of which was quite unnecessary as the delay was purely routine and I was attending classes just the same. Holland even sent my new play up special delivery for me to show Mabie. I had to send it back to him immediately as he had not finished having it typed. The Missouri credits have now arrived and I am fully registered. I only have to meet two requirements, two hours of science, probably astronomy which I will take next term. All the rest are electives, that is, whatever I choose to take. So my courses are all in the English and Dramatics Dept. The lectures here are far better than any I've heard previously. I'm studying Shakespeare and the Modern Drama, Stagecraft, Experimental Playwriting and a comprehensive survey of English literature. In stagecraft I get practical experience in backstage work, building sets, etc. Dakin would love this school as everyone is obliged to do some acting whether he wants to or not. The theater is the most completely equipped in the world and the rehearsals I have seen have been as good as professional.

The A.T.O. chapter entertained me twice this week, for lunch and dinner and want me to move in the house. They offer me room and two meals for $22. a month by which I would save slightly but the house is too far from the campus. It is considered one of the best chapters on campus. But I find the more interesting people are outside of frats. and sororities here. At our table here, for instance, we have mostly graduate students and English majors, a very cosmopolitan bunch, representing the Bronx, Manhattan, Canada, Pennsylvania, California, Mississippi, and Alabama. There is even a Russian, very communistic, who comes up to my room after every meal to talk art and politics.

I have learned of a private laundress who does shirts for 8¢ each which sounds fairly reasonable. I don't believe my laundry and cleaning expenses will amount to more than a dollar a month. I find that some people are getting rooms here for as cheap as five dollars a month - comfortable though very plain. So I may decide to move later on. The heating is the main consideration as it gets down to 25 below I am told.

I hope you have sent my new suit by now as I will be needing it. Also the shaving brush which I left at home. I have been lathering with my fingers which is not very efficient.

Marian Galloway, the young woman that Mr. Jennings introduced me to, by letter, is thinking of driving me down to St. Louis when my play is produced. I hope she will be able to. She has been marvelous about introducing me to people and aiding me in getting adjusted up here - a remarkably nice girl, from Virginia, about thirty-four years old. She has another protege, a very gloomy young man who is always threatening to kill himself, a writer - she and I have to work in shifts to keep him from getting morbid.

The letter with checks arrived. I am paid up for board and room to about the twenty-fifth of the month.

Prof. Schramm told me one of my short-stories had received the highest possible grade from the reader and so - if he likes it himself - he will accept it for <u>American</u> <u>Prefaces</u>. Luckily I have him as one of my instructors.

Tell Dakin to let me know how he is getting along at Washington. I hope you have been getting better news about Rose.

Lovingly, Tom

P.S. I forgot to return that Communist magazine to Evelyn Gross. Ask Dakin to give it to her. He'll find her address in Ternion in case he doesn't see her on campus.

[The " 'living newspaper' " was a staple of the Federal Theatre Project and an integral part of Edward Mabie's Speech 211, for which TW wrote several "skits" in the fall. Hugo L. Black qualified as a "current event" by virtue of his embattled appointment to the U.S. Supreme Court. On October 1 the senator from Alabama appealed to a national radio audience to judge him on the basis of his congressional record rather than membership in the Ku Klux Klan, which he had resigned.

Mabie may have delayed TW's admission and assigned probationary status, as Leverich concludes. The transcript, however, lists no special "Entrance Conditions" and shows instead that TW received probation on October 27 for "Deficient scholarship." The journal reveals the fall to have been a time of severe depression that occasioned poor academic performance and frequent absence from class. TW carried fourteen credit hours divided evenly between English Literature and Dramatic Arts.

Marian Gallaway, of Savannah, Georgia, was a graduate student in theatre who befriended TW and for whose textbook, *Constructing a Play* (1950), he later wrote a polite foreword. Gallaway received the Ph.D. from Iowa in 1940 and became director of theatre at the University of Alabama in 1948.

TW's promising submission to *American Prefaces* was "The Red Part of a Flag." Heavily revised in early drafts, the story deals with a sensitive young woman, loosely based upon Rose Williams, whose spirit has been drained by "the urban panorama" (n.d., HRC) of St. Louis.

This letter, first published in abbreviated form in *Remember Me to Tom*, pp. 89-91, was written on stationery imprinted with the name Thomas Lanier Williams and the address (canceled) 42 Aberdeen Place, Clayton, Missouri.]

70. *To Willard H. Holland*

[225 North Linn Street
Iowa City, Iowa]
Sat. P.M. [October 9, 1937]
[TLS w/ autograph marginalia, 2 pp. Brandt Collection]

Dear Willard:

Your letter with the encouraging news about the reading arrived at a perfect psychological moment as I was feeling quite low, due mostly to the fact that it is raining here and rain is definitely unbecoming to Iowa City. I can't understand how any town could be so dry in one sense of the word and so interminably wet in the other. Last night myself and some confederates toured the town in search of a whiskey label (one of those treasure hunts) and found nothing more exciting than Goetz Country Club Beer. When you feel like drinking up here you are supposed to make "needle beer" - which is near beer spiked with alcohol, the very description of which is enough to turn any one's stomach. So I am learning how to spend sober week-ends if nothing else in this region of the blessed.

Your new idea for the "return motivation" struck me as good but I would like to see the exact dialogue which will be inserted. The idea itself seems fairly logical although it might involve some anti-climactic exposition. I like the suggestion of them going off someplace "where it's dark". Clark Mills thought that their affair ought to be consummated in order to make its intensity more real. I did not feel that way about it at the time, but if you have the same feeling it must be right. The Neon sign is a beautiful touch!! In this boarding-house there is a young Jew who has spent several summers on the bum and he has given me a lot of information about the characteristics of transients. He has slept in flop-houses, jails, jungles, been deported, Etc., and so provides excellent material of the sort I am interested in. At the end of this letter I will append a few notes from his observations. The word "where" is effective I think. Also the avoidance of a protective "clinch" between Leo and Glory. After I have seen the script I will try to hit upon something different for the cigarette episode. Of course it could be done without dialogue.

I have already written McPherson a letter of thanks, quite a long letter describing the new theater building Etc. Of course I am very glad to be represented as a member of the organization. Shortly before I left I got a letter from Genevieve Albers inviting me to become an Honorary member. I wrote a letter of thanks which - in the rush of getting off - I probably forgot to mail.

I am having a play presented in the "laboratory theater" next Thursday. It is a dramatization of the Hunger Strike among convicts at the Stateville Illinois prison - in protest against new Parole policies which have reduced number of paroles from over 1300 last year to about 240 for the nine months of this year. These dramatizations are written in competition by the playwriting class. The three best are selected each two weeks and produced in what is called "a living newspaper". I was compelled to act in one of them last week - and took, because of my southern accent, the part of chairman at an African Methodist Episcopal Church conference, condemning Senator Black's appointment to the Court. Incidentally the play was written by a negro who shows real talent. It is astonishing the distance that people come to study in this Dramatics department. In my house, for instance, occupied mostly by dramatic students, four buroughs of New York City are represented, Queens, Bronx, Manhattan, and Brooklyn, as well as Saskatchewan, Canada, Philadelphia, Mississippi and Alabama.

Assignments keep me so busy I hardly have any time for independant work. However I am still planning to write the "Van Gogh" for which I have chosen the title "The Holy Family" suggested by an anecdote from his life. He took a prostitute to live with him who soon gave birth to an illeg. child by another man. V.G.'s friend, Gauguin, tried to persuade him to leave the woman but V.G. remained devoted to her. In disgust, as he left, the friend exclaimed, "Ah! The Holy Family - maniac, prostitute and bastard!" - Does that sound too profane? I think the real story of the relationship is rather beautiful and would make good dramatic material. But at the same time I am going ahead with "April Is The Cruellest Month" which stage facilities here would make possible and am also planning - if others are discarded - the study of an ordinary middle-class family in a city apartment, supposed to show the tragedy of bourgeois stagnation.

Would you like for me to have a new picture taken for publicity? They have some good photographers here. Glad you are softening the first act burlesque. I have had a short-story tentatively (almost positively) accepted by AMERICAN PREFACES, published here, which O'Brien (short story anthologist) rates as one of three best literary publications in country. The editor happens to be my professor in an English course.

This is all very diffuse and windy but I hope it makes sense - a football game is being broadcast in the next room.

Good luck - Tom

[Willard Holland had sent welcome "news" of the Mummers' enthusiastic first reading of *Fugitive Kind*. The "'return motivation'" proposed by Holland, who heavily revised the script in rehearsal, concerns the affair of Terry Meighan, the criminal outcast who hides in the flophouse, and Glory, the adopted daughter of the proprietor Gwendlebaum. Shortly before Terry is killed by the police, he and Glory consummate their love in a cheap hotel where you "just lay down your money an' go upstairs!"

Genevieve Albers served on the board of the Mummers and apparently had asked TW to be an honorary member of the organization.

"Quit Eating," TW's dramatization of a prison hunger strike, would evolve in 1938 into the full-length play *Not About Nightingales*. The talented "negro" play-wright is Thomas Pawley, later a professor at Lincoln University in Jefferson City, Missouri.

In January TW read the letters of Vincent van Gogh to Anthon van Rappard and thought them "full of rich, confident life" (*Journal*, January 12, 1937). *Lust for Life* (1934), Irving Stone's popular biography of van Gogh, may have been TW's initial source for "The Holy Family" idea. In surviving fragments of the play, a drunken van Gogh proclaims his loneliness to Margaret (Magda), a pregnant prostitute with whom he wishes to live and to treat "like a sister" (n.d., HRC).

TW's projected "study of an ordinary middle-class family in a city apartment" suggests, of course, *The Glass Menagerie* (1945), but it has closer affinities with such contemporary St. Louis stories of "stagnation" as "Blue Roses," "The Treadmill" (n.d., HRC), "The Red Part of a Flag," and with the play *Stairs to the Roof* (1945).

In the penultimate paragraph, as marginalia keyed to "AMERICAN PREF-ACES," TW added, "They have printed some of my poetry - which has appeared in Poetry , Voices & other leading poetry magazines - "]

71. *To Edwina Dakin Williams*

[325 South Dubuque Street
Iowa City, Iowa]
[ca. mid-October 1937]
[TLS w/ autograph postscript, 2 pp. HRC]

Dear Mother:

I only have time for a few lines before supper. I got your letter this morning and was pleased to hear the encouraging news about Rose. Does the Doctor also feel that she has improved? I wish that I could see the new Buick: I think they are about the handsomest cars on the market now.

I have had quite a dramatic time about my rooming-places. It happens that the Faculty Adviser, who supervises rooming-houses, is an A.T.O. I met him shortly after my arrival here and, hoping that I would move into the A.T.O. house, he got me out of my contract in the place where I was staying. It turned out to be rather disagreeable. They did not provide a study-lamp or clean the place properly. However I made no promise to move into the A.T.O. house and so when I was released from my contract I moved directly into the present place which is very satisfactory. Two nights ago a large delegation of A.T.O.'s called at the house and said they thought I was obligated to move in their house - they lowered their former price two dollars so that the room rent would now be ten dollars a month and breakfast and lunch for twenty-five cents which is extremely cheap - evidently they are in bad financial shape - but I still do not want to move in much as I am well-satisfied here and fraternity life no longer has the appeal it once had for me. However I may decide to move in with them if they can assure me of rides to and from the campus. The house is located rather far out.

I had a short play presented very successfully last week and another one will be put on next week, a satire on Hollywood producers. They are giving it the best director and a cast consisting of the university's best players and so I think it will turn out fine. It is about an ignorant Jewish movie-producer revising a great classic for the movies. American Prefaces are still holding my short-story. The editor says it is "going the rounds" which means I suppose that every one in the English faculty is passing judgement on it. They have also asked to see some of my short plays. There are several very well-known literary figures on the campus, all of which I have met. Prof. Mabie, head of the dramatics department, is a brilliant man but slightly unbalanced at times. He has been confined occasionally in the university hospital's psycopathic ward - he has terrible tantrums. On one occasion, when he attended the final dress rehearsal of a play, it displeased him and he threw his glasses at one of the actors: kept them all rehearsing from eight o'clock that night till noon the next day and made the author re-write the last act of the play.

I am glad Dakin got a part in the one-act plays: they will probably be pretty awful, but the experience will help him. Tell him I recently saw a book by Prof. Carson, "The Theater of the Frontier" in the University library - the girl who was reading it said it was extremely dry, but Carson would probably be flattered to know it is on the required reading list in one of Mabie's courses.

Holland wrote me a very encouraging letter about the new play. Said he read it to the Mummers and received "God! What a reaction!" It seems they are very enthusiastic about it and are going to give it all they've got - he is planning to run a feature article about me and the play pretty soon in one of the papers and wants me to have a picture taken.

When you send my next board and room checks, about the twenty-third, please make them out to me as I am planning to take my meals somewhere else. The diet at Scott's is too starchy: potatoes three times a day seven days a week. I find I can eat more reasonably and better food at the campus restaurants. I will buy a meal ticket to last me a month.

I have to buy some materials for stagecraft amounting to about three dollars - those are my only book expenses. I ought to buy them right away as we are supposed to be using them now.

Hope you are all well.

With much love, Tom

P.S. Will you please send me the stagecraft money by return mail as we are supposed to be using the materials now - for designing.

P.S. Yes, I got the suit and it fits fine.

[In an earlier letter to the Dakins, Edwina described Rose as so "fat" from insulin that she was "distressed to see her." More importantly the doctor "didn't seem to think she was showing enough improvement," although he added vaguely that "she was some better" (Monday {October 4, 1937} HRC). In later correspondence with TW, Edwina apparently described Rose as having been "reasonable" at the time of her last visit (as a journal entry on October 19 suggests) and probably withheld news of the doctor's rather bleak prognosis. Rose appears in the journal at this time as a source of ambivalent feelings: "I think of Rose and wonder and pity - but it is such a faraway feeling - how bound up we are in our own selves - our own miseries - " (October 9, 1937).

TW's forthcoming satire on Hollywood was entitled "The Big Scene," while the story still " 'going the rounds' " was "The Red Part of a Flag."

By all accounts Edward Mabie had a fierce temper, but his daughter, P.A.M. Stewart, has dismissed rumors of her father's instability and hospitalization as "'unmitigated nonsense!'" (qtd. in Leverich).

TW's resentment of William Carson, his former professor at Washington University (see letter #65), is evident in the slighting reference to Carson's book, *The Theatre on the Frontier: The Early Years of the St. Louis Stage* (University of Chicago Press, 1932).

This letter, first published in *Remember Me to Tom*, pp. 91-93, was written on stationery imprinted with the name Thomas Lanier Williams and the address 42 Aberdeen Place, Clayton, Missouri.]

72. *To Edwina Dakin Williams*

A.T.O. House
Iowa City, Iowa
Friday P.M. [October 29, 1937]
[TLS, 2 pp. Columbia]

Dear Mother:

I have had to read ten long plays this week and write a short one, which explains why I haven't written earlier. I am now very comfortably settled - in the A.T.O. house. They are giving me the room for ten dollars a month and breakfast and lunch for $11.50 which leaves me about nine dollars for evening meals. It is not a perfect arrangement but better than the former as the food I ate at Scott's was becoming rapidly indigistible, almost nothing but potatoes and ground meat. I only stayed in the second boarding-place two weeks, paid the amount we had agreed upon for that period and moved out. My landlady, however, felt aggrieved at my sudden departure and refused to let me have my trunk for several days. She demanded that I pay a full month's rent and in the end the fraternity had to pay her another three dollars - I naturally could not afford to - so now I have the trunk back in my possession. We had some very dramatic scenes, over the telephone, in the Dean's office - all of my manuscripts were in the trunk and I was determined to get <u>them</u> at all costs. We parted good friends, however, and she told me she hoped I would move back in when I'd had enough of fraternity life.

I have a room to myself and a bed in the dormitory here. The house is very attractive, on a bank over the Iowa river, and the members are considerably nicer than those at Missouri. It is considered one of the best houses on the campus. However I spend very little time here. I imagine I must walk an average of eight miles a day, as I have classes on both sides of the river and the fraternity house is on the outskirts of town.

An announcement of the <u>Mummers</u> play was posted on the Bulletin Board in the Dramatics building this week. I guess Holland must have sent it to Prof. Mabie. If any articles appear in paper, would you mind sending me a copy? Holland writes that the Mummers are going at it with great enthusiasm. I'm having a third short play presented next week. They are written in competition for the experimental playwriting class. I wanted to send "Candles to the Sun" to the WPA contest but am afraid I can't afford the postage as it would have to come out of my supper-money which is already depleted by laundry and incidental expenses. Olga should have given it directly to them instead of sending it back for corrections which I do not have time to make. <u>AMERICAN PREFACES</u> have definitely accepted a short-story and I think will publish it in two or three months. It was read and highly approved by the whole staff which includes some very well-known literary figures. Schramm, the editor, thinks it has a good chance of being chosen for the annual O'Brien short-story anthology, which would do a great deal for my literary reputation.

I hope you all can drive up here some week-end, perhaps Thanksgiving. I think Dakin would like to see this campus, especially the Dramatic Arts building which is the best of its kind in the world.

So far the weather has been delightful. I have a beautiful view from my desk - a long sloping lawn with big oak trees, down to the river and bridge.

Anxiously awaiting news of you all.

With love from, Tom

[The play announced was *Fugitive Kind*.

TW's claim of a "third short play" being presented in early-November is seemingly in conflict with a later report to Willard Holland (see letter #74). The discrepancy can be removed if the play in question is "Family Pew" and its presentation delayed until November 18, when it was acted by Professor Mabie's class. If not, then TW has enhanced his Iowa credits for Edwina's benefit.

Olga Becker had submitted *Candles to the Sun* to a New York producer who rejected it with the advice, "Eliminate the propaganda" (qtd. by Becker in a letter to TW, September 22, 1937, HRC). In returning the typescript, she enclosed her own lengthy notes for revision.

"The Red Part of a Flag," the story "definitely accepted" by *American Prefaces*, was first published by *Vogue* in 1974, with the alternate title "Oriflamme."

This letter was written on stationery imprinted with the name Thomas Lanier Williams and the address 42 Aberdeen Place, Clayton, Missouri.]

73. To Walter E. Dakin

[Alpha Tau Omega House
Iowa City, Iowa]
Nov. 18, 1937
[TLS, 1 p. HRC]

Dear Grandfather:

Today we are having our first snow, remarkably late for Iowa. It started last night and is still falling heavily this afternoon. I went to school this morning in my boots and riding breeches. They say the winters here are very severe. Last year it got down to thirty below and stayed in that vicinity for two or three weeks. So far the coldest has been twenty above but as I have to cover a good deal of territory every day that is cold enough for me. It is customary to sleep in an open dormitory all winter. But I intend to take my bed downstairs when the zero weather sets in!

Last night I heard the famous English novelist, J.B. Priestley, give a lecture. Two weeks ago they had Stephen Vincent Benet, a famous poet. The cultural opportunities here are remarkable for a mid-western school. They even have a fine free symphony orchestra. Also a radio broadcasting station - even television! Almost every evening there is an interesting public lecture, debate or round-table discussion in the Student Memorial Union -

which is a beautiful recreation hall containing a library, magazine room, cafeteria, dance hall, lounge and auditorium - furnished like an expensive hotel!

We are still putting on short "living-newspaper" plays in the Dramatic department. I am having a comedy produced this afternoon. Later in the year we will do some radio-broadcasting and produce a movie from student scripts. The facilities of this school seem to be unlimited. Evidently the Iowa farmers do believe in education - unfortunately it is the students from out-of-state that take the most advantage of it. Due to their home backgrounds, most of the Iowa students are pretty crude and intellectually corn-fed. They have fine, honest characters, are healthy and moral, but do not show a great deal of cultural interest.

From my two windows I now have a beautiful view of snow-covered hills and woods and a frozen river and receiving over my room-mate's radio a broadcast of classical music from the university studio. But unfortunately I have to put on my boots for another trip to the campus.

I was certainly pleased to get your letter and I know you are going to enjoy the Columbus Centennial. Give Dakin my congratulations for his successful stage performance. I would like to hear all the details.

With much love to you all, Tom

[On November 17 J.B. Priestley spoke to an audience of 1,500 on fourth-dimensional consciousness as a remedy for the "present deplorable state of the world."

For his grandfather, TW did not identify the forthcoming comedy as "Family Pew," a satire on religious piety set "in a Protestant church of a middle-western town." The Sunday morning sermon is an occasion for a family of four to indulge in "ruminations" (n.d., HRC) that recreate the personae and conflicts of the Williams household.

One Iowa student also not mentioned in letters home was Bette Reitz, a junior from Cedar Rapids with whom TW had an affair in the fall. William Jay Smith has recalled how "excited" he was at Christmas when he told the news: "I had never known him to speak with such passion about anyone," Smith wrote in 1996. In *Memoirs* TW described it as his "first and last and only consummated sexual affair with a woman" (p. 42).

This letter was written on stationery imprinted with the name Thomas Lanier Williams and the address 42 Aberdeen Place, Clayton, Missouri.]

74. To Willard H. Holland

A. T. O. House
[Iowa City, Iowa]
Thursday P.M. [November 18, 1937]
[TLS w/ autograph postscript, 2 pp. Brandt Collection]

Dear Willard:

Thanks for your letter. I am highly satisfied with the cast. I think on the whole Viola will fit the part better than Garrett although of course I had Garrett constantly in mind while writing Glory's lines. Viola is a more versatile actress and you have probably found her more dependable. I hope Sam's temperament does not prove too troublesome. I don't blame him for not liking the part - splendid that you have gotten [*deletion*]. I will probably get down for the Saturday performance. I don't envy you these early rehearsals - they must be ghastly things.

I have on my desk five volumes of Van Gogh biographies and letters most of which I have read - but very little dialogue written so far. Perhaps that is better because usually I plunge into dialogue before I have even formulated a plot which leads to a great deal of re-writing and general confusion. However I resent the fact that I am allowed so little time for independant writing up here. I have to write a short play on an assigned subject each week. I have been extraordinarily successful with this hack work - it is good practice - but I would much rather be devoting the time to a major work. The Van Gogh trouble is that there is <u>too</u> <u>much</u> dramatic material. It is hard to make a selection. Van Gogh was a great social thinker and artist - had a tremendous love for humanity and believed in the community of artists - he painted common people at work and tried to establish an art colony in southern France - but he was constantly misunderstood and persecuted - crowds gathered outside his window, shouting "Fou-roux" - "The red-headed madman" - that suggests a main theme - a man with a great love for humanity whom humanity rejected - he formed many disappointing relationships - his brother Theo was his only supporter - his work did not have any success till after his suicide in a fit of insanity. His story would be the story of an artist's relations to society - not one artist but all. I am desperately anxious to make enough money writing (or by any other honest means) to spend all next summer in the Ozarks doing nothing but writing on this play - I can live there for $12.50 a week and the conditions are ideal for work.

I feel that I am learning a great deal technically up here. Believe it or not, I can actually build flats and put up sets. Next term I will learn all about lighting. But the life here has many unpleasant aspects. For one thing my father is not contributing one cent to my support as he disapproves of all my activities - my grandparents send me thirty a month which is scarcely adequate for the barest living expenses. I get a bed in the frat. dormitory and breakfast and lunch in the fraternity house at reduced rates by coaching the Freshmen in their English and make a small commission selling tickets to the University theater - but have gone to bed numerous nights without supper. Such a stringent existence is probably excellent for the soul - but if some New York producer offers me a fat check for "The Fugitive Kind" I will certainly be in a receptive state of mind. Anyway you see I have some reason for disagreeing with Pangloss about this being "the best of all possible worlds".

I'm having another short play "The Family Pew" produced this afternoon. The others were "Quit Eating" on the prison hunger strike, "The Big Scene" satire on Hollywood and a fourth one "So Glad!" which will be produced later. Each two weeks three plays are chosen from the class for production. Despite the short-time for rehearsals the performances are usually letter-perfect.

I seem to have written a good deal and said practically nothing. So goodbye and good luck.

Tom

P.S. I am still looking for the "<u>progressive</u> Middle West" - and getting colder all the time.

Soon as I see "Bill" again I will ask him about the bum's money. I want to get play copyrighted before letting any Hollywood people get hold of it. Will have this done during Holidays - will be home and glad to help you with the medical opus -

[Willard Holland, Viola Perle, and Sam Halley, Jr., played leading roles in *Fugitive Kind*, while Jane Garrett took a lesser one. The censored deletion, whose source is unknown, may concern the part of Gwendlebaum, played by Louis Prince.

"So Glad!" is a dialect play set in "a negro dwelling in Nashville." Its title echoes the "religious fervor" of Marcus Deuteronomy Jackson, an obsessive and perhaps demented black carver of "nigger angels," whose visitation by "White folks" (n.d., HRC) is undefined in the fragmentary script.

"Bill" is probably the "young Jew" mentioned in letter #70 who had useful information about flophouses and transients.

This letter was written on stationery imprinted with the name Thomas Lanier Williams and the address 42 Aberdeen Place, Clayton, Missouri.]

75. To Walter Colvin McPherson

A.T.O. House
Iowa City, Ia.
[early-December 1937]
[TLS, 1 p. HRC]

Dear Mr. McPherson:

I don't want you to think I only thank people for favorable reviews so I am writing to say I appreciate your sincere and direct comments upon my new play. While temporarily painful, criticism of this sort proves of particular benefit to a writer in the long run, especially when his aim is toward technical improvement that may eventually enable him to say things he thinks worth saying rather than toward the enjoyment of a present success. Of course present success has its advantage: it removes some of the formidable odds that stand against an inexperienced writer. But if a writer goes on despite these odds and manages to survive without the luxury of a quick success - if he recognizes his failures and has an ideal of perfection - then the ultimate outcome in his case may be the better for those initial discouragements. If he does not do so - then the loss is not significant to anyone concerned.

My reason for inserting the young student in the play was to show a parallellism between his life and Terry's. Both are potentially strong characters, both rebels, the one taking a negative, the other a positive stand. Terry goes down through self-interest and those unpropitious circumstances which are apparently nobody's fault. But at the end of the play Leo is shown - or should be shown - choosing an opposite course. It was hard to bring these two characters together - convincingly - in one play and apparently I made a botch of it. It was hastily done.

Your sympathy has been too evident in the past for me to doubt its continuance. In my new work I shall be trying particularly to meet your exact standards and I'm sure it will be better on that account.

Yours very truly, Tom Williams

[On November 30 *Fugitive Kind* opened in St. Louis to disappointing reviews. Colvin McPherson (1906–1986), formerly well-disposed to TW, characterized the author as "merely loafing around" the set with little "to say" and dismissed the play as "weak" (*St. Louis Post-Dispatch*, December 1, 1937). Reed Hynds thought it marked "a step forward" for TW, but he found the play's thinking about the "chaos" of modern life to be "confused" and "inconclusive" and the author left "groping" at the end (*St. Louis Star-Times*, December 1, 1937). TW explained the parallelism of Terry, the criminal outcast, and Leo, the naive student radical, in answer to McPherson's charge that Leo's role was "not germane." Overlooked by the critic was TW's intention to use Leo as a poetic voice in the later scenes, where (as the stage directions indicate) the play is to "veer sharply upward" to "the lyrical plane."]

76. To Willard H. Holland

[ca. early-December 1937]
[AL draft, 1 p. HTC]

Dear Willard:

You understand me too well to think I am unappreciative of the sincere efforts you and the <u>Mummers</u> put into my play but since any good working partnership should be based on absolute honesty between the working partners - and since you and I both are profoundly absorbed in our <u>jobs</u> - I think I should tell you exactly what I thought of the play. Of course the weakness lay considerably if not mainly in the script - I wrote it too hastily and without sufficient reflection - but it seems to me that the whole burden was thrown on <u>me</u> - on the <u>lines</u> - in the latter half. There was hardly an effort at atmospheric build-up in the setting for that half. The lighting was all wrong - there was no large window to bring the city and the snow onto the stage - what became of the cathedral-like effect which we had agreed upon? The neon sign? And the lines - they were rushed ~~and jazzed and moaned especially~~ [*end of letter missing*]

[TW saw the December 4th performance of *Fugitive Kind* and was confirmed in his earlier doubts of Holland's direction: "In most things his instinct is amazingly sound but on some things we simply cannot see eye to eye - I don't think he likes my atmospheric touches - " (*Journal*, September 8, 1937; see letter #291). Colvin McPherson's review probably still rankled, especially his reservation of praise for the Mummers and their director, who deserved, he thought, "extraordinary credit" for trying to bring "experimental theater" to St. Louis.

This letter's place of origin is uncertain, either St. Louis or Iowa City or points in between.]

77. To Clark Mills

[Alpha Tau Omega House
Iowa City, Iowa]
[late-January 1938]
[TL draft, 1 p. HTC]

Dear Clark:

I guess it is typical of me that on the eve of my most crucial final - in a subject in which I have a delinquent average so far - I postpone note-reading till I have satisfied the more agreeable urge of answering your letter. After writing the letter I will probably go out and drink a couple of beers or swim a few lengths to further fortify my spirit. Really I am getting too old for an academic life. I can't take it seriously anymore. Here as elsewhere we are required to learn a terrific number of things that have absolutely no relevancy to our lives. And I have lost all patience with it. There is a surprising amount of liberality on this campus - and creative art - especially in the dramatics dept. but God knows what attracts it here. Everybody is talking about the literary "renaissance" at Iowa - there are five or six fairly prominent writers here, all of which are now working on novels [*end of letter missing*]

[TW was "delinquent" in Speech 135 (Advanced Technical Practice, i.e., Stagecraft), which he failed.

On February 19 *The Daily Iowan* featured four graduate students with novels under contract to trade presses. Each book had a strong regional bias, a signature of the Iowa creative writing programs to which TW was not closely attuned.]

78. To Edwina Dakin Williams

[Alpha Tau Omega House
Iowa City, Iowa]
[ca. early-February 1938]
[TLS, 2 pp. HRC]

Dear Mother:

It is quite a relief to be through finals and starting a new term. I got an A, two B's and two C's. This term my schedule is considerably heavier, sixteen hours, due to the necessity of carrying a science course. This is the only requirement for graduation which I have not yet filled. I am taking a course in advanced zoology, uninspiring but instructive. I am going on with my playwriting course in which I got an A last term. This term we are required to write two long plays, one a biographical play and the other an adaptation from a mystery novel. I am having a series of my short plays broadcast over the local radio station on the "Little Theater of the Air". I believe there is going to be an article about this new department in the St. Louis Post-Dispatch. One of their reporters has interviewed the director about it. They have four or five of my plays which they will produce each Tuesday night at seven-thirty. The first went over very well, although a revolver, used for sound effect, failed to go off.

They have had phenomenally warm weather in Iowa, only two or three really cold days since the holidays, this last week almost like spring. However it is always sloppy, either rain or snow, and usually a combination. Terribly hard on shoes and clothes as you can't walk a block without falling. Recently the fraternities had a snow-battle, concentrating on each other's windows. Scarcely a window left unbroken up and down fraternity row. Mine escaped as I have a back room.

Last week I got a card from Jack Pickering, editor of the Washington University Eliot, inviting me to act as judge in their poetry contest. They are going to send me about 15 poems to select the three best. I have had three poems accepted by American Prefaces. I believe they are going to publish my story and poems in a spring issue. I don't have very much time for writing except what is required for school work - which is considerable. Hope Dakin got through his finals okay. I was looking through our fraternity scrapbook today and noticed that a few years ago a Melvin Dakin, member of this chapter, was elected to the honorary senior's society. I'll try to find out more about him as he is probably a relative.

I was certainly relieved to get the checque which came about five days after my funds were exhausted - I had been forced to borrow several dollars to continue eating which is an annoyingly persistent habit, especially in these northern climates! Fortunately the boys in the house are unusually generous. I hate terribly taking so much money from you and Grand, which I know you can hardly spare. I live as frugally as possible but still money flies. I hope I shall manage to make some before long. I have to pay a three dollar laboratory fee for the science course this week and am supposed to buy a book for a dollar and a half. Perhaps I can dispense with the book.

Mrs. White called me a few days ago. Said she was writing you and wanted to be sure of your address. She repeated several times that she wanted you to be her guest if you drive up here. I hope you will soon as the weather gets nicer. Iowa City is going to be beautiful this spring. Dakin would like to see the performance of Henry IV which contains Falstaff - they have a marvelous cast for it and it will be a very elaborate production, using our new revolving stage. It will be performed April 5-8, which would be a good time to drive up.

I got a long letter from Clark in Paris. Seems to be having a fine time but doing little work. He sent me a long poem which I submitted to <u>American</u> <u>Prefaces</u> but they rejected it. However they are considering some poems by Bill Smith which he gave me at Christmas.

Have you visited Rose lately? I hope the new maid turns out somewhat better than the predecessors and things are getting along reasonably well at home. Business reports I see in the papers are certainly disheartening to say the least. It seems that the whole world is in a state of economic and political chaos for which there isn't any immediate solution. Very hard on these young people on campuses who are going to have to deal with it in the future.

With much love, Tom

[TW actually received B's in Shakespeare and Experimental Dramatic Production (Playwriting), C in a directed readings course, an incomplete in Modern Drama, and F in Advanced Technical Practice. He carried fifteen hours in the winter, and as he undoubtedly knew, was no longer on track to graduate in June.

The Little Theater of the Air broadcast adaptations of classical and contemporary plays, as well as original student compositions, on Tuesday evenings on WSUI. TW's anti-war play "Me, Vashya!" had the balky "revolver."

TW judged a poetry contest for *Eliot*, the student literary magazine at Washington University, and facetiously congratulated its editor upon having a female winner: "Everything possible should be done to discourage the male {poets}, for their own good" (letter to Jack Pickering, February 25, 1938, HRC). Of TW's own poems "accepted" by *American Prefaces*, none were published in forthcoming numbers of the magazine.

Edwina (and TW) last visited Rose at Christmas and would not return until April. The family probably did not see a summary report of December 16, 1937, that warranted little hope for Rose's "full remission" (qtd. in Leverich). In mid-January Edwina informed the Dakins that the first insulin course had failed and a second was needed (January 17, 1938, HRC). A delusional letter from Rose at this time confirmed the intractability of her disease and set the stage for Edwina's later visit by begging "to come <u>home</u>" (letter from Rose to Edwina, February 13 {1938} HRC). By April the second course had failed and Rose was "very much upset" to see her mother, who, she charged, had "put her into a 'charity hospital to be tortured'" (letter from Edwina to the Dakins, Wednesday {April 6, 1938} HRC).]

79. *To Edwina Dakin Williams*

[409 North Dubuque Street
Iowa City, Iowa]
[ca. mid-March 1938]
[TLS, 2 pp. HRC]

Dear Mother:

Your letter and the checks arrived yesterday. Thanks. I am now trying out something new - housekeeping! A young man who is a graduate in the dramatics dept. and I have rented a small apartment, two rooms and a kitchenette, which is located quite near the campus. We feel very elated about it. The place is only $24 a month, twelve dollars for each of us, and doing our own cooking we will save money. He is an expert cook. This morning we got six eggs for a dime and last night had a swell steak and spaghetti dinner for a total expenditure of forty cents. It is much cheaper and we can eat according to our own convenience and taste. The A.T.O.'s seemed to regret my departure but took it gracefully. Having a room to myself I find it much easier to work - especially since my former room-mate was pretty obnoxious. The complete quiet which we have here in the evenings is a relief. The place is nicely furnished. Gas amounts to about fifty cents a month, water and electricity are paid by the landlady - so on the whole it will be less expensive. On the floor below are some more dramatic students which makes a congenial crowd for us.

Spring seems to have arrived already in Iowa. I haven't needed a coat for several days and the air is delicious. Our front room has windows all around three sides so that I can bask in this sunlight while writing.

Sorry to hear of Dad's illness. Hope the vacation will prove helpful. I hope you don't take Mrs. Wells' offense too seriously - what else could you expect from a woman of her character? She probably thinks you have not been active enough in that idiotic campaign of hers.

It seems to me that I left the play Holland called about either on the desk in the attic or the small bookcase in the front room - it is called "Tomorrow We Live" and is in some kind of envelope or folder. Magic Tower arrived and will probably be broadcast when they have gotten through my other one-acts. The irritating thing about radio-writing is the ridiculous censorship. My latest show was cut all to pieces because of my realistic treatment of the dialogue. You aren't even allowed to say "damn".

Will you ask Dakin to tell Park Austin to send a transcript of my highschool credits to the Registrar's office here. For some reason they have to have an original transcript directly from the highschool.

I will stop now to cook myself some lunch. This is excellent domestic training! And I find it quite simple. But I must confess the garbage has not yet been emptied and there is quite a stack of dishes in the sink. We are going to invite some girls over to wash them for us.

Will be glad to get the renovated shoes.

With much love, Tom

[In *Memoirs* TW named his new roommate "Abdul" (actually Joseph Sofra, a Turkish graduate student) and described him as "a notorious girl-chaser" whose "intemperate tactics" (p. 45) had made him well known to the police. Edwina was not "very pleased with the idea of {TW's} 'keeping house'" (letter to the Dakins, March 16, 1938, HRC).

Mrs. Bernard O. Wells was running for the D.A.R. post of state regent and had failed to invite Edwina to a campaign luncheon. Cornelius advised his wife, the snubbed local regent, to put "'the hooks into her!'" (letter from Edwina to the Dakins, February 15, 1938, HRC). In *Spring Storm* (n.d., HRC), formerly *April Is the Cruellest Month*, to which TW had returned in his playwriting class, he satirized the D.A.R.'s veneration of ancestors and its narrow conception of class.

Rodney Erickson, a student director of the Little Theater of the Air, has recalled that a professor took exception to TW's scripts and nearly "'censored him out of business.'" One of the offending plays featured "'a mother-son relationship and the usual anti-feminine characters'" (qtd. in Leverich)—perhaps "Escape" (n.d., HRC).

Park Austin worked in the registrar's office at University City High School and was a close friend of Rose Williams. She has recalled (in an unpublished interview with Allean Hale) that TW and Rose often visited her nearby apartment on Enright Avenue to escape their unhappiness at home.]

80. To Edwina Dakin Williams

[409 North Dubuque Street
Iowa City, Iowa]
[ca. early-May 1938]
[TLS w/ autograph postscript, 2 pp. HRC]

Dear Mother:

This week I received some news from the Registrar's office which I am rather reluctant to communicate to you as I don't know how you will feel about it. It seems at the end of this semestre I will still be four hours short of the required thirty and to get a degree would have to stay for the 8-weeks summer session. It seems very silly and unreasonable since I already have far more credits than are ordinarily required for graduation, but they say it is a national ruling you must take at least 30 at the college granting the degree. Tuition would be $33, and I have been promised a board-job at Currier Hall which would take care of meals, working three hours a day, employment being very plentiful in summer because of fewer students. My present landlady says I could have a small room here for five dollars a month so the total expense would be about forty-five or fifty for the 8 weeks. I have been worried over the way you and Grand would feel about this. However it is better than it sounds, as there are some very definite benefits that I would get from the summer session even if it were not necessary for a degree. Extra credits would count toward an M.A. if I ever got one and the "Play Production" course I would take would be quite valuable. Also I could get my new play produced here. It is now finished except for a few revisions and was enthusiastically criticized by Dr. Conkle and the class. Holland has already printed an announcement of it on his programs for the next play. The summer term is from June 11 to August 5 with Commencement exercises on the last day. I took fourteen hours the first term and was intending to take sixteen the second to make thirty. I got a special permission to enroll for that many but after a few weeks I found that it was too much - I didn't even have a free afternoon for my writing - so I had to drop my Stagecraft course in which I was doing badly. It was nearly all carpentry, building sets and shifting scenery - and took far more time than it was worth. Dr. Conkle advised me to drop it and he said I could probably be granted a petition to graduate without the full 30 hours. But the faculty committee has not accepted the petition and I see no way, now, of getting my B.A. without attending this summer. I hope you don't think I've deliberately made things too easy for myself. I really haven't. I have been acting throughout the year with the utmost forethought and precaution - this academic red-tape has just crossed me up. Aside from this complication everything is fine. I made an excellent grade on my English reading review and have nothing to worry about the other finals, which commence the twenty-third. I believe I've gotten more out of this year than any years previous. I don't think two months delay should make much difference but I do feel quite badly about the additional expense it would incur, although it would be comparatively slight.

If I stay I would like to have my wash pants and khaki shorts as they say this town gets frightfully hot in summer. Fortunately my place is on the river and gets plenty of air. Why don't you drive up when Grand and Grandfather arrive the end of this month so we can go into the matter more thoroughly? Hannibal is mid-way if you wanted to take the trip in two laps. Miss Galloway and I made it in about 8 hours in zero weather in her slow Ford. She is going to be here this summer, too. In fact nearly all the important theater crowd are staying.

With much love, Tom

P.S. I saw the Dean this afternoon and he said there was a possibility they might re-consider my petition if I would promise to take a correspondence course. Will let you know later how it turns out.

[Failing Speech 135 in the fall, not "academic red-tape," had delayed TW's graduation. Edwina knew nothing of this circumstance, and while the truth was still
withheld from her, TW regretted the disappointment he would cause: "She has been
so marvelous, so lovely, so generous" (*Journal*, April 29, 1938).

When *Spring Storm* was read on April 27, it drew "hardly a favorable comment" from TW's playwriting class or from the instructor, Ellsworth Conkle, whose
play *Prologue to Glory* (1938) had recently opened in New York. TW was
"shocked" (*Journal*, April 29, 1938), having written a few days earlier to Edwina
that he was "very hopeful" about *Spring Storm*: "It is well-constructed, {has} no
social propaganda, and is suitable material for {the} commercial stage" (April 25,
1938, HTC). The play's setting at flood stage in the Delta, its portrayal of women
who despair of gentlemen callers, and its conjunction of disgust, cruelty, and suicide would become, respectively, the critical elements of *Battle of Angels* (1940),
The Glass Menagerie, and *A Streetcar Named Desire*, TW's first three commercial
productions. The Ensemble Studio Theater staged a successful reading of *Spring
Storm* in New York on October 26-27, 1996, and New Directions issued a first edition, prepared by Dan Isaac, in 1999.

TW's private "inventory" of the year at Iowa differed from his expression of
thanks to Edwina. Aside from a "passionate physical love-affair" with Bette Reitz,
the year, TW felt, had been "virtually wasted": "Yes, I know more about the theater but I don't see that my plays are any better" (*Journal*, April 29, 1938).]

81. *To Edwina Dakin Williams*

[126 North Clinton Street
Iowa City, Iowa]
Tuesday, June 21, 1938
[TLS, 1 p. HRC]

Dear Mother:

I'm ashamed of not having written a real letter in so long. The summer-
session keeps me busier than the regular term, especially with my hospital
work. I do not find it at all difficult, however, to combine the two and am
getting along quite well. I was transferred from the doctors' to the patients'
restaurant and the work in the latter is much pleasanter. I have more variety of things to do and there is not such a hectic rush. In my whole waiting career I have only broken one saucer and that occured when I was trying to learn to balance a tray on one hand - I think that accomplishment
would thrill me almost as much as having a play on Broadway.

I am getting all of my necessary four hours this term for just attending one playwriting class and reading my plays. I do a good deal of theater work besides that, but it is not required. Another writer and myself have been taking our typewriters down on the river-bank and working there in bathing-trunks. So I've acquired a nice tan already. Mr. Mabie is losing his best playwright next year so he has begun to take a special interest in me, possibly in hopes that I will come back. Of course I probably would if he could get me one of the Rockefeller scholarships. Marion is getting one hundred a month and a trip to Arizona to work on her thesis about the Indian ceremonies. It is amazing what Mabie will do for his graduate students, but he is a terrible tyrant and one doesn't dare show too much individuality around him. He is very emotional. He and Marion both wept when he told her that she had received the scholarship and could go.

Marcus Bach, the playwright who is leaving after this summer, is having his play produced first this summer. We have to take turns, in order of seniority with the dept., in getting our scripts put on. Grades have not yet come out but I know that I passed everything as the Registrar told me I needed only the four hours to graduate this summer. The commencement is August 5.

I'm glad you've received some encouraging news from Rose. I wonder if they would let her receive letters. I would like to write her if they approved.

Thanks for the checque. I had ample to pay my tuition and other expenses and really don't need as much as you sent me this month, since I'm getting my meals.

No hot weather so far!

With love to all, Tom

[TW satisfied the graduation requirement by concurrent enrollment in Problems in Dramatic Art and Edward Mabie's Experimental Theatre Seminar.

Marcus Bach was a graduate student in Dramatic Arts and, like Marian Gallaway, a protégé of Edward Mabie. *Calvario*, Bach's play treating primitive religious rites in New Mexico, had been announced on June 14 as the first production in the University's summer experimental series, with direction by Professor Mabie.]

Edwina Dakin Williams

82. To Edwina Dakin Williams

[126 North Clinton Street
Iowa City, Iowa]
[July 1938]
[TLS, 1 p. HRC]

Dear Mother:

Thanks for the checque and the box of clothes. The linen suit arrived just in time for me to wear to a first-night performance at the theater. Free tickets to all the shows are included in the summer tuition so I have been attending first nights regularly. Another one tomorrow. The first and third acts of my own play have finally been approved but the second act is still on the bench. Mr. Mabie is much less indulgent than Holland - since he knows a great deal more about it - so I have to have the script in best possible condition before he will consider it ready for production. I can't get through with it in time for summer production - which is just as well, as the summer productions are much inferior to the others, due to the shortage of acting talent and the crowded schedule. Mabie thinks I am coming back for a Master's - as all his writers do - but of course I would not consider it unless he offers me a job or a scholarship. Bach whose play was presented this summer has been engaged as a play-reader for the WPA theater in Chicago - gets $3000. a yr. - and he wants me to bring him some of my scripts for consideration. He had one of his own plays as the first production and it got a scorching review - the critic said that "no playgoer however complaisant or naive could help but brand it as a failure".

I received a woeful letter from Willard Holland last week. It seems that while he was in Hollywood with very bright prospects of crashing the movies - having a personal agent and all that - his salary was suddenly discontinued by the Mummers and he was stranded without funds. He had to come home immediately and there learned that a new board of directors had been elected in his absence and he had been discharged as director. They are willing to re-engage him provided that he surrenders his dictatorial powers - he urged me not to send them my script and says he is planning to organize a new company if they don't come to terms with him. They owe him a thousand dollars in back salary. Jane Garrett wrote me that the main objection was that he gave a few members all the best parts and was too autocratic. I don't know how it is going to work out. Willard said he was "nearly insane with the suddenness and injustice of it all".

I am delighted that Grand and Grandfather will have such a nice trip but am disappointed they won't come up for my graduation. I had looked forward to showing them about the campus. The date is Aug. 5, in the morning - which comes on Friday. I hope you can make it.

With much love, Tom

[Marcus Bach's new play, *Mister Jim*, opened in Chicago on July 4 and was indeed "scorched" by the press. TW's own play in preparation was *Spring Storm*.

Willard Holland and the Mummers were apparently reconciled and he directed their eleventh season (1938-1939). He then resigned to form the Town Square Theater of St. Louis before moving to Hollywood in 1943.]

83. *To Edwina Dakin Williams*

[126 North Clinton Street
Iowa City, Iowa]
Sunday morning July 31, 1938
[TLS, 1 p. HRC]

Dear Mother:

I am glad that you are still planning to drive up for the graduation ceremonies. They take place at 8 PM. Friday evening. The evening before, Thursday, there is a big dinner for graduates at the Union. Guests are eighty-five cents if you want to attend that also. I have an extra bed, upper-deck in my room that Dakin could occupy free and the landlady says that she will have a vacant room after Friday morning that she would rent to you. However I imagine you would want to get here before Friday morning. Let me know when you are coming and I will try to find a room nearby if not here.

Marian Galloway is planning to drive up to Chicago for a few days and return by St. Louis, she would leave here the sixth, and has asked Lomask (from St. Louis) and I to go with her. Lomask is trying to get a job there and I thought I might enquire around too. One of our St. Louis friends, Jack Conroy, is starting a new magazine in Chicago. We would see him. Also Marcus Bach who is new director of the Chicago WPA theater

has asked me to bring him some scripts and I would like to talk to him
about them and the possibility of work in his office. I would only stay a day
or two if I go and it would only cost a few dollars. But we can decide about
that when you get here. I have so many boxes of manuscripts and what not
I don't know what I would do without the car. My trunk is still at the fraternity house without a lock. I had the lock removed after Christmas when
I forgot my keys and haven't had it fastened on yet. As for money to get
out of town I will need about six dollars to pay a small dental bill and an
over-drawn mealbook from last Spring at the Union cafeteria. I owe my
landlady one dollar for the last week of the summer session. A total of
seven. That is all I can think of right now.

I have a small part in the final play of the season, only two lines - as a
page in <u>Richard of Bordeaux</u>. The closing performance is night of August
third. It would be nice if you could see that. It's an elaborate costume play,
using our new revolving stage. I read the final version of my new play this
week and will talk to Mr. Mabie afterwards. He probably won't make any
concessions until he knows definitely that I won't come back without them.
Usually he sends word the week before school starts that your application
has been accepted.

I look forward to seeing you very much.

With much love, Tom

[TW received a Bachelor of Arts degree on August 5, but for reasons that are
unknown (illness or transportation perhaps) no member of the family attended the
graduation exercises. Milton Lomask, TW's Iowa friend, was described in the journal as an "intellectual radical" who traveled with a "mulatto mistress" (October
16, 1938). Jack Conroy started *The New Anvil* (1939-1940) in Chicago in March
1939. The original *Anvil*, which he also edited, had been absorbed by the *Partisan
Review* in 1936.

In early-August Edward Mabie's playwriting seminar "quite finally rejected"
Spring Storm after finding the second act marred by "Heavenly's weakness as a
character" (*Journal*, August 2, 1938). Mabie is reported by TW (in a scene that may
be apocryphal) to have dismissed his class with an unusually tolerant statement,
"'Well, we all have to paint our nudes!'" (qtd. in "The Past, the Present and the
Perhaps," 1957). He referred no doubt to an alternate ending, prepared for an earlier draft of the play, that TW had labeled "too sensational for most non-professional producers!": Heavenly's "dress falls in a white cascade" before a "breathless"
Arthur, who is invited to "go out in the back-yard where you smelled those roses last

night" (n.d., HRC). When the play received its world première in Austin, Texas, on November 10, 1999, the alternate ending still proved controversial. The director complained to the press that he had been denied its use by representatives of the copyright holder (the University of the South), who were presumably intent upon censoring Tennessee Williams.

The rejection of *Spring Storm* meant the possible "defeat of everything" and led TW to mull his options: "I haven't the slightest notion what comes after this summer. Holland is about my last resource. If he likes {*Spring Storm*} and will produce that would at least give me a spar to hang onto for a few months. I would do better to come back here but how? Mabie won't get me a scholarship" (*Journal*, August 2, 1938).]

84. To Edward C. Mabie

[YMCA Hotel
826 South Wabash Avenue]
Chicago, Ill.
Aug. 8, 1938
[TLS, 1 p. HRC]

Dear Mr. Mabie:

Marian tells me that I should make a formal application for the NYA work which you mentioned at the last class period, so I am herewith making one. I am tremendously anxious to write a creative thesis for my Master's at Iowa but it is necessary for me to have work as my savings are exhausted and I can't expect any further help from my father who wanted me to remain in the shoe-business. I am an expert typist (worked as one three years) and could do anything that demanded office experience.

I haven't seen Bach yet but spent the afternoon at the Blackstone watching Edward Vail rehearse "Power" which opens there Monday. He is so hard-boiled that he has his stage-crew in a panic. I'm also spending a good deal of time with a notebook on the public beaches, taking down colorful idioms of speech and am stopping at a cheap South-side hotel to get authentic material for my flophouse play in case I ever get time to revise it.

I'm enclosing a list of projected new plays, some of which are already in progress, and will mail a copy of "Spring Storm" soon as I get it typed and bound.

Wishing you a pleasant vacation,

Sincerely, Tom Williams

P.S. This letter is not a fair indication of my typing ability as I am horribly jittery from lack of sleep.

[In addition to directing the University Theater and the department of Speech and Dramatic Arts, Edward Mabie (1892-1956) took a leading role in the development of community and academic theatre and had briefly supervised the Midwest region of the Federal Theatre Project. Neither *Spring Storm* nor apparently any other play by TW was staged at Iowa during Mabie's tenure. A long obituary in *The Daily Iowan* did not include TW in a list of his distinguished students.

TW spent nearly two weeks in Chicago without finding work on the Federal Theatre or Writers' Project. He was hampered no doubt by budget cuts and by a rule that 90% of the employees must be hired from relief rolls. Later in October TW wrote that he had "turned down a chance of getting NYA {National Youth Administration} work" (*Journal*, October 16, 1938) for which Marian Gallaway had urged him to apply.

Power (1938), by Arthur Arent, was a "living newspaper" production of the Federal Theatre that opened in Chicago on August 15. It was vigorously attacked by the *Chicago Daily Tribune* as a work of propaganda on behalf of "the New Deal's entire case against the public utilities companies" (August 16, 1938).

The "cheap South-side hotel" from which TW wrote to Mabie was probably the YMCA on South Wabash Avenue, whose imprinted stationery he had used in a preceding letter to Edwina (Sunday A.M. {August 7, 1938} HRC).]

85. To Clark Mills

SH: W. Dakin Williams
42 Aberdeen Place
Clayton, Missouri
[ca. mid-October 1938]
[AL draft, 2 pp. HTC]

Dear Clark:

I have just taken a sleeping pill to which I am likely to succumb at any moment so you will excuse the brevity and dullness of this letter. I'm glad to learn through your mother that you've found comfortable lodgings with a beautiful blond in such auspicious proximity.

Since you left I have been writing furiously - day and night - and all but completed my new play - there is something in what you said about the value of social isolation - I have seen nobody and done a great deal more -

but now I am paying the piper as the strenuous work has resulted in something like a nervous collapse - My blood pressure - which has always been my nervous barometer - jumped up alarmingly and I've spent several days and nights feeling like a smoking volcano - will probably have to rest completely for a while.

Jennings did a creditable performance in the play - which was nevertheless pretty awful. Poor Anne labored heroically to make the most of her "bit" part as a maid - Having practically no lines, she tried to compensate for this lack by an extravagant use of gesture and facial expression with a rather unfortunate result - She delayed her exits as long as possible and rolled her eyes and made faces for practically no reason. Given an important rôle she might be really good.

They're still stringing me along at KXOK and I've lost all interest - almost fully determined to go to New York soon as I can raise the funds - [end of letter missing]

[In September Clark Mills assumed his new duties as an instructor of French at Cornell University. TW planned to mark his departure from St. Louis with a feature story entitled "Return to Dust," in which he retraced their literary friendship and described Mills as "one of America's most promising younger poets" (n.d., HRC).

The "new play" is Not About Nightingales (1998). TW's impetus for incorporating and expanding its tributary sources—the prison sketch "Quit Eating" and a draft entitled "Hell" (n.d., HRC)—was a widely reported "atrocity" (Journal, October 16, 1938) at a model prison in Holmesburg, Pennsylvania, in August 1938. Striking prisoners were placed in the "Klondike," an isolation unit lined with radiators, where four died from temperatures approaching 150 degrees.

After completing a third draft of Nightingales in November, TW found the play "incredibly bad" and put it away with "other derelict scripts" (Journal, November 20, December 5, 1938), although he later described it as "the best" ("The Past, the Present and the Perhaps") of his early long plays. Nightingales received a successful world première in London on March 5, 1998, followed by its American debut (1998) at the Alley Theatre in Houston. The New York production (1999) at the Circle in the Square was highly regarded and nominated for several prestigious awards. In 1998 New Directions issued a first edition, prepared by Allean Hale.

Blandford Jennings and his wife Anne acted in the Mummers' production of Storm Over Patsy, an English comedy that opened on October 6. Later in the month she asked TW to write a publicity release for the Mummers' upcoming production of Sinclair Lewis's anti-fascist novel *It Can't Happen Here* (1935). The American people, TW wrote, should "know exactly what threats are constituted against them in the Fascist ideology" (n.d., HRC). He added in the journal that "I am at last becoming sincerely aroused in my social consciousness" (October 17, 1938).

In late-September TW submitted a "script" (letter from Edwina to the Dakins, Tuesday {September 27, 1938} HRC) to KXOK, a new radio station owned by the *St. Louis Star-Times*, but no position materialized (see letter #104).]

PART III

1939

NEW ORLEANS · CALIFORNIA
TAOS · ST. LOUIS

Overleaf: 722 Toulouse Street, New Orleans.

"In this old house it was either deathly quiet or else the high plaster walls were ringing like fire bells with angry voices."

—Tennessee Williams, *"The Angel in the Alcove"*

86. *To Edwina Dakin Williams*

431 Royal Street
[New Orleans, Louisiana]
PM: New Orleans, December 29, 1938
[APCS, 1 p. HRC]

Dear Mother:

This is most fascinating place I've ever been. Arrived late last night & spent morning finding room - very scarce on account of Sugar Bowl game. I am situated for a week at 431 Royal Street. Letter soon.

Tom.

[The closing months of 1938 found TW feeling "dangerously cornered, cut off, caught in St. Louis with nothing to do." The "shadow of what happened to Rose" (*Journal*, October 16, 1938), long a sign of his own stagnation and defeat, was present in November when he visited her at Farmington State Hospital: "She is like a person half-asleep now - quiet, gentle and thank God not in any way revolting." "New York will be exciting," he thought, in rousing himself from the fear that he might have "a touch" (*Journal*, ca. November 16, 1938) of his sister's disease.

TW left instead for New Orleans on December 26 and stayed the night with his grandparents in Memphis. From there he mailed several plays to a Group Theatre contest in New York that he apparently signed "Tennessee Williams." To conform with the contest rules, he subtracted three years from his age of twenty-seven and hoped that the Memphis postmark, reinforced by an authentic local name, would hide this deception from "'friends'" (see letter #102) in St. Louis who might otherwise expose him. He later offered several versions of how *Tom* became *Tennessee*, but these circumstances are a plausible source of the inspired creation.

With the financial support of Edwina and Grand, TW arrived in New Orleans on December 28 and set off immediately to explore the Vieux Carré: "Here surely is the place that I was made for if any place on this funny old world" (*Journal*, December 28, 1938).]

87. To Edwina Dakin Williams

431 Royal Street
[New Orleans, Louisiana]
Monday Jan. 2 [1939]
[TLS w/ autograph postscript, 2 pp. HRC]

Dear Mother:

The city has been wild with the football and sport carnival crowd - the big game was today so they will be gone tomorrow. I rented a room here in a cheap but clean hotel for four dollars a week. He would give me a month for twelve dollars - but I think I will find something better for that price soon as the crowd is gone.

The Lippmann's friends have been lovely to me. They invited me to a New Year's Eve party which lasted till day-break and traveled through about half-a-dozen different homes or studios and I met most of the important artists and writers. They are all very friendly and gracious. Roark Bradford, famous author of negro literature, and Lyle Saxon, who wrote Fabulous New Orleans, both live in the Quarter and I am promised introductions to them. I met Mr. Ashton, director of the WPA theater. Their program will be open after the first of March and so could use some of my plays. I'm going to submit Fugitive Kind soon as I've made a few changes. They have a swell theater, large as the American in St. Louis, and their plays run for a week or more - but apparently they lack good material as the play I saw was quite feeble in plot.

I'm crazy about the city. I walk continually, there is so much to see. The weather is balmy, today like early summer. I have no heat in my room - none is needed. The Quarter is really quainter than anything I've seen abroad - in many homes the original atmosphere is completely preserved. Today being a holiday, I visited Audubon Park which is lovelier than I could describe, blooming like summer with Palm Trees and live-oaks garlanded with Spanish Moss - beautifully laid-out. Also visited the batture-dwellers (squatters) along the river, and, for contrast, the fine residential district and the two universities, Loyola and Tulane. The latter appears to be a splendid school - it was closed today so I'm going to make another visit. The Quarter is alive with antique and curio shops where some really artistic stuff is on sale, relics of Creole homes that have gone to the block. I was invited to dinner Sunday by some people who own a large antique store. Their home is a regular treasure chest of precious objects.

Food is amazingly cheap. I get breakfast at the French market for a dime. Lunch and dinner amount to about fifty cents at a good cafeteria near Canal Street. And the cooking is the best I've encountered away from home. Raw oysters, twenty cents a dozen! Shrimp, crab, lobster, and all kinds of fish - I have a passion for sea-food which makes their abundance a great joy.

The court-yards are full of palms, vines and flowering poinsetta, many with fountains and wells, and all with grill-work, balconies, and little winding stairs. It is heaven for painters and you see them working everywhere. Mr. and Mrs. Heldner (Alice Lippmann's friends) say that if I get desperate I can earn bread as a model - but I trust something better will turn up. The Heldners live in two rooms with a baby girl - he is brilliant and very good-hearted. Showed me his canvasses which have won fine critical comment but during his whole sixteen years in New Orleans he has only sold four. They are very modernistic so are not popular as decoration for homes. He has a red beard and often forgets where he is going when he leaves the house - but not as bad as Mrs. Lippmann! There is a writers' project here and many of the writers I have met are on it - perhaps there is room for more. Lyle Saxon is at the head of it.

The fine weather and much walking have cured my cold and I am feeling splendidly. Will be here till Thursday and then will send my new address.

With love, Tom

P.S. My present money is holding out pretty good. I will write before it is exhausted and give you a more permanent mailing address.

P.S. Mailed my plays from Memphis in plenty of time.

[Alice Lippmann was an unconventional older woman, active in the arts in St. Louis, who had befriended TW. She later reportedly urged the *St. Louis Star-Times* to assign a young drama critic to interview him, initiating his friendship with William Inge.

"With a bang" the New Year's Eve party introduced TW to the "Bohemian life of the Quarter," which he found "interesting" and "utterly appalling" (*Journal*, January 1, 1939). In the play *Vieux Carré* (1977) he used the same festive occasion to date the homosexual initiation of the young writer whose career was closely modeled upon his own. No such event, however, is recorded in the journal or letters, nor does it appear in an early fragmentary draft of *Vieux Carré* entitled "Dead Planet, the Moon!" (January 1939, HRC). At a later date TW apparently used his own dramatic introduction to the Quarter to stage the unnamed writer's sexual initiation.

Roark Bradford won fame with his collection of African-American tales, *Ol' Man Adam an' His Chillun* (1928), which Marc Connelly adapted for his successful Broadway play, *The Green Pastures* (1930).

Fabulous New Orleans (1928), by Lyle Saxon, remains a standard purchase for visitors to the city. From 1935 to 1942 Saxon directed the Federal Writers' Project of Louisiana and was a generous friend to struggling artists.

Herbert Ashton, a roving trouble-shooter for the Federal Theatre Project, was assigned to the New Orleans unit at this time. TW informed Edwina that local officials liked *Fugitive Kind* (1937) "better than any {play} submitted so far," but feared that its "social message might be too strong for a southern city" and had sent it to Florida for the regional director's "judgement" (postmarked New Orleans, January 9, 1939, HRC). Such wariness may be attributed to the play's blunt attack on class and capitalism, a prime concern of the House Committee on Un-American Activities which had recently completed an investigation of alleged Communist ties to the Project.

This letter was written on imprinted stationery of the St. Louis Poets' Workshop. William Jay Smith has recalled that he, TW, Louise Krause, and Elizabeth Fenwick Phillips (who later married Clark Mills) fabricated such a letterhead to advertise their writing and create the impression of a "great poetic flowering" (*Army Brat*, 1980) in St. Louis.]

88. *To Edwina Dakin Williams*

[722 Toulouse Street
New Orleans, Louisiana]
[ca. January 18, 1939]
[TLS w/ autograph marginalia and postscript, 2 pp. HTC]

Dear Mother:

I just have time for a few lines. Am enclosing one of our printed cards which I composed and have been distributing around town. The slogan is my own invention and seems to be effective. We opened yesterday, business is extremely slow as the place has had no publicity except the cards, we haven't even gotten the sign up yet. However at each meal we have one more than before - and the meals are delicious, so if we can hold out a week or two I think it will go over fine. I serve as waiter, cashier, publicity manager, host - in fact, every possible capacity, including, sometimes, dishwasher. When not busy in the dining-room I stand on the sidewalk and try to drag people upstairs! It is really a great deal of fun. Besides myself there are three widows running the place. Mrs. Anderson, who owns it, is a perfect termagant - but the cooking is the best I've ever tasted - the cook is an old lady who ran a restaurant in Florida till the depression. We all conspire to keep Mrs. Anderson out of the way as her sharp tongue kills the trade. I usually find time to do some writing in between meals and of course my evenings are free. My play is still in Florida, being considered by the regional director of the WPA. I won't hear from it for another week, they say. One of my best friends here is on the staff of the Saturday Evening Post, gets $500. per story and sells one or two every month - but he says he hates writing because he is forced to satisfy popular demands. Since he has a car and many attractive girl friends, he has proved a very valuable friend to me. If I can get off Thursday we are going to drive over to Gulfport Mississippi to visit some girls he knows there.

My waiter's uniform is wash-pants, dark coat and bow-tie. Some time when you're not too busy I would like to have you send all my wash-pants with the checked spring suit - but don't go to any trouble about it.

I was delighted to get the shoes and the other package.

With much love, Tom

P.S. Business is picking up! - we served 10 suppers.

[The rooming house at 722 Rue Toulouse was the setting for several of TW's stories and plays, including "The Lady of Larkspur Lotion" (first published in 1942), "The Angel in the Alcove" (1948), and *Vieux Carré*.

Penned above the text of this letter is TW's "slogan" for the short-lived restaurant: "'Meals in the Quarter for a quarter.'" Mrs. Anderson became the model for one of his favorite character types, the callous landlady.

Two humorous travel sketches by TW's new friend Frank Bunce appeared in *The Saturday Evening Post* in 1938. They featured Dorrit Bly, a "giddily blond" legal secretary with a photographic memory and a penchant for quoting the law amid romantic misadventures. TW found it "amazing" that he and Bunce "should be friends" since their "viewpoints in art & life" were "so dramatically divergent." He considered writing a novel or play about such a friendship entitled "'Strange Companions'" (*Journal*, January 14, 1939).]

89. To Rosina Otte Dakin

[722 Toulouse Street
New Orleans, Louisiana]
Thursday. [ca. January 26, 1939]
[TLS, 2 pp. HRC]

Dear Grand:

I was so busy this past week I didn't have time to write. As you know, we opened a little restaurant here at Mrs. Anderson's called "The Quarter Eat Shop - Meals for a Quarter in the Quarter." - Well, it lasted one week. Tuesday morning Mrs. Nesbit, our cook, phoned and said her son would not allow her to come to work as she had been so exhausted the night before. She's 67 years old and was doing all the cooking and kitchen-work in the restaurant. She decided she'd better go down to Florida for a couple of weeks to be eligible for her old-age pension. So the restaurant is temporarily closed. It is too bad, as the food was excellent and if we had hung on a while longer it would have been a real success. We had a very nice clientele, mostly artists and writers and shop-owners here in the Quarter. Mrs. Anderson wants to sell-out for $350. - which would include the lease on the house and all the furnishings. The furniture all belongs to her and, while not handsome, contains a good many valuable antiques. She is going to keep up the rooming-house until at least the first of March, after which another lady will assume charge. If the restaurant is re-opened, Mrs. Nesbit will manage it. The restaurant would have been an immediate success except that Mrs. Anderson has made herself unpopular in the neighborhood. She is very good-hearted but has a sharp tongue and had antagonized a good many business-people through trying to run their affairs.

You will have no trouble getting a room here in the house. The one I described will be available at four dollars a week. I don't know if Mrs. Anderson will take boarders or not - that is, serve meals in the house - but there is a kitchen and stove you could use. I think you would find the room very comfortable and she will make reasonable terms.

Since the Eat Shop closed I've been applying for work on the Writers' Project here. The outlook is very promising as Mr. Lyle Saxon (author of "Fabulous New Orleans") is at the head of it and has promised to place me in the first vacancy. Today I got my social security number and went through a lot of other red-tape procedings and now I will just have to wait a week or two till Mr. Saxon can place me in his office. The work is pretty well paid - some men are supporting families on it.

I have started a new play with a New Orleans background. One of my good friends here writes for the Saturday Evening Post regularly, getting $500. a story. He has a car and has been fine about driving me around and introducing me to people.

I hope you will like the Vieux Carre. It is a very heterogeneous neighborhood. Some very wealthy people live next door to some who are destitute - it is all mixed up. The atmosphere is pretty Bohemian but it is perfectly safe to walk around by yourself, even at night. If you like quaint old places you ought to enjoy it. The neighborhood is teeming with antique shops, little restaurants, artcraft stores, Etc. Since I've been here the temperature has ranged between 40 and 80. It is usually about 60. The rooms have open-fire-places and gas grates. In the room next to mine there is a retired Professor from Northwestern University - he is painting down here. But I'm afraid he will only be here a week. The other tenants are musicians, artists, and salesmen - all quite respectable.

I have finished re-writing "Fugitive Kind" and am going to send it up to the Group Theatre with my other plays - even though it may be too late to enter the contest.

The Carnival preparations are already under-way here - the social life is very gay - but of course I am not participating very much in that. I have made some nice friends and enjoy living here more than any place I've been.

You could write either me or Mrs. Anderson about anything special concerning the room.

With much love, Tom

P.S. I'm not needing anything right now.

[The New Orleans play was a draft of *Vieux Carré* entitled "Dead Planet, the Moon!," a provisional title that TW derived from *The Letters of D.H. Lawrence* (Viking, 1932). TW appeared in the fragmentary script as Valentine, a young "literary not-quite who came to the 'Quarter' because he heard you could live without money, discovered his mistake - and is now waiting tables for room & board." In further use of his father's Sevier lineage, TW signed, and then canceled, a contemporary story entitled "The Lost Girl" (n.d., HRC) as Valentine Xavier of 722 Rue Toulouse.

The promise of the new play soon dimmed: "Can't seem to get going on it - Dull, dull! - I sit down to write & nothing happens. . . . What good's the old carcass when it's got nothing inside but a 25 watt bulb" (*Journal*, January 28, 1939). In reviewing this "crucial time," TW wrote later in the margin of the journal that it "might easily have ended in some form of disaster."

The "Carnival," of course, is Mardi Gras.]

90. *To Edwina Dakin Williams*

[722 Toulouse Street
New Orleans, Louisiana]
[ca. early-February 1939]
[TLS, 3 pp. HRC]

Dear Mother:

It is just as well Grand and Grandfather decided to delay their visit, as we've had a very hectic time at 722 Rue Toulouse. As I've probably mentioned, the land-lady has had a hard time adjusting herself to the Bohemian spirit of the Vieux Carre. Things came to a climax this past week when a Jewish society photographer in the first floor studio gave a party and Mrs. Anderson expressed her indignation at their revelry by pouring a bucket of water through her kitchen floor which is directly over the studio and caused a near-riot among the guests. They called the patrol-wagon and Mrs. Anderson was driven to the Third Precinct on charges of Malicious Mischief and disturbing the peace. The following night we went to court - I was compelled to testify as one of the witnesses. Mrs. Anderson said she did not pour the water but I, being under oath, could not perjure myself - the best I could do was say I thought it was highly improbable that any lady would do such a thing! The Judge fined her fifteen dollars. One of the other witnesses was the wife of Roark Bradford, who wrote Green Pastures, the famous negro play. Her dress was ruined at the party. I went to see her afterwards to assure her my part in the affair was altogether unwilling - she was very nice and cordial and assured me there were no hard feelings at least toward me. I also met Mr. Bradford and Sam Bird, a New York producer. As all my plays are in New York I had nothing to show him. I'm using my colorful experiences here as the background for a new play which is well under way.

The process of certification for the Writers' Project will be complete the fifteenth of this month and I expect Mr. Saxon will put me on at once, as he seems very much concerned and sympathetic about my precarious situation. He gave me a list of trade journals yesterday, that I might get temporary writing jobs from. I'm making a round of their offices. One of the radio stations is doing a weekly ghost story and they're going to produce my spook radio drama which I luckily got back from KXOK. They don't mention payment but of course it may lead to something - the radio-stations here are in a pretty bad shape, in fact everything is except the business which caters directly to the tourists.

I haven't heard a word from Rita Oberbeck about my Kansas City play. You might phone her that I am out of town and would like to know about it - I don't know her address but she lives on Euclid.

I hope I will get at least some encouraging news from the New York contest. It should be announced the fifteenth. I already know twice as many people here as I ever knew in St. Louis - some of them highly influential such as the Bradfords and Saxons - so I ought to get a break.

Mrs. Andersons unpopularity has wrecked the Eat Shop - I don't think she can ever re-open it. But Mrs. Nesbit plans to start a new one when she returns from Florida. - Mrs. Anderson plans to sell the place for $350. - lease on the house and out-right sale of the complete furnishings, many of which are valuable antiques. If you come down here, you might be interested.

I'm completely out of funds now - so could use a few dollars if you're not in the same predicament.

Hope you're all well and Dakin successful in his scholastic and social enterprises.

With much love, Tom

[The story of the indignant landlady is echoed in *A Streetcar Named Desire* (1947) and recast in *Vieux Carré*, where TW's equivocal defense of Mrs. Anderson, renamed Mrs. Wire, is closely paraphrased.

Roark Bradford wrote the stories that inspired *The Green Pastures*, but the play itself was written by Marc Connelly.

The "spook" radio drama is "Me, Vashya!" (n.d., HRC). Willard Holland, director of the Mummers, had condensed the one-act and renamed it "Men Who March" for broadcast in St. Louis. "Everyone," he wrote to TW early in the new year, "commented on our thrilling material and your name was mentioned 3 times in the broadcast" (n.d., HRC).

Rita Oberbeck had acted with the Mummers and was apparently trying to arrange a Kansas City production of *Candles to the Sun* (1937), which has not been documented.

An abbreviated version of this letter was first published in Edwina Dakin Williams's memoir, *Remember Me to Tom* (1963), pp. 101-102.]

91. *To Edwina Dakin Williams*

SH: Texas Hotel
San Antonio, Texas
Tuesday Night Feb. 21, 1939
[ALS, 4 pp. HRC]

Dear Mother:

No doubt you were surprised by my sudden decision to travel westward, I hope not too disagreeably. It seemed nothing was to be gained by remaining any longer in New Orleans - the cuts in the WPA made it uncertain when they could hire me and no other permanent work was available there. This fellow, Jim Parrott, was driving to the West Coast and invited me along free of charge. He's a swell young fellow - his family have a summer home in Lake George, New York, and winter home at Miami, Fla. He's a musician and has been promised work in Hollywood and thinks he could get me some scenario work there in the studios. We delayed our departure till Monday in order to see a little of the Mardi Gras - two days of it was quite enough. We are going over the "Old Spanish Trail" through southern Texas, along the Mexican border, New Mexico, Arizona and Southern Calif. to Los Angeles - we plan to visit a few Mexican towns and possibly find some work on the ranches. Our itinerary includes El Paso, Phoenix, San Bernardino and L.A. - you can reach me "General Delivery" at any of those Post offices. We may stop over a few days where work is available - I will let you know, at any rate, where I am. Jim's uncle owns a ranch near Los Angeles - we may work there a while. The trip is a wonderful experience for me - I'm collecting lots of significant material on the way - it is all very stimulating. There was practically nothing for me in New Orleans - still less in St. Louis - so I have nothing to lose by trying the West Coast. I had not heard anything from my plays in New York when I left. I'm writing them tonight to hold the plays till I get settled somewhere - I will want to have them in Hollywood - I hope they have at least some encouragement for me (at the Group).

We've been driving since sunrise so I'm dead tired. The air is delightful - dry and bracing - but makes me too sleepy to write.

As I mentioned in the post-card I hope you can send me a small checque to El Paso, Texas, "Gen'l delivery" - to provide me with living expenses on the way. We have a pup tent and a couple of army cots - intend to sleep in tourist lots along the "Trail" - but tonight it is too chilly for that - 28% - ordinarily my expenses will not run over about 50¢ a day as Jim is paying all the car expense himself. I think I was extremely lucky to get this chance - only hope you are not too disturbed about it.

Grandfather wrote me Jessie Watson was in N.O. - I called twice, found her out and left a card explaining that I was leaving for the West Coast and regretted I missed her.

I'm feeling marvelously well - the best I can remember. Contact with the world at large is very stimulating.

I want to write Grand a short letter now.

With much love, Tom

P.S. Will be in El Paso the 23 or 24 - & remain 2 or three days.

["Cuts in the WPA" followed congressional action in late-January that curtailed relief spending and set the stage as it were for the demise of the controversial Federal Theatre Project in June. Its director, Hallie Flanagan, defended the Project by reporting that some 64,000 performances had been given under its aegis, with a yearly average of 10,000 actors, writers, directors, and other theatre professionals employed in socially valuable work. The "Living Newspaper" units, which were active in New York and Chicago, employed innovative stage techniques and produced a fast paced, socially charged theatre that had a decisive effect upon TW, although his work was not selected by the Project.

TW and Jim Parrott began their "pilgrimage to the west coast" (*Journal*, February 26, 1939) on February 20. TW later described, and no doubt embellished, his departure from New Orleans: "I escaped owing $50 by sliding down from the second story on a string of bed sheets to a trumpet player waiting below who promised to drive me to California in his jalopy to what he described as his uncle's magnificent ranch. It turned out to be a run-down pigeon farm" (*Conversations*, p. 198).

Jim Parrott, the dissembling friend, was a high school English teacher from

Lake George, New York, trying his luck as an actor and musician. The plan, as revealed in a contemporary story, was for Jim "to star in" ("In Memory of an Aristocrat," 1985) the films that TW would write.

Jessie Watson, a partner in the Biltmore chain, had entertained TW and his grandfather in New York in 1928.]

92. To Walter Dakin Williams

[Villa Cuna, Mexico]
[ca. February 22, 1939]
[APCS, 1 p. Columbia]

Hello, Dakin -

We are in Mexico, just across the Rio Grande. Thought you might want one of these priceless old cards as a souvenir. They've been on sale about 50 years. Plan to spend night here in Villa Cuna and go to El Paso, Tex. tomorrow spend a few days there.

Tom.

[Dakin Williams, an energetic sophomore at Washington University, was immersed in "scholastic and social enterprises" and preparing for law school. The "priceless old" postcard shows a patrician couple embracing in a wooded setting.]

93. To the Editor

[El Paso, Texas]
[ca. February 26, 1939]
[TL draft, 1 p. HTC]

Dear Editor:

The author of these poems and his friend, Jimmy, a jobless musician, have run out of money and gas in El Paso, Texas. There is a terrific dust-storm raging and a sheriff named Fox who puts undesirable transients in the house of detention for thirty days. The author and the musician, a good tenor sax player, are not quite sure of their desirability and would like to continue westward to California where they understand that unemployed artists can make fifty cents an hour picking fruit. Their jalopy, running on kerosene or low-grade gas, could make Cal. on ten or fifteen dollars. If you like the poems an acceptance would aid materially in the author's survival.

He knows such appeals to an editor are unfair and in extremely bad taste and that a rejection slip would be a deserved rebuke.

Sincerely,

[The unknown "Editor" is perhaps a generic patron addressed in a facetious form letter. With its "choking" dust and "sterile" mountain scenery, TW found El Paso an undesirable place to be "stalled" by a "lack of funds" (*Journal*, February 26, 1939). Its watchful "sheriff" may have contributed to a similar figure in *Battle of Angels* (1940), a play that TW would draft later in the year.]

94. To Edwina Dakin Williams

SH: Young Men's Christian Association
Phoenix, Arizona
Tuesday March 1 [1939]
[ALS, 4 pp. HRC]

Dear Mother:

We are now stopping here in Phoenix for a few days. Jim has to recuperate his traveling funds by playing in bands occasionally and fortunately has found a temporary job here. I don't believe we'll stay more than 4 or 5 days, however, as we're impatient to reach the West Coast. In El Paso we met some lovely people, a girl who is secretary of the Junior League there and entertained us for several dinners. The town was disagreeable due to the terrible dust-storms, almost continuous. So we shoved off yesterday morning for Phoenix. The drive through the desert and the Gila Mountains was thrilling. It is like being on another planet, so totally different from the East. We have been cooking our own meals over open fires along the road-side. Tried sleeping in the car last night in middle of mountain range but it got too cold so we drove on into Phoenix, arriving here in early morning - got a tourist cabin, quite comfortable, for 50¢ a night (25¢ each). Jim spent some of his traveling money to replace a stolen clarinet which has slowed us down quite a bit but I expect we'll reach Los Angeles or Hollywood in about a week.

The air here is delicious, so fresh and pure it is a pleasure just to breathe.

I'm amazed by the number of destitute transients on the highways. You see them everywhere, fine, able-bodied young men who are unable to make a living anywhere, simply wander from place to place, begging for any kind of work. A few days ago we picked up a family of 3 on the road, including a little 4 year old girl. They shared our cabin with us and the wife cooked our meals - unable to make a living in their home town, they were headed for California - had to sell their car as they couldn't buy gas - it is pitiful to see even little children along the road, but a valuable experience as it gives you a very clear, unforgettable picture of the tragic dilemma in which many Americans are now finding themselves due to the economic mess we are in.

I will send you a card before I leave here -

Dad wrote me to see Sam Webb in Los. A. - I will do that as soon as I get there.

This Gypsy life agrees with me marvelously - I have a tremendous appetite, in fact bigger than is desirable, and feel quite well.

> With love to all, Tom.

[Edwina commented to her parents that "at last, Cornelius feels that he should be-stir himself a little for Tom, so he wrote him a letter at Phoenix and a letter to his salesman, Sam Webb, in Los Angeles to look out for him" (March 8, 1939, HRC). Webb, the Los Angeles representative of the Friedman-Shelby Branch, was one of several contacts provided by TW's parents to maintain supervision and ensure the "gypsy's" financial support.

Tuesday was February 28, not March 1, a familiar confusion in TW's dating of correspondence and journal entries.]

95. *To Cornelius Coffin Williams*

SH: Young Men's Christian Association
Phoenix, Arizona
Friday. [March 3, 1939]
[ALS, 3 pp. HRC]

Dear Dad:

We'll reach Los Angeles in about a week and I will certainly see Mr. Webb the first thing - it will be good to have a connection like that. Perhaps he can give me some leads on temporary employment till I find an opening in script writing. Parrott, the fellow I'm traveling with, has run low on funds so we've had to make a pretty slow trip, stopping off to earn gas money at various points along the way. We stayed several days in El Paso where he got work with a band. In Phoenix we've just about made enough to complete the trip. His clarinet was stolen in Texas, which accounts for the difficulties - he had to replace it with a large portion of the traveling fund. We're stopping at a tourist camp owned by an Indian squaw, Mrs. Cactus Flower, who collects her two bits at sun-up and says she's got a load of buck shot for anybody who tries to break camp without paying.

Phoenix is a great town - but I'm anxious to see the West Coast - if nothing else is available, they say you can make 50¢ an hour picking fruit. However I'm hoping for something a little better than that.

I could certainly use a pair of sport shoes if you have any in sample sizes - 7C - I've done so much walking lately I'm about on my uppers. Perhaps Mr. Webb could supply me with some of his sport samples.

Jim Parrott is O.K. - we've been through some tight spots on the road and he has been an awfully good sport. His Uncle owns a ranch near Los A. And he has some good connections in Hollywood, too.

Hope you're all well,

With love, Tom.

96. To Edwina Dakin Williams

c/o Fred Parrott
811 E. New Jersey
Hawthorne, Calif.
[ca. March 13, 1939]
[ALS, 4 pp. HRC]

Dear Mother:

I am now staying (of all places!) on a "pigeon ranch" in Los Angeles County. It's owned by Jim Parrott's Uncle. I arrived here with a terrific cold and they insisted that I stay with them and have treated me like a member of the family. I'm paying them $3.00 a week for room and board. They are not very well off so I thought I had better pay them at least the cost of feeding me. Jim is staying at another relative and both of us are looking for work. Sam Webb took me over to the Broadway Dept. Store where I met George Bessey, a friend of Dad's who is in charge of the Shoe Dept. there - I spent an afternoon pulling sticks out of shoes - for nothing! Sam did not even invite me out to lunch, which I thought rather surprising. Since Friday he has been sick at home with the "Flu" - I told him I would like to work at one of the retail shoe stores for nothing until I learned the line! He's going to get in touch with me, he says, as soon as there is an opening.

I haven't heard a word from New York concerning my plays. I left N.O. before I had a chance to hear from them. Sent them a card on the way requesting information about the scripts and that they be held until I had a mailing address - but no reply yet. I'm sending an air-mail letter to them this A.M. as of course I can't submit them to the studios till they're returned.

I won't stay here long unless I find work as I think L.A. is a thoroughly unattractive place to live unless you own a car and can drive about the beaches and the hills. Haven't seen the Lucados yet - my cold has made me pretty unsociable but is improving now that I'm out in the country.

Hope Dakin has recovered from his. I got the shoes Dad sent and will write him soon as I've had a little more contact with Sam Webb. I was awfully glad to get crepe-soled sport shoes - with so much walking to do.

With much love, Tom

P.S. Still have my typewriter - but am writing this in the Post office.

[TW stayed briefly at a YMCA after he and Jim Parrott arrived in Los Angeles ca. March 7. Parrott left to visit his family and to look for work at the film studios, and when he failed to return or call, a lonely TW took a bus to the pigeon ranch and was welcomed in from the rain "'like a wet dog.'" The hospitality of Jim's aunt and uncle gave "sublime relief," but it was nonetheless a desperate time, "rather like 'Custer's Last Stand'" (*Journal*, ca. March 15, 1939).

The Lucados were family friends and fellow Episcopalians.]

97. *To Edwina Dakin Williams*

SH: Friedman-Shelby Branch
Sam J. Webb
665 Hayward Hotel
Los Angeles, Calif.
Thursday [March 16, 1939]
[ALS, 6 pp. HRC]

Dear Mother:

I'm scratching this off while waiting for Mr. Webb - he left a message last night for me to see him and I hope he may have something lined up. Jim Parrott got a job in an airplane factory at $18.00 a week - his cousin is employment mgr. there - I also applied but they gave a rigorous physical test and my vision proved too defective. If you don't think America is preparing for war you ought to see the boom in plane-building out there! They're hiring workers daily and turning out planes at top speed.

I've almost recovered from my cold and like L.A. a little better. Where I'm staying is way out in the County - and they have no car - so I have some difficulty in getting around. If I start working I'll have to get a more convenient location. You can get rooms in beautiful homes right over the ocean for $8.00 a month at this time of year.

Jim's Uncle drove me into town this morning while delivering squabs. He sells about 60 a week - I spent yesterday afternoon picking them for him - in overalls and high rubber boots - quite an occupation for a writer! But I really enjoy working around on a "ranch" for a change.

I hope to rent a bicycle later on so I can see more of the country.

Some bad news! - I broke my glasses driving over the Mts. - I can afford to pay a down payment on a new pr. - they'll make them for $8.00

with an exam. thrown in and two dollars cheaper if they have the prescription - So you might phone Aloe's to send my right eye prescription out
here - I don't need a left lens as I can't read with that eye anyway.

Still no word from N.Y. about my plays - expect I'll hear in a couple of
days as I enclosed an air mail card.

Enclosing a couple of snaps taken on the way out. We have quite a few
more that I can send when developed.

I imagine Jim will get fed up on his factory job before long and want
to go back East - if I don't have any luck here I'll drive back with him. He
taught English in a high-school in Lake George, New York last year - wanted to rough it for a change so came West. In a month or two he'll probably be driving back and possibly can get me some work in that part of the
country.

I'm getting free art lessons here - Mr. Parrott's wife is a WPA art
instructor - I've made 3 oil paintings of scenes out here which are really
good - she says I have a remarkable talent so maybe I'll come back East in
a berêt.

Hope you're all well now.

                                        With much love, Tom

P.S. - Sam thinks he can get me work selling shoes during the Easter season,
though he feels I'd do better writing for the movies - So do I - but cannot
afford to be too selective at present. He bought me a 10¢ sandwich for
lunch - !!! He's a nice fellow if he gets me a job. Loaned me $6.50 to pay
for some glasses - that was the full price.

Will keep you posted about my activities - Still haven't seen the
Lucados - too busy at the Squab farm. Saw George Bessey at the Broadway
Dept. Store - he has 70 part-time clerks now.

It will take time to crash the studios so I'm awfully anxious to get any
type of work now.

You might send Grand the snapshots.

[TW's glasses were not broken in travel but lost in New Orleans (see *Journal*, ca.
March 15, 1939).

The "free art lessons" of Adelaide Parrott proved a source of delight and relaxation for the rest of TW's life. The Humanities Research Center has a sizable col-

lection of his early paintings, including landscapes, self-portraits, and portraits of Jim Parrott.]

98. To Anne and Blandford Jennings

[811 East New Jersey Avenue
Hawthorne, California]
[March 16, 1939]
[TLS, 2 pp. HRC]

Dear Anne & B.J. -

Well, here I am, of all places, on a pigeon ranch in Hawthorne, California - quite a jump from the Vieux Carre! I was offered a free ride out here with a highschool English teacher from New York State who was fed up with his profession and wanted to rough it a while. The idea also appealed to me so I joined in the reckless adventure. We had thirty bucks between us and an old V-8 - ran out of money in El Paso, Phoenix and Palm Springs but managed to work our way out - arrived here in Los Angeles after about 3 weeks on the road. I am boarding here on the pigeon ranch with his Uncle and he with his first cousin - I'm working for my board, killed and picked sixty squabs yesterday and drove them into the markets. We're about twenty miles out of L.A. - of course I had some interest in Hollywood but that expired after one disgusted look at the place. Perhaps I'll go back later but right now am content to rusticate for a while in this preposterous place. The owner gets dead drunk every night and one of my principal duties is to take him home and keep him out of communication with the local police. He drinks at one bar till they won't serve him another - and then staggers on to the next. When his resistance is sufficiently low I propel him homeward - while he sings "O Takki" at the top of his lungs - A Japanese song that he learned while in the Embassy over there. They're Eastern aristocrats gone to seed -

A very strange life for me to be living, even after the Vieux Carre! I seem to have a propensity for getting into fantastic milieux nowadays - when I write about them people will say it's ridiculous, such people and things don't occur!

The English teacher has started to work in an airplane factory, dipping canvas or something in banana oil - says it reminds him too much of the teaching profession but enjoys being a porletariat - so do I. Only I may start selling shoes Monday - one of Dad's salesmen in L.A. is getting me a job I don't want in a retail shoe store - but I need the money to pay some debts - I skipped out of New Orleans owing everyone. I still love that old town and want to go back - but probably won't for sometime. All of my plays are still in New York - I haven't heard a thing about them - Perhaps they're all lost in the mail - which possibility does not disturb me too much as I suspect I'm better at picking squabs than writing plays. Oh, yes I also shovel manure on the ranch - which should prove an excellent preparation for Hollywood if I go back there. Isn't Conroy working on his thesis somewhere in the West? Give me his address, if you can - I'd like very much to hear from you and Anne - what is Clark doing? The family wants to drive to New York this summer - mainly, I think, to entice me off the Pacific slope. Which won't be hard as I like my hills and trees together - not standing off and exchanging suspicious glances as they do out here.

Anxious to hear about the Greek daughters.

So long - 10.

[Anne (1895-1977) and Blandford Jennings (1897-1980) were St. Louis friends of TW associated with the Mummers. Blandford taught English at Clayton High School, while Anne did publicity work for the Mummers as well as local reviewing.

The leftist writer Jack Conroy lived in Chicago where he edited *The New Anvil* (1939-1940) and worked on the Illinois Writers' Project. He may have been on TW's mind after having reportedly rejected an unidentified story of his in February.

Clark Mills was completing his first year of teaching French at Cornell. The "Greek daughters" are Catherine and Mary Lois Filsinger, Washington University friends of TW.

In early-March Edwina informed the Dakins of plans for a summer trip: "Cornelius says we are going to the Fair in New York, probably in August. . . . Do you want to keep house for us, or, go along with us?" (March 8, 1939, HRC). She broached the same plan to a wary TW.

The signature "10" is used here for the first time in TW's known correspondence. Leverich reports that this letter was tipped into the pages of a manuscript and not mailed.]

99. To Unnamed Correspondent

SH: Friedman-Shelby Branch
Sam J. Webb
665 Hayward Hotel
Los Angeles, Calif.
[ca. March 18, 1939]
[AL draft, 2 pp. HRC]

So I amaze you, huh? Not half so much as I amaze myself! It has taken me about 2 weeks to recover from the shock of finding myself within spitting distance of the Pacific instead of the Gulf. From your letter I gather that you presumed Hollywood to be my chief objective - far from it! It was only in the back of my mind and that's where it still is. I took one disgusted look at the place & haven't been back.

All my plays are still in N.Y. - I got a card from the "Group" yesterday informing me that one of my plays had not yet been eliminated from the contest and I would hear from them probably within the next few days. I think it is beastly of them to tease me along that way!!! Of course when I get them out here I'll toddle up to Mr. Goldwyn and suggest he put them in the proper place. - "Incidentally" said the Group "your friend in New York did not give us '<u>Candles</u>'" - There were no tear-stains on the paper - but it shows they are getting Williams-conscious up there - I hope.

What am I doing? Well, I've been working on a pigeon ranch - shovelling manure which should prove a good preparation for Hollywood - picking squabs, Etc. But today I go out to Culver City (where M.G.M. Studio is locat- [end of letter missing]

[Leverich speculates that TW's unnamed correspondent was a recent New Orleans friend, perhaps the writer Frank Bunce.

Olga Becker, TW's liaison in New York, had lost her copy of *Candles to the Sun*. In a more critical aside to Edwina, TW described Becker's failure to submit the play to the Group Theatre contest as "outrageous" (n.d., HRC).]

100. To Rosina Otte and Walter E. Dakin

811 E. New Jersey
Hawthorne, Calif.
[March 20, 1939]
[ALS, 6 pp. Columbia]

Dear Grand & Grandfather:

I found your letter with the birthday present in the sample-room this morning, your complaint about the non-committal postals was a deserved reproach so I am sitting right down here, while waiting for Sam, to make a partial atonement. Things have been so unsettled that I scarcely had anything definite to write about. But now prospects are much brighter. Sam told me he would get me a job this morning, probably at one of the retail stores. I'll enjoy selling - it ought to be pretty entertaining and heaven knows I can use a salary, however small.

I got a card from the Group Theater saying that my plays had <u>not</u> <u>yet</u> been eliminated from the contest and that I would probably hear from them within the next few days. So I feel more hopeful. Soon as I get the plays out here I will submit them to an agent or studio. I would much rather <u>live</u> in the <u>East</u> so as soon as I've exhausted the possibilities out here - or made a little money - I'm going to check out - I <u>loved</u> New Orleans & that part of the country.

Mrs. Parrott is a WPA art instructor and has given me some free lessons - I've made <u>5</u> <u>oil</u> <u>paintings</u> (4 landscapes and a figure) which she thought were sensationally good - for a first attempt - they are really good enough to hang up - I will send you the best when I've made a few more.

She thinks I'm the most promising pupil she's ever had.

The Parrotts are Eastern aristocrats who have lost their money and gone rather to seed - but they have been marvelous to me - It's like home life on the pigeon ranch. I get a ride into town every morning with a neighbor. These Westerners are friendly but utterly & hopelessly <u>un</u>cultured. They hate good music, good literature - everything - jazz and hamburgers and the movies are their spiritual fare.

Perhaps later I'll meet a more congenial group - that is, when I get in contact with the literary crowd.

I imagine I will join you all on the trip to New York this summer.

<u>Get</u> <u>well</u> - I hate to hear about you and Grand both being under the

weather. For your birthday I'm going to send you a bunch of <u>oil</u> <u>paintings</u> - by <u>me</u>.

With much love - Tom

PS. My cold is <u>completely</u> <u>well</u>

101. *To Harold Clurman, Irwin Shaw, and Molly Day Thacher*

[811 East New Jersey Avenue
Hawthorne, California]
[March 21, 1939]
[ALS draft, 2 pp. Virginia]

Dear Judges:

Your telegram arrived at the zero hour. I had lost several jobs, spent several hectic weeks on the road getting out here - all I could find was temporary employment on a "pigeon ranch" at the above address. I had begun to feel like our hero in "The Petrified Forest" - except that <u>I</u> had <u>gotten</u> <u>here</u> - God knows <u>why</u>! - Sooo -

<u>Thanks</u>!!!

Another break occured almost at the same moment. Today I started work as a shoe clerk in a little retail store ½ block from M.G.M. Studios in Culver City. However I will retain the same address at <u>least</u> till after I get paid.

Perhaps I'll visit New York this summer with some works in progress -

Forgive this hasty scrawl - my typewriter's broken down & I'm using lunch hour to get this off.

Again many thanks - as sincere as they make them -

Tennessee Williams

[TW learned in a follow-up letter from Molly Day Thacher (1906–1963), playreader for the Group Theatre, that he had won "a special prize" of $100.00 for "the first three sketches in the series AMERICAN BLUES." (Ramon Naya won the first prize of $500.00 for *Mexican Mural*.) Judged "interesting" but less "completely realized" (March 20, 1939, HRC) were the two full-length plays that he had also submitted: *Not About Nightingales* (1938/1998) and either *Spring Storm* (n.d., HRC) or *Fugitive Kind*.

Founded in 1931 by Harold Clurman, Lee Strasberg, and Cheryl Crawford, the Group Theatre was an idealistic experiment in ensemble production that challenged the commercial tenets of Broadway. In 1932 Thacher married Elia Kazan, who had joined the Group as a stage manager and actor and who would later direct TW's major theatre. She took the lead in developing new writing talent and recommended TW to his future agent, Audrey Wood. The Group Theatre production of *The Gentle People*, by Irwin Shaw, opened on January 5, 1939, and was a modest success.

The five short plays published in 1948 as *American Blues* were in part at least different from the four submitted to the Group Theatre contest. "The Dark Room" (1948) and "Moony's Kid Don't Cry" (1941), identified, respectively, by TW (see letter #106) and by the editor Margaret Mayorga as original *Blues* entries, reappeared in the later collection.

Alan Squier, the wandering "hero" of Robert Sherwood's play *The Petrified Forest* (1935), was killed by the gangster Duke Mantee before reaching the metaphorical place of stone. The film adaptation (Warner, 1936), which TW doubtless saw, featured Humphrey Bogart in his first important role.]

102. To Edwina Dakin Williams

811 E. New Jersey
Hawthorne [California]
Tuesday Noon [March 21, 1939]
[ALS, 3 pp. HRC]

Dear Mother:

Some <u>good</u> news at last. Mr. "Tennessee" Williams got a telegram last night from the "Group Theatre" saying they were happy to make a special award of $100.00 for my group of one-act plays "American Blues"! - It was signed by Harold Clurman, director of the Group Theatre and probably the most important director on Broadway, Irwin Shaw, author of the current play "The Gentle People" & "Bury the Dead," & Molly Day Thacher, their play reader. I suppose the money & some more detailed information will come along later. This should give quite an impetus to my dramatic career - at least it should make the studios and producers pay some attention to me, as it is some degree of national recognition. I was over at Jim's cousin's house when Mrs. Parrott phoned that the telegram had arrived. They were more excited about it than I was. As I told them, for every bouquet in writing you get 10 kicks in the face - which prevents one from feeling too elated over an occasional honor.

If I go to New York city with you all I will now have an excellent point of contact through these people who are theatrical "tops".

Do not spread this around till the checque has arrived, as some of my "friends" in St. Louis such as W.G.B. Carson might feel morally obliged to inform the Group that I am over 25 - probably that wouldn't make any difference but I'd rather play safe.

I'm going to buy a new suit and put the rest aside.

I had already paid for my glasses. I started to work this A.M. in Clark's retail shoe store in Culver City, ½ block from M.G.M. studios. My boss is a young fellow - I think we'll get along fine. Salary - about $12.50 a week - hours - 9-6 - Sat. - later - which is pretty bad - but I can get more and better hours when I learn the trade.

I may as well stick at this till something better.

I bought an old bicycle for $10.00 Grand sent me - to ride to work on. There are no trolley connections between here & Hawthorne and the Parrotts are giving me such reasonable board I don't want to move.

My cold is well now.

For my birthday I would like a "Basque" polo shirt with two wide stripes in brown or blue.

The boy by the cactus is me.

With much love, Tom.

[Edwina was "bursting with pride" when she learned of the Group Theatre's "special award" and could "hardly wait" to "broad-cast" (letter to TW, March 23, 1939, HRC) the news locally. To her it was vindication of TW in light of his father's "horrid" criticism. Cornelius soon congratulated his son and promised to send him a pair of "woven shoes" in "D width" (March 31, 1939; qtd. in *Remember Me to Tom*, 1963, p. 106).

TW suspected that Professor William Carson, for whom he blamed the rejection of "Me, Vashya!" in 1937, might inform the Group Theatre of his true age of twenty-seven.]

103. *To Audrey Wood*

811 E. New Jersey
Hawthorne, Calif. ·
April 10, 1939
[TLS, 1 p. HRC]

Dear Miss Wood:

Having no acquaintance with agents I delayed answering your letter till I had communicated with Miss Thacher of the Group Theatre who has taken a very kind interest in my work. She recommends your office very highly and I am grateful for chance of such a connection. I have also been offered the services of Freida Fishbein and so it is not quite possible for me at this moment to definitely commit myself. No doubt you will also want to know more about me - so will you consult Miss Thacher or take a look at some of my scripts which may perhaps still be in her hands? Then write me again if your offer is still open - the sooner the better - and I will [be] fully prepared by that time to make this important decision. My personal affairs are in quite a muddle just now, I'm high and dry on the beach and may have to return back East or South within a short time - which accounts partially for my state of indecision. I would jump into the arms of any agent who could assure me the quick sale of anything - even my soul to the devil!

I want to thank you very, very much for your interest and from what Miss Thacher has written me about you I think the possibility of our association is very promising indeed.

Sincerely yours, T.W.

TENNESSEE WILLIAMS

[Audrey Wood (1905–1985) was a successful playbroker when she wrote to "the talented unknown" TW after learning of his Group Theatre award: "It seems to me, from what I have heard about you, that you may be exactly the kind of author whom I might help" (April 1, 1939, HRC). Her fame as the agent of William Inge, Carson McCullers, Robert Anderson, and many other successful authors lay before her, but the new firm of Liebling-Wood (founded in 1937 with her future husband, William Liebling) was respected and prospering, and she was amused that a dramatist without professional credits would take such a wary tone.

TW had been left financially "high and dry" in early-April when Clark's Bootery in Culver City released him after a downturn in business. He followed

Wood's advice and applied in June to the Rockefeller Foundation for a fellowship.

Elated by his recent award, and by Wood's "interest," TW resolved that his "next play" would "be simple direct and terrible - a picture of my own heart - there will be no artifice in it - I will speak truth as I see it . . . without concealment or evasion and with a fearless unashamed frontal assault upon life" (*Journal*, April 9, 1939).]

104. To Ellsworth P. Conkle

811 E New Jersey
Hawthorne Calif
[ca. May 4, 1939]
[TLS, 2 pp. HRC]

Dear Dr. Conkle:

I found your letter waiting for me when I returned here to the pigeon ranch after a ten-day bicycle tour of "El Camino Real", the beautiful coast-line highway, from L.A. county down to Tia Juana and as much further as the condition of Mexican highways would permit - which is about half a mile. I was very surprised and gratified that you had received news of my good luck in the Group Theatre contest. How did you associate Tennessee Williams of Hawthorne, Calif., with the rather undistinguished "Tom" you had in your class last year? - (rhetorical question - no explanation demanded!) - Well, anyhow, it pleased me tremendously and I thank you for your congratulations. Perhaps you are curious to know how I got out here. Well, I've rivaled the wandering Jew - or perhaps your fabulous hero, Paul Bunyan - in the extent of my peregrinations since last summer when I got honorably dismissed (with sheepskin) from SUI. First I went to Chicago where I spent several weeks and my small remaining funds in a useless effort to get on the Writers' Project. After that returned to St. Louis (my home) just long enough to bang out a prison drama and fail in a rather half-hearted effort to get a job writing radio continuity for a new station. Then went south to Memphis. Nothing available there. About Xmas time I reached New Orleans. Found a job as waiter in a little Bohemian restaurant in the old French Quarter. Here I collected loads of material and started a new play - but the restaurant closed. I tried once again to crash the Writers' Project - in New Orleans they treat you a bit more civilly - but that's all. Then about Mardi Gras, in fact just at that time, I was offered a free ride out to the West Coast - all possibilities being exhausted in the middle-west I took it, in much the same spirit as the hero of the Petrified Forest - only he didn't get there but I did! - the only work I could find out here was picking squabs on the pigeon ranch where I'm now staying - So when the Group award came it seemed providential, as I was really at the nadir of my resources. Since then I've had letters from two agents, Fishbein and Leibling-Wood, who have offered to handle my plays - I doubt that I have written anything saleable so far but the future prospects are at least somewhat brighter.

What I want now is something that will give me a little security in which to work hard and exclusively on one long play. As Miss Thacher says, I've been dodging the problem of craft (mainly through lack of concentrated effort) and it's time for me to take a pause and carefully plot out and prepare my next work - BUT HOW? One must have a modicum of stability in his life before he can "Carefully plot out and prepare" anything!

I may approach the Pasadena Community Theatre for a scholarship or something of the kind though my record at other universities is a definite hindrance to such a plan. I don't care for the academic life but it does provide a kind of shelter while doing creative work - of course universities resent being used for that purpose though I don't see why. Then I have some contacts with film-writers out here which may lead to something -

Excuse this garrulity.

There is a note of restrained but hardly concealed thanksgiving in the bare statement that you expect to leave "forever" at the close of this term, which I don't find too hard to understand. I hope you will form some new association which will allow more freedom. The class seemed to stop last year after it moved from your office and the meetings thereafter contributed more to a general confusion in my mind than anything else. I think the problems of playwriting have to be worked out individually though group discussions can be helpful. Sometimes.

Many thanks for your letter and best wishes -

Sincerely, Tom Williams

[Ellsworth Conkle (1899-1994) was a professor of Dramatic Arts at the University of Iowa and one of the more humane academics whom TW would meet. His cred-

Tennessee and the "lighthearted" Jim Parrott, en route to Mexico, 1939.

its included Federal Theatre productions of *200 Were Chosen* (1937) and the surprisingly controversial *Prologue to Glory* (1938), a sentimental melodrama about Lincoln's youth that was targeted by enemies of the Federal Theatre Project as unduly critical of politicians. In the fall he moved to the University of Texas and continued to follow TW's career.

TW recalls in *Memoirs* (1975) that he and the "lighthearted" Jim Parrott celebrated the Group Theatre award by setting out "southward on a highway called the Camino Real." After misadventures in "a border-town *cantina*," they returned, penniless, by way of Laguna Beach, where they settled later in May as the part-time custodians of a "chicken ranch." TW later wondered why he "was so committed to occupations involving poultry in those days; no analyst has ever explained that to me" (p. 5).]

105. To Edwina Dakin Williams

[811 East New Jersey Avenue
Hawthorne, California]
[ca. May 4, 1939]
[TLS, 2 pp. Columbia]

Dear Mother:

I have <u>not</u> decided to settle in Hollywood - how you got that impression I don't know! My original impression of the place still holds good - it is about the last place on earth I would want to live as Auntie's impression of it is just about right. It is full of sham and corruption and the atmosphere of the place is generally putrid. When you walk down Hollywood Blvd. you see practically nothing but rich Jews in dark glasses trying to impersonate glamorous movie stars. It is no wonder that the few really great artists out here - such as Garbo - remove themselves as far as possible from the film capitol except during working hours. Of course there is a great deal of money to be made in Hollywood - but they always exact their full pound of flesh and in the end the transaction almost invariably proves fatal to the creative worker. So far I have not been infected with the money-disease out here - I would still rather do my own kind of work and live in abject poverty than burn myself out in three years on a big salary, doing hack work.

What I <u>want</u> to do is live out here this summer in a little beach colony for artists and writers which I have discovered on my bicycle tour. It is an indescribably beautiful place - Laguna Beach - lovelier than anything I saw in Europe and you can live there very cheaply, little hill cabins being available for ten or twelve dollars a month with house-keeping equipment. The Group Theatre and my new agent, Audrey Wood, both urge me to devote all my time to writing one long, careful play as they feel I have been working too rapidly and without sufficient concentration on one thing. They are so enthusiastic about my possibilities that a production in New York will be almost automatic if I can get a good play written in about six months. But they don't seem to realize that I will need to live in the meantime. I have written suggesting they advance me loans on works in progress - possibly something of the kind will be forthcoming, as I could live quite a while on about fifty dollars out here - everything is marvelously cheap if you live out of the city. Miss Wood has gotten Rockefeller fellowships (of $1000 each) for four of her clients and she has advised me to apply for one which I'm going to do. I have an excellent chance of getting it - but it will take some time, of course, as the fellowships for this year were granted quite recent ly. I have sent her a bunch of short-stories - the few I have with me - which she may be able to market for me as, according to the letter I will enclose, she has good contacts with magazine editors in New York. She is a better agent than Fishbein, according to Miss Thacher, and placed such big successes as Room Service, Mamba's Daughter, On Borrowed Time, Etc. - I feel very lucky in getting such a woman interested in my work.

I think I may move out to Laguna this week and depend upon Providence to keep me out there. I still have about thirty-five or forty bucks left from my prize money which will keep me a month or two - and then there is probably some work - at least typing for other writers - to be had around the beach town.

Why don't you come out to the Frisco fair instead of the New York? The trip would be lovely and I could drive back with you if my play is finished. . . .

Glad you didn't get the house. You have one in Memphis, a farm in Georgia - and who wants a haven in St. Louis anyhow? ~~I think we should~~

With much love, Tom

[TW considered Audrey Wood's intervening letter of April 28, 1939, (HRC) to be confirmation of her agency. *Room Service* (1937), by John Murray and Allen Boretz, was Liebling-Wood's first hit, while *Mamba's Daughters* (1939), by DuBose and Dorothy Heyward, was a critical, if not a financial, success. The Harold Freedman Agency brokered Paul Osborn's comedy *On Borrowed Time* (1938).]

106. To Audrey Wood

[811 East New Jersey Avenue
Hawthorne, California]
May 5, 1939
[TLS, 3 pp. HRC]

Dear Miss Wood:

I have stalled Miss Fishbein off in the hope that you would come to a favorable conclusion about my work. Apparently you have and I am very glad of it.

I'm also pleased you submitted the scripts to Whit Burnett. When I first started writing I bombarded STORY magazine with my short fiction as they were the only ones in America publishing the sort of thing that I wanted to write. It was pretty bad amateur stuff that I sent them but Burnett and Foley both wrote me gracious and encouraging notes - till my itinerant mode of living and lack of postage made it too inconvenient to send things off. But perhaps it would be better not to remind Mr. Burnett that I was once a contributor as his recollections of my work may not be too favorable if he has any at all. From that period I have about five or six short stories of genuine merit, I believe - if you handle short-stories I would like you to see them - they are mainly psychological, lyrical or impressionistic stuff. One of the dramatic sketches in American Blues ("The Dark Room") actually was first in short-story form - I will send you a copy of it.

I'm awfully sorry to say that I have no other copies of the sketches. In fact I never have more than one copy of anything. I do all my own typing and would rather put in my time on new writing than recopying something old - I say 'rather', but it is actually not a matter of choice. Right now the exigencies of living give me only - with luck - two or three hours a day for creative work - so you see how hard it would be to make additional copies of old scripts!

About myself: I'm twenty-five, a native of Mississippi, descendant of Indian-fighting Tennessee pioneers. I've attended three universities, getting my B.A. degree last summer from the University of Iowa where, as Miss Thacher told you, I had the benefit of Dr. Conkle's teaching. I only became interested in writing for the theatre during my last year at the university so I had very little of the excellent dramatic training that is available at Iowa. While there I worked as a waiter in the state hospital - waiting tables is my chief subsidiary occupation although I've also been employed in a shoe warehouse, office and retail store for short periods of time in between my work at college. I've had two long plays presented in St. Louis by the "Mummers" of that city - they were "Fugitive Kind" and "Candles to the Sun" - the latter scored a big success but "Fugitive", as you might expect, was praised for its "Keen observation" and condemned for its lack of "plot" - reviews of these two plays are available if you want to see them. I think the critics were kind to "Candles" because it was a first play - it is really pretty old stuff, laid in an Alabama coal-mine and replete with such melodramatic episodes as a strike, collapse of a shaft underground, starvation and murder of union organizers - still it was not bad theatre, the audience reaction was good - I was amazed at its success as I considered it a rather "hammy" job of writing. There is only one very disshevelled prompt copy of "Candles" in existence but my kid brother writes me from home that he is engaged at spare moments in typing a new one - so you will eventually have it foisted upon you with whatever other works my family can discover around the old attic where I used to entertain the muses.

Of course I started out being very conceited about my work but that was rapidly kicked out of me - now I think I have a fairly complete humility. It surprises me a little when people take my work seriously at all - perhaps that is not a good thing, especially out here in the "Capitol of Blah" as the Mummers director calls Hollywood - but at least it makes me properly grateful when somebody like you shows an interest in my work.

I have two long plays in progress and another, probably the best, only in mind - as I have probably complained before, I lack financial security, some measure of which I believe is necessary to doing sustained creative work. For instance I have about thirty bucks and when that is gone I shall have to start writing desperate letters home, hocking my typewriter and my guitar - that kind of living is pleasantly exciting but not conducive to "emotion remembered in tranquillity" from which the finest art is supposed to spring! But perhaps under any circumstances I would still be a ham writer - so. . . .

During the last year I've lived in Iowa City, Chicago, Memphis, St. Louis and New Orleans before I came out here. My next objective is probably San Francisco where I hope I can meet William Saroyan. Then within the next year I want to visit New York -

I enclose a snapshot or two in case you may someday? God willing, have some use for publicity about this author. Right now I'm doing chores and picking squabs for my board on a pigeon ranch in Los Angeles County and have just returned from a 400 mile bicycle tour of rural Mexico and southern California coast-line - I would like to settle for a year in a cabin that I discovered in a lonely arroya down there, live a completely primitive, regular life and devote myself to writing one long, careful play. That is really my only ambition right now.

Thanks for giving me this delightful opportunity to talk about myself!

Sincerely, Tennessee Williams

["Deeply impressed" by the *American Blues* sketches, Audrey Wood informed TW on April 28 that she had taken "the liberty" of sending them to *STORY* magazine. *Fugitive Kind* she thought not ready for submission and commented that his "first problem is going to be how to sustain a dramatic idea in a full length play." She then set the tone for their relationship: "One of my virtues, unfortunately, is extreme honesty and I cannot at this point promise you any kind of a quick sale on anything. . . . You are not a finished dramatist although I do say I think you are highly promising" (April 28, 1939, HRC).

Among the stories sent to Wood at this time were "The Dark Room" (1985), "The Red Part of a Flag" (1974), "The Vine" (1954), and "The Field of Blue Children" (1939). One of the "long plays in progress" was probably "Dead Planet, the Moon!"; the play "only in mind" is cited in letter #108 as a biographical study of the poet Vachel Lindsay.

Misquoted is Wordsworth's famous statement that poetry "takes its origin from emotion recollected in tranquillity."]

107. *Rosina Otte Dakin*

General Delivery
Laguna Beach [California]
Wednesday [May 10, 1939]
[TLS, 2 pp. HTC]

Dear Grand:

I have moved again! This time only sixty miles down the coast to a little artist's colony known as Laguna Beach. It is the loveliest spot I could find anywhere along the coast in our bicycle tour down to Mexico so I decided to spend the remainder of my California sojourn in its vicinity. It is even prettier than anything I saw in Europe, including the Riviera and Sorrento. Richard Halliburton, who travelled all over the world, selected this place as his permanent home and has a big modernistic residence on one of the peaks overlooking the sea. Incidentally he has apparently met a tragic end in crossing the Pacific - I will enclose an article I just cut from the Laguna papers. I thought the sub-head about "County turns off water" added a rather grotesquely humorous touch. People around here say that Paul Mooney, mentioned as his collaborator, actually did most of his writing for him. They both went down in the junk - unless it all turns out to be a big publicity stunt.

Jim Parrott and I are renting a little cabin about two miles out of town, in a beautiful canyon - we've gotten it for fifteen a month which only makes $7.50 each. We both have bicycles to take us into town and Jim has a car. Then there are two beautiful twin girls we met in Los Angeles who entertain us frequently at their beautiful house on the beach - so we are ideally located. I have a nice out-door studio in which I do my writing and painting - Oh, yes, I'm quite an artist these days! Mrs. Parrott, who was a WPA art instructor, gave me a good start and I have completed about a dozen landscapes and portraits in oils - nearly everybody paints around here and there are a few really celebrated artists. They have a free art school and a large gallery and a fine little theatre and library.

Laguna is located on a bay surrounded by mountains - it is just opposite Catalina Island - you can see it plainly on clear days. The water is a marvelous blue and the hills thickly wooded and covered with gorgeous wild flowers. The coast along here is very rocky but we have a beautiful sandy beach for swimming. I wish you and Grandfather could have chosen a spot like this to retire to - the climate is superb and most of the population are refined elderly couples who have retired out here. The temperature is moderate all year round - the country is quite a resort for people afflicted with arthritis, Etc.

I'm hoping my agent will procure funds for me to remain out here a few months. She is pretty enthusiastic about my plays and seems to be making intelligent efforts to find a market for them. She wants me to apply for a $1000. Rockefeller fellowship which are distributed annually to needy young writers - but this would take quite some time to go through. In the meantime I can probably find some part-time employment around the colony to keep me going. We have a gas-range in the cabin, a shower and a hot-water heater so we do our own house-keeping and are very comfortable. It is close enough to Los Angeles for me to keep in touch with people there - a day's ride on bicycle, two hours by car - but hitch-hiking is the best mode of transportation out here! Next time I'm in the city I will try to get in touch with Virginia. Her home was at the opposite end of town from Hawthorne which made it accessible only by transferring on three or four different cars or buses. However I will make a point to see her before long.

Your letter was forwarded to me by Mrs. Parrott. My new address is General Delivery, Laguna Beach. The mail is not delivered along the Canyon but we call for it in town every morning.

Sorry to hear of Mr. Rhodes illness - give him my wishes for a speedy recovery.

With much love to you and Grandfather, Tom.

["Life here at Laguna Beach is like that haunting picture of my favorite painter Gauguin - 'Nave Nave Mahana' - The Careless Days." TW felt "like a perfect young animal . . . under the benign influence of this glorious sunlight, starlight and ocean." He also knew that "the great storms" would return and "with them the old lightning that I put into my work" (*Journal*, May 25, 1939).

In 1930 the author-adventurer Richard Halliburton discovered Laguna Beach and was also taken with its natural beauty. His "modernistic residence," aptly named "Hangover House," was regarded both as an architectural marvel and a laughingstock. As material for a new book of travel, he had sailed on March 4 from Hong Kong in a Chinese junk bound for the Golden Gate Exposition in San Francisco. He was assumed lost in a typhoon in the western Pacific ca. March 24 and declared legally dead in October. His editorial assistant, and companion, Paul Mooney, who also died at sea, had made a large contribution to the *Book of Marvels* (1937). Always adept at publicity, Halliburton had faked his death in 1925 while swimming the Hellespont, the source perhaps of TW's present skepticism. *The New York Times* eulogized Halliburton as a man "born to be a romantic in an age when there aren't many such."

In writing to Grand, and to Edwina as well, TW made strategic allusion to girl friends, but his first recorded homosexual encounter would occur in early-June: "Rather horrible night with a picked up acquaintance Doug whose amorous advance made me sick at the stomach." The experience briefly drove him back to Hawthorne with feelings of "spiritual nausea" and marked the first "downward turn" (*Journal*, June 11, 14, 1939) of the idyllic summer.

Peyton Rhodes was an academic friend of the Dakins who had befriended TW in Memphis in 1935.]

108. To Audrey Wood

General Delivery
Laguna Beach, California
[ca. June 19, 1939]
[TLS w/ autograph citation, 2 pp. HRC]

Dear Miss Wood:

Your "long delay in answering my long, descriptive letter concerning myself" is perfectly understandable. Perhaps you have known enough writers (I have) not to be too surprised when they show an unusual propensity for talking about themselves. Since I am now living in a lonely canyon with a minimum of social intercourse I see no promise of checking that tendancy in myself, as letters are just about my only means of advertising my ego at the present time. I have moved to a little cabin in back of a ranch in what is called "Bootleg Canyon" - my mailing address is Gen. Del., Laguna Beach, Calif. The owners have evacuated, allowing me tenancy of the shack in return for tending the poultry, cat, goldfish and garden. Written instructions say that I should "give the little chicks enough growing mash so that they will not be without it" which sounds simple but is horribly complicated by the fact that the little chicks eat continuously. Yesterday I came out, after a long seige at the typewriter, and found three of them legs upward in a state of rigor mortis - and as the food trough was empty I could not decide whether the poor little bastards had starved or foundered themselves! Do literary agents dispense any advice about feeding small chickens? I hope so. We also have a little bantam rooster, full-grown but tiny, confined to a coop with eight enormous red hens - his activities are a continual source of amusement and amazement to me and make me doubt, almost, the superiority of the human race! I suppose I'll come out some morning and find him in the same condition as the three small chicks, but if I do my "coroner's report" will be filled out with much less hesitation.

As I mentioned earlier, my most promising play is only "in mind" and I would like to know if you think it practical. It is a biographical play about

Vachel Lindsay but would concern, in large, the whole problem of the poet or creative artist in America or any other capitalistic state. Have you read Master's (Edgar Lee) biography of Lindsay? If you have you will know what a wealth of dramatic material his life contains. Nobody with a desire to create has ever put up a braver, more pitiful struggle against the intellectual apathy and the economic tyranny of his times! He was, as you know, for many years a tramp selling his poems for two cents - from door to door. But my play would center, I think, upon the closing chapter of his life - in Springfield, Illinois. That old yellow frame house intrigues me as a background for a poet's tragedy! The high-ceilinged rooms, the awkward, ugly furniture it must have contained - what marvelous stage sets they'd make! Then I'd weave into the plot the personality of a younger writer - some unknown like myself - who had approached Lindsay, perhaps, for confirmation and help. "To you from failing hands we throw the torch, Etc. - " (I'm "hamming" this dreadfully but I want you to get the idea!) - The play would terminate,* of course, with Lindsay's suicide - that awful, grotesque crawling upstairs on hands and knees at midnight! - but would strike some positive, assertive note - I mean I would not want it to be just another futilitarian tragedy about a beaten-down artist.

Perhaps this would be altogether too big for me to undertake, but since my personal experiences have given me some insight into Lindsay's problems, I find the idea very hard to dismiss.

Please do not feel compelled to rush answers to these effusions of mine, because, frankly, you are playing a very long shot when you take an interest in my work anyway. And I know, whether I hear from you or not, that you are doing what you can to promote my scripts and I'm extremely grateful for it.

Sincerely,

P.S. Please <u>do</u> submit whatever you think advisable to the Rockefeller foundation. How about my other long plays, SPRING STORM and NOT ABOUT NIGHTINGALES? As far as I know, they are still with Miss Thacher - unless she's sent them to my mother in St. Louis. Here in California I have no material but what I'm working on - should I write some kind of letter or application to the Committee?

Tennessee Williams

* Page 361 - Master's <u>Lindsay</u>

[TW's attraction to Nicholas Vachel Lindsay was rooted in the literary lore of St. Louis. A native of nearby Springfield, Illinois, Lindsay had courted the St. Louis-born poet Sara Teasdale, and his "awful" death in 1931 (he drank Lysol) may have contributed to her own depression and suicide two years later. To these well-known facts the Masters biography (*Vachel Lindsay: A Poet in America*, 1935) added a domestic history not easily lost upon TW: ill-matched parents and a frail, bookish son who was more his mother's than his father's child. Described by Masters as "an American story of the first importance," Vachel Lindsay's tragic life united the personal and social instances of the poet in a way that TW found inspiring.]

109. To Audrey Wood

[General Delivery
Laguna Beach, California]
[ca. June 25, 1939]
[TLS, 1 p. HRC]

Dear Miss Wood:

I'm almost deliriously happy with the news of STORY'S acceptance, since, as I've told you, I hitched my wagon to that star at the very inception of my writing career but had lately given up all hope of landing there. Well, I thank devoutly whatever accounts for my good luck in bringing us together as that accident seems to have had an effect on my fortunes directly opposite to that incurred by the wanton shooting of an albatross at sea!

I should be delighted to return the signed agency agreement if I had ever received it but it was either lost in the mail or was not enclosed in the letter you mention as I haven't seen hide nor hair of it. I have moved, you know, to Laguna Beach, Calif., so it is quite possible some of my mail addressed to Hawthorne has not reached me. The additional "American Blues" sketches you mention are <u>existent</u> - that, however, is about the best that can be said for most of them, as they are mainly in the first draft and were not bound with the others because they did not seem ready for professional consideration. I am slowly adding, however, to these dramatic cross-sections and will send you new installments from time to time. The old ones listed on the frontispiece are all packed away among my <u>Mss.</u> in St. Louis and the next time I pass through there I'll see what I can excavate in the way of finished scripts. Did you get the scripts I sent about a week ago, entitled "<u>The Vine</u>" and "<u>Death is the Drummer</u>"?

The twenty-five dollars looms quite large in my own perspective - in fact on the strength of it I'm having my typewriter repaired and am planning a trip to Frisco to see Wm. Saroyan and the World's Fair! I hope they're sincere about the early publication - I'll be waiting with bated breath.

I filled out an application for a Rockefeller fellowship mentioning the Vachel Lindsay play as work in prospect. The many grotesque elements in Lindsay's character, such as his purity complex, his indiscriminate missionary zeal and childish preoccupation with fairies and flowers make him a very complex and difficult subject for a psychological drama - perhaps you feel it is not a practical undertaking. In that case I hope you will let me know.

Sincerely, Tennessee Williams

[With "The Field of Blue Children," TW breached "the invincible fortress" of *STORY* magazine and profusely thanked the editor Whit Burnett: "I only want to say there are a great many circumstances in my present life which make this encouragement extremely opportune and I want to add my personal thanks to Miss Wood's" (June 25, 1939, Princeton).

"The Vine," a story about an actor's fading career and his wife's devotion, is related to a play idea described in letter #114. "Death is the Drummer" is an alternate title for the one-act play "Me, Vashya!"

TW hitchhiked to "Frisco" in early-July and visited the Golden Gate Exposition, but he did not meet William Saroyan at this time. His interest in Saroyan dated from the mid 1930s and was piqued no doubt by his recent Broadway debut as the author of *My Heart's in the Highlands* (1939). The play was produced by the Group Theatre on April 13 and criticized for its gossamer quality, further reasons for TW to feel kinship with Saroyan.]

110. To Audrey Wood

General Delivery
Laguna Beach, Calif.
July 16, 1939
[TLS w/ autograph addition, 2 pp. HRC]

Dear Miss Wood:

I received your letter of July 11 but the contracts have not yet come. I visited the pigeon ranch Friday and they were not there either so I suspect they've been lost - will be very glad to sign and return them when they reach me.

Very good of you to bear the typing expense for a while - it seems remarkably small but even so would more than obliterate my present funds. I'm busy preparing another <u>American Blues</u> sketch, this one contributing a coast-town bar-room to the gallery of American scenes that I'm trying to accumulate. Should be ready to mail in a few days.

I have shelved the Lindsay idea for a much more compelling impulse to dramatize D.H. Lawrence's life in New Mexico. I feel a far greater affinity for Lawrence than Lindsay and the elements of his life here in America are so essentially dramatic that they require little more than a re-arrangement to be transferred directly to the stage. Should I inform the Rockefeller foundation of my changed plans? - Probably not. I intend to run down to Taos, New Mexico, on my thumb before long - I understand Frieda Lawrence still lives down there, also Mabel Dodge Luhan and possibly Dorothy Brett who were intimates of Lawrence during this period. I want to take some pictures and absorb the atmosphere of the place and then start right to work if circumstances permit.

I'm also considering the possibility of spending some time in New York this Fall as I've never been really exposed to the professional theatre. I think I'd learn some craftsmanship - (badly needed) - by attending a lot of Broadway plays. Perhaps I could find some employment in New York that would make this possible. I probably would have gravitated that way sooner except that I don't like the crumby sort of Bohemian studio life that an impecunious writer is subjected to in a large city - I got too much of that in the "Vieux Carre" and it's taken five months of California sunlight to fumigate my soul. Also it is impossible to starve in rural California, with so many orchards and truck farms - though you can get an awful nostalgia for proteins - In New York I don't know. Somehow I think it is more dignified to climb a fence and steal avocados than to stand outside a soup kitchen. What is happening to the poor writers fired off the WPA? God help them. A play should be written about their dilemma! - Gosh, that's an idea! - Maybe I <u>could</u> write a play about writers on the WPA - I've known lots of them - Jack Conroy, J.S. Balch - some of them are among my best friends. . . .

I don't like novels - they seem purely esthetic, not <u>living</u> as plays are - (this in confidence!) - but I have several ideas for short novels and the temptation to wallow in words may some day impell me to write one. Do you market verse? I have a great mass of it, both modern and traditional, short and long, which I've only used so far as a lining for chiffonier drawers.

Miss Fishbein wrote me, dated June 25, "I have recently had a <u>request</u> for American Blues. Why it was sent to me I do not know, for I have surely not stated to anyone that I was representing you." - Do you suppose this request is fictitious or real? Probably the former - The letter just now reached me, being addressed to Hawthorne and of course I will write her at once that this is out of the question since you are now handling my plays. It is too bad she didn't state who made the request - but it sounds quite improbable anyhow. . . .

In a few weeks I can probably send you a scene-by-scene outline of the proposed Lawrence play.

I regret the rambling course of this letter.

Thanks for the encouraging message from Burnett.

Very truly yours, Tennessee Williams

IMPORTANT ADDENDA - Just this moment received following from Ann M. Paine of Dramatists' Guild. Quote: "On behalf, Etc., if you would be so kind as to send the Committee Mss. of two or three plays that you have written. Com. feels it would be in better position to pass upon your application if it had this further material. Would like to know in addition when these plays were written." - I will tell them that you are in possession of my play scripts and you can send them what you think best. All of my play scripts have been written in the last three years in the following order - Cairo, Shanghai, Bombay! (an undistinguished farce) - Candles to the Sun, Fugitive Kind, Spring Storm, Not About Nightingales - American Blues scattered throughout period and still in progress. ~~If you think more specific dates are demanded you might approximate them at random. I covered this information specifically in my application.~~ I have given dates in letter to Miss Paine.

[The "coast-town bar-room" reappeared as a dramatic setting in *Small Craft Warnings* (1972), including a character who resembles the nomadic Tennessee. With such a "gallery of American scenes," he struck the documentary note of the 1930s by attempting to unearth "the real America."

Audrey Wood's noncommittal reply (July 11, 1939, HRC) to "the Lindsay idea" had probably confirmed TW's doubts about the project. All that apparently remain are a one-page scenario entitled "Springfield, Illinois" (n.d., HRC) and the brief fragmentary play draft "Suitable Entrances to Springfield or Heaven" (n.d., Delaware). Neither has a hint of the social dimension that TW envisioned.

"Read from D.H. Lawrences letters {in the 1932 Viking edition compiled by Aldous Huxley} and conceived a strong impulse to write a play about him - his life in America - feel so much understanding & sympathy for him - though his brilliance makes me feel very humble & inadequate" (*Journal*, July 6, 1939). Frieda, Lawrence's wife, and Mabel Dodge Luhan, the patron who had invited the Lawrences to America in 1922, still lived in the Taos area, as did the Hon. Dorothy Brett, a deaf painter and English gentlewoman who was a persistent follower of the Lawrences.

TW remarked on the novel in reply to Wood's inquiry: "Have you any novel in prospect since Story Magazine has, as perhaps you know, a publishing tie-up with Harper's and would be interested in seeing whatever long fiction work of yours is coming along at this time" (July 11, 1939, HRC). Wood added in a following letter that she did not "handle" poetry: "You will have to fight the good fight on this yourself" (July 24, 1939, HRC).

Wood soon delivered *Fugitive Kind*, *Spring Storm*, *American Blues*, and *Not About Nightingales* to the Dramatists' Guild in support of TW's grant to the Rockefeller Foundation. The Guild, an affiliate of the Authors' League of America, administered the awards for the Foundation.]

111. *To Clark Mills*

[General Delivery
Laguna Beach, California]
[ca. mid-July 1939]
[TLS, 2 pp. HTC]

Dear Clark:

Mother writes that you are in St. Louis and that you were surprised to learn of my being in this remote corner of the civilized world. I believe the last communication I received from you, Professor McBurney, was a picture of a fat monk running upstairs with a bottle and beneath or behind this cryptic symbol some reference to my planned departure for New Orleans. Well, lots of water has run under the mill since then & I shan't attempt to describe it all. The important fact (or relatively important) is that I plan to leave here within the next week or two & am wondering if you are or will be still in St. Louis as that information would help me decide whether to actually go <u>there</u> or stop off some place on the way. I should have gotten my fill of strange places by now, having been so many since last winter, but yet I feel a curious lack of nostalgia for the parental roof.

Right now I'm in a little artists' colony on the South Coast known as Laguna Beach. Live in a little cabin two miles up a canyon from the town - which I share with a young fellow from Lake George, New York, who is the amazing combination of highschool English teacher, saxophone player and prospective movie actor. The life here is too perfect. The weather is invariably fine, there is nothing to do but write or lie around all morning & swim & lie around on the beach all afternoon and make a round of the village taverns at night. At first I was enchanted with this mode of existence: then it became a bit monotonous and now, finally, it has become quite unendurable. My social <u>milieu</u> is amazing - a bunch of jitterbugs and beach-combers and frantic week-enders! There is a famine of intellectual contacts out here.

I have had some good fortune, however. Through winning a GROUP THEATRE prize I acquired a very fine agent in New York, Miss Audrey Wood, and she has placed two of my stories with STORY magazine - (pay on publication, alas!) - and is trying to get me a Rockefeller fellowship for work on a new long play. I'm going to attempt a dramatic biography of D.H. Lawrence - his life in New Mexico. Do you know much about him? - A tremendously fascinating personality! - I want to stop off a short while in Taos, New Mexico on my way East to contact some of his friends there & get the background for the work.

Excuse me for writing such a tedious, factual letter. I am very tired, exhausted, have been writing all day as I have become all of a sudden so nauseated with the town & the beach that I could not drag myself out even for the afternoon dip.

I go everyplace on my thumb out here. Plan to go home that way as when I've settled various debts and gotten my more essential property out of pawn I won't have bus-fare left. Went up to Frisco on my thumb & saw the Golden Gate Exposition a couple of weeks ago. It is a very amusing and adventurous kind of travel.

This appeal for a letter is really urgent. Do you know I plan to spend next Fall in New York? Perhaps we could go East together. . . .

Best regards, Tom

[Clark Mills had completed his first year of teaching at Cornell and would soon return for a second.

TW's journal confirms the rapid exhaustion of Laguna Beach as a seaside refuge. By late-June the "perfect young animal" was feeling his "<u>normal</u> self again - full of neurotic fears, a sense of doom, a dreadful lifeless weight on . . . heart and body" (*Journal*, June 25, 1939). The summer's artistic work, apparently slight, was often impeded by "lassitude" and "nervous exhaustion," and in looking ahead, TW could see himself adding his own "peculiar note to the bedlam of a mad-house" (*Journal*, July 6, 1939). The patient and generous Jim Parrott could not relieve his friend's intellectual "famine" or loneliness.]

112. To Edwina Dakin Williams

[General Delivery
Laguna Beach, California]
Thursday [July 20, 1939]
[TLS, 2 pp. HRC]

Dear Mother:

This week has gone by in a flash and I just now realize that I haven't written to acknowledge your last letter and the checque. I've had a lot of other correspondence to take care of and some urgent writing. It looks like my Laguna period is drawing to a close quite rapidly as Jim has decided to go to Pasadena where he can work in the theater and it will be too expensive for me to remain here alone. So I will be ready to leave here at almost any time. Until this week Jim was planning to tour back East in his car the end of the month or the middle of August, but now his theatrical ambitions have decided him to remain out West indefinitely so I shall have to find some other means of transportation. I went to Frisco and back on my thumb - hitch-hiking - but rather uncertain about getting as far as St. Louis that way. As you can see by the enclosed letter from the Dramatists' Guild, they are considering my application right now and I may get some money from them before long. However I have no way of knowing when that will be. Also Mr. Burnett of STORY has accepted another short story. The first one will be published the end of August and the second about four or five months later. They want me to write them a novel as they have publishing affiliations with HARPERS & BROS. but I am absorbed in a play about D.H. LAWRENCE - I hope to go through Taos, New Mexico on my way home where Lawrence lived and meet his widow who is still living there.

Is Grand still in St. Louis? I hope so as I don't want to miss her. Too bad you don't have one of us to drive you around - I'll try to make up for it when I get home. What is Dakin's address in Colorado? I will drop him a card if I go through there on my way home. I would like to stay here longer as I love the West Coast but without a regular income it is too difficult. I regret to say that I had to borrow a few dollars on my suitcase this week to buy groceries - had to pay rent, you know, which put me "behind the eight ball".

I was glad to get Mr. Campbells' letter, though I don't think much could be accomplished through a meeting with Jimmie Fiddler. I might enjoy meeting him though.

Hope everyone is well.

With much love, Tom.

P.S. I will probably send things home in boxes as I have too much stuff for my two suitcases, neither of which is very large. If you have a capacious cardboard box there you might mail it to me with the summer suit that I could wear on the road - however that isn't necessary if it would be inconvenient.

[Before Edwina's "checque" arrived, TW was "really in financial hot water" and with a "Heigh-ho!" (*Journal*, ca. July 15, 16, 1939) had resigned himself to hocking his valise for rent and food. The "urgent writing" was not the D.H. Lawrence play but probably a one-act entitled "Intimations of Mortality."

It was not until 1945 that Whit Burnett published a second story by TW: "The Important Thing."

TW's guilty allusion to family was preceded by a similar journal entry containing the summer's only reference to Rose Williams: "God must remember and have pity some day on one who loved as much as her little heart could hold - & more! Why should you be there, little Rose? And me, here?" Thoughts of Rose led to Grand and TW ended the passage by blessing his "dear 'Two Roses'" (ca. July 10, 1939). Dakin Williams, eager for law school, was taking summer courses at the University of Colorado to hasten graduation.

W. Ed Campbell apparently knew the Hollywood reporter Jimmy Fidler and at the urging of Cornelius, a business associate, had written to him on TW's behalf. By the late 1930s Fidler's harsh film reviews and criticism of stars had made him an outcast in Hollywood and thus an unpromising advocate for TW. "Jimmy Fidler's Hollywood" was broadcast in St. Louis on KMOX.

Edwina forwarded this letter to her parents, adding a note that Cornelius was sending money to Sam Webb for TW's bus trip home, including a stop at Taos. The Lawrence project, one suspects, was not welcome news to Edwina. Her "purges" of indecent books, wryly noted by TW in later correspondence (see letter #128), were continued by Amanda in *The Glass Menagerie* (1945) with Lawrence as the chief offending writer.]

113. To Frieda Lawrence

Gen. Delivery
Laguna Beach, Calif.
July 29, 1938
[TLS, 1 p. HRC]

Dear Mrs. Lawrence:

Writing this letter is rather insane as I have no idea of your exact address, I am only vaguely persuaded that you are still living in New Mexico, in the vicinity of Taos. Briefly, I am a young writer who has a profound admiration for your late husband['s] work and has conceived the idea, perhaps fantastic, of writing a play about him, dramatizing not so much his life as his ideas or philosophy which strike me as being the richest expressed in modern writing.

I am now associated as a playwright with the GROUP THEATRE in New York, having recently received their national award for young dramatists, and have had plays produced in several large Middle-western cities, stories in STORY magazine, and a good deal of verse published. My New York agents are Leibling-Wood, Inc, 30 Rockefeller Plaza, in case you should wish to direct some enquiries about me. Frankly they have advised me against undertaking this play because of your possible opposition. However it doesn't seem likely to me that you would oppose it. I have read your deeply moving biography "Not I But The Wind" and am convinced that you would be entirely sympathetic toward any work undertaken to advance the world's knowledge and appreciation of your husband's genius. Provided, of course, that it accorded with your personal knowledge of facts.

I am leaving California in a few days and will pass through Taos on my way East. I'm writing to know if a meeting could be arranged between us.

Could you let me know by return mail? Excuse the abruptness of this. Geographically my life has been very much like your husband's - nomadic, restless, uncertain.

Even without this project in mind I should enjoy meeting and talking with you tremendously.

Sincerely, Tennessee Williams

[TW wrote to Frieda Lawrence (1879-1956) with Audrey Wood's warning in mind: "Mrs. Lawrence still lives and breathes in New Mexico" and "would be more than extremely difficult about a play concerning her husband" (July 24, 1939, HRC). His "admiration" for Lawrence was not feigned, but in striking the note of "genius," he adroitly echoed Frieda's view of her husband: "When I met other writers, then I knew without knowing how different altogether Lawrence was. They may have been good writers, but Lawrence was a genius" (*Not I, But the Wind*, 1934).

This letter, misdated and rife with exaggerated claims, clearly belongs to correspondence of 1939.]

114. To Audrey Wood

[General Delivery
Laguna Beach, California]
July 30, 1939
[TL, 4 pp. HRC]

Dear Miss Wood:

I'm experiencing quite a recrudescence of creative energy right now, writing so hard the past week or so that I haven't even gone down to the beach & suffered a badly bruised kneecap at the bowling alley (where I'm a pin-boy) as a result of "goofing off" (as the boss calls it) about a new play instead of elevating my limbs at the critical moment when the ball makes a strike.

Well, I am rather steamed up about the possibility of making a solid three-act out of a one-act that I have been working on. I have always wanted to write a <u>compact</u> drama instead of the rambling affairs I've done so far, one that adheres to the Greek unities of time, place, action. That is mainly why this idea intrigues me so much - and then it exercises a strong emotional pull (on me) because of the beauty & pathos of the characters & situation. Here it is - but please try to look beyond the hasty, hammy style in which this synopsis is written!

The play takes place during the course of July 4th in a cheap apartment at Long Beach, California. Mrs. Jonathan Melrose is dying of a lingering illness (cancer?), her husband has gone out to get drunk. They have no children, they live alone in a little 2 or 3 room flat. Both of them are fugitives from life. They live in the glorious expectations of the past. When Jonathan was young he was the golden-haired 'glamor boy' of a small lake town in northern New York. He was <u>the</u> <u>one</u> person of whom <u>great</u> things were expected. He had all kinds of talent, played beautifully on the saxophone and took leads in all the class-plays and was President of practically everything - yet because of his personal charm nobody was jealous of him, it was just the accepted, inevitable thing that Jon. should take first place in everything. Through his exalted ego, he lived in a rosy world of illusion, way, way out of this world - almost as though under the influence of a narcotic! - On the other hand IDA (later his wife) was rather plain, a shy, sensitive girl who wrote verse. She has a mad, hopeless devotion for Jon whose popularity is such that [he] is almost unaware of her existence. The two of them go off to college[,] the only ones out of the town's 300 population who go that year. At college the glorious myth of Jonathan begins to collapse. He doesn't do so well there, only gets a minor part in the dram. clubs presentations & his saxophone is considered slightly too corny for the collegiate dance band. He gets panicky with this strange & sudden reversal - begins to drink. But IDA is the only one that knows of his decline. She worships him - in order to enlist her in the conspiracy to preserve the legend of his grandeur back home, he begins to go out with her. They have both now begun their life-long construction of fables about Jonathan in letters to people back home. At the end of the year they are married & go west where it is understood back home that Jon will be a rising star in motion pictures. Success doesn't come so easily & Jon's panic is given an added momentum. His life slips more & more from <u>reality to legend</u>. From now on he lives almost entirely in the long, marvelous letters that are written back home. At first Jon writes them, then he gets 'Too busy with his picture work' & the task falls to IDA - she undertakes it with a devoted zeal & everyone knows back home about the really big things Jon is doing out here on the other side of the continent. This illusion is fairly safe since nobody in the lake town ever travels further than Albany or Glen Falls. - But Jon's actual business is mostly in bars. He picks up free drinks jamming on his sax & exercising the rather tawdry charm which hangs over from his youth. So fifteen years pass in this way - the legend back home is never allowed to grow dim - & we come to the point where the play begins, July 4 of this year - Jon out getting drunk, Ida suddenly stricken & dying. (All of the preceding is antecedant action, slowly unravelled through Ida's conversations with the neighborhood who gather about her like buzzards at the smell of death - these women act rather like a Greek chorus - that is, in their dramatic function) - In the first short scene she is discovered after a sleepless night (JON out) trying to straighten things up a little before he gets home. She collapses & the neighbor puts her to bed. The neighbor's daughter Thelma comes in - dressed for a beach-party - the talk is very trivial and gay and fire-crackers are popping [in] the alley below & there are shrill children's voices & the blare of radios from every window. - Ida asks for a sheet of writing paper & starts to compose her last glorious letter upon the legend of Jonathan - End of Act One. Act II - Mid-afternoon - Jonathan still out on his binge, Ida gradually slipping off into the past - She wanders deliriously in her talk to Mrs. Kramer, the neighbor-woman, who has come to watch her die. The tragic beautiful picture of her life's consecration to the myth of Jonathan comes out. His weakness, his failure have only deepened her love which has shut out all the rest of the world, even a desire for children that never came. Mrs. Jansen upstairs - who used to be a practical nurse - can see the poor woman is dying and so a search is organized for her husband, neighborhood bars are combed - but without success. At the end of this Act IDA realizes herself that she is dying - She begins a dramatic contest with time, a desperate struggle to hold on till Jon gets home - 'It would be so awful, him coming back and not finding her there!' - During the search of the bars a stranger overheard Jonathan's name - He wonders if this could be the Jonathan Melrose of Lake St. George where he used to live, who came out here about fifteen years ago and made a spectacular success as an executive in the motion pictures? - No, probably not - But he decides to investigate - So he goes to the address & calls from the walk below - 'Do some people name Melrose from Lake St. George live anywheres around here?' - IDA catches this & is terrified, dumbstruck - all she can think of for a moment is preserving the legend - 'No, no,' she whispers, 'for God's sake, tell him no! Tell him he's got the wrong party!' - This is done - 'I didn't think so,' calls back the stranger, 'I must have made a mistake.' Still not quite satisfied, he leaves for a while. - Ida wonders who it is - must be somebody from back home who has finally come to investigate the legend - Where is Jon? Jon must be warned - What's happened to him? - She lapses into coma & the neighborhood-women decide to summon an ambulance from the city-hospital. END OF ACT TWO. - ACT III. - It is dark & there is a beautiful fireworks display on the beach - You can see the rockets bursting through a maze of chimeneys & fire-escapes & roofs out the back window. IDA comes [out] of her sleep & her head is clear. Learns that the ambulance is coming to remove her - engages in a panicky struggle against it - She has got to hang on here till Jon gets home - The women marvel at her tenacious devotion. - Don't she realize a man like that don't give a goddam for anything but a bottle? - Here another legend is built up around Jon - but in the opposite direction - To the neighbor-women he is a monstrous symbol of male selfishness & cruelty & license - and it will serve him to come home & find his wife gone for good. - The ambulance comes & IDA is taken away, sobbing, still weakly struggling. The flat is left empty. There is a weird flicker of light from fireworks across the dark, ugly furniture & children scream distantly at play in the alleys - 'Fly, Sheepie, fly! Etc.' SHORT BLACKOUT OR CURTAIN. Act III - Sc. 2 - Late that night about two A.M. - Jonathan comes home - he has been on a two day binge, oblivious to everything - Finding Ida gone, he calls her - first querulously, then alarmed, then starts bawling her name out in terror - A neighbor-woman comes to the door - Like one of the Fatal Sisters in her long grey flannel robe - 'Where's Ida?' - 'Gone. She took a bad turn this morning and she had to be removed.' - 'Where?' - 'The city-hospital.' - 'Hospital?' - 'Yes. But she died before she got there.' —— Jonathan is stunned and the neighbor begins to reproach - 'Nobody around here is going to have much sympathy for you, Mr. Melrose. Your actions have been a source of gossip all over the neighborhood & it would probably be a very good thing if you was to find some new place to live after this.' (She starts to leave - turns at the door) - 'Oh, yes, there was a man that heard 'em calling your name at the bar - says he known you a long time ago in your old home town in New York - Benson or Bassett or something - he come around here several times

& he seemed to be absolutely dumbfounded to learn what the situation was here and about your wife dying and all. He said if he didn't get to see you to tell you how sorry he was - Bassett or Babcock or - something.' - The woman goes out. Jonathan is left alone in the room with two deaths, the death of Ida, the final death of his legend. - However it is Ida's name that he cries aloud in his ultimate grief. He crouches slowly beside the empty bed & covers his face in the crumpled sheets which still have the faint, sad smell of sickness and death - Fireworks from the beach make a fitful glow through the open window, the white curtains stir softly inward as the last curtain falls.

Soooooo! - I hope you will let me have a reaction to this before I procede in earnest. I have thought of calling it 'Death of a Legend' or 'Death: Celebration' - or possibly something less mordant as the real theme of the play is not death but <u>devotion</u> - rather similar to the theme of my short story 'The Vine'. - With its emphasis on atmosphere & character-touches, it should be the sort of thing for which I have a particular facility - Do you think the plot is strong enough to support a long play? Of course one's conception always enlarges during the period of actual writing. . . .

Sincerely,

P.S. - Who is this female of the canine species whose note you enclosed? Her clinical observations about 'some sort of psychological break' in the writer's personality were not very gratefully received. I've always expected to go nuts some day, but did not know it had happened already - This Barker is the first raven! - - - -

GOOD FORTUNE SMILES! - I have been offered a ride to St. Louis by way of TAOS, NEW MEXICO, where I can see Frieda & discover whether or not she is the ogre that you suspect her of being. I have always gotten along rather well with female ogres - so - I don't expect to write a Lawrence play <u>next</u> but am not willing to shelve the idea permanently just because his wife is still living. You are right about the WPA situation I suppose.

I will leave here in about a week or ten days - Send you a card at time of departure with a new mailing address. Thanks for showing my scripts to the GUILD & the other good work you are doing.

[The "Death of a Legend" scenario was based partly upon Jim Parrott's career, especially his desire to be "a rising star in motion pictures." Both the subplot of investigation and disclosure and Jonathan's "bawling" for his wife prefigure key scenes in *A Streetcar Named Desire*. TW's "quiet desperation" in late-July bespeaks the approach of summer's end and is reflected perhaps in the framing of Jonathan's dramatic situation: both have felt "the dreadful heavy slipping by of the days" (*Journal*, July 30, 1939) of their youth.

The "Barker" of "the canine species" is perhaps the same Margaret Barker mentioned in letters #128 and #149. An original member of the Group Theatre, she briefly left the stage in the late 1930s and appears to have taken an editorial or production position. Of the stories circulated by Audrey Wood at this time, "The Dark Room" is a likely source for Barker's "clinical observations" upon TW.

A briefer draft of this letter, dated July 29, 1939, is held by the Columbia University Library.]

115. To Cornelius Coffin Williams

[General Delivery
Laguna Beach, California]
[ca. early-August 1939]
[TLS, 2 pp. HRC]

Dear Dad:

I missed Sam's visit Sunday and was a little late receiving your letter due to the fact I have been spending some time in Pasadena attending the Maxwell Anderson Drama festival and visiting some studios in Hollywood. I just got back this morning and was very grateful for your letter and the money. I plan to leave here this week end - have to wait a few days to wind up some correspondance and await answers to letters I have written to people I want to meet in Taos, get a few clothes cleaned and my stuff packed. I have several possible sales for the bicycle - it's greatly depreciated in value due to constant use so I probably won't realize much on any transaction. I'm writing Sam to apologize for my absence and I presume he'll mail the money to me here as I can catch the bus directly from this point with only forty cents additional charge which will save taking all my stuff into L.A. I've accumulated more than I can hold in the two small grips so I am packing a box which I will either send freight or express.

I will spend a few days in Taos getting the background and informa-

tion I need and interviewing a few residents there. I'm sure it will be helpful and pleasant to meet Mr. Gusdorf there and I will get in touch with him
upon my arrival.

I will write you all the exact time to expect me when I leave here or
reach Taos.

I greatly appreciate the money and the trouble you've taken, and am
certainly glad that my return will coincide with Aunt Ella's visit.

With love, Tom

[Leverich doubts the truth of TW's itinerary. On Sunday, July 30, TW reportedly
hid while Sam Webb waited for several hours at the cabin. Webb wrote to Cornelius
(July 31, 1939, HRC) of his visit and added that he had left ten dollars and a note
for TW informing him that his father's check (sixty dollars) for travel had arrived.
TW did not, however, fabricate the Maxwell Anderson "festival" at the Pasadena
Playhouse, June 26 to August 19, and may have attended performances at the time
in question.

Alex Gerson Gusdorf, a prominent merchant and cultural figure in Taos, was
a regional salesman for the International Shoe Co. and another of the contacts that
Cornelius arranged for his son.]

116. To Audrey Wood

[General Delivery
Laguna Beach, California]
August 7, 1939
[TLS, 2 pp. HRC]

Dear Miss Wood:

Your letter regarding Mr. Knopf caught me almost at the moment of
departure for Taos. Of course I am very anxious to meet him but it is now
Monday P.M., I haven't heard from him yet and the situation here makes it
extremely difficult for me to wait around. I have given up my work at the
bowling alley and my time in the cabin is expired so I shall have to get in
contact with this gentleman very speedily if at all. If there is nothing in the
afternoon mail I will either phone him or write him special delivery explaining the necessity for quick action if he wishes to see me. My reactions to the
possibility of studio employment are rather confused. Pleased and excited,

yes, but also a little worried. Would getting this work preclude my chances of a Rockefeller scholarship? Naturally a year of independant writing would do me more good than hack writing for a film company. The energies of a writer are limited and it seems to me should be conserved as far as possible for worth-while objects. - I think I can trust your judgement in this matter so if anything comes of the "contact", please advise me frankly of what you think best. I would love to see the inside of Hollywood, it would certainly open a new social vista which might compensate even for temporary creative extinction. Not to mention the charms of a pay-check....

I have no doubt the contracts are perfectly satisfactory. I will get them off either in this letter or the next day or two. Will advise you by air-mail when I leave & my next mailing address, probably General Delivery at Taos, New Mex. I'm going there mainly to break up the painful descent from seacoast to Mississippi Valley. When I get to St. Louis will confine myself to an attic for a couple of months with typewriter & victrola & get the long play done which I outlined in my last letter. What did you think of its possibilities? -

It is marvelous what you are doing for me - I think it would surprise you a little to know the fabulous image that you have projected on my little cave of consciousness out here.

Cordially, Tennessee Williams

[Edwin Knopf represented the Samuel Goldwyn interests in Hollywood. In an earlier letter to TW (August 1, 1939, HRC), Audrey Wood explained that Knopf had been advised by Bertram Bloch, Goldwyn's eastern representative and a client of Liebling-Wood, to consider him for a writing job at the studio. TW later confided to Edwina that he "would like to work for one of the studios for a short time just for the experience - but of course I could demand a bigger salary after I'd had some success in New York." Wood's primary motive, he thought, was to get a "rake off" (Thursday Morning {August 10, 1939} HRC) on his salary by arranging a Hollywood job for him.]

117. *To Audrey Wood*

General Delivery
[Taos, New Mexico]
Wed. Nite [August 16, 1939]
[TLS, 2 pp. HRC]

Dear Miss Wood:

I waited a week to hear from Knopf and then had to leave Laguna Beach as I had given up my work there and my rent had expired. There was simply nothing to do but leave. I wrote a letter to him explaining my situation and suggesting that if he wished to see me he should make an appointment at his earliest convenience. But I didn't hear from him until today when his secretary's letter was forwarded to me, here at Taos. Now I don't know what to do. If the possibility of getting work there is sufficiently strong I'd be quite willing to return to the Coast - though how I'd manage it financially is again quite perplexing! The letter merely stated that he would be willing to see me at any time during the week. . . .

I've been very lucky making contacts here. I met the poet Witter Bynner in Santa Fe, an intimate of Lawrence's, who had just returned from a joint birthday celebration with Frieda. He was very cordial and gave me letters of introduction to nearly everyone here, such as the Honorable Dorothy Brett, Mabel Dodge Luhan, Spud Johnson & of course Frieda. It seems she is not at all unapproachable, in fact she has just gotten a new boy-friend, an Italian army officer, and is very much on the qui vive - I have a ride out there tomorrow to meet her. As I said, I don't mean to write the Lawrence play next but thought I had better get the background and material for it while I am out here. However I don't like it here. Frankly these people are like the country - which is like a dead planet, the moon! - They have a brilliance but it is not living. Whatever was living in them must have died with Lawrence - anyway it is certainly dead. They are a bunch of tired esthetes. Hollywood would be better - at least there is a commotion in Hollywood, an atmosphere of life!

(Perhaps I am just a little bit blue)

I don't think I will be here much more than four or five days. But you can reach me here General Delivery within that period if you wish to advise or direct me concerning Mr. Knopf. Then I'll head on to St. Louis. I have some completed short scripts that I will mail you as soon as I get more stabilized geographically. You haven't mentioned the play I outlined in my last letter.

I sent the signed contract - WOW! I'm still slightly punch-drunk from all that legal phraseology.

Very truly yours, Tennessee Williams

[Witter Bynner, a native of Brooklyn, New York, and a graduate of Harvard, settled in Santa Fe in the early 1920s and became a well-known poet of the region. No "intimate" of D.H. Lawrence, he resented being cast as the effete American socialist Owen Rhys in *The Plumed Serpent* (1926) and retaliated in his memoir, *Journey with Genius* (1951). For Edwina's benefit TW may have embellished his reception in Santa Fe, claiming to have spent the night as a guest in Bynner's "palatial estate" (n.d., HRC).

Willard "Spud" Johnson had studied under Bynner at the University of California and joined him in Santa Fe in the early 1920s before moving to Taos. He was also caricatured in *The Plumed Serpent* as Rhys's young friend Villiers. "Spud puzzles me, intrigues me a little" (August 20, 1939), TW wrote in the journal.

Frieda Lawrence's "new boy-friend" was Angelo Ravagli, an officer whom she met in Italy in 1925 and married many years later. It was he who transferred Lawrence's ashes to Taos amid seriocomic circumstances.

TW wrote at least three plays about Lawrence, but only one followed his original plan to dramatize Lawrence's life in New Mexico (see letter #110). "A Panic Renaissance in the Lobos Mountains" is a sexual farce in which Lorenzo, a garrulous reincarnation of Pan, is pursued by the adoring women of Taos, including figures based upon Mabel Dodge Luhan, Dorothy Brett, and "a rather exquisite female poet from, say, Chicago" (n.d., HRC)—perhaps a coy reference to Harriet Monroe. TW's glancing reference to the play's title in 1943 (see letter #261) may suggest a later date of composition.

TW's description of the art colony at Taos as "a dead planet, the moon!" adapts phrasing that Lawrence had used in a letter to Dorothy Brett (March 8, 1927). (Audrey Wood probably did not know that it had also been used as a provisional title for *Vieux Carré*.) TW followed Lawrence in dismissing the "tittle-tattle" (as Lawrence put it in 1924) of the "tired esthetes" of Taos.

Wood's discouraging report on the "Legend" play arrived in late-August. She noted its weak "story line," occasioned in part by the "hero's" prolonged absence from the stage, and feared that "it would emerge much more an emotional monologue than a full-bodied play" (August 31, 1939, HRC). TW agreed and soon shelved the project in favor of "more advanced scripts" (see letter #122).]

118. To Audrey Wood

General Delivery
Taos, New Mexico
Thursday Night [August 17, 1939]
[TLS, 2 pp. HRC]

Dear Miss Wood:

I had an unhappy accident this afternoon so I am writing to enquire if STORY has paid for my story yet and if you could mail my portion of the receipts to me here at Taos. I visited the Indian pueblo and was apparently too absorbed for when I left I left without my wallet - which possibly made some redskin five or six dollars richer, but myself infinitely poorer as it put a desperate crimp in my plans. If the checque has come through, please let me have my part by return mail - otherwise, forget about it as I shall manage somehow.

The Honorable Dorothy Brett is driving me out to Frieda's ranch Saturday for a picnic. She is really nice, in fact lovely, and her adoration of Lawrence is altogether sincere and touching. She says if the play is ever written & produced - she and the whole bunch will have to move en masse to New York for rehearsals to see that Lawrence is properly portrayed! - What an amusing situation that would create. . . .

In the Harwood foundation there are first editions, autographed, of everything written by or about Lawrence & I shall be one of the foremost authorities in two or three more days!

Sorry to trouble you about my colossal earnings but the Indian atrocity this morning makes my situation rather acute - I can understand now why my Tennessee progenitors had so little affection for the varmints.

Cordially, T.W.

[The scheduled publication of "The Field of Blue Children" on August 17 may give background and timeliness to TW's claim of Indian theft. The deed migrates from "afternoon" to "morning" in the course of this letter, and in a following one to Edwina, the "five or six dollars" stolen by "the varmints" has dropped to "four" (see letter #119). The "Indian atrocity" may have been a ploy designed to expedite Audrey Wood's payment of the STORY royalty.]

119. To Edwina Dakin Williams

[General Delivery
Taos, New Mexico]
Saturday evening [August 19, 1939]
[TLS, 3 pp. HRC]

Dear Mother:

I have just returned from Frieda Lawrence's ranch in the Lobo Mts. I met the Honorable Dorothy Brett and she invited me to drive up there with her. Some people on the next ranch were giving a luncheon which I crashed. Everybody was very cordial and I had a marvelous time. Frieda Lawrence was there, we had a long talk, and afterwards she invited me up to her ranch where we went in swimming. They treated me as though I had known them all their lives, the social atmosphere around here is the nicest I've found anywhere and yet the people are by far the most important I've ever met. Frieda is accustomed to entertaining people like Marlene Dietrich and Lillian Gish and Aldous Huxley. Their names were in the guest-book a few lines above mine - she speaks familiarly of Bernard Shaw! And the Hon. Dorothy Brett, who drove me up there, is the daughter of an English Viscount and the sister of the Ranee of Sarawak, the only Anglo-Saxon Rajah. She wears a cow-boy hat and blue denim trousers and is as simple as an old shoe. Tomorrow I'm going to her studio and afterwards she is going to take me to see Mabel Dodge Luhan, a very rich and celebrated woman writer who was responsible for bringing Lawrence to America.

This is the most beautiful country I've ever seen. Some of the valleys are checkered with green and yellow fields, others are deserts. The mountains over-grown with cedars and pinons and tremendous panoramas all around them spotted with little adobe ranches. The air is very pure, the altitude about 7000. It is pretty warm during the day but the nights are cold.

I got a room here for $3.00 a week so I will probably stay the week out. I have written Audrey to send me the checque for my short story so I will have to wait till that comes before I can leave. The Indians stole four dollars from me when I visited their pueblo! But I have enough left to get along till the story checque comes.

Mr. Gusdorf the salesman's daughter and wife both work in the Harwood Foundation which is the big museum and library. They are in

"*Spud" Johnson
at Taos.*

"Spud puzzles me,
intrigues me a
little."

—TennesseeWilliams,
Journal

Mabel Dodge Luhan, Frieda Lawrence, and Dorothy Brett at Taos.

charge of it and are very cultured people. I introduced myself to them and they called up the Brett and told her I wanted to meet her. The museum was Mrs. Gusdorf's old family home - she is a descendant of Spanish first settlers and very proud and aristocratic. In the library they have everything written by or about Lawrence.

I finally got a letter from the movie man, Knopf, inviting me to see him - but it is too late now - it was forwarded from Laguna. I told him to write Audrey if he had any position for me.

Frieda Lawrence spends her winters in Hollywood and is in the cream of society there so knowing her would be very useful if I ever worked in Hollywood.

I will probably leave here about Wednesday if I hear from Audrey.

I hope Aunty is still there. Give her my love and tell her to stay till I reach St. Louis which <u>will</u> be soon in spite of the delays.

I will try to write Grand & Grandfather but you might send them this letter as I may not have a chance for several days.

With much love, Tom

[Frieda lived on a ranch seventeen miles north of Taos that she and D.H. Lawrence had shared in the mid 1920s, a gift of Mabel Dodge Luhan. His ashes were later interred there in a small chapel, and the ranch itself provided a partial setting for the novella *St. Mawr* (1925). TW used the same mountain background for "Dos Ranchos or, The Purification," a brief verse play staged and published in 1944. Contrary to reports, he did not meet Luhan at this time or later at her fashionable salon in New York (see letter #144).

The single journal entry written in Taos found TW "<u>bored</u>" and "<u>lonely</u>" after the festivities at Frieda's ranch. He dreaded "going <u>home</u>" (August 20, 1939) and missed Jim Parrott, to whom he wrote with a prescient study of his career: "It's a slow, slow, bull-dog battle that we all have to fight—Good God, How many years have I been trying to write? Since I was eleven or twelve! And maybe five years from now I will begin to be known" (Wednesday Evening, August {23} 1939; qtd. in *Tennessee Williams Literary Journal*, Spring 1989).

Maggie, wife of Alex Gusdorf, was the daughter of Smith Simpson, an aid to Kit Carson during the Civil War. After her father's death in 1916, the family property was purchased by Burt and Elizabeth Harwood, and in 1923 the Foundation was established on the grounds by Elizabeth and several other local artists. It became a department of the University of New Mexico in 1935 and currently operates as a regional art museum. Literary holdings include a few books annotated by Lawrence.

The sixty dollars that Cornelius sent had been used in part to pay debts and retrieve "essential property" from pawn before TW left California, thus his present embarrassment of funds and implicit appeal to Edwina.]

120. *To Audrey Wood*

Gen. Del.
Taos, N.M.
8/24/39
[TLS, 2 pp. HRC]

AMERICAN BLUES

(In Taos)

Brett: And then Lorenzo said, 'Mabel - '

Tennessee: (rises abruptly)

Brett: (focussing ear-trumpet)   What's the matter, where are you going?

Tennessee: (frenziedly)   I've got a luncheon engagement!

Brett: (focussing ear-trumpet)   Who with?

Tennessee: Nobody! But I can't stand to sit here and listen to you when I'm half dead of starvation!

Brett: Starvation? Incredible! - What do you mean young man?

Tennessee: My agent hasn't sent me my STORY checque yet and I'm living on my landlady's trust in human nature which was exhausted last night.

Brett: Sit down. How do you like your eggs?

Tennessee: In large quantities. - Miss Brett, I'm not going to write a play about Lawrence, I'm going to write a play about YOU! - D.H. will enter in the last act and ask where the bathroom is....

CURTAIN.

(This play has a social message)

OR MORE EXPLICITLY - if my receipts from STORY (I suppose it was published, I haven't found the magazine out here) are not yet mailed, please, oh, please send by return Air-mail. This is an arid country and I haven't quite cultivated an appetite for cactus, though they do say it makes delicious candy!

I'm enclosing a story which might be converted into a play or a short novel if you think the material is interesting enough.

When I hear from you I'm going home and live on the folks for a while till I get a play finished. Please don't be annoyed by my importunities about that money but I am in a bit of a mess right now and even the smallest funds look very imposing.

Cordially, TW

[Upon arrival in Clayton, TW found that Audrey Wood's check had been forwarded from Taos. The story completed at Taos and probably mailed to Wood at this time was entitled "Why Did Desdemona Love the Moor?" (August 1939, HRC).]

121. To Rosina Otte Dakin

SH: W. Dakin Williams
42 Aberdeen Place
Clayton, Missouri
[ca. September 8, 1939]
[TLS, 1 p. HRC]

Dear Grand:

Well, here I am back in St. Louis, at least for a while. The heat and humidity seems very enervating after the 7000 feet altitude at Taos, so I haven't much energy right now. I've spent two days sorting out my old papers and deciding what I want to send to my agent. It seems that I may have a chance to meet her personally as I have an opportunity to drive to New York the middle or latter part of September. Clark is returning to Cornell University about that time and Frances Van Metre, a girl whom he is sort of semi-engaged to, is going to drive him up there and then go on to New York City - from Ithaca where Cornell is located. They have asked me to drive along with them which is a break. Dad said at breakfast (according to Mother) that he thought it would be a good thing and would help with the money.

The letter I sent Mother and asked her to forward to you all just about contains all the news at Taos. I was entertained by nearly all the people I wanted to meet and had a marvelous time there. I went to a picnic and swimming party at Frieda Lawrence's ranch in the Lobo mountains. Just before I left I became acquainted with a famous Cleveland artist, William Eastman who is a member of the Eastman kodak family. He was traveling with a Polish baronness, Hedvig Kraikow, and since it was right at the time of the German-Polish crisis, she was very distraught and gave a big dinner party to forget her troubles - at which I was a guest. We then went to a big casino and I watched her win several hundred dollars at roulette! By the end of the evening she was quite unconcerned about the foreign situation.

Mother says we are going to drive down for you some week-end. I hope you can come back here with us.

I'm too tired to write more - I think Mother is looking well and Dakin, of course, is engrossed in his fraternity rushing and other social commitments - although he has found time to type one of my long plays for me.

With lots of love to you both, Tom

[TW arrived in Clayton ca. September 6 after being stranded for several days in Dodge City, Kansas, "the least attractive town in the U.S.A.," or so he thought.

The artist William Eastman studied and later taught at the Cleveland School of Art. The "German-Polish crisis" refers, of course, to Hitler's invasion of Poland on September 1.

Frances Van Metre and Clark Mills were not engaged.]

Tom Anne Fred Don

PART IV
1939–1940
ST. LOUIS • NEW YORK
PROVINCETOWN • MEXICO

Overleaf: Tennessee, Anne Bretzfelder, Fred Melton, and Donald Windham toasting the Theatre Guild option on Battle of Angels, *Village Barn, New York, 1940.*

122. *To Audrey Wood*

42 Aberdeen Place
Clayton, Missouri
Monday September 11, 1939
[TLS w/ autograph postscript, 2 pp. HRC]

Dear Audrey Wood:

I found your letter and the checque forwarded from Taos on my arrival here yesterday. I was stranded for quite some while in Dodge City which I would like to nominate unhesitatingly as the least attractive town in the U.S.A. I think if enough people had ever been there it could be elected by proclamation as even Iowa City, Iowa (the Athens of the middle-west) would fail to give it very much competition.

My former plans have been completcly disrupted. Instead of being here for quite a while it seems I will have to leave in about two weeks or possibly less. A Cornell professor has offered me a ride as far as Ithaca, New York. I think I may go on from there for a very brief visit to New York City in which case I will drop in your office and see what can be done about patching up some of my scripts. I have gotten a polite personal letter from your Mr. Knopf at Goldwyn's so I feel that I ought to work my way back out to the West Coast and see if [I] can't make some connections there. As far as personal matters are ever desperate, it is desperately important that I should find something to give me some measure of security as well as freedom because the present regime leaves me practically no time or cnergy for my writing. Not that the writing itself is so damned important even to me, but I seem to be slightly better at that than oil-paintings or the clarinet.

Is there any hope of the Rockefeller fellowship? They have kept an ominous silence since receiving the plays. It would be such colossal good fortune that I feel instinctively it is quite beyond the range of possibilities.

I will try to send some new short articles.

Sincerely, Tennessee Williams

P.S. Your analysis of the Legend play was very accurate - until I have solved the antecedent action problem I will procede with more advanced scripts.

[A draft letter dated September 7, 1939, (HRC) includes similar details, but the urgent tone of the later printed version suggests that the "regime" of St. Louis had quickly proven intolerable. The brief period, following eight months on the road, was one of "physical uneasiness" and a "defeatist attitude toward work." New York, TW opined, "will have to be very good to give me a new impulse & straighten my troubled self out." He planned to leave Clayton ca. September 18, regretful that he had written "practically nothing" and would meet Audrey Wood "almost empty handed" (*Journal*, September 17, 1939).

Edwin Knopf represented the West Coast interests of the film producer Samuel Goldwyn.

TW's grant application to the Rockefeller Foundation had been pending since June.

Wood's intervening letter of August 31, 1939, (HRC) had identified a structural problem in "the Legend play" (see letter #114) that would continue to plague TW and require of his characters lengthy monologues to explain "antecedent action."

This letter was written on stationery imprinted with the name (canceled) of TW's friend Clark Mills and the address (canceled) 754 Westmoreland Avenue, Clayton, Missouri.]

123. To the Williams Family

SH: Young Men's Christian Association
356 West 34th St., New York, N.Y.
Monday Night [September 25, 1939]
[ALS, 6 pp. HRC]

Dear Folks -

I'm dead tired after a day of appointments so I will just scribble a few lines. Audrey has taken me right under her wing and made a succession of dates. Today we went to the Group Theatre together and had a long conference. They are going to try to get me work that will support me here while I study the professional theatre first-hand which they think is all that I need to make me a finished dramatist. Audrey says she will try to push the Rockefeller thing through but cannot say definitely when the verdict will be delivered. Tomorrow I meet the Actors' Repertory head and a Goldwyn man. Just to get acquainted. They (Audrey & her husband) took me to dinner & theater last night and I will eat with them again tomorrow night. They have certainly been marvelous to me and I feel very ashamed of the fact that I have only made them $2.50 so far but I guess they are hoping that I will increase my earnings later on.

I've had <u>terrific</u> expenses this week, getting settled and running around so many places. Down to about five dollars. Next week I <u>may</u> have a <u>free</u> room as a friend of Clark is leaving town & offered to let me occupy his <u>apt</u>. while gone. I leave here tomorrow. But write me care of Audrey only do <u>not</u> use <u>fancy</u> stationary as my circumstances are supposed to be desperate, you know.

I haven't even had time to visit the Fair and I don't know how I manage to get around, this town is so big and confusing. I haven't decided yet whether I like it or not - it is about like Los Angeles when I first got there. A lady who is an aristocratic Kentuckian has offered to rent me a room right around the corner from Columbia University - in a very nice neighborhood - Morningside Drive - for four or five dollars a week. I may go there - she is very genteel, has a son in the university, I met her through Clark at a literary meeting.

I left my hat in Frances Van Metre's car but <u>found</u> another one here in a telephone booth - you might phone Frances to return the hat - she is at Charles Lewis' residence, I think on Swon Avenue - in Webster Groves. Mrs. McBurney can give you her number.

Feeling quite well - will let you know my address wherever I move - the room here was 75¢ a night which is too much for permanent residence.

With love, Tom

P.S. Moved today to 57 Morningside Drive (the southern lady) - Had 6 appointments in one day. Will write later. Please send rest of money by return air mail as I am getting very low.

[Audrey Wood's first impression of TW was that he "spoke with a soft Southern accent, he was young, he was enormously gifted" (*Represented by Audrey Wood*, 1981). TW remembered meeting "a very small and dainty woman with red hair, a porcelain complexion and a look of cool perspicacity in her eyes" (*Memoirs*, 1975, p. 10).

It was a demoralized Group Theatre (1931-1941) that had just returned from a summer retreat on Long Island and faced the new season, the company's ninth, without strong dramatic properties or adequate financial backing. Key actors held the lead director, Harold Clurman, responsible for the Group's stagnant collective life and seeming loss of artistic vision.

The most successful venture of the leftist Actors' Repertory Company (1935-1938) was the première of Irwin Shaw's *Bury the Dead* in 1936. When TW met with the "head" (unidentified) of the company, plans were underway to revive Shaw's anti-war play, but the project never materialized and the struggling group ceased operations. TW may first have learned of the company through its production of *200 Were Chosen* (1936) by Ellsworth Conkle, his Iowa professor.

Bertram Bloch represented the East Coast interests of Samuel Goldwyn and was also a client of Liebling-Wood.

The "Fair" is the New York World's Fair, the original reason for TW's visiting the city. Frances Van Metre is the St. Louis friend who drove TW and Clark Mills to Cornell.]

124. To Rosina Otte and Walter E. Dakin

301 W. 108th Street Apartment 6A
[New York]
Monday Night [October 2, 1939]
[TLS, 1 p. HRC]

Dear Grand & Grandfather:

I'm appalled to think how long I have been here without writing you all - over a week - but all of my time has been taken up with meeting people, keeping various appointments and getting settled. In one day I had as many as six appointments and a dinner and a cocktail party so you can see how it has been. Most of the appointments are with theatre people who would be potentially useful to me. There are several theatre groups here that are interested in my work and a production by them this winter is possible but everything is still hanging fire. It is lucky I came to New York as being on the spot to make revisions and confer with producers seems to improve the possibilities quite a bit. Audrey Wood and Molly Day Thacher of the Group Theatre both want me to stay here for the theatre season to attend plays and study the theatre and they are bending every effort to find me some kind of work. The Rockefeller fellowship thing is still undecided but Audrey expects some action on it pretty soon now. She and her husband have been lovely to me. Had me out to dinner and given me theatre tickets to several plays. I haven't had time yet to meet Edwin but I think I'll get that done early this week. I'm living in a very attractive place now. It is sort of a club for young men and women - mostly college graduates, a very select group. The rent is just $4.50 a week which [is] cheap for New York and it is located within a few blocks of Columbia university and in view of the river. It is a big apartment hotel. The rooms are nicely furnished with pianos and social rooms available.

Of course the length of time I remain will depend on how successful Audrey is in finding me some remunerative occupation. As soon as anything definite happens I will let you know. I'm about to fall asleep now so will sign off temporarily. Possibly I will drop in to see Edwin tomorrow - Mother sent me his address.

I felt awfully lonely here the first few days but in this place I'll rapidly make friends. Of course I've met loads of people through Audrey but mainly for business purposes. The prospects here are quite encouraging. Everybody seems extremely interested in my work - they call me the "Gentile Clifford Odets" which is quite a compliment in the New York theatre. Well - I will keep you informed of developments and in the meantime -

Much love to you both, Tom

[TW's present address, his third since arriving in New York ca. September 21, may be the "<u>free</u> room" mentioned in letter #123. TW soon informed Edwina that he would move again because of complaints about his "typing at night" (postmarked October 4, 1939, HRC). Presumably this move led to the Men's Residence Club cited in letter #125.

One of the more successful Broadway plays that TW attended was *The Little Foxes* (1939) by Lillian Hellman. Whether the "alleged perversion and promiscuity" of its star, Tallulah Bankhead, were "filth" or "robust natural life boiling up to the surface" (*Journal*, July 6, 1937) had been debated by TW and friends in St. Louis. He chose the latter explanation in the course of a long friendship with the fellow southerner from Alabama.

The care of Molly Day Thacher and Audrey Wood could not avert TW's feeling of isolation: "Met lots of people here but nobody does me much good. They're all so involved in their own lives. I need somebody to envelop me, embrace me, pull me by sheer force out of this neurotic shell of fear I've built around myself lately. . . . I <u>hate</u> New York - long for the Taos desert or the Pacific" (*Journal*, October 3, 1939).

The flattering image of TW as the " 'Gentile Clifford Odets' " aligned him with the principal playwright of the Group Theatre, a socially conscious writer whose recent play, *Rocket to the Moon* (1938), would prove an important source for TW.]

125. To Edwina Dakin Williams

SH: Men's Residence Club
317 West 56th Street, New York
10/15/39
[ALS, 4 pp. HRC]

Dear Mother:

I hate to leave New York just now but of course appreciate the difficulty of remaining without funds. If nothing momentous occurs this week I will probably leave about Sunday. Mr. Liebling has spoken to a friend at Macey's Dept. Store - I'm going there tomorrow and Wed. I have another interview at Harcourt-Brace. There is such a whirl of activity with the season just starting that nobody has any time to look at Mss. seriously. The Czeckoslovakian actress is in town and wants to organize a company to star herself and produce my plays. She is charming. A number of other persons are interested and we have a meeting tomorrow with Audrey. I have finished the first draft of a new play - will have to work on it a good deal longer before I show it to anyone. Met Edwin and disliked him very much as he thinks he knows it all - just like Cousin Ned - and is very stiff in his manners. Lives in Conn. and spends his spare time gardening, he says. Did not ask me to visit him there - said Dakin had invited him to St. Louis but he knew how appalled you would be if he ever accepted! I told him that southern people, on the contrary, were usually gracious to strangers!

I have got a five-dollar-a-week room here with <u>free</u> swimming pool. New York is fascinating and I'm beginning to like it very much now that I've met more people. Some friends from U. of Iowa are here in theatrical work. One is in the Czeckoslovakia group meeting tomorrow - a scene designer who has made sets for 2 recent Broadway shows. Holland wrote me from Hollywood - he has nothing to do out there and wants my prison play. I may suggest he come to N.Y. if our plans progress well.

I guess I could use about ten bucks in Washington. I will leave here about Sunday if nothing happens. You really need to <u>push</u> your own work in N.Y. The agencies are perfect mad-houses, swarming with desperate, unemployed actors. I am always ushered in ahead of everyone else - to the private office - taking precedence in Dakin's threadbare top-coat over beautiful ingenues in Mink coats, which demonstrates the value of playwrights. But naturally they even forget what scripts I have given them. They are so rushed all the time. I have gotten things moving a little but still not enough. Last year they sold "Room Service" to the movies for $250,000.00 - so you see there is money in show business. When you get to it.

Much love - Tom.

P.S. - Have Dakin get gym locker at W.U. so I can swim there.

[TW's "new play," *Battle of Angels* (1940), may have evolved from "Dead Planet, the Moon!" (January 1939, HRC), an early draft of *Vieux Carré* (1977), and was perhaps continued intermittently in the spring and summer, especially during TW's unexpectedly long stay at Taos.

Edwin Franden Dakin, son of Horace Dakin, of Hannibal, Missouri, and great nephew to Walter E. Dakin, was the author of *Mrs. Eddy: The Biography of a Virginal Mind* (Scribner's, 1929). His coolness toward Edwina is unexplained. "Ned," Edwina's know-it-all first cousin, was Edwin M. Harford, a prominent businessman in nearby Webster Groves, Missouri.

Lemuel Ayers was the "scene designer" from Iowa whose recent credits included a revival of Sidney Howard's play *They Knew What They Wanted* (1924).

The "prison play" requested by Willard Holland is *Not About Nightingales* (1938/1998). No longer directing the St. Louis Mummers, he wrote a second letter from Hollywood in November lamenting his stalled career in films: "'What's the use'" (November 9 {1939} HRC).

According to Audrey Wood, RKO paid a "record" $250,000 for the film rights to *Room Service* (1937), the first Broadway hit of the new firm of Liebling-Wood.]

126. To Whitney Ewing "Whit" Burnett

[New York]
Saturday Afternoon.
[October 21, 1939]
[TLS, 1 p. Princeton]

Dear Whit Burnett:

I just called your office to tell you goodbye and with the slight hope I might see you for a short discussion of the possible book which I plan to write soon as I get the present play off my hands. Audrey returned me the "Desdemona" thing. It contains ample material for a long work but in its present form it is somewhat revolting, exactly as Audrey felt. It was undertaken mainly as an experiment in katharsis. I built up a deliberate series of harsh and shocking effects with the intention [of] "purging" them in a sort of transcendental last scene. The last scene was not realized, the shocking effects were left unrelieved. The thing requires a good deal more deliberation before a second attack.

Then I have another idea. A factual account of my experiences as an impecunious writer knocking about America. Not the usual "box-car and flop-house" saga which has been done to death, but a sort of picaresque, high-spirited narrative, rather in the nature of an old short story of mine you have seen called "A Tale of Two Writers" though the incidents in that were purely fictitious and the ones in this would be much stranger and more accurate. I would call it, satirically, "The Ivory Tower". I have had, I think, an extraordinary number of contacts with interesting personalities in the literary world - that is, for an unknown writer, and my very anonymity has made my adventures more colorful. For instance I appeared in night-court opposite Roark Bradford in New Orleans when the proprietor of a restaurant in which I was employed poured scalding water down on his studio party through cracks in the ceiling and several ladies too drunk to get out were considerably damaged. Then I spent several months trying to get a jalopy to California on ten bucks and a siphon and had lots of fun - in retrospect - on both sides of the Mexican border. I met a good deal of the Hollywood crowd, hitch-hiked and rode a bicycle all around California, spent a summer as a beach-comber with certain modifications, visited Taos and met all the old Lawrence crowd there - returned East by way of Memphis, St. Louis, Chicago. Well, it's impossible to indicate in a letter the material I could use in a work of this sort but I think, entertainingly written, it would make quite a book. The danger, of course, is the usual danger with factual material - stepping on the wrong toes! I suppose all names, including my own, would have to be withheld and a good deal of fiction inserted - I mean, as camouflage.

Stanley Young says I am running away but I prefer to call it just a "strategic retreat". I am going to Mississippi to finish my play. I have completed the first draft here in New York at the sacrifice of job-hunting. Nothing came of all my efforts in that line, I had a really extraordinary run of bad luck. But feel unusually well about it, as New York is terrifying. Even when motionless the people seem to whistle through the air like bullets - a fascinating illusion - so I am anxious to get back among my own kind of vague, indefinite folks.

Sincerely, Tennessee Williams

[Whit Burnett (1899-1973), a tireless editor, publisher, and anthologist, founded (with his first wife, Martha Foley) *STORY* magazine in 1931. Of the many unknown young writers whom he published, two would enjoy both literary distinction and friendship with TW: Carson McCullers and Truman Capote.

Among the "shocking effects" of "Why Did Desdemona Love the Moor?" were allusions to gay Hollywood and explicit sexual relations between a cynical young actress and a virile writer named David. The "transcendental last scene," a mountain avalanche, was intended to release the lovers' "thwarted tenderness" and create a balance of "equal beings" (August 1939, HRC). A draft of the unpublished story completed at Taos in August bears the clear imprint of D.H. Lawrence's love ethic.

Theodore Jackson, the "impecunious writer" in "A Tale of Two Writers" (n.d., HRC), was a model for the artist in the proposed travel narrative "The Ivory Tower" (later "Americans"). Burnett was blunt in dismissing TW's recent "adventures" in New Orleans and the West: "The public doesn't give a damn about impecunious writers" (letter, October 27, 1939, Princeton) and their travels.

Roark Bradford's role in the tale of the "scalding water" is described in letter #90.

A client of Audrey Wood, Stanley Young wrote the historical play *Robin Landing* (1937). TW's " 'retreat' " to Clayton, rather than Mississippi, came approximately one month after his arrival in New York. There he had reported four addresses, completed a draft of *Battle of Angels*, and upon departure apologized to Wood for resembling "the Seven Plagues of Egypt!" (Sat. Nite {October 21, 1939} HRC).]

127. To Molly Day Thacher

[42 Aberdeen Place
Clayton, Missouri]
[ca. late-October 1939]
[TLS, 1 p. HRC]

Dear Molly Day Thacher:

I am back in St. Louis, writing furiously with seven wild-cats under my skin, as I realize that completing this new play is my only apparent avenue of escape. My method of writing is terrifically wasteful. I have already written enough dialogue for two full-length plays, some of the best of which will have to be eliminated because it flies off on some inessential tangent. I wish to Christ I could write under some one's direction. That I could get back to New York. I have completed a first draft and part of a second but this process of weeding out is going to be terrific. For an intelligent writer this would not be much of a problem but I must admit I am not. My attack is purely emotional: under good direction could prove very effective but without it is in danger of spending itself in a lot of useless explosions.

However I think the play will work itself out. Because of the almost insane violence of my present attitude (loathing of St. Louis and humiliating dependance) I have to write everything over to tone it down, to eliminate the lunatic note, but eventually, perhaps in a month or two, the final product should emerge as something worth while and the author will then depart for one of three places, New York, the bone-orchard or the state sanitarium.

Of course all of this is a pathetically obvious play for sympathy. I am hoping that you will be moved to do whatever is possible to procure the fellowship for me. My whole life has been a series of escapes, physical or psychological, more miraculous than any of Houdini's but I do at the present moment seem to be hanging by that one thread: obtaining a fellowship and/or producing a successful play.

Short as it was, I came away from our last interview with a good many new ideas. I still write with all my old faults but at least I am now aware of them and capable, I think, of using more self-control.

With all the suitable apologies and thanks,

Sincerely, Tenn. Williams

[As playreader for the Group Theatre, Molly Day Thacher (1906–1963) had been instrumental in TW's receiving a special award for *American Blues*. She also recommended him to Audrey Wood, his agent, and would later urge Elia Kazan, her husband, to direct *A Streetcar Named Desire* (1947).

TW's "wasteful" manner of writing has produced massive archival collections that are largely unexamined by scholars. The Humanities Research Center holds some 500 bound and unsorted pages of *Battle of Angels*, concentrated in drafts dated November 1939 and May 21, 1941. An annotated prompt copy (n.d.) signed by the play's director, Margaret Webster, is held by the Library of Congress.

With reference to "the state sanitarium," TW alludes to his sister Rose and to his fear of repeating her illness. Apparently he did not visit her at Farmington State Hospital until late-December, two months after his return to Clayton.

TW's identification with Houdini prefigures "Malvolio the Magician" in *The Glass Menagerie* (1945). His escape from a nailed coffin was precisely the kind of delivery that Tom Wingfield and TW envisioned for themselves. To return once again to his father's house had been "humiliating, inglorious" (*Journal*, October 29, 1939).]

128. *To Audrey Wood*

SH: ~~W. Dakin Williams~~
42 Aberdeen Place
Clayton, Missouri
[ca. early-November 1939]
[TLS, 1 p. HRC]

Dear Audrey:

I'm sending you a very hasty, rough description of the play I'm working on. I've completed the first draft (Opus V, Written on Subways) and am half-way through the second but a tremendous [*omission*] of work is still necessary because of the violent, melodramatic nature of the material. It will require a great deal of smoothing out and toning down. I think I can partially anticipate your reaction. You won't like the pathological characters or violent theme but I'm hoping my final treatment of it will please you somewhat better. After I've married the banker's daughter or received the dramatic fellowship I may be in a mood to write something sweet and simple. Jesus, I hope so! If Mother doesn't launch one of her literary purges during my infrequent absences from the attic I should be able to complete a presentable script in a few more weeks. But I wish I could write under competent direction in New York. It might save a lot of revision in the later stages. I wrote Molly Thacher about the maddening situation here. My life is hopelessly circumscribed by the wholesale shoe business on one side and the D.A.R. on the other although I must admit there is considerably less anxiety about the next meal than there was on the Coast. But I am one of those noble animals who would rather starve in a jungle than grow fat in a cage. Molly in our last conversation said she would see what could be done about the fellowship. Does that mean she can exercise some kind of pressure? Please don't think I'm a whining spineless sissy. I'm really not - or _am_ I? Noooo! - I'm only thinking about my <u>ART</u>!!

(I suppose you can hear that horrible deprecating laugh of mine.)

Don't let this give you nightmares. Next time I promise to write a starring vehicle for Shirley Temple if you want me to. Prologue by Margaret Barker....

Best regards to Liebling and Austie and Georgette and the girl with the glittering eyes.

Sincerely, Tenn. Williams

[The "hasty, rough" scenario entitled "Shadow of My Passion" (n.d., HRC) offered a precise and rather detailed description of TW's fifth full-length play, _Battle of Angels_. Its "pathological characters" include a vagabond artist, Valentine Xavier, and two repressed older women, Vee Talbott and Myra Torrance, who look to Val for resurrection. The modern passion play comes to violent end on a rainy Easter weekend in the Mississippi Delta.

As recast in _The Glass Menagerie_, Edwina's "literary purges" were directed against the "insane Mr. Lawrence," especially _Lady Chatterley's Lover_ (1928), to which _Battle of Angels_ bears a strong resemblance.

TW's reference to Shirley Temple was prophetic of his stint as an MGM screenwriter in 1943. Reportedly asked to write for another child actress, Margaret O'Brien, he refused.

The death of the leading character played by Margaret Barker gave _The House of Connelly_ (1931) an excessively pessimistic ending, or so the directors of the Group Theatre felt. Wishing to give their inaugural play a more hopeful conclusion, they urged revision and Paul Green, the author, complied by allowing Barker's character to live.

Austie and Georgette were probably staff members of Liebling-Wood.]

129. *To Audrey Wood*

[42 Aberdeen Place
Clayton, Missouri]
PM: St. Louis, November 7, 1939
[APCS, 1 p. HRC]

Dear Audrey -

The fire motive in my new play has suddenly struck me as being atrociously silly so I am planning to limit play to action contained in first two acts, although the third act did have a terrific climax - still, it was sheer melodrama. This may be just a mood but will, at any rate, delay submission of script (which I had thought was finished) for some while longer. - Have you heard anything from the Fellowship Committee? -

Tenn. Williams

[The "fire motive" in *Battle of Angels* refers to Val Xavier's "obsessive dream" (see letter #150) of death by burning. The "terrific climax" described in the scenario (see letter #128) occurs when a lynch mob armed with blow torches storms the jail and Val "is borne off shrieking 'Fire!'"

"I wait! For the fates' decision. I mean the Rockefeller Fellowship Committee's. It seems a last chance of escape" (*Journal*, October 29, 1939).]

130. *To Audrey Wood*

[42 Aberdeen Place
Clayton, Missouri]
Saturday Nov. 11, 1939
[TLS, 1 p. HRC]

Dear Audrey:

I was relieved to find you were not too unfriendly toward the work in progress, which seems to be nearing completion. I have decided to stick, after all, to the present outline of action. I was faced with the problem of making the fire motive artistically justifiable or else eliminating it altogether, as I did not think it should be used simply as a melodramatic trick to add horror to the atmosphere. This gave me great worry for a while but in re-writing I think I have given the fire theme enough significance in itself to make its use excusable. I also have a new title FIGURES IN FLAME which does not smack quite so much of Macfadden publications. I started out, frankly, to write a commercial play but I now hope that the final result will have some artistic merit as well. The two things are not completely incompatible do you think?

Writing for me is a continual see-saw between rapture and despair which leaves me so exhausted, nervously and physically, that I actually believe each play reduces my life expectancy by several years. No, that's an exaggeration - but anyway I shall certainly have to run off somewhere as soon as this thing is finished, with or without the fellowship.

I presume the Donovan must have concluded that she could serve the stage best by providing it with material for possible melodramas through her own sensational disappearance. However she had already secured a high place among the immortals as far as I was concerned, - "They also serve" who only serve fried chicken! - with martinis and Scotch hi-balls. - Let the Matchek remember that. When she visits her broker.

Sincerely, T.W.

P.S. I may send you play in week or ten days.

[Audrey Wood was encouraged by the scenario of *Battle of Angels*: "If you can write a play with a violent theme well enough to make me think it is commercial, I will go screaming down the street like a mad woman and deliver you a sale as soon as I can get someone to go mad with me" (letter, November 8, 1939, HRC). The "fire motive" was retained in the November 1939 draft, as were the blow torches used by the Klan mob that lynches Val.

It was "Shadow of My Passion," the original title of *Battle of Angels*, that had smacked of Bernarr Macfadden's pulp magazine empire. Such titles as "The Price of One Girl's Folly" and "A Scarlet Woman's Heart" were typical fare in Macfadden's popular *True-Story Magazine*.

As TW revised *Battle of Angels*, he read and was perhaps reassured by William Faulkner's "mad book" *The Wild Palms* (1939). By "distortion" and "exagerration," Faulkner had realized the same kind of fugitive love that TW was trying to make "plausible" (*Journal*, November 10, 1939) in *Battle of Angels*. Both used the folkways of the Delta and its periodic flooding to ground their tales of extravagant love.

TW's journal reveals the same "see-saw between rapture and despair," but it was governed by a hearty optimism, even amid the frustration of living in Clayton: "Hi-ho! Better days are coming," he wrote on December 7, 1939.

Erica Donovan was apparently a producer who had shown interest in TW's work but then disappeared, Wood surmised, because she had "lost the money she thought she had" (letter to TW, November 8, 1939, HRC).

"'They also serve' who only serve fried chicken!" is TW's paraphrase of Milton's "Sonnet XIX": "They also serve who only stand and wait."

The heading (canceled) of the stationery used for this letter—Hotel La Fonda, Taos, New Mexico—may have prodded TW's memory of the western trip and led to a later journal entry: "I'd like to see Jimmie tonite. I'd like to ride my old bicycle up Canyon Road and look at the stars and hear the ranch dogs barking" (December 7, 1939).]

131. To Audrey Wood

[42 Aberdeen Place
Clayton, Missouri]
Thursday November 30, 1939
[TLS, 1 p. HRC]

Dear Audrey:

Well, here is the play - and I feel like Singapore Lou, waiting to see what color her baby will be!

This really wasn't intended for a final draft, as you can tell by the varieties of paper used, but the season is rolling along pretty fast and you say you are going out to the West Coast this winter, so I thought I'd better not delay shipment any longer even though the product is unrefined.

In our last talk in New York Miss Thacher said she wanted to see my play even in a rough draft. Even if it isn't her dish, she might be able to offer some helpful criticism, so perhaps it would be well to show her the script when you have read it. According to Billboard and The Nation, Thunder Rock is an onomatopoeic description of how the play landed on Broadway so it seems doubtful to me that they will be in the mood for another intensely serious play such as this is or is intended to be.

I saw Cornell and Lederer last night. I don't ordinarily use the word "exquisite" but I think I will on this occasion as it certainly describes the performances given and also Behrman's dramatic craftsmanship.

As soon as I can raise sixteen dollars (Travel Bureau rate) I'm going to barge back out to California as I have already exceeded the length of time in St. Louis which is even barely tolerable to me. There is a kind of spiritual fungus or gangrene which sets in here after the second or third month's residence. At the end of four you are pronounced incurable and committed to the wholesale shoe business for the rest of your life.

Best wishes for Liebling-Wood,

Sincerely, T.W.

[The November 1939 draft of *Battle of Angels* at the Humanities Research Center shows only one "variety" of paper and is probably a retyped copy of the original script. TW hurried to deliver the play to Audrey Wood before she left New York to open a new West Coast office of Liebling-Wood.

Thunder Rock, by Robert Ardrey, opened on November 14, 1939, and closed after twenty-three performances. Ardrey's concern with the approaching world war reflected the Group Theatre ideal of exploring serious contemporary issues, but reviewers found play and production uninspiring.

So impressed was TW with Francis Lederer in the road production of *No Time for Comedy* (1939) that he considered writing a play for him. It would be "an easy, careless thing that I may actually go through with if nothing else intervenes" (*Journal*, December 15, 1939). Katharine Cornell, who co-produced and starred in S.N. Behrman's comedy, was later approached by the Theatre Guild to play Myra in *Battle of Angels* (see letter #155). She was also the actress for whom TW "designed" (see letter #327) the first draft of *A Streetcar Named Desire* in early 1945.]

132. To Audrey Wood

SH: ~~W. Dakin Williams~~
42 Aberdeen Place
Clayton, Missouri
[December 1939]
[TLS, 1 p. HRC]

Dear Audrey:

The girl Irene in this story from my projected novel <u>Americans</u> will also be, most likely, the subject of my next full-length play, making a southern trilogy, Spring Storm, Battle of Angels, and this last one which I plan to call The Aristocrats. As you have observed by now, I have only one major theme for all my work which is the destructive impact of society on the sensitive, non-conformist individual. In this case it will be an extraordinarily gifted young woman artist who is forced into prostitution and finally the end described in the story. In "B. of A." it was a boy who hungered for something beyond reality and got death by torture at the hands of a mob - I hope that idea got across in the script. Your protracted silence has begun to disturb me, my dear!

When you have read the story (with play in mind) please pass it on to

Burnett as a sample of material to be used in novel which I have discussed with him.

I am still here in St. Louis by virtue of necessity - the <u>smother</u> of invention! All optimism has departed - I suspect and expect the worst!

I hope you are not the same,

Sincerely, T.W.

[TW's plan (unrealized) for "a southern trilogy" may distantly echo Eugene O'Neill's New England trilogy, *Mourning Becomes Electra* (1931). The "gifted young woman artist" intended for "The Aristocrats" first appears as Irene in a story entitled "In Memory of an Aristocrat" (1985). She is one of "the aristocracy of passionate souls" who may fail in their art but retain their integrity. In early drafts of the story, written perhaps in January-February 1939, her tragic "end" loosely follows the medical history of Rose Williams: after disrupting an art show in New Orleans, she is "railroaded" (n.d., HRC) into the state sanitarium and treated with insulin, which kills her. The story drew upon TW's experience in New Orleans and may be a partial study for Blanche DuBois in *A Streetcar Named Desire*.

By December 11 Audrey Wood's secretary had acknowledged receipt of *Battle of Angels*, but "Nothing else - Ominous indeed!" (*Journal*, December 11, 1939).

Only the "tittilating prospect" of an evening with "V" (a discreet kind of shorthand often used in the journal for homosexual contacts) could relieve TW's anxiety as he awaited the report of the Rockefeller committee. The much anticipated meeting on December 15 proved disappointing, however: "No dice with Va" (*Journal*, December 11, 15, 1939).]

133. *To Walter E. Dakin*

SH: W. Dakin Williams
42 Aberdeen Place
Clayton, Missouri
Tues. [December 12, 1939]
[ALS, 2 pp. HRC]

Dear Grandfather -

The letter you enclosed contained some good news for me, that the number of applicants for the fellowships had been narrowed down to 22 and mine was still among them and that extra copies would be made of my scripts to facilitate the decision.

Thanks awfully for your help in this <u>crucial</u> matter - And <u>will</u> you mail this enclosed letter <u>also</u> as quickly as you can. It is essential to keep my real address a secret at present as they investigate family finances and might be <u>mis</u>-led in thinking me the pampered son of the well-to-do!

I would like to visit you all for a little while if Grand is well and you'd promise to make <u>no</u> <u>trouble</u> and let me assist in things about the house.

With much love to you both, Tom.

[TW had asked the Dakins to mail an earlier letter to Luise Sillcox, executive secretary of the Dramatists' Guild: "It is to enquire about the fellowship. I don't want to mail it from St. Louis as I wish to keep my address here unknown" (postmarked St. Louis, December 5, 1939, HRC). Sillcox's return letter was forwarded to TW from Memphis and led to "a real resurgence of hope" (*Journal*, December 12, 1939).]

134. *To Walter E. Dakin*

[42 Aberdeen Place
Clayton, Missouri]
Thursday. [December 21, 1939]
[TLS, 1 p. HTC]

Dear Grandfather:

Your letter enclosed the glad tidings. I have been awarded the Rockefeller fellowship - $1000. I'm enclosing an air-mail acknowledgement which I wish you would get off to them immediately as I know they are wondering why they haven't heard from me yet. The announcement must have appeared in Wednesday's papers in New York. I'll try to get one and send it to you. This good luck changes my plans considerably. As soon as possible I will return to New York to continue contacts and try to sell plays and study the theatre. I want to get to Memphis sometime during the holidays however to see you all. I think I will run down there either the day after Xmas or a little later depending on your <u>own</u> plans. I don't want to interfere with any trip you have an opportunity to take. But I do want to see you all before I go back East. Mother and I are planning to take a big motor tour in the spring to the Natchez garden festival - you and Grand must come with us.

I also got a telegram from New York just before your letter came. It was from my agent Audrey Wood. She congratulated me on winning the fellowship, having seen the announcement, and said she had read my new play and liked it very much.

Have so many letters to write! Thank you for this invaluable assistance with my correspondence!

Much love to you and Grand, Tom

P.S. We saw Rose yesterday. She was about the same and was very pleased with her presents.

[In a letter dated December 18, 1939, (HRC) and mailed to Memphis, Luise Sillcox congratulated TW for winning a Rockefeller grant of $1,000. He was one of five national recipients chosen by a scholarship committee that included the playwright Paul Green. "Wow!" TW wrote in the journal, as Edwina "literally wept with joy" (December 21, 1939).

In her congratulatory "wire" Audrey Wood also expressed guarded enthusiasm for *Battle of Angels*: "Have read new play and like a great deal of it" (December 20, 1939, HRC).

On December 20 TW (and Edwina) reluctantly visited Rose at Farmington and was unnerved by the experience. Her "talk was so obscene - she laughed and spoke continual obscenities." Her doctor was "a cold, unsympathetic young man - he said her condition was hopeless - that we could only expect a progressive deterioration. It was a horrible ordeal. Especially since I fear that end for myself." Only the hope that art might give "some kind of poetic expression" to the "uncomprehendably brutal" aspect of life consoled him. He later wished that he "could share" his good fortune with his "little sister" and asked God to "bless all the tortured world" (*Journal*, December 20, 21, 1939).]

135. To Edwina Dakin Williams

Y.M.C.A.
5 W. 63rd Street, N.Y.C.
PM: New York, January 8, 1940
[APCS, 1 p. HRC]

Dear Mother -

I have just seen Audrey. She told me that I had come in <u>first</u> of all the Rockefeller applicants and introduced me to people in the office as "our sweet heart". One reader at the "Group" is excited about my new play (they now have it at their office) and is trying to get the head director to read it. My address is at the 63rd Street Y.M.C.A. Please forward this card to Grand & G. - I will be very busy the next few days.

Tom.

[As TW approached New York on the train, he was beset by the familiar "blue devils of defeatism" and braced himself for "success through failure, failure through success," his "method" being characteristically "oblique" (*Journal*, January 7, 1940).

The "excited" reader of *Battle of Angels* at the Group Theatre was probably Molly Day Thacher and the "head director" Harold Clurman.]

136. To Rosina Otte and Walter E. Dakin

SH: Young Men's Christian Association
5 West 63rd Street, New York, N.Y.
Jan. 19, 1940
[TLS, 2 pp. HRC]

Dear Grand & Grandfather:

I've seen and done so much I can scarcely believe I've been here less than two weeks. As before, I had a lot of people to meet - and just lately I've been attending daily re-hearsals at the Group Theatre of Clifford Odets' new play Night Music. This is the first time I've ever seen a professional play in rehearsal, of course, and since it is being directed by the finest director in the country and with some of the finest actors, the experience is tremendous to me. I met the author and also Irwin Shaw whom you may have heard of - another distinguished young Group theatre playwright. In fact I had a date with Odets sister, Florence. Unfortunately she is Jewish. But very nice.

Liebling and Wood took me out to dinner and to "John Henry", a new play by Roark Bradford who wrote "Green Pastures." It closed very shortly. Then a couple of nights ago they met me in front of another first-night theatre and gave me a box seat. I sat right over a number of celebrities such as Robert Benchley and Elissa Landi and Margaret Sullavan. I was the only person sitting in a box and felt very elated. It was a marvelous play, Sean

O'Casey's "Juno and the Paycock". The Group seem to be seriously interested in my new play - one of the directors said it was very vital and showed much progress in form. He is trying to get the main director to read it and I am busy making a number of changes - I don't think they will give it much attention till after the Odets play is finished (in rehearsal) as it is very crucial production for them.

I am staying at the "Y" - from my tenth floor window I have a beautiful view over Central Park to the towers along Fifth Avenue. There is a lovely cafeteria in the basement and it is within walking distance of the downtown theatres, Rockefeller center, Etc. The weather here has been milder than any winter that I have spent in St. Louis. The air is cold but very dry and exhilerating - I think it is healthful for me as I haven't had a sign of a cold since coming here.

Are you all going to Florida? After I leave here (probably in the early spring) I hope we can take a touring trip through the South - as Mother planned. I do hope you are keeping well as I am! If I didn't walk so much and have daily exercise in the swimming pool and gym, I would probably get fat as I have an enormous appetite here.

Three new plays are opening this week and I will try to see them - I spend about four hours a day watching these Odets rehearsals. And dreaming of that marvelous director working on a script of mine! Audrey and Liebling have been awfully nice to me - He had an appendicitis operation about Xmas time and she had to run the whole business so she hasn't had much time. I suppose Mother told you that the Executive Secty. of the Rockefeller foundation said that my work came in first in the contest and was the only work about which none of the judges had any argument - of course this improved my spirits and raised my stock with Audrey.

I hope to hear that you are leaving for Florida soon.

With much love, Tom.

[The production of Clifford Odets's *Night Music* (1940) was a "crucial" test for the Group Theatre, beset as it was by internal disputes and by an acute shortage of money after the failure of *Thunder Rock* in the preceding November. Odets's first comedy was directed by Harold Clurman, with Elia Kazan in the male lead.

Roark Bradford wrote the stories that inspired *The Green Pastures* (1930), but the play itself was written by Marc Connelly. Bradford's musical *John Henry* (1940) opened on January 10 and closed after seven performances. Audrey Wood later told

Edwina of TW's "elation" at a revival of Sean O'Casey's *Juno and the Paycock* (1924). His laughter, known to be braying, had "single-handedly carried the audience with him, he so obviously enjoyed the play," Edwina remarked in her memoir, *Remember Me to Tom* (1963).

Elia Kazan or Robert Lewis, directors of Group Theatre productions, may have tried to interest Harold Clurman, "the main director," in reading *Battle of Angels*.]

137. To William Liebling

SH: Young Men's Christian Association
5 West 63rd Street, New York, N.Y.
Nov. 19, 1940
[TLS, 1 p. HRC]

Dear Liebling:

I have obtained "Night of the Poor" from a lending library and am about half way through it - will finish it up at the Group rehearsal tomorrow. I can discuss it with Mr. Bloch, if he wishes, any time that is convenient for him.

It is a rambling novel about two young vagrants wandering over the country and meeting with a great number of other transient types - only none of them are very convincing to me. Phoney is the word I would use. The writing, however, is very good. Prokosch has an excellent prose style but in this instance is handling material which he doesn't know as well as I do. So I'm inclined to be rather severe with this novel. I cannot see - right now - its film possibilities though I do believe that material of this sort - the lives of the "fugitive kind" - is tremendous material for drama and should be used. This story, however, lacks plot development as well as convincing characters. When I have finished it I may have a different impression. At any rate, if Bloch is interested I would be very glad to talk it over with him.

I am doing some writing and attending rehearsals of Odets new play "Night Music". The play is full of brilliant talk and comedy.

Sincerely, T.W.

[William Liebling (1894-1969) was an astute and successful actors' agent when he and Audrey Wood began their agency in 1937. They soon married and worked in close professional partnership until the Liebling-Wood agency was sold in 1954.

Liebling had apparently asked TW to read Frederic Prokosch's novel *Night of the Poor* (1939) and assess its "film possibilities" for Bertram Bloch. Prokosch's "young vagrants" lacked the sense of artistic mission that Vachel Lindsay and others had taught TW to associate with the road, which may explain why the novel seemed unconvincing. TW and Prokosch later became friendly. There is no evidence that *Night of the Poor* was ever filmed.

TW inadvertently substituted November for January in dating this letter.]

138. To Audrey Wood

[Young Men's Christian Association
5 West 63rd Street, New York]
Mon. [January 29, 1940]
[TLS w/ addendum, 2 pp. HRC]

Dear Audrey:

It was very good of you to enclose the encouraging note from the A.M. editor. The date indicates it was written two months ago so I wonder if the iron is still hot for more material, or if you <u>have</u> any more on hand. Did you try the Miss. librarian on her - "Something About Him"? By the way, there are no other existing copies of any of these stories and what you and Liebling said about the danger of losing scripts has caused me considerable anxiety. This is sheer vanity, but I would almost rather lose my one good eye than anything I have written! Perhaps you had better make (at my expense) additional copies of those pieces which you wish to keep more or less in circulation among editors. There is no reason why I should not peddle them around a bit myself as I have so little to do right now and it would give me a pleasant illusion of activity. Did the stories come back from <u>Esquire</u>? <u>Story</u>? - Soon as they do I would like to call at your office and make arrangements to have additional copies typed of about three of these stories - to leave around editors' offices while I am here. Saves postage, Etc.

I am attending GROUP rehearsals daily. I think I have made some rather important changes in the third act of "Battle of Angels" though I was hampered considerably by the fact I had no script of my own to work with - had to reproduce from memory. Act three, Scene one, (Between the two women) was formerly the weakest thing in the play but I believe it is now the best scene with this re-writing which I have done. Audrey, I have a profound conviction that this play can be successfully produced - it's the first time I've felt that way about any long script, as I've probably told you. Clurman introduced himself to me and told me he had the play on his desk and <u>would</u> read it. But I wish we could make another copy to show the Theatre Guild, Etc., as it is not laden with social significance and would be equally suitable for any good producer who is not afraid of strong stuff. Would it be unpolitic to borrow the script from Clurman long enough to make another copy to show around elsewhere - or would this be likely to annoy them? God knows I don't wish to do that!

A friend of mine from St. Louis, Anne Bretzfelder, a gifted sculptress, is here in town and I wish we could meet you for cocktails some evening or possibly for lunch - she would not interfere with our discussion of things. If any convenient time occurs to you, will you leave me a message here at the "Y"?

Cordially - T.W.

(OVER) - On the back is a list of those scripts you now have, which may assist you in keeping track of them. I have two or three more short-stories available if you know of a promising market.

<u>Short Stories</u> (6)

"The Red Part of a Flag"
"The Lost Girl"
"The Dark Room"
"A Tale of Two Writers"
"Something About Him"
"In Memory of an Aristocrat"

<u>Short Plays</u> (not bound with American Blues)

At Liberty
This Property Is Condemned
Once In a Life-time
The Lullabye or Something Special for Special People

Long Plays

Battle of Angels
Spring Storm (Did this one get back from the Guild?)
Fugitive Kind
Not About Nightingales

[The story "Something about Him" (1946) has much the same dramatic structure as *Battle of Angels*. A sensitive young man arrives in a Mississippi Delta town, takes a job as a clerk, and touches the heart of a lonely woman. His departure at the town's insistence consigns Miss Rose, the librarian, to a life of "fox-toothed loneliness" (an image probably inspired by Katherine Mansfield's famous story "Miss Brill"). Audrey Wood wrote several days later that *Esquire* had returned four stories, including "The Vine" (1954), which was nearly accepted for publication (January 31, 1940, HRC).

At issue in Act Three, Scene 1, of *Battle of Angels* were Vee Talbott's denial of the flesh and her vision of Jesus on Easter morning, both derided by Dolly Bland in an exchange that TW probably found tedious as it appeared in the November 1939 draft.

TW's request that *Battle of Angels* be shown to the Theatre Guild coincided with a journal entry that Clifford Odets's play *Night Music* "seemed unusually weak" (January 28, 1940) and unlikely to save the Group Theatre. The Theatre Guild had prospered in its twenty-year history by building a large subscription list and by balancing art, commerce, and ensemble acting in such distinguished productions as *Saint Joan* (1923) and *Strange Interlude* (1928). After a string of failures in the 1930s, the Guild was restored to solvency, if not artistic distinction, by *The Philadelphia Story*, a light, sophisticated comedy (by Philip Barry) starring Katharine Hepburn that opened on March 28, 1939, and ran for 417 performances.

Anne Bretzfelder was a "glamorous" new friend whom TW had "not sufficiently explored yet" (*Journal*, January 7, 1940). In January he also met "a new crowd" of "starving artists from Georgia" (*Journal*, January 26, 1940) that included a nineteen year old named Donald Windham. Together they cruised Manhattan, as TW made decisive contact with the city's gay culture.]

139. To Audrey Wood

[Young Men's Christian Association
5 West 63rd Street, New York]
[ca. February 7, 1940]
[ALS, 2 pp. HTC]

Dear Audrey -

I dropped in to leave a couple of stories for "Esquire" but after a second glance decided to work on them some more -

I can afford $10.00 worth of typing this month - pay 22nd. Clurman took long play to Boston with him - Hope he doesn't <u>lose</u> it - think it should be copied soon as he gets back. And as many stories as can be included in that price.

Saw a <u>stinking</u> rehearsal of my one-act - Student actors at the School for the Feeble-minded! (Malicious remark). Hope no one I know is there unless it improves vastly. John wrote a soap-box oration himself and inserted it in script to give it a social message. Ah, well - I guess it isn't a crucial production, although my first in N.Y. <u>M.G.M.</u> phoned O'Shaugnessy they would be there. <u>Clurman</u> says he may do 1-acts if Odets play is successful - this spring - Afraid the "<u>if</u>" clause is a big one.

Did you send Esq. "A Tale of Two Writers"? Might be their dish -

<u>Hello</u>! (You are on the 'Phone) - <u>Goodbye</u>.

T.W.

[Harold Clurman was in Boston for the tryout of *Night Music* and had taken *Battle of Angels* with him to read.

"The Long Goodbye" (1940) opened in early-February at the New School for Social Research, with direction by John O'Shaughnessy. Apparently the student production did improve, for TW was "pleased" to hear "how good" (*Journal*, February 12, 1940) his lines could sound. The one-act play treats the familiar autobiographical situation of a young writer trapped in "the City of St. Pollution."]

140. *To Alice Drey Lippmann*

Y.M.C.A.
New York, N.Y.
[February 21, 1940]
[TTr, 2 pp. Private Collection]

Dear Mrs. Lippmann:

Freedom is ruthless because it makes us forgetful of other things. For the past few weeks I've been like a bird let out of a cage. I've felt as though I'd just inherited the sky. It has made me a little dizzy. And when you are dizzy things slip out of your mind. You really aren't yourself.

Now I have always told you, my dear, that I'm a selfish person. You persisted in thinking otherwise despite my frankness. So you see! Who was right? I don't mean to be selfish, I love people very deeply and truly and respect their gifts as much as I do my own. But I am wrapped up in my own little sphere too much - my own ideas, plans, desires - to be consistently thoughtful of other people. This is truth and truth in itself is worth something - so I give it to you as it is with all the suitable apologies and regrets. I am selfish and ignoble and am lying flat in the gutter with only a little side-long glance at the stars!

About Margaret and Albert. They are two charming people and they seemed to be very happy together. I have wanted to see them again, and am planning to, of course, but have been so busy I haven't even looked up Mother's first cousin despite her repeated insistence (and his) that I should do so. I've written a complete new long play, have attended daily rehearsals of Odet's Night Music (which opens tomorrow) and have helped in the production of one of my own little one-acts by the New Theatre League, all of which has completely usurped my freedom of action and will. Mother has exagerrated a little, as Mothers will, if she said I was running around with flocks of brilliant poets. As a matter of fact the only one of consequence I know here is Oscar Williams who knows Margaret and Albert - or at least Albert - as well as I do.

I went to hear W.H. Auden read his verse but did not get to meet him. A few minor poets were there as well as Oscar Wms. but I've seen none of them since.

Anne Bretzfelder has been up here from St. Louis and is leaving Sunday. I've only gotten to see her a few times but she has been extremely helpful in criticizing my new work and she's a person that I like immensely. I wish you would meet her, if you haven't already.

Do you see Bill? Tell him to write to me. I submitted his group of poems to Dorothy Hobson who is head of the new verse thing but haven't heard from her yet. I wonder if Bill has. I'm going to call her one of these days and check on the reaction.

Your own verse is here in my desk drawer and I am still cogitating upon some action about it. So far Harold Vinal is the only editor I've met who handles poetry. I intend to show him some of these, but I am wondering how much this will please you, as they make no payment. Clark Mills publishes there pretty regularly, you know, and so it is not a disgrace to appear in it.

I am going to return your original copies keeping some of (copies of) those which I think might be marketable here in case I meet just the right person.

I remember you sent me a post-card picture of a big bear once - in a supplicant pose. Asking forgiveness - for what I don't know! Unfortunately I don't have any bear pictures, supplicant or otherwise, but my contrition is no less genuine - nor my desire for pardon!

Auf Wiedersehen, (signed) Tom

[Alice Lippmann (1873-1971) was the wife of a St. Louis physician and reportedly the founder of a poetry circle that included TW, Clark Mills, and William Jay Smith. She had written to inquire about verse entrusted to TW and about her son and daughter-in-law, who were living a Bohemian life in New York. TW visited the couple in January and informed Edwina that he had found Albert "drunk," Margaret "in bed with rheumatic fever," and their "littered" room a "dump-yard" (Tuesday P.M. {January 16, 1940} HRC).

The "gutter" and the "stars," a partial quotation from Oscar Wilde's play *Lady Windermere's Fan* (1892), would reappear in *Summer and Smoke* (1948): "Who was that said that—oh, so beautiful thing!—'All of us are in the gutter, but some of us are looking at the stars!'"

Anne Bretzfelder Post has recalled for the editors a harrowing experience in early 1940: "I met {TW} at Audrey's one afternoon so he could give me some stories to illustrate. They were, I think, in an envelope addressed to Story Magazine. I left the envelope on the subway—went frantically to the Lost and Found Department, but no sign of them. Many years later I was at a PEN dinner party and met the director of Story Magazine. When I confessed my crime he said that the stories <u>had</u> been delivered to him. My husband then remarked that I could live the rest of my life free of guilt. Which I haven't, quite!"

As an informal broker of verse, TW sent William Jay Smith's poems to Dorothy Hobson, founder and director of The League to Support Poetry. He also met Oscar Williams, who became a prolific anthologist of modern verse, and Harold Vinal, who edited *Voices* and had published TW's own poetry in 1934.]

141. *To Audrey Wood*

SH: Young Men's Christian Association
5 West 63rd Street, New York, N.Y.
[ca. early-March 1940]
[TLS, 1 p. HRC]

Dear Audrey:

Enclosed ten dollars first installment of Typing Fund.

I think I'll shove off for California or Mexico soon as my checque comes in, about the twentieth. Will take new long play "Stair to the Roof" out with me for further work. Finishing a one-act "Portrait of a Madonna" which I think should be bound with the two other new ones, possibly under the inclusive title of "The Lonely Heart" as all 3 are about rather desolate people and nostalgic in atmosphere. Could use Tschaikowsky's beautiful piece as musical overture or background in a production.

I think a copy of "Battle of Angels" should go to the Theatre Guild, don't you? It is really more their sort of play than it is the Group's. John Gassner, their reader, is chairman of my playwrights Seminar at the New School and I might actually get him to read it if Playreaders actually do read plays.

I hope I can see you for some further discussion of the playwrights group. I am troubled chiefly by instinctive skepticism about the quality of work by Harvard boys like Rodell and would like to understand more thoroughly the advantages of being absorbed in a group with other unknowns. On the other hand, a production <u>is</u> a production. Though I believe a play like "Battle of Angels" would require the sensitive kind of production that an established acting company could give it. However in these matters I have faith in your wisdom, lady. . . .

Cordially, Tenn. Wms.

[TW described his new play, "Stair to the Roof" (1945), as "a rather promising idea about white collar workers" (*Journal*, February 12, 1940). "Portrait of a Madonna," related both to *Battle of Angels* and *A Streetcar Named Desire*, concerns the sexual-religious delusions of an aging southern spinster who is committed to a state asylum. The two short plays to be "bound" with "Portrait," first published in 1945, may have been "At Liberty" and "This Property is Condemned," which were published as companion pieces in 1941.

TW hoped to persuade Audrey Wood that *Battle of Angels* was more suitable for the Theatre Guild than the Group by virtue of its muted social content and commercial appeal. It was through her efforts that he received a scholarship to the Playwrights' Seminar at the New School, where John Gassner and Theresa Helburn became strongly attracted to the play and officially presented it to the Guild. Gassner later wrote that TW "participated only casually in the discussions {of the Seminar} and was self-absorbed. . . . He had a mind and a will of his own - he knew what he was after" (letter to David Staub, April 30, 1948, Southern Illinois). A fellow member of the Seminar was Arthur Miller.

The new "playwrights group" was apparently an attempt by Liebling-Wood to produce the work of young dramatists associated with the agency. Wood planned to raise funds on the West Coast later in the month, but there is no evidence that the venture was ever realized.]

142. To William Saroyan

[Young Men's Christian Association]
5 W. 63rd Street, New York City
March 4, 1940
[TLSx, 1 p. Private Collection]

Dear William Saroyan:

I read your article in this evening's (March 4) World Telegram with a great deal of sympathy and so much absorption that I had to walk back three blocks from the bus. Last summer I hitch-hiked from L.A. to Frisco to see you and the Golden Gate Exposition. I missed you. But I believe you are now in N.Y. and so am I. The implication is obvious.

By way of introduction, I'm also a playwright and a short-story writer. The only thing of mine you are likely to have seen is a short-story that was in the Oct. issue of STORY which I believe was also your first publication. I've been reading you in there and your other publications for y'ars and y'ars and I won't annoy you with adjectives about your work. But I like it a hell of a lot. Right now I'm living in New York on a Rockefeller Dram. fellowship and am more or less associated with the Group Theatre as I won their $100. (second) award for Young Playwrights' last spring and they are holding (AND holding!) a couple of scripts of mine. What you said about the indifference to the works of young playwrights by companies that are sensitive enough to help them struck very close to home. I have written six long plays and about twenty short ones in the last three or four years and only in the middle-west have I found productions for them. - Enough of all that.

I have a friend who is writing a book about your work. We would both like to meet you, Bill, and I have some things I would particularly like to talk over with you.

Could you suggest a time for us to drop in if you are not averse to dissipating your time on strangers; I am shoving off for Acapulco, Mexico, mainly because I like the sound of it and have been almost everywhere else - being one of those migratory writers so articulate lately! - Leaving about the twentieth of the month when I get my next checque so hope you can let me see you before then.

Cordially, Tenn. Wms.

[William Saroyan (1908-1981) had shown a flair for independence and publicity that was not lost upon TW. His long-running hit, *The Time of Your Life*, opened as a Theatre Guild production on October 25, 1939, and would soon be awarded the Pulitzer Prize, which he declined (see letter #159). His article in the *New York World-Telegram* coincided with TW's effort to bring *Battle of Angels* to the attention of the Theatre Guild. This "organization," Saroyan had written, "should be the medium of bringing out of obscurity the several new and valid dramatists this country is surely large enough to be expected to create inevitably every 10 years or so. . . . The idea is to get them to appear as little damaged and compromised by the disorder in the theatrical world as possible" (March 4, 1940).

The "friend" writing a book on Saroyan has not been identified and may have been a ploy to meet the rising celebrity. In any case TW did not meet Saroyan at this time.]

143. To Anne Bretzfelder

[Young Men's Christian Association
5 West 63rd Street, New York]
[ca. March 7, 1940]
[TLS, 2 pp. HRC]

Dear Anne:

Hope you're knocking out a good piece of rock in St. Louis. My desk is still cluttered with plays and fragments of plays and stray bits of short-stories. But it is now surmounted by an immense travel poster of a Mexican port. One of my sudden, Quixotic decisions. I plan to leave here for Mexico about the twenty second of the month. Sail second class (for $55.) to Vera Cruz. Then to Mexico City and on across to Acapulco where I'll spend the summer if it isn't too hot - and nothing develops to bring me home. Descriptions of that place have always haunted me. <u>Two</u> bays - one for swimming, one for breakers - emerald blue water, tropical jungles, pine-clad mountains (horrible travel-book style!). Hope you will stick to your intention of traveling down there.

Things are about as they were when you left. Audrey has turned Battle of Angels over to some mysterious people on whom the producing company is dependant - without even consulting me about it. Odets play will close this Saturday. Nothing is definite. I hope I will know more before I leave here. I may decide to leave from New Orleans so I can see my folks before sailing. If so will get you to join our party, which consists so far of a retired psychiatrist and two patients, man and wife, the woman having involutional melancholia and a constant attendant to prevent her from killing herself. Promises to be replete with dramatic material, huh?

Do you know I haven't mailed Mme. Lippman's verse to her yet?!

Saroyan is back in town and I have written to ask for an appointment to meet him.

Let me know your plans and what's going on in St. Louis. Sorry this is such a dull letter. I'm staying up all night to see the Queen Elizabeth dock at five o'clock in the morning.

So long. Tom

[In an earlier letter to Walter Dakin, TW described Anne Bretzfelder (1916–   ) as an "enormously wealthy young Jewish girl" whose "Hebrew ostentation" had occasionally made him "smile." "I like the Jews," he added, "but they do have some funny traits" (n.d., HRC). Before she left New York, they had "had a little love ~~sequence~~ episode in her Apt. one night but didn't mean much. Still I like her remarkably - for me" (*Journal*, February 24, 1940). Anne Bretzfelder Post later remarked that such advances had "displeased" and "pressured" her to "the extreme," but she now realized that TW "was probably profoundly being pulled in two directions" (qtd. in Leverich). She did not join him in Acapulco.

The "mysterious people" to whom Audrey Wood showed *Battle of Angels* may have been potential backers of the "playwrights group" that she hoped to form (see letter #141).

The Queen Elizabeth had departed secretly from England to evade German planes and submarines and safely entered New York harbor on the morning of March 7, "a creeping blur on a sunless horizon" (*New York Times*, March 8, 1940). New Yorkers cheered the daring maiden voyage of the world's largest liner.]

144. To Walter Willard "Spud" Johnson

[Young Men's Christian Association]
5 W. 63rd Street, New York City
March 14, 1940
[TLS, 1 p. HRC]

Dear Spud:

By way of identification, I'm the fellow who made such a pest of himself last August collecting information about D.H. Lawrence for a proposed drama. I have recently gotten a Rockefeller dramatic fellowship (with this as one of the projects) and am planning to make a longer visit, possibly all spring and summer. I know it is presuming on very slight acquaintance, but I wonder if you could tell me if a cabin, very small and reasonably inexpensive, or any other attractive living-quarters are available around Taos, preferably a little out of town. I don't mean hotels. I know you've been around there long enough to know. How about the cabin near Frieda's that the two Danish painters once occupied? Is that taken? I'm living on about a hundred a month so you can judge the sort of thing I can afford. I want to pay as little as possible and still live decently. Another fellow may come along, too, and we'd probably do some cooking.

Called to see Mrs. Luhan who has been having a 'salon' it seems at One Fifth Avenue - but too late. She'd left New York 3 weeks ago. So I still haven't met her. I've written two long plays since I saw you last, one was dedicated to Lawrence but neither is <u>about</u> him and Broadway productions are still some months in the future.

If you can't advise me on this residence problem, could you suggest a party who might? Taos got under my skin and I'm really anxious to get back there after this feverish period in Manhattan.

Cordially, Tenn. Williams

[TW met "Spud" Johnson (1897-1968) in Taos, New Mexico, in August 1939. A writer, publisher, and part-time secretary to Witter Bynner and Mabel Dodge Luhan, Johnson edited the provocative magazine *Laughing Horse* (1922-1939), which often published D.H. Lawrence material. TW's interest in revisiting Taos had been renewed by "disturbing reports" (*Journal*, March 11, 1940) of the summer heat in Mexico.

Mabel Dodge's famous "Evenings" in Greenwich Village had attracted a wide array of artists, intellectuals, and radical reformers from their inception in 1913 until Dodge left for Taos in late 1917. There she gained similar notoriety, married a Pueblo Indian named Tony Luhan, and lived principally until her death in 1962. The New York "'salon'" that attracted TW in early 1940 was unkindly dubbed "Mabel's comeback" by *Time* magazine and lasted only briefly.

The "two long plays" cited by TW are *Stairs to the Roof* and *Battle of Angels*, the latter dedicated to D.H. Lawrence: "Who was while he lived the brilliant adversary of so many dark angels and who never fell, except in the treacherous flesh, the rest being flame that fought and prevailed over darkness" (November 1939, HRC).]

145. To Audrey Wood

SH: Young Men's Christian Association
5 West 63rd Street, New York, N.Y.
Thursday P.M. [March 14, 1940]
[TLS, 1 p. HRC]

Dear Audrey:

I ran into Clurman on the way out and told him that I was removing a dark horse from his stables. He laughed and said that he had a lot more time now and wanted to read one of the typed copies.

I think the flood situation has eliminated the slightly implausible element in the last act, though in rehearsals I think we would still have to feel our way through it with blue-pencil, glue-pot and scissors.

However - I <u>do</u> think this play is <u>Commercial</u>! - Capital 'C' as in CASH! - I have been thinking about John Garfield as the male lead - Stella Adler as Myra - Sara Allgood as Vee! - I suppose, to be consistent, Shakespeare should have written the play!

Cordially, T.W.

P.S. I'm engaged in fitting together two different versions of ACT III. I think the resultant improvement will justify the little delay in getting the script to the typist. Ought to be done by Saturday.

[The "dark horse" refers to *Battle of Angels*, while Harold Clurman's new found leisure was probably a result of the closing of *Night Music* on March 9. The critics admired the Group Theatre production, especially Elia Kazan's performance, but the play itself seemed "minor Odets" and was dismissed as "foolish." TW recalled meeting Clifford Odets in the theatre lobby several days after the play's opening on February 22: "He was nice and I liked him for the first time - sympathy for the defeated. He nervously fingered his watch and looked deeply hurt - almost completely deflated. Ought to do him good as an artist" (*Journal*, February 24, 1940). Odets felt no such consolation and decried instead (in his journal) the "murder of loveliness, of talent, of aspiration" by "lean dry men who know little or nothing about the theatre." His sharpest critic was Brooks Atkinson of the *New York Times*, who would soon champion TW.

By exploiting the frequency of flooding in the Delta, TW intensified the mood of *Battle of Angels* and addressed the problem of plausibility by isolating Two River County and making Val Xavier subject to unchallenged mob action.

TW may have assumed that John Garfield, Stella Adler, and Sara Allgood, actors closely associated with the Group Theatre, were available now that the company had all but failed. Garfield would resurface as TW's first choice to play the role of Stanley in *A Streetcar Named Desire*.]

146. To Edwina Dakin Williams

SH: Young Men's Christian Association
5 West 63rd Street, New York, N.Y.
<u>Tuesday</u> [March 19, 1940]
[TLS, 2 pp. HRC]

Dear Mother:

My Mexican trip has been postponed, at least till the Fifth of April. The Theatre Guild has taken a sudden, unexpected interest in my new play. Audrey called up yesterday morning and said their play-reader, John Gassner who is also my instructor at the New School, was "tremendously excited over it" and wanted Elmer Rice, the playwright, to look at it soon as he got back in New York, April 2nd. I saw Gassner this afternoon and he confirmed Audrey's report and said it was the best play he had read in a year and if the other two readers, who took it to Nassau with them, liked it as well as he, there would be a production next Fall!! It seems that fortune is certainly with me, as this happens just when the Group Theatre has gone broke on Odets new play which has closed, a complete failure. The Theatre Guild has long been the outstanding theatre in New York, though lately the Group had challenged them. However they have had five straight hits this season, Katharine Hepburn in "The Philadelphia Story" which has been running a year and is now going on tour, Hemingway's the "Fifth Column" with Franchot Tone, just opened and a big success and Saroyan's "Time of Your Life" which is still running, Lunt and Fontanne in a new Sherwood play and a new play by Saroyan. If they should produce the play it would be the best possible production. So I am in a state of great suspense and regardless of the outcome, will certainly need a Mexican trip to relax me when things are settled. Audrey also sent me over to Harper's this afternoon - they are reading my short works and want me to write a novel. Said if I wrote fifty pages on one which they liked, they would give me a contract with advance payment. But I don't feel in a state to start a novel right now. I told them I would be very glad to sell them some short-stories to pay my boat-fare to Mexico. The writing and theatre world is a flock of sheep. They never get interested until someone else is. You have to distribute things around several places to work up any enthusiasm.

Spring is here today, I went out without a topcoat as the streets were quite warm and sunny. I suppose New York will be more pleasant now. I hope so as I have grown pretty tired of it in the last few weeks. The people here are all living such artificial lives - Indians would be a great relief!

There is no terrible rush about the box of things now but I would like to have them as soon as you have time, as I can use them all here now that it is getting warmer.

Forward this letter to Grand as I have [not] written them lately.

Much love, Tom.

If Mrs. Lippmann phones tell her I sent her poems to Bill as I didn't have her address. She has written twice in extreme anxiety about them.

[In late-March John Gassner confirmed the Theatre Guild's interest in *Battle of Angels* and informed TW that Theresa Helburn had told him not to send a copy to Elmer Rice, as she and Lawrence Langner wished "to reserve the play for discussion by themselves" (March 28, 1940, HRC). Gassner's encouraging note probably arrived shortly after TW had discounted the interest of the Theatre Guild: "I'm not banking on that little development" (*Journal*, ca. March 28, 1940).

Two of the Theatre Guild "hits" cited by TW opened in New York after this letter was written, and one, *Love's Old Sweet Song* (1940) by William Saroyan, was not a financial success. *There Shall Be No Night*, the Robert Sherwood play with Alfred Lunt and Lynn Fontanne in the leads, opened on April 29 and won the Pulitzer Prize.

An abbreviated version of this letter was first published in Edwina Dakin Williams's memoir, *Remember Me to Tom* (1963), pp. 114-115.]

147. To Edwina Dakin Williams

[Young Men's Christian Association
5 West 63rd Street, New York]
Tuesday PM. [April 9, 1940]
[TLS, 3 pp. HTC]

Dear Mother:

I am exhausted but very relieved as the preliminaries seem to be more or less settled. The Guild had a meeting at the class this afternoon, the play was thoroughly dissected and many changes were suggested, but Miss Helborn (one of the heads) took me home in a cab and said they would pay me one hundred dollar option on the play tomorrow which is the first step toward a complete sale. I haven't got the details straight but they may pay me this amount each month till the play is produced. In the meantime, however, I have to do a lot of revision to meet their requirements, many of which seem foolish to me at the present moment, but I am not telling them so. It appears that they are genuinely excited over the play and their intentions are quite serious. So I think we should come to some satisfactory compromise about changes. Of course I hate to go back to work on an old play when I want to write new ones. But you can't have cake and eat it. I told Miss Helborn I was planning to leave for Mexico and she thought that would be all right, as I need a change. A boat is sailing the day after tomorrow and if I can get packed in time I may catch it - I am so tired of New York, for a while, that I am really desperately anxious to get away as soon as possible.

It seemed like a very important occasion this afternoon. They had a photographer there who took flash-light photos of us all sitting about the table.

Well, at least they are paying my complete transportation costs to Mexico and something over - which is pretty big to me as I hated taking it out of the scholarship fund. Audrey has left town for California and this whole deal was executed without any help from her. In fact it was I who suggested letting the Guild see the script - nevertheless I suppose she will collect her ten percent.

I am dreadfully sorry to hear that both you and Dad have been ill. Hope this finds you both recovered. If I didn't need a complete change so badly, after these weeks of tension and scurrying-about making "contacts", I would come home for a short while before leaving. But a week on the ocean seems too marvelous to delay. And anyhow I will come back by way of St. Louis when the re-writing is done and work toward a production really gets under way.

I'm going to pack a box of winter things and mail them to you. I plan to leave by the Cuba Mail Line, landing at Vera Cruz and going to Mexico City for a while and then on over to Acapulco which has marvelous swimming, fishing and resting. They say it never gets hotter than 86 although summer is not the tourist season down there. And then one American dollar buys $3.60 in Mexican money so I can live very cheaply while down there.

Meeting of the Playwrights' Seminar at the New School, with Tennessee on the right taking notes and Arthur Miller on the left smoking a pipe, New York, 1940.

If I leave Thursday afternoon, I will send you a wire giving next address, probably care of Wells-Fargo in Mexico City or Vera Cruz.

Much love to you all, Tom

[Before his decisive meeting with the Theatre Guild, TW wrote that "tonight Germany seized Denmark and war was declared by Norway - but infinitely more important is the fact that my play will be discussed and perhaps a decision rendered by the Theatre Guild" (*Journal*, ca. April 8, 1940).

The recent "weeks of tension" left TW feeling that "something has happened to the fellow that's been writing in here lately. He doesn't sound like the guy that I used to know in the days gone by. Sounds listless and coarse. Needs a good emotional shot in the arm. Something exhilerating. Some spiritual champagne. - Maybe it's the end of youth, my dear . . . hope not - it <u>mustn't</u> be!" (*Journal*, ca. March 28, 1940).

An abbreviated version of this letter was first published in *Remember Me to Tom*, pp. 115-116.]

148. To John W. Gassner

SH: Young Men's Christian Association
5 West 63rd Street, New York, N.Y.
Thursday April 11, 1940
[TLS w/ addendum, 2 pp. Yale]

Dear Mr. Gassner:

Here are the notes I made at the seminar in a hastily digested form. I should like to see your notes also if they contain any suggestions that I missed. As I mention in this summary, I felt that the two parts of the play would be integrated by the continuous emotional drives of Vee and of Val - (perhaps Vee's name, selected because of its pubic design, should be changed to avoid this alliteration!) - and I feel that if this integration is not apparent it is mainly because the first two acts do not emphasize or dramatize those emotional drives clearly enough, such as Val's cosmic consciousness and Vee's sexual religiosity. Acting and direction can apply a good deal of this special stress, but some re-working of the script might assist also. To me the sharp division of atmosphere seemed a good thing, the contrast between Good Friday and Easter, dark and light, like two movements in music, returning to the dark with the final scene in the cell. God knows, however, I am not going to be obstinate about a thing like this with a possible production by the Theatre Guild impinging upon it. I shall make every human effort to transfer the action to the store without sacrificing anything essential or making the whole thing implausible or false. When working with amateur and industrial groups in the middle-west I was limited to one-set plays and managed pretty well - wrote a ten-scene play running three hours ("Candles to the Sun") that all took place in one miner's cabin and another play "Fugitive Kind" that all occured in the lobby of a flop-house, each of which was originally planned for several sets. So I have developed ingenuity in these matters though I still find them rather nerve-wracking.

There seems to be some complication, certainly not precipitated by <u>me</u>, about the reading option. The hundred dollars seemed like rain from heaven, but Miss Case who is pinch-hitting for Audrey Wood, and Miss Sillcox over at the Guild have found some technical objection which I do not at all understand, especially since I need the money at once so I can get to Mexico and begin concentrated labor. The life here is scattered in so many directions that complete absorption in one job is well nigh impossible.

I do hope we can get a satisfactory script in a short time as I have two other plays in progress which I feel that I am stealing from and the Rockefeller fund will only run a few months more - then back on the street - and each time the concrete seems harder!

I am still in a bit of a cloud over this fabulous good fortune!

Cordially, Tenn. Williams

[The distinguished critic, teacher, and anthologist John Gassner (1903-1967) joined the Theatre Guild in 1929 and two years later replaced Harold Clurman as its chief playreader. The seminar that he and Theresa Helburn conducted at the New School was affiliated with the Dramatic Workshop recently established by Erwin Piscator. TW's "NOTES FOR REVISIONS ON BATTLE OF ANGELS," printed below, confirms that Val Xavier and Vee Talbott were the leads and that Myra Torrance was a lesser figure who died at the end of Act Two. In later revision the conflict between "Val's cosmic consciousness and Vee's sexual religiosity" would be subordinated to Myra's sensuality and her premature death abolished. Only gradually, however, did TW accept these and other changes (including a transfer of action to the general store owned by Myra and her dying husband, Jabe) and redirect the play's abstract focus to the more dramatic search for love and sexual freedom. The play's lack of unity was partly a consequence of ill-defined or sharply competing female leads, a potential casting problem that was exacerbated by the playwright's being unknown.

The "other plays in progress" were *Stairs to the Roof* and perhaps "Dead Planet, the Moon!"]

NOTES FOR REVISIONS ON BATTLE OF ANGELS

by Tennessee Williams

Main criticism was that play seemed too sharply divided between second and third acts. It was suggested that the third act be laid in general store instead of jail to give a more unified effect and keep Myra and earlier action more clearly in focus at the end. I think this can be done, if necessary, by having "wake" at store which would motivate presence of other characters. All the incidental characters which appeared in first two acts could be brought back if this is considered desirable. Val could return voluntarily "out of love" for Myra - though this does not strike me at the moment as being as truly in character as his flight and capture in present script but could be logically motivated I suppose. First scene of act three will end with his return and possibly at the moment when the funeral party arrives - Vee's "portrait of Jesus" must be kept as this is an integral part of the play. I must motivate her painting the picture or rather the preliminary sketch in the store and this will present some difficulties but not insuperable. Vee must also still have power to set Val free. Val will be imprisoned in store with negro and Vee as guards while Sheriff attempts to get help from Jackson Springs as in present. No radical change in scene between Val & Vee but the other two prisoners will have to be eliminated I suppose. The negro guard can take the place of Loo Loon. What troubles me chiefly is how we are going to keep the "locked door" theme if Val is imprisoned in store - it seems to me one of most powerful things in play is his passionate exhortation to Vee to release him by unlocking the door which is a symbol of her own dammed-up passion.

Unquestionably this removal of third act to store will give a more close-knit effect but I think we should consider the advantages and disadvantages very thoroughly before we go ahead with it. While it is true the play splits in two separate parts in present form, I think the second part gets under way and is tense enough in itself to compensate for the division and the scene between Vee & Dolly strikes me as the most artistic single scene that I have written in any of my plays. The contrast is a natural one between Good Friday and Easter. The first part has the stormy blackness of the Passion, the last part seemed to be an appropriate counterpoint with its brilliant sunlit quality, the roccocco red and gilt of Vee's parlor, etc. -

I think the problem of knitting the two together could be solved otherwise by building Vee up in two preceding acts and emphasizing more directly Val's mystical preoccupation with the meaning of life so that these two elements will integrate the play without limiting it to the store. The division is less apparent when you consider that Vee has appeared in both the first and second acts and her religious illusions and frustrated sexuality are pretty well "planted" from the beginning. I think much could be done to draw the play together by merely stressing certain elements in these two characters. It can be done either way - I personally feel it can be done better this way, without actual removal to store, but I am willing to try both. Anyway I feel sure a satisfactory integration can be very easily worked out. Actually the theme is perfectly continuous throughout even as it now stands. Each character is following his own emotional drive straight through the play.

It has also been suggested that a new scene be written on Val's arrival at store. This <u>can</u> be done and would have the advantage of enlarging Myra's part in the script though it is really inessential to the story development. I will try to dramatize Val's mysticism more in terms of action - if this is possible. It may well be.

How about putting Act three scene one in store "wake" but keeping scene two in the jailhouse? - a very simple and inexpensive set and one could keep the barred doors and windows with their strong symbolic quality and of course Vee would be logical custodian of keys? - Off hand this seems better than in store at end and the two sets could be keyed together so closely - both dark and "passionale" - that it would have nearly the effect of a single set with only the addition of bars. . . . By the time I reach Acapulco we should reach some conclusion on these matters. Please consider it as carefully as possible and write me there your final feeling about it and I will go ahead as directed.

149. To Bertha Case

SH: En Route
"Spirit of St. Louis"
Pennsylvania Railroad
<u>Sunday</u> [April 14, 1940]
[ALS, 6 pp. HRC]

Dear Bertha Case -

I made tracks out of town as soon as that checque came through and if the deal is illegal, I'll probably be "South of the border" before anybody can stop me. No copy of contract was enclosed with the checque just a note saying here is $100.00 "advance royalty" on your play. And by G. I see no earthly reason why I should refuse it - do you? Does Audrey get 10% of this? If she does, let me know and I will instruct the D. or T. Guild to deduct it from next remittance.

Have a swell new idea for revision which I think should satisfy the T.G. and would not take more than a week or two after I get settled. Don't you think I ought to demand more payment, though, before I submit a revised script to them??

I collected my short plays from Endrey who claims they are not plays but sketches. I gave him a tremendous lecture which left us equally breathless. He did not get mad, nor did I, it was just a complete ideological impasse. I have asked a friend to return these scripts to your office, together with an extra copy of "Battle of Angels" and a couple of short stories. Another story, "The Earth is a Wheel" is in the hands of Felicia Sorel, at Margaret Barker's office, and I wish you would get it from her as I plan to make something of it when I return East. You might let Harper's (Mr. Aswell) see "Something About Him" or "Miss Rose" (same story) and "The Vine". And ask Mr. Altman at Goldwyn's if he could use that "Safety first" script I did at his wish. It was unspeakably awful but I thought he might like it. There was mention of money between us, 2 or 3 hundred, if the script was O.K. If time ever hangs heavy, you might try to track down that "Death is a Drummer" script as I think even Mr. Endrey would admit that was a genuine 1-act play.

Best of luck, dear lady, and if I can get you anything in Mexico, let me know!

Below is a list of addresses where you can reach me. As I procede, I will keep you posted.

Cordially, Tenn. Williams

(for several days or week)
42 Aberdeen Place,
St. Louis County, Mo.

<u>Thereafter</u>
c/o Wells-Fargo
Mexico City, Mex.

[Bertha Case (1909?-1984), substituting for Audrey Wood who was on the West Coast, issued a stern warning to TW: "You are, under no circumstances to accept the check you received from the Theatre Guild, which is, as was explained to you, a violation of the basic minimum agreement" (April 19, 1940, HRC). The "basic" agreement with producers had been forged by the Dramatists' Guild in the 1920s to standardize author contracts and set minimum royalties. TW later described the Theatre Guild as "a goddam cold-blooded bunch" for issuing a "phoney 'reading option' check" (qtd. in *Windham*, p. 14).

"The Earth is a Wheel in a Great Big Gambling Casino" became a line, and a pattern of imagery, in *Stairs to the Roof*. The unidentified story was drafted in late-January 1940.

TW briefly visited his family in Clayton before leaving for Mexico via Memphis and Clarksdale, Mississippi.]

150. To Theresa Helburn

42 Aberdeen Place
Clayton, Mo.
Saturday P.M. [April 20, 1940]
[TLS, 2 pp. Yale]

Dear Miss Helburn:

Received your wire just at the point of departure for Mexico and am now waiting over to hear from you further. You must think it strange that I bolted New York immediately upon receiving your checque, but my residence there had become a sort of endurance contest in which I felt myself to be rapidly losing out. I seem to be constitutionally unable to stay [in] one place more than three months and I had been in Manhattan nearly four and had an excruciating nostalgia for the beach again. These considerations aside, if it seems imperative to the good of the play that I return to New York, I am certainly willing to do so. I recognize this as my one big opportunity and I can assure you that I'm not going to neglect anything connected with it. If it's the last thing I do, I'm going to present you all with a satisfactory script! Of course I feel that I can do this best by following my own ideas, however it seems to me that they coincide, generally, with your own. Aren't I right in assuming the main objection to the play as it now stands is that there is not sufficient continuity between the first two acts and the third? I can see that myself - and I have thought of an entirely new way to correct it - by writing a new first act in which Val arrives in the county as a vagrant and seeks a night's flop, as vagrants often do, at the county jail. This first act would have the same background as the last and would have the effect of 'the fatal circle'. As a matter of fact I have completely written out a first draught of this new act - it occured to me while on the train and I stopped here to get it written. It seems to me we could use this first act to develop anything which you think is not sufficiently developed in the rest of the play. That is what I am doing with it - bringing out the more sympathetic traits of Val's nature and building Vee up so that she will be sufficiently important to balance with Myra and hold interest in the last act. Structurally this should make the play just about perfect from my point of view, it would have more poetic quality and force - Val's first and last nights in the jail-house. The first night he has one of his nightmares about fire - sees flame-shadows on the walls and wakes up screaming. VEE enters and lets him out as she does at the end of the play - when the obsessive dream is finally an actuality. Well - I can't make it sound very intelligible in a letter but can mail you a copy of it in a short while.

If I returned to New York now would you all be willing to take a regular option on the play with monthly payments? The reason I ask is that my funds were going twice as rapidly there as they would in Mexico and the prospect of returning to the pavement perhaps before even Next Fall was becoming nightmarishly imminent. I KNOW what happens to destitute writers in New York!!! - I have SEEN it happen. - I would rather go broke somewhere south of Suez - or Acapulco - than on the fabulous isle of Manhattan! Shortly before I left a literary acquaintance was evicted from his room in a snow-storm - quite like a bit of old-time melodrama - and if I had not given him mine and provided food for about a week, there would have been some difference in the census if not in the world of letters.

Please feel free to give me any orders which you think are essential - this is the most important thing in my life so far and I'm not going to leave the tiniest pebble unturned! - if I can help it.

Cordially, T.W.

[Theresa Helburn's "wire" reportedly reached TW in Clarksdale and led to his return to Clayton. By late-April he was back in New York, living once again at the YMCA on West 63rd Street and consulting with Helburn and Lawrence Langner, co-directors of the Theatre Guild.

The November 1939 draft of *Battle of Angels* opens with Val installed as a clerk in the general store. TW had not yet accepted the continuation of Myra's part in Act Three and the use of a single setting as necessary steps in unifying the play.]

151. To Lawrence Langner and Theresa Helburn

[Young Men's Christian Association]
5 W. 63rd Street, New York City
May 1, 1940
[TLS, 2 pp. Yale]

Dear Wardens of my Future!

Here is the new ACT ONE, in two scenes, and the insertion about <u>Vee's picture</u>. - Mr. Langner, this is such an obvious and delightful expedient that I am surprised it hadn't occured to me without your suggestion, but I am tremendously grateful for it, as I think the elimination of Vee's parlor-scene with Dolly - though a colorful scene - definitely halted the story-line and without it the play seems to rise in almost uninterrupted line toward the end. I am definitely pleased, to say the least, with how this insertion has worked out. Vee's removal to the back room - when prostrated by recognition of her self-deception - provides another nice symbolic touch, since the back room subjectively represents the physical domain. And with the new first act, I think we can now regard the play as completed from the structural stand-point. What remains is simply pruning down and some manipulation with glue-pot, pencil and scissors, a purely mechanical business which perhaps can be done most effectively with the cooperation of actors and director when the play is actually in rehearsal.

You know, this is not my first long play but my fifth. While two of the others, <u>Fugitive Kind</u> and <u>Candles to the Sun</u>, were successfully produced by the Mummers of St. Louis in 1937 - and incidentally got a splendid reception from both the audiences and the press - Still, this is the first of my long plays which I have actually submitted to professional producers: it is the first one which I have felt <u>completely confident</u> could be produced on Broadway with both a critical and a commercial success. I don't believe I am deceiving myself about this - as this confidence is something I never felt about the four preceding plays.

This sounds like I am trying to sell you a play. I am. - A production by you all is something more than just a production. As I told Mr. Gassner, the Theatre Guild has always had such a fabulous ring to my ears that I did not altogether credit the report that you might be interested in an untried play-wright. After talking with you all yesterday I felt an assurance of sensitive understanding and professional knowledge of craftsmanship which was completely new to me in my contact with producers. Miss Case has told me that several producers are interested in typing up this script, but she agrees with me perfectly that no other consideration should enter, not even for an immediate production, while you all are seriously considering the play. I mention this because I want you to see that there isn't any lack of confidence on my side. I can only wish that this were sufficiently mutual for you to take out - now - a regular option on the play. I can assure you - if you did - that these bones would turn to powder and this flesh to dust before I would allow you to be let down!!

Sincerely, T.W.

P.S. These new parts are in first draft and I have been more concerned with structure than lines so a considerable amount of polishing will probably be needed. I have no carbons or additional copies, so please don't let them get lost!

[Lawrence Langner (1890-1962) had served on the Theatre Guild's original Board of Managers, while Theresa Helburn (1887-1959) was a playreader and later its executive director. They emerged as a strong directorate in the late 1930s, when the Guild's ideal of group governance was undermined by debt and a string of failed productions.

In the prompt copy of *Battle of Angels*, the "insertion" suggested by Langner appears in Act Two and allowed for the deletion of the parlor scene between Vee Talbott and Dolly Bland. Vee's earlier religious painting had led her to identify St. Paul with an attractive boy who operated the local gas-pump. Her present "self-deception" occurs when the face of Val Xavier appears in her visionary painting of Jesus. The "back room" to which she is taken is "the physical domain" of Val and Myra's lovemaking.]

152. *To the Williams Family*

SH: Young Men's Christian Association
5 West 63rd Street, New York, N.Y.
[May 3, 1940]
[TL, 2 pp. HRC]

Dear Folks:

Just have a moment to type a few lines. I'm in the middle of very dramatic negotiations with the Theatre Guild. The changes they wished were relatively slight to what I had expected and I think have already been satisfactorily worked out. The Dramatists' Guild and my agent are now putting pressure on them to make a different type of contract with me as the one I signed does not give me as much money as I should get. There is quite a battle in progress between the Dramatist and Theatre Guilds over this point. Both Miss Helburn and Mr. Langner spent half an hour bawling at them over the telephone while I was there, and were practically besides themselves with fury when the D. Guild refused to yield a point. Mr. Langner [*deletion*] I think had selected me as an easy mark until the D.G. stepped in. I'm sorry it has created this hullaballoo but the outcome will probably be profitable for me, as it is quite obvious that the Theatre Guild want to keep hold of the play, especially since Miss Case says that several other producers are also interested in taking an option on it. Both Langner and Helburn woke me up a few minutes ago with a phone call. Their new Saroyan play laid a terrific egg last night, the reviews were merciless - I attended the opening night and the play was as sorry and absurd a spectacle as I have ever seen in spite of a very fine production. So they are more up in the air than ever, espec- [*deletion*] as he had invested in the play. The Lunt and Fontanne play which also opened under their banner is a big success, however. They are taking my changes out to the country for a reading tomorrow and I shall probably come to final negotiations with them a day or two later. They were both simply shouting over the phone so I suspect that they feel themselves on the verge of capitulation. The New York theatre is just as full of sharp practice and shysters and rug-peddling tactics as any other commercial racket in the country - it is fortunate I have some people to deal with it for me.

I hope Grand and Grandfather are with you now. Let me know so I will know where to write them. I will drop a card to Memphis, anyway, in case they're still there.

Will write as soon as things are settled here.

With love,

[*Love's Old Sweet Song*, by William Saroyan, opened on May 2, 1940, to reviews that were mixed rather than "merciless," but the play was not a financial success and closed after forty-four performances.

Attending Robert Sherwood's anti-fascist play *There Shall Be No Night* (the Lunt-Fontanne "success") led TW to reflect upon the "Holocaust in Europe": "It really does sicken me, I am glad to say. Of course my reactions are primarily self-ish. I fear that it may kill the theatre. But I dare hope that there is a considerable degree of altruistic sentiment also involved" (*Journal*, May 30, 1940).

TW soon informed his grandparents that negotiations with the Theatre Guild were "successfully concluded" and that he had "a regular dramatist guild contract" for *Battle of Angels*. He added with some dismay that Joan Crawford, a "film star" without stage credits, seemed to be the Guild's first choice to play Myra: "They want everything to be subordinated to her part and of course this is not altogether satisfactory to me and just between ourselves, Miss Crawford, if she takes the part, will have just as much of the play as I think belongs to her!" (n.d., Columbia).

Both deletions in this letter are the result of razoring by an unknown person.]

153. To Audrey Wood

Provincetown, Mass.
(for a week or two)
July 5, 1940
[ALS, 2 pp. HRC]

Dear Audrey -

I came up here without my typewriter as I wanted to have a real vacation. At long last and after many radical changes such as eliminating the whole 3rd act and writing a new first scene, "Battle of Angels" appears to be ready for production. Copies are being sent out now to various actresses. I was appalled to learn that Joan Crawford was being most seriously considered for Myra. She is such a "<u>ham</u>"! There is a chance, however, that they might get Miriam Hopkins who would be magnificent in the part. Of course I will just have to take what they give me. I like Langner and he is very pleased with my willingness to take criticisms and suggestions - Of course I would be a fool not to at this stage of the game.

I'm getting back to work on my new play "Stair to the Roof" - It doesn't have the strong sex theme but I think is a more serious, artistic piece of drama than "B.A."

I can't imagine <u>your</u> being <u>permanently</u> satisfied in Hollywood if you love the theatre, but if things do <u>not</u> go well financially for me next year, I would like to try some work out there myself. For a short time between plays. I <u>miss</u> seeing you in N.Y. Miss Case and I are <u>excellent</u> <u>friends</u>, though I rarely see her, or anybody that I don't <u>have</u> to see. I get along best by myself.

Sitting out in the sun all morning - half asleep.

Feel curiously indifferent to everything in N.Y. at the moment, though my fate is probably in the balance.

Hope to see you in Manhattan or L.A. - or <u>anywhere</u>.

Best regards to you and Liebling - Tenn. Williams.

[In June TW had taken an East Side apartment with Donald Windham and Fred Melton, the young Georgians whom he met earlier in the year. By the end of the month he was settled in Provincetown, on "the frolicsome tip" (*Memoirs*, p. 53) of Cape Cod, where he met "the most raffish and fantastic crew" that his "excessively broadminded" (qtd. in *Windham*, p. 6) self had ever encountered. Among the bohemian tenants on Captain Jack's Wharf were Joe Hazan and Kip Kiernan, aspiring dancers who had studied in New York. With "Kip" TW had an intense, if brief, affair.

The "radical" revision of *Battle of Angels* probably occurred in late-June when TW visited Lawrence Langner's farm in Connecticut. As the prompt copy reveals, the original three acts were finally reduced to two, the action was transferred to the general store, and Myra's now climactic death was reserved for the end of the play. *Battle of Angels* was ready for submission to a major star, but as TW later commented, the problem in casting the female lead was fear of "the other woman," Vee Talbott, who still had "a dangerously good part" (qtd. in *Remember Me to Tom*, p. 117).]

154. To Luise M. Sillcox

[Provincetown, Massachusetts]
July 8, 1940
[ALS, 3 pp. HTC / HRC]

Dear Miss Sillcox:

(I left my typewriter in New York to insure a real vacation -)

I welcome this opportunity to tell you, with the limited capacity of words, something of my feelings about the Rockefeller foundation's dramatic awards. In my case the award was particularly "dramatic". You may recall something of my situation when the award was given. I had actually hocked my typewriter, my fraternity pin and almost everything else of negotiable value. I was at the nadir of my resources, physical, mental, spiritual. Being told about my "possibilities" no longer encouraged me. I had heard it too often - so often that I was beginning to think it would make me a damned good epitaph someday! I had written the first draft of a new play "Battle of Angels" but I am not ashamed to say that the shock of it, coming upon a long period of terrific strain, unnerved me so that I could not get out of bed - or stop laughing and crying - for an hour or two!

Since then I have finished my play - sold it to the Theatre Guild - written a new one and conceived still another and my life contains a completely new vista of creative work and fulfillment. I am ~~reasonably~~ happy and well-adjusted and very glad to be alive.

Does this answer your question?

I would like to add that I have known so many desperate, struggling young writers that I may regard myself as an authority on their problems - I don't think a finer nor more constructive form of philanthropy is possible than that which the Rockefeller foundation is doing in helping these young people. They are all nice kids. Intelligent, tolerant, liberal-minded - the country's surest bulwark against the disintegrative ideas of ignorance and violence.

I hope and pray this fund will continue for a long time.

Sincerely, Tennessee Williams

[Luise Sillcox (1889-1965), executive secretary of the Dramatists' Guild, had apparently asked for a summary report or testimonial as TW's Rockefeller grant expired. He later quoted his friend Paul Bigelow on the bounty of "our Babylonian plutocracy": *The very rich have such a touching faith in the efficacy of small sums*" (*Memoirs*, p. 3).

This letter is held partially by the Harvard Theatre Collection (page 1) and the Humanities Research Center (pages 2-3).]

155. To Lawrence Langner

73A Commercial Street
Provincetown, Mass.
July 2?, 1940
[TLS, 2 pp. Yale]

Dear Mr. Langner:

I am back on the Cape but far from relaxed in mind, as I have considerable anxiety about the situation in New York. While I was there neither you nor Miss Helburn seemed disposed to tell me very much about your plans for the play. Miss Helburn told me over the phone, when I called her, that the play was being sent to various actresses and that was all she could tell me. To be quite honest, I regard it as an act of God that Miss Crawford did not find it suitable, though of course her criticism of the play as "low and common" is not within my little comprehension. Certainly the play is mainly a study of sexual passion, but serious rather than titillating, so I don't believe any responsible critic would find any validity in such a charge.

When Joan Crawford was first mentioned to me, I could not exclude the horrible suspicion that perhaps you all were buying the play solely as a starring vehicle for her - and now that she has rejected it, I cannot help wondering if this may not have knocked your production plans into a cocked hat. If this is the case, I would like to know - I prefer to face the situation squarely rather than go on living in a fool's paradise, which really isn't much of a paradise since it is fraught with so much uncertainty. Of course I would acquiesce in anything that you decided on, since I want above everything else a Theatre Guild production, but now I believe more than ever - since hearing Miss Crawford's criticism - that my fabulous luck is still holding, and that if your belief in the play persists also, we will have a great success with it.

I did not mention Miriam Hopkins to Miss Helburn over the phone, but I did go to see her performance at White Plains and was introduced to her after the show. Her performance was absolutely superb, she is every inch a stage actress with emotional power and technical equipment; her Hollywood commitments might get in the way, however, if you wanted to use her. She hasn't seen the play yet, but Mr. Bennet Cerf has promised to show her his copy of it and she told him she would read it promptly. As far as casting is concerned, however, I have no further impulse to influence your own judgement, since apparently the only thing I felt very strongly about is no longer existent. - My one concern at present is just how <u>actual</u> your plans for production <u>are</u>, and I do hope you can give me some information about this. - Naturally I have to think ahead if I want to avoid a recurrence of the nearly fatal situations that I have barely managed to squeeze through in the past. . . .

I am working on "Stair to the Roof" and a new group of 3 one-acts. If somebody else were writing it, I think the new long play might turn out to be the "great American drama" - there is so much amplitude in the theme - more cosmic than sexual for a change. Seeing "Night Music" all through rehearsal was a marvelous object lesson to me - since that experience I would never release a play - however profound in subject matter - till I felt it had sufficient theatricality to make it commercial. Any play that is not "commercial" - that is, "good theatre" - is necessarily still-born, isn't it? - My problem with this new play is to make it exciting theatre all the way through - the theme is big and definite enough to require very little more work.

I am sending a snapshot for your press Dept. in case they ever have occasion to use one. Makes me look like the author of a good sex play, don't you think?

I hope you and Mrs. Langner are well and that I may hear something from you soon that will relieve my jittery state of mind.

Cordially, 10.

[Lawrence Langner tried to relieve TW's "jitters" by facetiously thanking him for his "snapshot" and chiding his aversion to stars: "As to the idea of doing your play as a star vehicle, Heaven forbid that this should be the case. Under no circumstances would I have your play so defiled." He explained that the Theatre Guild's "actual" plan for *Battle of Angels* depended upon "finding the right lady at the right time." Miriam Hopkins and Tallulah Bankhead were "tied up until Christmas" and the Guild was "still waiting to hear from Katharine Cornell" (letter, July 31, 1940, HRC).

Bennett Cerf, president of Random House, would soon announce a "'gentleman's agreement'" (see letter #166) to publish *Battle of Angels* after it was produced. TW also hoped to use Cerf as an intermediary with Miriam Hopkins, who had recently appeared in Molnár's play *The Guardsman* (1910).]

156. To Edwina Dakin Williams

[73A Commercial Street
Provincetown, Massachusetts]
Thursday A.M. [August 8, 1940]
[TLS, 3 pp. Columbia]

Dear Mother:

I wish I could share this marvelous weather with you, it is warm and bright every day and delightfully cool at night. Sorry to hear it has been so bad in St. Louis. New York was also terrible the week I went back there. Fortunate that I could get away again. I think this is one of the nicest locations in town, a wharf right over the water. When the tide is in, I can swim right out from my front door and am getting ready to do that very thing in a couple of minutes.

My food is costing me <u>nothing</u> as a bunch of us on the wharf are eating on the community plan. One couple furnishes the money and does no work, while several of us do the work and contribute no money. My job is dish-washing. This economy not necessary but helpful and we enjoy working together. Of course I have to go on paying my share of the apartment rent in New York while I am living here, as the two fellows I was sharing it with are still there and the lease continues till October 1st.

There have been some newspaper items about me and my play lately. A nice little article under the caption "New Playwright" exclusively about me on the front dramatic page of the New York Herald Tribune, Sunday August 4th. You can obtain a copy of it at the newstand downtown near the post-office or at the bookshop (Foster's) on Washington Ave. - may have to send to N.Y. for it, though. I didn't get a copy myself, only borrowed a friends, but am sending for a couple.

Then there was an announcement of the Theatre Guild's production plans, including my play, in the New York Times the Sunday just preceding, also front drama page, and the little clipping which I am enclosing about Random House. They haven't paid me any money for it yet and no actual contract is signed - they call it a gentleman's agreement which seems to be more to their advantage than mine. However I am very glad to have formed this alliance with a good book publisher, as it may prove useful in getting other things done.

The play is still in search of a leading actress, Mr. Langner writes me. Miriam Hopkins, Tallula Bankhead, and even Katharine Cornell are among the ones who are reading it. I met Miriam Hopkins in New York for a short chat when I gave her a copy of the play. She was quite cordial and gave me a pass to her summer theatre performance of the <u>Guardsman</u>. It would be wonderful if they could get her, but I am afraid she is tied up with the movies till about Christmas.

I do some writing here every morning, go out to the beach in the afternoons, very much like the life in California, only I think the country is more picturesque.

Delighted to hear Grand and Grandfather have finally taken some definite action about their plans. Give them my love - I will try to get home for a while when things are more settled.

Love to you all, Tom.

[As described in the *Herald Tribune*, TW was a youthful "twenty-six" and "concerned with sociological problems." The *Times* "announcement" (July 28, 1940) outlined a competition for casting among five Theatre Guild plays, including one by the team of Bertram Bloch and Isabel Leighton, who were represented by Liebling-Wood.

As censored for Edwina, TW's daily regimen differed sharply from the one mailed to Donald Windham and Fred Melton in New York: He was "taking free conga lessons, working on a long, narrative poem, swimming every day, drinking every day, and fucking every night" (qtd. in *Windham*, p. 11).]

157. To Joseph Hazan

[151 East 37th Street, New York]
[ca. August 18, 1940]
[TLS, 8 pp. HRC]

Dear Joe:

I've thought about you a great deal since I left and it seems that I have said goodbye to my brother, or something closer than that, because all in all I seem to have felt more understanding with you than anyone else. What I would have done without you during that messy, neurotic interval just past I find it hard to imagine.

I had an awfully strange feeling as the Boston boat sailed slowly around the lighthouse point and then distantly - austerely - past the new beach and the glittering white sand-dunes. Saw P-town dwindling sort of dream-like behind me. Not real at all. The Pilgrim-monument getting smaller and smaller till it was just a tooth-pick - "mad pilgrimage of the flesh" is what it seemed to stand for. This awful searching-business of our lives. Freddie was standing at the rail with me. All of a sudden he pointed excitedly and cried out, "There's Captain Jack's Wharf!" And sure enough it was, very tiny, like a pile of little sticks, but clearly recognizable next to the old Wharf Theatre. My throat got awfully tight for a moment. Before I ever came there by accident one morning, that is the way Capt. Jack's Wharf looked, a pile of little sticks on the edge of the water - Now it looked that way again, just as though nothing at all had happened in the time between. It is terrible how impervious, how careless things are. Our storms of feeling don't touch them. When Denby left the sand-dunes for instance - they were just as glittering white as ever. Although you and I both had begun to feel they were inseparable - as though emanating - from that curiously brilliant white and blue smile of his. If everybody left P-town, it would be the same wouldn't it? I mean the physical aspects of the harbor. - No, I guess it would be better.

Leaving always makes you conscious of that fatal, inevitable forward motion in life which at other times can seem so curiously stagnant. When you see a shore-line recede behind you, you realize very keenly and bitterly and excitedly what is happening to you all the time of your life - the Long Goodbye.

I went to see Anne Austin. A nice cross-eyed old lady, very, very cordial. She said Jack Cole would not need you till he entered the Rainbow Room, Oct. 16, and that there was no point in your returning now as he was still in Chicago. She said she had thought of you only last week and reminded Jack to write you - but he was busy as hell and it had probably slipped his mind.

I have been to the travel bureau and paid ten dollars down on my fare to Mexico City. They have a private car leaving the twenty-second and the fare is $25. I haven't discussed this imminent departure with the kids but it seems fairly certain. I wish you were going with me. Some day we will have to take a long, adventurous trip together some place - when I have the money.

Manhattan seems empty. Full of the most horrible little worm-like people who merely seem to occupy space but who are no doubt very real to themselves and to their little circle of contiguous lives.

I know that most of them, perhaps nearly all of them, are happier than I am, but I don't envy them. You and I are snobs, Joe. We are always looking down on the bourgeois!

I haven't discovered that exciting quality which Emily finds here in the summer. I think it is some beautiful quality in Emily's soul that isn't in mine at the present moment.

I envy anybody's excitement right now. I am going forth on a desperate search for some in a very few days.

Goodbye, Joe. I'm going to see you again before very long.

10.

Do you need anything? Glad to perform any possible service for you and Kip before I leave here. Love to everybody.

[Joe Hazan (1916–   ) reportedly studied with Kip Kiernan at the School of American Ballet in New York and came to Provincetown, where he met TW, to pose for the painter Hans Hofmann. Hazan became TW's confidant in the affair with Kip, found him to be a "charming" and "generous" friend, but as he informed the editors, had no inkling of his talent and was later "amazed at his great success." He and TW shared an apartment in New York while *Battle of Angels* was being rehearsed and then drifted apart.

The "messy, neurotic interval" refers to an affair with Kip Kiernan that ended abruptly in mid-August, wrecked, TW thought, by "a stupid little girl" (*Journal*,

August 15, 1940) who persuaded Kip to resist the homosexual world. In *Memoirs* he described Kip as a beautiful young "Canadian" (p. 55) who was dodging the draft. His actual name was Bernard Dubowsky, "Kiernan" taken from a phone directory to hide an illegal status (as reported by Leverich). Kip's death certificate, filed on May 22, 1944, spells his name as Kipp, lists his occupation as artist and sculptor, and records his birth in Amarillo, Texas, on September 17, 1918—information given by his widow, Robin Gregory Kiernan. The Texas Department of Health, however, has no birth certificate for Kipp Kiernan (or Bernard Dubowsky), nor is the Social Security number listed on his death certificate a valid one. TW recalled visiting Kip before he died on May 21 at St. Clare's Hospital in New York City (not Polyclinic, as TW notes in *Memoirs*) from an apparent brain tumor. There is no evidence of a Bernard Dubowsky death in New York at this time.

TW confided to Donald Windham that "nobody ever loved me before so completely" (qtd. in *Windham*, p. 10), but he was also ambivalent and doubted his own constancy: "Why am I always restless, searching, unsatisfied?" he asked, amid "the great <u>real</u> thing" that presumably would make life "complete" (*Journal*, July 19, 28, 1940). Although brokenhearted when the affair with Kip ended, TW resolved "to see it through. No bug-house for me, baby" (*Journal*, August 15, 1940). He quickly returned to New York with "Freddie" Melton, hoped that "somewhere there is another rare and beautiful stranger waiting for me" (*Journal*, August 18, 1940), and prepared to leave for Mexico. TW's allusion to his recently produced play, "The Long Goodbye" (see letter #139), reveals the perspective of a literary mind amid disorder, one that would soon turn the bittersweet experience of the summer into material for art.

The original "Wharf Theatre" was the stage of the Provincetown Players (1915-1922) and the site of Eugene O'Neill's first performed play, "Bound East for Cardiff" (1916). His legendary residence at Provincetown in the early 1920s is unnoticed in TW's letters and journal.

Collaborations with Orson Welles and Aaron Copland and a dance column in *Modern Music* had made Edwin Denby a well-known figure in the arts, and of considerable professional interest to the dancer Joe Hazan.]

158. To Joseph Hazan

[151 East 37th Street, New York]
Tuesday A.M. [August 20, 1940]
[TLS, 8 pp. HRC]

Dear Joe:

Swell of you to write when I was so needing a letter! Don't write your letters over, send them just as they are, otherwise they might become a burden to you and so be discontinued. I want our correspondence to be a kind of mutual confession in the best sense, the same purpose we use our journals for, so let us keep each other's letters and write whenever we can. There is no barrier between us in expression as we share all secrets.

It is Tuesday morning, Paul hasn't called yet. Is he in town? I am leaving Thursday and did want to see him before. I like him immensely: he seems above things: a kind of "katharsis" to me. He is mistaken in what he said, but I can understand why he thought so.

Oh, if I only had this ability to lose myself in "beauty" which you speak of, but too often it only hurts me in that it makes me more conscious of my isolation, and I am afraid that I will always be casting myself against the stones of the world in an effort to be "absorbed, included" to escape from aloneness. I pray for the strength to be separate, to be austere. That is the best future for me - asceticism and consecrated work. But remember what an animal I am! And don't expect too much of me.

Still, I have started off on a rather disciplinary regime. Only one or two drinks a day, when very low, and a calm endurance of moods instead of a mad flight into intoxication and social distraction. When I feel like writing a little poem, instead I sit down and labor away on the long play. It is tedious to me for some reason. It is more monumental in conception than anything I have attempted, but the animal in me rebels against it and wants to do little, diverting things, such as sentimental lyrics or things about sex. But I see now that to grow or even to survive I must practise more discipline with myself and I am resolved to do this. I have also plunged into physical culture, swimming thirty lengths each day at the "Y" and working with weights. The motive for this is probably an ignoble desire to have a body like Kips, but since it is good for me, we may ignore the motive.

I am sorry about these carousals as they are scarcely the desirable out-let for either you or for Kip who spoke of wanting "new life". I am glad I am not there to witness such things and be confused by them. I am not worried about their effect, very seriously, however, certainly not for you as your reaction is clearly stated, and as for Kip, there is too much idealism in him to submit very long to trivial dissipations. I am more likely than either of you to be involved in these things, I have many times in the past - but always turned away in revulsion when it reached a dangerous point.

Keep your "aliveness", Joe, cling to it all you can, but don't let it turn you too far inward, away from the world, because if sheerly for commercial reasons, we must adjust ourselves superficially to society, learn to make a place in it through our work. Let the aliveness be a reservoir you go to at intervals to draw your strength, a secret sanctuary you have, but don't turn your back on people. Then, don't worry about your difficulty in finding a love-relationship now. Instinctively I know that you shall, and that it will be deeper and more satisfactory and thrilling than almost anyone else's, because of this potential excitement you have which other's don't have. Patience!

I am getting didactic. - Will you ask Kip to write me? No, don't ask him, if he wants to, he will.

After Thursday my address will be c/o Wells-Fargo, Mexico City. Will send you my home address there when I arrive. Both Langner and Helburn are out of town and there won't be any casting for two more weeks. It is possible Langner may demand I stay here, I am supposed to hear from him Wednesday. - Will mail three dollars to bicycle man on 22nd when check comes. Also sending you and Kip a couple of books as remembrances. What would you all like from Mexico? Besides my love? -

Tenn.

[TW had recently met the "legendary" Paul Bigelow, as he later described his close friend and confidant. He thought him "mistaken," however, in describing his love for Kip Kiernan as "purely physical." Joe Hazan had reported this view of the affair along with news of a recent "carousel" on Captain Jack's Wharf that led him to reaffirm "work & beauty" as antidotes to dissipation. He urged TW to "make a monk" of himself and to live with "people who are clean sincere and simple" (n.d., HRC).

The "blues returned with a vengeance" on the evening of the 20th when Bigelow visited TW and revealed that he and Kip planned to live together in New

York in the fall. TW suspected that "either consciously or unconsciously" (*Journal*, August 20, 1940) Bigelow desired his former lover.

The "monumental," and "tedious," play to which TW refers is *Stairs to the Roof*.

TW bought a copy of *Sonnets from the Portuguese* (1850) for Kip and marked Elizabeth Browning's famous verse for his "attention" (*Journal*, August 19, 1940): "How do I love thee? Let me count the ways."]

159. To Lawrence Langner

[151 East 37th Street, New York]
August 22, 1940
[TLS, 2 pp. Yale]

Dear Lawrence Langner:

A devastating thing has occured in my personal life and I am running away. To Mexico. My emotionalism is much too great for my intellectual capacity, it is like having sixteen cylinders in a jalopy. Ultimately this will lead to complete disaster, but let us hope that evil day is postponed until I have completed my stint of creative work in the world.

Miss Lewis says that I have your permission to leave. The moment that I am needed I can return by plane within twenty-four hours and I will keep you all informed of my address. Which at first will be care of Wells-Fargo, Mexico City. In Mexico I want to lose myself completely in my work and come back with a finished script which you will respect. I have a real faith in STAIR TO THE ROOF (A Prayer for the Wild of Heart that are Kept in Cages), - though at the moment my mood is not so affirmative as the play's. It must work up steadily to a big scene, which is at a carnival and represents "the bright, lost dream of the child" and should be the dramaturgic orgasm of the work, but is still too weak, too shallow for the rest of the play. I must wait till this scene tops the others before I finish the script. Anyway I intend to hold it in reserve until "Battle of Angels" has been produced.

Miss Wood shares my concern about your production plans. We are both on tenter-hooks due to the lack of any definite news. I see no reason why you should be afraid of this play, since I feel with sensitive acting it has every chance of commercial success - and the moment rehearsals commence I'll return to give my complete attention.

Audrey Wood has bet me a new hat that "Battle of Angels" will win the Pulitzer Prize, and if I were not afraid of reminding you of Saroyan, I would offer you the same wager.

Will you let me hear from you as soon as there is any news?

Very truly yours, 10.

[Lawrence Langner advised TW that "the best thing to do when you feel all steamed up . . . is to run away and use up the emotion in writing a new play. This is what all the great geniuses have done." He added that Miriam Hopkins had been "prodded" (letter, August 23, 1940, Yale) about *Battle of Angels* and that Tallulah Bankhead would soon receive a script. Langner did not, however, rise to the Saroyan bait. To the consternation of the Theatre Guild, Saroyan had interfered in their productions and in May declined the Pulitzer Prize for *The Time of Your Life* (he opposed any "material or official patronage of the arts," or so he told the Pulitzer board), which the Guild had co-produced with Eddie Dowling.]

160. To Kip Kiernan

[151 East 37th Street, New York]
[ca. August 22, 1940]
[TL draft, 1 p. HRC]

Dear Kip:

Fuck the whys and wherefores. Just write me a letter because you're my friend and you know I want to hear from you. The rest has gone under the bridge and way, way, way out to sea!

Five o'clock in the morning I leave for Mexico. Will you write me care of Wells-Fargo, Mexico City? Almost immediately after that I expect to go to Taxco and then on to Acapulco to resume my life on the beach with a slightly more tropical setting.

Everything comes at once. I discovered the present checque was the last I will get from the Rockefeller foundation and from now on I am at the tender mercy of the Theatre Guild. Still no definite news about play production, the same old song and dance about looking for leading ladies. God knows, perhaps I'll be stranded on the beach at Acapulco without a fucking penny twixt me and the hairless chihauhaus. In which case, will you come down there and keep me? No?

I will be a nice, lazy beachcomber the rest of my life, dozing under a big wide sombrero and in my dreams I will see entrechats, pirouettes and marvelous arabesques.

Celebrating my departure, little bit stewed. Doug is here and we are expecting a bunch of people I knew in New Orleans. Antique dealers, charmingly homolectual - you know the type. They had us over for cocktails this afternoon and had a marine in uniform, very butch with a chest full of decorations for expert marksmanship. We ditched the Aunties and came to our studio but just got a call that they are coming here, too.

The marine has rushed away so they won't find him here. As Doug says, Life can be beautiful. Or all this and heaven, too!

I'm sorry I can't be as monkish as Joe would like me to be. After all, would that be me? I feel right now a definite reaction against all sobriety, my nigger laughing and dancing which Joe likes is part of this me and not the other me and this is the me people like. Except you. Or do you?

I hereby formally bequeath you to the female vagina, which vortex will inevitably receive you with or without my permission.

But I love you (with robust manly love, as Whitman would call it) as much as I love anybody, and want you to write!

[TW's suggestion that Kip Kiernan (1918?-1944) "keep" him was a coy reversal of the financial support that he had "very likely" (*Memoirs*, p. 55) promised to Kip when their affair began. TW resolved not to write about Kip until he could do so "fairly" (*Journal*, August 15, 1940), but he soon began (perhaps before leaving for Mexico) a "play-sketch" entitled "Parade" (n.d., HRC), which he later described as "angry" (letter to Andreas Brown, March 19, 1962, HRC). "Parade" evolved into the play *Something Cloudy, Something Clear* (1981), in which Kip was invested with an apparitional beauty and pathos, while TW reëxamined the exploitative nature of his sexual desire.]

161. To Joseph Hazan

[151 East 37th Street, NewYork]
[August 23, 1940]
[TLS, 2 pp. HRC]

Dear Joe:

Gloom clouds have suddenly dispersed and I am the brighter side of myself once more, in fact with a new accent, a feeling of convalescence. Seems to be the beginning of a new period - especially since the air this morning is crisp and sunny like Autumn. I leave for Mexico in an hour, the future is pretty uncertain but I find it stimulating.

I have a bunch of addresses from Random House and the Theatre Guild so will probably make friends down there pretty rapidly and lead a gay-mad sort of life the first week or two in reaction to what I've been through. Then settle down on the beach and try to catch up with myself.

Do you know I started to call you long-distance one night and beg you to come up here at my expense? Felt like I had to see you. The kids were out all the time and I felt kinda blue. But then Doug showed up and life assumed a terrifically rapid pace, what with us running into all kinds of old friends on the street - pretty inane but it served a definite purpose. Now I will have to live in Mexico till the play goes into production as I no longer have money enough to live well in New York, the Rockefeller funds being used up and just option money, which fortunately goes up to one hundred next month. But when I do come back we must get an apartment together. Funny - in my wanderings about I have met a great many people, nearly all friendly, many of whom I was fairly intimate with in one way or another, but nobody has seemed as close to me in spirit as you are. That was why I thought only of you at those times when my life seemed in danger of falling to pieces. It was a cumulation of tension that I have gone through for months and months here in New York, constant suspense and nerve-wracking excitement, which I evaded with drink and with sex. It all came to a climax in this neurotic condition just gone through, but I think is now over.

You remember Clark Mills mentioned in my journal? He came over last night and told me quite seriously that he had decided to kill himself within the next year. He is tied to an academic job at Cornell which smothers his creative life and he sees no possible escape as his poetry, very fine but completely non-commercial, could never support him. I reasoned with him for a long time about the infinite value of life, of the miracle of simply being alive, and through this I think I convinced myself of it. More, I'm afraid, than him. I saw very clearly the central fact of life and all the rest as being little motes in the sun, circulating around it. I wrote this line yesterday at the beginning of a long poem - "I want to infect you with the tremendous excitement of living, because I believe that you have the strength to bear it!"

It does take strength to bear the excitement of life. Doesn't it? Especially when we live and feel very intensely when things are exploding inside us.

Somehow I feel very sure of a great power in me these last few days and I know it is only waiting - waiting a little while - to emerge in something constructive. A great dammed up emotional energy which cannot be entirely dissipated by little things. I know you have the same thing and we both will use it better as time goes on.

I must go down and talk to Doug as I am leaving shortly.

His lover is in town. Doug has been marvelous but I have missed you greatly.

Write to me regularly in Mexico about yourself and Kip and your activities and plays. You know!

Devotedly your friend, 10.

[The "kids" are Donald Windham and Fred Melton, and "Doug" a friendly presence in the journal at this time.

Clark Mills had taught unhappily at Cornell since 1938. In recalling his visit to TW's apartment at this time, he informed Leverich that he read a note that he thought intended for him. It was instead a love letter signed "10" and obviously addressed to a man. It was Mills's first knowledge of his friend's homosexuality.]

162. To Bennett Cerf

SH: Hotel Plaza
Monterrey, N.L. Mexico
August 28, 1940
[ALS, 2 pp. Columbia]

Dear Bennett Cerf -

I have told both Audrey Wood, my agent, and Ruth Lewis at the Theatre Guild to be sure you got a script for Mr. Nathan. Will you please remind them if it isn't delivered promptly, as I am very, very anxious for Mr. Nathan to see the script if he is willing to read it. Nobody's criticism could be more important to me, so if he has time, will you suggest he let me know his reactions? c/o General Delivery at Acapulco, Gro., Mexico. I intend to live on the beach, more or less, till some action develops at the Guild. The situation seems very indefinite and as my Rockefeller funds are exhausted, I feel more than a casual concern I may find myself stranded down here. But that experience would not, at any rate, have the shock of novelty about it.

Langner says he is "prodding" Miriam Hopkins.

I hope with some response.

Drove down in a jalopy with some Mexicans and a gallon of dago red which now is exhausted and the bottle re-filled with tequila. They drink and fight among themselves - I sit back and sing "God Bless America" so loud I can't hear them and utter an occasional prayer to "Our Mother of the Highways" when the road becomes very exciting. We are now in Monterrey. Everything fell out of the car at Sabinas Hidalgo - it is being put together if possible. Then we shove on to Mex. City. Two more days of all this - and heaven, too!

Cordially, Tennessee Williams

[As the publisher of Eugene O'Neill and William Faulkner, Bennett Cerf (1898-1971) was potentially an important contact for TW. His firm, Random House, had published *The Theatre Guild Anthology* in 1936 and was alert to new dramatic talent.

TW had written earlier to Cerf that it was "perhaps foolishly daring of me to expose my work to the fluoroscopic eye" (September 12 or 13, 1940, Columbia) of George Jean Nathan. He hoped, however, to gain Nathan's critical favor (now claimed by William Saroyan) and to shield *Battle of Angels* from the acid reviews of Theatre Guild productions for which he was famous. Nathan reportedly read the play and gave a qualified approval, which he later withdrew (see letter #262).

TW had availed himself of "a share-the-expense travel agency" ("A Summer of Discovery," 1961) and described to Edwina a sedate journey to Mexico City "in a private car with a nice Mexican couple" (n.d., HTC). He reserved both the reason for the sudden trip and the complaisant response of "the prostitute-bride" in the party to the news that he was homosexual: "'I guess you're lucky, honey. Female hygiene's a lot more complicated than men's . . .'" (*Memoirs*, pp. 57-58).]

163. To Joseph Hazan

[c/o Wells-Fargo
Mexico City, Mexico]
Tuesday Sept. 3, 1940
[TLS, 3 pp. HRC]

Dear Joss:

(I believe that I still prefer Joe). I am leaving in a couple of hours for Taxco and Acapulco. Mexico City is too big to take in one gulp so I am going away to the beach till my throat stops aching and then come back and try to swallow some more. At first I thought there was nothing here: mistaken: there is a tremendous lot but I am not strong enough for it right now. I go up and down, up and down the see-saw of moods, because my nerves are exhausted. I pursue stability: yes, the crisp, silent nights, the understanding stars, the katharsis of loneliness which is <u>aloneness</u> and not solitude among crowds. Last night, for instance, I was entertained at the home of Juanita, who is the queen of the male whores in Mexico City. They accosted me on the street and took me there. Such strangeness, such poetic "license"! We sat in a room with pale pink walls and enormously high ceiling, covered with pictures of nudes and pictures of Saints and madonnas. The bed was very wide to accomodate several simultaneous parties and was covered with a pale lettuce-green satin spread. Above it hung a handsome black and silver crucifix and Jesus with great sorrowful dark eyes looking over the pitiful acts of lust that went on there. No doubt thanking his lucky stars that he remained a celibate on earth, because if he had not - it is quite likely he would have been a fairy. Some of the whores were very, very lovely with eyes dark and lustrous as those of the Christ and smooth olive skins. But I stayed out of bed with them because I suspected they were all rotten with disease. I could speak no Spanish but "Manana es otro dia", they could speak no English, so there was none of that tiresome necessity for conversation which I despise so much. We laughed and drank together and three who had exquisite high voices and a feminine quality that was graceful and charming - instead of like Bobby of the Wharf's - sang a beautiful song called "Amor Perdida" - very haunting. They were like sad, wonderful flowers - <u>Fleurs de mal</u> - their price was two pesos, the equivalent of forty cents. And one was so lovely that when he kissed and embraced me, I had an orgasm, but I showed more than my usual discipline and kept out of any real mischief.

I also met a pitiful crowd of American drifters, one tubercular and living on hand-outs from chance acquaintances. Dropped them at once since they merely depressed me further and that would not do in the present circumstances.

This morning I woke up feeling very low, after Juanita's. Sick, neurotic headache that affected my stomach, old defeatist routine of thought. So I started packing and determined to leave at once for the coast. Acapulco. But before going went to see this woman whose address I got from the Theatre Guild. To show you how badly I needed human contact of the right kind, all my neurotic symptoms disappeared after her gracious reception. She seemed to understand intuitively the state that I was in and her whole manner was brimming with kindness. My nerves straightened out and my head became cool and quiet. It was like having a raw wound wrapped in a long white bandage. I feel now that it will be a woman I will finally go to for tenderness in life. They are drawn to suffering in men and know how to ease it. The sexual part - if there has to be any - would probably adjust itself in a while, since I am so easily directed in that way.

The mood that you were in when you wrote this letter is so much like mine! We are both standing on the outside of reality, looking in, and it appears all fantastic and empty. We are clutching at hard, firm things that will hold us up, the few eternal values which we are able to grasp in this welter of broken pieces, wreckage, that floats on the surface of life. Yes, it is possible, I think, to surround one's self with stone pillars that hold the roof off your head. It takes time to build them, time and careful selection of materials, infinite patience, endurance. We must make a religion of that last thing - endurance. Read the collected letters of D.H. Lawrence, the journal and letters of Katharine Mansfield, of Vincent Van Gogh. How bitterly and relentlessly they fought their way through! Sensitive beyond endurance and yet <u>enduring</u>! Of course Van Gogh went mad in the end and Mansfield and Lawrence both fought a losing battle with degenerative disease - T.B. - but their work is a pure shaft rising out of that physical defeat. A permanent, pure, incorruptible thing, far more real, more valid than their physical entities ever were. They cry aloud to you in their work - no, <u>more</u> vividly, intimately, personally than they could have cried out to you with their living tongues. They <u>live</u>, they aren't dead. That is the one ineluctable gift of the artist, to project himself beyond time and space through grasp and communion with eternal values. Even this may be a relative good, a makeshift. Canvas fades, languages are forgotten. But isn't there beauty in the fact of their passion, so much of which is replete with the purest compassion? And so we come back to the word "beauty" - which I thank God is significant to us both. Let us have the courage to believe in it - though people may call us "esthetes", "romantics", "escapists" - let's cling tenaciously to our conviction that this is the only reality worth our devotion, and let that belief sustain us through our black "tunnels".

Away from abstracts to practicalities. If Manhattan is unendurable, beg, borrow or steal about thirty or thirty-five dollars and come down here and live on the beach at Acapulco. We will work out some pattern down here which - if not perfect - will enable us to function freely within the necessary limits. There will be those symbols of universality around us, the beach and night skies, and we can select a few people whose presence are comforting to us while resting from work. Your work is individual, it comes out of yourself and not from any instruction. You could perfect it alone: especially in a primitive atmosphere with possibly the native dances to draw from - new patterns. I think I am going to love the Mexican people - later, when I grow calmer inside.

Kip wrote me a nice letter. He is living behind a wall without even a grated window for you to look through, you have to peek through the cracks, through the broken mortar, but when you do, you count more flowers than weeds on the opposite side. - Give him my best and also Paul. Devotedly your friend,

10.

["Joss Hassan" was the stage name of the "Hindu dancer" and student of eastern philosophy, Joe Hazan. TW spent "a lonely week" (*Memoirs*, p. 58) at the YMCA in Mexico City before leaving for Taxco and Acapulco.]

164. To Joseph Hazan

[c/o Wells-Fargo
Acapulco, Mexico]
[September 1940]
[TLS, 1 p. HRC]

Dear Joe:

This letter has been lying around here quite a while and in my tropical inertia I forget to mail it.

This last week I have gone back to work and am making fairly good progress. Started with a short story which is developing into a novel and may develop further into a play. Also a verse drama about the war and the usual lyric or two. Joe, if I sent you a bunch of my more marketable poems, would you like to try peddling them around town for me? I would give you a fifty percent commission on any sales. You look so goddam poetic that I think you could get right into the sanctum sanctorum of The Atlantic Monthly!

Nothing new here, except one new lover, a lovely native named Carlos who swims with me every night. Not knowing the language I have learned to be very direct. I dispense with all the tedious subtleties and merely say "Usted amor muchach<u>os</u> or muchach<u>as</u>!" - Carlos said "Non importe!" - So we go up on the "playa", under the moon and the whispering mango trees, and the restless beast in the jungle under the skin, comes out for a little air.

The writer is leaving soon for Mexico City: he is a spoiled creature. Son of the manager of the Pullman company and wealth has surfeited his senses so he can't find zest in anything. He raves continually about his sex experience which has been infinite and altogether with women, but horribly dull, and love is impossible for him. He despises women but wants to fuck all the time. He even says he finds their bodies disgusting when they take off their drawers. He is terribly lonely but too selfish to be absorbed in anyone but himself. He realizes this and is very miserable about it. He has written only for slicks and wood-pulps, popular stuff, but is now attempting a serious novel about his frustrations in life and in lack of love. You can imagine what a mess it is going to be. - I feel sorry for him but am rather relieved he is leaving. - I am inwardly strong and independant again. Not an admirable person in my way of living, but preserving my own kind of integrity through love of honesty with myself and with others. And so in contrast to Andy, who has never learned honesty and is now too old to learn it, my own situation doesn't seem quite so bad. - Things have had time to happen since you last wrote. What are they? I hope you are buzzing, buzzing, <u>buzzing</u>!

10.

[TW returned to work after a period marked by "heartbreak" and "the dullness and tedium of a mind that no longer particularly cares for existence." "Never, never," he was sure, would he "know the meaning of peace. But there is such a thing as relative peace . . . and that will return after {a} while" (*Journal*, September 8, 1940).

At Acapulco TW stayed at Todd's Place, a resort run by a drunken "Georgia cracker" and his "fat Mexican" wife and "occupied mainly by lizards - and Tennessee Williams" (letter to Lawrence Langner, n.d., Yale). He met the perennial travelers Paul and Jane Bowles and later became a close friend and advocate of their writing. Paul, who would compose the incidental music for *The Glass Menagerie*, remembered meeting a "sunburned young man in a big floppy sombrero" (*Without Stopping*, 1972) who had called at an inconvenient time.

The new work with novelistic and dramatic potential was a revision of "Why Did Desdemona Love the Moor?" (see letter #126). Its working title "The Bitch" refers to the cynical actress of the story, perhaps an early study for the Princess in *Sweet Bird of Youth* (1959). TW used the same provocative title for the story "Bobo" (October 1941, HRC), a draft of "The Yellow Bird" (1947).

Carlos did not care whether he made love with boys or girls. The sexual imagery of "the restless beast" was formalized in a "lyric" that TW composed at Acapulco: "When will the sleeping tiger stir / among the jungles of the heart?" (qtd. in *Windham*, p. 12).

TW identified the "spoiled creature" as one who wrote "mainly for slick publications under the name of Andrew Gunn" (fragment to an unknown correspondent, n.d., HRC). He claimed, in a letter to Donald Windham (see *Windham*, p. 16), to have had a tedious affair with him, a relation that was imaginatively recast in the story "The Night of the Iguana" (1947).

At Acapulco TW was reading a more talented and promising writer than Gunn, with whom he would develop a close friendship: "I brought one novel down here with me called "The Heart is a Lonely Hunter" by a young girl named Carson McCullers. It is so extraordinary it makes me ashamed of anything I might do" (letter to Bennett Cerf, September 12 or 13, 1940, Columbia).]

165. To the Theatre Guild

c/o Wells-Fargo
Acapulco, Gro., Mexico
Sept. 20, 1940
[TLS w/ autograph postscript, 2 pp. Yale]

Dear Theatre Guild:

Jesus Christ! Your monthly remittance is alarmingly delayed, I've been broke ten days, Todd and the Mexican woman and the crazy French refugee have all vamoosed, and there's nothing to eat on the place but cocoanuts and a pot of cold <u>frijoles</u>! If you decide to give up the "battle of Angels" I hope you will give me thirty days warning at least, so I can arrange to move the body some place where it can spill its hard luck stories in English.

We had a terrible time here the last few days. The French poet, Andre Genung, arrived by boat. He was a surrealist even before the war and the ordeals that he went through in escaping from France did very little to clarify his mind. After two or three days at Todd's place he began to believe himself to be Joan of Arc and started following the Mexican woman around with a big machete, which is a broad knife used in chopping the ends off of cocoanuts. As the Mexican woman has a very large bosom, the situation was fraught with considerable danger. Todd refused to take any action, so the woman went into town and brought back three Mexican soldiers. They all got drunk and still no action was taken. Then when I woke up the next morning the place was deserted, everybody was gone except two or three children - whose I have never discovered - who run around naked and climb the palm trees like monkeys.

I am doing a great deal of writing here now. Something extraordinary is happening to the long play. It is like one of those Chinese poems that are hard, round pellets of paper until you drop them into a cup of warm tea, when they open and blossom out like flowers so you can read the verse on them. - Apparently Acapulco or Todd's place was the cup of warm tea that my drama needed, because it is now unfolding at a surprising rate. I am packing into it practically all I have felt about life. It will probably take a good while after it's finished for weeding it out. But I feel it is going to be far and away my best piece of dramatic writing. At least from the literary point of view.

I noticed in the papers before I left that your and Mrs. Langner's play was going into production this year. Having read part of it out at your place, I am delighted to hear this - I don't need to wish you luck with it, the script struck me as being a natural.

Will you advise me about the checque if it's being held up for some reason? - Otherwise, don't bother.

You have two poems of mine I forgot at your country place - Will you please take care of them for me as I have no other copies? Just put them away somewhere till I get back.

Cordially, 10.

P.S. Checque arrived in this A.M.'s mail, thank God!

Thanks & best wishes! T.W.

[TW's monthly option check of $90.00 was "delayed" because he had not informed the Theatre Guild, or Audrey Wood, of his departure from Mexico City.

The "surrealist" poet Andre Genung has apparently left no trace in the avant-garde literature of the day.

Stairs to the Roof, the "long play" in progress, begins with a standard 1930s critique of capitalism and ends with Mr. E, a chastened god of creation, envisioning the colonization of a new star, by a new Adam and Eve, where sex is not required for procreation. Described by TW as a "serious comedy," the play drew upon his years at Continental Shoemakers in St. Louis and led him to reflect further upon the themes of urban stagnation, the exploitation of small wage earners by callous corporations, and the inherent tedium of domestic relations. The Theatre Guild held a reading option on *Stairs*, and as TW informed his family, he had "to make it as good as possible" (see letter #166).

TW probably read *Suzanna and the Elders* (1940), the Langners' comedy about utopian communities and plural marriages, while a guest at their farm in June. More candid reviewers panned the play when it opened on Broadway on October 29, 1940.]

166. To the Williams Family

SH: "Hotel Costa Verde"
Acapulco, México
Sept. 21, 1940
[TLS, 2 pp. Columbia]

Dear folks:

I've been in Mexico about three weeks now and find it a very good place to work. The picture at the top is a very bad one of the hotel where I'm staying. The situation is really the most beautiful I've ever known. The hotel is on a high cliff over the bay, which is blue as the Mediterranean. The beach directly below is the best in Acapulco. The water is very very smooth and almost too warm at this time of year, like tepid bath water. Hotel surrounded by palms and mango trees. Such exotic creatures as armadillas, ocelots, panthers, parrots, and even some monkeys are in the jungles nearby. In the lagoon there are alligators and safely outside the bay there are sharks.

My checque was late in coming but has now arrived. A slight crisis developed when ten American tourists ran out on their rent in the middle of the night. They had run up a big bill with drinks and other extras, so the Padrona became hysterical and refused to serve any more meals till all the other American guests had paid up in full. I can't get any American dollars here now but will be able to in Mexico City. I will go back there soon as my present writing job is finished. I am completing work on a new long play which the Theatre Guild took a reading option on last summer but haven't seen yet. I have to make it as good as possible. And this is the best place I've found yet for concentrated work. Another writer and myself have the whole back verandah to ourselves - and write and look out over the sunlit bay and relax in hammocks when labor is impractical. This is in the tropics, but I don't find it as hot as New York. There is always a breeze off the ocean and the nights are actually cool. I seldom go into town except for mail as the poverty there is depressing. The natives live under almost animal conditions. The pictures which I am enclosing were taken in Taxco, a picturesque town very popular with tourists between here and Mexico City. It is built on the side of a mountain. Mexico City is just about like any American city, only more beggars and fewer conveniences. Of course the climate is wonderful, like spring the whole year around, but the altitude, 8000 feet, gave me a headache, so I only remained a few days.

There is absolutely no talk of revolution down here. I'll probably stay till about the middle of October and then go back to New York, stopping in St. Louis for a week or two. I just don't know when the Theatre Guild is planning to put my play on and apparently they don't know either. They say it depends on when the right actress is available and that may not be till after Xmas. I am living entirely on their advance royalties now as my fellowship money is used up. They pay me a hundred a month now minus ten percent to Audrey Wood. Random House publishers have announced in the papers that they will publish the play after it is produced - they call it a "gentleman's agreement" and I am getting nothing out of it now. Everybody is very uncertain about what the war will do to theatre business especially in the case of serious, artistic plays. There is a great demand for musical shows and light comedies. Some critics think, however, that it may have an effect opposite to that expected, and people will have an unusual interest in plays that have some depth to them. As the season hasn't started, the question is yet to be answered.

Is there much talk of conscription, and would Dakin be involved? I guess my bad eye would let me out, so perhaps it has a beneficent purpose after all.

I'm awfull glad you are all settled in the new house. Grand, I hope you are well and taking care of yourself. I'm really anxious to get back for a visit - right down home-sick at times - but while I am working well here, don't think I should leave till the work's about finished. Did Aunt Ella visit you? - I will try to write her soon.

Life here very very quiet. I write all morning and part of the afternoon, swim before breakfast and again before supper. Spend the evenings in a hammock talking to the other Americans and drinking iced cocoanut milk right out of the shell - sometimes with a little rum in it.

Much love to you all, Tom.

P.S. - I bought you some beautiful Mexican photographs by the best photographer in the country, Moctezuma, and will either send them or bring them home with me when I come. They look beautiful in natural wood frames. - They are Mexican scenes, landscapes, Etc.

[After the Todds, the proprietors of the hotel, had "vamoosed," TW moved to the

Hotel Costa Verde, which would supply the off-stage setting for *The Night of the Iguana*. To promote the play's opening in 1961, he published an account of its origin in the tumultuous summer of 1940, linking his own emotional crisis to the stalled production of *Battle of Angels* and omitting any reference to Kip Kiernan (see "A Summer of Discovery").

TW later explained to Theresa Helburn that his mother had been "alarmed by reports of revolution in Mexico" (see letter #168) and exaggerated Grand's illness to hasten his return to St. Louis. To Bennett Cerf he further discounted "talk" of revolution and described the conflict between General Almazan and the Mexican president, Lazaro Cardenas, as "a totally unwarranted superfluity of grease! Graft has absorbed whatever wealth was released through the partial socialization. They work for two pesos a day and beer costs fifty centavos. Almazan would be worse, of course, but there isn't much to be said for the present regime" (October 10, 1940, HRC).

TW and his brother Dakin were subject to the Selective Service Training Act passed by Congress on September 16, 1940. Compulsory registration of males from twenty-one through thirty-five years of age began on October 16, with induction to be decided by a national lottery. TW was classified "IV F" and his "bad" left eye soon required cataract surgery. Dakin was studying law at Washington University and did not enter military service until November 1942.

The "house" at 53 Arundel Place, in fashionable Clayton, was the first one that Edwina and Cornelius owned in their married life. She has recalled in her memoir that a "chastened" Cornelius bought the Georgian Colonial for her after a drinking bout and then "regretted his generosity."]

167. To Joseph Hazan

SH: "Hotel Costa Verde"
Acapulco, México
Sept. 24 or 25 [1940]
[TLS with autograph insertion, 6 pp. HRC]

Dear Old Joe:

The Padrona just stuck your letter through my screen door. I had tied it closed with a string to exclude an inquisitive wasp - I threw up work on the play to read "YOU" who are really more exciting than work is.

Don't castigate yourself like that for criticizing people. It isn't to exalt yourself that you do it. It's just our inevitable function of looking at what is around us and making honest remarks. You don't spare yourself and neither do I. Each morning when I get up I look at myself in the mirror, and say with surprise and scorn and a kind of amused tolerance, "Well, here you still are, you old bitch!" - Now, that is definitely a ruder remark than anybody has ever addressed to me, besides myself. And I have heard you say things to yourself which are less gracious and more severe than anyone else would say to you. - So go right ahead, unembarrassed, with your analysis of the social world about you. It is an excellent thing. Tear your friends to pieces. I know you well enough to know that you will do it with a reserve of understanding and compassion and the realization that the whole idea of guilt is mistaken, that all of us are the little products of chance and so not to be chastised too severely for what we are or do or anything else.

Paul shrunk quite visibly when he visited me in New York after I left P-town, I particularly noted a dishonesty in his statements about Kip, his insistence that he felt no desire for him - but wanted to live with him in New York. So obviously a deliberate self-delusion! If not an out-and-out lie. - I think, however, that everyone shrinks in New York. Our faces and bodies get pale and the bustling about makes us little and nervous again. Lies come as naturally as flies at a church-picnic.

Despite this fact, I believe I am soon coming back. If not to New York, at least to the States. And all roads eventually lead back to Manhattan. For one thing, my Mother writes that my Grandmother is very seriously ill. I read between the lines that her condition is really critical. As I may have told you before, my Grandmother is the only relation I really care for. And though to see her in a lingering, mortal illness would be a terrible ordeal, still I couldn't stay away. So I will probably start back in a very short time perhaps this week-end. I have finished one phase of work on the long play. And it seems I might do the second better in proximity to the actual theatre. Then lights, theatres, city glitter and excitement draw me back like a moth, I can't stay away very long. A month or two and I'll be surfeited with that once more and wish to be back here.

The people here are of two classes, those who are waiting for something to happen or those who believe that everything has happened already. That is, the Americans and other outsiders. Their life is lying about the beaches usually in a hypnosis induced by strong drink and hot sunlight and lack of any exertion. Or sitting in a cantina on the square and carrying on light, trivial conversation about their fellow expatriates. Nothing surprises or interests them particularly, not even a world that is cracking up all around them. They grin and squint in the sunlight and squeeze a drop or two of lemon into their rum-cocos. And the dark, slow natives drift around them like figures in a dream. The juke-boxes play on every side of the plaza, furiously bright posters announce three bulls will be killed this week-end. So the life here is just as weird and grotesque in its way as the life in the industrial centers up north. - I am sure, now, that I will never find one particular place where I feel altogether at home, will just have to keep moving about and absorbing as I go. One definite thing has been accomplished which is what I set out for. To put Kip out of my blood. He's gone as completely now as if he had never existed. Except I still have a feeling of friendship for him and of course I would help him at any time that I could. - The human bondage is broken.

No, my advice was probably unwarranted. I cannot see you getting shipwrecked on any emotional reef right now. You sound pretty well stabilized in your work and your plans. I am sure, quite sure, that you are finding yourself a straight line upwards - and that it isn't the one projected by an erected penis!

Getting vulgar. - So long. I will send you a card to let you know where I'm going when I make up my mind.

- 10.

Later - I am in a bad humor tonight. There is a hard tropical downpour which has driven all the hotel guests onto the back verandah and me into my room to escape them. They are predominantly pro-Nazi Germans, coarse, loud, overwhelmingly arrogant, descended on the hotel in a swarm the last few days. I tried to speak to one of the girls yesterday and she said, "Excuse me, I don't speak Yiddish." Apparently she thought I was Jewish or else regarded all Americans as Jews - anyway the remark struck me as incredibly revolting in its racial nastiness and smugness, and since this crowd is in undisputed possession of the premises, I am probably going to leave in the next day or two. - Hitler has ruined the Germans, he has so thoroughly sold them on his lowest of bourgeois ideology. If the whole world falls into this state - and some people say we must be Fascist to fight

Fascism - it will be well nigh impossible to live in during the remainder of our generation. Gentle ideals were impotent enough before - what will become of them now? What will become of us? What will become of our passion for truth in this great Battle of Lies? Who can we speak to, who can we write for - what can we say? - Nothing but GOD BLESS AMERI-CA! - Oh, God, Joe - We have to get out and stay out of this damnable mess till it's over! - If only I can get my play on this year and make money, money, money! - Which is escape. - A yacht! Yes, that is a beautiful idea. - Where we can go places like this but stay just outside the stink of the people on shore. There are some British people doing just that. Mexico and Chile are the only countries that will admit them so they move between those two in their boat - which is a sailing vessel with an auxiliary motor - There are six of them, two of them writers - very charming young men - and all of them the wise, tolerant, gracious sort who are naturally exiles from this world.

Yes, if I get a good deal of money, that is what I will do, buy a boat and stay mostly off-shore till La Paloma flies back with the leaf of an olive! - However the things that I have to sell in my work - what little I can give to the world in the way of poetic truth - is going rapidly down on the war-time market, and lies and manic laughter and nationalistic hooopla are soaring dizzily up!

One of the German girls has just been bit by a scorpion and is screaming. I hope she dies.

The rain makes a loud, continual noise and the lightning glares balefully through my screen door. I think I will take off my clothes and go for a walk among the elements. Maybe God will be in a conversational humor tonight - for a change - and explain some things to me which I find most confusing.

I suspect that I don't have very much longer to live. A few years ago I was told that if I lived prudently, did everything in a calm and deliberate way, my circulatory system, which is considerably impaired from diptheria and Bright's disease as a child, might last till I was forty. But I have been doing all the things that I shouldn't and going as fast as I can, so probably that limit has been moved forward. - The Germans are going to bed - they grumble about my typewriter. Why do I write you this shit about my possible decease? Not for sympathy - I was congratulating myself -

Nevertheless it was stupid. You see I write you whatever comes into my dizzy brain and only afterwards think to censor the stuff - but leave it as it is and trust to your understanding.

Starting off again, probably tomorrow. Not sure where. Soon - St. Louis. Ultimately (perhaps soon) N.Y. - Do you still want to take a place with me? - Look around for something suitable and let me know. Will send my next address shortly.

10.

(Please save this for me)

STILL later:

Still here. The spell of this place is difficult to break. I have written home to enquire about my grandmother's condition and if it isn't immediately critical, I may hang on here till the middle of October, when my next checque comes in.

Joe, I'm going to give you a little lecture on the state of the world, partly because I wanted to clarify it in my own mind. I sat up all night talking it over with a man who has made the profoundest study of such things I have ever come in contact with.

First of all, Joe, we are being nailed between two horrible forces which are <u>CUPIDITY</u> on one hand and <u>STUPIDITY</u> on the other. It is hard to know which is worse. The cupidity is that of the owning classes and the stupidity that of the owned. In the past half-century or less something has happened which is still being kept a secret from the people. Namely, the collapse of the PROFIT SYSTEM on which CAPITALISTIC SOCIETY is based. For its success the profit system depended entirely on NEW FRONTIERS. For about forty years, now, the new frontiers have been exhausted, the world is all explored, colonized, industrialized, developed. What remains is negligible and not enough to keep the profit system going. You know what the profit system is. It is exploiting labor to produce and sell commodities for more than they are worth, the difference going into the pockets of the employers or CAPITALISTS. Where is this profit coming from? It is coming from the people, the laborers, the exploited masses. It is going <u>to</u> the capitalists. Now, as long as the capitalist had new frontiers to invest in, they kept their money going out again, re-investing it, keeping it active and constructive. But now that the new frontiers are exhausted, the capitalists have stopped putting money out in re-investments. Consequently the money is being tied up in their pockets. Consequently no new labor is being hired. Consequently the purchasing power of the masses has dropped. Consequently the factories cannot continue to operate profitable. Consequently they are shut down. Consequently there is unemployment, misery, depression, starvation, desperation for the exploited masses. WHY? Because the PROFIT SYSTEM IS DEAD BUT WON'T LIE IN ITS GRAVE!

The capitalists will not own up to their defeat, they cover it up desperately with all kinds of lies and makeshifts. The true monstrosity of this deception will make your blood run cold when you see it clearly and clearly think about it. CUPIDITY & STUPIDITY. The masses are so dumb they don't recognize what has happened & the capitalists are so cupidacious they won't tell them. Any thing to keep the profits a little while longer, although they are nearing the final impasse. The new deal has been a frantic effort to pump blood back in the dead system - an oxygen tank for an octogenarian - through government spending the masses have been given new money to pay the profiteers to re-open their closed plants. This is just a makeshift and the steadily increasing deficit makes it impossible to go on much longer. Then we will enter the last phase in which a final choice must be made. Between FASCISM and COMMUNISM, the only two feasible substitutes for the Democratic or Capitalistic system.

Fascism partially limits profits, say, to about six percent. Communism does away with the profit system altogether. Hence on this count alone Communism is preferable. But then there are many other advantages, such as the fact that it doesn't, like Fascism, take away the liberties of labor but rather enfranchises labor completely. Then Communism is not nationalistic or belligerent or racial. It is benign while Fascism is malignant. Fascism is an expedient of the Capitalist system to save itself at the last ditch. It is their shabby compromise, for self preservation. They give up some of their profits in exchange for security. This is Fascism.

Now about the WARS. Wars are a symptom of an exhausted and diseased capitalism. No longer able to sell their surplus at home, because they have exploited their workers to the point of absolute impotence to buy - they must obtain foreign markets on which to dump these surpluses. Hence - WAR. Competing with other nations for these foreign markets - substi-

tutes for the lack of new frontiers at home and buying power of own people - they come into sharp conflict - desperate struggle - finally a battle-to-
the-death which is now going on in Europe and Asia and is rapidly
approaching here. Dead capitalistic systems strangling each other in a
death-embrace.

Significantly Russia does not have to participate in this death-struggle.
Having no profit system, all her products are needed and used at home. She
has no surpluses to dump on foreign markets, does not have to fight for foreign trade - her territorial acquisitions are to protect herself and those ter-
ritories from the clutch of the others.

The prognosis is negative. Because Fascism is a better-working system
than Democracy it will probably triumph. The Capitalists will go and are
already going Fascist to save themselves. The people through their STU-
PIDITY will once more be sold down the river by the CUPIDITY of the
owners.

COMMUNISM and the WORLD REVOLUTION are the only ways
out. Complete abolition of the profit system, elimination of middle-man,
direct distribution of goods, state and communal ownership of all natural
resources and public necessities to eliminate slavery - these simple things
would create a new world order in which [omission] and war fare and
injustice and crime & want and almost every other social evil would pass
out of existence. This new order is not only possible, it is imperative. Every
visible sign demands it - But there is a gigantic and indescribably diaboli-
cal conspiracy to cover it up by those who would lose their special priv-
eleges if it came into being. Unfortunately the police power of the world is
still invested in these over-lords - the STUPIDITY of the masses enables
them to keep it.

So the world is now swinging toward Fascism - What can we do about
it? What will we? What do you think about this?

- 10.

[Earlier in August Joe Hazan criticized Paul Bigelow and Kip Kiernan for their
"inane" (letter to TW, n.d., HRC) behavior at Provincetown and threatened to
break off relations with them. Hazan's growing contempt for "civilization" led him
to imagine a wealthy benefactor upon whose "yacht" he and TW would "live beautifully in the tropics" (letter fragment, n.d., HRC). The coarse "pro-Nazi Germans"

at the Hotel Costa Verde made such escape momentarily attractive to TW and also contributed to the cultural setting of *The Night of the Iguana*.

News of Grand's illness stirred TW's own conviction of frailty. Leverich notes that TW "believed all his life, despite repeated diagnoses to the contrary, that his 'defective heart' was an organic condition" rather than one subject to "emotional and physical stress." He apparently distilled this fear into a story entitled "The Spinning Song," in which a vibrant young man learns of his heart condition and is advised by the family doctor "to cut down" (n.d., HRC) lest he too suffer his mother's premature death. Signed Thomas Lanier Williams, this early story may reflect TW's illness and hospitalization in 1935 (see letter #51). The same title was later used for a play draft that anticipates *The Glass Menagerie* (see letter #224).

The economic critique of the unidentified "man" should not have surprised TW in light of his exposure to radical politics in St. Louis. His friend Clark Mills, who briefly worked on the editorial staff of *The Anvil* (1933-1935), had once described "Capitalistic Society" as "a pyramid of boxes," an image of entrapment that TW promptly claimed for *Stairs to the Roof*.]

168. To Theresa Helburn

53 Arundel Pl.
Clayton, Mo.
Oct. 11, 1940
[TLS, 2 pp. Yale]

Dear Theresa Helburn:

This news about Miriam Hopkins is quite a shot in the arm. From the first I have felt a startling sense of affinity between her astral influences and mine. I went to see her out at White Plains and her brilliant acting made my blood run cold. I said to myself, 'Now here is a woman who could take my frequently over-written speeches and match them with an emotional opulence of her own that would make them not only natural but tremendously moving as well!' I met and talked to her after the show, Bennet Cerf had given her his script to read and she promised me she would read it. Now that you tell me she is definitely interested it seems but another in the uncanny succession of happy accidents I've had lately in my (professional) life. Can I do anything besides gnaw at my fingers and wait? Would even be willing to go out to the Coast and discuss the play with her, if that would do any good.

My mother was alarmed by reports of Revolution in Mexico so she wrote me that my Grandmother's health was failing. I came home to find she was merely recovering from a cold. Now they are both planning to go back to N.Y. with me, which brings up a lot of new problems as they are the most uncompromising of southern Puritans and seem to believe it my sacred and peculiar mission to eliminate sex from the modern theatre. - haven't read 'Battle of Angels'.

I'm polishing up the new script most of whose many dramaturgic problems appear to be solved. Can return to N.Y. any time, and not too reluctantly either, as the bright lights on the marquees seem attractive again. - Mendicancy has never proven much of an obstacle to motion in my life.

Another anthology, this one Margaret Mayorga's BEST ONE-ACTS OF 1940, is going to print one of my plays, <u>Moony's</u> <u>Kid</u> <u>Don't</u> <u>Cry</u>.

Jesus, I want to see this Hayes-Evans-Theatre Guild combination!!

Cordially, 10.

[While "gnawing" his fingers, TW had asked Bennett Cerf to exert his "influence, moral or otherwise," upon Miriam Hopkins. Anything "short of abduction from the studio lot" (letter, October 10, 1940, HRC) would be warranted, he thought.

The Theatre Guild's acclaimed revival of *Twelfth Night* opened on November 19, 1940, with Helen Hayes and Maurice Evans in the leads, and with direction by Margaret Webster, an Englishwoman who would stage *Battle of Angels*.

This letter was written on stationery imprinted with the name (canceled) of the Rev. Walter Edwin Dakin and the address (canceled) 1917 Snowden Avenue, Memphis, Tennessee.]

PART V
1940–1941
NEW YORK · BOSTON
KEY WEST · PROVINCETOWN · NEW ORLEANS

169. To the Williams Family

SH: The Ambassador, New York
Monday P.M. [November 18, 1940]
[TLS w/ autograph postscript, 3 pp. Columbia]

Dear folks:

These are very full, exciting days for me so you must overlook my lapses in writing. The trip to Miss. was pretty successful. We flew down to Memphis Tuesday morning, the first part of the trip as far as Washington was very rough, as were in a storm zone and I must admit I did feel somewhat uneasy, but after that it was beautiful and the flight a delightful experience. Mr. Ralston met us in Clarksdale Wednesday morning and showed us all about Moon Lake, Etc. Then Wed. night I called Mrs. Baugh and she drove us out to the cooperative plantation and various general stores the next day. Entertained us for lunch at the country club with Polly Clark and Tankie and the Rev. Malone. Delicious meal. Miss Webster got a lot out of the trip, took copious notes. We flew back Thursday night but were grounded in Nashville. The airlines sent us to a hotel where we stayed till the storm conditions improved - flew on about five o'clock Friday morning to New York.

Saturday night Miriam Hopkins had Miss Webster and I to dinner in her hotel. Everything I had heard about her in advance is true. She is the most temperamental person I've met, a regular hellion. Gave us a marvelous dinner in her hotel suite with champagne - then raised the roof for five solid hours about her part in the play. I think she wants to do a solo performance. Would like to cut everything in the play except her own speeches. Obviously this is impossible so we are going to have plenty of stormy sessions before the thing is over. She has a reputation for being a perfect hell-cat so this did not surprise me. However I must admit she is a brilliant actress and they say if you keep a firm hand she can be controlled. Both her Mother and her sister are mental cases so her temperament is probably unavoidable. We are going to pose together for Associated Press photographers in her suite Wednesday. I doubt if she lets me in the picture, though.

They are going to run a story about me in the Commercial Appeal, probably this coming Sunday. Mark Barron wrote it up here in N.Y. and has sold it to a number of southern A.P. papers. While in Clarksdale Miss

Webster and I were interviewed by the Daily Register and the reporter said she would send Grandfather the paper. Everyone I met down there asked to be remembered and they were wonderful to us.

The male lead has not been cast yet, due mainly to Hopkins. She won't have anybody not attractive to her, and is very hard to please. Fortunately she is amusing enough to be pardonable. During dinner, for instance, she suddenly jumped up from the table and shrieked, "I am old, I am tired, I am getting lines under my eyes!" I think that is her trouble, she is afraid of slipping.

Tell Dakin not to repeat any of these things - We have to be extremely careful in dealing with her.

Present plans are to have the play open the day after Christmas probably in New Haven and stay on the road for about two weeks before coming to New York.

Thanks for forwarding the checque and the clipping.

Love to you all, Tom.

P.S. Grand, I will be ready to join you all in <u>Florida</u> for a good <u>rest</u> when this is over.

[TW returned to New York with Edwina, who was dutifully treated to a day at the World's Fair, a ride on the subway, and dinner at the "'auto-mat.'" "You have to put money in the slot for each item" (October 25, 1940, HRC), she informed her parents, amazed by the modernity of fast food and self-service. With her departure TW "dived unwittingly into the little maelstrom" that *Battle of Angels* (1940) "had provoked" (TW, "The History of a Play," 1945).

TW later observed that the flying trip to the Mississippi Delta (November 12-14) was "a bit too much" for Margaret Webster, the self-described "English woman director who had never been farther south than Washington." She saw "just enough of this extraordinary country and its people to make them more mysterious than they were before" ("The History of a Play"). The people and the sites they visited—including a definitive general store at Sherard—were a familiar part of TW's childhood world and confirmed the importance of Clarksdale and the surrounding Delta in framing the Two River setting of *Battle of Angels*.

Miriam Hopkins was a Georgian by birth and in her late thirties when she played Myra Torrance in *Battle of Angels*. Her reputation as an accomplished Broadway actress led to starring roles in Hollywood, but as her career faded in the late 1930s, she returned to Broadway, hoping, as TW put it, that *Battle of Angels* would "bring her back" (see letter #174). Probably unknown to TW at the time was Hopkins's financial interest in the play. He was, however, sufficiently alert to avail himself of the imprinted stationery of the Ambassador Hotel, where Hopkins had an elegant suite.

Webster has recalled her first meeting with Hopkins and TW at the Ambassador: "We speculated about the author. It was three-quarters of an hour before he turned up . . . dressed in a shabby corduroy jacket and muddy riding boots. . . . He sat down on the spotless yellow satin chaise-longue and put them up on it. We started to talk about the play; he didn't seem much interested; once, when Miriam became a little vehement, he prefaced his reply with 'As far as I can gather from all this hysteria . . .' This is known in the language of *Variety* as 'a stoperoo'" (*Don't Put Your Daughter on the Stage*, 1972).

TW used his first major interview, an Associated Press release (November 24, 1940), to enhance the myth of a vagabond artist wandering the "48 states" in search of his vocation. Shunning fame and wealth, he told the interviewer, Mark Barron, that he planned to get out of New York "the minute" *Battle of Angels* opens, "and maybe sooner" (*Conversations*, pp. 3, 5). Only slightly less romantic was an earlier description of TW in the *Clarksdale Register*: "A southern gentleman, with a slight, but definite Eastern accent . . . whose travels include every major city of the United States and Europe" (November 15, 1940).

TW partly attributed the failure of *Battle of Angels* to Hopkins's displeasure with the casting of Valentine Xavier. It was probably she who demanded that Robert Allen be fired, leading the Theatre Guild to draft the journeyman actor Wesley Addy shortly before the play's opening (see letter #174).

Audrey Wood later opined that only a "deep collective death wish" could explain the Theatre Guild's decision to open *Battle of Angels* in Boston, a city whose reputation for "purity in the arts" (*Represented by Audrey Wood*, 1981) was all too well known.]

170. To Lawrence Langner

[New York City]
[ca. December 1940]
[TLS, 1 p. Yale]

Dear Mr. Langner:

I heard Grace Cotton (?) give a thrillingly beautiful reading of Sandra at yesterday's rehearsal, for the first time the part came to life and the end of the play was dramatic. Under the impact of her brilliant performance (she has precisely the right quality for this part) the play seemed to take on real meaning and poetic intensity, her scenes were really the high-spots. I am altogether convinced that she is the Quantity X we need to make this a <u>successful</u> production. Much as I like Doris, the play goes to pieces every time she comes on and I think it would be disastrous to open with her. I can't very well build up the part until I know we are going to have a capable actress in the role, otherwise it would be piling straw on a broken camel's back. So do let us make some immediate plans and decisions on this <u>vital</u> matter. Peggy is in complete agreement with me about this and I'm sure you will be when you've heard Grace read the part.

10.

["Peggy" Webster's frustrating experience with the Theatre Guild (she directed Guild productions of *Twelfth Night*, 1940, and *Othello*, 1943, in addition to *Battle of Angels*) led her to describe Lawrence Langner and Theresa Helburn, its co-directors, as "masters of miscasting" (*Don't Put Your Daughter on the Stage*).

"Grace Cotton (?)" has not been identified, but the "cruelly miscast" ("The History of a Play") Doris Dudley opened in the second female lead as Cassandra (Sandra) Whiteside, a young aristocrat whose name bespeaks her doom and corruption. TW later described himself as having been "dazed" by the chaotic production of *Battle of Angels*, but in advising Langner he spoke momentarily as an assured writer for the stage.]

171. To the Williams Family

SH: Hotel Bellevue, Boston
Sunday Night [December 29, 1940]
[ALS, 2 pp. Columbia]

Dear Folks -

We open here tomorrow night. Monday. Two weeks engagement, then a week in Washington before we go to New York. Gertrude Lawrence's new play is opening on the same night so we will have some stiff competition here. I will be kept frightfully busy with conferences and script changes as the purpose of these try-outs is to find the weak spots in the play and correct them if possible. Will try to write as soon as things settle down.

Love - Tom.

[Gertrude Lawrence's lavish "musical play" *Lady in the Dark* (1941) won raves in Boston and New York. The formidable team of Moss Hart, Ira Gershwin, and Kurt Weill provided book, lyrics, and music, respectively.

Margaret Webster has recalled TW's last-ditch attempt to "correct" the weakest spot of *Battle of Angels*: "The day before we opened Tennessee wrote a new last scene. Nobody had time to pay any attention" (*Don't Put Your Daughter on the Stage*).]

172. To Joseph Hazan

SH: Hotel Bellevue
Boston, Massachusetts
[ca. January 2, 1941]
[TLS, 2 pp. HRC]

Dear Joe:

I'm too exhausted to write much of a letter. The bright angels were pretty badly beaten in Boston - we are closing after the two weeks engagement for re-casting, re-writing and re-everything. Holiday crowds would not listen to poetic tragedy and the sexuality shocked the pants off the first-nighters and the critics who said they were "dunked in mire". Unfortunately all of the first-string critics went to Gertrude Lawrence's show which opened the same night and we got a bunch of prissy old maids to write our notices.

You will therefore notify Madame the Countess that the large room with the grand piano will be available for renters after the fifteenth. I will take what money I get, possibly between 500 or 800 dollars and lam out for Florida, Mexico or the Gulf Coast to re-write this play and finish the new one. Langner says he is going to continue payment of advance royalties as he intends to produce the play over again soon as it appears more commercial.

I am pretty sick over the whole thing but suppose I'll survive it. Oh, yes - will you do something for me which is absolutely imperative? I'm in trouble with the draft board. Please find out what is the name of the draft board closest to our apt. and send that information to Mr. Alden B. Parker, Selective Service Board #6, Clayton, Mo. and telling him that I will be back in New York in about two weeks. If it is necessary I can take the physical examination here in Boston.

Joe, you're a good boy and I love you - (spiritually!)

10.

[*Battle of Angels* opened in Boston on December 30, 1940, and closed on January 11, 1941. The first-night fiasco was complete when billowing fumes of smoke, intended to signify the conflagration of the set, obscured Doris Dudley's final curtain scene and drove the remainder of the audience from the Wilbur Theatre. The City Council denounced the play as "putrid" and ordered the censor to investigate its suggestive dialogue. To complete the engagement, the producers were forced to excise "practically all that made {*Battle of Angels*} intelligible, let alone moving" ("The History of a Play"), or so TW thought.

Reviewers agreed that the strange young author had furnished "the maddest night of melodrama" in recent memory and concluded that the play itself was either repugnant or amateurish, or both. The *Clarksdale Register* censured its "native" son for writing "DIRT," but it was more deeply offended by "effete" Boston's presuming to judge the Delta on the basis of such a "false" (January 8, 1941) report as TW had filed. He protested to Edwina: "Nobody of taste or understanding thinks my play dirty - unless life is dirty. I will write the Clarksdale Register to reassure them on certain points" (letter, n.d., Columbia).

By January 2 the Theatre Guild had decided to close *Battle of Angels* after its present engagement, and on January 20 the directors wrote a vacillating letter of apology to the Boston subscribers. They urged tolerance for "an occasional experimental play" but promised "sure fire entertainment" with the return engagement of *The Philadelphia Story* (1939) in February.

TW and his Provincetown friend Joe Hazan had briefly shared an apartment in New York, but when TW returned from Boston, he stayed once again at the YMCA on West 63rd Street.]

173. *To the Williams Family*

New York New Haven and Hartford Railroad
En Route
[ca. January 4, 1941]
[ALS, 4 pp. Columbia]

Dear Folks -

Our opening night stirred up quite a hullaballoo in Boston as many people in the audience who did not understand the play were terribly shocked by it and we have been having trouble the last three days with various clubs and leagues. I am returning to New York for conferences to decide what can be done to clarify the play for the non-poetic audiences. The Theatre Guild had several experts to see the try-out and they feel it is potentially a big hit but should stay out of town until the misconstrued scenes have been worked out differently. It may take some time. Everyone believes in the play, however. And I feel myself it is better to work on it longer than risk a bad press in New York with the present ending. This ending was one the Guild insisted upon to satisfy Hopkins who wanted to remain on the stage all the time and consequently twisted the script around quite a bit.

We are running 2 weeks in Boston with the present script and then will take time out for repairs.

We have played to capacity houses so far and Mr. Langner thinks I will get about $800.00 from the Boston engagement. Gertrude Lawrence and "Life With Father" are also playing there. I may go South for a while to work out the new ending - Maybe the Gulf Coast.

Sorry Dad isn't well.

Much love - Tom.

[The "twisted" ending of *Battle of Angels* saw Myra's death moved from the end of Act 2 in the November 1939 draft to the final curtain in Boston. After Myra is shot by her dying husband Jabe, her body is carried upstairs by Val with Sandra at his side. The store is aflame, fulfilling the prophecy of Val's death by fire and clearing the stage for Sandra's final speech of catharsis: "Don't be afraid, Snakeskin. (She clutches his head against her, closing her eyes with an expression of tragic exaltation) Those of our kind have flesh that is sacramental, not to be soiled by worms - but consumed by fire!" Sandra's following direction to Val, "Take the woman and bring her upstairs with us" (n.d., Library of Congress), could not have pleased Miriam Hopkins, who had fought to dominate the play's fiery conclusion (see letter #174).

Battle of Angels was less profitable, and the Theatre Guild less hopeful for its prospects, than TW led his family to believe. He noted in *Memoirs* (1975) that the royalties did not cover his advance (p. 63), and Audrey Wood has recalled that "the best" she could do "was an advance payment of one hundred dollars" (*Represented by Audrey Wood*) for revision.]

174. To Edwina Dakin Williams

SH: Young Men's Christian Association
5 West 63rd Street, New York, N.Y.
Monday. [January 6, 1941]
[TLSx, 2 pp. HRC]

Dear Mother -

Doris Dudley called from Boston this morning and said you were worried about me. I am o.k. - I was fully prepared for our difficulties in Boston - disappointed, of course, but feel that in the long run things will work out better. The play is not ready for New York, due mostly to my ill-advised efforts to make it a starring vehicle satisfactory to Miss Hopkins rather than to my own best judgement. It is sadder for Hopkins as she is really washed up in pictures and looked for this play to bring her back. But she messed things up herself by firing 3 leading men and finally opening with one who hadn't even had time to learn his lines.

The Theatre Guild has promised to continue my advance royalties until the script is repaired which is very decent of them I think. I will probably leave town in a few days to work in peace.

Much love - Tom.

[With reference to Miriam Hopkins's willfulness, TW anticipated the critic Elliot Norton's post-mortem analysis that *Battle of Angels* had been "done in by actor politics" (*Boston Sunday Post*, January 12, 1941), sharpened by Hopkins's financial interest in the play. Nonetheless Hopkins defended TW against charges of indecency and called for the City Council to be "flung into your Boston Harbor, the way the tea once was."]

175. To Edwina Dakin Williams

[436 East 73rd Street, New York]
[ca. late-January 1941]
[TLS, 1 p. HTC]

Dear Mother:

Can't write a long letter as I have to rest my eyes. Sent you a telegram soon as operation was over Wed. Did you get it? Entrusted it with a friend.

Reaction to the operation was pretty severe and painful - I had to stay in the hospital a week. Can't tell for about six weeks whether the sight will be restored but the Doctor thinks there is a good chance of it. Anyway the cataract will be removed. I have to stay here for treatments about a month. Sometimes a second operation is necessary if the diseased lens is not completely absorbed.

As the Doctor does nothing now but look in my eye and apply some drops I don't see why he should insist upon my remaining in New York, especially since it is so expensive for me here. The operation and hospital cost $169. so far and he is charging me five dollars a visit. I have it all paid for - that is, excepting the future visits.

If I can get away from N.Y. I will return to St. Louis for a month or two till my play is re-written, or visit the Parrots in Florida. They sent me a telegram inviting me to share a shack in the Keys - the squab ranch people are down there now. Must have seen that I was in hospital in one of the syndicated columns as they addressed telegram to St. Luke's.

Will let you know how I'm getting along.

Love, Tom

[TW wrote earlier to Edwina that "a fine opthalmologist" named W. Guernsay Frey had found a cataract on the lens of his left eye and recommended that it "be removed" (n.d., Columbia). The operation was the first of four such procedures and was reportedly done on January 22 at St. Luke's Hospital. TW recovered at the East Side apartment of Donald Windham and friends and by February 5 was en route to Miami, where he met his old traveling companion Jim Parrott.]

176. To the Williams Family

C. O. Trade Winds
Key West, Fla.
[February 12, 1941]
[TL, 1 p. HRC]

Dear Folks:

I should have given you some warning of this radical change of address but decided to go the day that I left. My doctor said no further treatments were necessary and I was free to leave town so I packed up immediately and took the first train to Florida. I met the Parrotts in Miami and Jim drove me on down here to Key West which will be my headquarters for the next month or two.

I am stopping in the 125-year-old house you see on the envelope. It belongs to an Episcopal clergyman's widow, Mrs. Black - he had Grace Church in Memphis. She is renting me the servants' cabin for eight dollars a week. The Theatre Guild is advancing me living expenses for the next two months in which time I am to complete my re-write of "Angels" and send it back to them. Then, if they are satisfied, they will renew the contract, and plan a second production. They are having a run of hard luck as their two new productions "Cream in the Well" by Lynn Riggs and "Liberty Jones" by Phillip Barry both got a unanimously bad press and are doomed to failure. I am going to rest for a week or two before I start any more writing as I am pretty tired out.

Unfortunately the weather in Florida is extremely bad right now. I don't advise Grand and Grandfather to leave till it changes. In Key West it has been so cold I have slept under blankets the past three nights since I got here - no sun at all. A cold rain and wind - but this is expected to break by tomorrow.

The doctor seemed satisfied with the result of the operation. I can distinguish light and dark much more clearly and there is some visibility of objects but it will take several more weeks to know whether or not the vision will return enough to be useful. The cataract absorbs gradually after the operation. Sometimes it stops at a certain point and a second "needling" operation is necessary to complete it. This can be done any time afterwards. Doctor said there was nothing in McGrath's report that would preclude the good possibility of sight being restored eventually - I am glad that I had it done though it was quite a bad ordeal. I suffered very severely for the first few days after the operation and they had to give me typhoid fever injections to combat the inflammation in the eye - it seems an artificial fever will accelerate absorption. The injections gave me high fever and chills that nearly shook me to pieces! I got wonderful attention at the hospital, though. They were in and out of my room every five or ten minutes, so there was absolutely no reason for anyone to come up. After I was released from the hospital I went to stay with some friends who gave me excellent care till I was able to look out for myself. Several columnists carried reports of my operation so I received a great many sympathetic calls.

Everybody in New York has been marvelous to me - considering what a hard-boiled town it is supposed to be.

I left all my summer clothes in St. Louis. As it will be very warm here when the wind changes, I wish you would send me my white linen suit and the dungarees which I wore in Mexico. Also any sport shirt which I may have around the house.

I think Grand and Grandfather would like it here. - Much love.

P.S. Mother, I got your letter before I left New York. Wrote a card but am afraid I didn't mail it.

[The southernmost city in the United States promised good swimming, sexual freedom, and artistic community. Among the celebrities whom TW met at Key West were Grant Wood, Max Eastman, Elizabeth Bishop, Pauline Pfeiffer (the recently divorced Mrs. Hemingway), and the aged philosopher John Dewey, who wore "blue rompers on the beach and look{ed} like a monkey" (letter to Theresa Helburn, Friday {March 14, 1941} Yale). In the 1930s Hemingway wintered, and wrote extensively, at Key West but left the island in late 1939 after breaking with Pfeiffer. In 1950 TW bought a small Conch house on Duncan Street, far removed from the center of tourism, and made Key West his official residence for more than thirty years.

Mrs. Clara Black ran "a very genteel boardinghouse" (*Memoirs*, p. 63) named The Trade Winds, a nineteenth-century landmark that was destroyed by arson in 1956. Edwina claimed her as "a lifelong friend" and TW fondly recalled this landlady as one "who knew when to be intrusive." In later years he became a close friend of her daughter, Marion Black Vaccaro, wife of Regis, reportedly "one of the principal heirs of the Standard Fruit Company fortune" (*Memoirs*, p. 65). Vaccaro served as the model for Cora in the story "Two on a Party" (1952) and is described in *Memoirs* as being "very loyal in her friendships" (p. 65).

Theatre Guild productions of *The Cream in the Well* (1941) and *Liberty Jones* (1941) had runs of 24 and 22 performances, respectively.

In the 1940s the "'needling'" operation described by TW was a common method of cataract removal for young patients. A "needle-knife" was used to incise the lens capsule and expose the cloudy cataractous material to the aqueous fluid in the eye. The material was slowly absorbed but often a follow-up procedure, using a needle and syringe, was performed a week later to flush out remaining lens material. In the absence of anti-inflammatory drugs, typhoid injections were used to produce fever and stimulate the body's ability to reduce post-operative inflammation and pain. TW's need for subsequent procedures, the next in January 1942, was probably due to retained nuclear and cortical lens material. He later explained in

Memoirs that his left eye had been injured "in a childhood game of considerable violence" (p. 74) and that it had assumed a milky cast by his twenties.

This letter was first published in Edwina Dakin Williams's memoir, *Remember Me to Tom* (1963), pp. 125-127.]

177. To Josephine "Jo" Healy

SH: The Trade Winds
Key West, Florida
[ca. February 12, 1941]
[TLS, 1 p. Columbia]

Jo dear:

I got all my stuff packed in about fifteen minutes Wednesday night and got down to the depot about five minutes before the train pulled out. Friday morning I was in Miami and Saturday night I was in Sloppy Joe's bar in Key West. This is the most fantastic place that I have been yet in America. It is even more colorful than Frisco, New Orleans or Santa Fe. There are comparatively few tourists and the town is real stuff. It still belongs to the natives who are known as "conks". Sponge and deep sea fishing are the main occupations and the houses are mostly clapboard shanties which have weathered grey with nets drying on the front porches and great flaming bushes of poinsettia in the yards. This is beginning to sound like very bad travel literature - but I do wish you were here. I am not having a wonderful time as I am still pretty knocked out from all I've been through but I think a few weeks of rest here will revive me. It is strange to be so completely removed from Broadway in such a short time and it is rather nice, although I miss people like you and Addie and Irene and the Theatre Guild, Inc. Sloppy Joe's is a far cry from Sardi's and even Ralph's. I am occupying the old servants' quarters in back of this 90-year-old house pictured above. I shan't do anything the next few weeks but swim and lie on the beach till I begin to feel human again. Then I shall learn how to fish. A good fisherman can thumb his nose at all commercial enterprise in the world.

The few reviews I got hold of of Liberty Jones (pardon the two prepositions) were not very good. What was the general reception? I will appreciate a little news of Broadway now and then if you get sufficiently untangled from those telephone wires to drop me a line.

My love to everybody, especially <u>you</u> ---

Tell Dick I'm sorry we couldn't get up to his place for some more steaks but they are a beautiful memory - one of the few.

10.

[Jo Healy (1904–1974), a switchboard operator at the Theatre Guild, had friendly Irish ways and an eye for talent, as noted by Celeste Holm: "She told me, 'I have a playwright friend—he's got a funny name, but he can write gorgeously. And I try to feed him. I can only afford spaghetti'" (qtd. in Leverich).

Ernest Hemingway's use of Sloppy Joe's Bar in *To Have and Have Not* (1937) helped to make it a landmark for writers and tourists. TW describes the bar in *Memoirs* as a part of the town's "authentic frontier atmosphere" (p. 65) and recalls dancing there with Marion Vaccaro to the music of a good black band.]

178. *To Lawrence Langner*

The Trade Winds
Key West, Florida
Wednesday, Feb.? [26] 1941
[TTr, 1 p. Yale]

Dear Lawrence:

I am occupying the slave-quarters in back of this 125 year-old mansion which is made entirely of mahogany and surrounded by palm trees which rustle and whisper constantly night and day like a Boston audience at a scandalous play. It is owned by a clergyman's widow who gives me lodging at a ridiculously low price because I remind her of her son who was an aviator recently killed in a crash. I lead an exciting double life here, writing all morning, spending my afternoon's in an English widow's cabana on the beach where I associate with people like John Dewey, James Farrell and Elizabeth Bishop and in the evening consorting, in dungarees, with B-girls, transients and sailors at Sloppy Joe's or the Starlight Gambling Casino.

I am pitting all of my strength, which is still considerable in spite of recent depletions, on this job of re-working the play. I know that the situation in which I now am is the opposite of strategic. I am right smack behind the 8-ball. And it is going to take plenty of luck to keep me out of the pocket. A few weeks ago I was a bright possibility. Now I'm just a bubble that burst in Boston! You all know that I'm something more than that. But nobody else knows it. Except the defunct Group Theatre. Therefore I am pretty completely at your mercy. My people were Tennessee Indian-fighters who never asked for mercy but lost their scalps whenever they lost a battle. I believe that you all are somewhat less implacable than the Redskins. But the theatre isn't. I expect to be scalped if I don't come through with a winner.

As for what I am doing, I am carving out slowly a more dramatic pattern of action in the first half of the play. I have written a new first scene which I think at the moment (still in the glow of composition) is the best I have done. I won't say that it's 'terrific', but I think that it creates a dramatic atmosphere which will be hard to top in later scenes. I can promise you this much: Val will be stronger and more exciting than he was before and Sandra a more understandable character. I am making her a virgin who has not given herself to any man because she found none with a capacity for feeling equal to hers - until Val. I am not so sure now that another act will be necessary after Myra's death. I've tried out several different endings and I am coming back around to the feeling that the play can be tied up more sharply with a conclusion in the store. The only problem is resolving VEE.

I have been following 'Liberty Jones' in the papers. I called the shot on that one when I saw the Pre-vue. A <u>beautiful</u> play as completely lacking in appeal to a general audience as anything I have witnessed. You are certainly an art theatre when you produce things like that but I wish for your sake and mine and all serious practitioners in the theatre an 'Art <u>audience</u>' could be created on Broadway. After I have had one commercial success I am going to sit down for five or ten years and learn how to write a play!

In the meantime, give Terry my love and tell her I am learning to fish so she won't have to "support me".

Best wishes always,

Cordially, 10 (Williams)

[Sandra Whiteside's virginity—an attempt perhaps to tone down the play's sexuality—was only a passing thought and one that may have warned Lawrence Langner that revision of *Battle of Angels* was not going well. Sandra's character reverted to a weary cynicism and dissipation in the revised draft that TW completed in the spring.

Reviews of *Liberty Jones*, by Philip Barry, bore out TW's prediction that realistic Broadway would not tolerate an allegorical fantasy interspersed with music and dance, especially in wartime. In a draft of this letter, TW pondered the politics of writing amid disorder and envisioned a time "when the permanent values that a serious artist deals with are not obscured by little details like the war. Our work can live in the future but unfortunately we must survive the present. I am learning how to fish. And how to be charming to widows. Practically the same thing" (n.d., HRC).]

179. To Audrey Wood

"Trade Winds"
Key West, Fla.
Thursday Feb. 27, 1941
[TLS, 1 p. HRC]

Dear Audrey:

When anyone's real nice in Mississippi they are described as "precious" and that is what you are. I hate for you to bother sending me those goddam little checques - God bless them! - with all the other nerve-wracking business you've got on hand. Would you rather send me the entire sum and let my land-lady act as the dispensor? Anyway let me know how much the Theatre Guild has come across with so that I can plan accordingly.

I'm working hard on the "Angels" and before long I'll probably have them jumping through hoops and balancing balls on their noses. Val is receiving daily injections of iron and beef extracts and should soon have hair enough on his chest to interest I.J. FOX. I'm trying to work out a more dramatic pattern of action in the first half of the play. Quite a bit accomplished in that direction. If producers are not too prejudiced by what happened in Boston, the play ought to be a pretty good "property" when I get through with it. For the first time in my life I am practicing self-discipline and doing what I know I ought to do rather than what I feel like doing.

The blue devils harrass me continually, however, so much has happened to discourage me about myself and my work. I feel sometimes like a piece of broken string. But you cannot give way to such feelings. And I don't. This is a one-way street that I have chosen and I have to follow it through with all the confidence or courage that necessity gives you.

I will enclose a one-act fantasy (light) which might do for the radio, Barrett Clark or even Miss Whozit (Blue Mt. lady) if the locale were changed to Miss.

Mail me the next checque ~~in a couple of days~~ now. I am going to leave on a hitch-hiking tour of the State to refresh myself for further operations on the play. - Eye shows gradual improvement.

My love to you and Bertha and Bobbie Barrett.

Sincerely, 10.

[Fearing TW's improvidence, Audrey Wood doled out Theatre Guild funds in a series of "little checques" that perilously followed her client's travels in the South.

A strengthened Val Xavier would have enough hair "on his chest" to interest the New York furrier I.J. Fox, well known in the 1930s for his promotions, stunts, and self-advertisement.

TW wrote of the "blue devils" besieging him in "the days A.B. - 'After Boston'": "God knows what will become of me if I don't meet the demands of the situation. And I am tired - dangerously tired - and not well. . . . I am afraid this town is bad for me - Water, water everywhere! - And I am not a voyager - any more. Bars alone - beaches alone - movies alone - I feel quite unable to speak to anybody - I wrote a 1-act and a few poems but do little on 'Battle'" (*Journal*, February 16, 25, 1941).

TW's "one-act fantasy," "The Case of the Crushed Petunias" (published in 1948), was set in Primanproper, Massachusetts, a delayed thrust at the censors of Boston. It was dedicated to "the talent and charm of Miss Helen Hayes" and submitted by Wood to the producer Cheryl Crawford. TW recommended as publishers Barrett Clark, head of the Dramatists Play Service, or "Miss Whozit," possibly Margaret Mayorga, editor of the annual *Best One-Act Plays*. "Crushed Petunias" is both a seedbed for future plays, especially *You Touched Me!* (1943/1945) and *The Glass Menagerie* (1945), and an echo chamber for more recent ones, including *Stairs to the Roof* (drafted in 1940) and *Battle of Angels*.

Bertha Case and Roberta Barrett were assistants at Liebling-Wood.]

180. To Audrey Wood

SH: The Trade Winds
Key West, Florida
Friday [March 14, 1941]
[TLS, 2 pp. HRC]

Audrey dear:

It is nice to be called Mr. Atlas but I fear your eye like that of the horse has a magnifying lens inside it that imparts a fictitious grandeur to all that it gazes upon.

Probable salvation appeared in the form of a WOMAN FROM WACO who is now worked into the play as a motivating force to take the place of Val's fire phobia which is pretty largely cut out to remove the psycopathic stigma. This Woman from Waco, which may be the play's new title, was one that Val became involved with in an oil-field near Waco Texas. She betrayed her husband with him and when he tried to break away she fastened an accusation of rape upon him which has hounded him all over the country. He hates her and dreads her as she has made him a fugitive outlaw. The revelation of this situation comes at the end of Scene Two, which is now scene three, and provides the dramatic "shot-in-the-arm" which that scene needed. I believe. The Woman from Waco herself appears in the last scene and precipitates the violent action, having finally tracked him down to Two Rivers. She is a symbol of the animal sexuality which has dogged Val's footsteps wherever he goes. - This is a very bare idea of what I am doing and I will send you a detailed synopsis as soon as things are ironed in and out more smoothly. Just about everything is in rough draft on paper. All the action remains in the store but there is not the big holocaust at the end nor the complete lyrical transition. It is all over-written. I will have to tone it down. But I think the dramaturgic pattern should be much improved by these changes. I also have written a new prologue or Scene One between Myra and Sandra the night before Val arrives to give the background of frustration more clearly and make the characters more sympathetic. Val is involved in a fracas with the men of the town when he defends a dispossessed negro. This also adds action to the first part of the play.

Now I am going to take a short trip around the peninsula (on my thumb) to refresh myself before I settle down to a final rewrite. Will you please mail Mayorga's checque right away to me, Air Mail, Miami, Florida,

General Delivery, as I may be away for more than a week and don't want to get broke on the road as they would pick me up for vagrancy and Langner would have to bail me out of the clinker. He once said to me in all seriousness, "The only thing that I am concerned with is genius!" - If the old fool still thinks that I am a genius he certainly wouldn't allow me to perish on a Florida chain-gang. - Or would he?

I am sure that Mayorga owes me twenty-five dollars because I signed a contract with her and it ought to be paid on publication. I'm writing a beautiful new short story but put it aside for the play.

I enclose you a very bad but good likeness that was taken for HARPER'S BAZAAR (before Boston). I was going to give it to Terry but I believe that I like you better. ---- After all.

Hello to Liebling and Bertha and the rest of your gang. Next season will be better than this one - that isn't bragging for any of us, is it?

Love, 10.

[Audrey Wood had told TW to "sit up straight, Mr. Atlas" and to "remember that the American theatre and Audrey Wood are depending on you to hold both of them up this next season" (letter, March 12, 1941, HRC).

An affair with a married woman from Texas is recalled by David in "Why Did Desdemona Love the Moor?" (HRC), a story written at Taos in August 1939. Her vindictive offspring, the "WOMAN FROM WACO," did not help to remove the "psycopathic stigma" from Battle of Angels, as the stage directions indicate: "She is a hard dyed blond in a dark suit. Her body is short and heavy but her face appears to have been burned thin by some consuming fever accentuated by the mask-like make up she wears" (May 21, 1941, HRC). Val's "fracas with the men of the town" and his defense of "a dispossessed negro" were attempts to give the play a further social dimension, although TW would later resist efforts by Erwin Piscator to turn Battle of Angels into a "sermon" (see letter #223) on injustice in the South.

Margaret Mayorga chose "Moony's Kid Don't Cry" (a revision of the 1932 college play "Hot Milk at Three in the Morning") for The Best One-Act Plays of 1940 (1941)—TW's first published play.

The "beautiful" new story, "Portrait of a Girl in Glass" (1948), contains the basic elements of The Glass Menagerie: the four principal parts of mother, son, daughter, and gentleman caller, the belated arrival of a suitor for "Rose," and "a third floor apartment on Enright street in St. Louis" (February 1941, HRC) to enclose the slight dramatic action. TW later observed to Wood that the eight-page story might "turn into a short novel, and I may use one or two others in your files as inter-relating plots - convertible into a play - title - 'The Voices In My Sleep'" (letter, n.d., HRC).]

181. To Audrey Wood

Miami Flo
1941 Mar 20 PM 9 11
[Telegram, 1 p. HRC]

AUDREY WOOD=

STRANDED - EVICTED HOTEL. BALKAN SITUATION COMPARATIVELY
NOTHING. IF ANTHOLOGY CHECK UNMAILED PLEASE WIRE TWENTY
DOLLARS WESTERNUNION IMMEDIATELY

LOVE= TENNESSEE WILLIAMS.

[TW's "trip around the peninsula" began in mishap when Audrey Wood sent the
"anthology check" to Key West rather than Miami. TW worked for several days as
a dishwasher and probably returned to Key West on March 23. He was soon back
in the Miami area, living in Coral Gables with Jim Parrott, who had entered a flight
training program at the University of Miami. On March 25 TW sheepishly asked
Wood to stop payment on the elusive check, "as it was either lost or stolen from
my wallet last night" (March 25, 1941, HRC).]

182. To Theresa Helburn

5475 SW 7
Coral Gables, Florida
[ca. April 4, 1941]
[TLS, 1 p. Yale]

Dear Terry:

Thanks for your note. I have suddenly bogged down on the home-
stretch or I would've gotten the rewrite to you before now. The real work
is about all done, it is mostly typing and patching together. But I have been
at it so unremittingly these past few months that I am breathless.

St. Louis Civic Theatre (professional) wants to do a try-out of revised
Battle. Director's wife sent me this wire. - What do you think? I told them
I couldn't agree without your approval. They do good work and have a big
following - play capacity houses, usually week or two weeks run, and the
St. L. critics are old buddies of mine. Everything I do is front page there!

Rockefeller foundation is granting me some money to "write a new
play". - Audrey just told me. - Audrey has been wonderful to me.

I am leaving here in a few days. Will visit my folks briefly and discuss things with St. L. Civic while there - if not Angels they want to do something else.

For God's sake "Send 'em solid" with these next two plays you're producing!

Love, 10.

[TW had promised to send Theresa Helburn a revised outline of the "everlasting" (letter, Friday {March 14, 1941} Yale) *Battle of Angels*. In her theatre memoir she made slight note of TW and none at all of *Battle of Angels*. She identified instead with Eugene O'Neill and his generation of dramatists, "the high point in the craft of playwriting in America" (*A Wayward Quest*, 1960).

In early-April TW received telegrams from Luise Sillcox of the Dramatists' Guild announcing an award of $500 by the Rockefeller Foundation "to write a new play" (April 2, 1941, HRC); and from Jane Garrett Carter writing on behalf of the St. Louis Civic Theatre and expressing interest in staging *Battle of Angels*, with *Spring Storm* (n.d., HRC) an alternate choice (April 4, 1941, Yale).

One forthcoming Theatre Guild production, *Somewhere in France*, by Karl Zuckmayer and Fritz Kortner, closed in Washington.]

183. To Audrey Wood

5475 S.W.7
[Coral Gables, Florida]
4/11/41
[TLS w/ autograph postscript, 1 p. HRC]

Dear Audrey:

Barely time for a note! Very, very happy and relieved about new funds.

Back on keys but leaving in a few minutes for Brunswick, Ga. Landlady's son-in-law, habitual drunkard, has run up gambling debts far in excess of his ability to pay - I have to smuggle him off the keys at once his life being threatened - to Georgia where I have instructions to keep him sober till his wife gets there in about ten days. What a job! But they have been so wonderful to me I can't refuse. - Driving his car up - leaving right away. - This done, I will probably come back north. To N.Y.

Tell Mr. Nickholson his suggestions sound beautiful and I thank him. -

St. Louis Civic Theatre wants to try-out Battle, too. Or another script of mine. Could we have two try-outs?

If you want to reach me quickly about something, General Delivery, Brunswick Georgia for the next six or eight days.

So long - 10.

PS. ONLY GOT TO MIAMI WITH CHARGE WHO IS NOW IN SANITARIUM. - SEND ME ONE MORE CHECQUE OF THEATRE GUILD - TO GET HOME ON. Will leave here soon as it comes and return East in a week or two after visiting folks.

(Play rewrite about ready for typist)

[Audrey Wood, probably the moving force behind TW's second Rockefeller Grant, wrote with congratulations from Liebling-Wood: "We both know how much it means to you" (April 3, 1941, HRC).

TW quipped in the journal that he had "the basic situation" for the new Rockefeller play in mind: "A Woman's Love for a Drunkard. Regis and Marion." This "melodramatic little interlude" (April 9, 1941) may instead have provided the dramatic situation for Cat on a Hot Tin Roof (1955): A wealthy heir who held the promise of providing a comfortable future for his wife, who was burdened either with controlling her husband's drinking or facing genteel poverty.

Audrey Wood reported to TW that Kenyon Nicholson would "be happy" to have him "near" (April 3, 1941, HRC) the Bucks County Playhouse in New Hope, Pennsylvania. When TW described this wary invitation to Fred Melton, it had been embellished: "Kenyon Nicholson has invited me to live as guest playwright at the Bucks County Playhouse, but I don't think I could take very much of that" (qtd. in Windham, p. 22).]

184. To Joseph Hazan

[5475 S.W. Seventh Street
Coral Gables, Florida]
[ca. mid-April 1941]
[TLS w/ autograph postscript, 2 pp. Columbia]

Dear Joe:

Awful, awful tired, been acting as sort of psychiatric nurse for an acute alcoholic, my landlady's son-in-law at Key West. His wife and I were trying to drive him up to a sanitarium in his home town in Georgia but only got as far as Miami with him and had to commit him to a ward here. Great nervous strain, no sleep.

I'm glad you have this beautiful soul and body companion, with that you should not worry much about anything else. Which is relatively unimportant. If you are set on Mexico, go ahead. Possibly a change would be just the thing for you if you are truly fed up with the life in N.Y. you should get away for a while. But I don't [know] what advice to give you about Mexico. Of course there is no professional dancing or art activity of any kind outside of Mexico City and the very chi-chi dilettante resort of Taxco. I did not like either of those places - you might on the other hand be very pleased with them. The more primitive places such as Acapulco are delightful in winter but how could you live? There is nothing for Americans to do - in fact the natives can't make a go of it. If you are with some one you care about greatly Mexico is much nicer - it is a lonely country. I can't help thinking you would get along better in the U.S. - I am coming back north soon as I get present affairs straightened out. I've got my play about finished and some more money from Rockefeller "to write a new play". Probably visit home first and then go on to N.Y. after a few days there. I will see you I presume before you run off anywhere with your mistress.

So long - 10.

P.S. I wrote Paul c/o A.S.L.

[The postscript cites Paul Bigelow and Andrew S. Lyndon, the latter a resident of Macon, Georgia, with whom TW would have a brief affair.]

185. To Audrey Wood

[5475 S.W. Seventh Street
Coral Gables, Florida]
Tuesday April [15, 1941]
[TLS, 2 pp. HRC]

Audrey dear:

I have decided to take the Georgia trip after all although the alcoholic case will remain here in the sanitarium. His wife has given me permission to stay at their farm as long as I want and eat all the fresh vegetables and eggs on the place. It is in the heart of the interesting Gullah negro country on the Ga. coast-line so I feel I should "take it in" for a while. Please mail Th. Guild checque #7 to General Delivery, DARIEN, GEORGIA. Put "Please Hold till Arrival" on envelope as I am hitch-hiking up there and exact time of arrival is uncertain though it shouldn't take me more than two or three days. I won't use any of Rockefeller money till I return to N.Y. A girl friend in St. Louis has promised to get my revised script typed and in order for me when I stop through there so I should have it all ready when I reach Broadway. - The world situation seems appalling right now. I am sending you and Liebling a FLOOGIEBOO, or LUCKY WORRY BIRD who is supposed to remove all anxieties from the reciprocant. I have been completely light-hearted since getting mine - hope it will have the same effect on you and Liebling. Very easy to take care of. Lives on radio news bulletins and interviews with actors and authors.

As ever, Tennessee.

[The "appalling" state of the world had darkened with Hitler's invasion of the Balkans on April 6. The German Blitzkrieg led Europe to stagger and launched what Hitler had described as a "year of decision" for the Axis powers. TW asked in the journal, "Will there be any decency, any peace, any reason, any sanity in our time? - In mine?" (April 9, 1941).

The "FLOOGIEBOO," Audrey Wood wrote, "looks exactly like Lawrence Langner's brother." She added, "Can't you find a bird that looks like Miss Helburn, I would like to mate them" (letter to TW, April 18, 1941, HRC).]

186. To Lawrence Langner

SH: Marsh Haven
Meridian Georgia
Sometime near the middle of April, 1941
[TLS, 1 p. Yale]

Dear Lawrence:

I am stopping here a while in "The marshes of Glynn" my cousin Lanier wrote about, to take care of an acute alcoholic while his wife closes the season in Key West. He wandered off in the marshes yesterday and has probably drowned. My only companion is an old Dachshund so old he doesn't scratch his fleas but just growls at them. Putting the finishing touches on the script. It looks good. A girl friend in St. Louis has promised to type it for me and set the pages in order which is a job I can never face alone. I should be back in New York with it all complete about the second week in May.

I hope that bird I sent you has taken your mind off the war. I have been completely light-hearted since acquiring one myself.

Cordially, 10.

[Marsh Haven was the Vaccaros' country home near Brunswick, Georgia. TW's "cousin" Sidney Lanier (1842-1881) visited the nearby salt marshes in 1871 and wrote of their "sweet visage" in a well-known poem entitled "The Marshes of Glynn" (1878). The tale of Regis Vaccaro's wandering off "in the marshes" is apocryphal, as preceding letters make clear.

TW returned to Clayton by way of Savannah and Atlanta and arrived at 53 Arundel Place ca. May 1. His "time on the road," as described to Donald Windham, had been "marvelous": "Everybody who picked me up was so interesting, from millionaires to lovely young truck drivers" (qtd. in *Windham*, p. 22). There is no reference to Rose in the journal at this time and no evidence that TW visited her at Farmington State Hospital. By May 10 he was en route to New York with a retyped draft of *Battle of Angels* for the Theatre Guild. "Accomplished some good work on Battle - hopeful about it" (*Journal*, May 9, 1941), he wrote before leaving Clayton.

The trip by rail was not without incident, however. TW did not check his baggage in St. Louis and a trunk containing clothes and scripts, left unattended in the passenger car, was unloaded in Pittsburgh. From New York he wrote in panic to Cornelius, hoping that his father's "position" might spur the authorities to "make an additional effort" (n.d., Columbia) to trace the missing luggage. On May 12 TW wired Cornelius that the trunk had been found.]

187. *To Lawrence Langner*

SH: The Moorland
Gloucester, Massachusetts
July 3, 1941
[ALS, 4 pp. Yale]

Dear Lawrence -

I felt considerably happier after our interview last week than I did before, as I felt that you were not, as I had supposed, simply fed up with me and all my works. As for the play, it is apparent that no definitive script has yet emerged though we now have a wealth of provisional and apocryphal material - one eventually <u>will</u> - and "Battle of Angels" can afford to wait, perhaps more than such plays as "Watch on the Rhine", "There Shall be No Night" Etc. which have to grasp at the fugitive present. Whatever its ineptitudes, I have made this play out of such enduring stuff as passion, death, and the spiritual quest for the infinite which are elements that time can only improve - So I am not worried about it. I will sell it to any producer who wants to buy it but would never allow anyone to give it a shabby production. I am especially distrustful of summer theatres, however well managed, and so for that reason I am relieved that you have given up the idea of a Westport try-out. I have always felt, Lawrence, that you are one of the few theatre people whose understanding I can count on in my efforts to bring a somewhat new kind of poetry to the realistic prose play. That feeling hasn't changed nor has my really deep gratitude to you and Terry. If this is the parting of our ways, please believe it is with the very friendliest feelings on my part.

Sincerely, Tennessee

P.S. A modern poetry anthologist is particularly anxious to get hold of that poem of mine called "Legend" whose only copy I left out at your country home last summer. Will you please, <u>please</u> try to find it for me?

10.

[In the late spring TW lived in New York at the West Side YMCA and the Woodrow Hotel and renewed his friendship with Paul Bigelow and Kip Kiernan. It was a time of "the most extraordinary . . . sexual license. . . . New lovers every night, barely missing one, for a month or more." It was not, however, a time of creative endeavor: "My main trouble is I cannot create. I am mentally torpid. And I do not even seem to care very much. Perhaps it is the excessive sexual activity. Perhaps I have really burned my daemon out. I don't think so. I think he is still a phoenix and not a cooked goose" (*Journal*, June 27, 1941). In early-July Bigelow packed a restless TW off to Gloucester, Massachusetts, to be diverted by a local theatre group.

TW's had speculated in earlier correspondence with Donald Windham and friends that his ideas for revising *Battle of Angels* would not "correspond with the Theatre Guild's" (qtd. in *Windham*, p. 21), and he was proven correct. Lawrence Langner rejected the current revision with a ponderous allusion to Mark Twain: "You have gone like the Leaping Frog of Calaveras County, you know, that Mark Twain story, I mean you rewrote it too much like the frog {that} jumped out of the county" (qtd. in *Memoirs*, p. 69). The Guild shelved *Battle of Angels*, including plans for a summer tryout at Langner's Westport (Connecticut) Country Playhouse. TW's respectful tone was absent in a coincident letter to Audrey Wood: "Spit in Langner's face for me" (July 2, 1941, HRC).

There Shall Be No Night (1940) and *Watch on the Rhine* (1941), by Robert E. Sherwood and Lillian Hellman, respectively, were award-winning plays that examined "the fugitive present" of fascism and world war.

In the "GENERAL NOTES" printed below, TW's summary of post-Boston work on *Battle of Angels* is keyed to a typescript dated May 21, 1941, and held by the Humanities Research Center.]

GENERAL NOTES ON REVISIONS

After spending about half my time on the original plan of having a final act in the lock up, I finally concluded, and I think quite correctly, that there was no way of preventing this play from being primarily Myra's since she is the character most fully realized and with the most sympathetic appeal and it would inevitably break in two after her death. Nevertheless it was necessary to dispose of the other characters, and without the general conflagration which had unsatisfactory results in Boston. So I hit upon the device of the "Tragic Museum", with a prologue hinting of events but not giving them away and an epilogue that would have katharsis effect of "emotion remembered in tranquillity" with also some ironical commentaries through the Temple sisters and mystery in the Conjure Man and offering a final account of all the main protagonists. It appears to me that this also has the advantage of establishing a somewhat non-realistic convention in the beginning of the play, which is necessary or certainly helpful in bringing out the lyrical qualities. It seemed to me that the action in the main body of the play would have an added suspense, poignancy, and richness, if played against a knowledge (in the audience) of some impending disaster, not as yet fully known but provocatively pre-figured in the prologue. To further enhance this effect I planned originally that the play should be enacted upon the stage as the store appeared in the prologue-epilogue, in other words among the "ruins", the souvenirs of violence, which followed the tragedy. So that the characters would be like "memories re-enacting experience" among the final effects of it. Thus the play would be done somewhat like "Our Town", practically without props, but this idea seemed to entail too many technical difficulties - so I put it on the shelf. It is still worth considering however, as it is a novel idea, and would certainly give a portentous atmosphere to everything that took place . . .

Structurally I think the play is much stronger. Discounting some of what happened in Boston as simply Boston, I nevertheless made note of the main structural flaws. The first two scenes went well enough but the audience did not grasp very clearly what the play was driving toward and the conversational length of the second scene wearied them. This scene obviously needed breaking in two and supplying with some more action to hang the talk on - a "dramatic shot-in-the-arm". Therefore I divided this scene into two scenes, morning and afternoon of the same day, with probably an intermission in between, and in each I injected a "scene of conflict", first between Myra and Val, when, disturbed and jealous over his obvious effect on the various women, she flies into a rage and fires him and he, to make her understand him, tells her his past life, omitting the fire phobia which is kept but much less obtrusively in the present script. The "bayous speech" is thus cleanly motivated here rather than popping out of no where as it did, more or less, in the original. Also there is progression in that Val regains his job. But the scene ends with suggestion of frustrated longing in both as Myra runs up stairs. The second scene rises cleanly and sharply to the climax of Val's conflict with the men of the community while defending one of "his kind", the dispossessed negro. The revelation of his being "Wanted" is definite progression and introduces warning and suspense.

The act closes with the "coming together" but with a much more substantial plot development than previously and with more interest excited in what is to come hereafter.

In ACT THREE, Vee is removed as an object of jealousy for Myra,

Sandra serving that purpose more logically. The "Jesus picture" scene is reduced to essentials.

Val's determination to break free which was only vaguely and subjectively motivated in the original, is now the direct result of action - the appearance of the Woman from Waco, who is and has been Val's nemesis for several years - personification of the animal sexuality side of his nature which has always dogged him and interfered with his idealistic pilgrimage through life.

From then on I think the play builds quickly and dramatically to Myra's death - and after that I have brought the curtain down as quickly as possible, eliminating the "fire in the cypress" brake and other things that confused and created a chaotic effect. Myra's death is handled more simply without the "Grandfather's book". There is nothing to tax credulity in the present ending as there was before and the Conjure Man's appearance with the jacket as the mob bursts in provides a clean, striking curtain, still on the realistic plane and leaving some denouement, or explanation of what happened afterwards, to the gentle, retrospective device of the epilogue.

The Conjure Man, if you are looking for a symbol, represents the dark, inscrutable face of things as they are, the essential mystery of life - "the one who knows things he isn't telling" - omniscience, fate, or what have you, of which death, life and everything else are so many curious tokens sewn about his dark garments.

T.W.

David Anderson's appearance in Scene 3 made Myra's early love and the wreckage of her life, before Val, a more tangible thing, - people believe what they see on the stage but often miss what is merely heard so I thought I would let them see David, before Myra's speech about her early heartbreak. I have not white-washed the characters, which would be to make this a flat, conventional play, but I have certainly added strength to Val in his conflict with the men and his social struggle and made his background more clear. I believe the play now has a social dimension with clearer picture of the whole community.

188. *To the Williams Family*

SH: The Moorland
Gloucester, Massachusetts
July 4, 1941
[ALS, 4 pp. HTC]

Dear Folks -

I have gone up here for a short visit to escape the terrific heat in N.Y. I was in a room on the top floor in N.Y. and it got so I couldn't sleep.

There is a summer theater colony here at this hotel and I have been given theatrical rates which is just half the usual price. A very elegant old hotel, on a cliff directly over the ocean. Extremely quiet, nearly all old ladies except for the actors. Ramon Novarro is playing here this week and he ate at the table with us last night.

I will only stay here about a week, then probably spend some time in Provincetown. I get more work done out of New York, especially when the heat there is so intense. I never felt anything quite so bad in St. Louis - that I can remember. Also I developed a carbuncle on my left shoulder. Had it treated almost free of charge at the city hospital but had to spend hours waiting in line at the clinic. It is practically well now and I am taking vitamin tablets as the doctor recommended.

You would probably like these New England matrons - but they are a little too formidable for me. They look aghast at the "theatrical crowd" - we are not even permitted to go on the beach in shirtless trunks.

I wish you would send me two play manuscripts if you can find them - particularly "Spring Storm" which I believe I placed in the top of one of my big manuscript boxes in the attic. Also the play which Dakin's friend did over the radio. That can wait till Dakin returns but I would like to have the other (Spring S.) this summer - I will let you know where to address it when I get settled again. Let me know if you find it - Write me c/o Liebling-Wood, 551 5th Ave. while I am away.

Love - Tom.

[With the Rockefeller grant TW felt increasing pressure to shake off the effects of Boston and begin a new play with commercial appeal. He may have recalled *Spring Storm* at this time because of the recent inquiry by the St. Louis Civic Theatre (see letter #182). In the following months he considered, and rejected, several additional ideas for a long play, including a return to D.H. Lawrence (see letter #204). A proliferation of stories, poems, and one-act plays would mark the remainder of 1941, with several works continuing to anticipate *The Glass Menagerie.*

Dakin Williams was enrolled in summer school at the University of Colorado, while the play adapted for radio was probably the 1937 one-act "Me, Vashya!" (n.d., HRC).]

189. *To Paul Bigelow*

[Cogan House
Provincetown, Massachusetts]
[ca. July 12, 1941]
[TLS w/ autograph postscript, 1 p. Massee Collection]

Oh, Paul -

What a mad-house I am in! I may return to New York before this letter reaches you as the situation here is intolerable. Joe has always had a genius for collecting the weirdest and most impossible bunch of pseudo-artistic crack-pots but he has now really exceeded himself. Our menage consists of a Russian Jewess with huge buttocks and a bleeding soul, a boy recently and prematurely discharged from a mental institution, who really seems the sanest of the group, a beautiful and hopelessly normal blond youth who sleeps in the bed next to mine, and two vaguely literary and hideous young men from the Village who stand over me while I am writing and snatch up each page I remove from the typewriter, everybody trying to surpass the other in quivering sensibility, a sort of thing which I have not found bearable since I quit the Vieux Carre. I have never encountered so much and such a bad sort of it. And at a time when I have a particular hunger for sane and simple surroundings. It is really too bad. I cannot get outside as it is raining - ever since I got here, and the ocean is too rough for swimming. Joe has got an album of primitive jungle music which he has going all the time - writhes and slithers about the place naked. Two corn-fed female art students, intoxicated by their contact with Bohemia, come in for dinner and stay all evening. - Oh, for a beautiful dull sailor or a drunk marine! - I think one of the cleverest cruelties of life is that it provides no convenient and pleasant form of self-extinction like fucking yourself to death. - How agreeable that would be right now!

I have kept everything packed up and I think I will just return to New York, take what money I still have coming to me and escape to Mexico right away. - Nothing else seems barely tolerable to me. - I wish you were free to go, too. - I know I should settle down <u>some</u> place and work intensively but it is no use trying in a place like this where there is no trade and no pleasant associations even. - I hope your Harpers affair has come to some satisfactory conclusion and that the weather in N.Y. is more tolerable. - If Freddie has gone into the coast-guards and you have room in the apartment, let me know by return mail and I will return instantly. - I may anyhow.

10.

P.S. The shoulder is about healed.

[In July TW made a second foray to Provincetown and lived in "a mad-house" of Joe Hazan's creation, rented from Edith Ives Cogan, a Boston physician.

Soon after meeting Paul Bigelow (1905-1988), TW described him as "<u>the</u> most stimulating, entertaining even brilliant companion I have ever had" (*Journal*, June 27, 1941). The "legendary" Bigelow was variously a journalist, a raconteur and friend of celebrities, an aspiring playwright, a production assistant for the Theatre Guild and Cheryl Crawford, and a night manager at the Franklin Arms Hotel in Brooklyn. In 1939 he and Jordan Massee moved from Georgia to New York, where they soon met TW.

The "Harpers affair" was Bigelow's attempt to find a publisher for the memoirs of Eva Gauthier, a Canadian soprano whom he and Massee admired. Fred Melton had entered the Coast Guard.]

190. *To Paul Bigelow*

"Cogan House"
[Provincetown, Massachusetts]
PM: Provincetown, July 25, 1941
[TLS, 2 pp. Massee Collection]

(Please keep this description of life in "Cogan House" - I want it in my memoirs)

Paul darling:

Your card and your letter were just fetched to our house by the dainty hand of one Ethel Elkofsky whom I have mentioned before. Apparently they were written a good while ago and I had not received them since they went to G. Del. and were merely collected by chance. Well, my dear, I have two reasons for remaining here thus long or perhaps several, but the most active right now is lack of funds to return as my last five dollars was just commandeered for house-rent - I have written off for my second-to-last Rocky check but doubtless it will not come before Saturday or even Monday. Be sure I will not procrastinate after it comes in getting away. - Though I must confess things have been somewhat better than I described them in my last letter and a certain element of fascination has crept into my horrified observation of activities under this singular roof. Joe and the Skeezo have both been trying to rape the Elkofsky but it seems that she is only physically attracted to homosexuals and all of her great, throbbing heart belongs exclusively to me! - She will only sleep in my room and abases herself to wash my feet, light my cigarettes, butter my bread, and even button my pants, but this, my dear fellow, is not my other reason for remaining Provincetown. - You have already guessed what it is. The impervious blond - the vast impervious blond of my thwarted libido! - I have declared my love and embraced him madly and he has laughed and said, Tennessee, you amaze me! - and that is how things stand - and I don't mean lay. It is kuite, kuite mad in this place. Most of our table talk yesterday was about orgasms - Elkofsky will have nothing of Joe or the Skeezo because it seems she had no orgasm with them the times they invaded her body and she has drawn great, metaphysical conclusions about the malevolent male universe from these misadventures in bed. She regards me with glittering, speculative eyes that make me shudder. Well, Friday nights we have great orgies with fifty cents admission to raise the rent-money. Of course I got kuite drunk and due to my frustration over the blond I carried on in a way that shocked everybody including myself. Four of us girls retired to an upstairs bedroom from which only occasional news-bulletins were issued to the party below till it ended. One of the women had come with one of the four and kept bawling at the locked door and shrieking downstairs that she knew her dear Eric was being held incommunicado against his will. At one time she wailed, Why does it take those bitches so long to come? I could have come ten times already since they have been up there! - All of this would have been very well (from all but the esthetic pt. of view) had it not been for the fact that better than half of the persons attending the party were strictly jam and of a character corresponding closely to Theatre Guild subscription audiences in Boston. Well, my dear, when I now appear in public the children are called indoors and the dogs pushed out!

Joe still dreams of procuring $150. back money on house-rent by the sale of his body - so far no takers, but he says that he has not really extended himself thus far. Yesterday he remarked that he needed a large mirror to dance in front of and that he would procure that, and also a canvas for the blond artist as soon as he had met a few people. Oh, dear, I said, I have met <u>so</u> many people and never received either a canvas or a full-length mirror. - Well, said Joe, it is different in my case. I'm a Hindu dancer!

At night an utter delirium settles upon the house. Like frenzied rats they go scuttling about in the dark on various errands, mostly profane or insane - there is a great shuffling about of bed-partners, only the blond remaining aloof from it all, and I who am fully content with singular slumber. - Every morning there is a mysterious new tension in the atmosphere

Cogan House "menage": Joe Hazan, Tennessee, Ethel Elkovsky, Walter Hollander, and an unidentified friend, Provincetown, 1941.

and the boding silence of the Hindu or the staring trance of the Skeezo or Ethel's hysterical animation cover up a great history of campaigns during the night. The household shifts in number from seven to twenty - we eat fish at every meal because we get it for nothing. My cumulated sexual potency is sufficient to blast the Atlantic fleet out of Brooklyn! - Perhaps I shall when I get back to N.Y. - I have [had] three affairs since I left and been trade in them all, so you know how interesting things are.

Langner just wrote me a honey-sweet letter - he says when he gets time he will sit down and make a great play out of "Battle of Angels". - I think that is very nice of him. - No mention of payment in the meantime. - I write every day, have started what may be a novel about a male prostitute, written a good short story and a remarkable <u>kuantity</u> of verse. -

So Freddie is in the coast-guard! Hurrah! - When I get back shall I park at your apartment till I am ready to leave for Mexico? - If I do I must have a place to fuck, because my dear I have never felt kuite so rape-lusty with all of this fish. p-- Tell Donnie he will not be safe with Freddie away. Nor will you, for that matter. ---You whore of Babylon - I mean Brooklyn!

Love to you all, and dear love to the boys in blue.

Tennessee

[Ethel Elkovsky was a visitor from Brooklyn, while "the Skeezo," or schizophrenic, reportedly feared that TW was trying to seduce him and later in the summer suffered a nervous breakdown.

The "novel about a male prostitute" may be an early draft of the story "One Arm" (1948), while the "good short story" is "The Malediction" (1945). Among the verse that TW wrote at Provincetown was "The Ice Blue Wind" (1944), typed on the stationery of Edith Ives Cogan, M.D.

A slightly different version of this letter (n.d.) is held by the Columbia University Library.]

191. To Audrey Wood

[Cogan House]
Provincetown [Massachusetts]
July 29, 1941
[TLS, 1 p. HRC]

Dear Audrey:

Here is a new short story which is rather too hastily written between other things, but I think might be interesting to <u>Partisan</u> <u>Review</u> and <u>Story</u>. I believe the editor of the first, which pays about as well as <u>Story</u>, is a man named Dwight MacDonald who may know of me through my friend Clark Mills who is a contributor of his. I think the Chaplinesque character of the little man and the universal theme of loneliness might be poignant enough to be worked into a short expressionistic play using music and projected settings like those the designer Leve showed me. If you agree about this, let me know.

I am returning to New York for a few days before probably leaving for Mexico where I can make what is left of my money go further. I have conceived a pretty good idea for a long play based on a famous refugée artist who has established a school here. So far I have not had energy enough for much sustained work, my experiences with the Guild have caused a tired, listless feeling which is slow to wear off.

I have asked Molly Day Thacher if she would be interested in anything of mine for their new theatre which seems to be becoming an actuality according to the papers. While the dollar-top idea may not be a good one commercially, they are certainly an intelligent group of people to work with.

I will see you before I make any radical departures.

Affectionately, Tennessee

[Rejection of "The Malediction" by Whit Burnett (*STORY*), John Tebbel (*American Mercury*), and other editors may have prompted TW to begin dramatization of the story in 1942. Lucio, the "Chaplinesque character," lives in a "strangely devitiated city" modeled upon St. Louis and shares with TW the "panicky" life of the lonely. TW's conception of the "little man" and his love for a stray cat (Nitchevo) owe much to a poem by Hart Crane entitled "Chaplinesque" (1921): "For we can still love the world, who find / A famished kitten on the step, and know / Recesses for it from the fury of the street, / Or warm torn elbow coverts."

Samuel Leve had recently designed "an amusing skeletonized old house" (as described by the *New York Times* reviewer Brooks Atkinson) for William Saroyan's play *The Beautiful People*, which opened in New York on April 21, 1941.

Hans Hofmann, the "refugée artist" who established a school at Provincetown in 1934, apparently intrigued TW as a subject for drama, as had several other artistic figures. He probably did not pursue this idea but later praised Hofmann as an innovative artist who had taken the "step" that "logically follows the historic advance of such a painter as Van Gogh" ("An Appreciation," 1948).

After the breakup of the Group Theatre, Elia Kazan and Robert Lewis attempted to preserve its ideals through the Dollar Top Theatre, with Molly Day Thacher as playreader. The plan to stage plays in a large house with each seat priced at one dollar seemed unpromising to TW, but in late-July he drafted a note to Thacher (written in the journal and probably not mailed) stating the availability of the "new" *Battle of Angels*, which he thought "a better play" for the "realistic revisions" he had made. The Dollar Top idea fell through when financial backing could not be found.

In August TW returned to New York but it was coastal Georgia, rather than Mexico, that he visited next, at the invitation of Paul Bigelow and Jordan Massee.]

192. To the Williams Family

SH: Golden Isles Beach Hotel
St. Simons Island, Georgia
[August 1941]
[ALS, 4 pp. HTC]

Dear Folks -

I think I will probably spend the rest of the summer down here. I came down at the invitation of some fabulously wealthy people I met through Mrs. Black in Key West. I was entertained like a prince at their mansion on Sea Island for a couple of days but have now moved over to this hotel on St. Simon's Island - it is just a few feet from the nicest beach I've ever discovered. Just before I left New York Audrey sold an option on my one-acts to a rich actor who intends to produce them some time. This will bring in fifty dollars a month, enough to live on in Mexico when my Rockefeller money runs out. Langner was pleased with Battle of Angels but so far has not taken any new option on it. They have practically no money as a result of last season's series of failures. Audrey and I felt that it would hurt the play's future chances to have a cheap and hasty summer production so that idea was given up. A man who has ~~an interest~~ money in "Life With Father" is now interested in my work and may advance some money on my next play if I can write him a very enticing synopsis.

What are Grand and Grandfather's plans? If I don't go to Mexico I might board with them in the South next Fall unless necessary for me to return to N.Y. - that is, if they are still thinking of Florida. Does Dakin have to go in the <u>army</u>? - I certainly hope <u>not</u>.

Love - Tom.

[The Massees were a prominent business family who lived in Macon, Georgia, and summered on Sea Island. Their son Jordan, who met TW in late 1940, has informed the editors that his parents were neither "fabulously wealthy" nor acquainted with Mrs. Black in Key West. With his imposing girth and white linen suit and tales of plantation life in the South, Jordan Massee, Sr., is often cited as a source for Big Daddy in *Cat on a Hot Tin Roof*. He reportedly enjoyed the company of his son's friend, if only because TW was such an attentive audience.

Hume Cronyn is the "rich actor" who held an option on TW's one-act plays, including "At Liberty" and "This Property is Condemned," both published in June 1941.

Lawrence Langner, of course, was not "pleased" with TW's revision of *Battle of Angels*. Martin Gabel, potential backer of TW's "next play," had been impressed by *Battle* and wished to meet the author, as Audrey Wood informed TW on July 11, 1941 (HRC).

Dakin Williams was completing law studies at Washington University and would not be drafted until late 1942. In February TW learned that he had been classified "IV F," unfit for military service, "until further notice" (letter, postmarked February 3, 1941, HRC).]

193. To Audrey Wood

SH: Golden Isles Beach Hotel
St. Simons Island, Georgia
[ca. mid-August 1941]
[TLS w/ autograph postscript, 1 p. HRC]

Dear Audrey:

I am enclosing the synopsis which Martin Gabel asked for and I do hope you will succeed in wresting some cash from this Croesus. Promise him everything including my soul! - if he is naive enough to purchase such intangibles as that.

It would probably be an excellent idea to have a couple of carbon copies of this synopsis made at my expense, one for our own files and the other for Miss Sillcox to look at, so she will see I have actually something to work on.

I have a much clearer line on the play as a result of writing the story down like this - I hope you think it is something to work on.

Cordially, 10.

I hope your blood-pressure is getting back up to normal. I wish I could give you some of mine.

Never mind carbons - I have made them myself - Mirabile Dictu!

[Audrey Wood was "impressed" by the synopsis (which has not been found) that TW hastily composed—presumably of *Stairs to the Roof*—but she was "disturbed" to learn, after searching the files, that the Theatre Guild held a "reading option" on her client's "next play." "So, my dear I'm afraid we can't take any of Mr. Gabel's nice money on this one" (letter to TW, August 20, 1941, HRC). TW had arranged the option in May 1940 when Wood was living in Hollywood (see letter #195).]

194. To Audrey Wood

SH: Golden Isles Beach Hotel
St. Simons Island, Georgia
[ca. late-August 1941]
[TLS, 1 p. HRC]

Audrey -

I thought I had better write Cronyn a thank-you note of some kind. If this will do, let him have it.

I thought to turn the new one-act over to you before now but it seems good enough to justify longer attention. It will be done this week-end, and I think it may be a very moving little play. "The Front Porch Girl", or "If You Breathe It Breaks".

If money cannot be extracted from Mr. Gabel, perhaps I had better try the synopsis on Gassner. He would like the material and might extort some further payment from the Guild.

Somebody has suggested I write a starring vehicle for Langner and Helburn in which he takes a bath in the last act in a tub of ass's milk, poured into the tub by Helburn wearing one of her most outrageous hats and nothing else. - I think that would have all the elements of good theatre, including social significance, and sex.

Shall I call on Whit Burnett or has he already returned my story?

10.

[Stage directions for "The Front Porch Girl" identify Miriam Wingfield as a fading ingénue of twenty-six who is "what is sometimes referred to in Mississippi as a 'front porch girl': a girl who sits hopefully, or perhaps despairingly, waiting for gentlemen who practically never drop in" (n.d., HRC). She has a cherished glass collection, brothers modeled upon Tom and Dakin Williams (one a sensitive artist, the other a pesky athlete), and a kindly gentleman caller at her mother's boarding house in Blue Mountain, Mississippi. With "Portrait of a Girl in Glass" and "The Front Porch Girl," TW identified the critical elements of *The Glass Menagerie* and began the experiments with tone, situation, and genre that would lead to a definitive script.

The Theatre Guild's playreader John Gassner liked "the speed" of the synopsis that TW had recently submitted, but he "worried about its being too light" (letter from Audrey Wood to TW, September 22, 1941, HRC).]

195. To Paul Bigelow

> [436 East 73rd Street, New York]
> PM: New York, August 27, 1941
> [TLS w/ autograph marginalia, 4 pp. Columbia]

Dear Paul:

I am pretty tired from helping the kids move in their new chateau - and incidentally <u>out</u> of yours - so will not write you much.

Nor will I try to tell you how embarrassed I was at having to send that frantic appeal for funds. I wired Criswell first but it seems Criswell had moved after a quarrel with Jack and Jack did not notify him of the wire till it had been delivered quite a while. In the meantime my panic reached such a degree - and also my appetite - that I felt compelled to appeal to you all. Criswell's money order came eventually and I left town with the instructions that Jordan's should be returned to him. - Was it? - I believe they sometimes wait 72 hours.

I was charmed by Charleston but naturally the time spent in seeing

Washington the <u>hard</u> way did not leave me with a too favorable impression of our national capitol, long may she wave, Etc. Patriotism <u>died</u> forever when I walked across town for the fifth time to the main post-office and still found no remittance from the Damnest Guild and came back out and saw the old glory still waving blithely on the capitol dome.

Cronyn has so far advanced two hundred dollars on the short plays, to be doled out by Audrey. She was "Tremendously pleased" by the synopsis but a rather serious hitch has developed because when she looked through the files she discovered that the Theatre Guild had already taken a "reading option" on my next long play which they paid only one hundred dollars for and which nevertheless is a pretty material barrier to the easy money of Mr. Gabel. We are trying to think of ways <u>AND</u> means! - Liebling ought to come in handy there.

Well, baby, I'm about as merry as old second day pan-cake. Sometimes I would just like to say about life - "The incident is closed!"

Carry on - yeah.

La Criswell is <u>here</u>. Taking a shower at the moment.

We went to Bianca's together last night. How dreary, my dear! The sailor's father had died and he's on a 20-day leave in Florida and I mean <u>no</u> one was <u>there</u>. But - a bunch of dessicated old queens who, as Criswell remarked, looked like their mothers had been scared by a mummy-case. At one point in the evening an alley-cat leapt off the fire-escape and scampered madly across the room and out the nearest exit - Criswell screamed: "TRADE!" - But nobody else was quite as amused as I was.

I will try to get the book off tomorrow. Except for one really good short story called "SUMMER EVENING" I was not too impressed by the Bowen. At her worst she is like a literary hybrid resulting from the unfortunate cross-pollination of Fannie Hurst and William Faulkner. At her best she is quite good, though.

This letter is also to Jordan and next I am going to write a letter to Jordan which will be also to you. My love to you both. - I hate to think how much trouble I was and I am - But no speeches, huh?

Won't you come home - <u>soon</u>? God only knows when I will be galloping off again - It's a disease and a progressive one, too.

My kindest regards to all, especially Emily and Mr. Massey - and Boom-boom!

10.

<u>Later</u>

Dear Paul -

I've left this fucking letter lying around here a couple of days. I've taken it out in my pocket several times intending to send it but brought it back home with me.

Baby, this place looks awful. The kids left everything in a terrible state, they took the bed in your room and they sold the big bed in the front room to that Jerry person. He took everything else but left the bed - so far. It has no covers on it and I just sleep on the mattress. Oh, God, it is <u>awful</u>-looking! There are scraps of paper and trash all over the floors and dust and complete disorder. I try not to look at it but it does creep into my consciousness somehow!

If this letter sounds funny, it is probably because I am drunk. I went out cruising last night and brought home something with a marvelous body it was animated Greek marble and turned over even. It asked for money, and I said, Dear, would I be living in circumstances like this if I had any money? It sadly acknowledged that it guessed I wouldn't. You can imagine how terrible looking the place is! No cover on the bed, just the awful bare mattress and practically everything removed from the apartment.

Last night after I sent the trade home I locked myself out, having left the key upstairs and had to stay on the street, leaning against lamp-powtw and car-fenders till four or five in the morning when the milkman let me in. I witnessed a strange little incident. One of the Chekoslovakian neighbors (phonetic spelling) chased his wife out of the house. She screamed, "You spit in my face, you leave me alone, my face is no punching ball!"

She hid behind a car and he walked all around looking for her. At last he came over to me and said, "Did you see the wife?" - I said, "No." and he said, "Excuse me, I got you wrong, buddy." Then he went back in the apartment and the woman came out from behind the ~~house~~ car and stood in front of the apartment as if rooted there for about an hour. Suddenly he dashed out again in his undershirt and she raced around the corner and hid behind the parked car again.

At this point the milkman arrived and I went in to bed.

As usual when drunk I am struck by the absolute enormity and monstrosity of living. I think I am going to leave very soon for New Orleans as living in this disorder is terribly upsetting.

(Editorial deletion)

This letter is awful so I will stop it before it gets worse. And go on out and do a little cruising. So long. Love.

1o.

[After layovers in Charleston and Washington, TW returned to New York in late-August and helped "the kids," Donald Windham and Fred Melton, move from their beleaguered apartment on East 73rd Street—the move probably occasioned by a falling out of Windham and Paul Bigelow. Bigelow, Jordan Massee, and Andrew Lyndon shared the apartment in the fall. Charles Criswell, a commercial artist and writer, would soon enter the service and leave New York.

TW may have found in Elizabeth Bowen's story "Summer Night" (1941) a character whose fear and isolation approached his own and whose haunting sister, deaf and unmarried, reminded him of Rose.

Deletion of the penultimate paragraph of this letter is intended to guard the privacy of friends whom TW observed in a scene of unrequited ardor and faltering relationship: "It really was a frightfully sad sort of thing. <u>Queens</u>! Oh, God, what a mess it all is!"

This letter was written on stationery imprinted with the name of the Golden Isles Beach Hotel, St. Simons Island, Georgia. Penned above the letterhead is the notation: "I <u>saw</u> Miss Wright - What a <u>fluff</u>!"]

196. To Whitney Ewing "Whit" Burnett

[436 East 73rd Street, New York]

[early-September 1941]

[TLS, 1 p. Princeton]

Dear Mr. Burnett:

I believe that Audrey Wood has sent you a story of mine called "The Malediction", something that boiled irresistibly out of my fingers, and also I hope from either my heart or my brain, during the forced labor on a new play. On reading it over I feel that it contains a good many of my usual ineptitudes of style and really should not have been submitted to you until I had done it better. I happen to be working against time which is why I rushed it off. The material seems to be a good deal more important than that of most of my stories, so it occurs to me that possibly you might be willing to let me work it over with certain specific suggestions from you.

That is, of course, assuming that you <u>do</u> like the material of the story. I know perfectly well that this is a presumptious thing to ask of a busy editor, but you must know how anxious I am to find some out-let for my short-stories which somehow never seem to be suitable even in subject matter for anybody but you.

I am leaving Monday for New Orleans where I expect to "dig in" for the winter: you can always get in touch with me through Audrey.

Sincerely, 10.

[Whit Burnett, editor of *STORY* magazine, returned this letter with a note at the foot (dated 9/8/41 and initialed) explaining his rejection of "The Malediction": "This has much that is good, but the total effect is one of sentimentality rather than the searching humanity I expected of it." As an attack upon American capitalism, "The Malediction" resembles *Stairs to the Roof*, whose revision TW was presumably considering at this time. The special importance of the story, apart from the bracing effect of publication, may lie in the presence of thematic elements that continued to boil "irresistibly" after their compromised treatment in *Battle of Angels*: sexually predatory women, cosmic religion, and the essential loneliness of the individual.

This letter was written on stationery imprinted with the name of the Golden Isles Beach Hotel, St. Simons Island, Georgia.]

197. *To Audrey Wood*

[436 East 73rd Street, New York]
Sept. 7, 1941
[TLS, 1 p. HRC]

Dear Audrey:

I am leaving in about an hour for New Orleans, address will be care of General Delivery till I get settled. And I do mean settled this time - if I have to chain myself to a bedpost.

Gabel's office was closed so I could not get the synopsis from him. When you do, please forward it to Gassner and Langner, and let me have a copy of it for my own reference. There are all three out now.

If you don't feel the "one-act" comes off in its present form, you might return it to me and I can work it over as I felt it had the possibility of considerable charm in production. I see where the violinist might suggest the end of "The Beautiful People". He does not have to appear if that would remove the resemblance. I suppose it is inevitable that some people will say I imitate Saroyan in spite of the fact that most of these one-acts were written before any of his plays were produced and I certainly did not have access to his unpublished manuscripts.

Please mail me twenty-five dollars of Cronyn's money care of Gen. Del. New Orleans right away so I will have something there if I arrive without money.

I did not see Burnett but wrote him a note. If he doesn't like the story, please try Partisan Review.

I may take little excursions around the South on a bicycle or my thumb, so do not be alarmed if I am temporarily out of touch at times. I will get as much work done as possible, but I do wish somebody showed a material interest in the synopsis before I concentrated on re-writing the stuff.

Have a good season.

Best, 10.

[The "violinist" in "The Front Porch Girl" is Miriam Wingfield's older brother Vernon, classified "Four F" in the military draft because of "deep psychic anxieties." Apparently Audrey Wood found this figure too reminiscent of a cornet player in The Beautiful People (as may be inferred from intervening correspondence). TW lived in New York in the spring of 1941 and had opportunity to attend William Saroyan's new play at the Lyceum Theatre, although he is silent on this point.]

198. To Paul Bigelow

c/o Mrs. Oglesby
1124 St. Charles
[New Orleans, Louisiana]
PM: New Orleans, September 15, 1941
[ALS, 5 pp. Massee Collection]

Dear Paul -

My second New Orleans period is under way - The Quarter has been cleaned up and become smart, respectable, and expensive so I have located in another part of town. I have a furnished room for $3.50 a wk. right across from the library and a block from the "Y" on Lee Circle - The whole building, one of these aimless fabrications of faded grey stairs and galleries, is likely to collapse any moment but my room has a sort of ridiculous charm with its tattered rose-covered wall paper and immense brass bed - full of sunlight, opening on a court with oleanders and morning glories and sunflowers. Well it is quite different from New York and that is something. It is not very genteel poverty but I am not particular anymore.

Well, darling, I met the Bultmans, they are sort of a multiple Bumbleshoot especially the sister who even jigs her Adams apple like his. She is what is known as an "ex-cellent conversationalist" - in other words talks your head off with absolute banalities. Classifies everybody according to ability as talker. For instance if she happens to like a person says "She is an ex-cellent conversationalist." Or if she didn't, as in the case of poor Sarah, says "She never opened her mouth except to say hello!" - Well, I only opened mine to yawn which I did constantly all evening.

The Secty. is cute, however, and would be a good lay and apparently they are rich enough to know just about everybody. Excuse the non sequitur.

Do please mail my laundry and remind Cris of typewriter. 1124 St. Charles - c/o Mrs. Oglesby.

The town is over run with soldiers, a few sailors. I presume I shall get my share of the trade around here, there is a back entrance to my room & it is right on the Circle. The house, incidentally, reminds me so much of the Bishop's poem about that strange pile of wood.

I am going to try to get a bike this A.M. and devote a week or two to recovering a somewhat dilapidated constitution.

Do take care of yourself - don't take anymore counterfeit bills.

Love - 10.

P.S. I have bought a used bike for $10.00 and am going to make a trip through southern Mississippi maybe next week. Send me Dale La Motte's address!

10.

P.S. Letter from Bumbleshoot indicates she may come down here.

[TW's "Second New Orleans Period" began on September 11 with a wry, if mis-dated, entry in the journal: "The much-bedeviled pilgrim - the fox who runs in circles - has returned to one of those places that failed him (?) before" (September 11, 1941). TW soon considered another "possible new play" entitled "Hawk's Daughter": "A man like my father. Sensitive, terrified children. Same two as in Portrait of a Girl in Glass" (*Journal*, September 14, 1941).

TW came to know "the Bultmans," who owned a mortuary service in New Orleans, through their son Frederick ("Fritz"), a young painter whom he had recently met at Provincetown. "We sat interminably in the Hotel Roosevelt bar and I drank to forget how stupid I was and they were" (*Journal*, September 11, 1941). It was Muriel Bultman Francis, Fritz's sister, who was "known as an ex-cellent conversationalist." The nickname "Bumbleshoot" alludes to Fritz's carrying a large umbrella that resembled a nineteenth-century bumbershoot.

The rooming house on St. Charles reminded TW of the ungainly wooden structure in Elizabeth Bishop's poem "The Monument" (1939): "'It's piled-up boxes, / outlined with shoddy fret-work, half-fallen off, / cracked and unpainted.'"]

199. To Ellsworth P. Conkle

SH: Hotel Monteleone
New Orleans, U.S.A.
September 17, 1941
[ALS, 2 pp. HRC]

Dear Mr. Conkle,

I have felt dreadfully unattached lately, wandering about the South, and it has suddenly occured to me that I might ask you if it would be possible for me to get a scholarship in your department at the University of Texas, on the basis of my creative work. I know it is very late to broach such a subject, but my chance meeting with an English instructor at the school, Oliver Evans, suggested it to me just this week. As you probably know, I got a B.A. at Iowa, summer, 1938. I am really too old to be going back to school but it might do me a lot of good right now to be tied down somewhere and so forced to stay "put" for a while. I am living on $50.00 a month, option money on some one-acts. I presume you know the sad story of my Theatre Guild play. I am working on several new scripts.

I shall vastly appreciate it if you will let me know what the possibilities at Austin are as soon as you can. Address = c/o General delivery, New Orleans, La. - (for the next few days).

Cordially, Tennessee Williams (Tom)

[TW's appeal to his former Iowa professor follows a period of bleak self-appraisal in the journal: "I have such an ordinary type of mind, only a little more sensitive than most others, only my longings and my critical faculty, my sense of my own unfitness, has any dignity. I feel stunted. I should have grown bigger than this. Certainly as an artist I should have grown much bigger and stronger and more durable" (September 14, 1941). When Conkle offered Tom a place to live in Austin and the possibility of his work being produced there, he replied that he was now feeling "much more settled" and praised Conkle for "doing some good red-blooded dramas" that showed "what the original 100% Americans really <u>were</u> and were <u>not</u>" (postmarked New Orleans, September 24, 1941, HRC).

Oliver Evans, whom TW reportedly met at Provincetown in July, held a master's degree from the University of Tennessee and would go on to teach at several universities. He and TW became frequent correspondents and close friends.]

200. *To Edwina Dakin Williams*

> [708 Toulouse Street
> New Orleans, Louisiana]
> [ca. September 22, 1941]
> [TLS, 1 p. HTC]

Dear Mother:

I have to go out to a dinner invitation in a few minutes. I have met a good many nice people here, including some of the original creole families and am fortunately entertained at dinner fairly often.

I am sorry you didn't like the plays. I know your conception of "'poetic truth'" is altogether different from mine but I am still a little surprised at the use of the words ugly and indecent in regard to these particular little plays that nearly everybody thinks are compassionate and moving. I don't care for the first one and am sorry it was included, but the second one I am very pleased with, and Mr. Cronyn, whose option money is supporting me now, was particularly delighted with it.

I am glad you mentioned the shoes - I can certainly use them. I believe I left a nice pair of black shoes there when I returned from Florida.

I am greatly relieved to hear that Dakin doesn't have to go in the army this Fall and can get his degree. Perhaps in another six months the world situation will not be quite so dark.

I do not think I will want to stay in New Orleans very long. Too much rain and I am always hankering for the ocean. I will probably move down to St. Petersburg when I get fed up with it here. I wish Grand and Grandfather were going down there this winter, though you will probably reproach me for making such a suggestion in view of Grandfather's needing so little persuasion to wander about. - Well, as long as there are pleasant places to visit and no particular reason for "staying put", I think that travelling around is a pretty sensible way of enjoying life. For me it is stimulating. When I feel stale I move to another place and it freshens me up.

The eye can wait till I get back to New York. I am saving up for a lot of dental work, though. Two huge cavities on either side of my mouth that give little experimental aches now and then.

I am working on what promises to be a pretty good play. But the war has certainly played the devil with Broadway. Nothing but silly, light stuff like "The Wookey". I don't think the desperate struggles and heartbreaking experiences of the British people, and people all over the world, can be or should be presented in such light fashion. What we need is writing that gets at the fundamental falsehoods and stupidities that makes the world such a nightmare for most of its people. Of course there should [be] light, diverting plays but nobody is producing the sort of things, right now, that will have lasting value because they deal seriously with fundamental things.

Love to all - Tom.

[The one-act plays that Edwina deemed "ugly and indecent" were "At Liberty" and "This Property is Condemned" (see letter #201). Collected by William Kozlenko in *American Scenes* (1941), they put their author in good literary company with Richard Wright, Irwin Shaw, and Paul Green. In a biographical note TW gave 1914 as the year of his birth and added the further misinformation that he did not leave the South until he "entered high school."

"Travelling around" was not merely "sensible" or "stimulating" for TW but an ingrained part of his defensive regime: "You have become, through practise, so horribly expert in the administration of palliative drugs - amusements, indulgences, little temporary evasions and escapes - you use them instead of warfare with the final, inner antagonist - maybe because you are not quite sure <u>what</u> he is" (*Journal*, September 17, 1941).

The promising new play was "The Voices In My Sleep" (see letter #201).

The Wookey, by Frederick H. Brennan, was a patriotic melodrama that opened on September 10, 1941, and ran for 134 performances. Reviewers noted the play's shallowness but none thought that it demeaned the wartime "struggles" of the British.]

201. *To Audrey Wood*

[708 Toulouse Street
New Orleans, Louisiana]
[ca. September 24, 1941]
[TLS, 2 pp. HRC]

Dear Audrey:

In spite of its rather fantastic assertions the slip which you enclosed had a more heartening effect than you can imagine. I don't believe anyone ever suspects how completely unsure I am of my work and myself and what tortures of self-doubting the doubt of others has always given me.

Well, as long as some people think well of my stuff I don't care terribly whether its printed or not as that makes me feel that it may eventually have some lasting place and not be wasted.

Please give Mr. Tebbel my heart-felt thanks.

You will be glad to hear that I am working on what promises to be a long, or at least a medium long, play which is straight realism, heavily emotional but not "out of bounds" so far. It is the sudden out-growth of several short-pieces. It is the nostalgic home-memories of a boy sleeping in a flop-house (for which I am using some of the material in "Fugitive Kind") on Xmas Eve, and scenes alternate dramatically between the home and the flop-house. I call it "The Voices In My Sleep" - Its present tendancy is to be a little too sad, though there is some wry humor in most of the scenes. - It will probably be of a length that will need one of my short plays to fill out the evening with it, as I want to make it as compact as possible. - Still it is too early to say much about it.

I am glad you showed Gassner that I still have a social conscience - after my Freudian detour. - There is very little sex in the new work. - Let us hope I can get along without it. - Oh, Christ, how I want to do something really worth while - Before some truck runs me down on my new bicycle. - If that should happen, by the way, you must tell my parents that I instructed copies to be made of everything at their expense (They will pay it) and please be sure that no single copies of anything falls in their hands as my Mother wrote me the other day that the plays in "American Scenes" were "ugly details about indecent people" and a disgrace to the kin-folk mentioned in the preface. I am afraid she would burn them in order to save my reputation. - The poetry and other scripts I carry around with me should likewise be kept from them and sorted out by you and Clark Mills and Paul Bigelow. - I bring this up because my defective vision and absent mind make an accident far from improbable sometime.

I am cultivating friends who give dinners.

Yours, 10.

[Tipped into Audrey Wood's letter of September 22, 1941, (HRC) was a note from John Tebbel, managing editor of the *American Mercury*, who described TW as "D.H. Lawrence and Hemingway and Thomas Wolfe rolled into one" but added that he might "be a better novelist than a short story writer" (qtd. in *Remember Me to Tom*, p. 130; see letter #202). The occasion was Tebbel's rejection of "The Malediction," sent next by Wood to John Mosher at *The New Yorker*.

TW's new "medium long" play was provisionally entitled "The Voices In My Sleep." The alternation of scenes "between the home and the flop-house" would reappear in drafts of "The Gentleman Caller," a later stage in the evolution of *The Glass Menagerie*, although not in the final version of the play.

It was probably a synopsis of *Stairs to the Roof* that Wood sent to John Gassner to keep her client's name current at the Theatre Guild, if not to vindicate his "social conscience."]

202. To Paul Bigelow

SH: New Orleans Athletic Club
New Orleans
PM: New Orleans, September 25, 1941
[ALS, 4 pp. Columbia]

Dear Paul -

I got reckless and invested half of my current checque in a membership at this rather exclusive Club, but it is worth it as there is a marvelous salt water pool, Turkish bath, Etc., and the prettiest Creole belles in town. I am already well-established in their circles and my particular intimate is a Bordelon, one of the oldest families in the city. Such delicate belles you have never seen, utterly different from the northern species. Everybody is "Cher!" - I actually pass for "butch" in comparison and am regarded as an innovation - "The Out-door Type"! - and am consequently enjoying a considerable succés.

The Bultman's, it seems, could do me more <u>harm</u> than good - they are <u>not</u> accepted. It seems the grandfather used to ride as a <u>footman</u> behind a <u>hearse</u>. - This explains a lot about poor little Bumbleshoot. - They only go out among the <u>nouveau riche</u>, and when I stopped to speak to his sister at "Le Petit Theatrê", the Creole belles I was with dispersed in a panic until she had disappeared. - Such nonsense! - Although I must admit she is not my dish.

In the past week I have started and nearly completed the first draft of a new long play - Medium long. Audrey sent me a marvelous letter from John Tebbel, Editor of <u>The American Mercury</u> - He had read "The Malediction" and tho he could not use it in the magazine, he described me as "Thomas Wolfe, D.H. Lawrence, and Hemingway rolled into one, and with a style that is far from eclectic!" - He is meeting Audrey at lunch, she says, to discuss my work further. - I badly needed some kind words like that, as the recent months have been pretty tough. - Gassner liked the synopsis but I am not doing any more work on that one till I have gotten the present thing done.

"Cher," I have a room on Royal, right opposite <u>the</u> gay bar - The St. James, so I can hover like a bright angel over the troubled waters of homosociety. And I have a balcony and everything but a mantilla to throw across it. But I <u>do</u> wish you would mail me my laundry. You don't want people to whisper - "The poor girl's putting up a very bold front, but actually doesn't have a <u>shirt</u> to her <u>back</u>!" - Dish, dish! - No kidding - please <u>do</u> mail it to me - 538 Royal Street -

I am so glad you are getting on with "The Luncheon" and you've <u>got</u> to write me about Fred's wedding and Donnie's nervous breakdown and Cris's attempted rape of Jordan and Andrew! - Etc.

Love - 10.

Got the typewriter o.k.

[TW stayed for a month at the Royal Street address, although he often directed his mail to 722 Toulouse where Eloi Bordelon, his "particular intimate," lived. In late-October he moved to "a horrible windowless brown cubicle" (*Journal*, October 27, 1941) after a dispute with his landlady who deplored the company that he entertained (see letter #208).

The juicy news from New York was the impending "wedding" of Fred Melton, Donald Windham's intimate friend, and Sarah Marshall, a girl from Macon, Georgia.]

203. To Edwina Dakin Williams

[538 Royal Street
New Orleans, Louisiana]
[ca. late-September 1941]
[TL, 1 p. HTC]

Dear Mother:

Just got your letter and many thanks.

I won't be leaving New Orleans for quite a while yet but when I do I will go to St. Petersburg and it would undoubtedly be good for you and Grand to meet me there. I am so anxious to see you both, but I think it is much better <u>away</u> from home. I just cannot live in the house with Dad, and you understand why. - You will not <u>show</u> him this, of course. I have nothing bitter against him but don't feel up to contending with the strain of his presence. - You need a change from it, too, so it would be nice for you to come to Florida for a while. I am hoping that it will be necessary for me to come back to N.Y. later this year for a production, either of the one-acts which Mr. Cronyn definitely intends to produce or something else. I am working on a new <u>comedy</u>. -

The enclosed note from the editor of "The American Mercury" may hearten you a little concerning my writing, as it did me. My work is hard to sell on account of not being written so much for commercial as artistic aims - always most profitable in the long run, even if posthumously - but you see it is occasionally appreciated by the right people, in the literary world. -

I am afraid the Theatre Guild is off on the wrong foot again. Even with Helen Hayes in a Maxwell Anderson play, they got very bad notices again in Boston - "Candle in the Wind".

I know you will be interested in hearing that the son of Dr. Richards of Columbus is living a few doors from me and I used his typewriter this morning as mine needed a new ribbon. He is an awfully nice boy - a painter - I cannot say whether his work is good or not as it is very modern and hard to judge. He said his parents remember you and Grand and Grandfather very well and spoke very highly of you. They are now living on the Gulf coast at Ocean Springs, Miss., and the doctor has been retired for quite a while it seems and is considered very dreamy and impractical. The mother would like to get back to Columbus but he refuses to go. - Excuse this typing - my machine is a little cranky today.

I have joined an athletic club here and so I get my swimming every day and I also have bought a second-hand bicycle to take little trips about the country. I like living here very much - have a room in the "Quarter" now, very spacious and light, for five dollars a week.

Much love to you all,

[Walter Dakin soon wrote to congratulate his grandson on the honor paid him by the *American Mercury*. It was also an opportunity for Mr. Dakin, now living with Edwina in Clayton, to protest Cornelius's hostility: "He don't even say 'good-morning' to me now. . . . If Grand were only well I wouldn't stay any longer." He added that "we are hoping Grand will have a thorough examination at Barnes Clinic - her cough continues bad and she is weak" (October 3, 1941, HRC). A cancer was suspected.

TW later identified the "dreamy and impractical" Richards as "the Doctor who brought me into this world" and his son Bill as "a congenial fellow-sufferer" (see letter #205) whom he was planning to visit on the Gulf Coast.]

204. To Audrey Wood

c/o Eloi Bordelon, Esq.
722 Toulouse St.
New Orleans, La.
[ca. October 7, 1941]
[ALS, 3 pp. HRC]

Dear Audrey -

Thanks for your prompt and trustful remittance. I did not know of Cronyn's misfortune nor that he had made such a small initial payment or I would not have lived so recklessly here. I lost one typewriter (mine), borrowed one from a friend and then hocked it for a meal-ticket at "Harry's". It will be retrieved this afternoon. I seem to do <u>more</u> writing with a <u>pencil</u>. Completed first drafts (practically) of <u>two</u> new plays, one, mentioned previously, is now called "A Daughter of the American Revolution" is predominantly humorous now, a sort of 'life with <u>Mother</u>'. The other a play about D.H. Lawrence which absorbs me more at the moment because of my long and deep interest in his work and ideas. - Maybe <u>Cronyn</u> would like to play Lawrence. Lawrence was a funny little man - a sort of furious bantam surrounded by large and impressionable hens - excluding Frieda who is truly magnificent. Both of these plays have scenes that could be separated as effective one-acts - And I have been thinking why not use the jail-scene in the original "Battle of Angels" - as a melodramatic one act - if something full of <u>action</u> is wanted for a program. - As you suggest, the theatre contains a great many surprises, delightful and <u>otherwise</u>, and a minimum of expectation is the best defense. - I have lived behind the mobile fortress of a deep and tranquil pessimism for so long that I feel <u>almost</u> impregnable.

I think I will give up this room and sort of live on my bicycle along the Gulf coast till we have more definite knowledge of Cronyn's reactions - leave my stuff with a friend - just take a notebook, toothbrush & extra shirt.

I enclose a little ballad, primarily for <u>your amusement</u>. Do you suppose "Esquire" would like it? Or is it too risqué.

Best - 10.

[Hume Cronyn's "misfortune" was closing in *Mr. Big* (1941) after seven performances on Broadway. When TW later signed contracts with Cronyn, he commiserated on their "sad experiences in the theatre" (October 21, 1941, HRC) and thanked him profusely for his support.

TW wrote "like mad" in the last quarter of 1941 and produced an astonishing number of sketches, stories, and plays. "A Daughter of the American Revolution" (n.d., HRC), a two-page dramatic sketch with the canceled title "APT. F, 3rd FLO. SO.," is an early source for Amanda Wingfield's telephone scene in *The Glass Menagerie*. In later correspondence with Audrey Wood, TW identified the Lawrence play as "The Long Affair" and cautioned her not to assume that "it isn't commercial": "It starts at D.H.'s first meeting with Frieda and ends with his death but the total effect is more tender than tragic and there is a good deal of humor in it. It might be something to interest the Lunts" (n.d., HRC). The one-act would evolve into *I Rise in Flame, Cried the Phoenix*, published in 1951.

The "risqué" ballad, "Cinder Hill" (1977), is about a whore named Mathilda whose retirement shocks "the boys" but whose equally sudden return to the profession is fatal: "The effort must have killed her."]

205. *To Paul Bigelow*

[538 Royal Street
New Orleans, Louisiana]
Friday Night. [October 10, 1941]
[ALS w/ illustrations, 4 pp. Columbia]

Dear Paul -

Many, many thanks for your sweet letter. I have just returned from a bike trip along the Gulf coast which terminated at Bay St. Louis a short distance outside of which I collided in the darkling hours before moonrise with a nervous cow who kicked the rear wheel out of line. I had to leave the wheel to be repaired & procede on my thumb; as I wore boots & khaki cap and appeared rather military I got along famously. I spent a night and day with the object of this pilgrimage, a youth named Bill who is the son of the Doctor who brought me into this world and apparently is trying to compensate for this injustice by providing me with such a congenial fellow-sufferer. Bill is an artist and a good one and the 24 hours at Ocean Springs were a nice change from the turbulent Quarter. I expected to stay longer but felt I ought to get on with my work. Cronyn's play closed on Broadway and I do not know how this will affect our artistic liason. Sort of holding my breath till I hear from Audrey. Well, I received an ecstatic, pulsing letter from Cris - the sort of stammering rapture that Juliet might pour forth to a worldly duenna, on the subject of Andrew. I assumed from the tone of the letter that the affair was <u>consummated</u> to say the very <u>least</u> and more or less eternal vows had been uttered. I was, in fact, reproached sternly for having suggested that he (regenerated by this love) might be interested in cruising New Orleans with me. As a matter of fact, I don't do much cruising myself - this is a rather peaceful period for me, for the first time in yrs. I find it not only possible but pleasant to sit at home & read & talk or meditate in the evenings. Darling, I am growing older - but a little more gracefully than the Maxwell I hope. Incidentally I am not amused that Dick has given her up, I am <u>sorry</u> - but <u>very</u> sorry for it is far more important somehow - or is this the cooperative vanity of artists? - what happens to Gilbert than what happens to Dick - Oh, Shit. Maybe that <u>isn't</u> what I <u>mean</u> - what I mean is that Gilbert has something in him that can be hurt very badly and I hate to see that happen. Be <u>good</u> to him! - The <u>hell</u> with Dick's handsome <u>soldier</u>!

You don't speak of yourself, damn you. How are you? - Will you have the operation? I think you must be getting well. Do you know I have formed the habit of burning holy candles for prayers and drinking Our Lady of Lourdes holy water? I will burn one for you and for me and for Gilbert and Cris all at once - a ten cent one! - And we will be purified and redeemed! - I work hard these days. For me there is either success or destruction sooner or not so sooner & so I work. I am talking like one of these volatile Latin bitches - excuse me. - In these ragged pages I send you the best little part of my heart. Goodbye!

10.

I am not really mad at the Bumbleshoot. I suppose undertakers are necessary and so are Bumbleshoots but I am not in a hurry to embrace either.

Hello to Jordan! - And Andrew. Oh, I do hope I will see you all here or in N.Y. before long!

[The bicycle trip (October 8-10) reunited TW with Bill Richards, who was visiting his parents at Ocean Springs, Mississippi. TW described Richards, to whom he was clearly attracted, as "27 and never had a real consummated affair" (*Journal*, September 28, 1941). The trip was a characteristic response to mounting pressure, as described in the journal: "The blue devils are massed for attack! - Well, let them - I'm ready for any assault the devils can conceive! - " (*Journal*, October 7, 1941).

The assorted hellos, prayers, and forgiveness for Paul Bigelow, Fritz Bultman, Charles Criswell, Andrew Lyndon, and Gilbert Maxwell summarize a "homosociety" in which TW now moved routinely.

Gilbert Maxwell was a native Atlantan and the author of a respected book of verse (*Look to the Lightning*, 1933) when he met TW in New York in 1940. He later published an informal biography entitled *Tennessee Williams and Friends* (1965), for which the main subject had considerable misgiving.

Paul Bigelow's jaw, reportedly broken in a Philadelphia mugging in 1940, became chronically infected and required surgery.

Tipped into this letter is a page with four "rather experimental sketches of G.B.S." The caricatures of Shaw, explained TW, were "not part of the letter. - intentionally."]

206. To Frieda Lawrence

c/o E. Bordelon
722 Toulouse
New Orleans, La.
October 20, 1941
[TLS, 1 p. HRC]

Dear Mrs. Lawrence:

You may remember me as a young writer who passed through Taos in August, 1939, just before the war started and met everybody who had known your late husband with the idea of collecting material for a play about him.

Well, in the meantime other work intervened. I wrote a play which was produced by the Theatre Guild with Miriam Hopkins last winter - it ran two weeks in Boston and created so much commotion with censors, club-women, Etc., that it was removed. - I think you would have liked it and so would Lawrence. It was, incidentally, dedicated to him. <u>Not</u> about him. "Battle of Angels".

Well, I am now well-along on the play <u>about</u> Mr. Lawrence, the first draft practically finished and it looks very good. - It is dedicated to you. No final title yet.

I should like to come to Taos to finish this play and have the benefit of contact with people who knew him. - Are you going to be in Taos this winter or late Fall, and if not, where? - Could I live around Taos on my present income which is fifty-dollars a month? I had been living on a Rockefeller dramatic fellowship but that ran out lately.

I'll be very grateful if you will let me hear from you.

Cordially, T.W.

Tennessee Williams

[TW's boredom after little more than a month in New Orleans made Taos an attractive destination: "Want excitement! - Move? Florida? - No. Taos? - Wish I could" (*Journal*, October 19, 1941). There is no record of Frieda Lawrence's replying to this letter, nor did TW revisit Taos until late 1943.]

207. *To Audrey Wood*

c/o Bordelon

722 Toulouse

[New Orleans, Louisiana]

Oct. 21, 1941

[TLS, 1 p. HRC]

Dear Audrey:

In response to the request for another one-act I have hastily banged out this little sketch of a spiritualist meeting I attended here in the quarter a few nights ago. - It did not end so dramatically as here represented but the characters are from life.

Incidentally the Spiritualist told me she saw a middle-aged lawyer passing out lots of money. - The only middle-aged lawyer I know is Langner and I suggest that we check on that right away.

I do hope you have already gotten my last appeal for money, mailed, I think, last week and that the check will arrive before this - I have had to borrow on my nice tan gabardine suit. When I leave New Orleans I shall write a song called "The Rampart Street Blues". Some day I expect to pass along there and see myself hanging in one of the windows - "Greatly reduced".

The Lawrence play is about ready to be re-written. It seems to go very well because of my great interest in him. - Walter Huston might like it or even the Lunts. - Might. - Shall I try to interest that <u>Life with Father</u> man in a description of it? - I think he manifested some interest in Lawrence on one occasion -

Sincerely, 10.

[The "spiritualist" sketch, which has not been identified, was an outgrowth of several chapel meetings that TW and Bill Richards attended in the Quarter. One was followed by a trip to a "Phillipine bar" where they "stared and stared" at a "lovely Polynesian" (*Journal*, October 27, 1941) youth. Lawrence Langner was both a theatrical producer and a specialist in patent law.

TW did not banter when he considered his poverty in the journal: "I want to have <u>money</u> again. I love the pleasures, the sensual pleasures so much. And how I loathe the squalor, the awkwardness, the indignity of being broke" (October 20, 1941).

The "<u>Life with Father</u> man" was Martin Gabel, apparently a lucky investor in the long-running comedy (1939) by Lindsay and Crouse.]

208. To Paul Bigelow

[538 Royal Street
New Orleans, Louisiana]
Thursday. [October 23, 1941]
[TLS, 1 p. Columbia]

Dear Paul -

Thanks for your letter. I was sorry about Gilbert but did not misunderstand your attitude to such an extent that you needed to clarify it so completely.

I am terribly distressed over my Grandmother who is in a St. Louis hospital, apparently fading gradually away, dear gentle yellow rose that she is - only eighty-eight pounds and would not give in till she collapsed. - The only member of my family I cared for very deeply so you can understand how I feel. I dare not go and dare not stay.

The problems of the Lawrence play which you mention are precisely those which I anticipated in advance of the undertaking. One must not presume upon his importance to <u>us</u> as an <u>artist</u> to make him theatre, but for the theatre must make the material itself intrinsically dramatic and interesting to people who think Lawrence fought Arabs. - Hence I make it primarily the story of a woman's devotion to a man of genius and a man's, a sort of modern satyr's, pilgrimage through times inimical to natural beings. - a would-be satyr never quite released from the umbilicus.

I am too sad to write much, darling. - Forgive me.

Too bad about the laundry - I had despaired of its arrival, there was no trace of it here, and determined to forget the matter. - It will be doubly welcome when it does get here.

Send it care of Eloi Bordelon - 722 Toulouse - or it can be forwarded from my present address. - I am moving. - A misunderstanding about some sailors who come in occasionally to discuss literature with me provoked a tedious little quarrel with the land-lady - I told her I could not live in such an atmosphere of unwarranted suspicion.

There were 550 Argentine sailors here on a good-will visit last week and I must say that no particular malice was displayed. Pan-American relations are much improved. - The lack of a common language had to be compensated by a good deal of prestidigitation. I rose admirably to that contingency assisted by the fact that they have only three top buttons and two on either side.

Christmas still seems remote. - I may be called to New York before then as Audrey writes that Mr. Cronyn, after the closing of Mr. Big, seems to have nothing but my one-acts on the shelf and apparently wants to take another beating. - Says she may have word for me "in the immediate future". - I am not at all eager for this to occur.

Darling, what can we produce from the tall silk hat of our esoteric fancy to cast a spell upon this sweating rabble? Even a trick deck can't have more than two faces on the card. - How sly and conniving we must be, sister witch!

Bubble, bubble, cross them double!!

Until the dark of the moon, dear Hecate - anon! 10.

[Edwina had written earlier of Grand's illness, to which TW replied: "I am dreadfully worried about Grand. Please let me know how she is getting along. Of course I will come to St. Louis if needed. I would come anyway but I just barely make ends meet and cannot afford trips unless necessary" (n.d., HRC). At the same time he wrote in the journal: "Love Grand but don't think of her except casually - say, for a moment or two once a day. - I'm sorry I'm so selfish" (October 21, 1941).

In earlier correspondence Paul Bigelow had identified "the problems" of writing a play about D.H. Lawrence: "His life is a series of dramatic climaxes to us, but they are climaxes of the spirit. . . . I don't think the visual and aural theater is a good medium . . . for the transfer of events and emotions that must be understood as much intuitionally and spiritually as directly through the senses" (n.d., HRC). Bigelow's own play, "A Theme For Reason," was reportedly written with the dancer Isadora Duncan in mind (see letter #240) and involved the same "problems" of dramatic form.]

209. To Paul Bigelow

SH: Royal Hotel Co.
Jackson, Miss.
Sunday Night [November 2, 1941]
[ALS w/ marginalia, 4 pp. Columbia]

Dear Paul -

I am on my way to St. Louis to see my grandmother who has been quite ill. Left most of my stuff in New Orleans so I will have to return there briefly - I am going to settle somewhere else, probably, for the remainder of my southern period. I had a violent and rather bloody matrimonial break-up with the Bordelon, and as she is the queen bee of the bitch society there, it would be unpleasant for me to remain during her displeasure which I must admit was somewhat justly provoked - Marriage is not for me!

The laundry has still not reached me - did you mail it again? - What a business!!

I am quite fed up with piss-elegant bitches (don't you love that phrase?) of the New Orleans variety, and wish to get back to nature. So maybe I will land in Florida if I can live there on my pittance.

If you write me at 722 Toulouse, the letter will reach me, or I will pick it up on my way back.

Very tired - I have a lovely lover in Baton Rouge I just left, and here I may try to get in touch with James Cox. So far I have traveled on my thumb - at Memphis will take the bus.

I love to be alone in a strange town at night - there is something cool and purifying about it. Does it give you that feeling? Isn't it pleasant to be lonesome sometimes?

Being with people is such a strain and there is so much unreality in it, unless you happen to like them very much.

I am taking the Lawrence script with me, hope to finish the first draft in Clayton.

The Bordelon became horribly vicious - hell hath no fury! - started cutting everyone she saw me with and threatened to fill her "black books", as she calls her list of enemies, with all who stuck by me - I could have put up a good fight if it seemed worthwhile but it didn't - merely tedious - and I long for the beach. - Hope it will soon be possible to get back to New York.

Isn't it nice that prissy little Miss Hayes got such a critical lambasting in her "Candle" number?

Kiss Jordan and Andrew for me - and <u>Cris</u> - and <u>Gilbert</u> - Oh, I <u>loved</u> the soldier anecdote - the sleeping soldier -

Love - 10.

[Before leaving for Clayton, TW summarized his second "New Orleans period": "None of my essential personality problems are solved. I have not found the sustained desirable lover. No new convictions - no new lamp-post on the dark road I am stumbling crazily along. - I think I grow steadily a little bit harder & emotionally tougher - Not what I want" (*Journal*, October 29, 1941).

If affronted by "piss-elegant bitches," TW had also been assaulted by "'dirt'" while cruising a bar in the Quarter: "For the first time in my life I was struck - not hard enough to hurt anything but my spirit. Close shave" (*Journal*, October 29, 1941).

TW later explained that his "bloody matrimonial break-up" with Eloi Bordelon followed an incident in which "a plaster blackamoor which she claimed to be of great value and several other articles were smashed in a little difficulty which arose among visitors and myself" (see letter #229). Apparently the "visitors" were unruly trade to which "The Bordelon" took jealous exception. The coincidence of this episode and the arrival of Edwina's check for bus fare to Clayton may have fortified TW's desire to travel, but it also caused a dilemma: "I would much prefer to escape to Florida and devil take the consequences" (*Journal*, October 31, 1941).

Candle in the Wind and its author, Maxwell Anderson, were "lambasted" by reviewers, but Helen Hayes received generally positive notices when she opened on October 22, 1941. The play's topical focus upon Nazi tyranny in occupied France nearly assured TW's lack of sympathy.

TW wrote "(Queen!!)" beneath the name of the manager of the Royal Hotel.]

210. *To Audrey Wood*

[53 Arundel Place
Clayton, Missouri]
November 13, 1941
[TLS w/ autograph postscript, 1 p. HRC]

Dear Audrey:

I'm awfully pleased you and Miss Mayorga liked the one-act. I did, but had no idea any one else would - it's impossible to tell how they will strike the reader. I enclose one more which I hope will be the last for a while as I <u>must</u> get some long plays finished.

As soon as I have my dental work done I want to leave here. I have to have a horizontally impacted wisdom tooth pulled. - Probably tomorrow. Then I will merely wait for Cronyns check to pull out of St. Louis as I am bored to death here. Back to New Orleans to pick up my luggage, then down to some quiet little beach-town in Florida - Sun! Ocean! Solitude! - The irresistible S.O.S. after a spell in St. Louis. Or any dirty big city.

I read Saroyan's play "<u>Jim Dandy</u>" in script form, sent to one of the local amateur groups. The maddest thing he has yet written. Still it has an unearthly charm. People go round and round for no reason in revolving door, walk with one foot in miniature coffin, sit in chair on table, dance, sing, change shoes, play cornet and pianola, recline on a Mae West bed, make rhapsodic speeches about the snow and the rain - all in a room of the San Francisco public library. In the end all kinds of bells start ringing - signifying death, I believe - and the characters wander off the stage continuing all their curious little practises as they go. - Undoubtedly a parable on the subject of LIFE - I cannot understand the symbolism, more than barely - But I read it twice and I must admit I was fascinated and moved by the strangeness of it and occasional speeches ring the bell of pure poetry. -

Success to Bloch and Leighton and Liebling-Wood!

10.

P.S. I have <u>another</u> new ending & some new ideas for "Battle of Angels" if anyone is concerned.

[TW's arrival in Clayton coincided happily with his father's absence on a business trip. He planned to leave before Cornelius returned, writing that "hatred of my father & <u>fear</u> - yes, fear - make it about as impossible as usual to live at home" (*Journal*, November 27, 1941).

Margaret Mayorga chose "The Lady of Larkspur Lotion" for *The Best One-Act Plays of 1941* (1942). The title refers to Cuprex, "'The Personal Insecticide'" used to treat "crabs," which TW needed but could not afford shortly before writing the play in October. It led him to pun upon, and to misspell, his own embarrassing infestation: "Literally a lousey writer, that's me. - A lousey guy" (*Journal*, October 19, 1941).

The published version of William Saroyan's play *Jim Dandy* (1947) was subtitled "Fat Man in a Famine" and set in "a transparent egg shell" containing the "majestic ruins" of the past.

Spring Again, a marital comedy by Bertram Bloch and Isabel Leighton, clients of Liebling-Wood, opened on November 10, 1941, and ran for 241 performances on Broadway.

Earlier in October TW drafted a letter to Lawrence Langner in which he enclosed still "<u>another</u> new ending" for *Battle of Angels*: "I have substituted dogs for fire and fox-skin for snakeskin and worked out a clean-cut finale without conflagration or regurgitation" (n.d., HRC).]

211. To William Saroyan

[53 Arundel Place
Clayton, Missouri]
[ca. mid-November 1941]
[TLS, 1 p. Todd Collection]

Dear Saroyan:

Like your character Jim Crow, I make a series of profound obeisances before your chair-on-a-table, having just finished reading your play <u>Jim Dandy</u> which rings in my head and my heart like the multitude of soft and musical bells that bring down the curtain. It is a beautiful little mystery of a play: I read it twice: first time I was too confused to enjoy it: the second time it began to glow and vibrate, coming out like a star in "first dark". - Well, I loved it. I got hold of the Ms. from the Little Theatre of St. Louis. - I am visiting here. The director didn't understand it, I am afraid, and seemed to think it needed understanding. - I hope I shall catch a performance some where. But it should be done in N.Y. because it should have an excellent professional cast to bring it out best. - I am crazy to see it.

I am returning to New Orleans in a few days. If chance should ever bring you down there, please let me know. - 722 Toulouse St.

Cordially, 10.
Tenn. Williams.

[The title character in *Jim Dandy* is served by a faithful black retainer named Jim Crow. A speech in the third act may have stated the rationale for TW's own defense of poetry in the theatre: "Poetry is *all* of the experience of *all* of the people," Jim Dandy proclaims. "Poetry is *all*. There is nothing which is not poetry."

Tryouts of *Jim Dandy* were staged by some forty-five member groups of the National Theatre Conference, including the Pasadena Playhouse. Reviewers of the Pasadena production, which opened on November 25, 1941, were puzzled by Saroyan's "soul gropings" but generally respectful and in several cases enthusiastic. There is no evidence of a St. Louis production at this time.]

212. To Audrey Wood

[53 Arundel Place
Clayton, Missouri]
Monday - Nov. [24] 1941
[TLS, 2 pp. HRC]

Dear Audrey:

I think I am sending you a really good little play. Perhaps rather shocking, but good. - Though very short, it has three distinct acts. I wish you would have it typed with the other two - I spilt coffee on some of the pages. You mustn't pay for this typing. Get it done as cheaply as possible and send the bill to me at 53 Arundel Place, Clayton. I will not be here, the family [will] open the letter and send you a checque for the typing.

I think I am leaving here tonight for New Orleans and then by bicycle along the coast of Florida till I reach that Never-never land where I can live cheaply - some little beach town I hope. - If I were a little more pessimistic or egotistic I might suppose that all this national defense was merely contrived to make my life more expensive.

I have not yet discovered what is wrong with the end of "The preacher's daughter" - I thought the wordless effect was more incisive. But I will put it away for another reading. Incidentally, Byron died in 1824 and I have him making love in 1827, which is a wee bit ghoulish - Better make that little change in the script. (Love Letter)

Thanks for the clipping about Eudora Welty - She and Carson McCullers and Wm. Faulkner and Katharine Anne Porter have practically got a deep southern corner on the best imaginative writing in America.

GILMOR BROWN (of the Pasadena Playhouse) was through here last week. The director of the St. Louis little theatre called me and said he wished to talk to me so I went down to his hotel and it seems that he had heard some favorable (!) reports on "Battle of Angels" and wished to read it. I am sending him my revised script from New Orleans with these latest changes which I am also mailing you for PISCATOR. - I have heard that Piscator intends to put his actors on flying trapezes in his next production. (Joke). - Any trial production would be a good thing.

From what I see in the papers the Leighton-Block play should be in the money. - I hope, for your sake mostly.

Yours truly, 10.

["Lord Byron's Love Letter" was mailed in late-October to Audrey Wood, who thought it "a commercial idea" (letter to TW, November 8, 1941, HRC) and considered sending it to Hume Cronyn for the program of one-acts that he was planning. It was first published in 27 *Wagons Full of Cotton* (1945).

The Eudora Welty clipping was related no doubt to the publication of her first collection of stories, *A Curtain of Green*, in November 1941.

The "favorable (!) reports" on *Battle of Angels* were reportedly those of Willard Holland, TW's former director, who was studying at the Pasadena Playhouse. In an earlier letter Audrey Wood informed TW that she was amused to have "interested" (November 19, 1941, HRC) Erwin Piscator, director of the Dramatic Workshop at the New School, in producing *Battle of Angels*.]

213. To William Saroyan

"In Transit"
Nov. 29, 1941
[AL, 4 pp. Todd Collection]

Dear Saroyan -

I am in transit and have no typewriter at my disposal so I will try to write largely and plainly enough to be read. - Many, many thanks for your letter. I did not expect it and appreciated it vastly. Your remarks about the theatre are correct. Your mistake is in assuming that every one of us new writers has your own rather prodigious energy that will enable him not only to write living stuff but blow, knock, blast, or scratch a hole in "the opposition" that will permit him to enter with his product. You have accomplished the impossible - the impossible for anyone else. I do not think I can do it.

I have the alternative of writing what I prefer to write - and keeping it in my suitcase, or writing what the theatre seems to accept regardless of how little I like it. Well, I can't do the second and my suitcase is getting terribly crowded. (A bleak situation). - Not with little neglected master-pieces, I know - but nevertheless with living material that ought to see the light - short stories, plays - long and short. "Interesting but not suitable".

Undoubtedly our artistic climate is going to change through the world situation. People are going to realize to their amazement that stupidity is no longer profitable, even the little people are going to learn (bitterly) the necessity of thinking.

I think there is going to be a vast hunger for life after all this death - and for light after all this eclipse -

People will want to read, see, feel the living truth and they will revolt against the sing-song Mother Goose book of lies that are being fed to them.

P.S. I am writing this on a bicycle trip along the west coast of Florida. If Hume Cronyn decides to put on some 1-acts of mine I will return to New York. I am living on $50. a month from these 1-acts!

[In answering TW's recent letter (see letter #211), William Saroyan commiserated over the failure of *Battle of Angels* and berated the show-shop mentality of Broadway: "If you want the truth, as I see it, there is no one in the American theatre who knows how to do anything other than the ordinary, banal, commercial and shabby—which makes writing plays a hopeless activity, unless one is one's self ready to put them on" (November 23, 1941; qtd. in Leverich). Saroyan had personally financed *The Beautiful People*, whose New York run was brief (64 performances) and unprofitable.]

214. To Audrey Wood

[St. Petersburg, Florida]
[ca. December 5, 1941]
[ALS, 2 pp. HRC]

Dear Audrey -

I feel like the backside of a donkey! - Got here with the flu, a raging fever & racking cough and it had not occured to my supercharged intellect that I knew nobody here to cash a checque for me. Consequence - I went to bed on the beach & probably would have perished but for the timely intervention of some friends from Calif. met by chance.

Well, I am going back to New Orleans - much too expensive here and too cold for swimming and I am too weak from the flu to camp out.

I am going back and tie myself down to one of the long plays and get it out, good, bad, or probably indifferent, within the next few weeks or bust - probably bust. - I feel like old King Lear, howling damnation on the moors! Only, alas, I have no daughters to curse. Only myself - and The Fool. -

10.

[TW left Clayton after Thanksgiving and reached St. Petersburg by December 4. His return to New Orleans coincided with the bombing of Pearl Harbor on December 7, "Our fin du monde," as he would later term it.

See letter #216 for a more candid description of the "friends from Calif."

The "long play" to which TW committed himself in his final weeks in New Orleans was *Stairs to the Roof*. His recent contact with William Saroyan may have been decisive. The play has the same eccentric quality that he admired in *Jim Dandy* (see letters #210 and #211), and it shares with Saroyan the vision of a world "plunging toward destruction" but still alive with "infinite possibilities" (*Stairs*) of spirit.]

215. To Edwina Dakin Williams

SH: New Orleans Athletic Club
New Orleans
Wednesday. [December 17, 1941]
[ALS, 3 pp. HTC]

Dear Mother -

I received both your letters - many thanks.

I am trying to finish my work on a long play before Xmas and have been writing all day to keep up with a schedule. Soon as I get it finished and in the mail I will probably leave here and return to St. Louis for the holidays. It is just cold enough here to be disagreeable.

The city is very dead because of the war - practically no tourists - business bad.

The Russian successes, very encouraging to me, would indicate that it may not last much longer. I don't think any of the Axis will stand up under defeat, and if the Germans crack up, the whole business will be practically over. I do hope before Dakin is called. He should try to get in the intelligence service or something like that.

Tell Grandfather to go further South than St. Petersburg if he goes to Fla., or wait till Spring. I had to pay a dollar a day for a room that the proprietor told me I could have for $2.00 a <u>week</u> in summer. And it was too cold to swim. But I liked the city.

I am living now at 722 Dumaine Street. Have a gas heater so it is comfortable.

Love - Tom.

["The Russian successes" followed a counter-offensive that claimed 85,000 German lives and recaptured many strategic points around Moscow. Dakin Williams remained a law student at Washington University.]

216. To Paul Bigelow

SH: New Orleans Athletic Club
New Orleans
December 18, 1941
[ALS, 3 pp. Columbia]

Dear Paul

Oh how tired I am! I feel a perfect wreck and what is worse, I look it. I put a work-schedule on my wall and stuck to it heroically but with all but fatal results. Play almost ready to mail to Audrey - "Stairs to the Roof" - I put the Lawrence in abeyance as it seemed less likely to interest producers.

Such a business! I took a trip to St. Petersburg on my thumb. Caught the flu or pneumonia or something on the way - arrived there with fever 104° and a racking cough. Check was waiting for me at P.O. but it had not occured to this dashing adventuress that she knew nobody in St. Petersburg who would cash it. Result I was stranded desperately ill on the beach and would doubtless have gone to my reward but for a providential meeting with Wm. Eastman of Cleveland (Kodak people) a wealthy Auntie whom I had met in Taos, who gave me refuge, and got me out of my worst difficulties.

Now I am back in New Orleans. The war has ruined things here, virtually broken up all gaiety. I hope to return to N.Y. after Xmas. How is it there? Have you moved? How is Jordan? Cris? Gilbert?

Please do write at once!

I sold a New Orleans one-act to Mayorga for her 1941 collection. Still living on Cronyn's $50.00 a month - barely!

10.

[In "Random Observations" TW claimed that *Stairs to the Roof* "was written involuntarily as a katharsis of eighteen months that I once endured (miraculously) as a clerk in a huge wholesale corporation in the middle west." Subtitled "A Prayer for the Wild of Heart that are kept in cages" (December 1941, HRC), the play follows the liberation of Benjamin Murphy, who has discovered the hidden "stairs" to freedom and is thus a threat to his callous employer—a thinly disguised substitute for Continental Shoemakers of St. Louis. The expressionistic effects of the play, Ben's naive pursuit of life everlasting, and his romantic adventures with "Alice" bespeak, respectively, the influence of Elmer Rice, William Saroyan, and Clifford

Odets. *Stairs to the Roof* has been performed at the Pasadena Playhouse (1945 and 1947) but not yet in New York, confirming TW's ever hopeful description of the play as one written more "for tomorrow than today" (letter to Audrey Wood, Monday {December 22, 1941} HRC). A first edition is planned by New Directions.

The lack of "gaiety" in the Quarter was the result of redoubled security in the aftermath of Pearl Harbor. Shore patrols and raids by MP's often targeted gay bars.]

217. To Paul Bigelow

SH: Hotel Peabody
Memphis, Tennessee
Dec. 30, 1941
[ALS, 3 pp. Massee Collection]

Paul dear -

I have just left New Orleans, my departure being almost coincident with Fritzi's arrival, though I did spend about 48 hours in their Mortuary establishment, long enough to dish all the latest in Orleans and York. I understand, my dear, that you have <u>acquired</u> some new <u>paintings</u> - <u>Less of that</u>!! Well, I burnt a cigarette hole in one of their finest old antique tables so I shan't lecture you too sharply - though I do think you should let her have some of her clothes back, you conniving old whore! I sometimes suspect that you were tutored in public and private relations respectively by W.C. Fields and Texas Guinan.

Incidentally, "Mother", have you been to see "The Maltese Falcon" - truly a screen miracle and one of the finest pieces of dramatic writing ever produced in my opinion. The acting, particularly by Sidney Greenstreet, is superb.

Now about my <u>papers</u> - you will recall that I left a considerable number of <u>Mss.</u> (ranging from <u>exquisite</u> to merely <u>superb</u>) in your care when I blew town last fall. Are <u>these</u> in the steamer <u>trunk</u> with the <u>alleged</u> laundry? They had damned well better <u>be</u> or you had better indefinitely <u>prolong</u> your southern <u>invasion</u>!

No - do please let me know where these papers are right away for I shall feel uneasy till you do.

I may go on to New York from St. Louis or I may return South. I may have another eye operation in St. Louis. If I go to N.Y. before Feb. 1st I will be delighted to take over the apt. though I'm sorry I didn't get to Andrew before the marines.

But what are <u>your</u> plans? You haven't left N.Y. for <u>good</u>? I hope not - I thought we might have another mad spring there.

Write me in St. Louis about the papers, old girl, but if you camp, be sure to sign it "Pearl". You know these old-fashioned families!! (Scream!)

10.

[TW mailed this letter to Macon, Georgia, where Paul Bigelow had joined his friend Jordan Massee. The adventure that led TW to identify Bigelow's tutors as W.C. Fields and Texas Guinan, a pugnacious actor and a brassy nightclub hostess, has not been identified.

John Huston directed and wrote the screenplay for *The Maltese Falcon* (Warner, 1941), while Sydney Greenstreet played the role of Kaspar Gutman in his first film appearance. TW later recalled this performance in drafting a one-act play entitled "The Last of My Solid Gold Watches" (see letter #253).]

PART VI
1942–1943
NEW YORK • MACON
ST. AUGUSTINE • JACKSONVILLE • ST. LOUIS

Overleaf: "I could see this little fellow with baggy pants and a torn sweater sitting all by himself and looking very nervous."

—James Laughlin on first meeting Tennessee Williams, 1942

The "gag" photograph celebrated Williams's subsequent award of $1000 from the American Academy of Arts and Letters (see letter #306).

218. To Paul Bigelow

[53 Arundel Place
Clayton, Missouri]
<u>Monday</u> [January 5, 1942]
[TLS, 2 pp. Columbia]

Dear Paul:

The merriment was genuine but the "pique" was not. You must have known that, my dear. (If you know Tennessee). I am relieved to hear the papers are packed with your things. I had a vision of you destroying them with many tears - great crocodile tears, while Jordan clasped your left hand and gave you from time to time a little sniff of ammonia to steel your nerves! All of my life I have suffered from the delusion that there was or is an organized conspiracy to destroy my work: I suppose it is based on the fact that self-appointed home critics sometimes did this. And even the wretchedest piece of doggerel I have produced (who have produced so many) becomes what <u>would</u> have been <u>deathless</u> the moment of its material destruction. So you really have kept the papers, darling? I bless you! As for the laundry it had long since ascended to the plane of the innocent fable. No more capable of rancoring my spirit than of protecting my skin. . . .

Blessings on thee, little man,
Bigelow with agile can!

How long will you be in Macon? I shan't stay here much longer, as you well know <u>why</u> (being no celibate either) and it seems feasible that I drop through Macon on my way either to Florida or New York and pick up the Mss.

I have not been well at all: caught a bad cold in Florida and it still hangs on. Will not leave till it is well, but it seems a lot better. As for the operation, I will either have it performed here immediately or soon as I get to New York. It is the same one I went through before.

The play - <u>good</u>! I have always felt that you should and Audrey will be delighted. I am crazy to see it.

I have just sent her one, The <u>Stairs to the Roof</u> and almost every day mail little changes to her which must be driving her to distraction, especially if she doesn't happen to like the play. I haven't heard from her yet. I think my next project will be a group of about seven more or less associated stories of Bohemian life in the <u>Vieux Carre</u> ending on December 7, 1941. Our <u>fin du monde</u>, as everyone feels too distinctly. Two are completed. I would like you to see them.

And Andrew? <u>Where</u>?

Do you seriously think I should come to Macon? I would like to.

Love, 10

[The new year led TW to ponder the future: "So I begin a new journal - appropriately in the house of my parents, always a place to start from and commence a new phase" (*Journal*, January 5, 1942). He was relieved to learn that "the Mss." entrusted to Paul Bigelow in New York were now in Macon, Georgia, where Bigelow's friend Jordan Massee lived.

TW's "home critics" were, of course, Edwina, who deplored the "ugly" and "indecent" aspects of her son's work, and Cornelius, who worried about the economic risks of the literary life. Of greater concern to TW were the "vicissitudes" of world war and the threat they posed to his faltering career. Predictably he had "no desire to participate in war work" (*Journal*, January 6, 1942).

Bigelow's play-in-progress was variously entitled "A Woman Who Came From a Boat" and "A Theme For Reason."

One of the "little changes" that TW mailed to Audrey Wood concerned the use of a "'Deus ex machina'" figure in *Stairs to the Roof* (1945). The "intervention" of Mr. E might be "effective" but it was also "probably cheating": "Do you see what I mean," he asked Wood, "and what do you think about it?" (Sunday {ca. January 1942} HRC).

TW had considered using "Vieux Carré" as the collective title for a trio of one-acts to be submitted to Margaret Mayorga or Hume Cronyn (see letter to Audrey Wood, October 27, 1941, HRC). The "stories of Bohemian life" to which he reassigned the title grew to nine and were later described as a "group" exhibiting "rather esoteric subject matter or treatment". Among the projected "Vieux Carré" stories were two of special merit: "Desire and the Black Masseur" (1948) and "One Arm" (1948).

TW met Andrew Lyndon when he visited Macon in June. "A charming little creature - breast of milkfed chicken!" (qtd. in *Windham*, p. 30), he found him to be.]

219. To Audrey Wood

[53 Arundel Place
Clayton, Missouri]
Jan. 6, 1942
[TLS, 1 p. HRC]

Dear Audrey:

Another re-inforcement for those rickety "Stairs". This hitches onto the carnival scene - just attach it with a paper-clip till I am able to polish the whole thing off.

Just came from the eye-surgeon who thinks my second "needle" operation ought to be done right away - I don't [know] whether to have it done here or by my original doctor in New York. Plans remain indeterminate.

How is the war likely to affect Tennessee? Perhaps he is one of those unlisted casualties at Pearl Harbor.

I have two more one-acts whenever you want them and a new story.

Ever, 10.

[The "rickety" *Stairs to the Roof* was nearly complete in revision and ready to be sent to "Potential Producers," for whom TW had prepared a descriptive circular: "This is . . . a criticism of those unlucky circumstances in our economic life which impose a virtual iron cage around the greater portion of our working population: specifically, the lower middle-class of so-called 'white-collar workers'" (n.d., Virginia).

TW's travel plans were instantly clarified, and his second eye operation delayed, by a telegram from Erwin Piscator of the New School showing interest in *Battle of Angels* (1940): "O let us be hopeful! What is it? A play production? Too lovely to believe - almost" (*Journal*, January 12, 1942). Soon he was living precariously in the Greenwich Village apartment of the painter Frederick ("Fritz") Bultman, his Provincetown and New Orleans friend.

The new story was probably a "Vieux Carré" piece, while the one-acts are unidentified.

Before sleeping on the 6th, TW communed with Proust, whom he had been reading: "We would have understood each other, my dear. How we might have 'dished' the world in that cork-lined room of yours" (*Journal*, January 6, 1942).]

220. To Clifford Odets

319 W. 11th Street
New York City
January 26, 1942
[TLS, 1 p. Indiana]

Dear Mr. Odets:

I was fortunate enough to see your new play last night and I must tell you that I am fearfully upset and annoyed by some of the critical reactions to this play, which I found to be one of rare beauty and power. I liked it, for instance, much more than "Night Music" which I was priveleged to watch through rehearsals. It is indeed discouraging to any practitioner of letters, to read such critical reactions from persons capable of exercising such a strong influence in the theatre. To call this play "dull" is almost to indict one's self of dullness. I know that Mr. Gassner liked it for he told me so, and I have read the relatively favorable reactions of Mr. Krutch and I know many persons of responsible judgement who were as profoundly moved as I was. Now it seems to me that there should be some concerted action by those who liked the play to defend it against this attack, which is really an attack against us all. This may seem a fantastic suggestion, but I think there might be something in the nature of a meeting or conference of writers and critics who liked it to organize a critical defense, before such a fine play is forced to give up.

Naturally I did not like certain things in the play, the last curtain, for instance, seemed to leave something wanted - perhaps a bit more of tragic katharsis. However a fine work must not be judged by its defects, as this play obviously was.

Please accept my own deep respect and best wishes,

Sincerely, 10. Wms.
Tennessee Williams

[TW's defense of *Clash by Night* (which had its première on December 27, 1941) did not lead to any "concerted action" on its behalf, nor is there any indication that Clifford Odets answered this letter. TW may also have been motivated by admiration for its star, Tallulah Bankhead, who won raves for her "sultry" performance in an otherwise "dull," "empty," "dead" domestic melodrama. Joseph Wood Krutch scolded the first-night reviewers for so harshly criticizing Odets and found "originality and power" (*The Nation*, January 10, 1942) in his new play.]

221. To Erwin Piscator

[319 West 11th Street, New York]
Monday. Feb. 2, 1942
[ALS, 3 pp. HRC]

Dear Mr. Piscator:

Things have come to the "dead end" here in New York. I can no longer impose upon the hospitality of my friend and my meager resources are all used up. Unless such an unexpected metamorphosis occurs that I am able to exist upon air, I shall have to leave. I wanted to see you to find out if I could read plays for you as Mr. Berghoff suggested I might. I have had no luck at obtaining other employment. And it appears that a production of my play is remote at best. Please let me know as soon as you can.

Cordially, Tennessee Williams.

[Erwin Piscator (1893-1966) directed proletarian theatres in Berlin and Paris before fleeing Nazi rule and emigrating to the United States in 1938. He led both the Dramatic Workshop (1940-1951) of the New School, whose first playwriting seminar TW attended, and its production arm, the Studio Theatre, which operated on a subscription basis and offered experimental plays not suitable for Broadway. Plans to stage *Battle of Angels* were announced in late-January and led to protracted negotiations on the script, which did not meet the requirements of Piscator's so-called "epic theatre," antidote to the theatre of introspection and private sensibility.

This letter was written on the back of Dramatic Workshop stationery that carries a typed note rejecting TW's application for a scholarship: "While we think that your work has much to recommend it, we do not feel that as yet it quite meets the extremely high qualifications necessary for such awards." TW was no more successful in applying to "read plays" for Piscator, as Herbert Berghof, an actor-director associated with the Workshop, had "suggested" he might do.]

222. *To Erwin Piscator*

[319 West 11th Street, New York]
Monday Noon. [February 9, 1942]
[ALS, 4 pp. Southern Illinois]

Dear Mr. Piscator -

I have just arrived at the hospital and will go under the needle in about an hour.

I am working on a dream-scene between Acts two and three in which Jonathan West, the negro preacher, appears to Val who has fallen asleep in the store, and in a ~~long and~~ passionate exhortation impells him to carry on "the torch" for the oppressed peoples. This will be done in poetry and with a background of choral singing (negro voices), and bells in the church tower. (Voices offstage)

I think if we use this we must do without a prologue - it would be unnecessary and I doubt more and more the artistic worth of the prologue.

This is positively the last and only major change which I am going to make in the script. I will be out of the hospital (Deo Volente) by Wednesday night or Thursday morning and I hope that you will have come to your final decision by that time as I will then either remain on account of a definite play production or return South at once - I cannot afford to stay longer and waiting and uncertainty are always so agonizing to me - they discourage me profoundly and drain my energies away. If you wish to go ahead with casting while I am in the hospital you may do that without me. Audrey Wood, my agent, can represent me in casting as she is an excellent judge of actors and knows the play from long experience with it. I could also interview actors here at St. Luke's. Then I have complete confidence in your theater in such matters.

Cordially, Tennessee Williams

[The "dream-scene" is consistent with a "New Outline" for *Battle of Angels* that TW wrote at this time to satisfy the "dictatorial" Erwin Piscator. Val Xavier, recast as a Negro sympathizer, returns to the Delta to carry on the work of Jonathan West, a "colored preacher" who gave him "his first intimation of a higher purpose in life" (n.d., HRC). Later correspondence with Piscator indicates that TW delivered the new scene to his office, but if extant it has not been identified.]

223. *To Edwina Dakin Williams*

[319 West 11th Street, New York]
[ca. mid-February 1942]
[ALS, 2 pp. HTC]

Dear Mother -

I am out of the hospital and my eye is reacting "exactly right" in Dr. Frey's opinion.

There has been so much disagreement and delay over the play production that I decided to use the otherwise wasted time in having the operation. Also it gave me time to rest and think things over. Mr. Piscator is a terribly dictatorial German, completely impractical, and is trying to force me to turn the play into a dry, didactic sermon on social injustice, representing the South as a fascist state. To comply with his demands will destroy the poetic quality of the play. Right now we are deadlocked and I can't say how it is going to turn out. I only know I am not going to make a mess of the play in order to incorporate his ideas. Either he will give in or the production will have to be called off. I am going out to his country place again tonight for another "battle". You can imagine how tiresome and discouraging this is!

I will let you know as soon as the issue is settled. Much love,

Tom.

[After his second operation TW was offered a weekend job as waiter at The Beggar's Bar in Greenwich Village. He reportedly wore a black patch upon which Fritz Bultman painted a surrealistic white eye, adding to his attraction as a waiter and a reciter of bawdy verse.

TW later informed Audrey Wood of a harrowing visit to Erwin Piscator's "palatial estate on the Hudson," where he again heard Piscator describe *Battle of Angels* as "a Fascist play" (see letter #232) devoid of social value or historical context.]

224. To the Williams Family

319 W. 11th [New York]
March 6, 1942
[TLS, 1 p. HTC]

Dear Folks:

I did not visit the New School for about a week so I was late in getting hold of the letters sent there. I will probably get mail earlier addressed to 319 W. 11th where I'm still staying.

Despite difficulties with Piscator and economic insecurity I am getting along very well here and enjoy being in New York. I have finished the first draft of another long play which I'm intensely interested in and the one just completed is being read with appreciation by the few groups I have submitted it to. Audrey has sold a one-act to an anthology (another one) for fifteen dollars on publication and while I haven't satisfied Piscator's absurd demands with "Angels", he is going to have a trial reading of the play by actors before an invited audience which may result in attracting other producers. A prominent actress has written from Hollywood to see the play, too - Helen Craig.

My eye shows continual improvement and I am now quite certain that I will have good vision out of it as soon as the cataract is altogether dissolved: this may take a good while yet. I've applied for a loan from the Dramatists' Guild to live on while completing the new play. If this doesn't go through, I can probably get some kind of defense work, though I would rather not have anything that takes up all my time as I think intellectual and creative-thought occupations are at least as valuable in these times as armament and one should do what he does best. Cronyn who held my one-acts has gone in the army, alas, and pays no more option-money. So many people here are interested in my work that I do not need to worry too much about the exigencies of living: I am sharing a friend's apartment and another friend has provided me with this excellent typewriter as long as I need it. The war seems to draw men of good will closer together and make the need for mutual kindness and humanity more apparent. If one can just survive this frightful cataclysm the times after may be the better for it.

Dakin must by all means stay out of the fighting end of it. I do not think he belongs there and his intelligence and education can be put to good use by home-services - besides some thinking people must be left for tomorrow.

Health - excellent. No colds since I've been here. What you say about the situation at home is my greatest distress and I only hope that you all have the inner calm that it takes to bear it.

Much love, Tom

[TW's "economic insecurity" became dire after he lost his job at The Beggar's Bar. A "noisy confrontation" with the proprietor, "a celebrated dance-mime" (*Memoirs*, 1975, p. 71) named Valeska Gert, led to the hurling of bottles, a call for the police, and TW's abrupt departure.

Earlier in March TW completed a first draft of "The Spinning Song" (n.d., HRC), a play "suggested" by his "sister's tragedy" (*Journal*, February 25, 1942). The play "being read" by potential producers was *Stairs to the Roof*, and the one-act sold to Betty Smith, editor of *25 Non-Royalty One-Act Plays for All-Girl Casts* (1942), was "At Liberty" (1941). In late 1941 the actress Helen Craig requested "not the rewritten version" of *Battle of Angels* but the "original script" (postmarked Van Nuys, California, November 24, 1941, Massee Collection).

Apparently Cornelius agreed that Dakin should "stay out of the fighting" and had promised to finance post-graduate study at Harvard. An advanced degree in business, the family thinking went, would make Dakin a more attractive prospect for Officer Candidate School and shield him from the draft.]

225. To Paul Bigelow

c/o Carley Mills
43 E. 50th Street, New York City
PM: New York, May 15, 1942
[TLS w/ autograph postscript, 2 pp. Columbia]

Dear Paul:

I have written you several times since coming to New York - and this is not one of those polite prevarications - and lost the letters. I know of at least two occasions on which Fritzi and I collaborated on letters to you. That household was so confused that nothing so systematic as getting a letter in a mail-box ever occured. Fritz and I have separated (and thereby hangs a tale or several tails) and life is relatively simple. Peut-etre trop simple - ah, well. At any rate, I am restless - planning, hoping, praying soon to leave New York. There are too many restrictions in my present situation and I was never one to brook very many restrictions. I have finished a comedy that I worked on - You may not believe this! - with Donnie. We delivered it to Audrey a few days ago and as soon as that and another matter or two is disposed of - I am going to leave the city. I dream of collapsing for a month or so on a beach in Florida, in which case I will pass through Macon and see you at long last. I cannot think of anything more agreeable at the moment. I have another play in first draft which I want to devote myself to completely for the rest of the spring and summer. But for several weeks I don't want to even look at a typewriter. - Ah, my God, what a time we have had in New York! It is quite beyond belief, but I was prepared for the incredible long before now and I seem to be all in one piece, if that is not bragging. I did not get a great deal out of Jordan about you but then I only saw him for an hour before breakfast. He looked wonderful and I thought it was awfully sweet of him to come. As there is too much to tell I won't try to tell anything at all. For now. Is your play finished yet? I do hope it turned out well. What are your plans? If I knew you were coming to New York I might arrange to stay on here. But I am bored with everything and do want to get away dreadfully.

Gilbert has his book finally coming out - James Decker is publishing it late this spring. Oh, dear, I haven't seen Gilbert since February when he created a frightful scene in a gay bar - spilt beer all over everybody making one of his dramatic gestures over a faithless lover. Donnie saw him recently in Central Park and said he looked like a "Withered apple" - The young are so unkind!

Donnie is living at the West Side "Y" and Fred is living with Sarah and her dog. I believe the dog is happy.

Write me, my dear Paul - Please!

Love, 10.

Writing this at 3 A.M. in case you observe discrepancies or dangling participles

[TW lived in a penthouse with Carley Mills, a composer-arranger of popular songs, after being evicted by Fritz Bultman in late-March, on a Friday "which was not Good." The provocation, as reported in *Memoirs*, was TW's recruitment of trade, presumably for Bultman's diversion, that turned "roguish" and stole several of his "prized" (pp. 71-72) possessions.

Donald Windham has observed that TW was attractive to what he called "'old aunties'" (qtd. in *Lost Friendships*, 1987, p. 182) but that he found such dependent relations to be uncomfortable. Of his two-month stay with the forty-five-year-old Mills, TW wrote in the journal: "I swim and live selfishly and cynically as a wise old alley cat. Integrity - I wonder" (April 26, 1942). For his novel *The Hero Continues* (1960), Windham drew upon Mills and his alcoholic circle of friends and based the main figure, a "lopsided" playwright named Denis Freeman, upon TW— not a flattering portrait, the subject thought.

In adapting D.H. Lawrence's story "You Touched Me" (1922), TW and Donald Windham had written "furiously" against their own destitution. Set in the aftermath of World War I, the story turns upon Lawrence's familiar plot of repression, awakening, and discovery. Windham has traced the origins of the project to an outline that he wrote independently, and in which TW saw "commercial possibilities" (see *Windham*, p. 26). Audrey Wood learned of the project in April and quickly sought dramatic rights from the Lawrence estate. From the beginning TW found his collaboration with Windham to be unequal, as he informed Edwina in March: "It is nearly done - unfortunately he is the brooding type and I do the writing while he sits and broods" (<u>Monday</u> {ca. March 16, 1942} HTC).

Gilbert Maxwell's current book of poems, *The Dark Rain Falling*, was published by James Decker in 1942.

Fred Melton, Donald Windham's companion, had surprisingly married Sarah Marshall of Macon, Georgia.]

226. *To the Williams Family*

[43 East 50th Street, New York]
[ca. late-May 1942]
[TLS w/ autograph postscript, 1 p. HTC]

Dear Folks:

I guess you're giving me a dose of my own medicine and not writing. I'm anxious to know what Dakin has done, if he is leaving for Harvard.

There's a little more news than usual here. A short play of mine, "This Property is Condemned" is being put on at the New School Tuesday evening on a program with Moliere and the Irish playwright Synge - audience by invitation. Some negro and folk-poetry of mine is being used in a play representing the American scene - It is called "American Legend" and will be done in the Fall. They have just bought me a copy of Mark Twain's

Life <u>on</u> <u>the</u> <u>Mississippi</u> which they want me to find incidents for dramatization in. And I have been asked to contribute some patriotic verse to a NBC radio program selling war-bonds - comes on for fifteen minutes once a week and they have top-flight artists and writers. The only patriotic poem I can think of that I have written is the one called "Inheritors", the only copy of which is in one of those little college verse magazines in the attic.

I don't know whether to ask you to send it here or to Macon Georgia, as I have been invited down there for as long as I care to stay by the family I visited on Sea Island last summer. I would alternate between Macon and Sea Island and probably find it a very stimulating change - the Masseys are the best family in Macon, so I have heard. And I am getting to be a sort of "professional guest". Audrey thinks I should go. She says she can raise the money for my bus-fare which is only $12.50 but I don't know if I will have anything besides that. I have never been so broke as I have been these last few months. I get work occasionally ushering in a movie-house - but I have been too busy writing to do much else. Next year may be my year as I will have three long plays ready, including the comedy just finished in collaboration - which Audrey likes very much. I have a little more filling-out to do on it and Audrey is negotiating with D.H. Lawrence's estate for a fair distribution of profits if it is produced - it is from a D.H. Lawrence short story.

No time for more now - Do let me hear from you soon,

Much love, Tom

Write me at 119 LeRoy Street   c/o D. Windham

["This Property is Condemned" was staged on June 2, 1942, at the New School and first published in 27 *Wagons Full of Cotton* (1945).

Plans for a sequel to "American Legend," a revue directed by Mary Hunter and produced by the American Actors Company on May 11, 1941, apparently fell through.

The patriotism of "Inheritors," by Thomas Lanier Williams, lay in the author's attempt to rouse a dormant pioneer spirit: *"Sound the horn, sentry! / The time has come to move on!"* (*College Verse*, April 1937; see letter #247).

Paul Bigelow, not the Massees, probably invited TW to visit Macon, if he did not invite himself.

The "long plays" being readied for production in 1943 were *Stairs to the Roof*, *You Touched Me!* (1943/1945), and perhaps "The Spinning Song."]

227. *To Audrey Wood*

[43 East 50th Street, New York]
Tuesday A.M. [June 2, 1942]
[TLS, 1 p. HRC]

Dear Audrey:

I find on reading this over that most of the adipose tissue has been cut away and the script is much more solid and hard-hitting than I had expected. I am perfectly willing to acknowledge it now as a legitimate offspring.

David Merrick of the Shumlin office asked to see me and it seems he wishes to be aware of my work. He says their office has a strong social spirit - I think we might show him this script if he'll be careful of it.

I regret to tell you that without my knowledge the New School decided to stage "This Property is Condemned" on their program this evening. I only heard of it accidentally - too late to prevent. I attended one rehearsal, last night, and I hope that nobody will see it as it is done with complete lack of feeling, against a projection from "War and Peace". Is it legal for them to cast and present a play without the author's knowledge and consent? - I think it is pretty raw stuff. - Makes you say, "Thank God for the Shuberts!" - ~~I am just about fed up with all of these little so-called art producers - they don't seem to have any better taste or feeling than the commercial ones~~. - - - - - - Bad temper.

I think I will leave town this week-end. Can you raise the transportation for me? The minimum is $12.50 but a few extra dollars would be useful - I think it is strategic to buy your first meal in a new town. I have loads of work for the summer - First I want to round-out the Lawrence play, then "The Spinning Song's" second draft - Then I want to prepare a group of short-stories to submit to book-publishers. I have about five of a similar type in various stages of completion and I think I will pick up the following at your office before I leave to work into the group - In Memory of an Aristocrat, Miss Rose and the Grocery Clerk, The Swan, A Tale of Two Writers, The Vine, The Red Part of a Flag, and, in the fairly certain event of its return from Story, Blue Roses and the Polar Star. With the five in progress, these should make enough for a volume and I may find that I can do a good deal more work on them now. - I also have a project with Mary Hunter which she will probably tell you about when it gets going. - Best.

10

[The "hard-hitting" play is *Stairs to the Roof*, as TW's reference to a "strong social spirit" would indicate. On June 14 David Merrick reported to Audrey Wood that *Stairs* was "interesting and beautifully written" but "unlikely" to be produced on Broadway without "a chorus of pretty girls and a part for Gertrude Lawrence" (qtd. in *Remember Me to Tom*, 1963, pp. 130-131). Merrick, a native St. Louisan who graduated in law from Washington University, was associated with the producer Herman Shumlin.

The staging of "This Property is Condemned" was an occasion for TW to advertise his talents, as he apparently did by inviting Donald Windham and other friends to its performance on June 2. Wood's professional representation had again been circumvented. In adapting *War and Peace* (1865–1869) for the small stage of the Studio Theatre (where it was performed in May 1942), Erwin Piscator used film projections and other scenic devices to convey the historical sweep of Tolstoy's novel.

TW continued to plan a collection of stories, while the "project" with Mary Hunter was probably the defunct "American Legend."

TW had queried Paul Bigelow (in a letter written earlier but postmarked Richmond, Virginia, June 5, 1942) about the amenities of life in Macon—swimming, "peace and quiet," a bicycle—and by May 6 he was living in a boarding house, in the company of his friend, "in the hottest little town in America." Their loquacious landlord was Dr. Rosser, a retired professor pleasantly reminiscent of Walter Dakin.]

228. To Robert Lewis

c/o Dr. Rosser
507 Georgia Ave.
Macon, Ga.
June 1942
[ALS, 2 pp. Kent State]

Dear Mr. Lewis -

The evening after I saw you at the New School I got hold of $30.00 and left town on the first bus out as I had been crazy to get away for a good while. I called you a couple of times that day without any luck. I wanted to talk to you about the one-acts as I hoped it wasn't just a momentary idea you had of putting them on. I know that you are the man to do it. I spoke to Audrey and I believe she has sent some of them to you. I turn them out, new ones, every once in a while and if you take an option on those now complete I will consider it inclusive of those I'm still working on. I think they are the best way of introducing my work and see no reason why a program of them would not be a commercial success.

I am intending to finish up a couple of long scripts this summer. - I am stranded down here in Macon, Ga., without a cent of money - it is better however than being broke in New York. I'll be back next fall, anyhow, as I have a job with the New School starting in September.

Best to you always, Tennessee Williams

[Robert Lewis (1909-1997) was an original member of the Group Theatre who met TW in New York ca. 1939-1940. His reputation as an innovative director—*My Heart's in the Highlands* (1939), *Heavenly Express* (1940), and *Mexican Mural* (1942)—no doubt impressed TW and led him to transfer his hopes for a program of one-acts to Lewis after Hume Cronyn entered the service (see letter #224). Lewis, however, could find no "backers" (*Slings and Arrows*, 1984) for the work of an unknown playwright and was forced to drop the project. Cronyn reported the same experience in his memoir, *A Terrible Liar* (1991), although in 1947 he directed Jessica Tandy (his wife) in one of the originally optioned plays, "Portrait of a Madonna."]

229. To Charles Criswell

507 Georgia Ave.
Macon, Ga.
[ca. June 21, 1942]
[TLS, 2 pp. HTC]

Dear Charles:

Paul and I have just gotten your address from Jordan and we are hastening to establish communication.

I never knew exactly where you were after you left New York and my life was too hectic to permit much reflection about it or investigation. Shortly after you left, in fact within a couple of days, my arrangements with Fritzi came to a violent termination and I was literally on the streets till, at the price of my virtue, I was ensconced in a pent-house in the East fifties with a middle-aged popular song composer. I remained there till a couple or three weeks ago when I fled to Macon and am now maintaining a residence with Paul in an attic in Macon, Ga. A brief and colorless chronicle it is! I will be here all summer, I guess, as I don't have penny one to get me anywhere else. In September I have a job at the New School handling publicity for the Studio Theatre there and I hope to have completed two new scripts including a commercial-looking comedy, by that time. The comedy is now winding up and was written with Donnie on a D.H. Lawrence shortstory.

Henrietta and Jordan both write that you want the typewriter back which you sent me in New Orleans. I may as well tell you the complete history of the machine which is about as dramatic as my own. Not having a place of my own for about a year now, I have been continually exposed to the whims and caprices of various bitches among whom was one Creole character I lived with in New Orleans. We shared an apt. and one night during her absence a plaster blackamoor which she claimed to be of great value and several other articles were smashed in a little difficulty which arose among visitors and myself. The Creole lady held me responsible for it and locked the door on me and my possessions (on opposite sides of it). Among these articles was the typewriter which, with my victrola and riding-boots, she refused to relinquish until I had paid for the blackamoor. Of course I could not pay for the Blackamoor. About this time my Grandmother took seriously ill and I was called to St. Louis. I trusted by the time I came back to New Orleans the situation would have cleared up. It so happened I did not return to New Orleans but to New York, at the call of Piscator. I wrote a number of letters asking for the typewriter to be forwarded, first to the lady and then to a friend I hoped might act as intercessor. I finally heard that the typewriter and boots were being shipped to St. Louis. This was late in the spring. I have not yet heard of their arrival there.

Now I have been without a typewriter myself all this time, since the confiscation, and since I cannot write except on a machine, this has been a most embarrassing deprivation to me - the only consolation I can give you is that if I <u>did</u> have the machine I would certainly refuse to surrender it to you. - I am utterly unscrupulous about such things. - And justifiably so - It is the law of the Jungle! However my brother is leaving for Harvard to work for a commission in the army this month - I believe he is leaving his typewriter at home. I will pass through St. Louis and if by that time the typewriter has come from New Orleans I will see that you get it. - I did not anticipate your wanting it back, however, at least for the time being.

I understand that you are going to be stationed around St. Louis in the near future. If that's so we must get together when I visit there, probably in late August. I can introduce you to some people, the few who are interesting in that part of the country. - Let me know.

The life here is endurable and sometimes better than that. Andrew and Paul and I are about the only society you would find interesting and perhaps not even us.

How is Jack? The last I heard he was having a nervous break-down, but then, so was I - more or less! - La vie est difficile! - (It always sounds more profound in French).

I hope you are not unhappy in the army, dear Charles, and do not be excessively troubled about the typewriter. You did a charitable deed and I am resolved to see that you do not suffer for it more than is necessary.

With love, Tennessee

[Charles Criswell (1910-1960), a native West Virginian, met TW in New York ca. 1941. He worked as a commercial artist, served in the Army Air Corps during the war, and married Henrietta Callaway, a Macon girl and a close friend of Jordan Massee. Criswell's collection of stories entitled *Nobody Knows What the Stork Will Bring* appeared in 1958. TW probably deceived Criswell about his return to New Orleans in late 1941 because he had not dared to approach his former companion, Eloi Bordelon, about the confiscated typewriter.

The casual reference to Andrew Lyndon belies the sexual turmoil that he created for TW: "Can it be that I love A. - and that's what does it? - Creates the block of fear? - And is it hopeless?" (*Journal*, July 1, 1942). In the late 1940s Lyndon became an intimate companion of Christopher Isherwood, soon to enter TW's circle of literary friends.]

230. To Jordan Massee

[507 Georgia Avenue
Macon, Georgia]
Tuesday June 29, 1942
[TLS, 2 pp. Massee Collection]

Dear Jordan:

Paul and I have been hoping you would get down here each week-end.

I'm sorry I didn't make it here before you left - I had to wait over for the production of a one-act - left the day after.

I was living under terribly trying - almost impossible - circumstances in New York and I came here in a state of nervous exhaustion which it will probably take me all summer to recover from.

The quiet life here is what I need and I hope it will have a pacifying effect, though I must admit I could sometimes scream with ennui, it is so hard to get accustomed to it after the turbulence of New York. My restlessness is probably harder on Paul than it is on me, as I pace around Dr. Rosser's attic like a caged tiger, scattering cigarette ashes and tossing papers hither and yon and being such a problem as only I know how to be. I am variously known (to Paul and Andrew) as Olympe, The Termite Queen, and God knows what else which they are polite enough not to call me out loud! - Well, if I ever have occasion to write my memoirs I will call it "The Victim of My Nerves!"

I have tried the society here and have decided that the milieu for me is definitely "Recreation" and Dr. Rosser's. I attempted the Gewinner's salon but it was a thoroughly indigestible mixture of such elements as Dr. and Mrs. Jones, some flaming Atlanta bells, Billie Fowler, Sue Myrick, and his absurdly naive maiden-Aunt Hazel. Only Holt would attempt such combinations and I have sworn off further inclusion among them. For the duration.

I work every morning. My play (the comedy with Donnie) will be ready for the typist late this week - It has been going well, I believe.

Paul has read me his play which I think not only fine but marketable. - I believe he plans to have it typed in about a week, too.

I will stay on here at least till I have money to travel. By the way, can you tell me if Carson McCullers is in Ga. and where?

The whole point of this letter is I wish you would come to Macon as soon as you can - Paul and I both miss you, every week-end expecting you and being disappointed. As the tired whore said to the drunk - "Do come!"

Cawjully - 10.

[Jordan Massee (1914-   ) was reared in a prominent Macon family and later worked in advertising in New York. He met TW in late 1940 at the East Side apartment of Donald Windham and Fred Melton and soon attended rehearsals of *Battle of Angels*.

TW's potential for scandalous behavior in conservative Macon troubled both Paul Bigelow and Massee. Bigelow informed Massee, who was staying with his family on Sea Island, that their restless friend had been instructed to behave "exactly" as he would if living "with his family in Clayton" (letter, qtd. in Leverich).

TW was dubbed "Olympe, The Termite Queen," for mimicking Lenore Ulric's affected performance in *Camille* (MGM, 1936).

Sue Myrick, a free-spoken reporter for the *Macon Telegraph*, was the most notable member of "the Gewinner's salon." A close friend of Margaret Mitchell, she had been the author's appointed "Southern Expert" on the film set of *Gone With the Wind* (Selznick International, 1939).

The Macon summer contributed details of setting and the residue of one memorable episode to TW's novella "The Knightly Quest" (1966). The fictional town of Gewinner, a center of military research, has a pervasive fear of spies and saboteurs. So too did Macon, site of a nearby defense industry, whose wary citizens reported TW and Bigelow to the police as "'suspicious characters.'" "Macon swell background" (July 3, 1942), TW wrote presciently in the journal.

"<u>Fear</u>," the "invented phantom adversary," dominated TW at this time and often blocked his "desire" (*Journal*, June 15, 1942) to write. He did, however, continue to revise *You Touched Me!* and learned in mid-June that Audrey Wood had acquired dramatic rights to the property, with 40% reserved for the Lawrence estate.

TW had already informed Wood that Bigelow's play "A Theme For Reason" was "about a refugee artist, very topical but unlike most topical plays, it has intellectual depth and artistic solidity" (n.d., HRC).

Carson McCullers, a third cousin of Massee, was spending the summer at Yaddo, the artists' colony in Saratoga Springs, New York, where she continued the previous season's rivalry with Katherine Anne Porter—whom TW was reading at this time.]

231. *To Jane and Gordon Carter*

[507 Georgia Avenue
Macon, Georgia]
[ca. July 20, 1942]
[TLS w/ autograph postscript, 1 p. Private Collection]

Dear Jane and Gordon:

I believe you asked me several times why I didn't write a comedy. Well, I have finally written two of them. The first, "Stairs to the Roof" is a fantasy and much too elaborate in staging for anyone but Billy Rose and he wouldn't like it. At least in these times. The other, however, might very well be what you want. It was written this spring and summer in collaboration with Donald Windham. I took it down here in Georgia to finish it and it is now finished and ready for the typist. It is a one-set play with six characters, three women and three men and was suggested by a short-story by D.H. Lawrence called "You Touched Me!" That is also the title of the play. We used the basic situation which is highly dramatic and packed into it a lot of comedy and a war-background which makes it topical. I haven't sent it to my agent yet or anybody but at a reading here it elicited much laughter in the right places and was considered very good. It occured to me that you might fit it into your summer plans, although I know it is pretty late in the season for that. Sorry I didn't think of it sooner. But if you have an open date for which you would like to consider it, let me know and as soon as I get it typed I will mail you a copy. It is a full length play, three acts, about average in length and it's the first thing I've written that I think your audiences would care for. That is not said disparagingly of either the play or your audiences.

I am having trouble about the typing. All the local typists are working at defense plants. I may have to mail the script to New York for typing. If I do that I will ask the agent to send you one copy - provided you have an open date.

By the way, a friend of yours, David Merrick, got in touch with me in New York and I have since had a couple of letters from him. He read the long fantasy and wrote very kindly about it. He thought it was beautiful but uncommercial - like me! It is about time I got commercial. I've had a hell of a time lately, living on doughnuts and right now I am living in an attic in the hottest town in America.

I had a one-act produced early this summer in New York. Libby Holman and Bobbie Lewis saw it and are planning, tentatively, to produce a series of them in the Fall with Libby singing. I have had to write her a singing play - She still has a wonderful voice.

I have a job in New York in September, doing publicity work for Erwin Piscator at the New School for Social Research. I will pass through St. Louis, probably, on my way north.

How are things going with you in the theatre, Etc.?

                                                    Best wishes always, Tom.

R.S.V.P.D.Q.!

[Jane (1916-   ) and Gordon (1903-1991) Carter had last shown interest in staging *Battle of Angels* for the Civic Theatre (see letter #182), a summer playhouse in St. Louis County directed by Gordon. TW was unaware, however, that the company's present season, its fifth, had been canceled in June as a war emergency measure. Before her marriage Jane Garrett appeared in the St. Louis Mummers productions of *Candles to the Sun* (1937) and *Fugitive Kind* (1937).

The blues singer Libby Holman had recently appeared in *Mexican Mural*, under Robert Lewis's direction, and apparently considered backing a program of TW's one-acts in the fall. A sexual and artistic rebel, Holman epitomized a raffish outsider's charm that TW found intriguing.]

232. To Audrey Wood

[507 Georgia Avenue
Macon, Georgia]
[July 29, 1942]
[TLS, 1 p. HRC]

Dear Audrey:

I am putting the 5 play copies in the mail this afternoon. Sending them by registered parcel post. I could find no suitable Ms. covers but you can replace the temporary ones I have used.

I have worn out several typewriter ribbons this summer but as usual I have produced very wastefully, sometimes writing only to escape ennui. I really must limit myself to fewer things as I don't have the ability to do more than one or two good things at a time. In fact if I do <u>one</u> good thing it is something for me to crow over.

Do you think I ought to take Piscator seriously about that job in September? We might get along better this time and again we might not. Did I ever tell you about my first interview with him, or rather - the second? I arrived at this palatial estate on the Hudson, admitted by a Prussian butler. After waiting half an hour I was conducted to his bedroom. He was slightly indisposed with a cold. He was lying up in bed with his dinner tray. Over the bed was a fur robe - I believe it was mink - and he was wearing peach-colored silk pyjamas. He looked at me mournfully and said, "Mr. Williams, you have written a Fascist play - all of your characters are selfishly pursuing their little personal ends and aims in life with a ruthless disregard for the wrongs and sufferings of the world about them." - A man that lacking in humor is not for me to deal with! Still, as I say - we might get along better this time.

The typist will start at once on Bigelow's play.

Cordially, Tenn.

P.S. I have that migratory feeling and will probably forsake this town for one of the Florida beaches after a while.

[With a second draft of *You Touched Me!* complete, TW wrote to Donald Windham that D.H. Lawrence would probably "be a little confused by all that has happened to his little story" (qtd. in *Windham*, p. 34). Substantial changes in Lawrence's original characters, especially Ted Rockley and Emmie, the addition of several new ones, including a pompous Anglican priest, and the invention of comic scenes to advance the romantic plot had succeeded in transforming Lawrence's ruthless "little" story into a quaint melodrama. The story's post-World War I setting was retained for the time being.

After receiving the script in early-August, Audrey Wood raised the issue of shares for the collaborators (so little did she seem to know Donald Windham that she called him "Dorothy"), who had agreed to an equal division. "May I suggest," she wrote to TW, "that if you've done all the writing, which I suspect, that you should get the greater percentage" (August 5, 1942, HRC). In Windham's novel *The Hero Continues*, an agent suggestive of Audrey Wood exhibits predatory instincts and a disregard for artistic integrity.

TW had written in early-July that a time "rich in neuroses," as was Macon, "is also rich in invention. I will probably get a good deal of work done this summer before the culminating disaster or the regeneration takes place" (*Journal*, July 1, 1942). The "wasteful" products of ten weeks in Macon included poems, a dramatic treatment of "The Malediction" (published in 1945 as "The Strangest Kind of Romance"), and a group of sketches about the deep South entitled "Dragon Country," a title that TW used in 1970 for a quite different collection of plays. There was also a hopeful journal entry that anticipated one of Blanche DuBois's speeches in *A Streetcar Named Desire* (1947): "I'd like to live a simple life - with epic fornications" (July 12, 1942).]

233. *To Mary Hunter*

507 Georgia Ave.
Macon, Ga.
Aug. 1, 1942
[TLS, 2 pp. HRC]

Dear Mary:

I guess it's about time I let you know where I am! I am in the hottest little town in America, known as Macon, Georgia, occupying a room in an attic, working nights as a bus-boy at a light-drinking establishment known as the Pig'n Whistle and spending my days at the typewriter and the lake. As for work, I have finally finished and just now sent off to Audrey the D.H. Lawrence short story play. The second draft of it took much longer than I had expected. I want Audrey to show you a copy when she is ready to send them about. But I have also had time to write a group of short plays about the deep South under the composite title of "Dragon Country". I haven't touched "The Spinning Song" since the first draft done in New York.

Well, it is good to be out of New York, Mary, under any circumstances, I never want to go back there unless I have a job or a play in production. Piscator offered me a job just before I left. I don't know how seriously to take him, however. If he still means it, I'll go back in September. Otherwise I'll stay here in the South which I hate and love so intensely. And manage to live somehow. What have you been doing, and what are your plans? My memories of you and your young and eager group of collaborators is the pleasantest recollection I have of that last period in Manhattan. And, incidentally how is Horton? The only playwright who doesn't remind me of a slightly putrescent fish. No, I take that back. I also liked Paul Green and E.P. Conkle, only they weren't really Broadway people. How about American Legend?

I have been corresponding with Robert Lewis who wants to do my one-acts next Fall with Libby Holman, but in his last letter he was working as dialogue director for Fox and seemed somewhat indefinite about the date of his return to New York.

I would like to hear from you, Mary.

Cordially, Tenn.

[Mary Hunter's "eager group" is the American Actors Company (1938-1944) that she, Horton Foote, and Helen Thompson formed with the intention of training young talent in an off-Broadway setting. The company chose the "American Scene" as its focus and showcased such indigenous writers as E.P. Conkle, Horton Foote, Paul Green, and Lynn Riggs. Hunter (1904-   ) also played the role of the insufferable Marge on the popular radio show *Easy Aces*.]

234. To Edwina Dakin Williams

[507 Georgia Avenue
Macon, Georgia]
[early-August 1942]
[TLS, 1 p. HTC]

Dear Mother:

I spent a quiet pleasant week on Sea Island with the Massees whom I visited last summer. They have a very remote section of the beach and we did nothing but play bridge, eat, sleep, and bathe in the ocean. My bridge was terrible but I did enjoy the swimming. I went there with a dreadful summer cold but the salt water has improved it.

I am waiting to hear from various people before I can plan for the Fall. I hope Mr. Piscator is still disposed to give me a job. If he does not retract the offer, I will go to work for him probably toward the end of next month. Then I have finally mailed Audrey the long comedy taken from the Lawrence story and I am waiting for her report on that. I felt it to be a commercial type of play. Robert Lewis writes me from the West Coast that he is working as a dialogue director for Fox film Co. and the date of his return to New York is still uncertain but when he does he wants to present my short plays.

I have been living in an attic here, the vast number of defense workers in town have put a premium on living-quarters. It has been pretty hot sleeping. But I like the town still and I have a lot of friends in it.

I will try to write Dakin this week. Don't worry about him. He is probably no busier than he was in St. Louis - He couldn't be! Every time I look at the dull, dispirited soldiers in the camp near here I have occasion to be thankful that Dakin is where he is. The life in these camps is all right for boys from farms and very routine occupations, but the spirited and active individuals, who have minds and want to use them, find the army life, as a private, extremely barren. I hope that Dakin will skip that part of it completely - apparently he will, if he secures a commission.

I am afraid you have been having a dreadful time of it this summer. I feel rather sick whenever I think of what you and Grand have to put up with. If I thought I could help I would come straight there, but I'm afraid my presence would only tend to aggravate matters, aside from the difficulties for me. However when I return to New York I will arrange to make a visit if you think it advisable.

Much love, Tom.

[The "week on Sea Island" was apparently the only time that TW and Jordan Massee met during the summer of 1942. The visit is problematic, however, and may be a fanciful tribute to Edwina's social aspiration for her sons. The journal reveals no trip to the Georgia coast, a three-hour journey for the penniless TW, while letter #245 can be construed as evidence that he and Massee did not meet during the Macon summer.

In answering Robert Lewis's letter, TW expressed a desire to work in films: "If anyone in Hollywood could use a dialogue writer, let me know. I've never done any work out there. Just now I'd like to try it" (August 1, 1942, Kent State). Later in August, in a follow-up letter written in the journal and probably not mailed, TW described Lewis's film work as "a painful subtraction from the theatre" but admitted that "the best pictures lately have been considerably better than 'the best plays.'" Audrey Wood, he added, had been his "good angel" and he "could never give her up for a Hollywood agent" (August 26, 1942), as Lewis had perhaps advised.

Edwina's life was indeed "dreadful" at this time, with Dakin away at Harvard and subject to the draft, Grand seriously ill, and Walter Dakin badgered by Cornelius, who was up to his old "devilish" (Journal, July 14, 1942) tricks. Earlier in July TW reflected upon his "psychological problems" and their relation to his family history: "I have to consider my family and their love - and be brave and enduring as long as it is humanly possible. We mustn't think about disaster. I'm afraid it could only be messy and prolonged - what happened to my sister. That way - No - I don't want it" (Journal, July 1, 1942).]

235. To Edwina Dakin Williams

[507 Georgia Avenue
Macon, Georgia]
[August 9, 1942]
[TLS, 1 p. Columbia]

Dear Mother:

I am sorry I was such an unconscionably long time in getting off a letter - I presume you have gotten the last one by now. I have been laid up with a very severe summer cold. It improved and then got worse again when it settled on my chest. I think I will have to leave Macon as it is very hot and humid here and sleeping nights in this stifling attic room is not beneficial. Providentially I have received a friendly note from Paul Green, the playwright whom I met in New York, inviting me to visit his drama department in North Carolina, the state university at Chapel Hill in the mountains. It is closer to both St. Louis and New York and the change of atmosphere will put me back in condition for what promises to be a busy year in New York.

I have gotten the enclosed letter from Audrey, which shows she is really enthusiastic about the new comedy I have just sent her. I think she feels that she will be able to sell it shortly, as it is, also in my opinion, the most marketable script I have given her.

The bus-fare to Chapel Hill is six dollars. I hate to speak to you of loans, but if you can provide this extra amount I think I can really reimburse you in the Fall. By that time, I will at least have work in New York. Audrey is negotiating with Piscator for a better salary than he intended to pay me.

It is dreadfully hot here and constantly raining which does not even cool things off - so I will leave at the earliest possible moment. Green is one of the best-known American playwrights as well as head of a famous dramatic school which specializes in southern material, and Chapel Hill is on the way North and just about opposite St. Louis.

With much love, Tom.

[When TW wrote next to Edwina from St. Augustine, rather than Chapel Hill, he begged indulgence for leading a "vagrant and indigent life" (n.d., Columbia). He spent a lonely fortnight there (August 12-28) before settling in nearby Jacksonville.

The "enclosed letter" from Audrey Wood improved TW's bleak "outlook" (*Journal*, August 10, 1942) when it was received on August 8. She was especially "happy" that he had written "a full-length script (for a change)" (August 5, 1942, HRC) and was already making plans to sell *You Touched Me!* to a Broadway producer.]

236. *To Erwin Piscator*

c/o General Delivery
St. Augustine, Fla.
August 13, 1942
[ALS, 5 pp. Southern Illinois]

Dear Mr. Piscator -

Excuse this pencil scribble on my notebook paper. The sickening, fetid atmosphere of interior Georgia became intolerable to me, physically and mentally, so I have run away to this little town on the ocean, which still appears clean in spite of all the horror which it has become the scene of. I am living on the beach and at the moment my residence is my suitcase - and an old over-turned rowboat. I have sent Audrey Wood my comedy - I believe she is pleased with it. It was written to make me some money to live on. A very inglorious aim, but not without practicality - do you think? Nevertheless I think it turned out to be a good play - so my artistic conscience does not blush at all. It is sort of a last, desperate throw of the literary dice in the direction of Broadway, and so I wait for something to happen and make a religion out of simple endurance. That, Mr. Piscator, is what I call the poor man's (or artist's) religion - Simple Endurance! It is <u>not</u> the <u>opium</u> of the people, it is their <u>bread</u> and their <u>wine</u>. It is what they live on, poor, damned sheep, and don't <u>know</u> it. This great blast of lightning, the <u>war</u> - I wonder if it will not stretch endurance too far - and force the human sheep to look for a new faith that is more rewarding!

What are we doing, we people who put words together, who project our shadows on stages - but trying to create a new and solid myth - or <u>faith</u> - or <u>religion</u> - in place of the old and dessicated and <u>fruitless</u> one of "simple endurance"?

But I didn't mean to deliver a sermon. - But to answer your question about my <u>plans</u>.

I did plan to return to N.Y. and work in your workshop. Apparently that plan has been cut off at the source. I have no other. I guess I am one of those improvident grasshoppers who make no "plans for the winter" but trust to luck and the benevolent ingenuity of their well-wishers.

I have much good material, I only want a stage, actors, a man to produce. Alas, I am not Saroyan - I understand he is providing himself with all these.

This scholarship you mention - would it provide me with a living in New York? - If so, I grasp it with the tenacious hands of a drowning man!

This sponsor - I hope you can find him, that he is not a chimera like most of my hopes have been.

Well, I am going to get back in the water - I am in and out of it like a turtle. I am sending you in the envelope some of the fine white sand of this beach. You can be a "Zigeuner" - put it in a shallow pan and blow your breath on it - and see the design of my fate!

Tennessee.

[The "horror" seen by the Florida coast was probably related to German submarine activity and the capture in July of four heavily armed saboteurs landed on a beach north of St. Augustine.

Apparently Erwin Piscator offered TW a publicity job with the Studio Theatre but withdrew it because he "had not heard" from him and was "forced to make other arrangements." He hoped, though, to find a "private sponsor" to fund a "scholarship" (see letter #240). In reply to TW's taunting letter of August 13, Piscator used uncommon tact and flattery: "As much as I would like to have you in the School in a definite capacity, I think it far more important for you to be perfectly free to write your own plays and that you have the opportunity to do so." He made no further mention of a scholarship and declined to play "Gypsy" fortuneteller with TW's gift of "fine white sand": "Every place I went with my briefcase I was reminded of you" (August 28, 1942, Southern Illinois).

Vanity aside, TW's appropriation of authorship suggests his close identification with D.H. Lawrence and the degree to which he saw his own psychological history reflected in You Touched Me! Several weeks later he changed tactics in correspondence with Donald Windham and asked to be kept "posted" on Audrey Wood's handling of "our play" (qtd. in Windham, p. 43).]

237. To Paul Green

[246 Charlotte Street]
St. Augustine, Fla.
August 17, 1942
[ALS, 1 p. North Carolina]

Dear Paul Green -

I suddenly rushed off to the beach, St. Augustine, and this pencil is the only practicable thing to write with. The trip north is delayed for a while, but I am intending to make it and whether or not I see the school in action, it will be pleasant to have a talk with you - although this solitary period in the jungles of Georgia and on the beach may leave me somewhat speechless. I want to see your habitat and Thos. Wolfe's - I wonder if you knew each other.

Cordially, Tennessee Williams

[TW had written to Paul Green (1894-1981) on August 9 to arrange a visit to Chapel Hill, but he left Macon before an invitation could be received. Green judged the Rockefeller applications in 1939 and recorded TW's flamboyant and probably unfamiliar name in his diary as "one of {the} recipients" (December 18, 1939, North Carolina). Author of the Pulitzer Prize play *In Abraham's Bosom* (1926), he had recently joined Richard Wright in adapting *Native Son* for a critical success on Broadway (1941). For many years Green taught a course in playwriting at the University of North Carolina, where (to answer TW's question) he and Thomas Wolfe had been friends and classmates. In 1937, in a diary note that has the accent of eulogy, he described Wolfe as "a big vital man in all ways" (January 23, 1937, North Carolina) and in the following year served as a pallbearer at his funeral.

"Speechless" echoes a recent journal entry of Laurentian invocation to the sun: "I will leave here with the sign of the holy author on my naked flesh. A sun child, a sun man. A savage. Lonely. Maybe speechless" (August 14, 1942). TW suffered a severe sunburn for his efforts and peeled throughout his stay at St. Augustine.]

238. To Paul Bigelow

[246 Charlotte Street
St. Augustine, Florida]
Tuesday P.M. [August 25, 1942]
[ALS, 4 pp. Columbia]

Paul dear -

I am distinctly surprised, in a way, by Audrey's letter. I suspect Liebling had a hand in it, smelled something non-commercial about the script. That is not surprising. We both realized it was not a script which commercial producers would devour with a sea-lion snap of the chops. But with so much basic beauty and thought, it will find a way into the Theatre. Definitely Cowl should see it, the Theatre Guild should read it; when we get to New York we will tend to these matters ourselves and less of it. I haven't heard anything from Audrey or Don since I got here and I have never felt quite so disassociated and remote. The cold hangs on. I have fever at night. It will not surprise me, when I get to St. Louis, if the family doctor slaps me into a rest-home or something. Oh, how I dread this apparently inevitable homecoming.

Daisy Mae is back in Macon. She saw that life in the big city was not for her and she concludes by saying "This ole Maid sends you her love from her decaying Mansion".

Well, I am glad she didn't wind up at Bar 13, trail's end for queens. She came. She saw - and she went back to Macon!

Miss Sally Akins is a horrid little person - venomous? My God! I talked to her for quite a while before I introduced myself and she thought it was ridiculous that a person with literary taste should like Tom Wolfe.

Had an exciting but exhausting bike trip to Jacksonville Beach. Will probably leave here this week-end. Will write you a card when my mind is resolved on that question. It will be distinctly more expensive to pass thru Chapel Hill. Is Criswell still in Illinois?

Love - 10.

Do you think one could dramatize "Don Quixote"? Selected parts of it? The death of the chivalric ideal - fall of knight-errantry, a play of the disaster of all ideals?

I am reading - starting the book - the Introduction by Geo. Woodberry to the Knopf (1926) edition is what gave me the notion - brilliant essay!

Saroyans plays were panned in Times and Herald Trib, only rev. I've seen. Goody! -

[The distinguished actress Jane Cowl was considered a potential star for Paul Bigelow's work-in-progress. She had recently been cast in a slight comedy entitled *Ring Around Elizabeth* (1941), which closed after ten performances. In later correspondence with Audrey Wood (see letter #240), TW shared her view of the "non-commercial" nature of Bigelow's play and foresaw the need for substantial revision.

Before leaving Macon TW read Thomas Wolfe's posthumously published novel *You Can't Go Home Again* (1940). Unlike "horrid" Miss Sally Akins, the undisputed mistress of Macon's public library, he thought Wolfe a "genius" who "has left his stamp on our human consciousness - and a very great stamp it is" (*Journal*, August 10, 1942).

George Woodberry's phrase "the grave of chivalry" and other such references to knight-errantry may have led TW to consider "the death of the chivalric ideal" as a subject for drama. He trusted nonetheless that "the immemorial Don Quixote of the race" would "rebel" (*Journal*, August 25, 1942) against the present smallness of ideals, a constriction that was felt once again in St. Augustine when he was stopped and questioned and asked for identification: "Disagreeable aspect here is suspicion of strangers because of saboteur scare" (*Journal*, August 13, 1942). TW used the Quixote figure at least twice in later work: *Camino Real* (1953) and "The Knightly Quest."

William Saroyan's self-produced and directed double-bill ("Across the Board on Tomorrow Morning" and "Talking to You") opened on August 17 and seemed to the *Times* critic Brooks Atkinson like "the compounding of a felony." The inaugural offering of the "Saroyan Theatre," corrective to a crass Broadway, was quickly withdrawn. After reading Saroyan's reviews, TW wrote in the journal, "Yes, I am envious and malicious," and added that "the son of a bitch had it coming" (August 19, 1942).]

239. *To Paul Bigelow*

[Jacksonville, Florida]
Friday Anno Domini
[August 28, 1942]
[ALS, 2 pp. Columbia]

Dear Paul -

Wrote you from St. Aug. but letter is still in my big valise which is now at bus depot. I am stopping in Jack. making a last ditch effort to avoid going home. This P.M. I am going down to U.S. Engineers office and apply for night work as a typist. An acquaintance of mine here tells me I should see a "Miss Trapp" down there. That failing, I shall grit my teeth and descend helplessly into the psychological <u>horrors</u> of home, for an appallingly <u>indefinite</u> period. Piscator writes that not having <u>heard</u> from me, he was "forced to make other arrangements" regarding alleged job, but that a scholarship from private sponsor might be forthcoming. He is now on the black list - our agents must liquidate him at once.

About your play - don't be too concerned about Audrey's letter. I think she really <u>likes</u> the play, at least she must surely feel its <u>basic</u> values, as I certainly <u>do</u>. It <u>will</u> find a place in the theatre. When we are both in N.Y. we will consider this matter more thoroughly and take personal steps. It is a <u>fait accompli</u>.

Oh, <u>Paul</u>, I am so tired, tired, <u>tired</u> - how many <u>centuries</u> have I lived so far? - At least a <u>thousand</u>! - but the war situation <u>does</u> look somewhat better.

"And in thy orisons, sweet nymph, be all my sins remembered!"

Love - 10

(I will let you know when <u>I</u> know where to write me.)

[TW had received bus fare from Edwina and was on his way to Clayton when he stopped at Jacksonville to delay a painful homecoming, "again unsuccessful, again dependant" (*Journal*, August 23, 1942).

TW quotes Hamlet's "To be, or not to be" speech in concluding this letter: "Nymph, in thy orisons / Be all my sins remembered" (Act III, Scene 1). His uncertainty also led him to petition Hart Crane, whose life and works he revered: "I am thy frail ghost-brother. Shy equal <u>wanderer</u>. Guide me" (*Journal*, August 23, 1942).]

240. *To Audrey Wood*

[Jacksonville, Florida]
[August 28, 1942]
[TLS, 1 p. HRC]

Dear Audrey:

I am writing from Jacksonville. This afternoon I am going to try to get a job typing in one of the military departments here. That failing I shall have to go back to St. Louis. In any case, if you want to reach me you had better address me there, 53 Arundel Place, Clayton, Mo.

Bigelow writes somewhat mournfully of your reaction to his play. Entre nous, I also felt that something [was] wrong and I think it was that woman, Erna, the dancer. Too much of the grande dame and not enough simplicity about her. The intellectual content, the basic situation, the highly topical and poetic background of the play made it intriguing to me and I hope that Bigelow can create a more appealing character and put it in more dramatic terms. There is the material there for a very unusual and intensely beautiful play, I think.

The pottery house is my little hope of salvation - How does it go? - I got a letter from Piscator saying that "Due to the fact he had not heard from me, he had been forced to make other arrangements in his office, but he hoped to secure me a scholarship from some private sponsor". - I suppose this means I am to continue my education - Heaven forbid!

I will let you know when I know where I will be definitely.

Best, Tenn.

[Undated drafts of Paul Bigelow's play reveal Erna Eddington to be an aging dancer, reportedly based upon Isadora Duncan, whose fame and fortune have vanished and whose innocence has been lost in the pursuit of a renowned career. As the play ends, she prepares for her death and redemption in a remote Pacific port named Suchiate. The three-act play, finally entitled "A Theme For Reason," is preserved in the Massee Collection and remains unperformed and unpublished.

The "pottery house" refers to *You Touched Me!* In the original story, the unmarried sisters Matilda and Emmie Rockley live with their dying father in "a square, ugly, brick house" surrounded by the family's abandoned pottery works.

In a draft of this letter (n.d., HRC), TW listed Carly Wharton, Martin Gabel, David Merrick, Hume Cronyn, and John Gassner of the Theatre Guild as potential producers of *You Touched Me!*]

241. *To Edwina Dakin Williams*

SH: Young Men's Christian Association
230 East Forsythe Street
Jacksonville, Florida
[ca. August 30, 1942]
[TL, 1 p. HRC]

Dear Mother:

I've been in Jacksonville several days looking for work, surprisingly enough, and I am starting a job tonight with the War Department, U.S. Engineers, a civil service job doing typing or rather, operating a teletype machine. I don't know how long I will keep it, fortunately there is no compulsion about length of service. The salary is very good, $120. a month, but I will probably find the work tedious and won't keep it any longer than necessary. I hope Audrey will in the meantime sell the comedy or make some other arrangement. I did not think it wise to count on Piscator as he has been so disappointing in the past and I have not heard from him this summer.

I am starting on the night-shift, at eleven o'clock tonight, but the hours are changed about and no doubt this is only for the beginning. I hope I can manage the machine: it is said to have practically the same keyboard as a typewriter. Very tired: had a medical examination, signed innumerable papers, took several oaths, and made out a will, besides standing around all day waiting for these various things to be done. I will write you in a few days how I am getting along.

I am staying at the "Y" temporarily - address above. I had bought my bus-ticket to St. Louis but I can get it cashed in: that will give me enough money till my first pay-check. Then I can pay you back. - Well, the trip to St. Louis is delayed, but I expect I will make it sometime this Fall.

Much love,

[TW continued to live at the YMCA and wrote next to Edwina at "five in the morning," on his second night on the job: "There are two others on the night-shift with me and we are all sitting around reading magazines and drinking cokes and listening to a radio so now you know what is being done with your taxes" (n.d., HRC).

TW had of course exchanged recent letters with Erwin Piscator but typically withheld bad news from Edwina.]

242. To Audrey Wood

[Young Men's Christian Association
230 East Forsythe Street
Jacksonville, Florida]
[ca. September 1, 1942]
[ALS, 8 pp. HRC]

Dear Audrey -

I have got to write in pencil as I am away from the office, but will try to be decipherable.

Mr. Collins notes are good. Fortunately I examined this script dispassionately a number of times during the writing and I have a good picture of all the valid objections. You know from past experience that I am not at all likely to be pig-headed about changes but I don't want to leap into them as precipitately as I did under the Guild Aegis with "Angels".

I do _not_ dismiss the possibility of putting the play in the 90's. Certainly that would add a picturesque flavor with costumes, Etc. I know why you and Collins suggest this, the background, the speech, the manner of the two sisters seems far removed from anything even as modern as 1919. The Victorian actually prevailed until the beginning of the 20's and is still prevailing in large middle and upper middle class sections of the South at least. I grew up, for instance, among just such characters as Emmie and Mathilda. In fact Mother and her friends around Columbus, Port Gibson, and Natchez would probably consider Emmie a little "advanced". You all forget how old-fashioned the _provinces_ _remain_, and that a shut down pottery house, especially, would preserve in amber the qualities of their mothers' society. Nevertheless if a _New York_ audience will not _accept_ this fact, the point will have to be _dealt_ with. I suppose the Boer war is a possibility but let us hold it a while in abeyance. I think I could make those girls, by direction, seem believably 20th century.

Anent Mathilda -

Her danger _is_ psychological. Without intervention, she would drift into that complete split with reality which is schizophrenic. The fear of the world, the fight to face it and not run away, is the realest thing in all experience to _me_, and when I use it in my work, I am always surprised that it does not communicate clearly to others. Perhaps that is the trouble with writing one's _self_ too much. The great psychological trauma of my life was

my sister's tragedy, who had the same precarious balance of nerves that I
have to live with, and who found it too much and escaped as Mathilda is in
danger of escaping. I want this danger to be clearly stated, but I do not want
her character to have an unhealthy <u>clinical</u> aspect as Val's did in "Battle"
and as Mr. Collins has suggested, a clarification would help. But there is no
reason why a thing so tragically common in human experience as simple
fear of reality cannot be feelingly communicated in drama and used as the
all-powerful motivation that it <u>is</u> in all too many lives. I want Matilda, more
than any other character, to be <u>understandable</u>, and I will do everything possible to get her across, but believe me, she is not "tour de force".

It is hard for a person with so many problems regarded as "special"
(they are not <u>really</u> so) to address audiences which are necessarily composed largely of extravert personalities - to talk to them about what is vitally <u>important</u> and <u>clear</u> to himself - <u>without</u> bewildering and offending them
with a sense of <u>exagerattion</u>. This, I suppose, is my great creative problem,
if I may be permitted to assume one; if I take the easy way out and simply
not deal with things I know <u>best</u>, I am being cowardly about it and really
precluding what might be an individual, special contribution. But this
problem is ubiquitous in my work. And the more I write from my inside
the more it will emerge. It is the purification, I guess.

The final scene of the play needs most revision, I agree. The marriage
<u>is</u> intended to take place immediately and the desire for a bridal bouquet is
an excusable whimsy. Is this the symbol Collins means? However I think
Mathilda's triumph can be presented in more dramatic, graphic fashion
and that is the question I think we should concentrate on.

I am extremely happy that Collins has taken this interest in the script
and he has the clear-headed, editorial faculty I need to circumvent certain
personal astigmata, or fixations mentioned before.

The 50/50 basis is okay with me, and all in all, since Donnie discovered the story which intrigued me so much (I don't think it is <u>slight</u>, for it
has all the suggestion of a lot more) he does have an equal proprietorship.
I want money, yes - but mostly I want an <u>audience</u>. If I get <u>that</u>, I am satisfied, for then I can throw in their faces the things they won't take till they
know me, all the little, helpless, unspoken-for crowd of sheep-like creatures
I seem to find in the world and wish Quixotically to be the equally little and
helpless voice of. I never, incidentally, hoped to do <u>all</u> of this, but a little is
better than none.

You are a patient Griselda if you wade through all this.

Give Mr. Collins my earnest thanks.

The job here is <u>bearable</u>. Not <u>good</u>. As I observed to Bigelow not long ago, "There <u>aren't</u> any good <u>plans</u> but there are a few acceptable <u>expedients</u>." He called it a silly aphorism but I regard it as <u>ultima dictum</u>, or something –

Always, 10.

I am damned glad Frieda did not see script. I think she is a lovable character, but I would hate to face the violations of the sacred Lawrence she and her attendants might imagine in the play.

[Alan Collins was a representative of Curtis Brown Ltd., agent for the D.H. Lawrence estate.

TW's family "fixations" were unyielding, even in adapting a fictional character for whom the "drift" into clinical schizophrenia was not germane. In Lawrence's story Matilda's inadvertent touch rouses Hadrian, her young adopted brother who has just returned from the war. She is frightened and repressed, "entranced," as Lawrence put it, but not tortured by the same pathological "balance of nerves" that afflicted TW and his sister Rose.

In adapting the original story, TW revealed insight into Lawrence's study of power and desire, as the play's final scene of "triumph" may suggest. But where the original ends ambiguously with neither Matilda nor Hadrian the clear victor, TW gives precedence to the woman—perhaps his chief violation of "the sacred Lawrence."]

243. To Paul Bigelow

SH: War Department
United States Engineer Office
[Jacksonville, Florida]
Sept 10, 1942
[TLS w/ autograph postscript, 2 pp. Massee Collection]

Dear Paul:

I guess you must be in New York by now, and I am anxious to know how you are getting along, especially as regards the medical consultation. Let me know what's cooking up there.

I don't remember whether I wrote you about my situation here or not. I am working at the office above, and the work is not bad. On the night shift and the work (receiving, copying telegrams for War Dept.) only takes up about three hours of the time and the rest is just leaning on the shovel. No boss, just another guy and myself. We take off for coffee or eats whenever we want to. Tedious, of course, but bearable. Only trouble is makes it impossible, almost, to do any writing, as I have to sleep nearly all day. I am living at the "Y". Have a room-mate, a blond moron not quite sixteen who wakes me up every few minutes during the day to ask how I like the new wave in his hair or some such interesting detail. The "Y" is managed by a sanctimonious couple, remind me of your missionary woman. The wife looks like Elsa Lanchester with her legs sawed off, only more pop-eyed and considerably grimmer. I always pass through the lobby whistling a church hymn, but piety lasts only to the turn of the stairs. I will try to steel myself against the desire to chuck job and lam out for New York - at least till something breaks up there. Audrey appears to be in action. In her last letter she enclosed a long criticism by Allan Collins of Curtis-Brown, Lawrence's publishers. He ended by saying the play was "damned good", but took particular exception to the character of Matilda, said she would not be believable even in hooped skirts - that her "fear of the world" was not explained nor understandable, should have some definite reason. I believe he and Audrey feel the play should be laid in the 90's. How do you feel about this? I don't. Nor do I see anything incomprehensible in Matilda. These successful Broadway people cannot conceive of anybody being afraid of anything but the Axis or a decline in the market. At any rate, they seem to be interested in the script and about to launch an offensive - but there will probably be a good many head-aches to come. Piscator and I have been exchanging sharp letters. He wrote that not having heard from me he was forced to make "other arrangements". I sent him an envelope full of sand from the beach at St. Augustine and suggested that he blow on it and tell my fortune. I received in return an irate letter saying the sand had spilt in his brief-case and he was unpleasantly reminded of me everytime he opened it. I replied that it was a privelege to be remembered at all. That I deeply appreciated his feeling that I should be "free to write" and so I had gotten a job copying telegrams for the government. No doubt I will hear from her again, as she is not one to relinquish the last word.

Well, my dear, Holt returned from New York - I heard from him before I left St. Augustine and also from Donnie who says that Woodrow practically deserted him - Or have I told you all that, already?

Then I got a letter from Lady Abdee, quite a long and philosophical one. She tells me that Bob Hope has sold his novel to Knopf. Isn't that remarkable? It sounded like such a strange thing.

Are you with Henrietta? Give her my love - And is Jordan coming up? If it is not inconvenient for him to remove my papers with his things, ask him to please do this and I will repay him the cost of transportation. In any case, the papers must not be mailed to my home address in Clayton because of the diaries and other intimate papers. I could get them in New York when I arrive there.

Very sleepy but I must go back to work as the teletype machine is clicking some more of its silly communications.

Today I read the following Ad in the personal column of "Saturday Review of Literature" - - - - "Pixie still afield in asphodel. Is there no gambling man? Reply such and such Box number." - Could this be Gilbert's sublimated tactics? - In lieu of the subway latrines. . . .

Tenn

Cold better. Nerves in bad shape due to lack of sleep. - Let me know what Audrey thinks of your play, and don't be discouraged whatever the initial reverses. You have the material for one of the greatest plays of our time.

P.S. Audrey mailed contracts signed by Frieda today. Mentioned your talk and said she liked you "enormously". Hoped she could be "helpful in one way or another".

[Paul Bigelow's chronically inflamed jaw required treatment once again.

With the "blond moron" an intimacy developed, as TW later informed Donald Windham (see *Windham*, p. 47).

The "sanctimonious" YMCA manager reminded TW of Miss Rogers, a dour missionary in Bigelow's play, and more vividly of Elsa Lanchester, an English-born character actor best remembered for her role as the monster's companion-mate in *Bride of Frankenstein* (Universal, 1935). TW's imagery recalls the famous birth scene in which her eyes are unbandaged and revealed as grotesque orbs.

Andrew Lyndon is "Lady Abdee," a contemporary British society figure upon whom he modeled himself, or so TW and Bigelow maintained. Bill (not Bob) Hope's novel has not been copyrighted. "Subway latrines" refers to Gilbert Maxwell's apparent promiscuity.

Audrey Wood not only mailed contracts at this time but also sent *You Touched Me!* to John Gassner, playreader for the Theatre Guild, who would make a decisive recommendation about the play's setting.]

244. To Paul Bigelow

SH: War Department
United States Engineer Office
Jacksonville, Fla.
Sept. 22, 1942
[TLS, 2 pp. Massee Collection]

Dear Paul:

I am taking a few minutes off among my onerous duties to answer your sad letter with whatever cheerfulness I can summon which isn't likely to be much. Do not decieve yourself that I am enjoying this little period of employment. I am just barely enduring it and come the first of the month I will in all probability plunge out of this town with more expedition than I have shown on any previous occasion. Last week they put me on the day-shift and I am telling you truthfully it was indescribable. I was banging out messages continually, yes - without a moment's let-up - for eight full hours in a room without windows and surrounded by clattering machines and an atmosphere of breathless frenzy. I just barely lived through it and at my earnest supplication was put back on the night shift starting today. I am definitely not in any condition for work of this sort, it is right down dangerous for me, and I shall not try to stand it longer than the first of the month. I haven't even gotten any good out of the money. I had to draw an advance on my first pay check as I was broke when I started to work and in an ill-advised burst of gallantry had informed Mother that I would need no more remittances. She was pathetically grateful for this information. It seems that the situation at home is all but intolerable. They can't get leather to make shoes anymore. My father's temper has hit an all-time high - or low - and the atmosphere of the house is tragic. Mother is thanking heaven that I have at last "settled down" and given up the "uncertainties of the theatre" - she is "so relieved for my sake" and even suggests that I may now be in a position to make a home for my grand-parents who are very unhappy because of father's nature. You see what a dilemma I am in? I now have to inform her that this job she is thanking heaven for is intolerable and I will have to give it up as soon as I get my first full pay-check. I would be willing to make almost any personal sacrifice to deliver my grandparents from my father's humiliating custody - they are too old and frail to live by themselves anymore - but it would serve no one for me to exhaust myself and probably colapse altogether. Poor Dakin, he is having a tough time of it, too. The Quartermaster studies are almost unbearably tedious - worse, he says, than anything in his law-course - and he also spends three hours a day waiting tables for his meals. My father is sending him no money whatsoever. Apparently the old man has gone completely over to the evil side of his nature - there was never much else. It is just as well I didn't go home for I am sure that I would have attempted to murder him - successfully I hope.

I recieved a sort of a letter from Jordan. It was a cartoon from "Esquire" showing a white degenerate embracing two native girls in front of a grass hut and blithely remarking "I really came here to write a play". Jordan added the caption that he thought this was almost applicable to my case. - Well-intended, I hope.

I am distressed about your situation in New York and that I am not able to relieve it any way at the moment. If I had been working longer I might at least send you some cash. As it is, I shall have to borrow till my first of the month check comes in. And then if I am to escape it will take about all of that to get me to New York. Yes, I am planning to go to New York rather than St. Louis. For reasons stated before. I feel that under the worst circumstances, I could get another job there. Those ominous words "Mitral insufficiency" appeared for the first time on my medical report when I was examined for this job, and they disturbed me a little. I think you and I both, however, are inclined to take a darker view of our prognosis than is probably justified because we are so little afraid of it. How well I know what you mean by the "Nirvana of non-existence!" I can hardly conceive anymore of those days when death used to seem fearful to me. It is a trick for imbeciles and infants - the difficulties are in the opposite state.

You would not approve of my social life here. My only close friends are a pair of whores, one male and the other female, named Buddy and Blondie, and they run interference for me on my round of the bars. Poor Buddy is the female of the pair, if such a distinction is at all admissible, and she has outlived her marketable charm and is now working as a waitress at a place called the Goodie Shop with a tyrannical old bitch of a woman making her scrub and pinch-hit for the plumber and all such odious things, in spite of which Buddy maintains a marvelous good humor. Blondie looks like one of those white rats that carry something like the Bubonic plague, but has an equally sunny disposition and I find them the only tolerable anti- dote to the overwhelmingly prosaic life in the office. Oh, and I have a large printed sign that I am intending to bring to New York for you to put up in your apartment. It is as follows: "Stop! You are Wanted! The Baptist Church is Ready to Give you Welcome!" There is more which escapes my memory. - I found it in the lobby of the "Y" which has no swimming-pool and is run by a sanctimonious couple like Dr. Rosser without the grace of his scholarly and venerable aspects and the woman looks like Elsa Lanchester with her legs sawed off and hyper-thyroid bulge of the eyes. They know I am up to something but are not sure what. I throw them off the track by whistling a church hymn when I pass through the lobby.

I hope some of this has had a cheering effect. Really, I did not like the tone of your letter, much as I understood how you must feel. It is not like you to be weighed down by these things - it is too much like me. And don't worry about your play. Audrey writes me that it needs more work in her opinion. But her statement was not at all damnatory, and even if it were, we are quite capable of forming our own judgement. At this distance I am inclined to think that if there is a formidable difficulty in the play, it is in the character of Erna. That if she came from the reading too much the "grande dame", it is because you have not altogether projected your own love for her into the script at this point. I think there are things that can be done without sacrificing the play's integrity to make her more appealing to such readers as Audrey and the all-too-pragmatic bunch that control the commercial theatre. And when we get together in New York maybe you will feel like discussing this again. In the meantime - No Mrs. Miniver speeches - What a revolting picture! - But carry on!

                                                    Tenn.

[The "well-intended" cartoon sent by Jordan Massee appeared in the July 1941 number of *Esquire*.

The "mitral insufficiency" noted in TW's medical report raised once again the question of a heart condition, in this case abnormal closure of the mitral valve that could lead to reduced function or failure.

However "revolting" its patriotism, *Mrs. Miniver* (MGM, 1942) was a great popular success and won six Academy Awards. In the film's final scene, which is set in a bombed-out village church, the vicar urged his beleaguered congregation to fight the war "'with all that is in us. And may God defend the right.'"]

"I really came here to write a play"

245. To Jordan Massee

SH: War Department
United States Engineer Office
Jacksonville, Fla.
PM: Jacksonville, September 22, 1942
[TLS w/ autograph marginalia, 2 pp. Massee Collection]

Dear Jordan:

I see what you mean, but the hero of your cartoon looks happierthan I ever felt in my life, including theMacon period. All of which adds further proof to my contention that the only working philosophy in contemporary society is containedin the American funny-papers and cartoons which show the triumph of the slap-happy and all the little delightful aspects of disaster.

Asaboteur has been at work on this government property which makes some of the words slide together.

I have heard from Paul and he soundspretty blue, poor boy. The doctor's report is not encouraging. I do hope that you will join him soon in New York, one can be so abysmally lonely there and I know how Paul dislikes these separations.

I particularly regretted the lack of chance to see you this summer. I feel that if you had been with us we would have presented a fully impregnable front to the world as seen from Dr. Rosser's attic, and there were so many things we could have talked over profitably, including our plays. I am afraid that Paul is becoming disheartened about the marketing of his. As you know, I admire the material of that play tremendously, and as I have told Paul, I consider it to be potentially one of the greatest plays of our time. The fault is in the character of Erna: she is a little too much the grande dame, not quite simple enough, to win immediate sympathy in reading. I have felt this more clearly at a distance from the play. I do hope Paul will not be downhearted and give up working on it. Once he gets the leading woman a completely lovable individual - she can and should be without doing any violence to the integrity of the play - I think he can overcome the inevitable obstacles to selling a really true and thoughtful piece of work. I hope you will buck him up about it, and by the time we are all in New York he may have the strength and courage for a new attack.

All in all I had an agreeable summer in Macon. Andrew was particularly sweet and charming: he touched me perhaps more deeply than I had any reason to suppose could happen. In some respects I am an emotional novice - still! I have been sort of dangling over the voidfor a good many months, clutchingat one little expedient after another, and I am afraid this does not make me easier to get along with. The job here is only barely bearable: I don't intend to stay here later than the first of October. Everybody has to make his own terms with life and mine just can't include a slaving occupation in spite of the fact that no reliable alternative seems apparent. Audrey likes my comedy, written with Don, and right now my hopes are pinned on something coming of that.

Do you know anybody in Jacksonville that I would like to know? I asked Andrew thatsame question and he didn't. So far I have met an Episcopal church organist who bores the be-Jesus out of me and two characters named Buddy and Blondie who form an escort when I make a round of the bars and are not the sort that Auntie [*deletion*] would boast of playing bridge with.

Incidentally one of the boys working here was a music student of [*deletion*] and said the students called him [*deletion*]. Horrid?

Now I must get back to work. If you decide to take a trip before you go to New York, I wish you'd drop by here, though I must confess Jacksonville is hardly more attractive <u>per se</u> than Macon.

Love, Tenn.

[TW was a reader of the "funny-papers" and himself an inveterate doodler. "One Arm," a story that he drafted in New York in the preceding spring, describes a simple-minded male prostitute who speaks and draws in the two-dimensional form of the comic strip. In *Camino Real* Kilroy was cast in the same popular format.

Andrew Lyndon wrote to TW after his departure from Macon: "I have the feeling of having always known you" (Monday night {September 14, 1942} HRC).

The deletions in this letter were made by an unknown hand to protect residents of Macon from indiscreet reference. The penultimate paragraph is also circled with the direction to "omit please."]

246. To the Williams Family

[Young Men's Christian Association
230 East Forsythe Street
Jacksonville, Florida]
Oct. 1, 1942
[TLS, 2 pp. Columbia]

Dear Folks:

I answered your last letter immediately but carried it around in my pocket a while and it disappeared. Not much lost, as the situation here remains unchanged, as they say in the war-bulletins. I was put on the day-shift for a week and if I'd stayed on it I would have been a nervous wreck. Luckily I am back on the night-shift again which is far more peaceful. During the day this office is an incredible bedlam, with all kinds of machines running at once, everything at fever pitch and everyone as cross as two sticks. I was gritting my teeth and holding my breath, determined to stick it out as long as I could in spite of badly shaken nerves - then, providentially, when I had done a week's time in that witch's brew, the manager, possibly sensing my distress, kindly asked me if I wouldn't like to go back on the night-shift and I have never been more grateful for anything. The contemplative mind of the poet is simply not adaptable to such circumstances. On the night shift where there are only two besides myself, I get along very well and get my work done. Naturally I do not intend to make a career of this business. It would be quite, quite impossible, even if I wished to. I have taken the job as an expedient, a stop-gap till something better comes up. It is just about the furthest removed from what I have any inclination or aptitude for, but I have made the best of it. Dakin and I are pretty much in the same boat right now. But it seems that a great many people are having to put up with worse things. I was distressed to hear of the situation at home, though of course I never imagined it to be at all pleasant. Still I do not think it necessary for Grand and Grandfather to tolerate that rudeness. I think Grand's health would improve if she were out of it. It is enough to make anyone miserable. I suggest that all three of you leave this year - and suggest it very seriously. I hardly see anything else to do. Grandfather is a gentleman and used to gentlemanly treatment and it is an unforgiveable and unendurable outrage that he should be forced to accept insulting treatment. Such things should not be permitted, and one must take a resolute stand at some point. You have the right on your side, and your first duty is to Grand and Grandfather, so if this rudeness keeps up I don't see what else you can do but take them out of it. I sincerely hope and expect that I will have a chance to return to New York sometime this Fall. I think it would be better for them to come there than Jacksonville. Jacksonville has turned cold already and the houses are not adequately heated. One could be very uncomfortable here in the winter, while in New York I have never felt any discomfort from the cold whatsoever. It is milder than St. Louis, and I think the atmosphere is healthier than any city I have lived in. I do hope Grand will have the strength to get away. I can't stand the thought of her being subjected to this ugliness, too.

I am feeling pretty well. Got completely over the cold I had for a couple of months. I swim nearly every day at the USO and have rented a bicycle that I ride to work and around town on. The salary is good but the cost of living here is worse than anywhere I've been. One cannot get a satisfactory meal for less than sixty cents. I do hope the President will succeed in curbing the prices of food, otherwise I hate to think what we will be reduced to. I am sure that he will take hold of things and stabilize them before they get completely out of hand.

I have no sympathy for the International - they - a few selfish men - have made fabulous fortunes through grinding the lives out of hundreds or thousands of little workers, and if they get it in the neck now, heaven knows they have it coming to them. Of course since one depends on these corporations for a living, their misfortunes are our misfortunes, too. Shouldn't be. - Much love -

Tom

[By describing his present job as "stop-gap," TW hoped to correct Edwina's impression that he had "'settled down'" and rejected the "'uncertainties of the theatre'" (see letter #244).

TW's lack of "sympathy" for corporations was evident in *Stairs to the Roof* and "The Malediction" (1945), the latter a project for dramatization begun in Macon and continued in St. Augustine. The vulnerability of the little worker at the center of the story echoes journal entries for both cities and indicates the extent to which TW identified with this "Chaplinesque" figure.

The International Shoe Company experienced wartime shortages of leather, further occasion, Edwina reported, for her husband's "temper" (see letter #244). In a coincident letter to Paul Bigelow, TW claimed to have written to Cornelius in "coldly passionate fury" (October 1, 1942; qtd. in Leverich, p. 467) over his rude treatment of the Dakins.]

247. To Robert Peter Tristram Coffin

[Young Men's Christian Association]
230 E. Forsythe Street
Jacksonville, Fla.
Oct. 5, 1942
[TLS, 1 p. Columbia]

Dear Mr. Coffin:

I have reason to believe we may be related and, having read your latest volume just lately, I would feel perhaps a pardonable pride if the fact could be established. My paternal grandmother, Isabella Coffin, comes from a New England family in which the name Tristram Coffin occurs more than once and she is descended directly from a Thomas Dudley who was, I believe, the first Colonial Governor of Massachusetts. If you are not averse to such enquiries, I'd appreciate it if you'd let me know whether or not any connection exists. On my paternal grandfather's side I'm related to Sidney Lanier whom you mention in one of your poems.

You once wrote some sympathetic comments on verse of mine appearing in "College Verse" (1937, I think). Most of my writing is dramatic. I've had short plays published in a number of volumes and had a couple of Rockefeller dramatic fellowships and a Theatre Guild production in Boston that stirred up a good deal more perturbation than was necessary among the more conservative witnesses. However I continue to write poetry - which does not leave home.

I get to New York pretty regularly, but right now I am working for the War Department, here in Jacksonville.

I'd be glad to hear from you.

Cordially, T. Williams
Thomas Lanier (Tennessee) Williams

[Robert P. Tristram Coffin (1892-1955), professor of English at Bowdoin College, was the prolific author/editor of some seventy volumes of poetry, history, criticism, and travel, virtually all concerned with New England. His collection *Strange*

Holiness (1935) won the Pulitzer Prize for poetry, while his "latest volume," to which TW alludes, was *There Will Be Bread and Love* (1942). No reply to this letter has been found, although Coffin did praise TW's poetry while judging a contest for *College Verse* in 1937. "Inheritors" he thought "the best single poem in the whole group": it had "entrails as well as fine bones, and that is saying much." Clark Mills won the first place prize with Thomas Lanier Williams a fourth runner-up.

Isabella Coffin (1853-1884), descendant of Norman Huguenots who settled on Nantucket Island in the late seventeenth century, married Thomas Lanier Williams II (1849-1908) and had three children. Cornelius Coffin, the middle child, was the father of TW.

This letter was written on stationery imprinted with the name of the United States Engineer Office, Jacksonville, Fla.]

248. To Paul Bigelow

SH: War Department
United States Engineer Office
Jacksonville, Fla.
Oct 7, 1942
[TLS, 1 p. Massee Collection]

Well, Paul dear - You must advise me, and as soon as possible, what action you deem wisest for me to take in this, my latest, dilemma!

Before I had risen from bed this morning my room-mate deposited in my lap a letter from Audrey so appalling that I barely had strength to get up.

She apparently wants me to come to New York and re-write "You Touched Me" as a modern play against the background of the present war, upon the bare possibility - or meagre likelihood - that it would then be suitable to show to Langner and Helburn of the Theatre Guild. This being the opinion of John W. Gassner.

Presumably you have already received some inkling of this, for she went on to say that you knew of persons who could give me data on village life in England during the present war, and that you even had a friend who would "put me up" while I was working on the re-write.

Now how does this jibe, in your opinion, with her previous feeling that Matilda and Emmie were too old-fashioned, too quaint for 1919? Really, I am hopelessly confused and about ready to ship out on the merchant marine!

I do not see how I could gather enough interest in the play to attempt another revision, and I do not see - do you? - how such a chronological shift could be made without having to give the play an altogether new slant. Audrey mentions the Gish girls as possibilities if the change is made. Now, I should imagine Lillian must be a good fifty years old by now! <u>Really</u>! - And how do we know which way the Helburn-Langner would want the calendar turned, backwards, forwards, or into another dimension? I am really painfully surprised at Audrey's writing me such a letter, and that she should suggest I give up my job to come to N.Y. for such a slight prospect. - What do you make of all this? Having seen her and talked to her, you may have a clearer impression than mine.

Naturally if I came to N.Y. I would have to find some means to maintain myself - Mother would be disgusted at me for giving up work here. - <u>Is</u> there a place I could stay you know of? And what appears to be the employment situation?

I think Audrey is sold on this present war deal and will not do anything unless I capitulate.

How did you make out with Bergner? Can you write me at once?

Love, 10.

[Audrey Wood's "appalling" letter advised that she could not develop a "definite interest" (October 5, 1942, HRC) in *You Touched Me!* until it was rewritten, and preferably along the lines suggested by John Gassner. In recommending a contemporary village setting, Gassner and Wood had no doubt consulted the popularity of *Mrs. Miniver* and other such topical fare. Although TW deplored the film, he would soon borrow one of its key romantic elements when he recast Hadrian as a flyer on leave from the war. Lillian and Dorothy Gish were 46 and 44, respectively.

The actress Elisabeth Bergner was reportedly interested in Paul Bigelow's play but chose instead the long-running comedy *The Two Mrs. Carrolls* (1943) as her next vehicle.]

249. To Audrey Wood

SH: War Department
United States Engineer Office
Jacksonville, Fla.
Wednesday morning
(After a night of reflection)
[October 14, 1942]
[TL draft, 1 p. HRC]

Dear Audrey:

In reading the play aloud last night it appeared very clearly to me that to be entirely congruous and charming it really ought to be laid at the turn of the century. The quaintness and earnestness of the characters, even the poetic quality of the writing are distorted by the unnatural effort to fit them into an immediate present. I feel doubtful that anyone reading the script with an eye to production will fail to observe this incongruity, which I am afraid is the one essential flaw of the play. Without it we would have a clear and beautiful play with all its meaning and message intact and the quaintness - with a period background - would only make it more charming. The turn of the century (the Boer wars were late in the nineties) was a natural time for looking at the future, at a new century which we are less than halfway through even now. The message of courage and fearless advance into change seems no less pertinent then than now - it is sufficient to have an unmistakable analogy to our times, unnecessary to have our times actually. When you first proposed the Boer wars I thought it might mean sacrificing the power plant but I find on investigation that power plants were in existence - the excitement of electricity and technological progress was very much in the air. If Hadrian's hopefulness would appear somewhat pathetic in the light of what occured in later history, I don't think that would defeat but might even give an added poignancy to the message.

If you agree with me about this - Donnie does - I'm ready to do it. I feel that Mr. Gassner's advice, on which the present changes were made, was probably very casually given and without much genuine feeling for the play or the authors.

Yours

[Apparently TW was unhappy with a preliminary attempt to update *You Touched Me!* and proposed returning to Audrey Wood's earlier preference for an 1890s setting (see letter #242). He was soon resigned, however, to the modernization of the play and informed Paul Bigelow that he was "back at work" and "making exciting progress." Hadrian was now "a flyer on leave" from the war, a topical setting, he said, that "brings out the corn in me which I think is the most useful quality of a contemporary dramatist" (postmarked Jacksonville, October 17, 1942, Columbia).]

250. To Paul Bigelow

SH: War Department
United States Engineer Office
Jacksonville, Fla.
[October 28, 1942]
[TLS, 2 pp. Columbia]

My dear Paul:

From your letter you seem to have misconstrued my remarks about your notes but <u>completely</u>. I found them extremely helpful and the term "officious" is quite the contrary of anything applicable to your kindness in making them out, and I am hoping to get all the assistance from you you're willing to give in preparing the final draft in New York. One of my new plans should be particularly up your alley, so to speak. I am introducing a new character, an English woman writer for whom the tea is being given, one Dame Shirley de Capet, sort of an amusingly ironical bull-dike who upsets Emmie and the Reverend no end by neglecting their intellectualities completely and being interested only in Hadrian's talk about the war, which Emmie had wished to exclude from the conversation. Also instead of going to the movies that night, the girls go out to a meeting at which the Dame is honored guest and at which Emmie is to read a paper on "Lawrence, Shaw, Wells, and Other False Prophets of Pragmatism". At the conclusion of which the Dame, in her little speech, politely derides an interest in such nonsense and states that a far more pertinent speech had been delivered that afternoon by the speaker's younger brother on leave from the air-force. All this is angrily related by Emmie and Matilda in their scene while Hadrian and the Father are hiding in the study. How do you feel about this material, and don't you think it hinges things up more firmly and convincingly? I am saving most of the actual work on it till we get together, my dear, for I feel that you will be invaluable in suggesting just the right crispness and pertinency it requires. I think if we are immured more or less in the artist's studio for about a week after my arrival, with our respective manuscripts for a sort of literary factory as Clark Mills and I once had, we will get everything thrashed out and ready to meet the world with. Then damn our eyes if we fail! Isn't that how you feel about it? Of course I put practically no faith in Gassner or the Guild, no more absolute faith than you are probably putting in La Bergner - But I think with re-writing we both can make scripts that will sell and pave the way for a joyful retreat to Guadalajara and some place equally and happily far removed from all the human torpedos on Broadway.

I have just written my very difficult letter of resignation to be effective, provided I can possibly be replaced, on the first of November. I expect I'll entrain at that time for New York and the prospect of living with this Free spirit delights me. I have accumulated a good deal of steam to blow off in New York and want to be some place where the explosions will not add too much to the existing havoc. I've been working nights and writing days and am about as thoroughly "done in" nervously as one could be and still remain at large. I am looking forward to seeing you, my dear, and am very glad Jordan will be around, too. - I hope this case of statutory rape brought against Errol Flynn in Hollywood has not sent Miss Maxwell post-haste into litigation. Herself such a frequent victim of statutory rape, which is defined as being with consent of a minor, I've been wondering if she would not find it unnecessary, provided a favorable verdict is rendered in the test-case, to spend any more time in the hotel business!

Love, 10.

P.S. - The English writer mentioned leaves the tea after Hadrian's speech and before the proposal scene.

[Cast in this letter as an "invaluable" collaborator, Paul Bigelow was recast as an editorial convenience in later correspondence with Donald Windham (see *Windham*, p. 54). The degree to which Bigelow's "crispness and pertinency" were involved in the Macon revision of *You Touched Me!* is a further part of the play's murky composition, as is his apparent complicity with Audrey Wood in leading TW along acceptable lines of revision.

Emmie's academic paper and literary "meeting" are ideas that TW probably derived from Edwina's early literary activities and which he used again in *Summer and Smoke* (1948). Windham was relieved that the writer Dame Shirley de Capet (also Dame Edwina and Dame Willoughby) "came out" of the final script of *You Touched Me!*

The "Free spirit" with whom TW was planning to live in New York was an artist named Karl Free.

Errol Flynn, a buccaneer of the film, was charged on October 16, 1942, with the statutory rape of a fifteen- and a seventeen-year-old girl. He was tried and acquitted in the following year. TW implied that "Miss" Gilbert Maxwell had also slept with older men for profit and that a verdict in favor of Flynn's accusers might lead him "post-haste" into profitable litigation.]

251. To the Williams Family

SH: COPY OF TELEGRAM RECEIVED
[United States Engineer Office
Jacksonville, Florida]
Oct. 28, 1942
[TLS, 2 pp. HTC]

Dear Folks:

The last few weeks I've been trying to make up my mind about a problem the enclosed letter will explain. Audrey wanted me to come back to New York right away to follow up this interest in the play. I thought it better to wait a while and see how the revisions worked out. So I have stayed on here and worked on the play during my spare time. Now I feel that the re-writing has progressed sufficiently well that I can safely take a chance on it and go back to New York, so that is what I am planning to do. If I can get a "release without prejudice", as they call it, from this office I will return to New York the first of the month. You may not entirely approve of this action, but I have considered from every angle and I know it is the right thing to do. This play is commercial, it is a romantic comedy of a sort that you and everybody else would enjoy, and I think I am wise in taking a gamble on it. Everyone else thinks so. I am not counting on the Theatre Guild, as I know they are unpredictable, but I and Audrey both feel that if we get a contemporary angle in the play it will interest any producer. But it is necessary to be in close touch with the New York theatre to do this right. Well, it will take me a couple of weeks to finish the work in New York and then if things don't turn out immediately as well as hoped, I will go back to work in some office. My boss here has promised to give me his personal recommendation for any job I apply for, and if I am released without prejudice, other government jobs will be open. I will have money enough to carry me through the uncertain period in New York, as I have put by a little and will leave with a full seventy dollar pay-check for the two weeks period. This job here was good enough, and it represented security, but it was stagnation at best. You never get anywhere without taking a chance on what is your real objective. New York is full of opportunities right now, in fact these seem to be the golden times for any man out of the army! I'm not at all worried about casting off, and hope you all won't be.

I wrote to thank you for the box of nice presents and left the letter at the office one night and it was never recovered. The cakes were swell, arrived in perfect condition and all the other articles very useful. I've gotten a lot of good out of my period here. Acquired a good deal of proficiency at this sort of work and the esteem and good-will of the people I worked for. They seem genuinely sorry I am planning to leave but agree that I am justified in doing it.

If all goes as planned, I will leave here about Sunday night. If you want to reach me before you get my new address, write me c/o Audrey Wood, 551 Fifth Ave., New York City.

Wish that you all were coming to New York. I would go by way of St. Louis if I had enough extra money. As it is, I will return south soon as I have a chance, maybe before Christmas and have a good visit.

I do hope you're all well, that the house is adequately heated and the atmosphere relatively agreeable.

Dakin looks marvelous in the snapshots.

Much love, Tom.

[TW requested a "release without prejudice" from the Engineer Office on October 28, and it was "accepted without delinquency or misconduct" (HRC) in a letter dated November 12, 1942. He reportedly told a different story to the "biographer" Gilbert Maxwell: "I turned out such poor work the boss practically used to get down on his knees, begging, 'Please, Williams, don't make me fire you in times like these when there just aren't any men.' The poor guy finally had to, though" (qtd. in *Tennessee Williams and Friends*, 1965, p. 62). The tale was further embellished in *Memoirs* to include TW's bungling of a "really important message" (p. 73).

By early-November TW began to live in various arrangements in New York: at first with Karl Free, for one disastrous night; in a furnished room; with Donald Windham at the Meltons' Greenwich Village flat; at the Hotel St. George in Brooklyn; and the familiar West Side YMCA.]

252. To Walter Dakin Williams

c/o Paul Bigelow
14 W. 48th Street, N.Y.C.
November 10, 1942
[TLS, 1 p. HTC]

Dear Dakin:

I am glad for your sake particularly that the war has taken such a favorable turn. I think in six months time the fighting will be about over.

I haven't had time to write home since I got to New York. I had to write on the revisions as fast as possible and today I finished up what I hope is the final draft. Audrey is very hopeful about the play as it is a comedy and it now has a very topical war background. We feel she will be able to sell it perhaps quite soon.

I got my "release without prejudice" from the U.S. Engineers which means I am eligible for re-employment in government service if I want another job with them. I couldn't do two things at once so I had to give it up while making the revised play.

The only good thing about the army is that nearly everybody is in it. I mean that is the only comforting aspect, and a uniform seems to be the only respectable suit of clothes nowadays. I know I felt a great deal more social poise with that War. Dept. badge on my lapel than I do without it.

Tell Mother I will keep you all posted on my goings on here, and that there is no occasion for any concern. I am working hard and living very quietly. I think I will have money enough to carry me through two or three weeks here and then will either have royalties coming in, or a good prospect of them, or another job.

Mother will heartily approve of this comedy. It is nearly all sweetness and light and would make the old ladies of Boston purr like cats drinking cream. Still it is not a bad play, in my opinion either.

My dear love to the two ladies of the house, and to you and Grandfather. "The rest is silence!" (Hamlet).

Tom

[Dakin Williams was drafted in November 1942 before he could enter Officers Candidate School. TW blamed Cornelius, telling Donald Windham that his brother had been forced to leave Harvard when "Father refused to pay his board" (qtd. in *Windham*, p. 56). Dakin has informed the editors that Cornelius funded his study at Harvard and that he left because he became subject to the draft as the fall semester ended. TW was not alone in thinking that recent news from the front—the retreat of Rommel's army in North Africa and new American beachheads in the Pacific—signaled an early turning point in the war.

TW's draft status ("IV F") had not changed but the advantage of military service was on his mind. In recent correspondence with Paul Bigelow, he noted

Drafted in 1942, Dakin Williams later served abroad as a flight-controller and legal affairs officer.

William Saroyan's induction and advised his friend that "it should be bruited about - before I return to New York - that I am in a branch of the military service. I think any success in the theatre is dependant upon such things at this time" (postmarked Jacksonville, October 17, 1942, Columbia).

With "the rest is silence," an allusion to the forbidding Cornelius, TW quotes the dying words of Hamlet in Act V.]

253. To the Williams Family

SH: Young Men's Christian Association
5 West 63rd Street, New York, N.Y.
[December 6, 1942]
[TLS, 2 pp. HTC]

Dear Folks:

The work on the play being all finished and the script started around producers' offices, I went out and got myself a job. I start working tomorrow at the "British Ministry of Supply" as a teletype operator, same work I did in Jacksonville and at the same salary, but I believe the office is somewhat quieter and pleasanter. I got the wire and the box - many, many thanks. The wind-breaker is particularly welcome as my coat needed cleaning.

Now that I already have a job, Piscator at the New School offered me another, reading scripts, but it wouldn't pay as well, so I won't take it unless the present one is unsatisfactory. I am living at the "Y" again, and it is swell to have a room of my own after visiting around so much.

The air in New York is very bracing after Florida. I think it is really healthier up here in the winter, at least I always feel better than I do in the South.

Tonight I am going out for supper to meet a publisher who is interested in bringing out a volume of my verse. He prints the best modern poetry and there is a very good chance he will do mine. I am polishing it up in my spare time. He is the editor of "New Directions" and I could not be printed under better auspices - I hope we get along amiably at this first meeting.

Audrey is enthusiastic about the long comedy and appointments for conversations about it are being made already. It usually takes several months to negotiate a sale, so it is a good idea for me to have this job to cover the interim. Also I have just sold a new one-act to the Mayorga anthology which comes out every spring. These anthologies are in public libraries all over country. In Jacksonville, for instance, I found two books with my work in it on the drama shelf.

The director of the Texas University drama Dept. was in the city this past week and she plans to put on "Battle of Angels" - to shock the South! That is, if the school authorities will let her. Personally I don't think it would be as shocking as she thinks it would, especially with a little expurgating. If this is done, the National Theatre Council would pay my transportation and living expenses while attending the rehearsals. This would be early in the Spring.

As soon as I am free - that is, have money enough to give up the job here - I will visit St. Louis. I hope it will be soon.

My dear love to you all.

I will keep you informed on my situation.

Tom.

[The "pleasanter" job with the British Purchasing Commission lasted for two days, as TW noted in the journal: "Could not sit still" (December 12, 1942).

James Laughlin, founding publisher of New Directions, recalled an amiable first meeting with TW at Lincoln Kirstein's apartment: "I could see this little fellow with baggy pants and a torn sweater sitting all by himself and looking very nervous. And I was a little nervous too, so I went over to talk to him . . . and we found out that we both loved Hart Crane, and we became almost instant friends" (qtd. in Leverich, p. 471).

Margaret Mayorga chose "The Last of My Solid Gold Watches" for *The Best One-Act Plays of 1942* (1943). In a biographical note she linked TW with folk dramatists Paul Green, E.P. Conkle, and Lynn Riggs and described the "etched characterization and psychology" of his selected play as "seldom found outside the best Russian literature."

Impressed by Sydney Greenstreet's performance in *The Maltese Falcon* (Warner, 1941), TW inscribed "The Last of My Solid Gold Watches" to the portly actor, for whom the role of the "superbly massive" Delta drummer Charlie Colton had been "hopefully conceived."

Margo Jones held a visiting position at the University of Texas and was not the "director" of its "drama Dept." Her enthusiasm frightened TW at first, but they became close friends, and she a fierce defender of his work. Jones returned to Austin with copies of *Stairs to the Roof* and several one-acts but soon informed TW that her "uncourageous" colleagues thought *Stairs* had "too many production problems" (letter, n.d., HTC) for a college tryout. Her plan "to shock the South" with a production of *Battle of Angels* also fell through.]

254. To James "Jay" Laughlin

c/o Lincoln Kirstein
637 Madison Ave., New York City
December 15, 1942
[TLS, 1 p. Houghton]

Dear Jay Laughlin:

Lincoln tells me that your name is Jay, not James.

I hope you remember our talk about my poems at Lincoln's Sunday night recently.

Well, I have gotten most of the long ones into fairly presentable shape, but of the short ones there is a bewildering number to choose among. I am wondering if you plan to be in the town (Manhattan) any time soon so that instead of mailing the only existing copies of a great number of poems only a few of which may be acceptable to you - It would not be better for us to get together and sort of go over and discuss them informally. With a sensitive poet in the grand manner, such a business might be a violent ordeal but with me I promise you it would be extremely simple and we would inevitably part on good terms even if you advised me to devote myself exclusively to the theatre for the rest of my life.

Any way that you want to do this is all right, just let me know. I might even be able to deliver them to you at your office in Norfolk if that seems a better plan.

Of course I am excited over the possibility and I do hope enough of the poems are sympathetic to you to make it work out.

Lincoln sends you his love.

Cordially, Tennessee

[James Laughlin (1914-1997), heir to a Pittsburgh steel and iron fortune, founded New Directions in 1936 while a student at Harvard. He went on to publish an incomparable list of modernist writers, including Ezra Pound, William Carlos Williams, Henry Miller, Dylan Thomas, and TW. He believed that "writing must remain an art and that it must not be degraded to the level of mass production business." TW's appearance in the anthology *Five Young American Poets* (1944) began a long and friendly association with New Directions.

A destitute TW availed himself of Lincoln Kirstein's address, typewriter, stationery, and influence with James Laughlin. Soon to be a massive figure in the arts, Kirstein was associated with George Balanchine in forming the American Ballet Company in 1935 and with the Museum of Modern Art on whose behalf he made several art-buying trips to Latin America. His influential magazine *Dance Index* began publication in 1942 and by year's end employed Donald Windham as secretary.]

255. *To the Williams Family*

> SH: The Museum of Modern Art
> Lincoln Kirstein
> Consultant on Latin-American Art
> [late-December 1942]
> [TL, 1 p. HTC]

Dear Folks:

I have been out doing a little Christmas shopping but I am afraid nothing will arrive before Xmas day. It was only today I could afford to buy anything. I have been engaged in hot disputes and negotiations with a producer who has finally come across with two hundred dollars to support me for the next two months while I make some further changes in the new comedy. A very happy outcome as it makes it possible for me to give up efforts to find a suitable job. The one at the British Ministry of Supply turned out to be dreadfully tiresome, much more so than the similar work I did in Jacksonville, so I gave it up after a few days and tried working nights in a hotel. Now I can devote myself to the important writing, and since everybody feels the new play to be a very valuable property, this is a fortunate outcome. The producer is a woman who has 80% of the financial interest in "Life With Father" which has been running for about four years and she is one of the wealthiest producers on Broadway, so if she is satisfied with my changes and puts on the play, it will be given a very fine, expensive production. I had hoped to come home during the holidays, but under the circumstances I think I had better finish the writing first so I will have it off my mind. Then I am sure I can get home for a visit. Transportation will be much easier after the holidays. Right now it is a terrible problem.

I have hardly been conscious of the holiday season, so many things on my mind. I will write individual thanks after Xmas, this is collective - Dad for his generous check which bridged the gap between my hotel job and the check from Mrs. Wharton, the producer. And Grand and Grandfather for theirs - the fact that Grandfather did not sign it was fortunate as it has kept me from squandering it. I am returning it for the signature. I hope to get Dakin some little present after Xmas, and I will certainly write him. I feel badly about him being away from home and doing all those disagreeable duties. Of course it will toughen him up, but I am sorry he has to go through it.

Xmas day I am having dinner with some friends and afterwards will go to the Philharmonic for some concert. Mrs. Wharton sent me a beautiful cashmere wool sweater from Lord & Taylor's as a Christmas gift, she is a real lady as well as a plutocrat. Has entertained me for dinner a number of times.

I am thinking of you all every day and am so eager to get home for a visit - I feel that I can pretty soon.

Much love and every good wish,

[TW was hesitant to visit his unhappy family: "It would hurt, it would be very sorrowful but I want it - to see them again. I should. After all, it is the only bond in my life. Otherwise I am just a loose plank on the flood" (*Journal*, December 18, 1942). The "generous check" from Cornelius suggests that TW may not have written (or mailed) the strong letter he cited in earlier correspondence with Paul Bigelow (see letter #246).

Carly Wharton's $200 payment was to support further revision of *You Touched Me!* Recent productions of the "plutocrat" Wharton and her partner Martin Gabel were *Medicine Show* (1940), a living newspaper play that called for socialized medicine, and *Cafe Crown* (1942), an ethnic comedy that ran for 141 performances and was directed by Elia Kazan.]

256. To Edwina Dakin Williams

Hotel St. George
Clark Street at Henry
Brooklyn, New York
Jan. 25, 1943
[ALS, 3 pp. HTC]

Dear Mother -

The Christmas box came this morning, just in time, as I am going to move back to Manhattan tomorrow. I find it too inconvenient living in Brooklyn and the hotel a bit too expensive.

I did not at all understand the news about Rose. What kind of operation was it and what for?

I have had to continue work on the play. Mrs. Wharton expects a lot of changes for her money and I can tell you it is quite a job satisfying her without making dangerous changes in the script. The Theatre Guild is also interested, so we now have two fish on the line, though neither is altogether landed. If an early production is not forthcoming, I may come home for a while. It seems dreadfully long since I've seen you all.

I'm ashamed to say I still have those silly little Xmas presents I was going to send you in my bureau. Now I think I will just bring them home with me when I come, as I am no good at wrapping packages and they are all kind of useless things anyway.

If I come home it will be in the next few weeks.

Please let me know exactly what was done with Rose and Dakin's address again -

I lost it.

I've never had so many things to attend to as just lately.

Love, Tom.

I loved all the things you sent in box. Eating the cookies right now - Still fresh!

[Earlier in January TW wrote of a sexual encounter turned violent: "This is the first time that anybody ever knocked me down and so I suppose it ought to be recorded. . . . Why do they strike us? What is our offense?" A few days later he began to see "richness" in the episode: "Not that I like being struck, I hated it, but the keenness of the emotional situation, the material for art" (*Journal*, January 5, 7, 1943).

Edwina's letter of January 20 brought the first "news" of a "head operation" performed on Rose Williams at Farmington State Hospital on January 13, 1943. Edwina had shielded TW from plans for the lobotomy and now quoted the doctors' report that Rose "shows 'marked improvement, and has co-operated through it all'" (January 20, 1943, HTC). TW later grieved in the journal: "A cord breaking. 1000 miles away. Rose. Her head cut open. A knife thrust in her brain. Me. Here. Smoking" (March 24, 1943). In each of their memoirs, Edwina, TW, and Dakin dated Rose's operation in 1937-1938, perhaps confusing it with the insulin therapy administered earlier at Farmington. In 1995 Leverich established an accurate calendar for her treatment.

The first lobotomies were performed in Switzerland in 1892 and aroused such criticism that the procedure was virtually abandoned for the next forty years. Animal experiments at Yale in the 1930s renewed interest and led Dr. Antônio Egas Moniz, a professor at the University of Libson Medical School, to pioneer the operation. His claims of having moderated symptoms of intractable psychoses by severing the lobes of the brain from the thalamus persuaded an American physician, Walter Freeman, to perfect the surgery and broadly institutionalize it in the United States. Between 1939 and 1951, 18,000 lobotomies were performed nationally and many more abroad. An influential study in 1947 cast doubt upon the therapeutic value of the procedure and, combined with ethical criticism, began to undermine the popularity of the irreversible operation.

On January 20 Carly Wharton found the fourth and latest revision of *You Touched Me!* unsatisfactory and withdrew from the project. TW declared himself a "veteran of discouragement" (qtd. in Leverich, p. 480) and hid the bad news from Edwina.]

257. To Andrew J. Lyndon

[Young Men's Christian Association
5 West 63rd Street, New York]
[March 1943]
[TLS, 2 pp. HRC]

Dear Andrew:

It is rather a shock to think that you are probably already out to sea and to be thought of in terms of Crane's "Voyages" and Melville's "Billy Budd". Excellent terms, both of them, and I hope you'll acquire an acquaintance with them, though I doubt if either item would be in a ship's library.

How kind of you and Harry! I am not at all prejudiced against a second Macon Period. It would probably be better than another period in Clayton, Mo.

Right now I have another job which I like somewhat better than the elevator job. I am an usher at the Strand Theatre on Broadway, one of the swanky movie palaces. I have a morning uniform, rather like an Eton scholars, and an evening uniform, midnight blue with satin lapels, and we are drilled like a regiment. I rather enjoy it. It is only eight hours, sometimes day, sometimes night; strenuous because one is constantly on the hoof, and has to deal with stampedes of old women crazy to see Humphrey

Bogart and Bronx kids crazy to hear Sammy Kaye. There is always a gang of standees that have to be held back in pens of velvet rope. An old woman slapped me yesterday. Another one broke through the rope and stampeded up the aisle. When I remonstrated with her, very delicately, she screamed, 'Don't you dare be impertinent to me! Why aren't you in the army?' To love the masses you must observe them only in the abstract, in solitude; right now I believe in autocracy: almost.

I must say that Paul and Jordan have been extremely nice to me lately. I had to collect a number of articles used in the new job, such as shirt studs, cuff-links, flashlight. They were extremely accomodating, Jordan even did some sewing for me, and very well done, too. I never mention them to Donnie any more or Donnie to them, so I think the friction will dissipate itself.

I found Laughlin awfully pleasant and there seems to be a genuine rapport between us. He is keeping all of the long free verse things (I have written a good deal more since you saw the collection) and plans to bring out a volume this summer called "Five Young American Poets" in which I will have forty pages. He has been bringing these volumes out annually for the past two years. He will also print the verse play in "New Directions" year-book, 1943.

Jordan took me to hear Jascha Heifitz play for a radio broadcast a few nights ago and it was almost unendurably beautiful, he played something by Saint-Saens, I think it was called, Rondo Capriccioso, and for I think the first time, music had the value of experience for me.

As for that unalterable opinion, I think that is true, because of rare honesty on one hand and deep interest on the other, but since it is the highest opinion I have concerning any that I know of, there is nothing that ought to be changed. As for the inarticulation, one always feels that even when it isn't there. One has to select certain things to remain loyal to unswervingly and among them are certain friendships. "Yet seldom was there faith in the heart's right kindness" is one of Crane's most personal and poignant lines: it is that faith which is most necessary to all whose lives are bound up with "the love of things irreconciliable".

Lincoln goes in the army this month and leaves Donnie in complete charge of the office and magazine. Today we had lunch together and he was wearing a light yellow corduroy suit and a red and white checked gingham shirt and he looked so much like a Modigliani crossed with a Matisse that

I couldn't keep a straight face. He was going to be photographed this P.M. by George Platt Lynes. The circumstances of his life, two years out of Atlanta, are so fantastic they ought to be serialized in a cartoon strip, 'L'il Abner of the Smart Set'. I think he sees the funny side of it, too, and that is the saving grace.

Life is more serious than all these things. D.H. Lawrence was the only [one] who realized how serious it was and his writing which is honest about it seems grotesque. Chekhov knew but also knew it would be grotesque if you tried to say it, so there is always the beautiful incompletion, the allusion and delicacy which Lawrence lost, with the sense of a deeper knowledge under it all. - Why this literary tangent?

I must go to bed. - I am on the night shift. - The ushers at the Strand ought to have football uniforms with catcher's masks.

Write me as much as you can about life at sea.

Always, 10.

[Andrew Lyndon (1918-1989), a native of Macon, Georgia, served as an officer in the Navy and settled in New York after the war. A friend to famous writers, including Truman Capote and Christopher Isherwood, Lyndon himself aspired to write but was not successful.

James Laughlin published TW's poetry and his verse play "Dos Ranchos or, The Purification" in 1944.

Introduction and Rondo Capriccioso (1863/1870), Camille Saint-Saëns's well-known composition for violin and orchestra, was recorded by Jascha Heifetz in 1971 (RCA Red Seal).

TW quotes a poem by Hart Crane entitled "A Postscript" (1933) that rues the inconstancy of friendship. The impetus for TW's own lecture upon friendship may have been his strained relations with Paul Bigelow: "Well, I am honest. Much as I like Paul, I don't believe he is. I hope this feeling is an illusion and will pass away. It frightens me" (*Journal*, December 16, 1942). The tension may have been aggravated by a recent unexplained "mess" (*Journal*, March 14, 1943) with Gilbert Maxwell that involved Bigelow.

Lincoln Kirstein entered the Army in March 1943 and left Donald Windham, the dandy in "yellow," in charge of *Dance Index* (1942–1948).

D.H. Lawrence and Chekhov were not TW's only "literary tangent" in March. In a preface to "Daughter of Revolution," a play to which he now returned, TW assailed Broadway for succumbing to "sham" wartime dramas that were "thrown onto the stage with a sort of opportunism which ought to make their perpetrators blush." Serious artists, he felt, would need the perspective of "a good ten years . . .

to absorb and integrate the experience of a war" ("Notes on Play and Production," March 1943, HRC)—a variation, in effect, upon the difficulty of artistic speech in Lawrence and Chekhov. "Daughter of Revolution" was "inscribed to Miss Lillian and Miss Dorothy Gish for either of whom the part of Amanda Wingfield was hopefully intended by the author" (n.d., HRC).]

258. *To the Williams Family*

SH: Hotel San Jacinto
Eighteen East Sixtieth
New York City
[March 1943]
[ALS, 4 pp. HRC]

Dear Folks -

You will understand why I haven't written lately when I tell you I have been trying out three different jobs. The first one was 14 hours a night entirely too much for me. Then I got a job at a Broadway Theatre, not enough pay. Now I am working at this fashionable East Side hotel which is much the most satisfactory job of the three, and pays adequately.

Mrs. Wharton and I had a disagreement about the play and she made no further advance on it. Now I have a <u>fourth</u> revised edition out, and she is interested again and so are three other producers but no action has been taken yet. So——I have to work!

The work is only from four o'clock in the afternoon till midnight; as I am used to staying up late, the hours suit me fine. Some of the rich old ladies here are regular dragons. They fight among themselves with incredible ferocity and it requires very tactful treatment and restraint to get along with them. But they are so amusing as characters that I can forgive their ferocity. A good many of them are in the social register but that does not prevent them from acting like Irish scrubwomen.

Mr. Laughlin plans to publish my verse (40 pages of it) this summer in a book called "Five Young American Poets". There will be <u>some</u> royalties, not very much, as poetry sells so badly.

If Audrey didn't want to keep me on hand for negotiations concerning the play, I would have left for a visit home. I hope things will work out so I can get away during the spring.

It is so easy to get work now, employers are literally begging people to work for them. But salaries are still not keeping up with the cost of living. When I was working at the Broadway theatre, strangers came up to me and enquired my salary and offered me higher pay to work for them. What a difference from the depression days! It is a pity it takes a war to create work for everybody.

Love to you all - Tom.

[Jobs were never too plentiful for Gilbert Maxwell or TW, who worked together at the San Jacinto Hotel and were fired after a series of comic misadventures. Doubling as night watchman and elevator operator, TW reportedly left the doors to the shaft wide open on the fifteenth floor. Maxwell later quoted one of the kindlier "dragons" as saying that the two were missed "but somehow the hotel seems a so much *safer* place to be in, now that they've gone" (*Tennessee Williams and Friends*).

"The great {Guthrie} McClintic" had succeeded Carly Wharton as a prospective producer of *You Touched Me!* He impressed TW when they met in late-March and seemed "to be rather substantially interested in the play" (*Journal*, March 24, 1943).]

259. To Edwina Dakin Williams

SH: The Museum of Modern Art
Lincoln Kirstein
Consultant on Latin-American Art
[ca. March 22, 1943]
[TLS, 1 p. HTC]

Dear Mother:

I have delayed writing till I could make some definite plans. Now I think I will probably leave the latter part of this week for St. Louis. The man I am working for does not approve of it, but I think under the circumstances he will acquiesce. At any rate, I have the money to make the trip. A few weeks rest at home would do me a lot of good. Of course I am terribly concerned about Grand, and I don't think it is right to remain away when she is so ill.

I will wire you when I am leaving. It may be Thursday. I am only waiting till then because Audrey returns to town on that date. However if you

would like me to come earlier (or later), let me know. I have put the money
aside for the trip and can actually leave at any time.

I won't try to make this a newsy letter since I will see you all so soon.
The producer seems pleased with my work on his story, more so than I am.
I only mind writing pot-boilers because it takes the time away from other
things I want to work on.

Much love, Tom.

[TW had received an "alarming" letter from Edwina with news that Grand was
"gravely ill" and would not go into the hospital. He deplored the "numbness" that
he now felt for his family: "Shameful that the news about Grand means so little. . . .
I've grown hard. . . . Turned into a crocodile" (*Journal*, March 22, 1943). He left
New York in late-March as the life there "converged into an aching wedge of noth-
ingness." No less painful, though, was the prospect of "meeting father" (*Journal*,
March 28, 1943) once again in Clayton.

Marion Gering was a producer who had hired TW to adapt a story entitled
"Heart on the Sidewalk," and from whom bus fare for the trip home had been
extracted.]

260. To Horton Foote

SH: Rev. W.E. Dakin
53 Arundel Place
Clayton, Missouri
April 5, 1943
[TLS, 1 p. Southern Methodist U]

Tovarich -

How are you doing on our Back-to-the-Farm movement? I am relying
on you to get the ball rolling as the more I think of a bucolic summer the
more it intrigues me. Let us if possible find one in the vicinity of a summer
play-house and a beach and let us determine to work on one big problem
(that is, one each) and not a lot of little pieces so that when the summer is
over we shall have something significant completed. When I was working on
the play in Macon last summer, I started out with a day-by-day schedule
which I tacked on the wall over my desk and would not get up from the typewriter each day till I had checked off the scene assigned. I think this disci-

pline actually works, when you have a free season. It would be an interesting experiment for each to supervise the other's revisions. I think good professional criticism is half the battle - and I have never really had it.

I am taking it easy here, not writing at all since I got here. Reading a lot of Lawrence, his letters and novels, and absorbing my Grandparents reminiscences. I have no friends here, see nobody, but every afternoon about five thirty or six I go down on the river-front and have a beer and listen to a juke-box in one of the dusky old bars that face the railroad tracks and the levee. That is the only part of St. Louis which has any charm. I feel much calmer. I want to continue this sort of life - quiet and contemplative, I mean - for about five months. By that time I should know what I want to do with my life from now on and have the resolution to do it.

Drifting is no good!

Horton, I have a horrid confession to make. I haven't yet returned those poems to your cousin. I left them in Donnie's office. I had lost the girl's address. Will you call Donnie and tell him to send them off? I wrote the letter and left it on the side desk. Ask Donnie to write her something, too. I feel very badly about it - I was in a very chaotic state those last few days in N.Y.

Write me -

Always. Tenn.

[Off-Broadway productions of *Texas Town* (1941) and *Out of My House* (1942) had impressed Brooks Atkinson and established the Texas-born Horton Foote (1916-   ) as a promising young playwright. "The cynicism, the ennui, the distrust" that TW associated with New York soon led to a city thought about Foote himself: "Horton is a nice boy but I wonder how sincere" (*Journal*, March 14, 1943). Suspicion born of rivalry, especially for production by the American Actors Company, was probably at work in this and other slighting references to Foote. The "Back-to-the-Farm movement" was detoured to Hollywood, where both "comrades" spent a "bucolic summer."

The relaxed tone of this letter probably reflects the absence of Cornelius on a business trip to the West Coast.]

261. *To Paul Bigelow*

[53 Arundel Place
Clayton, Missouri]
[ca. April 10, 1943]
[TL, 2 pp. HTC]

Dear Paul:

I've been home about two weeks and enjoyed it. It wasn't nearly the ordeal I expected. Grand's condition has improved. At any rate, she got out of bed to convince me she wasn't so ill and has remained out ever since and is perking up considerably. I've had a very quiet time, no entertainment, no people. Just reading in the attic and writing in the basement and trying to decide the next move in this baffling history of mine. A little contemplation does the soul no harm, though it isn't so good for figure. I have gained ten pounds since I got here due to no exercise and three enormous meals and a few snacks between. I have been reading Gorki's "Childhood" - what a magnificent book! And 'Lady Chatterley's Lover'. The non-sexual parts of it are Lawrence's best, though the fornicating sequences are pretty boring. Poor David must have pulled his beard out trying to think of something to have them do next! Like all of Lawrence's women except his Mother, Lady Chatterley is rather annoying. But the bitter portrait of Sir Clifford and the housekeeper is really terrific. - Dear me! This would make a good letter to Lady Abdy! - If I could think of something to say about Mozart.

I go down-town tomorrow to apply for a job at one of the defense plants. I plan to work a couple of weeks, save the money, and buy a ticket somewhere. Very probably New Mexico. It has been quite some while since the Indians have had the benefit of my association, and it is high time that Mrs. Luhan and I got together for a little Panic Renaissance in the Lobos and among the pueblos. Dakin has given me <u>carte</u> <u>blanche</u> with his civilian wardrobe which I find to include a new pair of brilliant red riding boots which fit me and an astonishing number of those breezy little sport-effects which, as you know, have always suited me so well. I haven't got Audrey's opinion on this proposed excursion, though I doubt that any-body on the East Coast will disapprove of it, with the morbid exception of Mr. Gering.

I took Mother to see the road company of "Eve of St. Mark" this week. She started crying two seconds after the curtain went up and never stopped, as my brother completes his training period in a few weeks, now, and will probably go abroad. Have you seen the play? It is an interesting thing. The final scene in which the two remaining sons "Join up", hard upon news of the first one's glorious end, is comparable to nothing but the vomit of a hyena. The reviews of the play in St. Louis were not good. I find that generally speaking reviews on the road seem much more intelligent to me. Our two reviewers in St. Louis both described the play as 'amateurish' and ineffective even as propaganda. Well, this is the twilight of an era in the theatre. God knows what's coming next.

We drove out to see my sister yesterday and found the operation on the brain had accomplished something quite amazing. The madness is still present - that is, certain of the delusions - but they have now become entirely consistent and coherent. She is full of vitality and her perceptions and responses seemed almost more than normally acute. All of her old wit and mischief was in evidence and she was having great fun at the expense of the nurses and inmates. She told me they were 'mentally lazy, interested only in menial accomplishments.' She herself is reading nineteenth century history and is particularly fascinated by Victor Hugo. Before the operation she was unable to read at all and was interested in nothing. She showed me about her building and I noticed the other girls regarded her very nervously. She said she had "publicly denounced them" that morning. She had the impression that I had been in the penitentiary and was sorry I wasn't, as she feels that an institution is "the only safe place to be nowadays, as hordes of hungry people are clamoring at the gates of the cities." It was curious to see these delusions persisting along with such a brightness and vivacity. To me mental therapy is the most intriguing work there is, and if I could make a fresh start, I'd take it up instead of writing. Unbalanced minds are so much more interesting than our dreary sanity is, there is so much honesty and poetry among them. But then, you wonder if there is such a thing as sanity, actually. Our own behavior, and especially our friends', does not provide a very good model, does it?

If I can remain away from New York, for a season, do let us keep in touch with each other. I regret we saw so little of each other. I think it is all but impossible, for reasons too obvious to mention, to maintain a real friendship there. They dwindle to acquaintances in spite of yourself. I think that is mainly why I dislike the city so much.

Tell Jordan hello, and if you see Miss Maxwell, tell her that [I] have it on excellent authority that she is infected with rabies.

Love,

[TW envisioned joining Mabel Dodge Luhan, D.H. Lawrence's former patron, for "a little Panic Renaissance" in the Taos pueblo, where she had discovered her fourth husband, Tony. The phrase echoes the title of a sexual farce ("A Panic Renaissance in the Lobos Mountains," n.d., HRC) in which Lawrence is cast as a reincarnation of Pan and besieged by the desirous women of Taos. TW did not return to Taos until December 1943.

Maxwell Anderson's war drama *The Eve of St. Mark* (1942) ran for 291 performances on Broadway and was named one of the "best plays" of the 1942-1943 season by the critic Burns Mantle. St. Louis reviewers found the road production (April 5-10) to be "non-professional" and the play itself marred by "lines {that} might have been lifted from an advertisement" (*St. Louis Post-Dispatch* and *Star-Times*, April 6, 1943). The final scene ends with the patriotic line, "Make a new world, boys. God knows we need it."

In a coincident letter to Donald Windham, TW was less sanguine about Rose's post-operative state and identified the "hordes of hungry people" as a phrase from a recent letter of hers that the family had implausibly found reassuring (see *Windham*, p. 56). TW's visit to Farmington was apparently his first since December 1939.

This unsigned letter to Paul Bigelow was not mailed.]

262. To Mary Hunter

[53 Arundel Place
Clayton, Missouri]
[ca. mid-April 1943]
[TLS, 2 pp. HTC]

Thanks, Mary, for your sweet letter. Home is such a wilderness that letters are absurdly cheering.

About "27 Wagons", I gave it to you because Donnie and I nearly died laughing at Flora when we read over the last scene aloud. Was that pathological of us, and can a sadistic play be presented validly or successfully as a comedy? I am afraid that plays of sadism are a symptom of emotional exhaustion, the sort of thing that artists with exacerbated nerves are peculiarly subject to. And I wonder if there is not going to be a wave of violent if not cruel writing after the war. I was shocked when I saw "Eve of St. Mark" to see them playing the horrible malaria scene in the cave for comedy and still more horrified that women in the audience howled with laughter. We are not soft people and the war is making us even harder. The subterranean ferocity - I wonder if it will continue to fool itself, I mean the owner, by the superficial sentiments that sentimental plays appeal to. There is a great deal of pity and tenderness in all of us, but when a certain balance is broken by things that create exhaustion, I think the underground devils come out - which makes for naked and savage kinds of creation. I have dug up the negro nativity play - I may send it to you, though it seems pretty sloppy.

Horton was probably referring to "The Gentleman Caller" which is still of indefinite length but bordering on a long play. It is admirably suited to a tiny stage as I am writing it with the sort of settings used in St. Mark - small areas spot-lighted in sort of a picture frame, intimate and sketchy. I am debating whether or not to work a good deal longer on it and make it considerably more serious. I am also debating where to go, but I think more and more longingly of New Mexico. If I've got to work some place, I might as well be choosey about the place. Wouldn't Mr. Gering be surprised? One could write a sadistic play on the subject! - If he got those tender sentiments sufficiently under control.

Well, I am glad the Theatre Guild scored a hit. Mr. Nathan's brutal article in "Esquire", with the parenthetical reference to my work, made me almost affectionate toward them.

If I get away from here, I will have a good deal to write you about - many adventures, no doubt.

En Avant! 10.

[TW felt a "curiously intense self consciousness" in the company of Mary Hunter, "as though all the inner organs" of his body "were visible to her." "Self conscious," he realized, "whenever I like much. A bad fix to be in" (*Journal*, March 17, 1943).

Before leaving New York TW worked on a dramatization of "27 Wagons Full of Cotton" (first published in 1945), thinking it "not worth much - amusing but a little nasty perhaps" (*Journal*, March 24, 1943).

The "malaria scene" (Act Two, Scene III) in *The Eve of St. Mark* is set in the Philippines and draws upon the gallows humor of soldiers who are beset by enemy fire and malaria fever: "I begin to feel chilly around the edges."

"The Gentleman Caller" was, of course, a working title for *The Glass Menagerie* (1945), which TW wrote now against the background of his sister's operation. Its "intimate and sketchy" form recalls an earlier journal description of "'the sculptural drama'" that he aspired to write. *The Glass Menagerie* was to be a "play of short cumulative scenes," of "statuesque attitudes or tableaux," whose "poetic" form would replace the "conventional three-act play" (*Journal*, ca. April 1942) in the post-war theatre.

The Theatre Guild's new "hit" was *Oklahoma* (1943) with settings by TW's Iowa friend, Lemuel Ayers. The Guild's nemesis George Jean Nathan had written a scathing review of the company's quarter-century of production, including reference to "Tennessee Williams' cheap sex-shocker, *Battle of Angels*" (*Esquire*, April 1943)—which the author found "unreasonably depressing" (*Journal*, March 28, 1943). Nathan's provocation was an anniversary sketch of the Guild (*New York Times*, November 15, 1942) written by its co-director, Lawrence Langner.

"En Avant," apparently used here for the first time in TW's correspondence, would become a familiar closing for letters and journal entries, as well as a declaration of the writer's indomitable will. Although a common expression, it may have been suggested by a quotation from Rimbaud—"Ce ne peut être que la fin du monde, en avançant"—that was printed as an epigraph in *The Collected Poems of Hart Crane* (1933). TW had recently used the phrase "fin du monde" (see letter #218) to describe the watershed effect of Pearl Harbor.]

263. To Audrey Wood

[53 Arundel Place
Clayton, Missouri]
[ca. mid-April 1943]
[TLS, 1 p. HRC]

Dear Audrey:

Things are in a bad shape here. I won't go into the wretched details but it is like a Chekhov play, only sadder and wilder.

I haven't been able to get away yet. In fact I will probably have to remain for two more weeks, due to my Grandmother's condition and other factors present. Please assure Mr. Gering that my dereliction is only apparent and that justice will be done in the end.

I have been able to do some sustained writing for the first time since last summer. The Gentleman Caller is developing into a full-length play and should be ready for you to look at when I return to New York.

Give Liebling my affectionate regards, and Bigelow if you see him.

Tenn.

I haven't got Gering's address, so will you forward this enclosed letter to him, please?

[TW's Chekhovian reference to his family may have been prompted in part by the Katharine Cornell revival of *The Three Sisters* (1901) that he attended before leaving New York. Rose's intractable illness, the decline of Grand, and the constant tension in the Williams household formed a kind of Chekhovian impasse in which the same hopes and fears and antagonisms were repeated without end.]

264. *To Horton Foote*

[53 Arundel Place
Clayton, Missouri]
April 24, 1943
[TLS, 2 pp. Southern Methodist U]

Dear Horton:

Is the island of Manhattan trembling with the rage of Mr. Gering? I feel as though it were. I suspect it is even registered on the seismograph in St. Louis. I was supposed to be back in New York two weeks ago and the date of my departure is still not definitely set, though I must certainly leave before May 2nd when my Father returns from the West Coast.

I am very excited by the news of the company plans. They sound excellent to me and you may certainly count on any support I can give. My only question is concerning the change of name. Since the American Actors Company has received so much honor under its present title, I wonder why you want to change it. It seems to me that the word "Playwrights" is too exclusive in an organization that also contains characters like Mary Hunter and Helen Thompson and Jane Rose. The emphasis should be on a brilliant concert of direction, management, acting, <u>and</u> playwrighting. I wish you could think of a title that would mean "Art Theatre", as distinguished from commercial, without exactly saying "Art Theatre". The most palpable and discouraging fact in the New York theatre is that no art theatre is in existence at the present time. You promise to establish one and you have already taken notable steps in that direction - Why not let the emphasis be modestly but plainly focussed on that object and accomplishment?

I have been working with tigerish fury on "The Gentleman Caller", it has become a fully-developed play almost of usual length. It has at least one part in it for you and maybe two, if you can imagine such a thing.

Did I tell you the pay-off with Gering? I had told him I would have to drop the war play. Then I discovered I hadn't money enough to get home on, so I had to tell him I had changed my mind and get another fifteen dollars out of him. Now I must pay back the fifteen or go on with the wretched business. When I think of it I could blow my brains out!

Listen, if you can get a farm-job that is only for you, for God's sake, take it! I mean don't make my employment conditional, because it may easily be impossible to find anybody who would want <u>both</u> of us. That would be wonderful, but you mustn't pass up a good chance holding out for it.

I have to be very careful this summer, live as quietly and healthfully as possible, as I am terribly tired and run down and can't get rid of my cough. If I don't take it fairly easy, I will be doing "Camille" next season at the Provincetown. Wouldn't that be something!

Are you going to let me see "Michael Strahan" when I return? I am very anxious to see what you have done with it. I have great faith in the ultimate script and think you should devote the summer to it if it isn't right yet.

How about contacting Naya for a script? Disagreeable as he is, he is like a box of roses in the luminous dark and ought to be reclaimed from that munitions plant. I cannot believe that he is through with the theatre. At any rate, I don't think the theatre is through with him. There is a primitive power in his writing that immediate criticism cannot destroy. He may be the Rimbaud of American drama.

We must remember that a new theatre is coming after the war with a completely new criticism, thank God. The singular figures always stand a good chance when there are sweeping changes.

Keep your ear to the ground and concentrate on honesty till you know what else is coming!

All these people are going, going - GONE!

Maybe we are, too, but -

<u>En Avant</u>! 10

[The failure of *Only the Heart* in 1944 led to the demise of the American Actors Company and made "plans" to restructure and rename it irrelevant. When TW later signed contracts for a McClintic production of *You Touched Me!*, he commented that Mary Hunter had erred in producing Horton Foote's drama before his own (see *Windham*, p. 167).

"Marcus Strachen" is listed as a "Never Produced Script" in the Horton Foote Collection at Southern Methodist University.

Ramon Naya wrote the experimental play *Mexican Mural* that Robert Lewis staged in 1942.]

265. To Audrey Wood

St. Louis Mo
1943 Apr 27 PM 5 51
[Telegram, 1 p. HRC]

AUDREY WOOD=

OKAY THANKS FOR WIRE WONT LEAVE TILL YOU WISH=

TENNESSEE.

[TW complied with Audrey Wood's telegram advising that he remain in Clayton until further notice. On April 30, 1943, she wired again: "COME AT ONCE TO NEW YORK. HAVE ARRANGED WRITING DEAL PICTURES WHICH NECESSITATES YOUR LEAVING NEW YORK IN TIME ARRIVE CALIFORNIA AROUND FIFTEENTH OF MAY. FARE TO CALIFORNIA PAID BY PICTURE COMPANY. ADVISE WHEN ARRIVING NEW YORK" (HRC).

The film company was Metro-Goldwyn-Mayer, and TW's salary as a script writer was a "fantastic" $250 per week for the six-month contract period.]

PART VII
1943–1945
CALIFORNIA · TAOS · ST. LOUIS
PROVINCETOWN · CHICAGO · NEW YORK
MEXICO CITY

266. To the Williams Family

SH: New York Central System
En Route
[May 8, 1943]
[ALS, 4 pp. HRC]

Dear folks -

I am ensconced in a compartment on the crack transcontinental train and travelling like rich folks for the first time. It is fun. When I think how often I've travelled on my thumb this elaborate transportation seems a little fantastic.

I will get in Hollywood Monday morning. I won't try to write much about it as I know very little. It seems they want me first to dramatize a long novel called "The Sun Is My Undoing," and I will work with Pandro Berman at Metro Goldwyn Mayer. I get $250. a week, the first term expires in 6 months and may be renewed at a higher salary. Audrey has appointed herself my "power of attorney" and all funds go through her. She will give me $100. a week and put the rest in an account she opened in my name at the Chase National Bank. She said she was afraid I would spend or give it away if it went directly into my hands. She is thoroughly trustworthy so I guess it's a good arrangement.

I got no sleep last night because of farewell entertainments lasting all night and can hardly hold my eyes open. Will write soon as I get there.

Love - Tom.

[TW left New York ca. May 8 and traveled to the West Coast on trains renowned for luxury and style: the Twentieth Century Limited to Chicago and the Super Chief to Los Angeles. During a lay over in Chicago, he visited the Art Institute and proclaimed de Chirico's *Conversation among the Ruins* to be his "favorite" (qtd. in *Windham*, p. 63).

The Sun Is My Undoing, by the prolific Marguerite Steen, ran to 1,176 pages of picaresque romance and adventure. Set in eighteenth-century England and the West Indies, the novel so abounds with "murders, piracies, abductions, insurrections, storms, tortures, and a few dozen assorted romances" that it led one acerbic reviewer (Clifton Fadiman) to say that he knew of "few books that combine as much activity with as little life." Steen's "long novel" was not filmed.]

267. To the Williams Family

SH: Metro-Goldwyn-Mayer Pictures
Culver City, California
[May 11, 1943]
[TLS, 2 pp. Columbia]

Dear Folks:

My first official act in this new office of mine is to write you this letter, which I am sure you are waiting for. I have a private office in the MGM administration building with desk, typewriter, phone and two easy chairs and a view over a pretty flower garden and the foothills of the San Bernardino mountains. I came West in grand style. I had a compartment as far as Chicago and from there on, a lower berth on the Super Chief. It was a lovely trip and I rested and enjoyed it. We went through a snow-storm in Arizona and New Mexico which made the mountain scenery very beautiful.

It is really a problem finding living space around Los Angeles. I spent all yesterday and half of today finding a place. Now I have a little two room kitchenette apartment one block off the beach in Santa Monica. I could afford something much nicer on my $250. a week, but I preferred a simple place to the pseudo-elegance that these Hollywood people go in for. It costs me only $45. a month, furnished. Furnished in very bad taste with such articles as a plaster model of Mae West and bathing-beauty pictures, but I was extremely lucky to get a place at all, due to the terrible over-crowding of defense workers.

I think I should tell you the financial arrangements I made with Audrey. She wished to have power of attorney over my funds as she felt I might squander them or give them away, so rather than oppose her, I went to the bank with her and made that arrangement. Now all my money goes through her. She deducts one hundred and fifty a week to deposit in an account at the Chase National Bank in New York, so that if I give up my job after the first six months' term, I will have something saved up. She sends me a hundred a week for living expenses. This, of course, is minus her ten percent agents' fee. If she were not a scrupulous person, this would be a dangerous arrangement, as she has control of my funds as power of attorney, but I feel sure that Audrey is completely honest and won't take any unfair advantage of her control. She has done so much for me, and this is such an unusual break for a fairly unknown writer to get, that I thought it better not to oppose her wishes about anything. I think she is motivated entirely by a real interest in me. I am going to have all my scripts typed up now that I can afford it, and will make out a will naming Mother and Dakin as beneficiaries with Audrey as executor, or literary executor, as I think if anything happened to me, the scripts should remain in Audrey's care as she can best judge and handle them.

I will get a phone call any moment from Pandro Berman who is the man I am going to work for here. He probably wants me to handle the dramatization of some new novel they have purchased. I will try to sell him an original script of my own, as that would be much easier to work on.

I haven't even looked around the lot yet, and have only seen one star, Katharine Hepburn. If Mr. Berman doesn't keep me too long in our first conference, I will go out and inspect the lot and probably watch some filming.

The rainy season is over here and it will probably be sunny till Fall. There is a fog every morning, especially along the beach, but by noon it clears off and the air is fresher and more invigorating than Florida. There is a great deal of aerial activity all the time and the display of search-lights at night, spotting planes over the ocean, is very impressive. There is much more alertness for enemy attack here than there was even in New York, and I suppose some attack is not unlikely due to the great concentration of defense plants and barracks around Los Angeles.

If any of you plan to visit California this summer, and I certainly hope you will, let me know a week or so in advance so I can get a better place. It is hard to find one, but you can always do it given sufficient time, and price ceilings keep rents down to what they are other places.

Just got back from seeing the producer and he has put me to work on a script for Lana Turner. Will write you more about it later.

Where is Dakin?

My address is 1657 Ocean Ave., Santa Monica, California.

Much love, Tom

Better write me c/o Scenario Dept., M.G.M. Administration Bldg. Office 223.

[TW described his new quarters in a sketch entitled "The Mattress by the Tomato Patch" (1954): "The Palisades is a big white wooden structure with galleries and

gables and plenty of space around it." He wistfully identified it with "the summer
hotel" in *The Sea Gull* (1896/1897), but when Christopher Isherwood (whom TW
met soon after arriving in Hollywood) visited in August, he found his young friend
living in "a very squalid rooming house" and typing like a "meditative sage" amid
"a litter of dirty coffee cups, crumpled bed linen and old newspapers" (*Diaries*,
August 18, 1943). Later in the spring TW considered moving to a nearby "residence
club," which he also recommended to his family, should they visit him in California.
It is "strictly Gentile," he added, and "right on the ocean" (n.d., Columbia).

Audrey Wood's banking plan did not succeed. The MGM payroll checks were
issued directly to TW, who claimed to an indignant agent that he had not done the
"foul" deed of "rescinding" (letter, n.d., HRC) her arrangement. Wood's provident
plan notwithstanding, TW preferred to cash his checks locally and send a portion
for saving to both Wood and Edwina—the system that prevailed.

Drafted in November 1942, Dakin Williams had completed basic training,
graduated as a second lieutenant from Officer Candidate School, and was currently stationed in Orlando, Florida, training as a flight-controller in the Army Air
Corps.]

268. To Audrey Wood

SH: Metro-Goldwyn-Mayer Pictures
Culver City, California
[ca. May 21, 1943]
[TLS w/ enclosure, 2 pp. HRC]

Dear Audrey:

I am grateful that the news about Lana Turner made somebody happy.
It is an ill wind that blows no good!

I think it is one of the funniest but most embarrassing things that ever
happened to me, that I should be expected to produce a suitable vehicle for
this actress. Poor thing, she is now having a baby and at the same time, her
next picture is supposed to be written by me! As misfortunes usually come
in pairs, if not triplets, this coming child of hers seems likely to be a monster.

It would be useless for me to describe the script I have to work with, a
scenario prepared by Lenore Coffee. It contains every cliche situation
you've ever seen in a Grade B picture. They want me to give it "freshness
and vitality" but at the same time keep it "a Lana Turner sort of thing".

I feel like an obstetrician required to successfully deliver a mastodon from a beaver. A bad comparison, as the beaver is a practical little animal who would never get herself into such a situation.

I am working mostly with Jane Loring, Berman's assistant, who is an awfully sweet person and giving all the help possible. Berman is a nice guy, too - obviously knows a hell of a lot more about show-business than writers.

My wages are still tied up by the Wage Stabilization Board. Do you understand about that? One is not supposed to get salary increases. Since I am entering a completely new field, I think it is only a technical obstacle - but in the meantime I am having to borrow money from MGM to live on. At present I owe them $110., sixty of which went to pay for a motor-scooter which was necessary to get me to and from the studio. The street-car takes interminably - as I live in Santa Monica and it runs about every half-hour. (I had the motor-scooter five days when both the tires blew out! Also the violent motion ejected my reading-glasses on a concrete pavement and shattered the lenses!)

If my first pay-check goes to you, my dear, you will have to be lightning-quick in forwarding my allowance if you want me to avoid more complicated accounts with the cashier. I will be so broke in a few more days!

I no longer feel any compunction whatsoever about the huge salary I am getting, as I shall certainly earn it.

Christopher Isherwood warns me that I must not take to drink, as most Hollywood writers do. - I am not going to.

I intend to leave here as sane and able-bodied as I arrived, which is not expecting too much.

With affectionate greetings to you all - Tennessee

Lem Ayres tells me Margo Jones of Texas is coming to the Pasadena Playhouse this summer and plans to put on "Battle of Angels" there.

In payment of Gering, be sure of a simultaneous exchange of money and manuscript (Stairs to the Roof).

Keep hold of the checque (in your right hand) till he has released the script from his left hand - his right hand will undoubtedly be free to clasp the check!

Have Liebling stand over with ruler in case knuckle-rapping is necessary.

[TW added his name to an impressive list of Broadway imports who had written for MGM: Zoë Akins, Philip Barry, Marc Connelly, Noel Coward, George S. Kaufman, Robert Sherwood, and P.G. Wodehouse, among others. His description of the Lana Turner project echoes a classic Wodehouse witticism: "I altered all the characters to earls and butlers with such success that they called a conference and changed the entire plot, starring the earl and the butler." Earlier news of the Turner assignment had "met with ribald laughter" (May 18, 1943, HRC) at Liebling-Wood, as Audrey teased in an intervening letter to TW.

The trite script was based upon Judith Kelly's novel *Marriage Is a Private Affair* (1941), winner of the 1941 Harper Prize, and released under the same title in 1944 with Lana Turner in the role of Theo Scofield West. (TW's allusion to the birth of Turner's daughter, Cheryl Crane, was prophetic: if not "a monster," she nonetheless created a sensational incident in 1958 when she stabbed her mother's abusive boy friend and was exonerated by a finding of justifiable homicide.) The film's producer, Pandro S. Berman, became a legendary figure at MGM, his well-known tolerance of writers sorely tested, one suspects, by TW: "I throw little cheesy scraps to the movie producers and they remain curiously patient" (*Journal*, June 16, 1943).

The National Wage Stabilization Board arbitrated labor disputes considered threatening to the war effort and passed on the adjustment of certain wages and salaries.

Christopher Isherwood had warned TW away from motor scooters as well as "drink." He recalled that after lunch at the Brown Derby on May 12, "we went to a dealer's, and he selected a very junky old machine which is obviously going to give trouble" (*Diaries*, May 13, 1943).

Lemuel Ayers, TW's Iowa classmate and a client of Liebling-Wood, designed the sets for *Oklahoma!* (1943) and was in Hollywood to capitalize on his success.

Apparently Marion Gering once considered producing *Stairs to the Roof* (1945). He was to be reimbursed for an advance on a project that TW had not completed.

As requested by Wood, TW enclosed an extensive list of his literary properties. On June 2 she filed an amended copy with "the Legal Department at Metro," having added "The Gentleman Caller" to the document and labeled it "not complete." It was "wise," she thought, "to establish the fact that you had written this before you went with Metro" (letter, June 2, 1943, HRC). MGM later claimed rights to the play as one written under its aegis.]

269. *To Paul Bigelow*

SH: Metro-Goldwyn-Mayer Pictures
Culver City, California
23 May 1943
[TLS, 2 pp. Columbia]

Dear Paul:

I truly meant to write this sooner. The period of adjustment is not over yet and it has been pretty tough.

I don't want this to be a gloomy, Russian sort of letter so I won't dwell upon the daily necessity or obligation to whip myself into the pretense of being vitally concerned about a certain character named Theo - Theo Scofield - destined to be immortalized by Lana Turner as soon as Lana recovers from her present condition of pregnancy. I haven't forgotten how to spell, or read too many letters from Donnie - I am just too tired to hit the right keys. I have not been at all well since last winter - a cough that hangs on and on - and the strain of this new position has left me quite enervated. But I shall pull myself together - soon as I get used to it here, and get on some healthful regime.

As for the studio itself, I have nothing but nice things to say. Everyone is lovely to me, almost embarrassingly nice and cordial. I say embarassingly because I keep thinking how they are cheating themselves. I am not their dish anymore than they are mine. But at least one of them, Pandro Berman's assistant Jane Loring, is really delightful. Looks like a weary lion with a flaming bush of red hair and always lounging around in Oriental-looking trouser outfits. We understand each other, thank God, and I can be honest with her about my feelings about Theo, Etc.

I have a really lovely little private office. An easy chair and a lamp table besides the business appurtenances - good big typewriter, cream-colored walls and Venetian blinds that can let in any degree of the usually terrific California sun. Right now I have a sort of Chekhovian twilight effect, which may account for the gently melancholy tone of this letter - well, I am still a bit lonesome, too. The visit home was such a nice change, but the very niceness of it - was sad. It seemed so final - my grandparents, you know, both so old, and Grand so lovely and delicate, a leaf on a window-sill.

Tout changes! (All changes)

Lemuel Ayres has arrived to work here. He says Margo Jones is coming to Pasadena playhouse. By the way, I wish you would forward the letter she wrote me, it may have some reference to her plans which Lem says involve some of my work.

If you were here - though I have foresworn gossip - I would probably divert you with a lot of funny stories. One simply can't do it in letters.

Are you really coming to California and when? Of course you could stay in my apartment if I am still in it. Though it would not please you at all, being the sort that contains a plaster model of Mae West on the mantal piece and a picture of Saint Theresa over the sink. Living space here is virtually impossible to obtain and it was a choice between this sort of place and one of those ghastly pseudo-elegant pseudo-modern Shangri La sort of apartments which Santa Monica is peppered with. I chose the cheaper and less offensive sort first mentioned. - It reminds me of the frightful little flat that Dad selected for poor Mother when we first came to Saint Louis. She looked at it and laughed and cried. But it is in view of the ocean - well, with a little craning of the neck. And the land-lady has already provided material for an amusing one-act. She belongs to "the movement" but confuses it with sex. We get along fine - her first name is Zola and on her table she has Zola's book "The Human Beast". When she entertains soldiers she tells them it is her biography and the fools believe her - Well, she is rather beastly-looking, you know. Drinks a quart of beer for breakfast - usually in my kitchen.

I am being very good, and you know what I mean.

Our friendship was a bit languishing in N.Y. - which is not the place for any sustained relationships - but you know I think of you always with much affection, though you may be a little baffling at times.

Give Jordan my greetings and take care of yourself - and write me.

Love, Tennessee.

[Between TW and his landlady Zola (renamed Olga Kedrova in "The Mattress by the Tomato Patch"), there were no secrets "as the summer wore on" at The Palisades. The one-act play that she inspired was entitled "Two Conceptions of Movement," a reference to her confusion of sexual and ideological motives in espousing Communism.

Coincident with this letter is a journal entry stating that Paul Bigelow "is destroyed as a friend to trust," presumably because he was not "frank" (May 23, 1943). In earlier correspondence with Audrey Wood, TW had urged her "to keep" Bigelow from visiting California: "As soon as he got here I am sure he would require the attention of specialists." The prospect of a visit by Donald Windham, whose friendship also seemed in doubt, was no more welcome at this time: "Some day I will found a colony for dissatisfied writers, but the time is not ripe" (n.d., HRC).

As a "tired" TW observed, this letter has more than the usual number of spelling errors, strikeovers, and typos, many of which have been corrected or removed by the editors.]

270. To James "Jay" Laughlin

SH: Metro-Goldwyn-Mayer Corporation
Culver City, California
[ca. May 29, 1943]
[TLS, 2 pp. Houghton]

Dear Jay:

Your letter from Utah traveled back and forth across the continent before it reached me. What a pity they didn't book me through Salt Lake City. I am sure that skiers are the opposite of writers and both of us must be reaching corresponding degrees of satiety though I can't help thinking yours is better than mine. I would love to have gone there but they put me on the Santa Fe, through a beautiful blizzard in Arizona and New Mexico but way off the track of your skiers.

I could not decide between the two prefaces either. There is a paragraph about Joyce at which point the two could be joined - or if you like the serious and frivolous angle - that would do just as well, I think. Certainly I would be pleased to have them both printed if you can give me that much space in the volume.

This celluloid brassiere that I am making for Lana Turner is not un-amusing; I have gone to movies so much, even ushering at them, that the script is almost automatic. I was somewhat disconcerted the other day - after writing many fiery dramatic speeches I thought I had better refresh my memory of the girl's technique, so they ran her latest picture for me in the projection room - I discovered she talked baby-talk! - but nicely.

Do you know Christopher Isherwood or like his work? I visited him last night in his monastery. He has gone into one in Hollywood, of all places. It is a miniature copy, architecturally, of the Taj Mahal and when I entered about eight girls and three men, including one Hindu, were seated on cushions in a semi-circle about the fire-place, all with an absolutely expressionless silence. Which made me so uncomfortable that I turned to one of them and said, "Why is it that the word Krishnamurti comes into my mind?" It was the only thing Hindu I could think of, and I had no idea who or what it was. Turned out to be dreadful blunder, as they acidly explained that he was the follower of Amy Besant and she not hardly mentionable in their circles. The dead-pan atmosphere became even thicker - and Isherwood suggested we go out for a walk. I cannot surmise his real attitude toward "the family" - he is English enough not to speak his mind very frankly - but I am wondering a little if he is not going to write a wonderful story of what is going on there.

I would like very much to meet the designer you mention and I am hoping you will make the trip to L.A. Call me at the Studio when you get here.

If my teeth were not in such a bad condition already, I would have appreciated the 17th century couplet more deeply. At any rate, it reminded me to make an appointment with the dentist.

En Avant! 10

[James Laughlin, TW's publisher, wrote from his ski lodge at Alta, Utah. He would print "Frivolous" and "Serious" versions of TW's "Preface to My Poems" in *Five Young American Poets* (1944).

In February 1943 Christopher Isherwood began to live at the Vedanta Center in Hollywood as a student of Swami Prabhavananda, a monk of the Ramakrishna Order of India. TW's humorous staging of his visit is not confirmed by Isherwood's memoir, *My Guru and His Disciple* (1980), which merely records the ill-timed arrival during "a meditation period" and notes a silent exchange of the "necessary psychological signals" for a later meeting. With variations and embellishment, TW described the scene in a coincident letter to Sandy Campbell (see *Windham*, pp. 71-72), in *Memoirs* (1975, p. 77), and in *Conversations* (pp. 352-353). One product of Isherwood's discipleship was a translation with Swami Prabhavananda of the *Bhagavad Gita*.

Jiddu Krishnamurti, a rival Indian teacher to whom TW made blundering reference, was a protégé of the British theosophist Annie Besant.]

271. To Audrey Wood

SH: Metro-Goldwyn-Mayer Corporation
Culver City, California
5/31/43
[TLS w/ enclosure, 1 p. HRC]

Dear Audrey:

I am sending you herein a hastily prepared synopsis or film story treatment of "The Gentleman Caller". I have worked this out in spare time since I've been here, but as you know the stage version, in a rough draft, is already written before I signed here.

I feel that this could be made into a very moving and beautiful screen play - much better than the stage version could be - only it would have to run unusually long, about as long, I should think, as Gone With The Wind - I think the theme and treatment is sufficiently big in scope to justify such a length and long films are better anyhow.

I'm showing this to you first and would like your opinion about presenting it to Berman or other producers on the lot or elsewhere.

The sooner I can get into material like this and out of celluloid brassieres for Lana Turner the better! (for everybody concerned, especially, I think, Miss Turner.)

Now of course this story or play would have to be purchased outright, it certainly is not included in my services under contract. I don't mind writing the film treatment on the basis of present salary, but first they would have to purchase the play from me, I mean buy the material.

As you can see, a lot of work and time would have to go into this script, but it would be a labor of love.

The stage version, as it now stands, is not up to the potentialities. It is still too rough to turn in. I think I should get that into shape first, before I tackled the screen scenario in full.

Margo Jones writes me that she is in a froth over 'You Touched Me' and wants to do it at the Pasadena where she will direct this summer. She wants me to get a copy for Gilmore Brown to read right away. Could you send one to him? - I think this idea sounds very good indeed and we should give her every encouragement to work on it.

I am too busy to be unhappy out here - otherwise I probably would be. Will have to take another advance on salary today.

Yours, 10.

[The "Provisional Film Story Treatment of 'The Gentleman Caller'" opens with the shot of "a sleepy southern town in the Mississippi Delta . . . a few years before the beginning of World War I." After summarizing the impulsive courtship of Amanda and Tom Wingfield in Blue Mountain and the family's subsequent decline in St. Louis, the scenario describes the arrival, in 1938, of a gentleman caller for the daughter Laura and her inevitable disappointment in love. For the film version TW planned a "more cheerful conclusion" than the one reserved for the stage. After Laura's brother Tom leaves the family, repeating his father's desertion, she and Amanda return to Blue Mountain, where they are reunited with Laura's grandparents and where she, grown into "a woman of strength and character" (May 31, 1943, HRC), will receive her own callers (young soldiers) as did Amanda many years ago. In a later draft TW devised a "more cheerful conclusion" for Amanda as well, with a closing shot of her nomadic husband, Tom, Sr., returning to Blue Mountain, valise in hand, and she "rather weakly, helplessly" (June 28, 1943, HRC) primed to forgive the long absence.

In June TW showed the evolving film treatment to Lillie Messinger, the MGM executive primarily responsible for his hiring.]

272. To Paul Bigelow

SH: Metro-Goldwyn-Mayer Corporation
Culver City, California
PM: Culver City, June 9, 1943
[TLS w/ enclosure, 2 pp. Columbia]

Dear Paul:

So glad to hear from you after all this time and to know you are still in command of the situation at 66 Orange street. And by the way, the subtle indication of a strictly normal juxtaposition of figures in that address is nicely done. Also the specific mention of color precludes the less wholesome alternative explanation. So I feel sure that you are in a safe place and will not require a duenna. I envy this security. You may have seen from the papers that there has been a great deal of violence here between service-men and zoot-suiters. The warfare on other minorities is not yet organized, but the L.A. queens - I am told by those who should know - have nearly all "gone underground" anticipating its out-break. I have been making public appearances in the Palisades of Santa Monica only at noon, and in a cast-off costume of Carmen Miranda's. Happy to say that I have passed unmolested. The Palisades, by the way, are very amusing. They are a long park on a bluff over the ocean. There are two winding pathways, among palm trees and summer-houses and verdant arbors - and during the long twilights or when the moon is in its brighter phases - (there is an almost complete electric black-out on the coast) - a great many solitary figures stroll about them - nature-lovers and admirers of the ocean - pausing frequently to lean poetically against the balustrade or muse in solitude among the tangled vines - all of them so deeply moved by beauty that it has actual internal repercussions and they have to retire with amazing frequency to the rest-room, a pagoda-like building nestling among palms and bushes in the middle of the park. These influences make residence along the Palisades very elevating and would bring out the poet in one less impressionable than I. One might also observe that a love of nature is one of the most enduring passions, as the vast majority of these solitary admirers of the ocean appear to be fairly superannuated, even in the dark of the moon. Matings beneath a palm-tree are frequently very suddenly dissolved under the first arc-light, on the inland side of the park, by mutual agreement. My front room window is a fine observation post and I find it better than going to the movies. - Once in a while, when some intrepid blue-jacket crosses into the park, the palm trees sway and the very earth is shaken. A gregarious instinct suddenly develops in the solitary strollers and the white cap on the dark path is like a candle in the center of many capriciously flitting moths.

I think it unwise to leave so colorful an exposition on my desk over night so I will hastily wind it up with usual assurances of faith and devotion.

As for the innocuous blandness of the glass of water, I have seen stage magicians who could do marvelous things with them.

Whatever you are, my dear, you are neither bland nor innocuous, but though one regards you warily, it is not without love.

Tennessee

[TW's sexual innuendo refers to the street address of the Franklin Arms Hotel in Brooklyn, New York, where Paul Bigelow worked as a night manager. TW enclosed the headline and lead story of the *Los Angeles Times* for June 8, 1943: "Downtown Riots Flare in L.A. Zoot-Suit War." Dressed in flashy attire—tight-cuffed trousers, heavily padded shoulders, wide lapels—gangs of young zoot-suiters reportedly caused the rebellion by molesting citizens on the street.]

273. To Christopher Isherwood

SH: Metro-Goldwyn-Mayer Corporation
Culver City, California
[ca. June 9, 1943]
[TLS, 1 p. HRC]

Dear Isherwood:

I wrote my poetry editor James Laughlin IV (New Directions) that I had encountered you under strange and exotic circumstances in a Hollywood seraglio and he wants me by all means to write an article about you and "The Movement", whatever it is. So I wonder if you will grant me another audience - so to speak - either in the sacred precincts or something more profane, like the Brown Derby? Somehow or other I anticipate a refusal. I don't think you like me particularly, or perhaps you distrust me, or you would not be so cagey. Ordinarily I only like people who like me (vanity, you know) but the attachment and sympathy I felt for Herr Issyvoo in Berlin has even withstood the intensely Anglican cold-shoulder which he has given me in Hollywood.

It seems that Laughlin would like to run an account of you and your new way of living along with an article by Henry Miller on Dali. You may not regard this as a flattering juxtaposition, nor do I think it a very congruous one, but I would be glad to undertake the job if being in the New Directions gallery would amuse you.

10.

[After meeting TW on May 12, Christopher Isherwood (1904-1986) described him as "a strange boy, small, plump and muscular, with a slight cast in one eye; full of amused malice" (*Diaries*, May 13, 1943). He answered TW's present letter on June 10 and attributed the apparent "cold-shoulder" to his new and unaccustomed reserve as "a monk" (June 10, 1943, HRC). When a "bored" Isherwood later surprised himself by "hunting up Tennessee Williams" at The Palisades, they had "supper" on the pier and "talked sex the entire evening" (*Diaries*, August 18, 1943), confirming TW's impression that "Isherwood seems strangely like me - his mind, his attitude" (*Journal*, March 21, 1943). Isherwood soon gave up his plan to become a Hindu monk, if not his reverence for Vedanta, and TW appears not to have written an article on "'The Movement.'" He later claimed "great friendship" (*Memoirs*, p. 77) with Isherwood and ranked *The Berlin Stories* (1935/1939) of "Herr Issyvoo" (as Frl. Schroeder pronounces the name of her English boarder in *Goodbye to Berlin*) with Chekhov's work. After TW's death Isherwood acknowledged the sexual part of their relationship: "It was not a big deal, we just found each other very sympathetic, and we went to bed together two or three times, I imagine" (qtd. in Leverich).]

274. To Audrey Wood

SH: Metro-Goldwyn-Mayer Pictures
Culver City, California
[June 12, 1943]
[TLS w/ autograph marginalia, 1 p. HRC]

Dear Audrey:

Glad to get your wire and know there is a script on the premises. Lillie is not in her office right now. The building is so quiet I guess it must be Saturday. I never really know what day of the week it is out here, for I write all the time (<u>Not</u> <u>always</u> for Lana Turner) which keeps me a bit hazy about other things.

I had dinner at the Brown Derby with Margo the day she got here. Cost me ten dollars but it was worth it as she did the Mad Scene from Lear as only she can do it. Such ravings! And called me desperately because no script had arrived for Gilmore to read. So I had to wire you. We had drinks with Lem Ayers whom she wants to design a set - but so far Gilmore, whom I haven't talked to, has only committed himself to the use of the subsidiary stage (in an auditorium that only seats 100).

I have completed a long short story, 28 pages, which is another use of the material of "The Gentleman Caller" and may give you a clearer impression of what will be in it, the stage version. As you will see, the climactic dinner scene has great possibilities for a quietly impressive sort of drama, though you may be terrified at my attempt to project so special a character as the sister is. However the person who tells the short story also acts as a narrator in the play and his comments - memories - give a clarification and dramatic emphasis to the action. I will not enclose the story with this letter, want to read it over and maybe get it typed here.

I feel a little guilty about the time I <u>don't</u> spend on the Turner script but there are days when just looking at it brings on amnesia, anemia and the St. Vitus dance! I am sure you understand!

Always affectionately yours, Tennessee

P.S. The checks persist in coming to me. I write you another on the Culver bank in which I deposit the whole sum as last time. I will faithfully get after them about it.

[After completing her first year as a visiting professor at the University of Texas, Margo Jones accepted a position as summer school director of the Pasadena Playhouse. She planned originally to direct *Battle of Angels* (1940) but was "sold" on *You Touched Me!* (1943/1945)—for whose script TW had wired Audrey Wood—and negotiated with Gilmor Brown, supervising director of the Playhouse, for a main stage production.

The "long short story" was a revision of "Portrait of a Girl in Glass" (1948), first drafted in 1941 (see letter #180) and now expanded to nearly four times its original length. The "climactic dinner scene" refers to the visit of Jim, the gentleman caller, and to Laura's halting expression of love. When TW read the typed copy later in June, "Portrait" seemed "a failure - dismal. Worse than the thin little story it was before." For comparison he re-read "The Malediction" (1945) and opined that "the artist would seem to have dwindled" (*Journal*, June 23, 1943).

Penned above the letterhead is the notation: "The Messenger is not so bad when you know her. We have lunch Monday."]

275. *To Audrey Wood*

SH: Metro-Goldwyn-Mayer Corporation
Culver City, California
June 18, 1943
[TLS, 2 pp. HRC]

Audrey dear:

Got the play from Lillie Messenger okay. Delivered to Pasadena.

I think I am working out a satisfactory adjustment to the life here. One thing I have to learn is to keep my gorge down when writing stuff that doesn't have the inner compulsion. Why I should find that so hard I don't know. Probably because I've just never done it before. But they are very patient with me here, extremely kind and friendly, almost embarrassingly so, and don't seem to mind when I go off on other material for a while, as I've been doing with the long short story and "The Gentleman Caller." Of course I don't tell them what I am working on, but have to acknowledge it isn't always studio material.

Just got your letter about the film story treatment. Yes, the central and most interesting character is certainly Amanda and in the writing the focus would be on her mainly. A conventional woman, a little foolish and pathetic, but with an heroic fighting spirit concentrated blindly on trying to create a conventionally successful adjustment for two children who are totally unfitted for it. The stage play ends in defeat - which she rejects at the very end and prepares to continue beyond. The film story would have a softer ending, I think. But I must warn you that Lana Turner is no where figured in my calculations. The part of Laura is the most difficult to write and the hardest to portray and would take somebody more like Teresa Wright or possibly some very sensitive young actress discovered through a stage production of it. I think that ought to come first. The boy would be used as narrator from beginning to end, the play is his memory and reconstruction of past through the Mother's nostalgic reminiscences and his own intimations of it. The play is still expanding, the stage version of it, and a final draft would be premature at this point. Naturally I can't give all the time to it that I ordinarily do to a play that holds me emotionally. It will have to evolve through the usual see-saw of under and over-writing, till it gets an even keel.

I have a carbon of film-story treatment so keep yours. We may not need it for years! (Until stage version has been produced - it will be an ace-in-the-hole.)

Windham has been angling for an unqualified invitation to join me here but I hope I may have scotched the idea in my latest letter, which told him quite honestly that any feeling of responsibility I might have for his support on the Coast would be limited to about two weeks. Don't say anything to him about it, the letter will serve the purpose if anything will. I feel sorry for Don and for any young writer who has to make a living at things which don't interest him, but my first obligations are to my mother and grand-parents and any extra money I have goes to relieving their insecurity and dependance, which he must understand. Then, also, I have to look beyond my term here.

The situation at home is that my father has always used his money-control as a humiliating despotism over all in the house.

I'm ashamed to tell you I haven't gotten down to have that talk with the accounting department about mailing the checks. I just don't get around to it. Until I do, I will send you these checks for all but my $100. a week.

I don't need to tell you I keep extremely busy. Having been knocked off the scooter twice in all too rapid succession, I figure the percentages are against me and will probably get rid of it in favor of some more reliable vehicle.

Always, Tennessee

[The script delivered to the Pasadena Playhouse was *You Touched Me!*

The film scenario of "The Gentleman Caller" (see letter #271) has "color and mood," Audrey Wood wrote, but lacks sharp focus: "I strongly suspect you mean this to be Amanda's story but I'm only surmising at this point." She also warned that the probable assignment of a limited film actress to Laura's role, "one Lana Turner" perhaps, would require "general clarification" (June 14, 1943, HRC) of the delicate part.

TW warned Donald Windham that he could not be responsible for guests for more than a few weeks (see *Windham*, pp. 75-76). Wood approved of this discouraging tactic and urged TW not to run "an institute for weary New Yorkers" (July 7, 1943, HRC). Neither Windham nor Paul Bigelow made the uncertain trip west, confused perhaps by invitations that were given and withdrawn in the same letter.]

276. To Katherine Anne Porter

SH: Metro-Goldwyn-Mayer Pictures
Culver City, California
June 22, 1943
[TLS, 1 p. University of Maryland]

Dear Katharine Anne Porter:

Through the agency of Donald Windham and the photographer I have come into possession of a photograph of my favorite living American author, one Katharine Anne Porter, and I want to thank you for being the subject of it. You are sitting, or perhaps I should say curled up, in what appears to be an enormous chair of straw that is practically a cabana and you appear to be looking out at the world from the shadowy recess of this big chair with a smiling warmth and knowingness that is very endearing.

Well, I am putting the picture up with the other two on the walls of my study. You will be a triumvirate that includes Hart Crane, and Anton Chekhov, besides yourself. I hope you approve of your company as much as I do!

I will ask Donald to forward this note as I have no idea where else you are - that is, beside the big chair in the sunny afternoon!

Cordially, Tennessee Williams

[TW read Katherine Anne Porter (1890-1980) in Macon, Georgia, during the preceding summer, perhaps with the encouragement of Paul Bigelow, who reportedly met and became friendly with her in Mexico in the early 1930s.]

277. To Audrey Wood

SH: Metro-Goldwyn-Mayer Pictures
Culver City, California
[ca. June 26, 1943]
[TLS, 1 p. HRC]

Dear Audrey:

This will be a brief jotting down of recent developments. First of all, I am removed, or shall we say liberated, from the Lana Turner script. I have never received any reverse of fortune with greater complacency, though I commiserate with whatever degree of heart-break it <u>may</u> occasion at Liebling-Wood! Lillie Messinger and Berman got together and concluded it was not the assignment for me. Lillie has introduced me to Arthur Freed and it is understood that my next assignment will probably be with him and probably on something I select myself as material. I have done some more work on the film story treatment of "The Gentleman Caller" and am showing it to Lillie as potential material. I am enclosing some changes made in the treatment which you can insert at proper places in your copy.

I kept at work on the Turner script, however dispiritedly, and the change was entirely their decision as I felt duty-bound to do what they gave me.

While new assignment is pending, I will get back to work on stage version. And I am also involved with Lem Ayers and Eugene Loring on a short subject of "Billy the Kid". I am doing dialogue and poetry sequences. Lem is reading "You Touched Me" and Margo hopes he will design a set for it.

I think it would be well to give McConnell okay on Cleveland production as one can never tell how amateur productions will turn out. The one
here might not be as good a showing as he could arrange.

Lillie promises to get a lot of MGM people to see the local production.

Must run to bank with pay-check and get your check in this letter.

Always, 10

[However welcome, TW's removal from the Lana Turner film was shaded with self-
reproach: "I'm afraid the ego was too ambitious and optimistic. I'm not much of
an artist, even at best" (*Journal*, June 23, 1943).

TW tried to interest the MGM producer Arthur Freed in "Billy the Kid," but
he was preoccupied with the career of Margaret O'Brien, a more deplorable child
star than Shirley Temple, or so TW thought. Eugene Loring would soon do the
choreography for *Carmen Jones*, the Oscar Hammerstein hit which opened in New
York on December 2, 1943.

Frederic McConnell, director of the Cleveland Play House, was negotiating for
a production of *You Touched Me!* to open the fall season.]

278. To Audrey Wood

SH: Metro-Goldwyn-Mayer Pictures
Culver City, California
July 9, 1943
[TLS, 2 pp. HRC]

Dear Audrey:

Thanks for your comment on the story. I made a carbon of it so it
won't be necessary to type it over unless it looks too messy. You know I
never expect magazines to buy my stories, that isn't what I write them for
at all, so I am not particularly concerned if they don't. Any work that has
honesty and a sufficient degree of craftsmanship or power eventually finds
an out-let, I do have faith in that, but don't care how long it takes. So let
one or two people see it, then put it away in our little savings account.

In the list of stories I gave you I check-marked a number of items of
which there were only single copies that I thought should be typed up to

guard against loss. I wish you would have one or two of those typed each week, and send me the bill for it. I would like to pay it out of my own spending account. Might begin with the "Cat Play" and then the better short stories like "The Vine" and "Memory of An Aristocrat", "Red Part of a Flag", Etc.

Margo, Gilmore Brown, Lem Ayers, and possibly Miles White and I are all meeting for supper at Margo's to have a round-table discussion of the play production. Gilmore has finally committed himself to a production, some time, some place. I understand the difficulties quite well, as I know the hierarchies that have to be appeased and finnagled around little theatres, and I must say that I did not expect Margo to pull it off. Nor am I too excited about it. There is a curious sterility about the Pasadena set-up, their plays, the ones I have seen so far, have been sort of emotionally lifeless, worse than Broadway. I have a feeling that Mary Hunter, with her relative detachment and her more objective approach, is more likely than Margo to do something really important with the play. I know that she wants to do it, and I really don't think there is a director in New York who would do it so lovingly or intelligently as she would, and it needs a woman's warmth. I know that, for curiously it is the women who like the play, or at least those with some womanly virtues. It ought to do very well at matinees if it gets on Broadway.

Margo has gotten a letter from Carl Benton Reid asking to see the script and has sent him a copy.

I think Margo will write you about the Pasadena system and its manifold complications.

Margo is a rare character, an Alice in Wonderland no matter where she goes - When I think that she has spent a year in India and turned out a book on Hindu philosophy, gone around the world, and directed plays for seven years in Houston - and hasn't lost one bubble of her original effervesence, I feel that I should go out and build a shrine in the hills for her spirit. - She is a little worried about my air of detachment, she expected me to be a much more vital person, I believe.

Horton Foote has arrived out here. It was not very smart of me to introduce him to Margo, for he is just as ingenuous as she is and I think he is much closer to her idea of a playwright. I regard Mr. Foote with a somewhat uncharitable reserve. Rivalry has something to do with it, I'm sure, but I find his great warmth and ingenuousness seeming a little spurious beside Margo's. - She doesn't. - The three of us get on well together, but I'm afraid I act like a Boston audience much of the time.

Yes, Lem and Loring and I have been hatching the Billy idea. Mr. Freed is supposed to call me in for a conference on it. I see it as a sort of folk-opera with a fresh approach to the western material, songs and ballads and dances, predominating, with Loring as Billy. Possibly a use for my folk-poems, as lyrics. The story is beautiful and epic and could be given a very fresh and tender treatment if we were given a free hand with it.

In the meantime I am grateful for being left alone in my lovely white office.

Bigelow writes me letters that make me howl with laughter, and I am still sparring with Windham about his trip. It is understood, if he comes he will pay his own expenses, getting a vacation with pay from the magazine. So I feel no great concern one way or the other.

Affectionately, 10

[In late-June TW mailed "Portrait of a Girl in Glass" to Audrey Wood, describing the revised story as "a minor excursion into the same material I am using for the stage version of 'The Gentleman Caller'" (June 29, 1943, HRC). She replied that "Portrait" was "enormously" interesting but would not be an "easy {story} to sell" (July 7, 1943, HRC).

The "Cat Play" is the dramatic version of the story "The Malediction," published in 1945 as "The Strangest Kind of Romance."

Lemuel Ayers caused one of the "difficulties" by making his sets contingent upon a main stage production of You Touched Me! at the Pasadena Playhouse and his continuing employment as designer should the play reach New York or London. TW advised Wood that such a plan was impractical and might "rule out" (July 15, 1943, HRC) a production by Mary Hunter, director of the American Actors Company, and she agreed.

Carl Benton Reid originated the role of Oscar Hubbard in The Little Foxes (1939). He left New York for Hollywood in 1943 and had a long career in films and television.

Soon after Horton Foote arrived in Hollywood, TW wrote that "Margo and Horton {are} fairly drooling over each other" and that he had probably "been supplanted in her heart by the starry-eyed ingenue, Mr. Foote" (Journal, July 9, 1943). Wood facetiously reassured TW that while Jones "admires Horton Foote's work she still feels that yours is definitely the greater talent. So Williams still has first place in her affections" (July 15, 1943, HRC).

"The Billy idea," which survives in a typescript entitled "The Ballad of Billy the Kid" (n.d., HRC), was soon dropped, as TW concentrated upon *You Touched Me!* and "The Gentleman Caller."]

279. *To Paul Bigelow*

> SH: Metro-Goldwyn-Mayer Pictures
> Culver City, California
> July 15, 1943
> [TLS w/ autograph marginalia, 1 p. Columbia]

Dear Paul:

Margo and your namesake and I all join in thanks for your gracious extension of hospitality to the Texas prodigy. I have seen his picture and am sorry I won't be there to make him feel more at home. He is just 19 and Margo feels that he is the tender and suggestible type who should not be exposed to wrong influences. It is a pity I can't personally keep his interests in the right channels, you know how strongly I feel about the preservation of innocense in the young. But I feel that in my absence you are the logical person to undertake this care.

Margo was very, very touched by your wire and letter, and I think she will write you when the lamb arrives, or get him to.

Chop, chop! Dribble, dribble! - Mmmm. (Reflections inducing over-activity of the salivary glands.)

I took your suggestions for beach costume quite seriously, but am afraid such voluminous garments might be hazardous in the water, so I have modified the design a little. As for venturing into the Palisades after sun-down - Surely you don't suppose a girl of my character and experience would do anything so imprudent! I feel that one should never go unescorted - both ways. I always stop and consider what you would advise me to do, and act accordingly. I have my books, I have my little victrola, and what with evening psalms and prayer and meditation, I find that the hours pass quickly. Only I wish, dear sister, that you could be here to accompany me at the organ, as you used to do those evenings at the Woodrow. What beautiful devotionals we used to have in those days!

One of these days I am going to settle down, maybe a ranch in New

Mexico, maybe a place in old Mexico. That is really what I am hoping to do, to be able to make myself a permanent place. Then you must come and spend your declining years with me. We will paint tea-cups and have an Indian to carry our market basket, maybe two of them with two baskets!

Margo and I will probably soon get to work on the Pasadena production of "You Touched Me". It is also being done early next season at the Cleveland theatre. I do hope you will get to see it somewhere, having been such a devoted and efficient obstetrician at the long delivery, I think you should.

Always lovingly, Tennessee.

[The "namesake" and "prodigy" entertained by Paul Bigelow was probably Paul Moor, a student at the University of Texas with whom Margo Jones had a brief affair.

In recalling their "devotionals" at the Hotel Woodrow, TW evoked a scene of sexual license that he and Bigelow had shared in 1941. "Remember the New York days," he wrote in the journal after leaving the city for uncertain quarters in New Orleans, "the plush days when I had a room at the Woodrow - that pleasant little penthouse room that looked over Central Park. The portable victrola by my bed and always money enough to eat or smoke or fuck or almost anything else that I desired to do" (October 20, 1941). He continued to treasure "Eros" in the summer of 1943, especially anonymous, "brutal" sex, but also admonished himself, "I must invoke another. One involving more of the retiring heart" (*Journal*, July 13, 1943).

Penned above the letterhead is the notation: "I will write you soon a more sensible letter. Hope you are happy in new job, and all."]

280. *To the Williams Family*

SH: Metro-Goldwyn-Mayer Pictures
Culver City, California
July 20, 1943
[TLS w/ autograph postscript, 2 pp. HTC]

Dear Folks:

I've been getting together and arranging my papers which is an all-day job and tires me more than anything else and puts me into a terrible humor, so I really shouldn't try to write a letter. But I think of you all waiting to hear from me, so I can't put it off any longer. You know I would write much oftener if I didn't get so sick of the typewriter by the close of the day when there is time for letters.

I haven't had a picture assignment for the last two weeks and have been happily devoting myself to my own work. It has been marvelously bright and warm every day, like a continual ideal spring season, only the nights very cool. How I wish you all could get away from the awful summers and winters in Saint Louis! Really the middle-west doesn't seem fit to live in after California. No wonder people are sick so much in that part of the country, and so well out here, apparently. I hope some day you will get rid of all property out there and settle in this country. I will always travel around, I guess, but this or New Mexico is the place to have a home.

With Margo Jones here and Horton Foote from New York working at another studio, I have been going out more and meeting more people. Something doing almost every night. Margo is going to produce "You Touched Me" at the famous Pasadena Playhouse. Right now it seems the production will be postponed till November when the bigger stage and better actors would be available. She is planning to give up her $300. a month job at the University of Texas just to stay out here and put on this play, she is so crazy about it. Hopes that she will obtain financial backing to transfer it to the stage in New York. It is a big gamble for her to take, and of course I appreciate it enormously. She is a very remarkable person. Had seven years experience as director of the theatre in Houston, Texas, traveled around the world, spent a year in India and written a book on Hindu philosophy. And is just thirty years old.

I got a letter from Rose, in addition to the one you sent me. It is obvious that she still has her delusions, and I don't see how she could live outside an institution of some kind. She asked me to send her ice-cream and chocolate candy, or some money to buy it, but also said that she and all her friends were dying. I will try and find a suitable present for her and send it out there.

The sinus trouble has cleared up entirely, and I am feeling quite well.

I will probably have a new picture assignment in a few days.

Love, Tom

I think the war will be over before Dakin gets through training.

[Earlier in the spring Walter Dakin visited Rose at Farmington State Hospital and described his granddaughter's condition to TW: "We found Rose about as <u>you</u> saw her, only little heavier - too bad, she is too fat" (letter, June 19, 1943, HRC). In July she wrote (apparently from Farmington) in answer to TW's recent "nice letter": "I'm trying not to die, making every effort possible not to do so. . . . The memory of your gentle, sleepy sick body and face are such a comfort to me. . . . If we have to die I want to be cremated my ashes put in with yours. Go to church for the sacrement & pray for your sister's body that it will be made thin & strong & given a husband as good as I am" (July 8, 1943, HRC). Rose reportedly spent a part of the summer at a rest home in North Carolina, the first instance of TW's ability to help his sister financially, which he found "a satisfaction" (qtd. in *Windham*, p. 87).

In August TW would receive a six-week furlough without pay rather than "a new picture assignment."]

281. To James "Jay" Laughlin

SH: Metro-Goldwyn-Mayer Pictures
Culver City, California
July 23, 1943
[TLS, 2 pp. Houghton]

Dear Jay:

It is wise of you to recognize the astringent value of life in the snow and the mountains. Every artist needs such a place of refuge. New York makes you hard and grubby, California relaxes you too much. Reading back through my journal to the summer I was here before, Laguna Beach in 1939, just before the war broke out in Europe - those far-away days - I find myself observing that life here, on the beach, is like Gauguin's picture <u>Nave Nave Mahana</u>, "The Careless Days". I was disturbed at the time that life was too indolent and pleasureable and that I would almost welcome the return of interior storms after so much dreamy peace. Well, plenty of storms came along and I experienced, later, quite a nostalgia for the <u>Nave Nave Mahana</u>. During that summer I was care-taker on a chicken-ranch while the owners were away. For days I would forget to feed the chickens, life was so dreamy, then I would make up for it by feeding them too much. About half of them died, fell on their backs with their feet sticking rigidly up, and I left the ranch in disgrace for New Mexico.

When you first mentioned "The Ecuadorean Carrion" I thought it was the title of a long poem and it intrigued me immensely. Isn't it a good title? I feel a keen desire to see this material, Latin American poetry is so much softer and yet stronger than ours, they are not afraid of tender feelings and lavish color nor of the cruelty that goes with it, like the bull-fights in Mexico where the fighters have an almost feminine or tender grace but destroy the bulls so remorselessly, with much wonderful music and brilliant colors. I think the cold British influence has done us in a little. We ought to look South of us, since we can't follow Crane with intensity enough to make it worth while.

I did not know you had relinquished your copy of the verse play until Margo Jones showed up with freshly typed copies of it in a very mysterious way and has gotten everybody at the Pasadena Playhouse very excited over it. I think she intercepted it on the way to the typist in New York, then fled for California with it. She has come out here to try out my plays with the hope of obtaining Hollywood money for New York productions. I will see that you get a fresh copy, and apologize for the agent.

I have a little picture gallery in my office of persons of importance in my life, such as Crane and Chekhov and Katharine Anne Porter and this amazing new sponsor, Margo Jones. As my first real publisher, I would like to include one of you, if you have one to send me, preferably on skis.

My next picture assignment will probably be a folk-opera, the lyrics and libretto for it, on the saga of Billy The Kid. They despaired of getting me to write for Lana Turner, suitably, and until the right assignment comes along I am left to my own devices, happily.

I hope you haven't given up the trip out here entirely. There may be parts of my longer poems that you think need revision, such as the end of "The Dangerous Painters" which I think may slacken a bit in the end. If so, I have time now to do further work.

<u>Salud</u>! Tennessee

[Discussion of "Latin American poetry" arose no doubt from James Laughlin's plan to publish a selection in the 1944 New Directions anthology. TW's "verse play" entitled "The Purification" appeared in the same number and was also staged in 1944 by Margo Jones at the Pasadena Playhouse. The "Ecuadorean" Alejandro Carrión would become a contributor to *Five Young American Poets*.]

282. To Katherine Anne Porter

> SH: Metro-Goldwyn-Mayer Pictures
> Culver City, California
> July 30, 1943
> [TLS, 1 p. University of Maryland]

Dear Katharine Anne Porter:

Crane and Chekhov look gently sad this morning, in this California sunlight, but you are still smiling in it, ineluctably, so I look at your picture more frequently even than theirs, and it always gives me a lift.

What a happy surprise your letter was! Now I know where you are and what you are doing, and the favorite picture has even more reality. The picture I have is facing, not the profile, which I should love to have also. You made another mistake when you mentioned your possession of some informal pictures of Crane in a happy mood. I am wondering if you have any copies of these to spare. Not only would I love to have one, but I feel sure they would be of great interest to all the few who love his poetry.

I know you are quoted to some extent in the fine biography of the poet by - what's his name! But I wish that you would sometime write about him yourself as you knew him in Mexico, and say something about those more endearing characteristics which you found in him. That is, when you have finished the novel.

Do you ever hanker for Mexico? I do, and am planning to go back there when my term here expires - and write under "that tree".

It is not really good here, in spite of all the sunniness and relaxation. The atmosphere is too thick with a striving and opportunism that is even more offensive, somehow, than the ordinary American type. It begins to be almost visible, between you and the landscape or ocean. In Mexico it wasn't like that, at least I didn't feel it.

> Salud! Tennessee (Williams)

[In an intervening letter Katherine Anne Porter wrote that she was "pleased" by TW's interest in her photograph (a "birthday" picture reportedly taken by Paul Cadmus) and by the literary "company" in which she had been placed. She recalled photographing a "jolly" (June 30, 1943, HRC) Hart Crane in her garden at Mixcoac in 1931 and regretted her inability to care for him in his illness. In *Hart Crane: The Life of an American Poet* (1937), Philip Horton quoted Porter's "random recollections" of Crane's visit to Mexico, a report quite at variance with the experience she bitterly described to friends, and which naively led TW to assume that Porter had "endearing" memories of Crane that she wished to share.

Porter's story "That Tree" (1934) describes a bootless American type whose dream of being "a cheerful bum lying under a tree in a good climate, writing poetry" appealed to TW.

In later years Porter avoided TW's company and in correspondence with Seymour Lawrence (January 20, 1961) repeated a slur of Allen Tate's upon his homosexuality.]

283. To Audrey Wood

SH: Metro-Goldwyn-Mayer Pictures
Culver City, California
Aug. 2, 1943
[TLS w/ autograph marginalia, 2 pp. HRC]

Dear Audrey:

About Pasadena: I am also sorry it is not set for the big stage. According to Margo it <u>could</u> be done on the big stage, but about a month later than the Oct. 24 date in the little one. I think the time element is even more important than the stage, however. Lem refuses to design for the little (intimate) theatre, and as I explained to you before, would only design for the big one if he were given a contract assuring him the job for any subsequent Broadway and London production - which rules his participation out altogether.

Margo and I showed the script to Ruth Ford, the actress, and she has actually duplicated Margo's enthusiasm for it. She will probably play Matilda. I wonder if you know her or her work. Her Broadway experience was with Orson Welles and she has played in 22 movies, but never gotten a real break out here, her featured parts being in Grade B films - I have seen her on the screen and thought her a very fine actress but had no idea how beautiful she was till I met her. She doesn't screen at all like herself. Margo and I both feel she has the right quality for Matilda, and her vitality and enthusiasm for the script may be of great value in putting it over. I have given her a script which she is showing to various people she thinks might be potential backers of a Broadway production - she has great charm and a world of contacts out here.

I wish the play were being done out here entirely independant of

Gilmore Brown and his rather snide organization. They have the same attitude as Lem Ayers, strictly one of personal advantage, and the delay in getting it started and the controversy over which theatre is due to this lordly and patronizing point of view. I think it best, however, to leave the whole thing in Margo's hands. It is her project, so to speak, and she has invested so much effort and feeling in it, that the less interference she is given the better. Such as Orson Welles.

Carl Benton Reid has read the play and says the Captain's part is highly suitable to him. He would like to play it, but like Ayers, he wants a contract assurance that he would have the part in a Broadway production. It remains to be seen if he will do it without that. Well, I see his point of view, for to do it well he would have to invest a lot of time and effort - naturally he wants some assurance.

In the next few weeks something entirely new may develop for the play, but in the meantime I think we may as well leave everything in Margo's hands - and Ruth's, on the promotion end of it.

As for "The Gentleman Caller", I have devised a new ending for it, considerably lighter, almost happy, and am having to re-write the earlier scenes to jive with it.

As for Metro, by the time my six months are up here, I hope that I will have been gripped by some really <u>big</u> theme for a long play, one deserving entire devotion - In which case, I would retire to Mexico and live on those savings until it is finished.

Let's face it! - I can only write for <u>love</u>. Even then, not yet well-enough to set the world on fire. But all this effort, all this longing to create something of value - it will be thrown away, gone up the spout, nothing finally gained - If I don't adhere very strictly to the most honest writing, that I am capable of.

Happily I think that in the long run the most materially as well as spiritually satisfactory course for me to take is to follow my heart with absolute willfulness where work is concerned. If you lose on that kind of deal, and you very well <u>may</u>, you know it wasn't because you cheated or walked out on anything superior to yourself. - So endeth the lesson for today! Tomorrow's Text - "Repent or ye Shall Perish!"

Affectionately, 10

[Gilmor Brown directed the Pasadena Playhouse from its founding in 1917 until his death in 1960. With five performance areas, a School of the Theatre, and several thousand subscribers, it was a preëminent community theatre when it produced TW's work in the 1940s. The main stage seated 800, the Playbox, an experimental theatre, fifty. Bankruptcy forced the closing of the Playhouse in 1970.

Ruth Ford had both theatrical and film credits when TW met the fellow Mississippian and sister of the surrealist poet Charles Henri Ford. Her friendship with William Faulkner, also toiling in Hollywood at this time, would lead to the role of Temple Drake in the dramatic adaptation of *Requiem for a Nun* (1959).

The "almost happy" new ending may be one in which Laura and her gentleman caller are pointed toward love and Amanda apologizes to Tom for her "scolding tongue" as she helps him to pack: "And when you've found whatever it is you're after - Then come home and I'll be waiting for you - no matter how long!" ("The Gentleman Caller" {A Gentle Comedy}, n.d., HRC). In other dramatic, narrative, and film versions, Rose/Laura is invariably deserted by her gentleman caller and her brother, Tom, secretly leaves the family.

Penned above the letterhead is the notation: "The enclosed check anticipates pay-day but will be covered by the time you get it."]

284. To Audrey Wood

SH: Metro-Goldwyn-Mayer Pictures
Culver City, California
[August 9, 1943]
[TLS, 2 pp. HRC]

Dear Audrey:

The lion is showing his claws! Tennessee is not cowering in a corner, but he is considerably confused and taken aback.

I have just received a note informing me that I am to be laid off for six weeks without pay because there is no present assignment for me. This came up without any warning. The lay-off starts today - Monday. I have no copy of my contract but I assume the action is legal or they wouldn't take it.

As you know, I was taken off the Lana Turner horror-play when Lillie Messenger talked to Berman and told him I was not happy about it. Since then I have had only one contact with officialdom here, which was an interview with Arthur Freed. He seemed quite sympathetic, and it was agreed that I would try to work out a story-outline on Billy The Kid as a sort of folk-opera. This I have been doing somewhat desultorily for the past couple of weeks, waiting for Lem Ayers who has an equal interest in the material to have time to confer with me about it and give me his suggestions. As you know, I have had plenty of my own work to occupy my time here, and felt that I was very gainfully employed from any reasonable point of view.

The Scenario department, however, says the tentative Billy The Kid idea does not constitute an actual assignment. And just now a very curt young man has entered my office, without even knocking, to inform me that I should move my stuff out as I could not hold this office during the lay-off - which is extremely inconvenient because of the large store of Mss. books, Etc. that I have here. I shall have to give up my Santa Monica apartment, as I will have one week's pay to live on during the lay-off period and could not afford to keep that place.

This puts quite a dent in our savings plan, doesn't it? As well as our Amour Propre!

I have just now talked to Lillie Messenger about the situation and have made an appointment with Fadiman, Story head, for tomorrow.

Where I shall go during this period I am not sure yet. I may take a little trip, Frisco or some place, and will use the completely free time advantageously to get this work of my own out of the way.

I have already mailed Dramatists Guild fifteen dollars on my debt to them and have promised them the remainder, which I will send as soon as I get back on the pay-roll here. The bill they sent you does not acknowledge the fifteen I paid them - you might call them about that, as the bill is the same amount as originally presented to me here, before my remittance.

I will have a heart-to-heart talk with Lem Ayers, assuming that he has a heart! One is never quite sure of that organ in other people around here, and perhaps it is vanity to be sure of it in myself.

Don't be excessively troubled by the situation here. I will try to be properly penitent for my natural waywardness and act more like a Hollywood writer the rest of the time here.

McConnell and Margo have both written you, I think, about the Cleveland and National Theatre Conference plans, which sound good to me.

Have a nice vacation!

Affectionately, Tennessee

[With Audrey Wood on "vacation," William Liebling (Wood's partner and husband) probably offered first condolences upon learning of TW's "lay-off," to which he replied: "Don't worry about my Russian moods. They come and go. At times I am Slavic and other times Chinese. My mother was frightened by the Moscow Art Theatre and Pearl Buck" (August 20, 1943, HRC).

The National Theatre Conference was an association of non-profit community and academic theatres. Recently the group had sponsored national release of William Saroyan's play *Jim Dandy* (1941) and Maxwell Anderson's *The Eve of St. Mark* (1942).]

285. To Frederic McConnell

SH: Metro-Goldwyn-Mayer Pictures
Culver City, California
Aug 10, 1943
[TLS, 2 pp. Cleveland Play House Collection]

Dear Mr. McConnell:

Margo Jones showed me last night your letter, for which I say ALLELUIA!

About a national release of YOU TOUCHED ME! - as far as I am concerned the answer is not yes - but YES YES YES!

The only reason all of my plays aren't done all over the country is because nobody all over the country has asked for them. I'm not a New York character and God knows I'm not a Hollywood character. I hail from the South and the middle-west, and while I won't say my out-look is cosmic, it is certainly country wide! - With all its faults in mind, I feel that YOU TOUCHED ME! has something affirmative to say to people all over the country, wherever your conference reaches, and I would like them to hear it.

Now about Margo -

Margo and I have never signed any kind of papers with each other. It's just an affair of the heart (and I don't mean body!) She burst onto me last winter, which was really the winter of my discontent - I was running elevators and ushering in theatres while completing this play - with all her warmth, energy, and enthusiasm - she gave me a new lease on life. This was before she saw this particular script. When she did see it, she fell in love with it, head over heels, as only Margo can - do you know her? Well, I think any good play is polygamous, it ought to have lots of affairs, go to bed with dozens of people every night of the world! But this particular play's virginity - I think it belongs to Margo! - Don't you? - Because she gave herself to it so quickly and completely, and has worked her heart out promoting its production. - Pasadena means nothing to me, frankly, but Margo means everything!

So I feel that Margo <u>ought</u> to do the first production, whenever or <u>where</u> ever that is. I would love for it to be at Cleveland, because I know through Audrey Wood and many other people what a fine creative theatre you have there. - But do let's give little Margo the first crack at it! - There or anywhere.

Many many thanks for your letter, and all it means to me!

> Cordially, T.W.
> Tennessee Williams

[During Frederic McConnell's tenure as director (1921-1958), the Cleveland Play House staged more than 600 productions, including 40 American premières and 150 revivals. On July 31, 1943, Margo Jones had written to ask McConnell (1890-1968) for a fellowship—he chaired the fellowship project of the National Theatre Conference—so that she could take leave from the University of Texas and direct *You Touched Me!* at the Pasadena Playhouse. She also recommended that the Conference nationally release the play, which McConnell apparently seconded and TW heartily endorsed. In later correspondence McConnell informed TW that he himself hoped to direct *You Touched Me!* at Cleveland and only grudgingly agreed that the play "belongs to Margo": "Not because she is by any means the most competent person to do it but out of sentimental loyalty and justice to her" (August 14, 1943, Cleveland Play House Collection).

In late-August Wood cautioned TW not to sign "any kind of contract that may be submitted to you by the National Theatre Conference, the Pasadena Playhouse, the Cleveland Playhouse, or Margo Jones, personally" (August 30, 1943, HRC) for production rights to *You Touched Me!* She knew her client's impulsiveness and did not wish to repeat the contractual fiasco of *Battle of Angels*.]

286. To Edwina Dakin Williams

[1647 Ocean Avenue
Santa Monica, California]
August 24, 1943
[TLS, 1 p. HTC]

Dear Mother:

During my lay-off I've been busier even than usual as Goldwyn Studios phoned me they needed a vehicle for Teresa Wright and wanted me to submit any suitable material. I thought of Spring Storm, and so I wired for it, and prepared a film story treatment which has kept me busy. I turned it in a couple of days ago. If sold out-right it would mean a good deal of money, anywhere from five to twenty-five thousand, but I won't look for that till it happens. As a stage play, I think it was not very good, so I have nothing to lose. The nice thing about it is that anything written during my lay-off period is my own property, not Metro's. So they will have no claim on the script.

I've got my rent paid and still have about sixty dollars from the last pay-check to last me till I go back on salary, not later than Sept. 24th. If I run short of money I will have Audrey send me a little from my N.Y. savings account. I am sorry this interferes with my contributions to the fund in St. Louis. I will try to make up for it later.

Of course I am shocked by what you've been going through in Saint Louis. I think you should hire a maid, even at a higher wage, and hope I can soon help out. Have you had the operation on your nose? You mustn't delay about that.

Margo Jones is leaving for Cleveland, Ohio. She is going to produce the new play there and then in Pasadena. And as you can see from the enclosed letter, arrangements may be made for productions in other cities. This ought to result in transference to Broadway - that's what we're hoping for.

Don't worry about me not liking commercial writing. I feel about it the same way that you would about being paid to give up Christianity and go to the synagogue instead of Saint Michael's. However this doesn't mean I won't make a living out of writing, it might mean the opposite.

I have to see Margo off on the train, so must hurry.

With much love to you all, Tom.

Also enclosing a note from the poetry man.

[TW had probably last considered *Spring Storm* in April 1941, when Jane Garrett Carter expressed interest in a St. Louis production (Civic Theatre) of the play.

Family legend has it that Edwina's "nose" was bruised when Cornelius slammed a door in her face. In earlier correspondence she informed TW that she would "have it attended to soon and your father will pay for it. I'm simply going to have the bill sent to him after it's done" (June 22, 1943, HRC).

Proximity to New York reviewers and producers weighed heavily no doubt in the decision to open *You Touched Me!* in Cleveland rather than Pasadena. Margo Jones left California in late-August with plans to visit her family in Texas before reaching Cleveland on September 13. TW reported to Donald Windham that she had "wangled" a fellowship from the National Theatre Conference to direct both the Cleveland and a later Pasadena production. "The girl is rather monumental in force of character" (qtd. in *Windham*, p. 101), an awed and somewhat relieved TW observed after her departure.

James Laughlin, "the poetry man," had recently informed TW of poems selected for *Five Young American Poets*.]

287. To Audrey Wood

1647 Ocean Ave.
Santa Monica [California]
Sept. 14, 1943
[TLS, 2 pp. HRC]

Dear Audrey:

Laughlin has written me that he has received the verse play from you and will get it into the anthology NEW DIRECTION 1943. This year-book represents the best creative writing, internationally famous names going into it such as Thomas Mann and Jules Romain, all the advance guard people, and so I was terribly anxious to get the little play in for its prestige value. A certain percentage of sales or an out-right anthology fee goes to the individual contributors, I believe, and Laughlin will give you some statement about that if you ask him. I presume it is made on publication. As I think you know, Laughlin is also bringing out 40 pages of my verse in his YOUNG AMERICAN POETS, for which he has recently sent me a twenty-five dollar advance. Your two-fifty may be deducted from my next check to you. Laughlin is a rara avis, a very rich boy with a good heart and ready sympathy. He seems to be particularly interested in my work right now and will be a good friend to keep as his publishing house, New Directions, specializes in work that doesn't fit into other usual places, in other words - creative material. We need somebody like him in case we turn out something now and then worth printing.

McConnell writes me today about his arrangement with you, which I think is very good. I think I will be able to arrange with Metro to spend a couple of days in Cleveland to see the show and would like that visit to coincide with the presence of any N.Y. people who may get down to see it. McConnell writes that he thinks considerable cutting is needed to tighten up the show and strengthen Matilda. I have asked him to send me the cut or altered copy well in advance of production so I can approve it or do some work of my own. I agreed pretty much with what he felt was wrong with it.

Today Case returned the script I submitted for Teresa Wright, saying that Duggan wanted it but couldn't sell it to Goldwyn. She suggested I make some changes and return it to her for submission to other studios. I have just now done this, building up what I think is the best selling-point. Will suggest to Bertha that she have copies typed up and send you one, as I think it makes a pretty good film story. Now I haven't any agent's agreement with Bertha and don't want one covering more than this script as that would mean splitting all fees between you and her which I think unfair to you. If this script is sold at one of the studios, could you and Bertha make an arrangement affecting that deal alone? I don't need Bertha or want her for anything but this - with all due respect.

I have had a good rest from the studio. Lately a distant relative of mine Jane (Lanier Brotherton) Lawrence who had the ingenue lead in 'Oklahoma' has been visiting me with her fiance. She is a wonderful girl and will probably make some pretty big pictures out here with Columbia. Both I and the fiance were broke for a while and Jane supported us both with the most cavalier attitude - now I have your check and Tony a job so everything is okay. I presume I go back to the studio next week.

Today I received a manuscript I wish I could show you. It's from somebody called B. Eden in Dallas Texas - how she got my name I don't know but she has sent me a script complete with magazine illustrations which she says look like the characters in the story and ten lullabies which have some obscure connection with it. There is a lullabye for each of the allied nations and she thinks it would be nice to also have one for the enemy nations, Japs, Germans, and Italians. Only one lullabye nation is not represented, the Jewish and on the page for that she makes the following note:

(This will kill you!)

"Jewish Lullaby, yet to be obtained."

"I should rather like Sam Goldwyn, that man of great vision and fore-thought, to select in his own word and air, the Lullaby for this number."

Incidentally, the script was addressed to me in care of Sam Goldwyn at Metro-Goldwyn-Mayer!

Where magazine advertisement sections have failed to provide her with the right illustrations, she has turned undaunted to her own hand and paint-box - Also beneath the illustrations she gives the exact height and weight of the characters, the hero being 6' 2½" inches and weighing 192 pounds, hair coal-black and slightly waved.

Commenting on these illustrations, she says, 'Diligently I searched and I have found, as all agree, a very close resemblance to the main characters.' Concerning the heroine's picture, however, she apologizes, 'I have never seen her in this shade of red. If you will please change the skirt to a green and tan plaid-like, and the shirt to a tannish affair, it will be a bit more appropos.'

Concerning another female character - 'Here is a true prototype copy of Dolores. Her very black hair is long and curled and a blue ribband always is pinned at a vantage point. Her eyes are very black and as is the wont of the invalid-woman, she generally wears a long, clinging white or light-blue silken something. She is fair-skinned to the dangerous point. I give you Dolores!'

Here is 'The Primeval Lullaby' which seems to be in the same genre as my 'O Tahki Sahn'.

'Hi - i - ri - i - kil - Ri-eeek!

Repeat.

Oo - o - roo - rrr - uffff - ooo!'

Repeat first two lines. This is accompanied by hand-drawn study of a ghastly nude female figure clutching a baby that has a watermelon head and a chicken body, as near as I can make out!

Shall I give this Texas woman your name and address?

Affectionately, Tennessee

[TW's poetry and his verse play "The Purification" were not published until 1944, an early instance of delay and apparent disorder in James Laughlin's handling of manuscripts.

Frederic McConnell had recently informed TW that *You Touched Me!* "is much too long and in many cases repetitious. . . . Everybody who has read it here feels very strongly that Matilda must be made more credible and sympathetic and much less flabby in order to establish a sounder conflict in the first place and to justify Hadrian's struggle and desire." He added that contractual "terms" made with Audrey Wood were "simple enough. Royalties are to be waived, but we are assigning two hundred dollars to her to be used as you and she see fit" (September 10, 1943, Cleveland Play House Collection). The play would have its première on October 13 and run until the end of the month.

The film "script" that Bertha Case returned was *Spring Storm*. Drafted and revised in 1937-1938, and first performed in 1999, the play fared no better in Hollywood than it had in playwriting classes at the University of Iowa (see letter #83). Case, a past employee of Liebling-Wood, had joined the A.S. Lyons Agency in Hollywood.

Jane Lawrence and Anthony Smith were married shortly after arriving on the coast, with TW as their witness. Lawrence played the featured role of Gertie Cummings in *Oklahoma!* and was under contract to Columbia Pictures. TW met Tony, later a distinguished architect and sculptor, in New York ca. 1942. The three remained close friends.

B. Eden, of Dallas, Texas, had sent TW a story entitled "Fear." When he did not respond, she wrote, "Has something happened, or are we here in Texas, the 'slow south-west,' too fast?" (October 1, 1943, HRC).]

288. To Audrey Wood

[1647 Ocean Avenue
Santa Monica, California]
[ca. September 28, 1943]
[TLS, 1 p. HRC]

Dear Audrey:

Mary Hunter wrote me to find out exactly what commitments had been made regarding the play and I told her that legally none existed but that I felt it morally owing to Margo not to release the play to anybody until about a week had elapsed after her productions so that she would be given every fair chance to reap the reward of bringing it into Broadway herself. Now I've never made this commitment to Margo even verbally but have kept it in my own mind as the fair thing to do in view of her extravagant efforts and devotion. I mentioned it to Mary because she wanted some direct answer about the play's availability and as you know I have a very deep regard for Mary's ability, in fact I would esteem her a director probably better than Margo.

I am planning to attend one or two performances, opening, at the Cleveland show. I think a lot remains to be done on the script and I want to see and approve the changes that McConnell is making and the play in performance. I will need round-trip fare out of McConnell's money for that purpose. I assumed that Donald would already know of the money, and that in any case it would be better not to conceal anything from him and provoke his suspicions. So I wrote him that funds had been allocated for traveling expenses but that I was afraid it would take nearly all of it to get me to and from Cleveland which I knew he would agree was more important than getting him there. I said if anything is left over he could probably use it. I feel that Windham will be reasonable about this, although we both know he is not a young man exceptionally prone to overlook his own advantage.

I am back on the pay-roll at Metro but still at home. I get my first check Wednesday. I owe you all two weeks commission from this check, to cover also the last check before the lay-off. I will ask them directly or through Bertha to lay me off for about five days while I cover the Cleveland try-out. I don't suppose there'll be any objection.

Don't worry about me making any commitments without you - never! You're a wonderful girl and I never forget it.

Yours, 10

[Audrey Wood had learned from Mary Hunter that Margo Jones held an option on *You Touched Me!* which ended after the first week of its Cleveland run. "Is this actually true?" she asked in an intervening letter, and again implored TW not to "make any commitments at all on your work without consulting me since you know full well that I constantly have your interests at heart and that I know much more about all business matters than you want to know" (September 23, 1943, HRC).

TW's preference for Hunter had not changed since early-July, when he informed Donald Windham that she has "the inside track" on a New York production of *You Touched Me!* Her credits and contacts, and her intelligence, he thought, exceeded "the energy" (qtd. in *Windham*, p. 84) of Jones.

In recent correspondence Wood asked TW not to inform Windham of the $200 assignment by Frederic McConnell, which she hoped to use for "our joint expenses re covering this play" (September 23, 1943, HRC). TW, however, had already told Windham of the expense money and later urged him to request payment from Wood (see *Windham*, pp. 107, 109). Eventually she reported paying $30 to cover his "expenses to Cleveland" (letter to TW, November 20, 1943, HRC).]

289. To Margaret "Margo" Jones

[1647 Ocean Avenue
Santa Monica, California]
8/29/43
[TLS w/ autograph postscript, 2 pp. HRC]

Dear Margo:

I had a feeling before you left here that the Cleveland deal was not going to be a happy one for you, that it would be, as you say, bloody difficult because it was already apparent to me that this man McConnell was a pretty high-handed Joe. Well, honey, the next best thing to being there with you and fighting it out in the same fox-hole is feeling the way I do this morning, almost as aware of your feelings as if I'd been through it all myself. Well, I have been through a good deal of that sort of thing with people like Piscator, Etc. Win, lose, or draw, you know my faith and affection are yours!

I hope you understand how I couldn't pitch another long speech into that spot without understanding its purpose. When things go badly we are inclined to clutch at straws and that only makes it worse. I wrote speeches like crazy in Boston while they were slashing and twisting around the script and all that resulted was the destruction of the good qualities already present and the substitution of schmalz. When a play has gone through as many rewritings and as much consideration as 'You Touched Me' it is extremely unlikely that anything is left out that ought to go in.

I must say to you confidentially that I do not at all like nor countenance the fact that McConnell made radical cuts and changes in the script, apparently affecting even the story-line, without consulting me about them at all. Writing and production are two such different departments, but producers never seem to realize this! - I got a brief letter from McConnell this morning in which the croak of the raven was only thinly disguised, but he said that you and he were working nicely together and in agreement about everything. How true is this?

I am glad you indicated, and he also, that the outlook was not very bright. I prefer to know such things and be prepared for them. Under the circumstances, if I were you I would not issue any more publicity about the play than necessary and unless things appear much more favorable than your letter indicates I think it would be better to concentrate on selling the play in Pasadena after I have seen it and done what I can to rectify the script. I have great faith in what Ruth and Henry Morgan and maybe Agnes Moorhead will do for the play here, and also in the happier job you would have working by yourself.

I will go downtown today to make my train reservations on whatever date is necessary to get me there opening night. Let's you and me just run away from them all, with maybe one or two of sworn allegiance, and get good and roaring drunk, I mean really piss-eyed, and wash the slate clean with whatever laughter and tears are suitable to the occasion, then catch a train back here the following day and start all over again! Anyway things work out, dismally or gorgeously, you are my Girl Friday, or I am your boy Monday. I don't know the rebel yell, but a reasonable facsimile will be served in the patio!

With all faith and love, 10

About New York: if any producer wants to bring the play in there on the strength of a Cleveland production, you may be damned sure I'll put up all the fight I can for you as the director. Honey, I'm going to be in a peculiar position the middle of November. I will almost undoubtedly be let out of MGM, to all intents and purposes except the salary going on, I'm out of there now. I have a long fight ahead of me as a writer and if this play doesn't do anything I will be in a mighty bad spot again. Naturally, this being so, I could not afford to turn down a New York production if, in spite of all arguments and cajolery and a determined bluff, the manager persisted in demanding a New York director. Audrey wouldn't let me do that even if you and I thought it the right thing to do. Survival, literal survival, is going to be as much of a problem, and maybe more, as it has ever been in the past. Now if the play turns out much better than it now looks, our hands will be a lot stronger and we'll be in a far better position to name the terms to any possible buyer. So let's cross that river first and don't ever doubt my intention of standing by you as far as we can possibly go!

P.S. better not use the article I sent you if things continue to go badly. It would look silly.

[Margo Jones (1911-1955), the so-called "Texas Tornado," directed community theatre in Houston before taking a visiting position at the University of Texas in 1942. Her tenure at Cleveland was "bloody difficult" from the beginning, as she informed TW in an intervening letter. Before Jones arrived in Cleveland, McConnell advised her by telegram that he had cut twenty-five pages from *You Touched Me!*— a warning that he would not be a passive producer. In earlier correspondence with TW, in which "the croak of the raven" was detected by the apprehensive playwright, McConnell claimed that he and Jones were "working closely together and are in agreement about everything" (September 24, 1943, Cleveland Play House Collection).

TW had recently warned Jones not to request additions to *You Touched Me!*: "The play is already over-loaded with speeches plugging the theme." At issue was an expanded curtain speech for Hadrian in Act Three after he wins Matilda's love. Such moments, TW claimed, needed "lightness and grace" (postmarked September 24, 1943, HRC) rather than declamation.

The all-star cast that TW envisioned for the Pasadena production of *You Touched Me!* included Ruth Ford, Agnes Moorehead, Henry Morgan, and Carl Benton Reid.

This letter, misdated by TW, is postmarked September 29, 1943. Jones did not arrive in Cleveland until mid-September 1943.]

290. To Frederic McConnell

[1647 Ocean Avenue
Santa Monica, California]
Oct. 4, 1943
[TLS, 2 pp. Cleveland Play House Collection]

Dear Frederic McConnell:

Or Mac, as they seem to call you. The bird of ill-omen was flapping his wings between the lines of your letter! This was a devilishly hard play to write, such a delicate balance had to be struck between the serious and the light elements. It could easily have been a very heavy drama in the Strindberg tradition, but I think it was wise to leaven the dough with comedy as I did, for otherwise even our brave little theatres wouldn't have touched it. So I put in comedy, not of the contemporary smart-crack kind but in the robust Elizabethan manner. Altogether it is a play of our times, but not in our manner. I am sure that it requires for production an approach and technique all its own and that a bloody struggle was inevitable to find the right key for it. I understand that last act is your main trouble. It should be kept in mind that the melodramatic acts of Emmie in this act are those of an hysterical spinster, nothing more. Her locking of Matilda and Hadrian in the bedroom, separately, are a comical allusion to such persons' faith in the locked door. Locks and keys, flimsy wooden panels, hedges and vines are the spiritual paraphernalia of such people - as I have just now written Margo - it is what they think in terms of. I sincerely believe that nobody does anything in this play that is not thoroughly credible and in keeping with the character. Granted Emmie's actions are foolish - but if presented as they are meant to be, hysterical spinsterish reaction to the big problems of life, a childish inability to face facts and deal with them in an adult way - they need to present no strain on credulity nor be terribly hard to play. Now I feel it would be definitely better to give the play a fair chance the way it is written rather than make hasty changes which cannot be given the necessary consideration. Surely there is nothing appalling dangerous in this play! I have written plays that were potential TNT but this isn't one of them. It won't take the roof off your theatre one way or the other, all it requires is a workmanlike performance to be at least - shall we say - clean entertainment. The use of comedy keeps it on a wholesome level - the devices may be apparent and not as dignified as the matter of the play. But there is the magic of the theatre to compensate for this. We younger playwrights lean too heavily on this magic, but we need it and it ought to be placed more generously at our disposal than at that of the older commercial playwrights. Sometimes the illusion, the <u>trompe d'oeil</u>, which is what I mean by theatre magic, is justified by the essential matter of the play, but in many instances I've seen there was no such justification. Win, lose, or draw I think we are all agreed that a play advocating a grave and aggresive approach to a new solution of affairs in the world is eminently worth our pain and trouble to put on. I feel it was worth mine to write it.

(This is supposed to be my little inspirational message for the day. I hope it hasn't had the opposite effect - that would be ironical!)

I am sure you are looking forward to the day as I am when the present octupus has been cut loose from the theatre. It belongs in the hands of the people and their artists but now like the radio and the screen it is all but universally controlled by the entrepreneurs. No wonder the pure ideal is so hard to find, relegated usually to the dustiest corner of the prop room!

I want to get there for opening night and will try to come with the many hands and arms of Shiva to spread comfort and faith among all! I believe Audrey Wood and perhaps Donald Windham will come from New York. I wish that Frieda Lawrence could see it but I am afraid she is still in Taos.

Cordially, 10. Wms.

[The "bird of ill-omen" in Frederic McConnell's recent letter brought news that *You Touched Me!* was "being altered from day to day" in rehearsal and thus a "completed script" (September 24, 1943, Cleveland Play House Collection) could not be sent for approval. TW was reminded no doubt of *Battle of Angels*, whose script was revised incessantly and its cast divided by politics. TW's "inspirational message" was probably honed by correspondence of Margo Jones cited in letter #291. It is unclear whether TW is addressing fears that the sexual farce of Act Three may be too "robust" for Cleveland, or that it is too contrived to be staged effectively—or perhaps both.

Reference to the Hindu god Shiva suggests that if Christopher Isherwood had failed to save TW from buying a "junky" scooter, he had at least widened his range of allusion.]

291. To Margaret "Margo" Jones

[1647 Ocean Avenue
Santa Monica, California]
[ca. October 4, 1943]
[TLS w/ autograph marginalia, 1 p. HRC]

Margo dear:

Your long letter just received and read over my breakfast coffee. It is sort of heart-breaking, I mean what you have been through. It is lucky I wasn't there for I just wouldn't have had the patience you have had. Nobody is as savagely critical of my work as I am, and yet - the kind of negative reactions you describe are intolerable to me, they just destroy me. They don't come from an honest desire to help or improve but just an inert mass of antagonism and ego, conscientous againsters. It takes so much faith to write a play, I don't see how you can put one on without it. I don't see how you get your actors to give anything after all they've gone through. No, I couldn't have stood it. I would have raged and stormed and torn the script to pieces! - You have never seen me in one of my rare fits of insanity. Once in Saint Louis, when <u>Fugitive Kind</u> was put on, that happened. The whole play was built around a big window overlooking the city - I was out of town and when I arrived at the dress-rehearsal I found my window was a little transom at the top of the back wall! I fled from the theatre and walked along the street, literally tearing the script to little pieces and scattering it on the sidewalk.

Regardless of what I see in Cleveland, I will promise not to make a public exhibition of my feelings, that is, to anyone but you.

I have just written McConnell and hope I've given him more faith in the last act. Naturally I know the devices are a little insubstantial. But I do honestly and sincerely believe none of them are incredible. Emmie's actions are just about what an hysterical spinster would do. They are foolish but perfectly in character. They're not supposed to be regarded as anything but foolish and hysterical acts of a woman not adult enough to solve the big problems of life with anything but locked doors and the Constable. I will study that act hard when I see it and try to figure out some more angles.

I will probably have to travel by coach to Cleveland but will time my departure so I can get a good sleep before the opening performance. Right now I've got a dreadful cough and a fever, but unless I get very much worse, I will make the trip. I am sure glad you prepared me for the situation there. All I can say now is Keep up the good fight. - Gilmore phoned me yesterday. A Lt. Norvelle wanted to know if the play was available for NTC and Gilmor wished me to write him. The old boy also gave me two tickets to Othello which I saw last night. Carradine played Iago - but unbelievably bad! Onslow Stevens was superb as Othello and that last act revived my faith in poetic tragedy - God, what drama! David says he can't write the article till you send him some facts. Do you want him to do this? - For the first time Gilmor spoke real sweetly of the play last night.

So many people don't like my work! It's a wonder to me that I am even the 'Best Known of the Unknown Playwrights'.

Love, 10.

[TW wrote to Lt. Lee Norvelle, U.S. Naval Reserve, and expressed continuing interest in a National Theatre Conference release of *You Touched Me!* He warned that the play was neither "easy" to stage nor universally admired, but "it has a definite message for our time" and "is worth the trouble" (October 4, 1943, HRC).

Onslow Stevens would play Captain Rockley in the Pasadena production of *You Touched Me!* He replaced Carl Benton Reid, whose earlier association with the Cleveland Play House led him to originate the comic role.

The "thick, juicy slab of a summer" (qtd. in *Windham*, p. 103) came to an end amid complaints of illness, fatigue, and lack of creative interest: "With virtually no will and little enough consciousness I drift from one day to another, with energy that ebbs and flows within a shallow estuary. For quite a while I have had the same thought or feeling every night, that the shroud is already cut, that this period is sort of a final temporizing" (*Journal*, October 3, 1943).

Penned at the head of this letter is the notation: "Here is a tiny change - Emmie: You've run your Jolly Roger on the rocks! (instead of pirate vessel)"]

292. To Audrey Wood

[1647 Ocean Avenue
Santa Monica, California]
10/21/43
[TLS, 2 pp. HRC]

Dear Audrey:

Just got your letter and am stopping mid-way in story about a one-armed killer condemned to the chair to write you.

I am going to give you some fairly forthright information which I hope
you are spiritually prepared for as I was. You know me, how I drift through
the world and nothing that happens to me makes much difference except
the odd little world that I make on paper! - Well, Metro has phoned that
my option will not be renewed. "Things have not worked out as well as we
expected." I felt no kind of emotion, I merely thought, I wonder how dear
little Audrey will feel about this? If you feel all right about it, then I do!
After the Lana Turner thing petered out they paid me no more attention,
seemed to forget I was there. So I went on with my own creations, which
are two plays that I ricochet between and a group of stories I'm preparing
for Laughlin to maybe publish. Incidentally, I do want you to have three or
four of my best stories <u>typed up</u> right away and sent to me to add to this
collection. Something very, very good may come of it, as Laughlin regards
me as you and Margo with an affectionate blindness. The ones I want are
The Vine, The Red Part of A Flag, In Memory of an Aristocrat, Miss Rose
and the Grocery Clerk, The Lost Girl, A Tale of Two Writers. Keep copies
and send me carbons. And <u>bill</u> me for it.

About You Touched Me. I gave it up as a lost cause when I read
Margo's last letter five hours before I was to catch the train. I know the
impossibility of creating anything without an almost fanatical faith in what
you are doing - when I heard the circumstances surrounding the production I knew that nothing but lifeless exercises upon the stage could come
from it, and that too much of my dearest feelings and thoughts were bed-
ded in that awkward little play for me to enjoy looking at such a mutila-
tion. Incidentally I was never shown a revised copy and had no idea that
all the third act complications had been neatly removed and nothing put in
their place. How could it or did it even pass muster as a three-act play? The
reviews are acts of God under these circumstances and I am religiously
moved. I have made no objection to McConnell, nor shall I. But I am working out a new third act. I share his distrust of the dog and the door business
in the original script and am trying to have a real dramatic scene without
their use. But what he concocted was altogether without dramatic substance
as I look at it. (Margo has shown me the cuts.)

My plans - I find that I have accumulated a nice little savings account
at this end of the line, too. About three hundred. And with that and the
N.Y. account I can live for about six months in some frugal manner in some

remote place like New Mexico or Old, finish up one of the two plays and only emerge when the trumpet is blown somewhere. There is a curious sort of spiritual death-ray that is projected about the halls of Hollywood. I sensed it first in the writers I met out here. All spiritual Zombies it seemed to me. Don't think I am about to take the veil or robes of any holy order, but I do feel that I must grow as a personality, achieve some balance and synthesis as an individual in order to give anything. I was frightened by the emotional deadness of these people, all superior craftsmen and many with really fine talents, but seeming all withered inside - the kiss of Lana Turner? I don't know! But it is alarming. - This is all very Russian and the wine of sour grapes! - But I _am_ looking for something.

Yes, please deposit a share of the transportation money in my Ny. account but if necessary pay Windham his round-trip Cleveland fare out of it, too. My coach fare round-trip would have been Ninety-three dollars and I am willing for you to deduct Donnie's fare from that amount. In my dealings with Windham I want to bend over backwards in absolute scrupulousness because the situation is so fraught with possible resentments. Windham's chi-chi crowd in N.Y. are merciless gossips and I don't want them saying that poor little Donnie was robbed by that wolfish Mr. Williams! Ironical, huh? Donnie is only the victim of circumstances, mostly happy ones!

I believe my option expires in early Nov. and till then I will add my savings to the account at this end as I will need quite a bit to travel and get settled before I start drawing on what you have in N.Y. and I loathe writing letters for money.

I am glad you still believe in "You Touched Me". So do I. It only needs intelligent handling and really home-cooked actors.

My love to you all, Tennessee

In your opinion is it dangerous of me to concentrate on comedy in the last act, all but the final love-scene between Hadrian & Matilda? I feel the ideas of the play are all stated by the end of Act Two.

[The story in progress is "One Arm" (1948).

For nearly a month (see journal entry for September 30, 1943), TW suppressed the news that MGM would not renew his option. His hand was forced when

Audrey Wood wrote on October 16 to say that Lillie Messinger, of MGM, would soon visit New York and she planned "to talk to her primarily about you" (October 16, 1943, HRC).

The two plays upon which TW worked alternately may be those identified in letter #293 as "The Gentleman Caller" and "The Columns of Revelry." None of the stories cited for retyping would appear in TW's first collection, *One Arm and Other Stories*, issued by New Directions in 1948.

The Cleveland reviews of *You Touched Me!* were generally positive. William F. McDermott "put it down as one of the best of untried dramas the Play House has presented. It has one paramount and indispensable theatrical value—it holds your interest and it earns your respect." He also paid tribute to the "exceptional sensitiveness and understanding" (*Cleveland Plain Dealer*, October 14, 1943) of Margo Jones's direction. In a coincident letter to Frederic McConnell, TW was politic but expressed dismay over the radical cutting of Act Three, which he had rewritten and promised to mail "within the week" (October 21, 1943, Cleveland Play House Collection).

Wood attended the first two performances of *You Touched Me!* and was so "encouraged" that she sent "notices" (letter to TW, October 16, 1943, HRC) to a long list of prospective film and stage producers. In excusing his absence, TW had advised Wood that "gloomy reports" from Jones and travel "circumstances too costly" (telegram, October 12, 1943, HRC) would keep him on the coast.]

293. To Frederic McConnell

> [1647 Ocean Avenue
> Santa Monica, California]
> November 15, 1943
> [TLS w/ autograph marginalia, 1 p.
> Cleveland Play House Collection]

Dear Mr. McConnell:

I was happy to get your letter and hear that the results of the play are not so disappointing to you. I know that you undertook the production against the advice of others in the company, and that it was also embarassing and difficult to have another director, even Margo. Believe me, I am capable of vicarious experience and have a clear idea of the position you were in. As I have told you, I would have preferred for Margo to stay here and concentrate on the Pasadena production. But she had done so much to promote the play, locally and abroad, and her heart was involved in it so deeply that I could not conscientously stand in her way, though I felt instinctively that it was unwise. Of course we have talked it over thoroughly and I can assure you that there is no bitterness about the differences of opinion. They were inevitable. Being a true woman, Margo is ruled more by the heart than the head and it was harder for her to see flaws in the play's construction than for you or I. Both of you were right. Only the play was wrong. If that is not contradictory!

Well, we are trying it again. I am doing almost as much cutting as you, although in a different way, as my cuts do not alter the story line quite as much as those in Cleveland but are more directed at eliminating the diffusion you mention. I am attending the rehearsals here and Margo is allowing me to take a hand in the direction. It is a lot of fun, I have never done it before. Margo and the cast are a little shocked by the way I throw things out of the script, but rehearsals reveal so much dead matter in it that I am appalled. I had re-written the God damn thing so many times - that is why it has all those repititions! And redundancies. I forgot that I had said things before. I was in and out of borrowed homes and temporary jobs and life was too confused for craftsmanship! Even if I were a craftsman.

Please do send me some pictures. I have none at all. And if you can get hold of a certain article - I believe it was in the editorial page of one of the papers - based on Hadrian's "Frontiers" speech - I would like to have that. Margo will not part with any of her momentos and that article is the one thing I most want.

I am glad you are still interested in my work. I am working on two things alternately, a quiet little picture of middle-class family life called "The Gentleman Caller" and a tragedy in verse called "The Columns of Revelry", neither the sort that the Shuberts would bet their shirts on. Then there is the new "Battle of Angels", which I regard as my best work. The Theatre Guild put on a first draft of this play in Boston, but the later version has never been tried. It is a tragedy, the theme is powerful but not as broadly or popularly appealing as "You Touched Me". However it is a richer and solider piece of drama.

My connection with Metro terminates this week, and my next move is still in the dark. Margo leaves for Texas the day after our Pasadena show opens and I will leave also for somewhere. We open the 29th.

Cordially, Tennessee.

[TW wrote in answer to Frederic McConnell's letter of November 9, in which he defended heavy cutting of *You Touched Me!*, admitted that the production had been "a little disturbed" toward the end when he replaced Margo Jones's direction, and closed with a curt invitation "to send me your next opus" (November 9, 1943; Cleveland Play House Collection).

Hadrian's "'Frontiers'" speech in Act One envisioned a post-war search for peace based upon daring new patterns of thought and action.

Penned at the head of this letter is the notation: "Moving - address c/o Margo at P. Playhouse."]

294. To Rosina Otte and Walter E. Dakin

[1647 Ocean Avenue
Santa Monica, California]
Nov. 15, 1943
[TLS w/ autograph postscript, 1 p. HTC]

Dear Grand and Grandfather:

I have been commuting between Santa Monica and Pasadena ever since the play rehearsals started there which has made me even worse than usual at correspondance. I think of you all every day even though I so rarely have the leisure to write. I should have moved to Pasadena but the town is so crowded with war-workers there was literally not one vacant room. The trip is two hours each way and my attendance at rehearsals is necessary as I am still revising the script. While it was pretty successful and attracted a good deal of favorable attention, the Cleveland production showed some weaknesses in the script which I have to patch up during the present production. I think it will come out a lot better. The producer in Cleveland cut thirty pages out of the last act, including one whole scene, without consulting me which made the last act rather inconclusive. Margo couldn't do anything to stop him without getting fired. However the affirmative spirit of the play was highly praised by everybody and passages were even quoted in the editorial sections of the Cleveland paper, one editor basing an article on "twelve great lines" from one of the speeches about the post-war world. Margo has the only copy of this but I am writing for another so I can send it to you. I am hoping the play will be sold to Broadway, but the interested producers are waiting to see what happens at Pasadena and get the final revised script following that try-out.

I have received a letter from Dakin at Fort Dix. He is certainly getting around. I am sure all this is very good for him, and it now looks as though the allies are in a position to end the war before he has much chance for participation. - Reassure Aunt Ella about Hollywood. Everybody here is too busy to get into mischief. Actually it is the quietest place I've lived. All the night-life stops at midnight, people stay at home more than they do in Saint Louis. I personally have too much to do and think about to be influenced by Hollywood society even if it had any dangerous charm.

My plans are not certain yet, and won't be for a couple of weeks. If I decide to return East, I will get through Saint Louis for a visit.

Dear love to you both, Tom

New address - c/o Margo Jones, Pasadena Playhouse - I will, or <u>may</u>, find a place there this week.

[The prospect of commuting from Hollywood to Pasadena helped to deprive *You Touched Me!* of its all-star cast, including Ruth Ford, who surmised that TW "'never forgave'" her the defection. "Hollywood people," he said at the time, were "all bitches and liars and degenerates in the true sense of the word" (qtd. in *Windham*, p. 112). Rehearsals continued with local players, Onslow Stevens the only film actor in the cast.

After training as a flight-controller, Dakin Williams was assigned to a unit in Philadelphia responsible for air defense of the Washington-New York corridor. On more than one occasion, he recalls, they sent the Roosevelts to the basement of the White House with false alarms.

TW's exchange of family news did not include Cornelius's business trip to Los Angeles in late-October. Of their "arduous meetings," TW wrote that his father appeared "very chastened and today we made talk alone for the first time in probably ten or fifteen years. A pathetic old man but capable of being a devil - " (*Journal*, October 26, 1943).]

295. To Audrey Wood

[c/o Jane Lawrence
1652 North Harvard
Hollywood, California]
11/30/43
[TLS, 1 p. HRC]

Dear Audrey:

Play opened last night and I am completely happy about it. It was a complete vindication of all the elements in the play that McConnell distrusted and cut out in Cleveland. In fact that eliminated portion of the play was what seemed to entertain the audience most thoroughly last evening. The production had great warmth and charm and held the audience all the way through, the comedy and love-scenes being greatly appreciated, the whole thing having a warmth, a lightness and a heart-touching reality which I had never guessed it could have. This is the first time anything of mine has been done to my own satisfaction so you know how happy I feel about it. Unfortunately no reviewers come to the playbox - that is an edict of the management. However we think - since it went off so well - it should have a press coverage and we will try to finagle some press people in for later performances. I am sure - as Margo says - that it was superior in every way - to the Cleveland production.

Mary Hunter has sent a check for typing up the revised scripts. I feel sure she will divide them with you. The changes are not radical from the one you now have. It is tightened up a great deal through cuts and re-arrangements of speeches but except for the elimination of one device - Emmie locking Matilda in her bedroom at the Act Three Scene One curtain - the story line has not been changed. One weakness is apparent, a certain abruptness in the resolution of the love-story, a sort of arbitrary change of character in Matilda at the end. I think that can be straightened out, and we are making certain little changes in the production here to give it more validity. However the comedy in the last scene and the touching curtain with the departure for church seem to successfully disguise the slieght-of-hand in the elopement so that the audience wasn't bothered by it.

James Laughlin is on the coast and attending the show tonight. Margo leaves in the morning. I cannot go back to Santa Monica as the Sheriff is after me there. I am being sued by the motor scooter company as I refused to pay them for the scooter after it proved a Jonah. I had signed an un-read contract that held me responsible for the entire sum even with scooter returned. The Sheriff has been seiging my Santa Monica apt. trying to serve papers on me but I have successfully evaded him so far. He hasn't tracked me to Pasadena yet. I intend to return at midnight, pack up and be out before daybreak. I understand that if he doesn't touch me with the papers I can escape the suit. I think I will leave in about a week for Saint Louis, have my teeth fixed up and maybe another eye operation, then decide on a new sanctuary. The Mexico deal is attractive as I had Mexico in mind as a place to go. I have a copy of the Purification which I will get off to you. Send the stories to me and I will edit them for Laughlin. The books, he says, are coming out in six or eight weeks. That is, the New Direction anthology and the poetry book.

Margo did a beautiful job on the show in everybody's opinion and I can't praise her work too highly. She has a vitality that is truly amazing and no script was ever given more loving attention. - Bertha Case and Dickinson did not show up at the opening. Maybe will later.

Best, 10.

[After the Pasadena opening on November 29, TW informed Donald Windham of studio interest in *You Touched Me!* and of Mary Hunter's renewed search for backing in New York (see *Windham*, p. 120).

TW was mortified when James Laughlin visited his apartment unannounced and presumably saw his photograph, requested in July, tossed carelessly on a table while Chekhov, Crane, and Porter hung serenely above the litter. Laughlin apparently enjoyed *You Touched Me!* but did not publish it.

To elude "the Sheriff" TW stayed with Jane Lawrence and Tony Smith in Hollywood. The tale of the motor scooter featured at least one serious accident and failure to continue payments after TW either abandoned or returned the "junky old machine" to the dealer.

The "Mexico deal" refers to a new film company sponsored by the director Dudley Murphy. He reportedly admired TW's work and had been encouraged by Audrey Wood to use her now unemployed client as a script writer. She also hoped to interest Murphy in producing "The Purification."

In the director's note Margo Jones repeated her praise of TW's "beautiful and important play" and editorialized upon the need for regional theatres (such as the Cleveland and Pasadena Playhouse) to test "'unproved'" works rather than await "Broadway approval" (playbill, *You Touched Me!*, Pasadena Playhouse, November 29-December 5, 1943, Huntington Library).]

296. To James "Jay" Laughlin

Taos, N.M.
Dec. 20/43
[ALS, 3 pp. Houghton]

Dear Jay

I have retreated like you to a place of snow, the snow-covered desert of Taos. Washes Hollywood off. In Hollywood I am a <u>worm</u> - prostrate - crawling - here I feel alive again. Frieda Lawrence has promised me a piece of her ranch in the Lobos to build on when I am ready, I will be ready this spring if the play sells. Frieda is helping me with it. Removing the Dame and all the war shit which isn't Lawrence or me. Frieda is still a Valkyrie. The ~~most~~ only exciting woman I've known!

It is lovelier here in winter than other seasons. Cold but so dry it feels good. Makes the blood run again - and brighter. I was all, all gone on the coast - this is my predestined home I believe. But I must leave to be home in Clayton for Xmas to see the kid brother off on a hop to China - & comfort the family.

There I will try to get some stories in shape for you, while waiting news from N.Y.

The Creole Palace was fun, the most I had off the beach the whole time I was in Calif.

I have just read an article by Henry Miller in a mag. Frieda has, called "The Phoenix" - 1938 - He damns Proust and Joyce as dead writers of a dead world. A cruel allusion is made to Joyce's blindness as symbolic - which I find odious. However the article has a macabre brilliance. I met Miller before I left - Red beard and I went out there. He seemed very spry. Alert. Highly conscious.

Having read nothing but that unfortunate attack on Joyce - and Proust - I should reserve my judgement, but I suspect he is too heartless to be a great artist. I will try and get hold of his works.

Strange that he admires Lawrence. Lawrence would hate him, I imagine.

They tell me there is some good skiing around here.

Ultimately we may compare notes.

<u>En Avant</u>, 10.

If I get a home here, I will form a hospice for poets - St. Bernard dogs with brandy flasks and everything! But God pity them when they get there! Evanoûit!

[TW returned to Clayton by way of Santa Fe and Taos, his first visit since August 1939.

Henry Miller's essay, "The Universe of Death," appeared in *The Phoenix* (1938-1940), a quarterly edited by James P. Cooney and Miller and published in Woodstock, New York. While D.H. Lawrence had struggled heroically "to escape a living death," Joyce and Proust, Miller claimed, merely "*reflect* the times. We see in them no revolt: it is surrender, suicide, and the more poignant since it springs from creative sources." The "cruel" allusion to Joyce's blindness led Miller to describe him as only "technically" alive in 1938. Miller's long editorial relation with James Laughlin began auspiciously in 1935 when Laughlin, then an "enterprising young man at Harvard" (as described by Miller in a contemporary letter), reprinted a selection of Miller's work in the *Harvard Advocate*, in a number that was seized by the police.

"Red beard" is TW's friend Tony Smith.]

297. To Mary Hunter

53 Arundel Place
Clayton, Mo.
Dec. 27, 1943
[TLS, 2 pp. HRC]

Dear Mary:

All of us home for Christmas, all of us still alive - the blush of immortality is certainly on us! Grandmother is radiantly beautiful, all warm and white and shining, and Grandfather is getting his second sight and his hearing has improved. Mother and father are bravely continuing the quarrel that must have started the first time they found themselves in a dark room together. My kid brother is home on his final leave before sailing with a convoy for some place where he will need mosquito netting - that is the only hint given.

Did you get the scripts I mailed you from the Coast or the letter I dropped on the street in Santa Fe? Did I write you from Taos? I spent a week there in the enchanting company of Frieda and her Italian lover. They run a pottery plant! Frieda is even more amazing than I remembered. Huge. A cap of bob-cat fur on a head of wild yellow straw and eyes lit with lightning. She has been following the progress of 'You Touched Me' closely and is more than satisfied with the play. She objected only to the Dame Willoughby and some of the war-talk which she felt would be distasteful to Lawrence. She did not ask for any changes, but after my talks with her I had some new ideas which I proceded to work out. There are now some important changes in the script. A new curtain for Act three Scene one - which was badly needed - Act one sc. two (the tea-scene) written over without Dame Willoughby and Hadrian's speeches (Frontiers) written over and finally relieved of the editorial flavor without losing their context. The scene between Hadrian and Matilda in the last scene is also rewritten and has more natural warmth I believe and the breathless quality I wanted but never quite captured in other versions. It is fantastic and ridiculous the amount of time I have spent on this play - for thirty percent! - but the Pasadena production convinced me that it is a real property and I feel it would be a great pity for it to fall short of the finished professional production which it has not yet been given. Since Cleveland I have been looking mainly to you. In fact I have always felt that you and this play were natural selection. So write me now how things stand as exactly as possible. Audrey has wired me for copies. Unfortunately I could only get four copies made for thirty-eight dollars! Hence I could only send you two. That left one for me and one to give the Hollywood agent for the studios interested. Poor Audrey has gotten none! I do not know what other interest she has developed in the play in New York, nor what has come of Bertha and the studios. But I am not intending to make any commitments until I have heard from you. Naturally I hope you can crystallize something quickly. I know that a final script will be helpful and will get this new material off to you this week. The script situation is certainly very confusing. I think what I will do is send my script with Taos changes to Audrey with instructions to have copies made again. Now I haven't cashed your fifteen dollar check so if you wish to apply it to these final copies, write me to that effect. I think that would pay for about half the copies, typed in N.Y., so you and Audrey could split them. Unless I have lost it, your check is in my trunk which hasn't gotten here yet. I will let you know. I hope all this makes sense. My departure from the coast was fraught with much haste and many complications, not the least of which was a Sheriff seeking to serve papers on me in connection with a law-suit brought by a motor scooter company! So I am still in confusion.

I see that our friend Carley is backing a Margaret Webster production of the Cherry Orchard. Those two fine ladies! - This is not sarcasm, but tinged with sorrow. In the first place I think Carley might very well back your production of the Cherry Orchard - or even better, The Sea Gull - and in the second place I don't see Nazimova mentioned. In the third place - Mr. Chekhov is dead and I am the living author of one reasonably good play which I think might make her a lot more money. Does this sound childish? Yes - I do know better. My faith in Carley is not really affected, but the Webster is still a red flag. She always makes me think of what Peg of Old Drury yelled to the mob that stopped her coach mistaking her for the king's mistress - "I am the Protestant whore!"

10.

[TW's homecoming is described in "Grand" (1964), with the fragile Rosina Otte Dakin welcoming her grandson for the last time. She died on January 6, 1944, the Feast of the Epiphany, from a lung hemorrhage. At the time Dakin Williams was en route to northern Burma.

Frieda Lawrence may have reminded TW that her husband's original story had little if any "war-talk" and that the post-war optimism of Hadrian's "Frontiers" speech had no basis in Lawrence's own acute despair after World War I. It was the war's approaching end, however, that dictated the cutting of "war-talk," lest it ironically date the updated setting of You Touched Me! The published version of the play (1947) has only a trace of the writer Dame Willoughby, a late addition to the script.

Carly Wharton's long-running revival of The Cherry Orchard (1904) opened on January 25, 1944, with staging by Eva Le Gallienne and Margaret Webster. TW cited Alla Nazimova's performance in Le Gallienne's 1928 revival of Chekhov and was apparently still smarting from Webster's failed direction of Battle of Angels. Just as the actress Nell Gwyn, mistress of Charles II, declared herself "the Protestant whore" when mistaken for the king's popish mistress, so Webster (TW implied in a strained analogy) was prone to shift blame for her own artistic failures.]

298. To Margaret "Margo" Jones

[53 Arundel Place
Clayton, Missouri]
1/12/44
[TLS, 2 pp. HRC]

Dear Margo:

I have been thinking of you continually, but when I tell you all that has happened you won't wonder that I am just now writing.

I left California about a week after you did. As far as I could tell, nothing at all had happened concerning You Touched Me. I think I went to about all the performances except the last two which Gilmore Brown attended. Somehow I did not want to run into him. I heard afterwards, I forget who told me, that he was very pleased with the show and was more than usually warm in his comments to the actors. I know they must think me awfully cold-blooded for my disappearance but I was exhausted and had to reserve my strength for the awful business of pulling up stakes, which I did with Marjorie's and David's help. I wrote Gilmore from Taos. I spent about ten days there. It was just what I needed. My blood started running again and I was revived. I saw a good deal of Frieda Lawrence. She read the play for the second time and was very pleased with it. Talks that we had stimulated me to do some more work on it and I began a revision which I am just now finishing up. It affects mostly the last two scenes and the second one. I will send you the new foreword and a copy of the scripts when typed up in New York. I am sending the material to Mary who will have scripts typed there. Her interest appears unabated and while she is still indefinite about the financing, she assures me that is making good progress. Donnie has acquired a 4-room apartment in a very effete neighborhood, the east sixties, and invites me to stay with him in New York. I haven't yet decided to go there.

In the meantime, I arrived home and saw my brother off. He sailed over-seas. Then all of a sudden my grandmother, to whom I was very devoted, had a lung hemmorrhage and died in two hours. Then - mostly to avoid the funeral which I have always dreaded - I went in the hospital and had my eye operation. It was performed by a medical professor before an audience of students and accompanied by a lecture which I found exceedingly unpleasant. But the results were very successful this time. Through a thick lens I can see about as clearly as with my good eye. It magnifies the eye and gives me a somewhat terrifying appearance, but so much the better! If the lens does not correct the divergence, another operation may be done later on the muscle.

From Audrey I have heard nothing but a telegram wanting to know where I am. I wired back where. From Case and the West coast I have heard nothing at all. Only a Xmas card from David and a couple of wires from Marjorie concerning my luggage which finally got here. I have had many laughs thinking about that rooster. Mlle. had it wrapped in chiffon the last time it came on! - Looking back on Pasadena it all seems such fun and probably the most satisfying experience I've ever had in the theatre. If I were a professional writer I suppose I would be disappointed that nobody bought the play there, but I guess I'm just not professional enough to care much about that. Especially since I see now that for all its warmth and sparkle here and there the play needed heavier timbers to hold the last act up. I hope I've supplied them. We certainly made the most of what we had to work with, and all in all we set those people a pretty high example of theatrical sincerity. I don't think either of us will ever forget some things: Houseley's performance and Mary's, and Marjorie's gallantry - and the second Act. - and that rooster, that pitiful, proud bird, bloody but unbowed! I am not a sentimental nor very articulate person, but I'm sure you know how much all your work meant to me and those things it created.

Jay has sent me the proofs of Purification. There was your name right under mine - I was proud to see it there. Isn't Jay an angel? One of the best! His allegiance and yours give me something to work for in this weary old world!

But I am pretty happy here, at home right now. For the first time - maybe because the old folks are old and lonesome and I feel like I'm doing something for them - it seems real good to be here. Anyhow I think we ought to keep in touch with the lares and penates.

I must stop now and go swimming so I won't get fat on all this home-cooking - Yes, I've found a pool here!

In a few days I can tell you where I'm going and when - well, in a week or so anyhow. If I head for Mexico I will sure as hell go through Austin. If anybody else planned a Playwrights theatre I would doubt it, but you have a way of putting those dreams into action. So go to it! And give me the details.

Love, 10.

["Mlle." Jene Cannon, officious Playbox stage manager (or so TW thought her), delivered the "bloody but unbowed" rooster that Emmie shoots accidentally while guarding the hens, evidence of TW's borrowing from D.H. Lawrence's novella "The Fox" (1923).

By dedicating "The Purification" to Margo Jones, TW recalled their loss of sisters (Stella Nell Jones died in 1925 from influenza) in circumstances which aroused guilt and self-recrimination in the survivors.

One of the declining "lares" was Cornelius, with whom TW "sat up" (qtd. in *Windham*, p. 128) on a night of illness and remorse in Clayton.]

299. To Audrey Wood

53 Arundel Pl.
Clayton, Mo.
1/16/44
[TLS, 1 p. HRC]

Dear Audrey:

We've had a rough time of it here. First my brother sailed over-seas with the air-force: then my Grandmother, who had seemed unusually well, suddenly had a lung-hemmorrhage and died in two hours. I was very fond of her and it was pretty shocking, although she was very old and the quick and relatively easy death was a merciful way to lose her. I went ahead with my eye operation, mostly to avoid the funeral. I hate them. The operation was quite successful. Now with a thick lens I have 20/30 vision in the bad eye, which is certainly a great improvement over total blindness. In spite of all this I managed to do a very extensive re-write of 'You Touched Me'. However I could not find a typist here and Mary Hunter was yelling for it, so I sent her the re-write with instructions for typing and told her to see that you got a copy soon as ready. She is paying for the typing herself. Now if you want more than the one copy, - Have some more made at my expense. We haven't discussed Mary's plans for putting the show on. How do you feel about it? Of course Mary has not gotten all the backing yet but declares the progress good. I would rather have Mary put it on - provided she had the money - than anyone else in N.Y., mainly because she wouldn't over-ride my own very clear conceptions of how it ought to be done. Pasadena was just right in spirit and interpretation but badly handicapped by student and amateur actors and Mlle. and bad lighting. Nevertheless the happy audience reaction surprised me and made it pretty apparent that the show has strong appeal when properly done. The re-write strengthens the last act mainly - and brings the war background up-to-date.

Laughlin has sent me proofs of 'The Purification' and I am busy writing and re-modelling a group of short stories for him. Laughlin sent me a check [for] $32. for "The Purif." anthology rates. That is $3.20 for you. Take it, from N.Y. account.

I hope circumstances will permit me to see you in N.Y. soon. Otherwise I will drift south and pin myself down to some new project.

All best, 10.

300. To James "Jay" Laughlin

[53 Arundel Place
Clayton, Missouri]
1/31/43
[TLS, 1 p. Houghton]

Dear Jay:

Here is the list of books I wanted. All you have of Rimbaud, the Kafka, anything you recommend by E.M. Forster. Lately my enthusiasm has divided between Crane and Rimbaud but I don't think Crane would resent the division. Crane would drunkenly declare himself the reincarnation of Christopher Marlowe but I think it is more significant to observe that he was born less than ten years after the death of Rimbaud. A restless spirit like Rimbaud's wouldn't wait longer to find another earthly residence, though I wonder if he would choose to be a poet again - maybe as expiation - No, he wouldn't need that, not after that horrible last chapter of his life. Do you think one should write a play about him? A motion picture would be the ideal medium starting with 'Morte a Dieu' and ending with the pitiful conversion in the hospital at Marseilles. Not with pious implications, however.

I am at work on your stories. In fact so intensely that when I stopped this evening I had a regular crise de nerfs. Vertigo, so that I couldn't stand up, a crazy feeling of panic, palpitations, nausea, chill - then finally an absolute drowsy peace with a wolfish appetite. I am now in that last phase, thank God. When I read the stuff tomorrow it will either be in my best vein or else pure gibberish. Unfortunately the ~~subsequent~~ paroxysms could signify either.

I will probably leave here in less than two weeks, for N.Y. if I receive favorable news of the play, otherwise for New Orleans or Mexico - but I will send you an address when I leave.

Letters from Margo and David, both raving of books you sent them. You have acquired two fanatic admirers in them. With your Lincoln-like aura it must be hard to avoid idolatry of this kind. People like David and Margo, too intelligently skeptical for the church and with more emotional excitability than they can put into social or sexual relationships and with professions not quite creative enough to absorb it, have need of discovering a modern Saint or Buddha, and sooner or later your mountain lodge will inevitably be a citadel of holiness.

10.

[Hart Crane's boast was quoted in Philip Horton's biography (*Hart Crane: The Life of an American Poet*), with Katherine Anne Porter as authority: "'I am Baudelaire, I am Whitman, I am Christopher Marlowe, I am Christ.'"

In his fascination with the death of artists, TW added Rimbaud to the necrology of van Gogh, D.H. Lawrence, Vachel Lindsay, Sara Teasdale, and Crane, who drowned himself at sea in 1932. The "horrible last chapter" of Rimbaud's life transpired in Marseilles, where he was hospitalized for a tumor that required amputation of his leg and that led to a painful death in 1891. TW's biographical source was almost certainly *Rimbaud: The Boy and the Poet* (1924), by Edgell Rickword.

James Laughlin's height and reserved bearing led TW to describe his publisher as Lincolnesque.

TW misdated the new year.]

301. *To Margaret "Margo" Jones*

[53 Arundel Place
Clayton, Missouri]
2/12/44
[TLS w/ autograph postscript, 2 pp. HRC]

Dear Margo:

Your letter and the Curtain Club's came together. I have just written them, mostly about the innocent fallacy of trusting Broadway producers to cooperate in anything that would build up a decentralized theatre. Their program is a splendid one both for them and playwrights and ought to be made a regular yearly thing. I am sure it would become a famous institution if carried out wisely and if they don't [make] discouraging mistakes at the out-set. Regardless of whether they use my work or not, I am cordially for it and anything that takes a chop at the octupus arms of Broadway. Laughlin has sent me a copy of "Purification" so you needn't have mailed yours. I think I will have another script ready before the contest closes, beside the one-acter. Will write you about that later. Of course I can't wait around here till the contest is decided. Just not possible, I am too restless and circumstances here too distressing - - when prolonged. I think I will go on up to New York early next week. Mary Hunter called long-distance a few nights ago. Long-distance calls are always confusing to me, I don't get much out of them as they make me too nervous to hear distinctly, but I believe she said that some definite news would be forthcoming in a week or ten days. I am just a bit suspicious of goings on up there. She and Donnie were both delighted with the re-write I did here and in Taos. It seems to me that something definite ought to be done about it more quickly. They are putting Horton's play on <u>again</u>, but it has been postponed several times for casting difficulties. Apparently that is what holds up action on mine. At least that's how I figure it. Which hardly seems fair or intelligent. In the first place Horton's play was already given practically a Broadway production last year - was fully covered by reviewers and producers - and was given the best possible production. It was a good enough play but not really exciting. It should <u>not</u> be given precedence over 'You Touched Me' which has never had a chance in New York and which I modestly regard in its final form as a much stronger script. - Entre nous! Sooo - they have yet to prove by their actions that they are sincere about wishing to create a

(PLURAL) playwrights' theatre. I'm going up there and size up the situation and see what I can do personally. I have been dreaming lately of going to England, perhaps with the Red Cross or some other agency of the kind. I am hungry for something really new. Then I might find the London theatre more hospitable than Broadway. I'm sure it is less superficial and finicky. Such plans are really too visionary to mention, but I shall investigate the chances of it in New York. Knowing you has made me more visionary, I guess! One has to be. - I have heard nothing directly from Audrey since I got here, a mysterious lapse in communication. A long letter from David, full of gags but nothing from Jane or Tony. Wonder if they are still together. The situation between them was a bit strained when I left. Quelle Menage! as Rimbaud says at one point. Such a quiet life I've been leading! My society consists of one lady sixty-years-old, whose poetry I revise. I swim at the Y and go to movies and work - last week I addressed a small poetry group on Hart Crane's poems, two old queens and eight middle-aged women were the audience, appreciative but mystified.

Love - 10.

P.S. Here is something else for you to read if you can get hold of it. It is a long story (Condensed from a novel) that came out in an anthology of before-unpublished creative writings in 1936, published by W.W. Norton, edited by Kreymborg. The story is badly titled - Vain Voyage - It is by a man I have never heard of before although the biographical notes credit him with three novels and a book of short stories. At the time this anthology came out he was on the Federal Writers' Project in New York City. His name is Fred Rothermell. Ever heard of him? I go to this length about it because it is probably the most amazing piece of American fiction I have ever seen, as fine in style and execution as Katharine Anne Porter and with a more vital content. The dialogue, of which there is much, is in my opinion the finest dialogue - well, finer than any I've heard in the theatre! And the characterization of the old man, the central character, is the subtlest, most penetrating, heartbreaking thing outside of Chekhov - if, indeed, Chekhov ever did one that poignantly! And you know how I feel about Chekhov. It is appalling to me that an artist and a story of this calibre should be - apparently - so unknown. I intend to enquire about him in New York - of the anthology publishers. This is the sort of artist and material that should be going into a new American theatre. As a matter of fact, his story could almost be transposed to the stage without change - four sets, however. But they could be very sketchy: the action is mostly psychological, except for the scene in the stock exchange. The story is of an old man losing his life-savings in 1929 crash. Just when he was about to retire from book-keeping job and go to Java which he had always dreamed of. Sounds like a common tear-jerker but reserve your judgement till you have read it. I would want to adapt it except the dialogue is really all there.

I will mail my Mss. from N.Y. as there is a bit more to do on one - & the typing. Cheerio!

[The later Broadway critic Stark Young organized the Curtain Club in 1909 while teaching at the University of Texas. The Club's "program" of staging plays in relative independence of Broadway was one that Margo Jones and TW would associate with the growing movement toward a decentralized national theatre. TW learned in March that "The Purification" would not be staged at Texas, due perhaps to its requirement of music and ballet.

Only the Heart was "not really exciting," the critics agreed, and Horton Foote's Texas play closed after forty-seven performances (April 4-May 13, 1944). The failure of their first Broadway venture hastened the demise of the renamed American Actors Theatre.

The poet "sixty-years-old" was probably Alice Lippmann, a family friend and early supporter of TW.

"Vain Voyage" (*The New Caravan*, 1936) is a classic 1930s tale of economic exploitation and defeat. Henry Button, the abused little man in Fred Rothermell's story, anticipates Lucio in "The Malediction."]

302. To Margaret "Margo" Jones

[53 Arundel Place
Clayton, Missouri]
3/2/44
[TLS, 1 p. HRC]

Dear Margo:

This is just a note to let you know what I'm doing. I meant to leave for New York a week or so ago but became engaged in a new enterprise and am waiting now till it's near enough finished to be safely put aside for the interim of travel. It is the wickedness of fate, as Emmie would call it, that I didn't get this under way in time for the Texas contest - Nothing was finished so I had to just send the Purification. But I think I will be able to get a <u>very</u> rough first draft of the present work off to you in a week or so, as I want you to have an early look at it. It is luxuriously romantic, gorgeously pictorial, set in medieval Italy and based on Browning's famous monologue "My Last Duchess". I once did a 15-minute sketch on the subject at the University of Iowa. I cannot imagine how I happened to pick it up again. All of a sudden one morning I was just writing about the Duchess of Ferrara - and have continued furiously for the past five days! It now runs 60 pages with one scene not yet written. With a little poetic splurging here and there I can stretch it to full-length, if necessary. The title is "A Balcony In Ferrara". The setting is like a painting by Matisse of a room with a balcony over the Mediterranean. A dazzling contrast of hot and cold colors. Rose colored and cream walls and throbbing blue outside. And medieval costumes and pageantry. That is what excites me, I suppose, the pictorial richness. And the chance to be violent. - again . . .

During this stay at home I also did a complete re-write of the nauseous thing I read you in Pasadena, The Gentleman Caller. I was afraid to leave anything in that condition, so I did it over. Better I'm sure - but if enough better I don't know. I was going to send it with the Purification when I became engaged in this and let it go for a while.

Two weeks ago I wrote everybody in N.Y. that I was leaving immediately either for there or Mexico. I suppose they assume I went to Mexico - all except Donnie. He insisted upon an explanation so I told him I had the 7-year Itch. Which is true, I did have it - there is an epidemic of it here. But I got over it in three days, by remaining in a coat of grease and long underwear for that period. - (You can imagine the unpleasant sensation this created in the family!)

Well, I must stop and go swimming. It always pulls me together after a hard day like this has been. Saint James the Second, affectionately known as Jay, has submitted my name to some Academy that gives thousand dollar endowments to deserving artists - I haven't heard anything from them yet. If I do - Viva Mexico! A bas les Shoo-bare!!

- Love - 10.

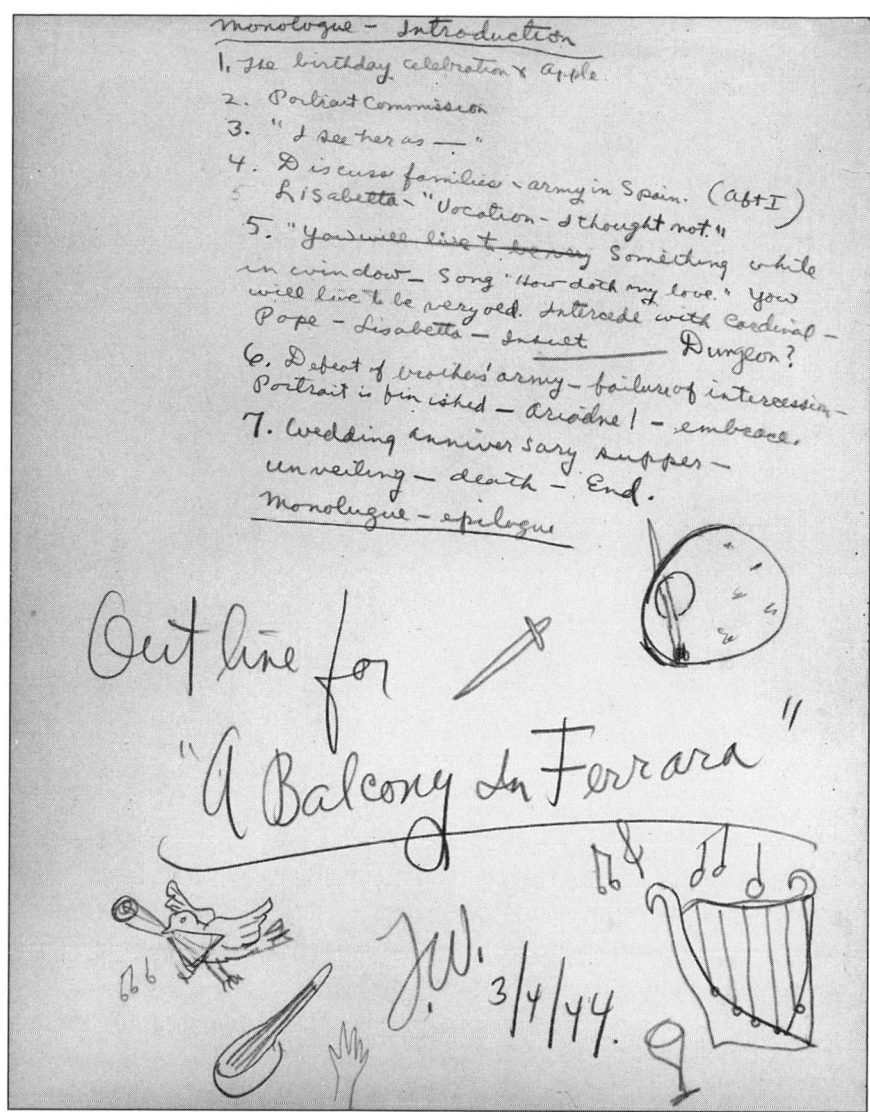

Tennessee's illustrated cover sheet for "A Balcony in Ferrara."

[TW's first motive in drafting "A Balcony in Ferrara" was "purely romantic." The second, he explained, was "to capture the spirit and quality" of the Italian Renaissance, "probably the most dynamic and brilliant and appalling period in human history - next to our own" (author's note, n.d., Columbia). The original sixty-page script was "stretched" to 140 (including revised and fragmentary pages) and seems to have briefly furnished the "strong theme" (*Journal*, ca. September 11, 1943) for which TW had searched since the failure of *Battle of Angels*. In adapting Robert Browning's famous monologue, he may have been guided by the earlier play, the love of Myra and Val and the blocking action of Jabe forming a tragic pattern for Browning's more obscure dramatic conflict. With its aura of poetry and theme of forbidden love, "The Purification" (soon to be staged by Margo Jones at the Pasadena Playhouse) may also have been influential in the "Ferrara" undertaking.

To TW's embarrassing "7-year Itch" was added "a crise de nerfs" brought on by the "gloom" (qtd. in *Windham*, p. 130) at home following Grand's death and the uncertainty of Dakin's military assignment.

In recommending TW to the American Academy of Arts and Letters, James Laughlin described him as "the most talented and promising young writer whom we publish." He knew of "no one with equal talent who has not yet received full recognition" (letter to Felicia Geffen, February 14, 1944, American Academy of Arts and Letters archive).]

303. To Audrey Wood

[53 Arundel Place
Clayton, Missouri]
3/4/44
[TLS, 1 p. HRC]

Dear Audrey:

Are we having a silent argument over something? If so, what?

My conscience is unusually clear, and if I should die in Saint Louis, unlikely as that is with so little going on even in the way of mortality, I am sure my soul would go straight to heaven!

If we are all in the same state of grace there is nothing to argue about.

Evidently there were two opinions about the state of my soul, however, as I was afflicted lately with scabies or the 7-Year Itch! There is an epidemic of it here, but the family are sure a gentleman would not have caught it. I got rid of it in a week, but only by remaining in a coat of grease and long underwear without bathing for three days and nights.

The colored lights are on, and I have been hard at work. Sixty pages of a play, and a couple of scenes still to go. At the first break in the weather I'm leaving here and most likely for New York.

I hear from James Laughlin continually about wonderful things he is going to do for me. He has recommended me to the Academy of Arts and - Is it Sciences? - for a thousand dollar subsidy - Then yesterday he wrote that his <u>wife</u> is starting a magazine and wants to devote the first issue of it entirely to "Battle of Angels" at $2. a page. - Somebody is dreaming - Margo - Mary Hunter - all of my friends are dreaming! - Only I remain coldly rational thinking only in terms of experience and probability. - - ?

How are you? Tenn.

[If Audrey Wood and TW were having "a silent argument," his backdoor brokering of *You Touched Me!* would have been ample provocation. Along less quarrelsome lines, Wood had complained in her last letter to TW that the press of agency business made it "impossible to carry on a polite correspondence with the rest of the world" (November 20, 1943, HRC).

The "colored lights" were on for "A Balcony in Ferrara"—here a term of literary inspiration and energy that would be recast sexually in *A Streetcar Named Desire*.

Although scheduled for publication in July 1944, *Battle of Angels* did not appear in *Pharos* until the following spring.]

304. To Frieda Lawrence

[Young Men's Christian Association
5 West 63rd Street, New York]
March 20, 1944
[TLS, 2 pp. HRC]

Dear Frieda Lawrence:

I should have written you a long time ago: but actually it wasn't till now that I had anything at all specific to tell you, except the changes made in the script since you last read it. I am sure you would find it a good deal more to your liking as I conscientously removed those elements you, and I feel sure, Lawrence, disapproved of: the emphasis on military matters. All that section has been rewritten and while a general indictment of war remains, the discussion of Hitler, Etc. is out. Also the last act has considerably more dramatic power with the girl running out of the house instead of again to her room, and the situation consequently much more in doubt till the end. The producer, Mary Hunter, is highly pleased. As soon as we have a free script - one not making rounds of backers - I will get one to you. Here is the money situation: the play is budgetted at $35,000. That is the amount we must raise to put it on. I can not say exactly how much of that is now in sight - certainly not more than half. I have just arrived in N.Y. from the South to try my hand at interesting financiers. I remember you mentioned the Baronness Guggenheim. Do you think she would be a prospect? Or can you think of anyone else? The play is to start rehearsals right after the opening of another play the Actors Company is doing. It opens April 4th. If we have our money by that date we would go right into production. Any suggestions you can give on persons to contact would be helpful.

I had an eye operation in Saint Louis - my German grandmother died suddenly of a hemmorrhage of the lungs - a quick and beautiful death with no preceding sickness at all - my brother left with the air-force for India - all this while I was doing the re-write and the first draft of a new play - so you will understand why I have not had a chance to write you earlier as I should.

I no longer have the least doubt about the value of the play as an investment. I think with the type of understanding, sensitive direction Mary Hunter would give it, success would be assured. But it is not so easy to convince backers - they seem to shy away from anything that has the quality of literature unless it is signed by someone like Maxwell Anderson. So we have a fight on our hands. For all our sakes I hope we make the grade. It will be another act of homage to one of the truly bright angels of our time - Lawrence.

With kindest regards, Tennessee.

[TW arrived in New York in mid-March and stayed at the West Side YMCA for at least the remainder of the month. He soon wrote to his family, reaffirming confidence in Mary Hunter's production of *You Touched Me!* but citing her "mistake" in "putting on Foote's play first. If that goes badly it would make it harder for her to raise the $35,000. which 'ain't hay' - " (n.d., Columbia).]

305. To James "Jay" Laughlin

[Young Men's Christian Association
5 West 63rd Street, New York]
[ca. March 24, 1944]
[TLS, 1 p. Houghton]

Dear Jay:

The old fish-peddler Liebling woke me up early this morning on the phone saying he had a letter to read me. I was very indifferent as I supposed it was from the scooter people in California or something equally fatuous but disagreeable. Consequently I was a little thunderstruck when it turned out to be from Walter Damrosch of your estimable society informing me that they were going to present me on May 19th with a thousand dollars, at a suitable ceremony which they hoped I would attend by person or proxy. Words are a bit inexpressive about such feelings but I will venture to say that I am happy about it. And that I am grateful to you for your part in this dispensation. I am quite certain it was more your recommendation than whatever it was Liebling saw fit to send them. Audrey was out of town and while Liebling is a smart Broadway character, somewhat nicer than most, I doubt that his selections were very strategic. I think I've already told you what I will do. I will go to Mexico! - I have been here about a week, making the dizzy rounds of theatre people and shows but somehow feeling totally unoccupied, while in Saint Louis, where I saw no one and only went swimming, I felt horribly busy. Mother writes me that she has mailed "Battle" to you. I left it for her to do as she is one of those conscientous Puritans who never leave undone what ought to be done. They may drive you crazy but they are never lazy. I have written Peggy Webster. She is about to succeed Le Gallienne in the leading part of "The Cherry Orchard" so she may beg off. To write about what happened in Boston is a frightening assignment but I will undertake it. It will be hard without stepping on sensitive toes. The whole thing was an explosion of which nobody got a very lucid impression, least of all myself. I will try to describe the chaos, ambiguously enough to avoid offense. All of us who came with the company meant well: it was Boston that was dirty.

Don and I are courting backers for "You Touched Me". It may go on late this spring or early Fall. Sometime when I have a play that I am absolutely sure of, I will offer you a piece of it. But not this one. It will not offend anybody but I can't see it making anybody a Croesus.

After the turmoil of this week and the next I may get back to work but
don't expect I'll really do much till I retire on my thousand to some quieter
precincts. - Robeson as "Othello" made my blood run cold. Christ, what
majesty! - All the rest here is piffle. Even the Cherry Orchard seems a little
wilted. But life -- life is good and exciting!

Tennessee

[The old "flesh-peddler" William Liebling read a letter of notification dated March
22, 1944, and signed by Walter Damrosch, president of the American Academy of
Arts and Letters.

In earlier correspondence TW had suggested to James Laughlin that Margaret
Webster write a preface for the forthcoming edition of *Battle of Angels*. Hers is "the
most literate mind on Broadway" (March 7, 1944, Houghton), he wrote in recommendation, while harboring a fear that she might evade or shift blame for the play's
failure in Boston.

TW repeated his praise for Paul Robeson's Othello in correspondence with
Margo Jones. This was "the first really <u>majestic</u> presence" that he had "known
since Nazimova on stage" (March 30, 1944, HRC). Webster directed the Theatre
Guild hit, which opened on October 19, 1943, and ran for 280 performances.]

306. To Walter Damrosch

[Young Men's Christian Association]
5 W. 63rd Street [New York]
March 24, 1944
[ALS, 1 p. American Academy of Arts and Letters]

Dear Mr. Damrosch:

This grant is really an act of God! I have just finished the first draft of
a play in verse but doubted I would have the leisure to push it through. My
Hollywood savings had dwindled to a point where the need was imminent
of getting another job. Jobs mean the virtual secession of creative designs.
Hence the almost supernatural atmosphere of this good fortune!

Many, many and most sincere thanks to you and the Academy. You are
true benefactors in a time when the kind are rare.

I will be in New York this spring and will of course be present at the
ceremony. I plan to leave for Mexico afterwards to finish the project.

Cordially, Tennessee Williams

[On May 19 TW and Donald Windham attended the Academy Ceremonial and reportedly "got the giggles" while observing the "*'immortels'*" (*Windham*, p. 133). The Committee on Grants, which included Elmer Rice, William Rose Benét, and Henry S. Canby, presented a Merit Medal to the seventy-two-year-old Theodore Dreiser for his pioneering work in American realism. In addition to TW, Eudora Welty, of Jackson, Mississippi, received a citation and grant.

The verse play in progress is "A Balcony in Ferrara."]

307. To James "Jay" Laughlin

[New York]
4/2/44
[TLS, 2 pp. Houghton]

Dear Jay:

I hesitate to send you this, because while the story of this play is interesting to me as a dreadful crisis in my life, I am afraid it will seem like much ado about nothing - especially the way I have written it up - to other people. You must judge about that, and don't print it if you think it will give a disgusting impression of vanity or martyrdom.

I saw poor Peggy Webster last night. I say 'poor' because she has just replaced Eva Le Gallienne in "Cherry Orchard" and is having, I think, a ghastly time with it. She has none of Le Gallienne's delicacy and charm on the stage. In fact, she has gotten heavier, her body and movements are rather masculine, she looked almost like a Princeton Triangle ingenue, and the loose flowing garments that Le G. wore so bewitchingly appeared on her incongruously like maternity garments. You see how mean I can be? For an essentially kind person? The only justice is that the part should have been given to a deserving actress who needed it - Peggy is a director. Well, we were both a bit embarassed as this was the first meeting since "Battle". Peggy seems willing to write a preface but cannot say <u>when</u>. I said, knowing your printers dilatory habits, eventually might be soon enough. However if necessary I think she could be prodded into fairly early action. Since this crap of mine is so wordy, you may want only a short piece from her. Peggy loathes failure and her work on "Battle" was. What a failure!

About the mag's name - as you say, names don't matter much. The difficulty with Pharos is that phonetically it has antique sound of Egypt, a bit musty sounding, you know. Otherwise it is excellent. But Margaret is such a lovely name. Why not call it Margaret's Magazine? Or "Nerves"? No - that's awful! I give up. But try and find something with a green quality if you can.

I am beginning to hate N.Y. again already - I spent night before last in the Federal Pen. I was picked up crossing the park after midnight and didn't have my registration card on me. In fact I didn't possess one. Was turned over to the FBI and incarcerated for the night. I am now out with a sub-poena while my cards are being sent from Clayton. The night in the Pen was fearful! But I have made some good friends at the FBI - they are really very gentlemanly. New York is sweltering with suspicion and prurience and petty malice. It is sad to see one's friends caught here and becoming infected with it, especially when they came here as such fresh and sensitive individuals. I want to get them all out!

The publicity woman for the "Academy" asked for some pictures: George Platt Lynes offered to make some free of charge. If they turn out good - he is a wonderful though somewhat chi-chi photographer - I will send you one for Margaret's Mag.

The Acad. ceremony is May 19th: after that I will be at liberty. I will leave here and get back to real work.

God Bless you! Tennessee.

[TW's "History of a Play" was printed as an afterword to *Battle of Angels*, without any sign of editorial concern or intervention.

Margaret Webster's so-called "ghastly" performance in *The Cherry Orchard* (she entered the cast on March 30) set off alarms for TW. He warned James Laughlin that her preface may be "stupid," for "her object will be defense of her failure" (April 14, 1944, Houghton) in Boston, now presumably compounded in New York.

Pharos (lighthouse) was a short-lived magazine (1945-1947) edited by Laughlin's wife, Margaret Ellen Keyser. Each number was to be devoted to a single long work and would be "published intermittently at the pleasure of its editor."

TW's arrest does not appear in his FBI file as released under the Freedom of Information Act. Included are four censored reports, dated 1952, 1954, 1956, and 1964, and supplied to such government agencies as the Department of State, the Coast Guard, and the United States Information Agency. Worthy of note were TW's sending "greetings" to the Moscow Art Theatre, his being "sympathetic" to the

"'Hollywood Ten'" (suspected communist film writers and directors subpoenaed in 1947 by the House Un-American Activities Committee), and his "reputation of being a homosexual" (also of concern to Naval Intelligence, which had "secured statements from individuals who admitted participating in homosexual acts with Williams").

The "chi-chi photographer" George Platt Lynes was well-known in the 1930s and 40s for his surrealist-inspired portraits of fashion, dance, and celebrity figures. His extensive collection of male nudes was sold to the Kinsey Institute and exhibited in New York in 1993.]

308. To Edwina Dakin Williams

SH: The School of American Ballet
Lincoln E. Kirstein, President & Director
George Balanchine, Chairman of Faculty
May 10, 1944
[TLS, 1 p. HRC]

Dear Mother:

I am only staying on here for the award presentation the nineteenth. Then I will either come home for a while, or go first to one of the nearby beaches. I have been thinking of taking a summer course in a university, maybe Washington and in the Italian Renaissance which is the period setting of the play I am working on now. I'm going to write for the Washington summer catalogue and see if they offer such a course. Sewanee might also be suitable.

Money is coming in slowly on the play. The chance of a spring production is quite off now. If Foote's play had been successful the backers would have been much less cautious. Foote's play is still running but not making money and the backers are pretty resentful about it, as they are being called upon to put more money in that play to keep it going and so far have not realized a penny on it.

I want to buy some white shoes here, so if you have an extra shoe coupon you might send it to me. I have gotten several very respectable looking portraits from Mr. Lynes which you will like much better than the one I sent. In fact, I look quite elegant in them and might pass for a member of cafe society. I don't believe my picture got in any of the papers - perhaps will later. I send you the invitation. Wish you would be here to attend it. It will apparently be very impressive. Eudora Welty, who got one of the awards, is from Jackson, Mississippi.

Where is Grandfather spending the summer?

Love, Tom.

[TW did not study the "Italian Renaissance" but rented a cottage on Fire Island and for the next few weeks led a "retreat" that was neither "Christian" (see letter #309) nor restful.

The George Platt Lynes photograph which Edwina disliked may be the one that shows a mock-pensive TW wearing a torn sweater—selected for the cover of this edition.

Kip Kiernan died on May 21, 1944, in New York City, reportedly from a brain tumor. In *Memoirs* TW recalls visiting him in the hospital and sadly reflecting that the young dancer "had never looked more beautiful" (p. 60). TW gave the impression that the visit occurred in March and that Kip died shortly thereafter, but the death certificate requires a later chronology.]

309. To Margaret "Margo" Jones

SH: Hotel Woodrow
35-37 West 64th Street, New York
[ca. June 9, 1944]
[TLS, 2 pp. HRC]

Margo honey:

This is the third time I've written you since the last letter you received but I have been shuttling back and forth between here and my cottage on Fire Island and the letters disappeared. I had the place for three weeks, a lovely five room cottage on an island in the Atlantic. I meant to get away from the world but actually had more society than usual as all my New York friends, and most of Donnie's, flocked over for week-ends that lasted all week. It was fun but hardly describable as a retreat, Christian or otherwise.

I hardly think you need my encouragement as to your plan, but let me go on the record as endorsing it without qualification. I think it magnificent, and very thoroughly thought out. I haven't a doubt in the world that you will put it through or something mighty close to it. The prospectus contains one mis-spelt word - sould for soul but is otherwise flawless. David expects to see you in Pasadena so is waiting till then to give you his reactions which I am sure will be more practical than mine. He has a comedy he wants you to try out for him with your student group. I haven't seen it but I feel sure it will prove amusing. I got to see very little of him as I left for my island soon after he got here and he didn't have a chance to join the migration.

Jane Owens and Paul Moore did. They came the same week-end as Mary Hunter and everybody seemed to like everybody. I have decided that Jane is second only to you as a verbal spell-binder. Her anecdotes and reminisences kept us entertained the whole time. As if that wasn't enough, she and Paul washed a whole week's accumulation of dishes and got the place looking better than any time since I struck it.

I can't give you this as an address as I am about to shove off again. I think I will spend a month or two on the Cape, probably at Provincetown, to get in better physical shape before I go South. I had told the folks I'd spend the summer at home, but just don't feel well enough to endure the summer inferno that Saint Louis is.

"YTM" has been making the rounds about three weeks and the reactions have been "very favorable" according to Mary and Helen Thompson. I really do think the changes made in the script built it up a good deal, particularly in the last two scenes where it was most needed. Don't worry about Emmie. The leopard still has her spots. The different interpretation will be mostly in staging - and different only from Cleveland, not Pasadena. Mary was frightened by the gloomy atmosphere of that production, not by the play itself. Most of the money now offered is contingent upon assembling the proper cast. That is, the backers are willing to put up big money if we have a big name in the cast. A star in one of the romantic leads, Matilda or Hadrian. Or someone like Gish for Emmie. About $20,000 has been offered so far on that contingency. It is a tough game, getting the cast before the money, and the money before the cast, and will take quite a bit of doing. But Mary and Helen seem optimistic about it. Could you look around for us on the coast, and would getting a revised copy of script help you? You have worried over the goddam thing so much already I hate to even mention it to you again! But if you bump into the perfect Hadrian or Matilda on Sunset Strip some evening - don't let it get away! --- I am getting some new material typed up shortly - mostly short plays and short-long plays - which I will mail to you. <u>Cock</u> <u>Crow</u> is suspended till I get settled somewhere. This is a bloody mess of a letter. I will do better when I light for the summer. I am writing on one of those public machines, dime for half hour - and the God damn clock ticking like a time-bomb underneath the machine is about to make me delirious - Your picture is on my dresser. The inscription is a trifle embarrasing - but the picture adorable! It will go with me always.

- Love - 10.

[Margo Jones's "prospectus" was submitted to David R. Stevens, Director of Humanities, Rockefeller Foundation, in support of her plan for a decentralized national theatre: "I believe in a dramatic map for America that will include great native playhouses in every town large enough to want one." With a reported grant of $150 per month and expenses (awarded in August), Jones began to travel in search of models for a professional theatre in the Southwest—Dallas in all likelihood, she thought—that would break the "bottle-neck" (letter to David Stevens, May 20, 1944, Dallas Public Library) of New York and Hollywood. TW repeated his support for the idea in a 1945 radio interview with George Freedley (see *Conversations*, pp. 20-24).

Jones would soon be in Pasadena to direct "The Purification" (or "Song for the Guitar"), which TW did not attend and apparently had forgotten was slated for July 27-29 in the Recital Hall.

Paul Moor later published a factually-flawed profile of TW entitled "A Mississippian Named Tennessee" in *Harper's Magazine* (July 1948).

"Cock Crow" was an alternate title for "A Balcony in Ferrara."]

310. *To Audrey Wood*

General Delivery
Provincetown, Mass.
Monday July 3, 1944
[ALS, 4 pp. HRC]

Dear Audrey -

I am moving into a little shanty in the dunes where I can avoid the summer crowd. I find this a good place to work and think I will get a play off to you next week, "The Fiddle in the Wings" which used to be "The Gentleman Caller" all done but the <u>first</u> scene which is a very tricky one, as it must establish all the non-realistic conventions used in the play - I call it "a play with music", as like "The Purification" it will have a string accompaniment.

Please mail me a $100. check soon as you get this, for I have to pay my rent in advance. I will try to make it last through July. When I get through the N.Y. savings I will go home. The $1000. check is in a savings account there.

Mayorga wants me to adapt a one-act of Gogol's. I haven't read it but it seems to me the job is worth more than the usual anthology fee. I will write her to send me a copy of the play ("The Gamblers"). It isn't in the local library. Unless it particularly interests me there's no point doing it for that small amount.

Do see if you can interest Fitzgerald in "YTM".

Mail check immediately, please.

- Love - 10

P.S. Webster wrote a lovely preface for "Battle of Angels" which comes out in Laughlin's new mag.

[In mid-June TW returned to Captain Jack's Wharf, where such practiced Bedlamites as Joe Hazan and Fritz Bultman had forgathered. At the time he wired Audrey Wood for a $100 check and signed it "Love?" (June 14, 1944, HRC).

"'The Fiddle in the Wings'" may first appear in "Prologue: The Wingfields of America" (n.d., HRC), a lengthy verse preamble that drew upon TW's poem "Inheritors" (1937; see letter #226) and was intended to give epic background to the Wingfields' cramped life in St. Louis. The provisional title survives, of course, in Tom's opening speech in *The Glass Menagerie* (1945): "In memory everything seems to happen to music. That explains the fiddle in the wings." Later in August TW wrote to Margo Jones that finishing "The Gentleman Caller" (the earlier working title to which he reverted) had been "an act of compulsion, not love. Just some weird necessity to get my sister on paper. Thank God it is done, however inauspiciously, and I can resume the Renaissance play. . . . It has exciting material, at least" (August 1944, HRC).

Barry Fitzgerald was the quintessential stage Irishman whose success in *Going My Way* (Paramount, 1944) made him good box office for *You Touched Me!*

Before writing "A Note on 'Battle of Angels,'" Margaret Webster queried TW from Martha's Vineyard about his own remarks, so that she "'would not repeat or contradict'" him (qtd. in a letter from TW to James Laughlin, n.d., Houghton). To TW's evident relief, she lauded his "gift of poetry" and described the "mess" in Boston as "nobody's fault and everybody's fault."]

311. To James "Jay" Laughlin

[Provincetown, Massachusetts]
[July 1944]
[TLS, 2 pp. Houghton]

Dear Jay:

Just between us, the play was never copyrighted. I always put copyrighted on my Ms. though they never really are. I think it will suffice to follow that procedure - just put "protected by copyright" and lightning won't strike us for lying - I hope.

This is a very unreal sort of summer. Do you ever have periods like that in which reality seems to have entirely withdrawn? It is not necessarily unpleasant - it creates irresponsibility, more vagueness than usual - a new sense of proportions or the lack of them. - Usually it only occurs in summer and on the ocean. - It happened to me once in California - Laguna Beach just before the war - I called it Nave Nave Mahana, after the painting by Gauguin. It doesn't interfere with work - I have done a good deal on a long play - but it makes your work seem more smokey, more cloudy than it even is. And you are impatient with words. They seem the most unreal things a man can work with. Sometimes a storm blows up and enormous birds rush over - that's what you are waiting and enduring for. In between times everything is unbelievably pink shrimpish. What comes, what is coming?

I have just returned from the beach and a fish supper - maybe I am writing in a sun-stroke.

I am still living here on my Hollywood savings, the one grand intact - I'm saving it for a probable flight to Mexico in the Fall. I may need the money for the play late this summer. When I do, I'll wire you for it.

Saw Charles and Chilly Death and Charles' mother - one day they drove up the Cape and took me to lunch. First time I ever saw a thoroughly intimidated southern matron. Chilly was on his high horse, complained so bitterly about lunch that Madame paid the entire bill to conciliate him. - This was the only high-society incident of my season and I greedily absorbed enough of it to last me a while. Yes, I find the same charm you do in Charles - a negro charm I call it. I think he is rather like a piss-elegant mulatto, which is really quite charming. Since there is a heart underneath.

As for printing Charles book, of course that is entirely a matter of your own discretion and choice. I find his work phenomenally uneven. I have read things which were right out of heaven and others - there is Broadway term "from Dixie" which means real corn. However I think he is an important literary figure - mostly through his magazine. If only he were not so biased against anything non-magical VIEW - because of its exploratory ardor - might be the only exciting magazine in America. (PHAROS being still at the mercy of the Mormons). I have great hopes for resurgence of experimental writing and journals and theatre after the war - VIEW might have a prodigious future, if only Charles could achieve a more comprehensive taste and less ego-centricity - I liked the last issue. If I go to Mexico, how about letting me dig up some Mexican material for an issue of PHAROS, if you can get it past the Mormons? Would I have to know Spanish? - I don't. But plan to study it.

I am planning to stay here through September, except for a week of library research at Cambridge (Harvard) - It is too expensive to return to New York before I am ready to leave the East Coast. Perhaps you will come up on the Cape? I will have a cabin and could put you up here. Practically the entire lunatic fringe of Manhattan are among the summer colonists at P-town.

10

[The uncopyrighted play is *Battle of Angels*.

The imperious visitors were the poet-editor Charles Henri Ford and the painter and stage designer Pavel Tchelitchew, "Chilly Death," whose gloomy themes TW spoofed. James Laughlin published books by Ford in 1938, 1942, and 1949— apparently not the one that TW cited.

Under Ford's editorship *View* (1940-1947) gradually modified its surrealist principles and became a diverse, richly illustrated magazine of contemporary literature and painting. Among the contributors to the first three series were André Breton, Marcel Duchamp, Henry Miller, William Carlos Williams, Wallace Stevens, Kenneth Burke, and Lawrence Durrell. The current number had a cover by Georgia O'Keeffe and an "anthology" by Donald Windham entitled "The Eyes of Ulysses" (May 1944). An article in the first number, September 1940, would have cheered the author of *Battle of Angels*, had he read it: "Poetry—the Only Hope of the Drama."

The editorial address of *Pharos* was P.O. Box 215, Murray, Utah, near Laughlin's ski lodge at Alta. Local printers reportedly found *Battle of Angels* to be a "'sinful text'" (qtd. in *Windham*, p. 143) and had slowed its production.]

312. To William Cannastra

Old Whaler
[Provincetown, Massachusetts]
[ca. early-August 1944]
[TLS, 1 p. HTC]

Dear Bill:

By brief I guess you mean the leather zipper case. I hope you do. I didn't miss it till I got your letter, thank heavens, or I would have been very anxious about it. I don't know what all it contains, but no doubt some unfinished scripts I would be broken-hearted to lose. If you come the 19th do bring it with you. Otherwise I can pick it up when I pass through Boston. Just keep it out of sight, for I know it must contain things I would be embarassed to have read.

The bath was horrible! For three dollars I got a ghastly little room decorated with the most revolting pictures. On the wall was the following inscription which I have committed to memory as it was such a jewel of its kind. "Had Wonderful Night of Fun! Sucked 14 cocks, all big fat ones, and took the four biggest up my ass!" After a glance at this and other flora and fauna, I said my prayers and went to bed, but off and on all night creatures out of Steinberg cartoons kept creeping into my room and waking me up with slimy caresses. About four A.M. I decided to leave, as my nerves were cracking. On the way out I bumped into a lovely sailor coming in. I turned around and went back in. We descended together to the steam room and he was just picking up the soap when the nasty little masseur, whom I had neglected to tip, barged in and threatened us both with ten years in the Pen, hoping to get money. I told him to go fuck himself, and dressed and left, spending remainder of time till boat sailed walking around Boston in a stupor.

I am now back at the Old Whaler, though as usual I spend nearly every evening at Bill & Julian's. The sailor Troy visited us and the fisherman Valentine is back in town for a week. Today Joe Hazan and a pretty German girl, Mady, and I drove over to Wellfleet. Swam in the lake, then visited Tchelitchew and Charles Henri & the View crowd. They are on a great hill overlooking the Bay, the loveliest location I have seen on the Cape. God, how I could kick myself for not going there or to Truro!

Baby, you are silly to stay in the damn law-school if you hate it so much! Fuck it and get to hell out of there! The world is a brilliant place to live in "If you have the Viking spirit in life and a Robust Conscience!" (That is from Ibsen's "Master Builder") You are needlessly tormenting your soul. I know it is fun to be Hamlet, to wear sable - but it becomes a debilitating habit that sooner or later you will have to break yourself from. Do it early! Don't droop, don't pine - not with your brain, your charm, your beauty! The world is your oyster, so put some horse-radish on it and swallow it down!

I seldom give pep-talks to anyone but myself, who needs them most.

Let me know definitely if you are coming the 19th and in the meantime find something new and stimulating to take your mind off Law, if you feel you must stick at it.

Love - Tennessee.

[Bill Cannastra (1922-1950) was "a beautiful gangling kid with dark hair and light eyes and a stammer" (*Memoirs*, p. 83) who reminded TW of Kip. TW met Cannastra in Provincetown and later visited his Harvard dorm, where again he played the imperfect guest: "You left unteen things here in Cambridge including your brief," Cannastra wrote, and added that he had been inspired by TW's "pounding away" as he retyped "The Gentleman Caller." He also pointed out "the steam place" where TW spent an eventful night before returning to Provincetown: "I hope that you managed to find it" (n.d., HRC). Cannastra graduated from Harvard Law in 1945, attracted a circle of literary friends in New York, including Allen Ginsberg and Jack Kerouac, and remained in touch with TW until he was killed in 1950 in a bizarre subway accident. A drunken Cannastra had leaned out of a train to wave to friends and was struck by a column that nearly decapitated him. He is obliquely memorialized in Ginsberg's poem "Howl" (1956): "What sphinx of cement and aluminum bashed open their skulls and ate up their brains and imagination?"

The "fisherman Valentine" had dictated a personal love story to TW that he in turn hoped to publish in *View* as an instance of primitive art. Magic, however, was in vogue and Charles Henri Ford apparently rejected the project (see *Windham*, pp. 135, 140).

TW roughly quotes an exchange of Solness and Hilda in the third act of *The Master Builder* (1892). Constrained by family "duties," Ibsen's characters explore the ethical "right to set aside" such impediments to love and happiness.]

313. To Margaret "Margo" Jones

SH: ~~Lincoln Kirstein~~
637 Madison Avenue
New York City
Sept 1944
[TLS w/ autograph postscript, 2 pp. HRC]

Dear Margo:

I am only stopping in New York about a week, then on to Clayton till the crystal ball becomes less cloudy. Darling, I could never send out the first draft of any play of mine, not even just to be typed, though I thank you a million times for the offer. <u>Soon</u> as it is reasonably presentable, I will certainly take you up on that - and may need to! However I shall send you the synopsis. <u>However</u> please don't show it around, especially around Hollywood. I think it is a good story-plot and I don't want it coming out in pictures vaguely or definitely similar before I have finished the stage version - which is going to take a long time. I wouldn't be surprised if I were still working on the final draft next summer. Laughlin and I are little ruled by the calendar.

I am having "The Glass Menagerie" (formerly The Gentleman Caller) typed up here right away and will send you a copy. It has some interesting new techniques and all in all I am not displeased with the out-come. That is, when I consider the terrible, compulsive struggle it was to do the thing and what a frightful, sentimental mess it might well have been, and was at some stages. It needs a good deal of pruning, condensing, possibly some re-arranging even in this version - I would like to know your opinion of it - I think it contains my sister, and that was the object.

I am more than a little disappointed in the way that the Actors' Company here is handling "YTM" - I wouldn't mind the lack of accomplishment if there was just less obscurity about it. They never really tell Donnie or me what is going on - for instance, we have no idea exactly how much money they have raised, and questions are evaded with cheerful generalities. Mary is such a sweet person, that I find it impossible to be exacting in my questions. It seems to me that the play has gotten a lot of favorable publicity and it should not be all this difficult to raise money on it, though Horton's play certainly did the company no good. - Well, I don't think we should wait around forever for Mary unless we are shown some tangible prospects - I see her tonight and perhaps will learn a bit more. (Please don't write Paul Moor or anyone about this - everyone talks so much here!)

Does this job you mention mean that the Margo Theatre Project is really on the way? I can't think of anything nicer for me than such a position would be. Nor can I think of anything that would seem more promising for a theatrical revival. Right after the war there is bound to be terrific resurgence in the arts, so your theatre would be starting at just the psychological time. Many, many boys will come out of this war with a desperate thirst for creation instead of destruction! - There is your chance, Margo! - I believe that you are a woman of destiny!

- Love, 10.

Do stop by Saint Louis - My address there is 53 Arundel Place, Clayton, Mo. - phone listed under Cornelius C. Williams. I think my strange little family will interest you. The book of poems is out but I have not yet received my copies. You shall have one - from me or Laughlin. - Love - 10.

Horton is engaged - met fiancée last night - nice, fairly pretty -

[TW returned to New York in early-September and remained there for approximately six weeks. Writing from California, Margo Jones had probably reminded her forgetful friend of his intention to send her "a very rough first draft" (see letter #302) of "A Balcony in Ferrara." She also kept him apprized of plans that she and John Rosenfield, drama critic of the *Dallas Morning News*, were mulling for a professional repertory theatre in Dallas with Jones as director. In late-October she met TW in Clayton, as she toured the Midwest on her self-described "'survey-study fellowship.'"

Although replaced in early-July by "'The Fiddle in the Wings" (see letter #310), "The Gentleman Caller" was restored as working title in August correspondence with Donald Windham and Jones. Its replacement in September by *The Glass Menagerie* has only one precedent known to the editors: a cancellation recorded in May 1943 while titling the "Provisional Film Story Treatment of 'The Gentleman Caller.'" The famous title may have been suggested by Hart Crane's poem "The Wine Menagerie" (1926). Collected in an edition (1933) of Crane's poetry that TW knew and treasured—indeed had "appropriated" from Washington University in St. Louis—the poem is a cryptic study of the power of alcohol to "distill" the visionary "competence" of the poet. A menagerie of "glozening decanters" lines the mirror behind the bar and "conscripts" the wary poet "to their shadow's glow."

Five Young American Poets was published by New Directions, belatedly TW thought, on September 3, 1944.]

314. To Edwina Dakin Williams and Walter E. Dakin

637 Madison Ave. [New York]
Wednesday Oct. 11, 1944
[TLS, 1 p. HTC]

Dear Mother and Grandfather:

Thanks a lot for the checks which arrived in the nick of time. Several things have happened to keep me here. First I had to have the new play, written this summer, typed up and distributed, which took about ten days. Then Laughlin, of New Directions, came in town. I had to wait for him to arrive and see him on several occasions, as he had proofs of "Battle" for me to check. Now there are two remaining things I have to remain for, at least through this week. Friday evening Mary Hunter is giving a reading of "You Touched Me" for a group of potential backers. I have to be on hand for that. Then the New School is thinking of opening a new class or department, called New Plays In Progress. They are considering my appointment as the head of this department, which would be a very interesting job for me. I am not counting on it, as they have tentatively offered me jobs before which didn't go through - but I am to see Mr. Piscator tomorrow and should be able to tell whether or not this one is truth or fiction. If it looks sufficiently authentic, I think it would warrant my staying here another two weeks to give it full chance to materialize. Piscator claims that I move around too rapidly for him to keep up with me, or he would have found a permanent place for me on the school faculty. If I get the job of course it will pay me enough to live here. However if it doesn't look reliable, I will leave immediately after the reading Friday evening. In that case I think I will have money enough to get me home. If I have to remain longer, I don't see how I can avoid using some of the fellowship money - not more than a hundred dollars of it - to take care of me here till the New School thing gets started. I will wire you this week-end if I have to stay and will need that amount. I hope you would have no difficulty getting it out of the bank, if I should have to have it.

In a recent letter you said Dakin was in a hospital in India. Is he sick? That was the only reference you made to the matter.

I do hope Grandfather's treatments are satisfactory. If I leave this week-end I will certainly be there before he starts on a trip.

Much love - Tom.

[Once again a position for TW at the New School seems not to have materialized.

Dakin Williams served briefly at an air field in northern Burma before being hospitalized with malaria. Reassigned to Calcutta, he was reportedly put in charge of legal cases arising from the presence of American troops in India.

This letter was written on stationery imprinted with the name of the American Ballet Caravan (canceled) and its director, Lincoln Kirstein.]

315. To Margaret "Margo" Jones

637 Madison [New York]
Oct 18, 1944
[TLS w/ autograph postscript, 2 pp. HRC]

Margo dear:

I hope that my good news will not seem bad news to you. I am sure it won't, really, if it strikes you as being good for me. Any good thing for one of us is good for both!

This news just broke yesterday, I had no previous intimation of it, in fact never dreamed that any commercial manager, even one with Dowling's superior sensibilities, would think of doing the Caller on Broadway. I guess it's a sign that the theatre is changing. Before Dowling decided, he sent the script to Nathan and Nathan liked it. I guess that's why Dowling is getting Hayden. Everybody has liked the script so far, the first time this has happened with any of my plays, and it surprises me completely. Of course I liked the material because it was so close to me, but for that very reason I doubted that it would come across to others. It was such hell writing it! Dowling plans to play the narrator himself. He explained to me that he will look much younger on the stage. Even so I think that will mean setting the play further back in time. I had thought of someone no older than myself playing the narrator. But of course Dowling is a grand actor and can get away with anything! As for Hayden, she is so physically and temperamentally right - has such a lovely quality - that her limitations as an actress don't seem important in this instance. Eddie will play her like a fiddle! He told me he didn't think the play would go on before late winter - he has another play to do first, one he doesn't like much. In the meantime I think I will get out of town. I don't feel like being involved with a Broadway crowd, and you always are when a play is coming up. Then if I am not in telephone reach, they won't plague me so much about little changes that occur to them. If you were here now I would probably stick around, as your presence would give me a certain moral support in dealing with them, but as it is I feel safer at a distance. Not that I anticipate much trouble, but having been through the mill with Langner and Helburn I am twice shy! I hope you will be around when the production gets started. I could certainly use you. Perhaps by November fifteenth I will be ready to come back here. If you pass through Saint Louis we might leave together. You know how frightened I am of everybody! Especially people in the theatre. So - I need you!

I will probably leave here this week-end for home.

Love, 10.

PS. Got letter from Schnitzler at U. of C. wanting release on play. Of course I can't give it now. Wrote him nice reply today. And do appreciate his interest. Most of all, yours! but you know that.

This month in N.Y. has been a strain and my nerves are shot. Again. Can't seem to take very much. Suppose a quiet period at home will do me some good.

Mary still working on "YTM". Do you think a production of that first would hurt the Caller? because of similarities between Matilda & Laura?

Want you to meet Dowling. Wish there was some way you could work with him on the show.

Probably see you in Saint Louis.

En Avant! - 10.

[The "good news" that *The Glass Menagerie* would be staged by Eddie Dowling might seem "bad news" to Margo Jones, TW surmised, because they had reportedly discussed using it to open her projected Dallas theatre.

Audrey Wood has recalled that Dowling, then forty nine, was the first producer to whom she sent *The Glass Menagerie*. His direction of William Saroyan's *The Time of Your Life* (1939) and other such imaginative theatre was qualification, she thought, for a play that also seemed deficient by Broadway standards of realism.

The critic George Jean Nathan, who would marry Julie Haydon (the original Laura), reportedly advised Dowling to accept the play, and legend has it that Dowling's wife applied the final pressure: "'You may not like it and it may not make you any money, but if you don't read it now, and someone else should buy it, I'd never hear the last of it'" (qtd. in *The Best Plays of 1944-45*).

Henry Schnitzler became interested in staging *The Glass Menagerie* at the University of California after Jones visited the campus on her fellowship.

Dowling wrote to Jones on November 2, 1944, and invited her to be his "co-director," as "Tennessee seems to feel that you would fit that capacity one hundred per cent" (HRC). Jones was granted leave by the Rockefeller Foundation, signed a contract dated November 15, 1944, and joined the cast of *The Glass Menagerie* on December 1.

This letter was written on stationery imprinted with the name of The Museum of Modern Art (canceled) and its Consultant on Latin-American Art, Lincoln Kirstein.]

316. To James "Jay" Laughlin

[53 Arundel Place
Clayton, Missouri]
Nov. 1, 1944
[TLS, 2 pp. Houghton]

Dear Jay:

It is quiet and sunny here, Fall just getting started, big rooms full of yellow light, sounds of women puttering about, all very reassuring and agreeable in this appaling world. Just before I left N.Y. I saw a picture "The Rainbow" (Soviet film) at the Stanley in Times Square. Such a powerful study of hatred and horror! I suppose this is an authentic picture of what is happening outside "the belvedere" and I felt quite shaken by it. If you have a strong stomach, see it! It is really an apology for hatred. With such savagery unleashed in the world I don't see how there can be peace again for hundreds of years. Those are the things one should be writing about. How to reconcile my world, or the world of - say - Charles Henri Ford - tender or private emotions or rare, esoteric fancies with what's going on outside. Micro with macro cosmos! Should one even try? Or blandly assume, as I suppose Charles does, that we are the really important ones with the significant concerns? - Have you read Parker Tyler's dissertation in the new VIEW? There is where a superlative is reached in esthetic distance! - It is a good issue, incidentally, especially the "folk" pieces.

The work on "menagerie" may start in two or three weeks. Just before I left town I had a frightening conversation with Dowling. He proposed that a happy ending be flashed on the screen at the close of the play - Laura with the brace removed ("orthopoedics do such wonderful things!") and the gentleman caller standing again at the door! - That is the sort of thing the most intelligent producers spring on you! - He said it was just a suggestion, not a demand, "There is so much unhappiness in the world, Etc." that the audience shouldn't go away feeling depressed. - I am working out at the "Y" so I will go back in condition to fight off all such assaults. Fortunately Margo will be there. She will arrive in N.Y. in a few days.

Great distress here as we have received a 15 page letter from my brother in the Burma jungle announcing and justifying his conversion to Roman Catholicism. My grandfather, an Episcopal minister, has packed up and returned South. Wouldn't you think this generation would at last and at least be done with theological dogma? No! - my kid brother writes a long dissertation from the fighting front on "Transubstantiation" (accepts it literally) and "The Infallibility of the Pope" which he says has not been disproven! - Believe it or not, I am the bright one of the family!

Maybe I will get back before you leave - if Dowling wires me.

Hope you get back at Schwartz and all writers who bore each other. Don't let them do all the talking!

I talked to a woman who works for Vanguard at a cocktail party. She says you don't circularize the book-dealers enough. How about that?

I have to write a critique for next VIEW. Think it will be on Lorca and Ramon Naya and "The Plastic Theatre". - not on Shapiro. I could think of nothing pleasant to say about his V-Letter so I just won't do it.

Tennessee

["Powerful" images from *The Rainbow* (1944, dir. Mark Donskoi) had reached TW's own "'belvedere,'" a place of refuge from the "mutilations" ("The Summer Belvedere," 1944) of world history, as described in a recent poem.

Parker Tyler's essay "The Erotic Spectator: An Essay on the Eye of the Libido" (*View*, October 1944), is a far-ranging, and still incisive, study of visual perception in modern art.

Eddie Dowling's request for "a happy ending" had been anticipated by TW in the "Provisional Film Story Treatment of 'The Gentleman Caller'" (see letter #271) and in earlier drafts of the stage play itself.

Dakin Williams has recalled for the editors that his conversion to Roman Catholicism "caused Grandfather to panic and run," while Cornelius, "never the religious one," said "'it could be worse - he might have become a Hindu'"—hospitalized as Dakin was in India.

From 1941 to 1945 New Directions collaborated with a number of fine presses in publishing "The Poet of the Month" series. Vanguard was not one of these, but its representative had perhaps informed TW of advertising problems associated with the project.

TW was interviewed in St. Louis by William Inge, wartime replacement for Reed Hynds on the local *Star-Times*. "Another name to add to the already elongated list of St. Louis' literary sons and daughters is that of 'Tennessee' Williams" began an article rife with misinformation, including the whopper that *Battle of Angels* "closed after two weeks in New York" (November 11, 1944; rpt. in *Conversations*, pp. 6-8). Inge and TW became friends, occasional lovers, it seems, and in the 1950s competitors on Broadway. TW introduced Inge to Margo Jones, who produced his first play in 1947, and to Audrey Wood, who became his agent.]

317. To James "Jay" Laughlin

[New York]
Dec. 15, 1944
[TLS w/ autograph postscript, 1 p. Houghton]

Dear Jay:

We catch the train tomorrow afternoon for Chicago and probably the most hectic week of my far from pacific career, so I am snatching these few relatively tranquil moments to say hello - When I think of you on your mountain, among the everlasting snows, - well, it is like Kilimanjaroo from the pestilential jungle! Stay on your mountain, boy!

I won't try to tell you how things are going. It's just in the lap of the gods. Too many incalculables - the brain-cells of an old woman, a cold-blooded banker's reckoning of chances, enigmas of audience and critics. It is really a glass menagerie that we are taking on the road and God only knows how much of it will survive the journey.

I have one great thing to be thankful for - and that is Margo, in whose apartment I'm writing. Without her in on this adventure I wouldn't have gotten this far along with it - she has been heroic.

Have just said goodbye to Audrey - she mentioned that she is getting in touch with your man Brecht and seems highly interested in him.

Anything new on "Battle"? Incidentally, Dowling is enthusiastic over it and has sent a copy to Tallulah Bankhead. IF the menagerie is successful, I think he would try to interest her in an early production of it and I think she'd be damned good as Myra. Maybe a little short on tenderness but plenty of richness and drama. If this materialized I would try another version of the script - eliminating two features that have always troubled me, the vague "book" and the prologue-epilogue. I hope you are making that suggested division in Act Two - that would help.

I have seen only one review of the poems, in the Herald Tribune. It was pretty condescending but not really evil. - as the View would have been. But I think View has killed their review - for lack of space in the Christmas issue.

Regardless of how things turn out on the present venture, I will be grateful for a chance to retire from the world and get back some composure. It has been months since my heart beat quietly!

Yours ever, Tennessee

Best to Margaret. We open Dec. 25

[Chief among the "incalculables" was Laurette Taylor, the legendary actress who had come out of retirement to make a seemingly uncertain adjustment to the part of Amanda. Her lines, if remembered at all, were delivered in a southern accent that resembled "the Aunt Jemima Pancake hour" (qtd. in *Windham*, p. 155), or so TW thought at the time. A long history of alcoholism, not entirely overcome, added to the risk of Taylor's casting. The "cold-blooded" backer and co-producer, Louis J. Singer, was a worried, meddlesome presence, who would soon demand that a happy ending be drafted to protect his investment. And George Jean Nathan, no patron of TW, tried to manipulate the production through his friendship with Eddie Dowling and his romantic attachment to Julie Haydon.

In September TW asked James Laughlin (who complied) to insert "a dim-out" (September 25, 1944, Houghton) between intimate and busy scenes in Act Two of *Battle of Angels*. Val's "'book'" still troubled TW because he could not give this work-in-progress definition or credibility. The "prologue-epilogue" device had appeared in the May 1941 revision of *Battle* and was retained in *Pharos*.

The "evil" notice of *Five Young American Poets* was not "killed" but delayed until the March 1945 number of *View*. Philip Lamantia deemed the anthology to be "of hardly any consequence," and TW none at all. Both versions of his preface were "inane," Lamantia thought, and his poetry showed an "obvious lack of talent." Any plan that TW had of writing for *View* ended with these harsh remarks.]

318. To Walter E. Dakin

[Hotel Sherman
Chicago, Illinois]
[December 25, 1944]
[ALS, 1 p. HTC]

Dear Grandfather -

Know you understand how busy I've been - What a hectic time! But the play is now pulling together and the outlook is bright. Mother is here for the opening tomorrow night.

How I wish you were!

I will write you all about it, anyhow.

Much love and a very merry Xmas to you -

Tom.

[Edwina also wrote to assure her father that *The Glass Menagerie* was "bound to be successful" (December 25, 1944, HTC). The many "incalculables" of rehearsal, the technical challenge posed by a play whose "*scene is memory*," the bitter cold of opening night, the superb reviews, the pleas of Ashton Stevens and Claudia Cassidy that Chicago save an endangered classic remain a vital part of the play's lore after more than fifty years of production. Perhaps no praise more assuaged TW's long and bitter struggle than the postscript of Ashton Stevens's opening night review: "From neighboring seats I heard William Saroyan mentioned, and Paul Vincent Carroll, and Sean O'Casey, and even a playwright named Barrie. But the only author's name I could think of was Tennessee Williams, whose magic is all his own" (*Chicago Herald-American*, December 27, 1944).]

319. To Jo Mielziner

[Hotel Sherman
Chicago, Illinois]
[ca. January 11, 1945]
[TLS, 1 p. HRC]

Dear Jo:

Many thanks for your note - I guess you know by now that your light-ing job is the first thing on every one's tongue in connection with this show.

It is nothing less than sensational - and now that the crew is working smoothly, it is far more effective than when you saw it. Now it goes like clock-work and is inestimably and very integrally a part of the play. I want to thank you for your patience - endurance is a better word - Margo is sending you a clipping about Mr. Singer's assistance to you that I think will give you the final sense of fulfillment!

Well, business has picked up considerably - I am still going through hell with various dissenting opinions about the end of the play - but most of Eddie's mugging and ad-lib has been cut out - and of course you know that Taylor <u>did</u> know her lines - and gave a performance so astonishing that none of us still quite believe it! Hope I see you in New York soon, Jo - and that you'll stick with us - with or without Mr. Singer's expert assistance. . . .

Cordially, Tennessee

[Shortly before opening night, Ashton Stevens quoted a breathless description (by the company's business manager, Alex Yokel) of Jo Mielziner's preparations to light *The Glass Menagerie*: "Jo Mielziner has just arrived to start the lighting job of his luminous life. Jo dopes out an electrical scheme that is tremendous because I can't think of a bigger word. Where an ordinary show has one switchboard, Jo has seven. He has 57 sets of lines hanging from the fly gallery, 150 feet up, and is using every line to hang the electrical equipment" (*Chicago Herald-American*, December 24, 1944). It was, Mielziner said, his "most difficult" job to date, and one that had been complicated by the penny-pinching economies of the backer, Louis J. Singer. The "clipping" that Margo Jones sent to Mielziner was probably Claudia Cassidy's col-umn of January 8, 1945, in which Eddie Dowling was quoted as saying that Singer "couldn't get enough of watching Jo Mielziner work. He even offered a few sug-gestions" (*Chicago Tribune*).

TW called upon the talents of Mielziner (1901-1976) for at least eight other productions, including *A Streetcar Named Desire* (1947), *Summer and Smoke* (1948), and *Cat on a Hot Tin Roof* (1955). Prewar credits for *Strange Interlude*

(1928), *Street Scene* (1929), and *Winterset* (1935) were the foundation of a career in theatre, ballet, opera, and film that transformed American stage design from a business into an art form.]

320. To Margaret "Margo" Jones

SH: Hotel Sherman
Chicago, Ill.
[ca. February 2, 1945]
[TLS, 1 p. HRC]

Dear Margo:

Things are about the same here, box-office still booming - for instance last night was five hundred dollars more than a week ago. Only one trouble has come up since you left - Laurette's voice. She had a "relaxed throat" or something and has been extremely hoarse the last four or five performances. Only treatment is rest and of course she has no chance to rest it - and she won't stop talking even after the show! I have been sharing her responsibility with Tony, spending every night with her in various bars and she seems to be getting about as fond of me as she is of him, which is a blessing but not unmixed. Anyhow she's a grand old girl.

I guess you know we are booked for N.Y. on March sixth. I haven't sat out front lately but think I will tonight and if I notice anything amiss will let you know. Eddie still comes out with some dreadful ad-libs in the drunk scene. One night he started singing "Blue Birds over the White cliffs of Dover" - which came out five years after the period of the play. And he calls Julie "Old Timer" and the menagerie "little glass guys". But then you know that problem!

I have rented this big typewriter and am stretching my literary muscles a bit, just to keep in shape.

I left Dad with Laurette while I ran off to a late party - the night he was here. She was furious as she couldn't stand him. Called me up next morning and yelled, "How dare you leave me alone with that dull old man!"

Mary Hunter called long distance to say she had money to buy play and "about all the money for the production and was ready to go ahead with it" but a wire from Audrey advised against any immediate commitment - said you had attended a conference of the money people. Did you, and what is the situation? Would appreciate your version of it. I've written Mary to give me a complete detailed statement on the financial set-up before I can enter into a contract and so far no answer. I can't let Mary down on this deal and I'm not going to - but Audrey is right about needing the best and most professional set-up and real assurance of it before we start.

If you don't hear from me it's only because nothing important comes up and I'm so damn busy keeping Laurette happy, Etc. But I think of you and miss you all the time, baby.

Much love - 10.

[By late-January Margo Jones had returned to New York and resumed the Rockefeller grant. *The Glass Menagerie* would run for thirteen weeks in Chicago's Civic Theatre and earn a reported gross of $188,300. It began to meet operating expenses in the third week and by the end of January business was "booming." On March 1 TW informed Edwina that the 850 seat house was still near capacity and earning royalties of $1,000 per week (Thursday Evening {March 1, 1945} HRC), which Audrey Wood banked in New York. Edwina savored this decisive victory in TW's long "fight with his father; he was a success in the field he had chosen." The "literal" Cornelius, Edwina also reported, did not believe that she was Amanda or that the family "portrayed" on stage resembled "ours in any way" (*Remember Me To Tom*).

TW's "stretching" of "literary muscles" would soon eventuate in *A Streetcar Named Desire*, to be announced to Wood in late-March 1945 as a work-in-progress.]

321. To Audrey Wood

SH: Hotel Sherman
Chicago, Ill.
[ca. February 5, 1945]
[TLS w/ autograph postscript, 2 pp. HRC]

Dear Audrey:

James Laughlin came through town and saw the show and is very anxious to publish the book right away. In view of Jay's kindness to me and the fact he has already published my work and will continue to publish it I am firmly persuaded that he should do the book. He is willing to pay Random House the one hundred dollar advance which he says was only for "Battle" - that is, the terms affecting a contract for one book cannot be made applicable to another. In the years since Cerf made that payment he has not shown one spark of interest in my work or existence and while I don't feel any resentment of this - he had no reason to - I don't think I should now favor his firm instead of Laughlin's, especially since to be published by New Directions is far more of an honor to my way of thinking. Of course we must have Laughlin's assurance - and I think we will - that the book will come out speedily enough and will be properly distributed among the book-dealers. I believe in dealing with people who have shown sympathy and faith in you - which isn't merely sentiment but also sound business practise. So please work with Laughlin on this and see what can be done to extricate me gracefully - without unnecessary offense - from the Random House commitment. Should I write Cerf myself or can you and Laughlin handle it? Here is the contract Laughlin left here with me.

I am glad we are going into New York next month. Worried about Laurette. She got terribly drunk at a party night before last. Literally passed out cold and fell on the sidewalk - first time this has happened and she was okay for the next performance. But I know she is terribly lonely here and the sooner she gets back to N.Y. the better. Know you won't talk about this - I wasn't at the party but heard about it. I believe she restrains herself a little when I am around and that is one reason I'm staying

- Love - 10.

- Just got your letter -

I feel <u>positive</u> we're going in March 6th - Friday & Sunday nights showed our first drop in attendance and I suspect even Eddie realizes we can't milk Chicago beyond that date - especially if he has any concern for <u>Laurette</u>. Think we may safely procede on assumption of that date - Eddie is full of blarney! - Margo is sometimes fallible even from my point of view. I think Mary will do something beautiful with "YTM" - I will work right along with her more than I could with anyone else! Send me revised "YTM."

[In late 1940 TW had signed a contract (for an advance of $100) that gave Random House publication rights to his "next work," which became *The Glass Menagerie*.

Although surprised to learn of the agreement (made during Audrey Wood's sojourn in California), Wood found it desirable and had pointedly informed TW that Bennett Cerf handles plays "better than any other publisher in New York at this time" (January 25, 1945, HRC). Nonetheless TW wrote naively to James Laughlin to assure him that "Audrey will extricate me from Cerf" (February 6, 1945, Houghton).

Eddie Dowling's "blarney" that all Chicago was calling for *Menagerie* to remain in town through Easter (April 1) was actually a shrewd prediction in light of the play's closing on March 24 (see letter from Wood to TW, February 3, 1945, HRC). The final decision to open in New York on March 31 was timed to capitalize on the Easter weekend and to qualify for the 1944-1945 round of theatre awards.

Margo Jones had expressed concern to Wood and Donald Windham about Mary Hunter's post-Pasadena revisions of *You Touched Me!* TW described the changes to Windham as relatively minor and complained of Jones's meddlesomeness and inability to read a script accurately (see *Windham*, pp. 161-162).]

322. To the Editor, Chicago Herald-American

[Hotel Sherman
Chicago, Illinois]
[*Chicago Herald-American*,
February 25, 1945, p. 19]

Dear Sir:

In the United States there is a little band of drama critics whose tenets of faith in a certain type of theater—or certain types—have been largely responsible for holding that misshapen thing within certain bounds.

I say misshapen because of the many distortions that have taken place since businessmen and gamblers discovered that the theater could be made a part of their empire.

Once they made that discovery—being vital souls—they proceeded to enlarge their grasp upon it till finally very little remained outside.

But when they swallowed the theater they also swallowed these critics—this little band of a dozen or so—here and there in America, who did not regard the theater as a business or a slot-machine or a concession at a carnival or a race-horse.

The theater seemed to lie sweetly on their stomachs, but often the drama critics—or a certain number of them—kicked up a fuss and gave them indigestion.

Ultimately it is my hope that the indigestible morsel will prove an emetic powerful enough to remove the whole mistaken banquet from their bellies.

They had no business, these businessmen and gamblers, gobbling up the theater, for it was never marked for their consumption: They got hold of it because the ones that should get hold of it were not very quick at the table. Their boarding-house reach was exceeded.

I am not speaking bitterly of businessmen and gamblers. Gamblers are exciting personalities and businessmen are not only respectable but often desirable members of any society. I am only speaking bitterly of them as custodians of an art which to me is religion.

All of this is prelude to a remark that was recently made by Mr. Brooks Atkinson, and which was quoted to me recently by Mr. Ashton Stevens. Mr. Atkinson and Mr. Stevens are members of the same profession and also of the small division of the profession which doesn't rest quietly on the stomachs of commercial entrepreneurs of the stage.

They are among the select few of American drama critics who insist that the theater have another purpose than entertainment and profit.

Being human, they believe in entertainment and they believe in profit. But they also believe in the power and the glory that a resurgent theater could have in a resurgent American democracy.

Mr. Atkinson's remark was made when he retired, temporarily, from his position as drama critic of the New York Times to become a war correspondent in China. He justified this change by saying that criticism of drama was "an ignoble profession at best."

Whether or not he meant it seriously, the remark deserves some examination.

I disagree.

Any profession becomes ignoble when it is practised by charlatans. A quack doctor makes an ignoble profession of medicine.

If theater itself is important, the criticism of it is equally so. For it is the attitude of the critics that determines the direction of change in theater. And change is imminent. Always after a great shaking up of world society, as the present war has been, changes occur in all of its reflecting institutions and arts. With the war now speeding into its final phase in the Orient and Europe, the Pacific fleet bombing Tokyo, and Russian troops at the gates of Berlin, we are just about face to face with a new world which is either craven or valiant.

The dice are poised half-way between the box and the board.

In the meantime normal activities go on, and certainly not least among these is the theater.

The theater is expression and nothing is more powerful, now, than expression.

Then how can you call a profession which determines the way that theater will likely go "ignoble"?

It is squarely up to the critics to make their profession noble or not. They sit in the cab of a locomotive whose power may be tremendous, and if they refuse to let it turn in the direction of falsity and prostitution and dullness, if they insist upon truth and liveliness, Mr. Atkinson's remark is proven an ill-timed jest!

But you don't have to prove it to me. From now on I'm from Chicago!

(Even polishing the apple is a noble profession if you mean it!)

TENNESSEE WILLIAMS

[Published in Ashton Stevens's column, TW's letter to the editor reportedly drew the wrath of Eddie Dowling and Louis Singer, the latter the shady entrepreneur of the production. TW later informed Donald Windham that Dowling had instructed his New York press agent to remove the playwright's name from all releases about *The Glass Menagerie* (see *Windham*, p. 163).]

323. To Donald Windham

SH: Hotel Sherman
Chicago, Ill.
[ca. late-February 1945]
[TL draft, 1 p. Private Collection]

Dear Donnie:

With money rolling in at the rate of a thousand a week, all impulse toward action has been short-circuited in me. I have no reason to stay here and I can't think of any reason to go. I am neither elated nor depressed, just feel sort of dissociated from everything past or future. I mosey around town, usually with Tony and Laurette or the university kids, till five or six in the morning - go to bed and sleep till about four in the afternoon. Have breakfast sent up. Work desultorily. Smoke cigarettes, have cocktails sent up, answer the phone, finally go for a swim, then to a movie, then call for Tony and Laurette at the theatre. What a useless existence! But this overwhelming security has made all plans or effort suddenly pointless and given life an air of extreme unreality. What shall I do with myself? I don't [know] whether it's a fool's paradise or purgatory! But I shall have to decide on something extraordinary soon or I will turn into a jelly-fish.

[Two later essays by TW closely follow the lament of this draft letter. "On a Streetcar Named Success" (*New York Times*, November 30, 1947) was timed for the première of *A Streetcar Named Desire* and thus served the dual function of advertisement and confession. It was expanded and published in *STORY* magazine under the well-known title "The Catastrophe of Success" (1948).]

324. To Audrey Wood

[53 Arundel Place
Clayton, Missouri]
Thursday March 8th 1945
[TLS, 2 pp. HRC]

Dear Audrey:

I fully participate in your happiness over the McClintic deal though I feel somewhat guilty and embarassed over its effect on Mary.

She woke me up at ten o'clock this morning with a long-distance call which went on for at least five minutes. She had received your letter which she said took her completely by astonishment and wanted me to explain as you were not in town. Having just awakened I was in no condition to cope with her verbally, that is, with any finesse, so I simply told her the facts as I understood them - that you and Mr. Collins had not obtained her agreement to the contract, or were not in accord on terms, and so you'd had to go ahead with another management. I am afraid I mentioned McClintic - involuntarily. She said she had always been willing to combine forces with another management on the play and that she would be willing to work on that basis. I said I hoped some way might be found to work that out. Then she said she must have some assurance it would be, not just wishes, or she would have to stick to her guns - or something like that. Sounds ominous! Then I told her, although I appreciated all she had done and was extremely anxious not to let her down altogether - still my investment in the play was so great that I felt justified in acting quite objectively about it and choosing whatever producer I thought could do most for the script - naturally McClintic would be my choice, I told her. Reminded her also that I had only 1/3 interest and that Windham and Lawrence - represented by Collins - had to be considered. - Well, we were getting nowhere fast and Mary becoming more and more excited - so I said, finally, I will get in touch with Audrey and find out what is happening - meanwhile do not be nervous or unhappy about it! The conversation ended with her imploring me not to consummate any deal till we had talked it over in New York - I said nothing definite to her. I tried to be gentle and reassuring without actually misrepresenting anything to her - but of course I felt like a heel! Though actually I don't suppose any playwright would act differently under these circumstances. - Do you suppose McClintic would give her some part in the production, co-director, assistant, or anything like that? That would certainly avoid a lot of unhappiness and disappointment for Mary and embarassment to all of us - for I am sure Mary and Mary's friends will never regard Tennessee as anything but a snake if she is left out cold! - I am putting all this in your hands! Can you hold it?!

Regarding Windham's percentage, I thought a contract had been drawn up a long time ago making that definite. There was some correspondance concerning it the summer I was in Macon and at that time I wrote you that if Windham wanted a fifty-fifty arrangement I did not want to antagonize him by holding out for more, though certainly I should have it. Since that time, however, - as you know - I have re-written the play repeatedly, worked on it always entirely without his assistance - since the first two months when collaborative effort on it was getting us nowhere - Actually at this time the whole play is my creation, dialogue and all inventions not drawn from the Lawrence story - which Windham had wanted to follow exactly to its death-bed conclusion. He never really liked what I was doing to the play and after I started making it a comedy, he seemed to lose interest in everything except its possible sale.

Windham's attitude is understandable, however. He discovered the short-story and it was his idea to make it a play - I volunteered to assist him - it just happened we couldn't work together and the final result was totally my own product.

Obviously the percentages are unfair, but I would prefer for any adjustment - if any is still possible - to be by friendly agreement rather than any pressure put on him. A fair arrangement would be for Frieda Lawrence and I to have equal shares and Don the remaining twenty, which is about as large a price as anyone has received for his amount of effort or contribution. If the matter were coming up for the first time, I would insist upon this division - because of all I've done on the script, and the fact that "Menagerie's" success is the only reason this one is sold. If he won't agree to change percentages, perhaps he would consent to smaller credit on the program. - one or the other - I think it would be all right to talk this over with him and see if he is inclined to be unselfish. - We have been good friends a long time and I wouldn't like to antagonize him. Let me know your opinion.

I have some revisions on the last scene of "YTM" which I will mail you before I leave Saint Louis - want to go over them once more.

I'm intending to leave this week-end, back to Chicago, as I've kept my room there - Unless you've already mailed my check, please send me an extra hundred this time ($200.) as I am going to buy some new clothes to gladden the eyes of Broadway.

Perhaps I will need an armed body-guard when I get there, with Yokel and Hunter both feeling betrayed!

Love, 10.

[TW wrote from Clayton, where he submitted to a week of family inquisition relieved by nightly forays with Bill Inge.

Enclosed in this letter was a note for Guthrie McClintic in which TW expressed "happiness" over their "alliance on 'You Touched Me!'" and confidence that his direction would realize the "plastic" elements of the play. It should, TW wrote, "have great lightness and charm and pictorial beauty" (March 7, 1945, HRC).

McClintic's $750 advance for *You Touched Me!* led Audrey Wood to query TW once again (see letter #232) about the distribution of royalties: "Won't you think about this and let me try to make a better deal with Windham" (March 6,

1945, HRC), she urged. Donald Windham has noted that she asked him on March 12 to rescind the 1942 contract that gave equal shares to the collaborators and accept a 40/20 division instead. He declined, pending discussion with TW. Apparently the terms of the original contract remained in force (see *Windham*, pp. 166, 169, 178).

TW described his "new clothes" to Windham as "a race-track suit! - loud black & white check job," and quoted Eddie Dowling's disapproval: "Are you gonna wear *that* to the Opening?" (qtd. in *Windham*, p. 165).]

325. To James "Jay" Laughlin

[53 Arundel Place
Clayton, Missouri]
Sunday [March 11, 1945]
[TLS w/ autograph postscript, 2 pp. Houghton]

JAY!

How silly of you to think I was letting you down about the "menagerie" publication!

I didn't answer your letter because Audrey wrote me that "everything was settled" and you were putting the book in print, that is, getting the type set up in preparation - so I assumed it was all ironed out. She did say, however, that Cerf had turned down your hundred and that nothing could be done till after the opening - that is, definitely.

I know I should have gotten the final script off to you by now. I enquired a couple of times for a copy but the script girl put me off saying there was only one which she needed - I have none at all. And Dowling's drunk scene still only exists in his voice-box: he destroys paper copies for some reason. Can Audrey give you a script or must you get one through me, and how soon? I guess we must get legally disentangled from Cerf before actual printing can start, but I have every intention - if your printers can give you a reasonable date on it - of taking any action necessary to get clear of Cerf. I want no part of any commercial publishers now or ever! Not as long as I am eating without them. Once you get tied up with one you become, for better or worse, a professional writer which shouldn't happen to anyone!

I have let other things slip lately because I've been amusing and torturing myself with a group of somewhat surrealist poems, loosely connected under the general title of ELECTRIC AVENUE, mostly with a southern background: might fit in with THE COUPLE which I sent you last Spring. My main aggravation is inability to break from the five beat line or slight variations of it: it has become a fixation, monotonous and inescapable. In this connection I have been studying St. Jean Perse as he has the most flexible cadences of all. Crane is not really good at cadence, though he is powerful enough not to need it. He usually has either five-beats or machine-gun bursts that only he can get away with. Except in the prose-poems like ETERNITY and HAVANA ROSE in which I think he reached his pinnacle of style, or form.

I left the "menagerie" in a state of chassis. Pandemonium back-stage! Intrigues, counter-intrigues, rages, smashed door-panes, - quelle menagerie! I was in the dog-house with nearly everybody - with the backer because I wrote a Sunday paper column on business-men and gamblers in the theatre which he took as a personal affront. With Tony and Laurette because Tony has developed an alcoholic persecution-complex and has convinced Laurette of God knows what imaginary offenses of mine! Things are so tense all the time you never know when the whole company will just blow up and vanish! Actors are just not believable - so fantastic! especially the good ones like Laurette and Tony.

I am sorry about the disappointment in N.Y. though I might have told you, for I have been through it continually. A thing like that is so firmly rooted in one time or place, in one set of circumstances, that try as you will you can't breathe life into it the second occasion. But why should you want to, as it is not <u>duration</u> that gives it <u>value</u> really.

The evils of promiscuity are exageratted. Somebody said it has at least the advantage of making you take more baths. But I think one picks a rose from each person, each of a somewhat different scent and color. Each affair can make some new disclosure, and whether it builds or reduces your range of feeling and understanding depends pretty much on yourself. Of course you pay for it with something - perhaps a cumulative distrust of what is called 'real love'.

As for hurting people who love you - nothing is less avoidable! I have been home for a week - every night this week some feeling of compulsion sent me out of the house from about five in the afternoon till after two in the morning - any excuse just to get away and escape talk and questioning!

Though I knew I was insulting and hurting them. Tonight I came in at ten - the earliest - and was greeted with a flood of tears and reproaches - and how could I explain or excuse myself except by saying - Yes, it's true, I can't stand it here, not even one night out of one week out of one year!

I will be in New York about or on the 24th. If Audrey permits, let's call on Cerf together and have it out with him. - Have been reading the 1942 Annual - many thanks - the stuff by Alvin Levin has brilliant patches - I can't follow Goodman, he is so abstruse or intricately intellectual - I like the W.C.W. play to read but I question its plasticity, its stage values - but I haven't finished it yet.

Returning to Chicago tomorrow evening.

A riverdici, 10.

P.S. Audrey is sweet.

Read "Maiden Voyage" by Denton Welch - to understand Charles Henri Etc. - a lovely book!

[Bennett Cerf had "turned down" James Laughlin's offer to repay the advance on *The Glass Menagerie*. Cerf would await the play's reception in New York before making a decision to publish.

The "surrealist poems" underway are probably those which TW completed in Mexico in July 1945 and published in *New Directions 9* (1946). "Camino Real" and "Recuerdo" make reference to "Electric avenue," which "stops for NoooooBODY!—who doesn't believe one number comes twice in two throws."

The backstage "chassis" ("the whole worl's in a state o' chassis!" opines a character in Sean O'Casey's *Juno and the Paycock*) was a product of Laurette Taylor's preëminent notices, her repeated censure of Eddie Dowling's mannered style of acting and his age (too old at fifty to play her son, she thought), and Dowling's own sullen resentment. Ashton Stevens is reported to have chastised Taylor for endangering the play's chances in New York by allowing a feud to develop, and she bowed at least momentarily to his warning.]

326. To Eddie Dowling

[Hotel Sherman
Chicago, Illinois]
[March 1945]
[TL draft, 1 p. HTC]

Dear Eddie:

I am enclosing two items for your perusal - one is a hasty synopsis of the play I mentioned to you last night which is being tried out at Pasadena and which I think might have exciting possibilities for you as it is your sort of play. (Not that any good play isn't)

Also a new draft of the drunk scene. I have been studying the audience reaction to the material in it and I am trying to select those parts which go over and weed out what doesn't. Perhaps this is something which we should work out together before we open in New York - there is no question in my mind now about the rightness of your having this scene and I am grateful to you and Nathan for thinking of it. I am only troubled by the fact it hasn't entirely solidified - that is, acquired a final, definitive written form, and think we should have one - word for word - before we open. Phrasing - exact phrasing - ought to be <u>set</u>. Half of comedy rests in the cadence and accent of a line - only half in the line's meaning! That's why I think we should select just what material we want to use and for you to commit it exactly as phrased. I think this can be your <u>top</u> scene in the play and want to make it that!

You may think my new idea of the "peeping Tom" too vulgar - my idea was that it suggested the general indignity of the life forced on him as well as being a funny start to the scene. Your best laugh in the scene is on "rise and shine" so I am keeping that, but have a new idea for the end which would use the father's picture effectively and bring in the idea of the father-son pattern.

I am unhappy over the new tag-line <u>Where your imagination begins</u>. I think this is fully implied in 'where my memory stops' and the addition is too obvious and unnecessary. The end of a play - the final spoken line - is too important to admit what is obvious. If you are still dissatisfied with the final lines, let me know and I will work on alternatives. Among my notes I found this:

'Goodbye to you, Mother and Laura -
Old worn-out music of the past, goodbye!'

Don't think it adds anything but you may consider it.

[*Stairs to the Roof* was slated to open on March 25, 1945, at the Pasadena Playbox with direction by Gilmor Brown. TW considered Eddie Dowling (1894-1976) a likely producer-director for the play, if only because *Stairs* resembled William Saroyan's work in subject matter and technique. He later sent production stills to Dowling and described plans for further revision but nothing came of his desire for a New York opening (letter, n.d., HRC).

Dowling's continued ad-libbing in the "drunk scene" (Scene Four) concerned TW as the play's transfer to Broadway approached. The scene, probably suggested by George Jean Nathan, was intended to enhance the parts of Dowling (Tom) and Julie Haydon (Laura) and to give *The Glass Menagerie* an element of comic relief. TW has noted in *Memoirs* that Nathan and Dowling composed their own scene, which included "a song for Eddie—'My Melancholy Baby'—and other unmentionables." The final draft, for which TW accepted "no collaboration," did "the play little harm" (p. 82), he admitted in retrospect. In fact it gave Tom and Laura their only stage time alone and thus confirmed the intimacy of brother and sister. The draft status of this letter suggests that TW may have felt some awkwardness in presenting Dowling with the "definitive written form" of a scene for which the irrepressible performer still claimed authorship.

The "peeping Tom" idea may have originated with Bill Cannastra's voyeurism as described in *Memoirs* (p. 84). It does not appear either in the reading (1945) or acting (1948) versions of *The Glass Menagerie*, nor does Dowling's suggested elaboration of the end of the play.]

327. To Audrey Wood

[Hotel Sherman
Chicago, Illinois]
Friday, March 23, 1945
[TLS, 3 pp. HRC]

Dear Audrey:

Just got your wire about contracts and am worried about them. I distinctly remember signing and mailing them in the envelope which you provided the very day that I received them. I sent them Air-mail. The address - already on the envelope - was Kiowa Ranch, San Cristobal, New Mexico. This was at least a week ago and they certainly should have reached Frieda by this date. Of course these New Mexico ranches are a bit remote from airlines and perhaps mail-deliveries are irregular. If you don't hear affirmatively in the next day or so I would rush through another copy of the contract.

I have been buried in work the last week or so and am about 55 or 60 pages into the first draft of a play which I am trying to design for Cornell. At the moment it has four different titles, The Moth, The Poker Night, The Primary Colors, or Blanche's Chair In The Moon. It is about two sisters, the remains of a fallen southern family. The younger, Stella, has accepted the situation, married beneath her socially and moved to a southern city with her coarsely attractive, plebian mate. But Blanche (the Cornell part) has remained at Belle-reve, the home place in ruins, and struggles for five-years to maintain the old order. Though essentially decent and very delicate by nature, she has gone for protection to various men till her name is tarnished. She teaches English in a small-town highschool but loses the job when her name is involved with a married man's. The place is finally lost, Belle-reve, and Blanche, destitute, gives up the struggle and takes refuge with Stella in the southern city. She arrives broken by the failing struggle (arrival first scene of play) and is at the mercy of the tough young husband, Ralph. A strong sex situation develops, Ralph and Blanche being completely antipathetic types, he challenged and angered by her delicacy, she repelled and fascinated by his coarse strength. His friends are similar types who meet Saturday nights at the house for poker. One of them is attracted to Blanche and in her desperate need for an outside strength she accepts his attentions. She is about to make the adjustment that Stella has made, accepting the coarse for protection, when Ralph - who has unconsciously fallen in love with Blanche - learns of her reputation in the small town, the scandal that forced her to leave the school. Blanche has been pretending that she still has the school job and will return to it in the Fall and has concealed the loss of Belle-reve. Ralph exposes these facts to Stella on the night of Blanche's birthday - and as a birthday gift he presents Blanche with a bus-ticket back to the small town she is exiled from. It turns out that he has also informed his friend Mitchell (the one that Blanche has decided to marry) - Mitchell fails to arrive for the birthday supper. (Last act of the play) Blanche, desperate, calls him and insists that he come. He makes it plain that now he will have her only as a mistress. She tries to explain her life to him but he can see only the details of promiscuity, not the underlying panic and need for protection which had forced this upon her. Blanche sends him away. In the second scene of this act she is alone in the flat (two-rooms by the freight-yards, big windows overlooking, intermittent roar of locomotives, Etc.) - Ralph enters, Stella being still out. He comes into Blanche's room. There is a violent scene at the end of which he takes her by force.

There are at least three possible ends.

One, Blanche simply leaves - with no destination.

Two, goes mad.

Three, throws herself in front of a train in the freight-yards, the roar of which has been an ominous under-tone throughout the play.

I know this is very heavy stuff and am writing it with as much lyrical and comedy relief as possible while preserving the essentially tragic atmosphere. The comedy comes mostly from Ralph's friends, and the sex theme dignified and relieved by a poignant characterization of Blanche. Treatment is everything in a play of this type, but some of the scenes already have a good deal of dramatic texture, so I think I will go on with it.

This is my only copy of the synopsis so please keep this letter. If you agree it might interest Cornell, have another copy typed for her and McClintic to look at.

Blanche is about thirty-four, Stella and Ralph thirty. There is one set, interior of two room flat and important exterior view. There are four big parts, and four small ones. Period indefinitely modern.

Tony is back in the play. I will leave with the company Sunday afternoon, but don't know where I will stay in New York - at some hotel with a swimming-pool if such is available. Have you any influence with The Shelton? That would be my choice, but they are awfully hard to get into. Mother plans to visit New York about the middle of April - I will make her a present of the railroad fare.

Love, Tenn.

[TW was to sign and mail contracts for *You Touched Me!* to Frieda Lawrence in New Mexico.

Guthrie McClintic may have encouraged TW to write a play for his wife, Katharine Cornell, when he saw *The Glass Menagerie* in Chicago. After attending a performance in June, "Kit" wired TW asking that he "write her one" (see letter

#330), to which he replied, "If I am lucky that is exactly what I will do, and most want to, but it takes some doing" (June 15, 1945, HRC). Had Cornell originated the part of Blanche DuBois in A *Streetcar Named Desire*, she would have been in her late forties. The only important elements not mentioned in the synopsis, a virtual scene-by-scene projection of *Streetcar*, are Stella's pregnancy and the story of Allan Grey.

In a late interview (1972), TW described a halting first approach to *Streetcar* as well as a calendar that differs from his report to Audrey Wood: "My first idea for the title was 'Blanche's Chair in the Moon.' But I only wrote one scene then. She was waiting for Mitch, and he wasn't showing up. That was as far as I got then; it was December of 1944. I felt *Streetcar* so intensely that it terrified me. I couldn't work for several months I was so terrified. I said, 'I can't cope with it; I can't carry this off.' I didn't go back to it until 1947, when I was in New Orleans" (qtd. in *Conversations*, p. 215).

Anthony Ross, the hard-drinking Gentleman Caller, was hospitalized for dysentery (TW diagnosed the real problem as "alcoholic") and replaced by Randy Echols, the production stage manager. He played the part "<u>not good</u>" (letter to Audrey Wood, Wed P.M. {March 14, 1945} HRC), TW thought, and both he and Laurette Taylor resisted a plan by the producers to use Echols permanently.]

328. To Bennett Cerf

Hotel Brevoort
New York City
March 30, 1945
[TLS, 1 p. Columbia]

Dear Mr Cerf -

I have reported our phone conversation to Laughlin and he feels that anxious as he is to publish THE GLASS MENAGERIE he could not very well repay the kindnesses you have done him by taking the book if you want it terribly badly.

Therefore I shall be willing to sign with you for it on your usual terms, provided they are satisfactory to my agent, Audrey Wood; and that you exercise your option by Wednesday, April 4th. The play opens tomorrow night and that should give you ample time to study the reviews and decide whether you can afford to risk your reputation on so dubious a venture.

One further provision would be that the contract contain no option on future plays or books. I have definitely decided that I wish to have my books published by New Directions because of my sympathy for the writers in that group and what they stand for.

Sincerely yours, Tennessee Williams

[Following its "smash success!" (letter from Bennett Cerf to TW, April 2, 1945, Columbia), *The Glass Menagerie* was published by Random House on July 31, 1945. It was one of the few books that TW offered to a publisher other than New Directions until Doubleday issued *Memoirs* in 1975.

New York reviews of *The Glass Menagerie* were enthusiastic, if marked by fairly serious reservations. George Jean Nathan's report went beyond reservation, however, and angered TW by insinuating that Tom's "wooden" part had been "rewritten," presumably by Eddie Dowling, into "some living plausibility" (*New York Journal American*, April 4, 1945). "No line," TW thundered in rebuttal, had been written by anyone save the playwright. He ended "A Reply to Mr. Nathan" with the statement that he was "very, very, very, very - - - MAD!" (April 9, 1945, HRC) and then withheld the piece from publication. TW's nemesis notwithstanding, *The Glass Menagerie* won every major theatre award save the Pulitzer and ran for nearly 600 performances.]

329. To Guthrie McClintic

SH: Hotel Adolphus
Dallas, Texas
5/23/45
[TLS w/ autograph postscript, 3 pp. HRC]

DEAR GUTHRIE:

This place is no good for my purposes and I am pulling out almost immediately - as soon, in fact, as I can make pullman reservations to Mexico City, which will probably be Friday or Saturday morning. I would appreciate it vastly if you could send me those addresses you mentioned right away. I always get the most awful feeling of desolation the moment I get into Mexico, though it fascinates me, too. The last time I nearly went crazy the first few days - from loneliness - and picked up with some characters on the streets through a mutual smattering of French - I don't speak a word of Spanish! - and got embroiled in situations from which I barely escaped with my life. So it would be lucky to have a few of the non-throat-cutting variety to get in touch with when I arrive there. And if I have any urge for violence I can go to the bull-fights instead.

This place is not as I had visualized it. It is too industrial to be really southern and it smells of reaction. I am trying to hide this from Margo, but I do not feel the atmosphere here in which anything really progressive is likely to happen. It is steeped in the sort of things that make America an ideal backdrop for another Hitler. For instance the real power in artistic circles here is John Rosenfield of the Dallas News - Margo's chief supporter - and in discussing Martha Graham he says "I don't care for that kind of showmanship!" - And you are not supposed to have negros on the same stage with whites! - and all that sort of hog-wash. I haven't a doubt in the world that Margo will establish a theatre here and that it will be big like everything else in Texas - In Mississippi where there is a genuine heritage of liberalism - believe it or not, among the cavalier descendants - a progressive southern theatre might have a better chance. I know that is what Margo wants, heart and soul, but I suspect that this place is a creative booby-trap, just from a day's encounter with it. I may be mistaken and I hope I am. At any rate the theatre will be started and Margo will make some kind of success with it, for she is really indomitable - but it will not be the seat of a southern renaissance!

You should have seen the place they had prepared for me - a five-room house with panelled walls and Persian carpets! While it was being completed I was supposed to occupy a room in "the big house" of the estate. The bed was nearly as big as the room which was enormous and I was told reverently that Emperor Franz Joseph had slept in it! - It seemed to epitomize the whole tragedy of the Hapsburgs and just at the sight of it I decided to leave at once for Mexico City.

So I am stopping at a down-town hotel and diplomatic relations are temporarily severed. I have not had a single phone-call since I checked in and room-service seems to be my only friend in Texas.

I hope you will seriously consider the question of having some music for "You Touched Me". I don't think it needs original compositions - though I'm a firm believer in the use of such - but there are several scenes where music would be enormously useful. In Pasadena for instance we had faint organ music throughout the lyrical breakfast scene in which the boy speaks of tenderness, Etc. - which is called for by the line "Miss Tyler is running over the Palm Sunday music". It was so effective. And in the "mad scene" - the one where the boy is locked in the bedroom and there is all that running up and downstairs, Etc. - I think music from the carnival in the village would accent the feeling of spring madness, incipient out-break, young confusion and delirium. There are moments when it is definitely called for - when Matilda opens the door and mentions hearing it - but there are other places, throughout the scene, where I think it would make a lovely sometimes lyrical and sometimes satirical counterpoint to the action. I know that Paul Bowles is terribly interested in working on the music if you decide to do anything about it. About Matilda's dresses - make them dreamy and lovely! Perhaps faintly Elizabethan in style, in soft May-pole colors. I hope you get really good actors in both the young parts - I know you will have them in the older parts. The girl ought to have delicacy and distinction as well as looks, but above all and everything she ought to be able to act, for it is not the easy part of the play as Matilda is a fairly complex young woman and is shown going through a real emotional upheaval. It is the only part I feel anxious about at the moment, for none of the girls we have considered so far seem right for the part - that is, none that I saw. Frances Waller was very, very pretty but appeared to have no relation to "Mist and cloud". But with actors you are the most resourceful man in the theatre so my nervousness is more anticipation than dread. . . .

I am so glad there is not a Singer in our wood-pile.

On that happy note, - Au revoir! 10.

Address me c/o Wells-Fargo in Mexico City. I will let you know address soon as I land.

[By 1945 Guthrie McClintic had produced and/or staged more than fifty original Broadway plays and revivals, many with Katharine Cornell in a leading role. His reputation as a director who easily blended commercial and artistic values (especially in the award winning production of *Winterset* in 1935), and who had produced several hits for clients of Liebling-Wood, made him attractive to the firm. In 1940 McClintic had rejected *Battle of Angels* and three years later chose not to produce *You Touched Me!* when first offered the script. He made only passing reference to TW in his theatre memoir, *Me and Kit* (1955), and none at all to *You Touched Me!*—scheduled for a fall production in New York.

Later in July TW wrote in support of Margo Jones's "Dallas Theatre idea."

Howard Barnes presenting the New York Drama Critics' Circle Award for The Glass Menagerie, *best American play of 1944–1945 season.*

The occasion, an article solicited by Jones and published in the *Dallas Morning News* on July 22, 1945, allowed TW to extol his friend's project while saying little about Dallas itself that was laudatory: "Margo and I are southerners, most of the people that will be working in the Dallas theatre have sprung from the South, and it does not seem surprising or unnatural to any of us that the location of such a theatre should be in the heart of the South. We believe in the emotional richness and the vitality of this part of the country which is ours by birth and breeding." With more candor and less reservation, he stressed that "something has to be done to dramatize and enrich" the post-war society, to satisfy its "vast cargo of heart-hungry youth."

TW wrote later that he had been "snatched out of virtual oblivion and thrust into sudden prominence" following the critical and financial success of *The Glass Menagerie.* The experience, peculiar to Americans whose "favorite national myth"

is the Cinderella story, gave security at last but also left him feeling cynical and isolated and without powers of recovery: "I no longer felt any pride in the play itself
but began to dislike it, probably because I felt too lifeless inside ever to create
another" ("On A Streetcar Named Success"). A fourth eye operation, performed in
early-May, gave brief anonymity and with it restoration to the world of the living.
TW spent an unhappy few days in Dallas with Margo Jones, who was planning at
the time to open her theatre with a revised *Battle of Angels*, and then flew to
Mexico, "an elemental country where you can quickly forget the false dignities and
conceits imposed by success" ("On A Streetcar Named Success").

TW deferred to McClintic in casting the role of Hadrian in *You Touched Me!*:
"PRACTICALLY A TOSS UP CLIFT HAS MORE EXPERIENCE AND CHARM BROWN
HAS MORE FOXY UPSTART QUALITY I HAVE DYSENTERY YOU DECIDE"
(Telegram, June 9, 1945). Montgomery Clift originated the role of the charity boy
in the play's disappointing run of 109 performances.

With "not a Singer in our wood-pile," TW rejoiced that such an unsavory figure (or so TW thought him) as Louis J. Singer, co-producer and backer of *The Glass
Menagerie*, would not be involved in the production of *You Touched Me!*]

330. To Audrey Wood

[Mexico City]
6/20/45
[TLS, 1 p. HRC]

Dear Child of God:

I wrote you a very gloomy letter the last time for I had swallowed one
of those Mexican bugs that prey on American tourists and I was feeling
very low indeed. But I found a little Mexican doctor who gave me shots
and pills, enough to kill a horse with - but I survived the treatment and
have been feeling exceptionally well ever since.

Disregard the instructions affecting prize money in last Memo. Won't
need it as I have wired Chase Natl. to let me draw $500. through Banco de
Commercio in Mexico. This will, I hope, see me through the Mexican jun-
ket and perhaps even back to the wilds of Texas and New York.

I have met the following here: Leonard Bernstein, Dolores Del Rio,
Rosa Covarrubias, Norman Foster (Now directing Mexican films), Romney
Brent's sister, Balanchine, Chavez, and many lesser notables of the Inter-
national Set (!) all of whom have invited me places. But it is not like Chicago

and New York, that is, the society is not at all exhausting and I have plenty of time to work. And I love Mexico, I think it is really and truly my native land! I will stay here till it is almost time to go back for "YTM".

Guthrie has sent me several wires about casting and I also got a wire from Katharine Cornell (Signed Kit) saying she had seen "Menagerie" and wanted me to write her one. And today - having pinched myself, I know I am wide awake! - I received a letter from Lawrence Stanislavsky Langner, the one who operates that famous Art Theatre on E. 56th Street - saying that he still has the scenery of "Battle" stored at Westport and has a new director in mind for it! This was profoundly touching, but also a little funny I thought - so I am mentioning it to you and Liebling!

One cannot help loving people who make you laugh! And I think the Guild has been favored by the Gods because their serious antics have even gotten a chuckle out of Cothurnus! - Imagine enticing us with the news that that horrible old brown set, probably all webbed and molded, was waiting for us in a store-room at Westport! Of course my instinct is to wire Lawrence, "You should have stood in Miami!" But instead I shall write him one of my nicest testimonials of affection, for this last communication has completed the cycle, often observed in life, from deepest tragedy to lightest farce!

Love - 10.

INDEX OF RECIPIENTS

Letters are cited by reference number in the following Index of Recipients.

GENERAL INDEX

WORKS BY TENNESSEE WILLIAMS